ach., 2/2/98

From the library of

Charles Nauert

With appreciation
for your scholarship
and for your
openness to the
potentialities of
humanity

[signature]

SEEDS OF VIRTUE

AND KNOWLEDGE

SEEDS OF VIRTUE AND KNOWLEDGE

Maryanne Cline Horowitz

PRINCETON UNIVERSITY PRESS

PRINCETON, NEW JERSEY

Library of Congress Cataloging-in-Publication Data

Horowitz, Maryanne Cline, 1945–
Seeds of virtue and knowledge / Maryanne Cline Horowitz.
p. cm.
Includes bibliographical references and index.
ISBN 0-691-04463-5 (alk. paper)
1. Seeds (philosophy)   2. Seeds—Religious aspects—History of doctrines.
3. Ethics—Europe—History.   4. Knowledge, Theory of—History.
5. Education—Europe—History.   6. Europe—Intellectual life.   I. Title.
B105.S43H67   1997
128'.09—dc21   97-18580

This book has been composed in Galliard Typeface

Frontispiece: Sandro Botticelli, *Primavera*, the propagative/creative breath of Zephyr
and the vegetative language of Chloris, Uffizi, Florence, Italy.

Printed in the United States of America

1   3   5   7   9   10   8   6   4   2

TO

JAMES EDWARD CLINE AND ETHEL ELLIS CLINE

ELLIS HOROWITZ

RUTH RACHEL, EDWARD GLENN, AND

IRA STEVEN HOROWITZ

• C O N T E N T S •

THE TITLE *Seeds of Virtue and Knowledge* draws attention to a significant optimistic and inclusive pattern of thought in Western philosophical, theological, educational, and ethical writings: the human mind nourishes seeds of virtue and knowledge, which may flower into human wisdom. An intellectual cluster of words and phrases for the natural law within—*seeds, sparks, reason*, and *common notions*—coalesces in Stoicism and spreads through the Stoic sentences of Cicero, Seneca, and Quintilian. A spectrum of theologians from Augustine to Thomas Aquinas and from Marsilio Ficino to Jean Calvin consider the God-given natural seeds and natural light in relationship to divine illumination. The Stoic epistemology is particularly influential on the Christian humanism of John of Salisbury, Petrarch, Guarino dei Guarini, and Desiderius Erasmus and impacts medieval, Renaissance, and Reformation educational curricula. Raymond Lull, Pico della Mirandola, and Jean Bodin explicitly draw on living traditions of Jews and Muslims; they exemplify the ecumenical Christian tradition of seeking in humanity the God-given seeds of virtue and knowledge.

As there are no books about specific aspects of the idea of seeds of virtue and knowledge, I shall expose and trace the identification of seeds with reason, common notions, and natural light of the intellect, ideas that are important in histories of epistemology, theology, moral and political philosophy, and pedagogy. In this first history of seed and spark imagery I connect and juxtapose different discourses to show their assumptions, continuities, and intertextual resonances. For example, in examining texts elaborating the idea that seeds of virtue and knowledge grow into trees of wisdom in the soul, I discovered that the Senecan image that thought sprouts from seed to treetop coalesced with biblical tree imagery in Philo's allegorical commentary on Gen. 2.8–9: "And God caused to spring out of the ground every tree fair to behold and good for food, and the tree of life in the midst of the garden, and the tree of knowledge of good and evil. Moses now indicates what trees of virtue God plants in the soul" (see ch. 8, nn. 81–83). I prove the direct impact on Bodin of Philo's metaphor of an internal mental garden, which I label "the garden of the soul," and suggest that through Ambrose and early Augustine this garden of the soul (*hortus animae*) influences medieval and Renaissance verbal and visual imagery.

Histories of manuscript illumination, wall decoration, painting, woodcuts, engravings, and emblems provide evidence of visual vegetative imagery, which I apply to elucidating textual vegetative imagery. Parallels between botanical and ethical discourses and between visual and verbal imagery provide abundant historical evidence of the broad cultural context of the analogy between horticulture and culture and of the importance of belief in seeds of virtue and knowledge for faith in the possibility of a renaissance.

Manuscript and book illustrations and wall decoration supplement textual commentary in opening our eyes to some broader cultural configurations. Like Pascal comparing the tiniest grains of sand with the most majestic and brightest stars in the heavens, we take a linguistic and symbolic turn from the minuscule seeds to the grandiose trees. In civilizations around the globe there are trees of life at the center of culture ascending from the earth below through the air above and reaching as high as the North Star. Medieval tree symbolism includes such trees of ascent as well as trees of virtue and vice and of the arts and sciences. Consideration of those images expands our sensitivity to the resonances, associations, meanings, and applications of the imagery of seeds that propagate thought: from the Latin *semen* (seed) and *seminare* (to sow) come *seedling, seedbed, seminal,* and *dissemination,* and from the Greek *speirein* (to sow) come *sprout* and *shoot.*

The fifteenth and sixteenth centuries self-consciously "blossom" in their symbolic images. Amid debates on nature and grace the visually evocative Stoic metaphor of seeds of virtue sprouting into the deeds and words of a virtuous sage fuses with the Psalmist's comparison of the righteous to "a tree planted by the streams of water, that bringeth forth its fruit in its season" (Ps. 1.3). On one hand there is the image of an aged tree deeply rooted in ancient Mediterranean soil, growing abundantly in natural sunlight (see fig. 3.6); on the other hand there is the image of the *sefirot* from the Hebrew Kabbalah, a tree of divine emanations rooted in God spreading downward into branches by which humans may ascend (see fig. E.1). Medieval and Renaissance readers alike know from Plato's *Timaeus* that humans are upside-down trees with their roots located in their souls, which stem downward from the divine Creator. Vegetative images, as well as light symbolism, suggest the divine origin of humanity.

Embedded in texts influential in Italian and Erasmian humanist circles and taking on diverse applications, the "seeds of virtue" or "sparks of divinity" are effective and consequential rudiments in the writings of such humanistically educated individuals of the fifteenth and sixteenth centuries as Leonardo Bruni, Costanza da Varano, Aeneas Sylvius Piccolomini, Cassandra Fedele, Laura Cereta, Jacopo Sadoleto, Guillaume du Vair, Justus Lipsius, Michel de Montaigne, and Pierre Charron. In the most optimistic formulations in advanced rhetoric, poetics, law and government, and theology the telic phrases for divine potential in the human mind are instrumental, pragmatic, and rhetorically effective and play a vital role in the educational curricula for knowledge and character development that mold the foundations of the modern world. For example, Pico gathers the sparks of wisdom scattered among a variety of world cultures; Bodin considers by means of a seven-voice ecumenical conversation the common notions that grow in diverse minds; and Fedele and Montaigne find seeds of virtue flowering in commoners, that is, "noble" behavior among male and female common folk.

The assumption that there are "seeds of virtue" and "seeds of knowledge" in humanity contributes to Western confidence in the moral and intellectual agency of women and others who are subordinated or enslaved by society. The ancient Stoic school is remembered for its open membership, including slaves and women, and its cosmopolitan view that all humans share, through their reason, in a world community governed by natural law, a view that is in opposition to Aristotle's belief in a hierarchy of deliberative capacity corresponding to natural slavery and female inferiority. Even though Stoics stress the rarity of sages, they recognize the universality of human potential; through the ages, many have been empowered by the thought that divine sparks and seeds of virtue and knowledge bless each human mind, enabling the propagation of learning, civic ethics, and religion. Sermons and educational addresses still delight in the *imago Dei*, the image of God shared by all humans, and encourage the blossoming in our lives of creative flowers of wisdom and of fruitful acts for the benefit of the human community.

While some Christians seek to gather together the sparks of religious insight implanted in all humans, believing that diverse readings from multiple cultures may aid the ascent to the Divine, others focus more narrowly on the Christian religious tradition and the one unique incarnation of the divine seed. Innocent III, Martin Luther, Marguerite de Navarre, and the Council of Trent are concerned to uproot the tree of vice growing in each sinner's soul, and they evangelically advise that one open one's soul to Jesus.

The vegetative symbolism of the age of the Renaissance and the Reformation is not without "crowns of thorns": theology, literature, and detailed historical records attest to the trees of alleged "vice" to be cut down (Matt. 7.15–20; fig. 6.3). The expulsion of the Jews from Spain and their continued exile from England and France, Catholic accusations against Protestants that they are "Judaizers" and reciprocal Protestant accusations against Catholics that they are "legalistic Pharisees," the battles in the streets of German towns and in the French countryside in which some Christians kill other Christians in the name of religion, the enslavement and pressured conversion of Amerindians and Africans in the Americas—to moralists such as the essayist Montaigne and the priest Charron all these phenomena indicate that a rethinking of natural-law theory and of ethics separate from specific religions would be wise. "Que sais-je?" ("What do I know?") is Montaigne's famous question; in Stoic fashion he answers, "Naturam sequi" ("To follow nature").

Humanists, philosophers, theologians, artists, and emblem compilers seek to revive and cultivate the natural seeds of virtue and knowledge and to ignite the spark of divinity in order to bring about a "rebirth" of culture and a reawakening of religion through art as well as "reform." By focusing on humanist applications of Senecan epistemology, including Quintilian's pedagogy of transplanting seeds from the wise, this book reaffirms the cultural movement of the renaissance as expressed by botanist Pierre Belon: "The minds of men . . . have put in evidence all kinds of good disciplines which to their so happy and desirable renaissance, all as the new plants after a season of winter regain their vigor in the heat of the Sun" (see ch. 7, n. 7). The printing press speeds up the internal cultivation of seeds of virtue and knowledge by transplanting the most beautiful and most wise flowers of moral wisdom via florilegia of classical sayings and examples and books of emblems, adages, and essays.

Fifteenth-century Italian humanists, reading newly discovered full manuscripts of the rhetorician Quintilian and the outstanding botanist Theophrastus, believe that one should nurture, nurse, prune, fence, and cultivate a child or sapling from infancy to adulthood. Renaissance humanists take the association between horticulture and culture that is "deeply grounded" in language and symbolism and transform it into a major defining motif of their age: humanist vegetative symbolism permeates philosophy, theology, botany, art, and pedagogy.

It is surprising that previous scholarship on the origins and expansion of the concept *renascità* has not discussed the seeds to be reborn. In order to draw attention to the multifold aspects of seeds of virtue and knowledge, this book interweaves several approaches. The introduction explains my plan to treat the image cluster of seeds, sparks, common notions, and reason as an epistemology of common notions, an educational strategy of implanting and sparking, a paradigm of the mind growing like a plant, a literary intertext of unquoted quotations, a vegetative metaphor related to several visual images—in fact, a language of vegetative growth and a continuing controversy on assessing humanity. Readers are welcome to turn to a later leaf to begin.

In the sixteenth century, symbolic trees in visual illustrations come to the aid of the educational theory of nurturing the seeds of virtue and knowledge: Andreas Alciati's emblem showing an olive tree entwined by a grapevine proclaims that "the prudent must abstain from wine"; the Stoic motto "One must be steadfast under pressure" accompanies a picture of a date palm bending to withstand a weight; an emblem of a mulberry tree provides sympathy and hope for the student who is a "slow bloomer" (see fig. 7.3). Images as well as texts contribute to what I interpret as the premodern scientific paradigm "The mind develops like a plant." From Cicero, Seneca, and Quintilian in Roman antiquity to Petrarch, Guarino, Ficino, Sadoleto, Erasmus, Du Vair, Bodin, and Charron in the Renaissance, humanist strategies for education build upon analogies of a pupil to a young tree and the educator to a gardener. To us they bequeath the idea that under proper educational cultivation the human mind might attain the full flowering of wisdom.

I AM GRATEFUL for the generous sabbatical leave policy for faculty at Occidental College and for the hospitality of the Center for Medieval and Renaissance Studies at the University of California, Los Angeles. My appreciation extends to the Renaissance Society of America and its constituent societies for their annual interdisciplinary conferences; and I also acknowledge the contribution of numerous colleagues who provided scholarly responses to my presentations of specific chapters at meetings of the Medieval Association of the Pacific, the Society for Emblem Studies, and the American Historical Association.

The National Endowment for the Humanities and the Ford Foundation contributed summer stipends that aided this research. An American Council of Learned Societies travel grant and a Université de Bordeaux conference stipend allowed me to participate in international colloquia on Jean Bodin and Michel de Montaigne, respectively, and the Louis and Hermione Brown Humanities Support Fund helped cover some of the material costs. I would like to thank the staffs of the Occidental College Library, the libraries of the University of California, Los Angeles, the Huntington Library, the Houghton Library of Harvard University, the library of the University of Wisconsin, Madison, the Bibliothèque nationale, and the libraries of Avignon, Bordeaux, and the Université d'Angers. I thank graduates of Occidental College, especially Morissa Rosenberg and Angelica Salas, and UCLA graduates, especially Robin Hardy and Lora Sigler. I extend my thanks to members of the Occidental College staff and administration, in particular Luisa Reyes, Cecilia Fox, and David L. Axeen.

For numerous dialogues on book drafts at significant turning points in this research I warmly thank William J. Bouwsma, Robert M. Kingdon, Marion Leathers Daniels Kuntz, and Richard H. Popkin. I appreciate the valuable suggestions of readers Anthony Grafton, Donald R. Kelley, and Marcia L. Colish. For editorial assistance I thank Carol D. Lanham and Simon Varey. I thank the editors Lauren Osborne and Brigitta van Rheinberg; the manager of the editorial production group, Jane Low; as well as the full staff of Princeton University Press. I appreciate the thorough work of the copyeditor, Joanne Allen, and the indexer, Roberta Engleman. Although I alone am responsible for the overall scope of this work and for errors that may remain, I would like to thank specialists whom I consulted on specific chapters: on chapter 1, David Blank; on chapter 2, Richard H. Dales; on chapters 4 and 5, Michael J. B. Allen and Paul Oskar Kristeller; on chapter 7, Virginia W. Callahan; and on chapter 8, Ann L. Blair. I would like to acknowledge the late Julius Weinberg, with whom I explored Stoics and scholastics, and the late Gerhart Ladner, whose articles on vegetative symbolism broadened my vision. I thank William E. Engel and

Daniel S. Russell for their encouragement of my research into emblems and Eric Frank for references in art history. For bibliographical suggestions on Philo and other Jewish sources I thank Arthur Lesley. I appreciate numerous French literary scholars who commented on my previous articles on Montaigne, Bodin, and Charron.

I thank the following publishers for permission to include revised and expanded versions of previously published articles: for chapter 1, the *Journal of the History of Ideas*, with permission of The Johns Hopkins University Press; for chapter 9, *Renaissance Rereadings* (University of Illinois Press) and *History of European Ideas*; and for chapter 10, the Renaissance Society of America. And I thank the Princeton University Press for permission to include selections from *Seeds of Virtue and Knowledge* in my talks and future publications.

In addition, I appreciate the many ways in which Occidental College faculty have sustained this scholarship: in particular I am appreciative of Margaret E. Crahan, Wellington K. Chan, Nina R. Gelbart, Jane S. Jaquette, Barbara S. Kanner, C. Scott Littleton, Mary Elizabeth Perry, Marla S. Stone, and Jean Wyatt for sharing at several stages thoughts about our books; Eric M. Frank and Michael R. Near for our interdisciplinary team teaching of the Renaissance Culture Core; and the entire Department of History for providing a milieu of cross-cultural exploration across the centuries. In the interludes of writing this book I conversed with my students on the beautifully landscaped Occidental College campus, walked on pathways at The Huntington Library and Botanical Gardens, and contemplated the treetops from library windows of the University of California, Los Angeles. I dedicate *Seeds of Virtue and Knowledge* to my family, who have nourished my optimism on human nature; together with loved ones, each season brings new growth.

SEEDS OF VIRTUE

AND KNOWLEDGE

As a plant or tree grows from a seed, so do thoughts, images, and deeds sprout from human beings. This book is a historical analysis of texts and images from antiquity to the Renaissance that assert or suggest that there are seeds of virtue and knowledge in the human mind that enable a child to learn, an adult to become wise, magistrates to ground law codes, and their civilization to flourish. I interpret this overall cluster of images and ideas, which assumes the paradigm "The mind develops like a plant" and the equivalence of *seeds* with *reason, common notions*, and *natural light* in the human mind, as both an "epistemology" and a "vegetative language" of seeds of virtue and knowledge.

Belief in an epistemology of seeds of virtue and knowledge accords with the classical dictum "Live in accordance with nature." *Natural* is both a value term meaning "moral and true" and a descriptive term meaning "inborn in human nature."[1] The goal is clearly inclusive of both knowledge and virtue. Desiderius Erasmus, whose sixteenth-century educational books influence Protestant as well as Catholic schools, exemplifies the tradition. Pages of balanced, cadenced Latin sentences define the goal: "Est vir tum eruditus, tum probus" [He is a man both learned and good].[2]

The scholars of the ages from antiquity to the Renaissance, so different from one another, collectively seem different from those of our own age, especially in their concern for developing a combined moral and intellectual teaching. In the Renaissance as in antiquity, educators create anthologies of righteous and rhetorically effective sayings to arouse the reason and the will of their students to contribute to the public realm of great words and deeds.[3]

We shall focus on the vocabulary introduced by the ancient Stoics for claiming human access to natural law, that is, their concept of *ius naturale* within human nature; this book contains some surprising evidence of the prevalence in education, religion, literature, as well as moral philosophy, of premises that are foundational to Western normative political philosophy.[4] I provide evidence for delving further into the humanistic and neo-Stoic movements of the late sixteenth and seventeenth centuries in seeking out how *ius naturale* was transformed from traditional *natural law* to modern *natural rights*.[5]

Bodin is known to apply divine natural law in his *Six Books of the Republic*, but he is often viewed as an inconsistent thinker. Yet as we shall see in chapter 8, he in fact builds a consistent epistemological foundation for his wide range of works upon a natural-law epistemology of "seeds of virtue, knowledge and piety," and he forthrightly declares that slavery derives not from natural law but from human greed. In Bodin's view, cultivation of the seeds generally supports obedience to political regimes, yet "seed of reason" can support radical politics, as in the resistance to tyranny of Étienne de la Boétie's *De la servitude voluntaire*.[6] Montaigne, the subject of chapter 9, is an interesting example of a thinker who carefully disputes natural-law language yet resorts to "la semence de la raison universelle" to explain the virtue of peasants and to the internal natural law to condemn cruelty and torture. Seeking the origins of "natural rights," Richard Tuck is on an important track when he suggests that we look at late-sixteenth-century texts and at the uses of natural-law language as a response to Skepticism;[7] and chapters 7–10 of this book show Guillaume du Vair, Justus Lipsius, Jean Bodin, Michel de Montaigne, and Pierre Charron each in his own way applying natural-law language in response to doubts and to religious discord.

The main focus of this book is the diverse applications of belief in seeds, sparks, reason, and common notions among Italian humanists of the fifteenth century and French humanists of the sixteenth century. To achieve an explanatory analysis of the works of major Renaissance authors, my first three chapters give background on representative and authoritative texts from Graeco-Roman antiquity and the Hebraic-Christian traditions. In order to indicate the cultural significance and the complexity of the web of influences between writers and illustrators, in this introduction I suggest the broader metaphoric implications of my discovery of the vegetative images of seeds, flowers, and trees of virtue and knowledge. Throughout this book we shall consider visual images, especially illuminations within manuscripts and illustrations in printed books, that correspond to the literary images in the texts.

Those who have long been interested in thoughts and images from antiquity to the Renaissance, as well as those who long to reclaim once again optimistic, inclusive strands of European thought, will find visual and textual evidence of the widespread belief in the West that human wisdom, like a grove of trees, grows from seeds of virtue and knowledge. In this reinterpretation of significant aspects of Western thought, I emphasize the cumulative impact on the Italian and French Renaissance of Cicero, Seneca, Quintilian, Philo, Augustine, Aquinas, visual vegetative imagery, and the expanding humanist curriculum. Those whose work primarily involves contemporary thought might be surprised by the continuing relevance/irrelevance of the ideas analyzed in this study. The example of the phrase *seeds of virtue* and of the images of flowers of virtue and trees of virtue may be of interest as "a datum of Western consciousness"—one very basic to the tree structures in modern linguistics,[8] to the issues of referentiality and representation, and to Derrida's bold call for a deconstructing of "la dissémination."[9] Likewise, seeds of virtue and knowledge in humanity in relationship to the vegetative and divine realms exemplify "correspondences," the *episteme* Foucault considers characteristic of the sixteenth century.[10]

With regard to enduring philosophical and literary concerns, the thinkers discussed in this work reflect upon the human problems of explaining how ideas develop in the human mind and validating concepts that they deem essential for civilized life. They too face quandaries concerning the criteria for truth and the foundation for ethics. Plato contends with the rhetoricians; the ancient Stoics rival the Academy during its period of Skepticism. Montaigne and Charron themselves uphold many of the arguments of Academic and Pyrrhonian Skeptics, and each in his own way is a rhetorician, using words partially for oratorical effect; nevertheless, both resort to the Stoic seeds of virtue and knowledge as epistemological grounding for their notions of human wisdom. Skeptical and deconstructive philosophies are—and remain—a challenge to both opponents and followers.

Multiple approaches are helpful for understanding the roles variants of *semina virtutis* (seeds of virtue) and *semina scientiae* (seeds of knowledge) have played in the Western tradition. In fact, applying one approach would misleadingly uniformly label changing phenomena. Several categories of analysis are necessary because authors treat the phrases in different ways. For example, according to the Greek Stoics, the material/spiritual *spermata* (seeds) from the pantheistic material/spiritual divinity are within us. Their interpretation of the seeds as both physical and formative makes such seeds precursors of *genes* in twentieth-century vocabulary. Alternatively, according to Augustine, the immaterial *rationes seminales* (seminal reasons)—which are formative but not physical—are implanted in our minds through God's illumination of the Platonic ideas of justice, truth, and beauty.[11] The Greek Stoic theory will concern us briefly because of the concrete original imagery it provides, but illumination and participation theories, in either the Augustinian or later versions, are an enduring alternative. I label the Augustinian view a "divine path to wisdom" in contrast to the Senecan or Ciceronian model of a "natural path to wisdom."

Throughout the medieval and Renaissance period illumination theories vie with theories of the natural potentialities of the growing human being. We shall view the development of what God gave humans at the Creation as "natural paths to wisdom," since premodern Jewish, Christian, and Muslim thinkers nearly unanimously accept the revelation of Genesis declaring that nature was divinely created. There is a startling difference between theorists who defend natural paths to attain "human wisdom" (*scientia*), knowledge of good and evil and of the arts and sciences for living in communities on this earth, and theorists who defend natural paths to attain "divine wisdom" (*sapientia*), knowledge and contemplation of divine things.[12]

In chapter 3 I discuss two dichotomies: between "natural paths" and "divine paths" and between "human wisdom" and "divine wisdom." Medieval illustrations of trees of the arts and sciences, growing from the seeds of knowledge, indicate natural paths to human wisdom. Lull's tree diagram for the principles of medicine presents the tree both vertically, with subfields indicated by labels on the branches, and in cross section, by means of the circular rings on the trunk of the "core curriculum," the base from which the branches derive (see fig. 3.4). The circle of knowledge (from Greek *enkyklios paideia*, "course of general education") continues to function in the Library of Congress, where the library's rotunda, the circular main reading room, provides the core for exploring the branches of knowledge.[13]

Other tree images are arborescent representations of the Divine in which the onlookers are encouraged to ascend. However, although the illustrator, like the author, is attracting the onlooker's gaze upward, he or she may be intentionally obscure about whether one may ascend to divine wisdom by one's own efforts; in terms of theological orthodoxy, that obscurity is one of the values of symbolic language and imagery (see fig. 3.2). The ambiguity of verbal or visual metaphoric imagery has particular power. One might interpret Ficino, Pico della Mirandola, and Cardinal Sadoleto as applying vegetative symbolism for natural paths to divine wisdom. In chapter 6 the issues involved in diverse tree symbolism provoke Reformation and Counter-Reformation controversies.

How one interprets different authors' images and conceptualizations of seeds of virtue and knowledge in part depends on one's interpretation of their seed theories. Aristotle, Galen, and the Bible share a common focus on the seed as the source of embryological and plant growth. In Aristotle's biological and botanical framework, plants, animals, and humans derive from seed (although he resorts to spontaneous generation to explain some simple forms of life). The Greek Stoics do not accept Aristotle's belief that semen from a male of the human species is formative and telic in the embryo but provides no physical material.

The English word *conception*, derived from the Latin *conceptio*, appropriately connotes the *double entente* of the explanatory metaphor of mental conception modeled on biological conception of an embryo: the emergence of a mental picture or understanding of an idea has resemblances to the emergence in an inseminated female womb of the first stage of embryonic development. For example, Hildegard of Bingen's illustration physically represents God's implantation of the immaterial soul, with its divine sparks, in the female womb (see fig. 2.4). The divine implanting of seeds of virtue and knowledge, or sparks, in the human soul, as in the Stoic *logos spermatikos*, may invoke a gendered, organic, developmental image as an explanatory metaphor for the human grasp of concepts. We gain a deeper comprehension and appreciation that possibly scholars implore distinctly female muses to help nurture and cultivate the seeds growing in the wombs of the scholars' minds (see, e.g., figs. 4.2 and 10.1).[14]

Generally, however, the analogy is not between biological and mental conception but between seeding the soil and seeding the soul. From classical antiquity until well into the seventeenth century (before studies of pollination) it is generally accepted that the key difference between plants and animals is that plants develop asexually from seed. There are, in fact, the asexual vegetative phenomena of plants regenerating through runners, off-shoots, cuttings of root stems, and grafting of two plants, which Virgil poetically describes in *Georgics* 2 (see fig. 5.5).[15] A vegetative representation is particularly appropriate for representing the divine source of the uplifting human characteristics of knowledge and virtue. Hildegard of Bingen's illustration shows the link between the divine and human realms as a vinelike umbilical cord, a vegetative offshoot provided by God (fig. 2.4).

The complex parallels of plant propagation, human procreation, and divine insemination appear in Botticelli's *Primavera*, a painting often interpreted since the nineteenth century as symbolic of the age of the Renaissance. The ideological ties between the assumption of seeds of virtue and knowledge and the emergence of the dominant metaphor created by humanists and artists of the fourteenth and fifteenth centuries, namely, the renaissance of arts and letters, are explored in chapter 5, in my reinterpretation of Botticelli's *Primavera*, especially the arborescent, mythological detail of the pagan wind god Zephyr inseminating the nymph Chloris (see frontispiece and fig. 5.2). There I explore the practical, experiential role the concept seeds of virtue and knowledge plays in humanist educational practice.

My task as a historian is to try to present each of the major versions of seeds of virtue and knowledge within its own intellectual context. The phrases, meanings, implications, and overall significance change of course; but the authors view themselves as being in a succession of historical continuities through a common belief that the human mind is predisposed to develop certain notions and through a tendency to overlook the differences between their notions and those of their sources. Most importantly, the eclectic flexible possibilities of the phrase *seeds of virtue and knowledge*—its visual associations with botanical and biological life and its metaphoric power to evoke the iconographic meanings of vegetative symbols in art and religion—are the very source of its longevity. In response to the multifaceted aspects of seeds of virtue and knowledge, we shall have opportunities to study the concept as (1) an epistemology, (2) a strategy, (3) a paradigm of science or of folk psychology, (4) a literary intertext, (5) a metaphor related to several visual images, (6) a language of vegetative growth, and (7) a continuing controversy on assessing humanity.

Epistemology. From the perspective of the history of ideas and the history of philosophy, the cluster of seeds, reason, common notions, and sparks functions logically within carefully delineated systems of thought as a fundamental idea (an assumption, a preconception, a premise) that is central to theories on how humans attain knowledge.[16] This book examines several varieties of such carefully constructed epistemologies: among ancient Stoics such as Seneca and Cicero, as well as in the works of theologians such as Augustine and Thomas Aquinas, systematic philosophers such as Ficino and Lipsius, and philosophically educated humanists such as Erasmus and Bodin. *Semina virtutis* and *semina scientiae*, the hard-to-notice topos, are diminutives phrase describing a seminal potency that is in fact claimed to

be the seat of all cultures; that claim is made directly by Pico della Mirandola and Ficino, as well as by Bodin. This is a very appealing universalist
application of seeds of virtue and knowledge that proclaims the worldwide
potentiality for human dignity.

Strategy. The epistemology underlies the whole Renaissance pedagogy
of gathering commonplaces in a notebook (or, later, an emblem book), a
process that reaches a highly complex cultural level in Erasmus's *Adages*, as
well as in Montaigne's *Essais*. As a shortcut to asking questions to draw out
the natural notions, scholars gather the very best sentences of the greatest
thinkers and implant these "flowers of wisdom" in the student's mind. The
technique is already fully amplified in antiquity in Quintilian's *Institutio
oratoria* (The education of an orator), whence it influences each revival of
the ancient humanities curriculum. I shall do my best to discern whether an
author is discussing the emergence of inborn seeds in the mind or the
transplantation of seeds of virtue and knowledge from the wise to the student; yet we must remember that those who believe in the natural paths to
wisdom think that the sentences of the wise ring true because they correspond to the shared common notions.

Thus, the epistemology of seeds of virtue and knowledge functions in
educational strategies; it can be strategic in legitimizing a particular curriculum such as the scholastic Thomist natural-law ethics or the Greek-
Hebrew-Latin humanist curriculum of Catholic and Protestant universities. The concept seeds of virtue and knowledge is particularly evident in
many Renaissance educational treatises, epistles, and orations, where it is
viewed by some historians today as "mere rhetoric" and by others as the
"foundation-stone for civic ethics."[17]

The historical and political debate on Leonardo Bruni, chancellor of
Florence, is central to the controversy on whether humanism is especially
supportive of the civic ethics of republics. This book allows one to place in
a long chronological sweep to our own times the contrasting strategies of
cultivation of the virtues through human means and their cultivation
through God's grace. Thus, in the fifteenth century the humanistic praises
of the human virtues of Florentines and their republic in Leonardo Bruni's
Laudatio[18] contrasts with the eschatological call for divine grace of Savonarola's preaching: "In Savonarola's sermons we may clearly read the realisa-
tion that the republic is possible only if all men are virtuous, and that all
men can be virtuous only if they deserve, and receive the divine gift of
grace."[19] As I document in chapter 10, a dichotomy in strategies is evident as well in the contrast of the third book of Pierre Charron's *Les trois
veritez*, which validates only the fruits of faith in Roman Catholics, and the
third book of his *De la sagesse*, which says that seeds of virtue and knowledge in a citizenry may bear the fruits of prudence, justice, fortitude, and
temperance.

A key issue of the civic-humanism controversy is whether there are ties
between a humanist education and expanded capacities for political partici-

pation;[20] in both republics and monarchies of the Renaissance the issue is who has sufficient rank to participate. In the fifteenth- and sixteenth-century controversy concerning whether true nobility is based on one's birth or on one's virtue, citation of Senecan and Ciceronian passages on seeds of virtue (rather than seeds of lineage) tends to increase the ranks of those who may be considered capable of self-governing; in Castiglione's *Book of the Courtier*, some traditionalists respond to the possibility that a virtuous and talented commoner might be trained to be a courtier by defending the seeds of lineage, while others argue that ancestry and upbringing provide the necessary soil for the seeds of virtue to flourish, "for no evil is so bad as that which springs from the corrupted seed of good."[21] In *The Fruit of a Liberal Education* the Englishman Richard Pace, a friend of Thomas More and Desiderius Erasmus, advocates the idea that good studies lead to virtue and that furthermore "true nobility is surely created by virtue, and not by a long and famous line of ancestors."[22] Chapter 5, below, documents the egalitarian implications of Stoic seeds of virtue among some fifteenth-century Italian women humanists.

Although scholars dispute the commitment of a particular Renaissance writer to republicanism or to princely rule, it is indisputable that humanists throughout Europe and its colonies apply their crafts to serving a wide array of political and ecclesiastical governments.[23] There is rarely "mere rhetoric" in the sixteenth century, for the humanistic subjects grammar, rhetoric, history, ethics, and moral philosophy serve important societal purposes. We shall see that vegetative images of virtue blossoming serve as civic strategies for encouraging loyalty to regimes ruled by one, the few, or the many. Directing citizens to a tree diagram of Aristotle's three forms of government that serve the people and pointing citizens away from the tree diagram of such governments turned bad or self-serving, Guillaume de la Perrière's *Le miroir politique* and the English version, *The Mirrour of Policie*, encourage civic virtue in the citizenry—service for the good of the people (see fig. 7.6).

Paradigm. It is not surprising that from antiquity through the seventeenth century, when Europe has mainly an agricultural economy, we find abundant vegetative imagery. Commenting on the rural atmosphere of urban homes in sixteenth-century France, whose floors are strewn with flowers or leaves in summer to keep them sweet-smelling and cool, Lucien Febvre notes, "The country made its presence felt even in everyday language, which was filled with allusions to the fields. Season began with the singing of the cricket, the blooming of the violet, the ripening of the wheat."[24] What has not been noticed sufficiently is that in premodern Europe it is a functioning paradigm to consider the growth of the mind to be comparable to the growth of a plant and the growth of a righteous person to be comparable to the growth of an upright tree. Biblical moral imagery drawn from the agricultural Hebrew society in Palestine reinforces Stoic epistemology. The notion that each human being has seeds of virtue and knowledge from which virtue and knowledge can blossom is to some extent a scientific paradigm of human development.[25] It functions as an explanatory model in scientific treatises such as Bodin's *Universae naturae theatrum*. The epistemology rings true because the comparison of a child's growth to a plant's is part of a persistent model of folk psychology.[26]

We are accustomed to viewing as paradigms the alternative mechanistic models, such as in the familiar neoclassical analogy of the brain and a clock or, today, the analogy of the brain and a computer. Although the comparison of the human to a machine is based also on precedents in classical antiquity, it does not attain significant influence until the seventeenth century;[27] what precedes the paradigm of the mind functioning as a machine is the paradigm of the mind developing like a plant. A palm tree visibly sprouts forth in an eighteenth-century image of the soul's growth by the mystic William Law (see fig. E.4). The political implications of choosing a machine paradigm or a plant paradigm are primary to John Stuart Mill (1806–73); in *On Liberty* he writes, "Human nature is not a machine to be built after a model, and set to do exactly the work prescribed for it, but a tree, which requires to grow and to develope itself on all sides, according to the tendency of the inward forces which make it a living thing."[28] In favor of the cultivating and unfolding and against the uprooting and dwarfing of either trees or people, Mill advocates spontaneity, individuality, and full liberty of expression.[29]

Intertext. Sometimes the writer whose vocabulary includes *seeds of virtue* or *seeds of knowledge* has not fully considered the logic or evidence for its use but accepts such a phrase as a truism; from the perspective of literary history, therefore, it is helpful to realize that a phrase sometimes functions as an intertext, a classical unquoted quotation, within a later text that reverberates with allusions of which the author may be only partially aware.[30] The phrases describing the "sprouting" or "growth" or "flowering" of ideas are often unacknowledged quotations (the assertion resting on authority). The perspective of literary history is most helpful in analyzing the common refrains on the "rebirth" of the age in Renaissance humanist dedication letters and oratory; nevertheless, the refrains are significant since unexamined assumptions or phrases treated as commonplaces become implicit structures of thought that play very powerful roles in cultural traditions.[31]

Metaphor. It is common knowledge that a mature plant generally derives from a seed; thus one gives immediate assent to the idea that the good deeds and wise statements of a mature person derive from seeds of virtue and knowledge.[32] There is ample plant and tree symbolism throughout the world;[33] Paul Friedrich has found evidence from the third millennium B.C.E. of the religious importance of oak trees associated with lightning among Balts, Teutons, Greeks, Italics, and Celts, as well as a relation between the semantic system of tree names and religious belief and ritual.[34] Such anthropological evidence[35] suggests that the authors and image-makers studied here are working not only within a narrow, traceable tradition of texts and images but also within a broad cultural continuum that resonates in language, religion, art, gardening,[36] and herbal remedies. For example, a Renaissance banquet is not complete without a cornucopia, a goat's horn overflowing with fruit and ears of grain, and the symbolic resonances are also cornucopian—plenitude, the biblical first fruits, and the harvest of the grain goddess.[37] Starting in chapters 2 and 3, we shall consider several traditions of visual images with the purpose of "seeing" the live metaphors in the texts and expanding our vegetative visual vocabulary.

Language of vegetative growth. The functional omnipresence of symbolic light and tree imagery, which often is not consciously perceived or analyzed by observers or even practitioners, is the background to Ficino's viewing ideas as "sparking" from one "brilliant" person to another and as "sprouting" from our minds. Western visual images that represent structures produced by the human mind as trees suggest that the references to seeds of virtue and knowledge and trees of virtue and knowledge are part of something larger, namely, symbolic vegetative language and metaphor.[38] In the beautifully illustrated and documented *Landscape and Memory*, Simon Schama suggests the multifaceted ways Europeans and Americans have seen, trimmed, and created their vegetative environment and how these remembered landscapes pervade cultural expression, appearing in woodcuts, paintings, architecture, photographs, descriptions, histories, narratives, and flashbacks.[39] Exposing the landscape within mind, heart, and aesthetic sensibilities, he points out many trails through the forest; yet he does not approach our groves in philosophy, theology, mysticism, humanism, science, and government, where sprout the seeds of virtue and knowledge.

The opening of our eyes to visual imagery has been aided by Christian iconographical studies, as well as by the newer studies of political iconography; nevertheless, in presenting the language of vegetative growth that has influenced individual and civic ethics and spirituality, one is challenged to overcome the religious/secular dichotomy evident between the Princeton Index of Christian Art and Raimond van Marle's *Iconographie de l'art profane au Moyen-Age et à la Renaissance*.[40] One should look to such guides for fuller discussion of the Christian images of the Virgin as the enclosed garden or of the tree of Jesse or, alternatively, for pagan images of tree worship or of gods born in trees; in contrast, the focus of this book is humanity. This is the first historical inquiry into pagan, Jewish, Christian, and secular manuscripts and books for the seeds, buds, flowers, trees, and fruit of virtue and knowledge.

Fascinated by finding the phrase "seeds of the great virtues and knowledge" in a work by a so-called Skeptic, Pierre Charron, I sought to reconcile aspects of his thought and then to trace the origins and the philosophical equivalents of such seeds (see ch. 10, n. 14). Having documented the Stoic idea of natural law in humanity—reason, common notions, seeds, and sparks—I sought further examples in philosophy and theology. Not yet attuned to the literary and visual ramifications of the metaphor, I was interested in the history of the normative tradition of natural law and virtue. My own linguistic and symbolic "turn" occurred concomitantly with my enjoyment of literary and art historical studies and my involvement in conference planning for the Renaissance Society of America. Within the interdisciplinary endeavor of preparing *Renaissance Rereadings: Intertext and Context*, Julie A. Smith's woodcut illustrations of poet laureates and university masters wearing laurel wreaths and Paul F. Watson's evocative essay "To Paint Poetry" initiated my vision of this book as a visually documented work.[41]

Seeking the visual evidence directly accompanying literary images of trees of virtue or knowledge, I turned toward mystical works, herbals, rhetoric, book illustration, especially emblems. It was then that I noticed in texts that I had previously examined the treetop to which Seneca's seeds grow and the agricultural analogies in biblical commentaries; as my search broadened to include the vegetative metaphors in Western language and the visual imagery of mental vegetative growth, I interpreted anew Philo's allegory on Eden, Botticelli's *Primavera*, and the Chambre du Cerf in the papal palace in Avignon.

This book is evidence of the linguistic "turn" in history-of-ideas scholarship, not a turning of phrases into mere words but a reinvigoration of the symbolical and referential meaning of texts and images by elaboration of the linguistic and cultural contexts of their origins, permutations, and transformations. Quentin Skinner's seeking for new patterns of meaning and J. G. A. Pocock's inquiries into the history of political discourse have stimulated important studies within moral and political philosophy;[42] and within intellectual history, William J. Bouwsma appropriately draws attention to creative historians writing in dialogue with the neighboring disciplines of literature, linguistics, the arts, and anthropology.[43] The linguistic "turn" among historians of ideas, as announced by the executive editor of the *Journal of the History of Ideas*, Donald R. Kelley, "aims at the recovery of the rhetorical dimension of ideas." Kelley sums up: "To put it briefly and for present purposes, authorial intention connects text with historical context, while language, or a more particular political idiom, ties text to tradition, or canon."[44]

John E. Toews, expanding upon Martin Jay's recognition that the linguistic turn depends on the particular linguistic theory of meaning the historian adopts, views historians today as willing to consider " 'signs' whose meanings are determined by their relations to each other, rather than by their relation to some 'transcendental' or extralinguistic object or subject," and yet historians' main concern is to study "worlds of meaning . . . as responses to, and shapings of, changing worlds of experience ultimately irreducible to the linguistic forms in which they appear."[45] That insight directs us to the breaks and continuities between cultural traditions and challenges us to contextually approach the sign theories of the authors we study, theories that may in fact assume metaphysical ideas or physically visible referents.

Contemporary linguistic theories problematize the historical study of medieval and Renaissance signs designed to refer to the great book of nature revealing God's providence. In elaborating meaning for a time when analogies of microcosm and macrocosm were not metaphors but both theology and natural philosophy, we expose a variety of instances in the literary and visual arts of belief that the pattern of growth in the vegetative world signifies the pattern of growth in the human mind. The canon division that the scientifically minded associate with the scientific perspectives of the mid-seventeenth century makes it difficult to understand the preceding medieval and Renaissance viewpoints,[46] as well as to understand the persistence of theological and humanistic viewpoints, including what I interpret as the "language of vegetative growth," into our own times.[47] Through the ritual giving of flowers as gifts, the signs related to the virtue of friendship budding and blossoming resonate in our lives.[48]

Intrigued by the presence of the internal natural-law tradition in private and public spheres—for individual and civic ethics—I hope this book will contribute to the current quest to elucidate and improve upon the historical languages of Western moral and political philosophy. Within the language of vegetative growth, Cicero's tracing the foundation of the commonwealth to "gregarious impulses" or "seeds" is an important application to political philosophy, just as Seneca's view that "nature could not teach us this directly; she has given us the seeds of knowledge, but not knowledge itself" is a basic application to epistemology and ethics. The contributors to *The Languages of Political Theory in Early-Modern Europe* provide excellent examples of what Anthony Pagden labels the four "most important, most easily identifiable languages of political theory in use in early-modern Europe": "the language of the law of nature and what has become 'political Aristotelianism'; the language of classical republicanism; the language of political economy; and the language of the science of politics."[49] Examples may be found in this book of the complex interweaving of the political languages, for the language of vegetative growth permeates the early modern political languages.[50]

While chapter 1 attributes the vegetative language of natural law to the Stoics, chapter 2 exposes Stoic vegetative aspects of the Aristotelian-Thomist language of natural law. Distinguishing between the political and theological implications of these two natural-law traditions on household and state is especially important because Cicero asserts deliberative reason (*recta ratio*) in humans—men and women of all ranks and cultures—whereas Aristotle asserts nonlimited deliberative reason (*bouletikon*) only in citizen men.[51] The influence of Ciceronian vegetative language on humanists and on humanist discourse on republics is evident especially in chapters 1, 5, 7, and 8. Two applications to political economy are Ficino's praise of human productivity and Jean Bodin's argument for increased foreign trade, that "the light of virtue is so bright that not only does it chase away vicious gloom but also it gleams the more it is communicated."[52] Explicitly trying to aid the science of politics, Bodin contributes the hope that the seed of knowledge will transform comparative study of law, history, and government into a science; Montaigne suggests that the likeliest truly natural law is self-preservation and affection for offspring. The eclectic Stoic phrases, indeed, enter into what J. G. A. Pocock calls the "languages employed by specific communities in their professional discourse," for one will find here numerous examples from the "language of medieval scholastic, of Renaissance emblematic, of biblical exegesis."[53]

In this history of the idea of seeds of virtue and knowledge I shall show, when appropriate, how seeds and sparks function as epistemology, paradigm, and educational and civic strategy; I shall have occasion to view important intertexts (accepted on authority)[54] and visually evocative metaphors, as in Bodin's and, through him, Charron's borrowing of Philo's garden of the soul. Linguistic issues help to clarify the cluster of metaphoric images that serve as a mode of Western thought and perception: a language of vegetative growth. I ask my reader, who is welcome to turn to any leaf, Is the phenomenon of seeds and sparks of virtue and knowledge best understood as an idea, a strategy, a paradigm, an intertext, a metaphor, or a language?

Historians have neglected the topic of seeds. There is no work on the two millennia of Western ideas of seeds, sparks, common notions, and reason, nor is there a work that elucidates the particular importance of seeds of virtue and knowledge in the French Renaissance. It is not simply a question of "missing the forest for the trees" but one of not recognizing the worldwide forests created by the human mind as we pursue a particular branch, or rather twig, of knowledge. Trees and their fruit have received more attention; the forests of books claiming that seeds of virtue and knowledge are scattered in our minds have not been assessed until now. And now is a good time, for the turn toward the twenty-first century is a time of gene research and speculation about genes. While medical research focuses on genetic defects, genetic diseases, and mental disorders that may be a factor in antisocial behavior,[55] it is most appropriate to reconsider the tradition among natural philosophers, theologians, and humanists of strategic belief in seeds of social behavior.

The usage of the terms *seeds, sparks, common notions*, and *reason* provides an important clue to an author's epistemology. One can seek clues in texts and in images to find common patterns, such as the "favorite words and phrases . . . most people introduce into their speaking and writing unintentionally, often without realizing it" (by which computers test authorial authenticity today) that Giovanni Morelli in the 1870s compared to the "material trifles" in an artwork by which he determined authenticity.[56] There is evidence in this book that the specifics of an author's vegetative and light symbolism are a clue to the author's functional epistemology. This introduction, in clarifying the limitations of this particular study in the context of its broader ramifications, suggests some important implications of this omnipresent yet relatively neglected ancient commonplace.

Is the conceptual framework of seeds blossoming into wisdom an antiquated relic of the past or a continuing functional way of thinking? On one hand, the phrases *semina virtutum* and *semina scientiae* are artifacts of a bygone era. In the fast-paced twentieth century we often participate in cultural lag, the experience of clinging to ideas or attitudes in one area of life that our convictions or scientific understanding in another area of life or discipline have undermined. On the other hand, considering these phrases' close correlation with some others, there are remnants of premodern approaches to education in our current semantics (from the Greek *semantikos,* "significant," and *sema,* "sign").

Not only in seminaries (*seminarium,* "seed plot," "seedbed," "nursery") but mainly in colleges and universities, students meet in seminars (Greek *seminar,* Latin *seminarium*), as did their medieval and Renaissance predecessors, and that is where seminal ideas (Latin *semen,* "seed") are to pass from professor to student or, in more triangular fashion, between students and professor for the dissemination of knowledge (Latin *disseminatus,* from *disseminare,* "to sow"). There is no way one may overlook the connotation of potency in this imagery in premodern times for all male educational institutions; the Renaissance women scholars we shall discuss pursue their studies in a cultural environment that views them as *viragos.* Nor may one miss the fertility evident in the vegetative decoration, however purely ornamental and routine, that colors the "leaves," or folios (Latin *folium,* "leaf"), of medieval and Renaissance manuscripts and books. *Foliate* (leafy) ornament abounds.[57]

Today, we apply for *seed money* from granting agencies to gain funding to develop *seminal* ideas. Those who no longer contribute new ideas are jokingly referred to as *dead wood.*[58] To avoid such a fate, we *nip* bad habits *in the bud,* and try to *turn a new leaf.* We pursue the various *branches* of learning in hopes of contributing to the *flowering* of culture. And this latter hope links to our thinking in the organic and vegetative symbolism of historical periodization, a leitmotif of Renaissance humanists that I shall show to be closely allied with epistemologies of seeds of virtue and knowledge— the *budding* graduate student, the *sprouting* of genius, the *flourishing* of a city, the *roots* of the age's greatness, the *rebirth* of culture after an *infertile winter.* Would I go *out on a limb* if I suggested that today a student meditating on the biblical psalms of David on a beautifully landscaped college lawn might awaken the vegetative language of spiritual growth?[59]

The vegetative symbolism takes on new applications for aesthetic theory and for theories of genius in the romantic movement of the late eighteenth and nineteenth centuries.[60] In the philosophy of education, educators such as Johann Heinrich Pestalozzi and Jean Piaget have influence and keep

vegetative analogies vibrant in modern educational theory; for early childhood education we place students in *nurseries* and, since Froebel, in gardens for children, *kindergartens*. Vegetative imagery still abounds, perhaps
sometimes dissociated from organic growth, even in references to the *trees*
by which data are organized in computer science.[61]

Although the Stoic, Platonic, and abundantly eclectic epistemological
foundations (seeds of virtue and knowledge divinely implanted in our
minds) may have declined, the verbal form of ideas growing, flourishing,
and dying is applied in theoretical discussion of language. Generally, it is
not hard to find examples of the vegetative and procreative imagery currently in use.[62] One example will suffice: under "Metaphor in Philosophy"
in the *Dictionary of the History of Ideas*, S. C. Pepper sums up his "Root
Metaphor Theory," which is not about plant images but about the origin
and development of schools of philosophy, by discussing "pregnant" experience and a "fruitful" world hypothesis. The four "root" metaphors discussed are formism, mechanism, organicism, and contextualism.[63] While
the organic metaphor we are studying does not fit into Pepper's category
"organicism," the exact form of the organic metaphor we are seeking
abounds in his labels and in the description of how metaphor emerges!
Influenced by Quentin Skinner's questions on historical agency and history
of ideas, I expose some of the intellectual origins of the organic language
for describing an idea "born" or "gaining ground" and try to refrain from
the mythology of treating ideas as organisms developing toward an ideal
type.[64]

Continuing controversy on assessing humanity. The themes discussed historically in this book continue to echo in books teaching religiously based
ethics with titles such as *Clusters of Grapes: Sow a Character and You Reap
a Destiny* or *A Living Tree: The Roots and Growth of Jewish Law*.[65] Viewing
human conscience as the voice of God is a commonplace of modern Reform Judaism, as well as of Protestantism: "In fact, conscience is the voice
of God, and when you hear the voice of conscience within you, you are
really hearing God speaking to you; and if your conscience tells you you
ought to do something and you do not do it, you are really disobeying
God."[66] In the controversies surrounding contemporary mores and morality, we find the issues of how to teach ethics without theological dogma-
tism (so prevalent in the texts discussed here from the Middle Ages, the
Renaissance, and the Reformation) alive in contemporary life.[67] It is encouraging that both philosophers and theologians are seeking "a vocabulary for moral discourse in which Christians and non-Christians can participate equally."[68] Meanwhile the gap between popular and elite cultures may
never have been greater than it is today, ironically an age of mass culture.

Intentionally writing disruptively, Jacques Derrida in *La dissémination*
attempts to sound the death knell for Western beliefs that words might be
seedbeds for the dissemination of knowledge, that there are trees of ascent
to the Divine, that the common occurrence of an idea reflects its truth.

Although he does not cite any examples of the phrase *seeds of virtue* or *seeds of knowledge* per se, Derrida exposes the traditional analogy between words and flower buds, between term (*terme*) and seed (*germe* or *semina*), and plays with the lack of referentiality in texts to any true Platonic Number or true Idea. From a Derridean perspective, all texts, whether quoting or not, are recombinations of words built from other texts, whether quoted or not. Such unquoted quotations (intertexts) contrast with Derrida's citations of Philippe Sollers's *Numbers*, which Derrida both italicizes and quotes.[69]

While the authors we shall study are influenced by the embryological theories derived from the Bible, Aristotle, or Galen, all of which teach that any one living being derives from one seed, Derrida's phraseology reflects the twentieth-century embryological theory of the combining of genes from one ovum with those from one sperm of the many sperms available in semen.[70] He talks of the human incapacity to trace ultimate origins of either species or cultures:

> It is a singular plural, which no single origin will ever have preceded. Germination, dissemination. There is no first insemination. The semen is already swarming. The "primal" insemination is dissemination. A trace a graft whose traces have been lost. Whether in the case of what is called "language" (discourse, text, etc.) or in the case of some "real" seed-sowing, each term is indeed a germ, and each germ a term. The term, the atomic element, engenders by division, grafting, proliferation. It is a seed and not an absolute term. . . .
>
> If this in itself were intended to mean something, it would be that there is nothing prior to the group, no simple ordinary unit prior to this division through which life comes to see itself and the seed is multiplied from the start. (337–38; 304)

Derrida derides the worldwide tradition of the mystic's internal ascent through a column, a pole, a tower, or a tree (figs. 3.1, E.4); Derrida views the tree at the center of the soul or of a culture as air, hot air, which is assumed to rise! He spoofs such images as a tree rising to its divine source by the image in his text of *i*, the letter's upper dot always suspended like a head displaced from its body. "The column is nothing, has no meaning in itself. A hollow phallus, cut from itself, decapitated (i), it guarantees the innumerable passage of dissemination and the playful displacement of the margins" (381; 342). All writing is commentary on other writing and thus is on the margins. To Derrida, medieval and Renaissance Christian and Jewish authors who read nature as the book of God or who utilize mystic texts to ascend are looking at mirror reflections of mirrors, merely commenting on previous linguistically produced texts. Many of the authors discussed here would not disagree that their works are commentaries on previous ones; however, they cherish ancient texts that they believe are divinely inspired, and they read the evident repetition of nature as evidence for the natural law written into human nature as well. Like Derrida, our premodern authors struggle with the criterion for truth, but unlike him, even such Skeptics as Michel de Montaigne and Pierre Charron believe that God has left traces of the truth.[71]

All these images of transplantation of citations lead to Derrida's double image of "rootlessness" in trees and in number theory: "The tree is ultimately rootless. And at the same time, in this tree of numbers and square roots, everything is a root, too, since the grafted shoots themselves compose the whole of the body proper" (396; 356). Among ancient Pythagoreans, Platonists, as well as medieval natural-law theorists, mathematics is the model area of self-evident truths: for example, from the self-evidence of the equation $2 + 2 = 4$ one might point out the self-evidence that it is always good to flee evil and seek good. Likewise, if one squares the square root of any number, one will return to the number. Derrida hits logocentricity at its roots, so to speak, quoting Sollers's novel *Numbers*, with its numbered passages: "4.80. . . . *Desire appeared first, wandering about over everything. It already existed before the germ of any thought /* . . . *Germs, seeds sown innumerable number.*" Citing another passage, he goes on: "1.81. . . . *past and future germs.* . . . *Germs, grouped and disseminated, formulae that are more and more derivative*" (376; 338). Spoofing the tradition of the commonplace book (which I discuss in chapter 5) by making the following words dance across the page like a great saying, Derrida discloses that axioms or commonplaces ring true only on account of familiarity and repetition: "it is only by virtue of two texts being repeated that one can enjoy any one part whole or by virtue of the turning around of the same text" (365; 329).

The epistemology of seeds and common notions and the metaphor of the tree at the center are important targets of Derrida's contemporary criticism of the Western tradition. From a postromantic, relativist, historicist perspective, the idea of seeds as an inborn potential for wisdom has several bizarre yet nostalgically attractive features: the implication that concepts bloom like flowers within humankind, the authoritative appeal to universal agreement, and the claim that there is a universal, timeless true wisdom. In addition, from a postmodernist perspective, *seeds of virtue* is a figurative organic metaphor that falls within Derrida's category "mythology in philosophy," a linguistic fiction basic to the historic relic of *logocentricity*, the Heraclitean notion, adopted by the Stoics, that logos (reason) within the human mind corresponds to the logos inherent in reality.

From contemporary Continental as well as Anglo-American writings on the history of discourse, rationality—including knowledge and law—would reflect agreement of a group. These postmodern questions echo the debates between Plato and the Sophists and between the Stoics and the Epicureans on whether there is more to knowledge or law than the agreement of a group.[72] The methodologies by which one confirms or creates knowledge likewise would move forward through group consensus or meet disruption through crises in agreement on methodologies. Within the continuing controversy surrounding Arthur Lovejoy's *Great Chain of Being*, my inquiry explores a "tiny grain of being" wherein the Stoic and eclectic modifications of Platonic ideas have been hiding from Skeptics and even within some Skeptics for centuries innumerable.[73]

With our twentieth-century limits in mind, let us inquire into the enduring folk psychology evident in our languages and in our theorizing of assuming that the mind develops like a plant or a tree. To expose the full-scale theory and images may be either deconstructive or constructive:[74] authors are not empowered to control the application of their work. In fact, the process by which an assumption becomes an idea available for a historian's analysis already indicates a social process of cultural deconstruction well under way: one might think of World War I, which shattered European social optimism, the context in which J. B. Bury wrote the *History of the Idea of Progress*.[75] My hope, however, is that greater understanding of the history and diverse applications of a cluster of phrases and of their accompanying educational and civic strategies will be constructive for reaffirming human dignity.

In contrast to the post–World War II fascination with theorists of human evil and the traditional overemphasis on the Christian idea of original sin, this book joins others in providing evidence that the idea of human potential for knowledge and virtue is a key idea in Western culture. Such works contribute to the ongoing reassessment of Western philosophical anthropology.[76] In chapter 6 I show the impact of both biblical and philosophical vegetative language during four centuries of consideration of the dignity of human nature. It is particularly important to focus in depth on these two rival and overlapping strands of thought during the Renaissance, the Protestant Reformation, and the Catholic Reformation, for in the sixteenth century the doctrine of original sin clashes head-on with the epistemology of seeds of virtue and knowledge. The results have significant impact on developments in humanistic education, legal practice, state politics, church politics, ethics, and natural philosophy, as well as theology. Much more has been written about ideas of original sin and of Christian redemption than about ideas of natural potential for virtue and knowledge; in correcting the imbalance, I explore relationships between individual thinkers and between historical movements.

A book on seeds of virtue and knowledge is especially appropriate given the ecumenical accomplishments of Vatican II, reaffirmed in 1993 in Pope John Paul II's *Splendor of Truth*. The sources in classical, Hebrew, and Christian civilization for belief in a human capacity for virtue may aid ecumenical efforts for building mutual respect and community among peoples of diverse faiths and traditions. The Second Vatican Council, opened by Pope John XXIII in October 1962 and completed by Pope Paul VI in December 1965, published within its final Latin report "The Declaration on the Relationship of the Church to Non-Christian Religions," "The Declaration on Religious Freedom," and "The Decree in Ecumenism." The

Synod of Bishops, called by Pope John Paul II in 1985 to reevaluate Vatican II, affirmed the important principles of the above documents: "The Second Vatican Council affirmed that the Catholic Church denies nothing which is true and which is holy in other non-Christian religions. . . . The Council also affirms that God does not deny the possibility of salvation to all men of good will."[77] More poignantly ringing in the contemporary conscience is a Jewish woman's diary entry of 15 July 1944: "It's really a wonder that I haven't dropped all my ideals. . . . Yet I keep them, because in spite of everything I still believe that people are really good at heart."[78]

This book focuses not on the issue of salvation or justification but on the issue of people of goodwill. Notwithstanding the plentiful evidence here of ancient Greeks or Romans proclaiming natural paths to virtue and Jews providing guidance for the righteous life, my main focus will be the evidence of several traditions of Christian belief in the capacity of non-Christians to attain virtue. This trend within Christianity is the view that I label "inclusive" and "ecumenical."

In presenting a history of seeds of virtue and knowledge from ancient Stoicism to the neo-Stoic movement at the turn of the seventeenth century, a span of almost two thousand years, I am drawing attention to an enduring and significant human thought and image pattern. I hope to make apparent and available to those who consider themselves religious and to those who consider themselves secular, as well as to those still searching, some of the beliefs found in Greek, Roman, Jewish, Christian, humanist, and philosophical texts that it is possible—because all human beings share a common potent source for wisdom—to cultivate in oneself, children, students, and the human community a garden of beauty, truth, and goodness.

Stoic Seeds of Virtue and Sparks of Divinity

MANY MORAL TREATISES of the Renaissance have as an underlying assumption that God-written natural law is within human nature, providing the potential to become virtuous. Some Renaissance writers emphasize the role of God's grace in actualizing the potential; others emphasize the role of the liberal arts in the development of human nature. A Renaissance author's implicit belief in the existence of natural law in us is often revealed by his or her use of various images: human *reason* is said to be a part of the reason governing the universe; the *notion* of goodness is said to be common to all people; *seeds* implanted by God in us at birth blossom into true virtue; *sparks* kindle in humanity, enlightening the mind with wisdom.

Reason, common notions, seeds, and *sparks* represent the sources of virtue in human nature—male and female.[1] They express how humankind is linked to God's universal law by a natural law within. These ideas may be traced to their original synthesis in the writings of the ancient Greek and Roman Stoics. Although the Stoics borrow some of these terms from their philosophical predecessors, they do the work of synthesis themselves, weaving these words into a coherent doctrine of human natural law.

Without the benefit of modern critical scholarship, which has assembled and categorized the fragments of the Stoics, the ideas we shall discuss now in their full synthesis come down to Renaissance scholars often without precise authorship and often via later authors. Ficino and, following his guidance, Bodin are to attribute many of these Stoic ideas to the Platonic Academy; in fact it is hard to distinguish Stoicizing Platonism from Platonizing Stoicism. The two ancient authors from whom Renaissance authors gain most of their knowledge of these doctrines are the Platonizing Stoic educators Cicero and Seneca, whom I shall discuss more thoroughly than I do other Stoics.[2] Other classical authors who are important for the Renaissance absorption of the Stoic "natural path to wisdom" include the Latin authors Quintilian and Virgil and the Greek authors Diogenes Laertius, Epictetus, Plutarch, Philo, and Plotinus.

REASON

The concept reason is integral to the Stoic doctrine of natural law. Cleanthes (ca. 305–230 B.C.E.) teaches that virtue is "living agreeably to nature in the right exercise of reason," which he holds to consist in the selection of things in accordance with nature.[3] Virtue emerges from right action, which is a product of *orthos logos*, "right reason." In the "Hymn to Zeus" God's reason flows through the universe, giving order and direction to all things. Humankind, distinct in this from all other things, has a unique reason through which the divine *logos* flows: we may spurn this divine gift and lead a wicked life, or we may be guided by reason to God's universal law and accordingly lead a life of righteousness.[4] Chrysippus (ca. 280–207 B.C.E.) explains the different paths by which animals and humans live "according to nature": animals follow impulse; however, humans, endowed with natural reason, follow not impulse but reason. The ruling part of the human soul, *hégemonikon*, is important to sixteenth-century French authors, who translate it as *l'esprit*, that is, mind including reason and will. In following reason, humankind acts in accord with the right reason of the universe, which for Stoics after Chrysippus is identical with *nomos koinos* (universal law).[5]

The extant fragments attribute the identification of God with divine and natural law to the founder of the Stoic school in Athens, Zeno of Citium (ca. 336–264 B.C.E.).[6] Those teaching in the Stoa Poikile (Painted Porch), on the northern side of the Athenian agora, participate vigorously in the controversies between the schools. The Stoics build upon the linkage of *physis* (nature) and *nomos* (law) in the Heraclitean notion of a *theios nomos* (divine law).[7] They also borrow from Plato, who argues that justice exists by nature (*physei*) and in nature (*en tê physei*), to discredit both Sophists and Epicureans, who argue that *nomos* (law) is relative and contingent.[8] Ironically, it is a Skeptical director of Plato's Academy, Carneades, who in 156 B.C.E. presents in the Roman Forum the Stoic theory of justice, and the next day he presents his Academic Skeptic rejection, arguing that humans cannot achieve certainty. Cicero reverses the order of Carneades' two speeches and gives the final word to the defense of Stoic natural justice.[9]

As if stating a commonplace, Cicero (106–43 B.C.E.) defines law as *ratio* (reason).[10] When human reason is developed, it becomes like God's and is rightly called wisdom.[11] Since by definition law is "right reason applied to command and prohibition," we have received with God's gift of reason the gift of law.[12] Cicero concludes: "Hence we must now conceive of this whole universe as one commonwealth of which both gods and men are members."[13] It is significant that both gods and humans are members of this commonwealth: the law of justice is not handed down from gods to humankind but is present in both kinds of beings in the form of right reason. Both Cicero and Philo of Alexandria (20 B.C.E.–ca. 50 C.E.), a Hellenistic Jew reading and writing in Greek who has a significant impact on early church fathers and, as we shall see, on such Renaissance authors as Pico della Mirandola and Bodin, present as Stoic their own distinctions between God and nature and between God and his law. Like Cicero, Philo affirms that "this world is the Megalopolis or 'great city,' and it has a single polity and a single law, and this is the word or reason of nature, commanding what should be done and forbidding what should not be done."[14]

Cicero's definition of law as the reason that exists in nature allows him to found his concept of justice on his concept of law:

> Well then, the most learned men have determined to begin with Law, and it would seem that they are right, if, according to their definition, Law is the highest reason, implanted in Nature, which commands what ought to be done and forbids the opposite. This reason, when firmly fixed and fully developed in the mind, is Law. . . . Now if this is correct, as I think it to be in general, then the origin of Justice is to be found in Law, for Law is a natural force; it is the mind and reason of the intelligent man, the standard by which Justice and Injustice are measured.[15]

Passed down through Lactantius and cited often in medieval and Renaissance texts, Cicero's passage clarifies that what makes law natural is its presence in human nature; it is the fully developed reason.

COMMON NOTIONS

The Stoic epistemology explains how human reason comes to know the dictates of natural law. The starting point is the Epicurean theory that repetition of *phantasiai* (perceptions) inductively brings about a *prolêpseis* (notion, or preconception) in the human mind. Epicurus's (ca. 341–270 B.C.E.) contemporary Zeno uses the term *ennoia* to express the concept notion. Although it is not exactly equivalent to Epicurus's term, it is close enough for Diogenes Laertius to use the term *ennoia* to define *prolêpseis*: "By preconception [*prolêpseis*] they [Epicureans] mean a sort of apprehension of a right opinion or notion [*ennoia*], or universal idea stored in the mind."[16] The term *prolêpseis* is borrowed from the Epicureans and incorporated in new ways in Stoic teaching by Chrysippus.[17]

In the early Stoic view, certain *phantasiai* force the mind to assent to them. These self-evident perceptions or presentations reveal the truth about things and are called *phantasiai kataléptikei* (comprehensive presentations). These irresistible perceptions, carrying the power of true conviction, are the possession of the wise man or woman.[18] Despite the attacks of the Academic Skeptics, who doubt the reliability of sense data and therefore question the validity of both *prolêpseis* and *katalêpsis*,[19] the Stoics remain firmly convinced that there is a criterion of truth.[20]

The issue of the criterion is to be particularly relevant in the sixteenth century. Stoic concern about whether the criterion of truth is in the senses, in reason, or in both is made apparent by Aëtius in a passage precedent to medieval scholastic debate and to epistemological passages in Bodin, Montaigne, and Charron:

> The Stoics say: When a man is born, the ruling part of the soul is like a sheet of paper suitable for writing. On this he writes off each single thought. . . .

> That which comes through the senses is the first thing written down. . . . But
> of thoughts [*ennoiai*], some arise naturally in the ways already mentioned,
> without technical skill, while others come by our teaching and conscious ef-
> fort. These latter are called thoughts only (*ennoiai*) but the others are also
> termed preconceptions [*prolêpseis*]. Now reason [*logos*], because of which we
> are called rational, is said to have received all its preconceptions by the time a
> child is seven years old. And a notion is an image of the mind of a rational
> living being—for when the image strikes a rational soul, then it is called a
> notion, taking its name from that of mind.[21]

The Aristotelian opening statement that the mind is a blank tablet appears
to be contradicted later by the statement that some thoughts arise naturally. The beginning of this passage gives ample evidence of the Stoic emphasis on sense knowledge; the end gives ample evidence of the Stoic
emphasis on rational knowledge. This apparent contradiction, however,
can be partially resolved. Seneca (3 B.C.E.–65 C.E.) writes: "Every living
thing possessed of reason is inactive if it is not first stirred by some external
impression; then the impulse comes, and finally assent confirms the impulse."[22] Sensation is thus necessary for the development of reason. When
Aëtius writes that some thoughts "arise naturally in the ways already mentioned," he is referring to the natural development of thought from the
accumulation of sense perceptions in the mind.

The description of the mind as "a blank tablet" is transformed as the
materialist Stoic tradition becomes Platonized. Chrysippus gives as an example that the mind in receiving the image of a triangle would take on the
shape of a triangle but modifies the doctrine so that *impression* may mean
a qualitative change in the soul.[23] His term *prolêpseis* refers to perceptions
penetrated by reason. The common notions, such as the idea of God or of
goodness, arise in the spontaneous reasoning of all people.[24] Aëtius says
that the Stoics conclude that there are gods from their observations of the
beauty and order of the universe; Cicero points out that the Stoics arrive at
the notion that there is goodness from their observations of the many acts
perceived to be good. Through this inductive procedure, certain notions
arise *physei ou technêi*, "by nature not by art."[25] Stoic epistemology thus
reflects the tension between the influences of Aristotle's Lyceum and those
of Plato's Academy; during the period of the Middle Stoa, Panaetius
of Rhodes (ca. 185–110 B.C.E.) and Cicero's teacher Posidonius (135–
51 B.C.E.) increasingly Platonize Stoic thought.

Cicero supports the doctrine of common notions through his belief in
inchoata intelligentia, the rudimentary beginnings of intelligence: "With
no guide to point the way, she [Nature] starts with those things whose
character she has learned through the rudimentary beginnings of intelligence, and alone and unaided, strengthens and perfects the faculty of reason."[26] The direction in which a child's rudimentary intelligence will develop is universal, for "those rudimentary beginnings of intelligence to

which I have referred, which are imprinted on our minds, are imprinted on all minds alike."[27] The Stoic materialist imagery of imprinting remains in Cicero's terminology, indicating that the structure of the rudimentary knowledge is common in all humans; the process of attaining truth is an *enodatio*, or unraveling, of this rudimentary knowledge.[28]

The doctrine of common notions appears also in Seneca's *Epistles*, where he defends it on the grounds of *consensus gentium* (universal assent):

> In our eyes the fact that all men agree upon something is a proof of its truth. For instance, we infer that the gods exist, for this reason, among others—that there is implanted in everyone an idea concerning deity, and there is no people so far beyond the reach of laws and customs that it does not believe at least in gods of some sort. . . . I make the most of this general belief: you can find no one who does not hold that wisdom is a Good, and *being wise* also.[29]

The common occurrence of such beliefs indicates that they arise spontaneously and naturally, that they are common notions. Seneca appears to be quite proud of the argument from universal consent despite the criticism it received from the Academic Skeptics. Even though Cicero presents Carneades' arguments against the proof of universal consent,[30] he still believes that rudimentary intelligence is imprinted in all minds alike, that true law or right reason applies to all, and that "on every matter the consensus of all peoples is to be regarded as the law of nature."[31]

Many ancient philosophical schools teach that humans have an innate desire to know and an innate eudaimonistic desire for the good, but only a few philosophers, most preeminently Plato, teach that there are innate ideas in the mind that may be recalled. Nevertheless, the Stoic concept common notions has sometimes been confused with the concept innate ideas as defined and rejected by John Locke in the seventeenth century.[32] Locke's definition goes as follows: "It is an established opinion amongst some men, that there are in the understanding certain innate principles; some primary notions, *koinai ennoiai*, characters, as it were stamped upon the mind of man; which the soul receives in its very being, and brings into the world with it."[33] Locke is attacking the doctrine of innate ideas while utilizing the Stoic vocabulary of *koinai ennoiai* (common notions) and Stoic imagery of impressions stamped on the mind. The merging of Platonic and Stoic epistemology that Locke refutes in preachers, pamphlets, and tracts of his day has intellectual origins in fifteenth- and sixteenth-century texts.[34]

The Stoics believe that the mind is born predisposed to certain ideas that are not yet held. These ideas are evoked and developed through the stimulus of sense impressions and the development of reason. According to Seneca, "At our birth, nature made us teachable, and gave us reason, not perfect, but capable of being perfected."[35] The mind thus contains the potential for knowledge but not knowledge itself.

The one ancient Stoic who openly uses the term *innate* is Epictetus, translations of whose works influence the neo-Stoic revival in sixteenth-century France.[36] His strong belief in common notions may very well be the foundation for his adherence to the early Stoic idea of a world-state founded on natural law. In his *Discourses* the most important human faculty is reason—the one faculty that contemplates itself and makes correct use of external impressions. Observing that all human beings assume good to be profitable and worthy of choice and that all assume righteousness to be beautiful, he argues that these assumptions are preconceptions. From the argument of universal consent Epictetus comes to the view that "preconceptions are common to all men, and one preconception does not contradict another."[37] Conflict arises not concerning the preconceptions but concerning their application to particular cases. Education involves learning to apply our natural preconceptions, *physikai prolêpseis*, to particular cases and learning how to distinguish what is within our control from what is not. Our own moral behavior is the one thing within our control.[38]

Philosophy thus builds on the foundation of human preconceptions. We are particularly predisposed to moral preconceptions: "Who has come into being without an innate [*emphyton*] concept of what is good and evil, honorable and base, appropriate and inappropriate?"[39] Epictetus does not specify how much these ideas need to be developed in order to be consciously present in the mind of a child. He does indicate, however, that the natural preconceptions are often hidden by false opinions, which frequently supplant the truth of the innate concepts. Opinion needs to be replaced by an articulate organization of our preconceived notions. Philosophy thus begins with an examination of terms. Our notions need to be analyzed, systematized, and classified in proper relation to observed facts.[40] Epictetus gives elaborate examples of reflection on vague preconceptions, making them articulate and organized so that they may be used as a standard for judging actual experience. For example, the vague notion of evil does not lead everyone to conclude that death is no evil. The development of this conclusion can only be made with the aid of philosophy and the subsequent development of reason.[41]

The Stoic *koinai ennoiai* play an important role in Stoic epistemology. While no passage directly states that the common notions are the foundation of our knowledge of natural law, this assumption is implicit. Through the common notions we naturally and spontaneously come to know the good, the wise, the just, the beautiful, and God.

SEEDS TO TREES

In Stoic cosmology the whole universe is viewed as a living being. The identification of God with matter extends the previous philosophic tradition of the world as animate. Reason is said to pervade the universe as the soul pervades the body: "The whole world is a living being, endowed with soul and reason, and having aether for its ruling principle."[42] As an organism, the cosmos has both a natural birth and a natural death. God, or Logos, when referred to as the creative force of this animate universe, is called *logos spermatikos*, translated as "seminal reason," "seminal principles," or "creative reason." This term shows with striking clarity the biological framework within which the Stoics view the world.

Recent research has uncovered the Aristotelian biological basis of Stoic cosmology. Let me briefly explain and also stress how important and impressive it is in this context that the Stoic theory of seeds of virtue and knowledge contributes an inclusive generic philosophical anthropology supporting the moral and intellectual agencies of women and men. According to Aristotle, there are four categories of causes of anything coming to be—material, efficient, formal, and telic. In the case of the human embryo, the mother contributes the material and place for development; the father's semen provides no material contribution but is the impetus (the efficient cause), the coding, structure, or pattern (the *logos*, the formal cause), and the direction toward the form (the telic cause) of the embryo's development. In his unawareness of anything as minuscule as an ovum and his unwillingness to hypothesize a human equivalent to animal eggs, Aristotle attributes to the visible male semen the source of human generation. The male principle is spiritual and active; the female is material and passive. Furthermore, imprecise about whether he is talking about the father or the semen, Aristotle views the father as *homo faber*, the maker, working on inert matter to bring forth a child in the form of his own soul.[43]

Seneca is to struggle with the problem of Aristotle's four-cause theory in epistle 65. He utilizes Aristotle's theory to proclaim that for an artist making a sculpture the bronze is the matter, the workman the efficient cause, the formal cause the shape emerging, and the final cause the purpose of the artist, perhaps fame or money. There is a fifth cause as well—the pattern upon which the art is molded—which corresponds to the father as exemplar in Aristotelian biological theory. Seneca thus helps overcome Aristotle's ambiguity between father and semen as craftsman of the child. By adding to Aristotle's four-cause theory a significant fifth cause, which Seneca attributes to Plato, he allows later thinkers to argue that the father as exemplar is to mold the child through education. Renaissance educators such as Sadoleto are to apply the following Senecan passage to educational theory.

> To these Plato adds a fifth cause,—the pattern which he himself calls the "idea"; for it is this that the artist gazed upon when he created the work which he had decided to carry out. Now it makes no difference whether he has his pattern outside himself, that he may direct his glance to it, or within himself, conceived and placed there by himself. God has within himself these patterns of all things. . . ; he is filled with these shapes which Plato calls the "ideas,"— imperishable, unchangeable, not subject to decay. And therefore though men

die, humanity itself, or the idea of man, according to which man is moulded, lasts on, and though men toil and perish, it suffers no change.[44]

Wesley Trimpi points out that Seneca reduces the significance of the formal and final causes by squeezing between them "the exemplary model." Arthur Kinney labels this fifth cause the "Senecan original," and he elucidates many examples of its importance as a path taking Renaissance rhetoric away from sophistry into a stable realm wherein the Renaissance literary and visual artists may create.[45] Seneca's last sentence in the quotation above implies an application to education: a youth can imitate an exemplary human being and through that imitation come to recognize humanity itself. Sadoleto is to share with Seneca a lack of concern whether the pattern, or exemplar, is internal or external in humans—as writers, both participate in literary prescriptions meant to be internalized.

The Greek Stoics, well aware of Zeus's traditionally alleged sexual pursuits, adapt Aristotle's theory of fatherhood to the divine progenitor of the cosmos. In taking this theory over to his cosmology, or more precisely, cosmobiology, Zeno shows how the living organic cosmos emerges from the *archai*, the principles of genesis—efficient, telic, and formal principles combined—acting upon matter.[46] As Diogenes Laertius states, "Nature is defined as a force moving of itself, producing and preserving in being its offspring in accordance with seminal principles [*logous spermatikous*] within definite periods, and effecting results homogeneous with their sources."[47] As Zeller explains, "Generative powers in the plural, or *logoi spermatikoi*, are spoken of as belonging to Deity and Nature; and in treating of human nature, *logoi spermatikoi* denote the generative powers as a part of the soul, and must be thought of as bearing the same relation to the individual soul as the generative powers of Nature do to the soul of nature."[48] According to seminal principles, the offspring are similar to the *logos spermatikos*, or God, and thus the world and human beings in particular are of the nature of God.

The fullest explanation of the genesis of the world through the *logos spermatikos* occurs in Diogenes Laertius:

> God is one and the same with Reason, Fate, and Zeus; he is also called by many other names. In the beginning he was by himself; he transformed the whole of substance through air into water, and just as in animal generation the seed [*sperma*] has a moist vehicle, so in cosmic moisture God, who is the seminal reason [*logon spermatikon*] of the universe, remains behind in the moisture as such an agent, adapting matter to himself with a view to the next stage of creation. Thereupon he created first of all the four elements.[49]

Of the two principles of the world, the active one, *logos*, is viewed as existing in the beginning. In acting upon the passive principle, substance, *logos* is in fact acting upon the other aspect of itself in a pantheistic world. As becomes clear later, the substance that exists in the beginning is fire. In

Heraclitean fashion, fire turns into air, air into water, and water into earth.[50] The stage of water creates a moist fertile field from which God as seminal reason may create the various parts of the cosmos.

The combination of the terms *spermatikos* and *logos* implies both the matter and the form of things. God is seminal in that he is the original seed or germ from which all originates. God is reason in that he contains within himself the determination of the shape and qualities of all things that come to be. The *logos spermatikos* is the source of all matter and the source of the pattern of all that happens. Matter constantly changes its material form but always retains a permanent identity, an inherent law of process, the *logos*.[51] The phrase appears again, this time in Proclus, "And the Stoics believed that the seminal reasons . . . were imperishable."[52] The seminal reasons' imperishability explains how the same world may be created after each general conflagration: the determination of the pattern of world occurrences is contained in God as *logos spermatikos*, dwelling in primary matter.[53]

In Stoic doctrine the Greek term *spermata* and the Latin term *semina* (seeds) often substitutes for the phrase *logos spermatikos*. The origin of this substitution appears to be in the analogy of God in the universe to the seed in the womb: "The primary matter of all things is reality, is all eternal, and neither increases nor decreases. Its parts, however, are not always arranged in the same way, but are separated and are again conjoined. Throughout, this matter is arranged by the universal reason, which some call fate, and which is similar to the seed of the womb."[54] Stobaeus thus makes it clear that God as *logos* is the creative force of the universe, providing the plan for the changes in matter. But given the materialistic framework of the Stoic thinkers, *logos* itself is corporeal. The appropriate materialistic imagery appears to be *spermata*, for seeds contain within them the plan for future growth.

The Greek Stoics in a materialist manner absorb Heraclitus's and Plato's view that virtue exists by nature. In a Greek fragment concerned with comparing Stoic to Aristotelian ethics and to Empedocles' materialist view of good and evil derived from a mixture of elements, the Stoic virtue is presented as developing in accord with nature: "And finally it is by nature that we are all born according to virtue, in accordance with how we have our origins."[55] From the Greek Stoic concepts of *logos spermatikos* and virtue in accord with nature emerge the distinct Stoic Latin phrases *semina virtutis*, "seeds of virtue," and *semina scientiae*, "seeds of knowledge." These phrases are scattered throughout Stoic writing.

The Stoics Cicero and Seneca create the full-fledged theory of seeds of virtue and knowledge as a natural path to wisdom; and as major authors studied by medieval and Renaissance students they are a fundamental source for the transmission of the theory. Cicero uses the phrase *semina virtutum* to refer to the social nature of humankind. After accepting the opinion that men and women originally founded societies because it was in their nature to be social, he attributes the agreement of civil society to "certain seeds, as we may call them, for (otherwise) no source for the other virtues nor for the State itself could be discovered."[56]

Various threads of Stoic educational theory are expressed by Cicero:

> But that faculty which is highest and most excellent in man she [Nature] left lacking. It is true that she gave him a mind capable of receiving every virtue, and implanted at birth and without instruction some small intimations [*notitias*] of the greatest truths, and thus, as it were, laid the foundation for education and instilled into those faculties which the mind already had what may be called the germs of virtue [*elementa virtutis*]. But of virtue itself she merely furnished the rudiments; nothing more. Therefore it is our task (and when I say "our" I mean that it is the task of art) to supplement those mere beginnings by searching out the further developments which were implicit in them, until what we seek is fully attained.[57]

Cicero expresses pride that human reason naturally contains some notions of truth and some elements of virtue, and he exhorts humankind to utilize its arts in fulfilling what nature has left incomplete. Education is needed to cultivate human reason and bring it forth into wisdom.

The logical link between the concept *logos spermatikos* and the concept *semina scientiae* is best made evident by Seneca, who states: "The Stoics believe in one cause only,—the maker. . . . It is surely Creative Reason [*ratio faciens*],—in other words, God. For those elements to which you referred are not a great series of independent causes; they all hinge on one alone, and that will be the creative cause."[58] *Logos* becomes *ratio*, "reason," in Latin. Often the context implies reason as it is seminal in human nature. For Seneca, discussing the teachings of wisdom, says, "Then she goes back to the beginnings of things, to the eternal Reason which was imparted to the whole, and to the force which inheres in all the seeds of things, giving them the power to fashion each thing according to its kind."[59] Here *ratio* is clearly identified with the *semina* in all things: pervasive eternal reason is the source of all creativity.

In the gods reason is perfect; in humanity it is capable of being perfected.[60] Since perfect reason is called virtue,[61] the gods are virtuous by nature. There are also some exceptional men and women who attain virtue after only very short training, but most require more extended training to develop their reason and consequently their virtue. The very possibility that we may attain the virtue of the gods rests on the fact that we are derived from the gods and retain some divinity within us.[62] The part of divinity that exists in us—the *logos spermatikos* or *ratio*—is sometimes called *ratio* and sometimes called *semina scientiae*. The same message is repeated through the two kinds of Senecan imagery: "At our birth, nature made us teachable, and gave us reason, not perfect, but capable of being perfected."[63] "Nature could not teach us this directly; she has given us the seeds of knowledge, but not knowledge itself."[64]

Seneca explains how the seeds are developed in us. In our observation of the world we see analogies between things; thus from the observation of good acts we gain a notion of virtue. Hence, general notions are gained through inductive observation and reasoning. Both notions and seeds need to be developed before a student gains wisdom. Seneca's rejection of the doctrine of innate knowledge is evident as Seneca believes that virtue is not a gift of fortune but an achievement that requires training, teaching, and practice: "For the attainment of this boon, but not in the possession of it, were we born; and even in the best of men, before you refine them by instruction, there is but the stuff of virtue [*virtutis materia*], not virtue itself."[65] *Virtutis materia* is an expression very similar to Cicero's *inchoata intelligentia*; both expressions derive from Greek Stoic materialism. The stuff or beginnings of virtue are well described by the imagery of seeds.

In his epistle 124 Seneca extends his concept of seeds of virtue into an analogy of the child to a plant. He argues that goodness cannot be present in the delicate frame of the human infant,

> no more than in the seed. Granting the truth of this, we understand that there is a certain kind of Good of a tree or in a plant; but this is not true of its first growth, when the plant has just begun to spring forth out of the ground. There is a certain Good of wheat: it is not yet existent, however, in the swelling stalk, nor when the soft ear is pushing itself out of the husk, but only when summer days and its appointed maturity have ripened the wheat. Just as Nature in general does not produce her Good until she is brought to perfection, even so man's Good does not exist in man until both reason and man are perfected. And what is this Good? I shall tell you: it is a free mind, an upright mind, subjecting other things to itself and itself to nothing.[66]

It is important to understand Seneca's vegetative analogy, for it elucidates the Stoic theory of seeds of virtue, the rhetorician Quintilian's analogies of a student to a sapling,[67] and many Renaissance texts and images. Seneca's tree analogy has two purposes: to clarify the processes of reasoning as well as to clarify what it means for humans, in contrast to plants or animals, to live in accordance with nature. Thought growing from roots to treetop parallels a human developing from a sprout to an upright tree. To think that at birth we are already good, rather than at the beginning of becoming good, is to place "the tree-top where the root ought to be."[68] The development of the obvious upright human physical physique is necessary but not sufficient. Seneca, as we have seen, draws a parallel between the physical development of an upright plant or tree and the development of the *liber animus, erectus*, "the free upright mind." True goodness is not found in trees and grass or in dumb animals, because only humans and God share reason. "Indeed, to sum up, that alone is perfect which is perfect according to nature as a whole, and nature as a whole is possessed of reason."[69]

Sparks

In their pantheistic and materialistic outlook the Greek Stoics look upon God as the *logos spermatikos* and as the primary element *physis*. They accept Heraclitus's identification of *physis* with *pyr* (fire). As in Heraclitus, primary fire is distinct from the fire of our experience. Unlike ordinary fire, which consumes, *physis* is characterized by a warmth that preserves. In fact, fire is the one element in the universe that is never consumed; it remains eternal throughout the cyclical conflagrations and creations of worlds.[70] Saint Augustine states, "For the Stoics thought that fire, i.e., one of the four material elements of which the visible world is composed, was both animate and intelligent, the maker of the world and of all things contained in it, that it was in fact God,"[71] so that fire has the same characteristics as *logos spermatikos*—intelligence, animation, and creativity.

Discussions of the creation of the world use the concept of fire, or sometimes the concept of seminal reason or seed. In fact the view that fire is a self-generating seed explains how matter becomes the basis for the multiplicity of things. In the following accounts the two concepts are combined: "Now the primary fire is like a kind of seed, containing the reasons of all things and the causes of everything past, present, and future";[72] "Zeno, Cleanthes, and Chrysippus used to say that reality changes into fire like a seed, and again out of this the same kind of arrangement, such as formerly existed, is achieved."[73] By using the concept of fire Stoics stress the material source of the universe, and by combining it with the concept of seed they stress the identity of the passive material source with the active creative source: both are God.

Just as the imagery of God as *logos spermatikos* is the logical basis for the imagery of *semina virtutum*, the imagery of God as *pyr* is the basis for the imagery of sparks of divinity. Cicero speaks of an *igniculus*, a spark or little flame: "And in this whole discussion I want it understood that what I shall call Nature is (that which is implanted in us by Nature); that, however the corruption caused by bad habits is so great that the sparks of fire, so to speak, which Nature has kindled in us are extinguished by this corruption, and vices which are their opposites spring up and are established."[74] Nature, as the primary element fire, implants sparks (*igniculos*) in human beings. They are "kindled" by Nature, but they can be "extinguished" by bad upbringing. The concept of a spark is used by Cicero in the same way as he uses the concept of seeds, to indicate the element within that contains divine reason and virtue.

The versions of the Stoic creation story in which *pyr* plays an important role parallel the Stoic creation stories in which *logos spermatikos* plays the key role. As Censorinus reports, "Zeno of Citium, the founder of the Stoic School, believed that the origin of mankind was established out of a new world, the first man having been generated from the soil, by aid of the divine fire, that is, the providence of God."[75] Humanity is thus created out of the earth, which is the fourth element created from the primary fire; and the divine fire directly animates us. As Cicero summarizes, "Their doctrine is that all force is of the nature of fire, and that, because of this, animate creatures perish when their heat fails, also in every domain of nature a thing is alive and vigorous if it is warm."[76] Thus, for the Stoics fire or heat is a source of the vitality of human nature, a source that derives from human-kind's linkage to God the divine fire.

In Virgil's *Aeneid*, seeds and sparks are mixed together in an expression of the Stoic view of the world and of humankind. All of nature is nourished by one spirit (*spiritus*) and one mind (*mens*). This divine force is the motive power of all, the source of all living creatures.

> Thence man's race, and the beast, and the feathered creature that flies,
> All wild shapes that are hidden the gleaming waters beneath.
> Each elemental seed has a fiery force from the skies,
> Each its heavenly being, that no dull clay can disguise[77]

Living beings retain within themselves native seeds (*semines*), which have a fiery force (*igneus vigor*) from heaven. In this passage Virgil links the concepts of God as *logos* or *mens*, *semina*, and *igneus*. What living beings retain of the divine Creator is expressed as "seeds" and a "fiery force," revealing the influence of the Stoic concept of God as *logos spermatikos* and *pyr*. The cyclical theory and the conflagration also appear, for the souls of the dead are awaiting the time when all will return to fire.

> . . . Few reach to the fields of delight,
> Till great time, when the cycles have run their courses on high.
> Takes the inbred pollution, and leaves us only the bright
> Sense of heaven's own ether, and fire from the springs of the sky.[78]

Virgil expresses the Stoic and Heraclitean view that when the soul returns to its complete fiery state, it regains its purity and becomes godlike. In chapter 5 we shall see that female and male Italian humanists often cite the sixth book of Virgil, line 730, "Each elemental seed has a fiery force from the skies," to indicate powers of the human mind distributed among all of humankind as divine gifts.[79]

In Stoic thought, humans are intimately linked to God through the substance of their souls that they share with God. Humankind thus has direct access to natural law, which contains the precepts of individual and communal governance. The Stoics have several different ways of expressing this link between humankind and God. Law exists in nature as *logos*, *nous*, or *ratio*. We come to know this law through the *ratio*, the reason within us. Our reason is directed in its development by the *koinai ennoiai*, the common notions, which give us the potential to attain certain knowledge of the general notions God, goodness, justice, and beauty. A more figurative expression of the link between God and humanity is the idea that God as *logos spermatikos* leaves within us *spermata*, seeds of knowledge and virtue. The relationship may also be expressed in the conception of God as *pyr* (fire) leaving *igniculi* (sparks of divinity).

In Platonized Stoic texts, such as those of Cicero and Seneca, the phrases are transmitted to posterity in such a way that they are later interpreted by Jews and Christians as figurative images expressing the divinely created contribution to the human mind. This gift gives a human child not the full-blown knowledge of natural law but the potential to attain this knowledge. The goodness of a child is not fully developed at birth but, like a plant, develops gradually. Just as the goodness of a plant is visible when it has grown tall to maturity, a woman or man's virtue is visible when a full, upright mind (*liber animus, erectus*) has developed. The Stoic synthesis of the doctrine of natural law carries the conviction that all men and women may develop their God-given potential for knowledge and virtue.

The Challenge to Christian Theologians

STOIC LANGUAGE asserting that *ius naturale*, translatable as "natural law" or "natural right," is within human nature appears in a wide variety of medieval theological, philosophical, literary, and legal works.[1] In this chapter I will show that reason, common notions, seeds of virtue and knowledge, and sparks of conscience function as interrelated clusters of epistemological concepts within two distinct theological positions, most fully elucidated by Augustine (354–430) and Thomas Aquinas (ca. 1225–74). My elaboration of Ciceronian and Senecan images in Thomas Aquinas supplements the extensive studies of his "Aristotelian" natural law.[2] While this book is the first history of the epistemology of seeds and sparks, it does not treat that topic in isolation; this chapter documents that these literary images in theological texts correlate with important visual renditions of seeds and of trees of light and are equivalents of the well-known theological, philosophical, and legal concepts of reason and common notions.

Just as the Justinian Code, the sixth-century *Corpus Iuris Civilis*, strategically adds dignity and validity to Roman law by founding *ius gentium* (law of peoples) on natural law, Gratian declares at the beginning of his *Decretum* (1140) that "mankind is ruled by two laws: Natural law and Custom. Natural law is that which is contained in Scripture and Gospel"; the fifteenth-century *Corpus Iuris Canonici* continues Gratian's merger of natural law and biblical divine revelation to officially support church law.[3] Recent scholarship has documented that Stoic natural law influences medieval Western thought mainly through Cicero and other Roman orators rather than through Roman jurisprudence. Nevertheless, a wide spectrum of sixteenth-century thinkers, including Jacopo Sadoleto, Jean Bodin, Pierre Charron, and Jean Calvin, do cite the natural-law claims of Roman law and revealed law; for example, Sadoleto refers to the Roman Twelve Tables as "that seedplot of all equity and right," and Calvin refers to the essence of the Ten Commandments—loving God and one's neighbor—as "some seed in us, which proceeds from nature without ruler or legislator."[4]

The applications of the natural-law tradition have received more attention than have the epistemological foundations. From the mature Augustine on,[5] a major question is, Are humans so corrupted by original sin that they require divine illumination or biblical divine revelation to attain knowledge and virtue?[6] Among Christians the phrase *seeds of virtue* or *seeds of knowledge* is a clue to the enduring belief in natural and universal human potential provided by the divine Creator. Although the concepts reason, common notions, seeds, and sparks are truly commonplaces, this study of the meaning and application of these words shows significant variations in belief concerning the natural human capacity to be knowledgeable or virtuous.

In the first section below, I suggest the broader issues of the language of vegetative growth and of plant and light symbolism. The transformation of a pagan pinecone illustrates how classical notions of seeds are appropriated and Christianized as they pass into medieval civilization. Likewise, the Roman and Christian appropriations of a Jewish menorah, a "tree of light," and of Philo's Hellenistic readings of the Jewish Scriptures exemplify the Christianization of Jewish ritual and of Hebraic-Graeco ideas.

In the second section, I compare and contrast the usage of the Stoic phrases in the texts of Augustine and Thomas Aquinas, for they provide two poles of thought to which other medieval, Renaissance, Reformation, and later Christian authors refer. The intent here is to show that the differences between Augustine's and Aquinas's reformulations of the "natural law within" are consistently based on their differences of epistemology and to suggest that each theologian inherits ultimately from the Stoics the synthesis of "reason," "common notions," "seeds," and "sparks" as equivalent figures of thought.

My case studies of pagan and Jewish images and ideas elucidate the challenges facing Christians as they wrestle with the mystery of distinguishing divine wisdom (*sapientia*), cognition of divine or eternal things, especially as revealed in the New Testament, and human wisdom (*scientia*), knowledge of good and evil and of the sciences and arts helpful for living in society. On the one hand, the distinctively Christian path to wisdom through participation in the Logos, Jesus Christ, becomes among the church fathers a unique Christian way of transforming the Stoic vocabulary; on the other hand, the absorption of Stoic natural-law theory into the Justinian Code provides a practical vehicle for applying the Stoic vocabulary for the wise functioning of society.

Christians struggle to determine what the human mind derives from the gifts at Creation (*natura*) and what emerges from divine illumination or grace. The Stoic images, derived from a Greek pantheistic expression of the divine presence in nature, are adaptable to either theological or natural application or both. A complexity derives from Christians' considering the philosophically based Stoic definition of "wisdom as knowledge of divine and human things"[7] or the revelation-based Hebrew literature on wisdom, which teaches divinely revealed wisdom for a righteous life on earth.[8] The dialogue among Christians includes the very issue whether to proceed on the assumption that divine immanence allows for no isolation of natural potential or on the assumption that the distinction between Creator and created allows for theological precision concerning natural versus supernatural processes. Let us look first at some artifacts that suggest the challenges inherent in the appropriation and Christianization of ancient cultures, for the Renaissance artists and writers are to struggle again with how to construct syntheses.

CHRISTIANIZATION OF PAGAN AND JEWISH IMAGES AND IDEAS

Two first-century Roman objets d'art show how seed and light symbols become integrated into both Jewish and Christian thought, whence they become images of human potency in the Roman Catholic Church. Since my intention is to present mainstream Western thought, I discuss very conspicuous objects—the giant bronze pinecone in the Vatican (fig. 2.1) and the rendition of the temple menorah on the Arch of Titus (fig. 2.3).

Pinecones as seeds of virtue. The very large bronze pinecone is from the pagan first century. The three-and-one-half-meter macrocosmic replica represents a pinecone containing propagative seeds, and by its location it encourages virtue. It has stood since 1618 in the Cortile della Pigna, in the wing of the Cortile della Belvedere. A whole section of Rome, Rione Pigna, is named for this pinecone. In medieval times people thought the pinecone originated from the pinnacle of the dome of the Pantheon or from Hadrian's Mausoleum. These attributions show medieval Christian recognition of a pagan origin of the symbolic figure.

St. Peter's church, planned by the first Christian emperor, Constantine (306–37), for the bishop of Rome, had an atrium in use by the late fourth century and was completed by the early sixth century. Possibly under Pope Damasus I (serving from 366 to 384) but definitely before Pope Symmachus (498–514),[9] the gilded bronze pinecone was placed within a fountain, the Cantharus, at the center of Constantine's atrium in St. Peter's.[10] Until the dismantling of the forecourt by Pope Paul V (serving 1605–21) for the rebuilding of the nave of St. Peter's in 1605, the fountain remained a centerpiece; our first record of it as a fountain comes from the *mirabilia* of the twelfth century.[11] From openings both in the pinecone and in gilded peacocks where the wind creates musical sounds, a feature of many pagan fountains in antiquity, "water gushed ablutions of the faithful."[12] Not surprisingly, given the association of vegetative growth and water in lush literary and artistic renditions of the Garden of Eden and of Paradise,[13] the forecourt becomes known as the "*Paradiso* by the time of Dante."[14]

This pinecone is a vivid visual example of how ancient renditions of explanations for potency, that is, seed theories, are Christianized by the Roman Catholic Church. The pinecone's flamelike shape resembles that of the human phallus and takes on magical properties for fecundity in Assyrian monuments, Etruscan sepulchral urns, as well as on the gates of Rome in antiquity.[15] There is usually a small pinecone at the tip of Bacchus's wand, and pinecones are thrown into the sacred vaults of Demeter to cause fertility in women.[16]

We may appropriately feel awe before this antique image of potency enduring over the centuries in an indisputably Christian setting.[17] When the bishop of Rome placed the pinecone in the Cantharus, there were still pagans nearby to convert, and plants connoted to Christians innocent asexual propagation; by the time post-Trent Paul V relocated it in Michelangelo's

2.1. Christianization of a pagan seed of virtue. Ancient bronze pinecone
from the first century C.E, placed in old St. Peter's and relocated
in 1618 to the Cortilla della Pigna, Vatican.

new St. Peter's the papal library had commissioned the published translation of Theophrastus, the best ancient botanist, who contradicts his
teacher Aristotle in distinguishing male from female evergreen trees but is
openly perplexed by plant reproduction, and experimental botanical gardens had been set up to transplant seeds from newly discovered lands and
experiment on plant propagation.[18] Yet, much earlier any reader of the
Hexameron of Ambrose (339–97) might learn that the pinecone has a
sheath that protects its fruit and seeds within: "In this pinecone nature

seems to express an image of itself; it preserves its peculiar properties which it received from that divine and celestial command and it repeats in the succession and order of the years its generation until the end of time is fulfilled."[19]

In its use in ablution, the fountain represents a Christian adaptation of a variety of temple purification rites, reminiscent of the ritual baths for men and women that archaeologists have uncovered outside the outer wall of the Second Temple in Jerusalem. Gen. 1.28, "Be fruitful and multiply," in the allegorical interpretation of Clement of Alexandria (d. ca. 215), pseudo-Clement of Rome (third century), Eusebius of Caesarea (d. ca. 339), and later Isidore of Seville (d. 636) departs from its Jewish literal meaning of perpetuating God's creation of man and woman to become a declaration of taking on the life of celibacy and working to increase the spiritual membership in the specifically Christian church.[20]

The pinecone may likewise indicate the fruitfulness of spreading Christianity to new believers. For Christians one of the strengths of vegetative symbolism is the commonplace that plants propagate asexually.[21] Furthermore, in Rome the pinecone was associated with the eunuch priests who carried a sacred pine tree through Rome on the day of the Festival of the Great Mother Cybele, 22 March, and "eunuchs for the sake of Heaven" (Matt. 19.12) came to be interpreted as meaning celibacy.[22]

The viewing of a pinecone as "the fruit of Cybele" is illustrated by a Renaissance emblem in which a macrocosmic pinecone appears in a landscape (see fig. 2.2). The theme of the Stoic motto "Virtue is difficult but fruitful" is continued in the poem, which explains, as does St. Ambrose in his *Hexameron*, that the tough outer tufts of the pinecone hide sweet fruit within.[23] A sacred stone in Rome dating from the second Punic War shows Cybele carried by the priests.[24]

Another aspect of the association of the pinecone with Cybele is the story of Attis, who is imprisoned by the Great Mother Cybele in a pine tree, from which he is reborn in the spring.[25] Also, as Plutarch informs us, the son of the goddess Isis, Osiris, is reborn from a pine tree, and pinecones appear as offerings to Osiris on several monuments. A Judaeo-Christian version of such a tradition would make the pinecone imply resurrection of body and soul.[26]

Tree of light. Whereas the pinecone's location in the Vatican illustrates Christian appropriation of pagan art, the Arch of Titus commemorates the Roman suppression of the Jewish state of Palestine and Roman destruction of the Second Temple in the year 70. And whereas Christian authors discuss as a model for "appropriation" the Hebrew slaves stealing goods from the Egyptians for their exodus from Egypt, a more typical exemplum of appropriation is this poignant Roman bas-relief of the original ancient gold almond tree of light, a treasured ritual object commanded by Mosaic law to stand near the Holy Ark of the Torah (see fig. 2.3). The Roman stone carving of the menorah of the Second Temple in Jerusalem carried by newly

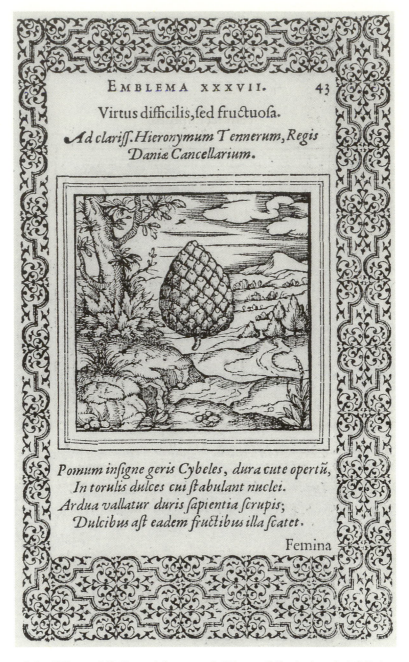

2.2. "Virtus difficilis, sed fructuosa" (Virtue difficult, but fruitful), in *Hadriani Iunii Medici Emblemata*, 1565. "You bear the fruit of Cybele with honor, / Fruit, hidden in a hard skin for which seek kernels / Have a stall in the tufts. Hard wisdom in protected by / Sharp stones but it likewise teems with sweet fruit."

2.3. Tree of light, Arch of Titus, the menorah being carried in a triumphal procession by the Roman soldiers after the conquest of Jerusalem in 70 C.E. Replica by Beth Hatefutsoth, Museum of the Diaspora, Tel Aviv, Israel.

enslaved Hebrews as booty for their Roman conquerors becomes an object familiar to the Christians in Rome after the year 81. Exod. 25.31 commands the cultural creation of a "candlestick of pure gold" with "cups" and "knobs" and "flowers." The seven-candle menorah is to have on each of two branches "three cups made like almond-blossoms." The original carved tree of light accompanies the Ark in the desert, and in abundant imitations it continues to light up synagogues with a light that is literal and resonates with symbolic, ritualistic, and political meanings.[27] The seven-candle menorah increases our wonder at the ways in which Western civilization amalgamates Hebrew, Greek, and Roman cultural traits in order to Christianize them.

Menorahs combine vegetative and light symbolism; candelabras become ritual objects in churches as well as in synagogues. After the appearance of the *Zohar* in the thirteenth century, the Hebrew symbol of the tree of light combines with symbolism of the Kabbalah. In numerous ways Jewish light symbolism for God and for the spark of the divine in humanity enters Christian thought. The almond tree of light, an important image in Pico della Mirandola's *Oratio*, brings together both vegetative symbolism, to which seed imagery belongs, and light symbolism, to which spark imagery belongs.[28]

Light symbolism is found in so many religions that it is difficult to identify when Stoic light imagery is the source except when the imagery is closely associated with phrases unique to Stoicism, such as *seeds of virtue*. Some Christian texts intentionally merge associations between the natural light from the sun and the spiritual light of the Divine and between the natural light of the created human intellect and that of the divinely illuminated human intellect. The notion that the natural world is a book of divine revelation encourages thinking of the natural as a sign of the spiritual.[29] I therefore view references to the more unusual and originally Stoic phrases *seeds of virtue* and *seeds of knowledge* as my best proof-texts for direct or indirect Stoic influence.

Philo of Alexandria. The Hellenization of Jewish thought by such Jewish authors as Philo of Alexandria (20 B.C.E.–50 C.E.) influences the early church. Contributing a Hebraic perspective to Stoic natural-law theory, Philo views the Hebrew God as the Divine Light of ancient philosophical and religious quests, as the Logos containing the Platonic Ideas, as the author of the natural law implanted in the first human being and of the revealed Mosaic law, which is a superior expression of natural law.[30] Before Aquinas makes precise distinctions between eternal law and divine, natural, and human law, it is common in medieval thought, as in Philo, to discuss divine law or eternal law rather than the Ciceronian natural law;[31] influenced by Philo, Jean Bodin returns to the prescholastic merger of natural law with divine law.

Besides Origen, who borrows much of Philo's allegorical reading of the Five Books of Moses, Christians who borrow from Philo's commentaries on the Greek version of the Hebrew Bible use Philo as a way of supplementing, not replacing, a literal biblical reading. Ambrose makes extensive use of Philo, citing him in *Paradise* 4.24 and indirectly in 2.11. Augustine, departing from his spiritual counselor Ambrose when the latter relies too much on allegorical meanings, contributes significantly to the multilayered hermeneutics of interpretation that retains the literal rendering of the Hebrew Bible and of the Greek New Testament.[32]

For example, an influential aspect of Philo's biblical interpretation is that in the first archetypal human being (*anthropos*, corresponding to the Hebrew word *adam*, "human being") Adam refers to reason or upper reason and Eve refers to sense perception or lower reason. To become a man means to apply one's upper reason to control one's lower reason and to conduct oneself in accordance with the divine Logos. Philo is well aware that the rule of *adam* parallels the rule of *hêgemonikon* over the human being in Stoic thought. Augustine views Adam and Eve as literally the first human couple but uses Philo's allegory to diminish the sexism in Paul's 1 Cor. 11.7–8. Augustine clarifies: "As we said for the nature of the human mind, that both in the case when as a whole it contemplates the truth it is the image of God. . . . But on the side whereby it is directed to the cognition of lower things, it is not the image of God."[33]

The presence of Stoic concepts in Philo of Alexandria's texts influences Greek fathers, Ambrose and then Augustine.[34] In Stoic thought, God is both the *logos* (reason) and *pneuma* (spirit or breath), through which we share in the divinity. *Logos* particularly refers to God as natural law, and thus the human reason and the seeds from the *logos spermatikos* are natural law within. From Gen. 1:26, which describes the human made in God's image, Philo concludes that the image of God is the Logos and that the human so created in God's mind is an archetype.[35] The Logos is an intermediary between God and the world that contains the Platonic forms. God creates the world on the model of the Logos, *sophia*, wisdom of the Jewish wisdom literature.

Philo's philosophy is inclusive, appreciative of the development of reason in Greeks, Romans, and Hebrews. Christian identification of Philo's term *logos* with Jesus Christ does not necessitate religious exclusivity. After studying under Stoics, Justin Martyr (d. 165 C.E.), who becomes a Christian in 130 C.E., identifies Logos with Jesus in a way that includes all rational people. To Justin Martyr, Jesus is as ubiquitous as Stoic reason in humanity and in the universe: "We have been taught that Christ is the first-born of God, and we have declared above that he is the Word of whom every race of men were partakers; and those who live reasonable (i.e., according to 'logos') are Christians, even though they have been thought atheists."[36]

Participation and illumination. Continuing a Christian reading of Philo's texts by identifying the Logos with Jesus Christ, Origen, Marius Victorinus (d. after 363), Augustine, and other church fathers are to find support in John 1.1 and 14: "In the beginning was the Word. . . . And the Word became flesh and dwelt among us." Philo's notions of logos as wisdom, logos as the container of the Platonic form, and logos as human reason all come to describe Jesus.[37] In the Christianization of the Stoic vocabulary in the New Testament and among the church fathers *pneuma* becomes identified with the third member of the Trinity, the Holy Spirit, and *logos* becomes identified with the second member, Christ. The divine presence in the human soul becomes apparent as *logos* continues to refer to reason and *pneuma* becomes a word referring to the highest part of the soul, to the "spirit."[38] In the following chapter, we see Philo's vegetative symbolism for the Logos—a macrocosmic tree or vine—illustrated on the walls of Dura Europos Synagogue. New Testament comparisons of Jesus to a vine are to clinch the Christianization of Philo's imagery.

Although Augustine appropriates the Stoic vocabulary for the natural law within, his attention to human participation in the Logos, or Christ, permeates his epistemology. One comes to know eternal law and its subordinate natural law, the "law written in the heart" of Romans 2, through illumination by the Logos.[39] According to Augustine, everything is what it is on account of its participation in the Logos, for Christ is the divine exemplar on which everything was formed. Wisdom involves the participation of the human soul in the eternal reasons, the ideas in the Godhead.[40] For Augustine the doctrine of illumination explains how one participates in the eternal reasons. As the Joannine Gospel declares, Christ is "the true light that enlightens every man."[41] One finds Christ by looking into one's own soul, where the "inner master" resides. Augustine interprets Matthew's statement "One is your master, Christ," to mean that humanity has one master, the inner truth presiding over his soul, Christ.[42] Knowledge thus is a process of remembering God, who is a transcendent presence in the soul. Although Augustine usually refers to God's presence as the Logos or Christ, sometimes he refers to it as Spirit: "But when it rightly remembers its own Lord, having received His Spirit, then because it is so taught by an inward teaching, it becomes fully aware."[43] As Christ or as the Holy Spirit, God is thus the very life of the soul, the source of its ability to know truth: "Our illumination is the partaking of the Word, namely of that life which is the light of man."[44]

Thus, the concept of participation in the Holy Spirit or in Christ provides a source of human knowledge of divine wisdom. In such a way is the whole concept of natural law reformulated in Christian attempts to reconcile it with the beliefs that reason is impaired by original sin and that the supreme human good is not virtue but salvation. Interestingly, the Stoic vocabulary is flexible and ambiguous enough that it could be preserved, transformed, and utilized by Christian writers. For example, the *seeds of virtue* and *sparks of divinity* by which the Stoics explain human self-sufficient ability to achieve goodness become useful "diminutive" terms for explaining the remnant of goodness that survives original sin and makes one responsible for wrongdoings.

ECLECTIC STOIC PHRASES IN AUGUSTINE AND THOMAS AQUINAS

Medieval writers in general agree that natural law is within; they disagree, however, on the method by which one comes to know it. Whereas Saint Augustine suggests that one belittles God's power if one attributes to the intellect a sufficiency to produce truth, Saint Thomas Aquinas thinks that one praises God's power in recognizing the creation of a being who shared in rationality. Augustine emphasizes our dependence on God's illumination and denies that we are capable of goodness without grace, and Aquinas emphasizes our God-given natural capacity for acquiring virtue and knowledge and accepts that we are autonomously capable of attaining natural virtue, the cardinal virtues of prudence, justice, temperance, and fortitude (restricted virtue, that which is directed not to the proper divine end but to the natural end, a good life on earth) (*Summa theologiae* 1–2, qu. 65, art. 2). The Augustinian and Thomist poles of thought create two distinctly different Christian formulations of the Stoic concept of natural law within humanity. The Thomist viewpoint is closer, though not very close, to the original Stoic in the efficacy granted to human nature.

Reason. There is one distinct reference to human natural law in the New Testament, where Paul says: "When Gentiles who have not the law do by nature what the law requires, they are a law to themselves, even though they do not have the law. They show that what the law requires is written on their hearts, while their conscience bears witness."[45] Whether this passage reveals Stoic influences or not, the church fathers interpret *lex scripta in corde* (the law written in the heart) to be *lex naturalis scripta in corde* (the natural law written in the heart). Saint Hilary of Poitiers (ca. 310–68), Saint Ambrose, and Saint Augustine establish this interpretation, so that soon *lex naturalis scripta in corde* becomes a fundamental assumption of medieval thought. When the doctrine of natural law appears in Christian writings, the reference is generally Romans 2.[46]

By identifying the concept heart as the seat of moral judgments, Paul is following Hebrew tradition; one advantage of this tradition is that in Hebrew *lev* (heart), implies the coordination of both reason and will (see fig. 5.4). Paul's term is the Greek *syneidésis*, a word that appears about thirty times in the New Testament.[47] In Cicero and Seneca *syneidésis* indicates an internal witness to guilty actions committed in the past. In Paul *syneidésis* is not only a source of remorse but also a witness to positive moral acts. Church fathers cite Paul to indicate that natural law is available to human reason through conscience.[48] The concept of conscience thus synthesizes Hebrew, Stoic, and Christian sources.

It is a commonplace in medieval thought that natural law is a function of human reason. Augustine views the natural law, the human participation in the divine law, as a function of reason.[49] Following the Ciceronian view of cosmic harmony and order, to which the rational creature should conform, Augustine defines *virtue* as "the disposition of the mind whereby it agrees with the order of nature and of reason."[50]

Disregarded minority opinions include that of the Roman legalist Ulpian, who believes that natural law is "what nature has taught all animals." Ulpian did gain another hearing, during the revival of Epicurean thought, as we shall see in Michel de Montaigne.[51] A related minority opinion, of Anselm of Laon (d. 1117), teacher of Peter Abelard (d. 1142), emphasizes that natural law is the golden rule functioning in primitive humanity. In this version, the source is still rational, but for some like Abelard, the doctrine heads toward perfectionism through the belief that in some people natural law would be sufficient to allow them to achieve salvation without revelation.[52]

When twelfth-century canon lawyers and scholastic theologians discuss natural reason, they focus on the exact place and nature within us of natural law. They question whether natural law is a faculty, a *habitus*, or an act. Likewise, theologians debate the relationship between conscience, reason, and will.[53] The position that eventually is to dominate church thought is the Aristotelian Christian position, which views synderesis as a *habitus* of the intellect. Saint Bonaventure's opposing position views conscience as part of the practical reason and synderesis as part of the will. Conscience becomes the natural judge, directing human knowledge of justice, and synderesis becomes the natural weight, inclining the human will to realize the virtues.[54]

Aquinas clarifies the relationship between natural law and reason: "Now the guide and standard for human activity is reason. . . . For it is reason that arranges things for an end, and in Aristotle's view (*Eth. Nic.* 7, ch. 8) the end is the chief director in what is to be done. . . . So law is a function of reason."[55] Law, then, is an expression of practical reason, since it guides us to the individual end of happiness and the common end of the common good. Aquinas calls the habit in the practical reason that enables us to know natural law *synderesis*. Associating Aristotle with the statement that "synderesis does not regard opposites, but inclines to good only," Aquinas defines *synderesis* as "the law of our intellect because it is a habit containing the precepts of the natural law, which are the first principles of human actions."[56] Synderesis thus provides to the practical intellect practical principles of natural law comparable to the Aristotelian first principles of the speculative intellect.[57]

Although natural law is an object rather than a natural habit, it is still intrinsic to human nature. Using Aristotelian principles, Aquinas clarifies Gratian's statement that natural law began with the creation of the rational creature. Natural law directs humans to their natural ends; it guides them toward perfecting themselves and thus realizing the human "form." According to Dom Odon Lottin, Thomas Aquinas's merit lies in "having put in its full light the intrinsic character of natural law. Natural law is none other than human nature expressing itself rationally. It is the Aristotelian dynamism applied to the moral order: man perfects himself in realizing in his conduct his condition as man, but as a beginning by expressing his condition through the dictates of his natural reason."[58]

Aquinas's description of natural law as a function of right reason is generally accepted in late medieval thought even by nominalists such as John Duns Scotus or Gabriel Biel. In the nominalist school, *synderesis*, or *scintilla conscientiae* (spark of conscience) is defined as "a natural inclination toward good and away from evil. This is not an act or habit of the will but the voice of natural law speaking through the dictates of right reason."[59]

The voluntarism of nominalists does not apply to the method by which we acquire natural law, for they follow Aquinas in viewing synderesis as a part of reason.[60] Like Aquinas, Scotus distinguishes synderesis, which gives us intuition into the first principles of natural law, from conscience, which applies these principles to particular situations. Gabriel Biel follows in viewing synderesis as a vestige of our pure nature, enabling obedience to natural law.[61]

The various schools of medieval thought agree that human reason is an internal source of knowledge of natural law. Augustine and Aquinas disagree, however, on how reason attains this knowledge. The two different methods are apparent in their use of the concept common notions. The epistemologies underlying their uses of seed and spark imagery are expounded based upon their concepts of common notions.

Common notions. Augustine talks of the mind possessing *notio impressa*, an imprinted notion of blessedness and wisdom.[62] He declares that "notions of morality are among those imprinted on the mind, for we should not be able to say that one [good thing] was better than another . . . unless there were imprinted upon us a concept of good itself."[63] Thus, we attain the concept of good and the ability to make moral judgments from impressed notions.

Augustine relates common notions to his doctrine of illumination in his *De Trinitate*: "God is wholly everywhere, whence it is that [the mind] lives and moves and has its being in him and therefore can remember him."[64] Augustine distinguishes his doctrine of illumination from the Platonic doctrine by pointing out that the soul does not exist before the body. In the Augustinian sense, the mind "remembers" God, who is the interior master of the soul. To clarify how the rules of justice pass from God's "book of light" into the heart of the just person, Augustine utilizes Cleanthes' and Chrysippus's figurative image of the seal on wax. The rules, that is, the laws of nature, are transcribed on our minds.

Augustine presents the view that the notions are not innate but are impressed on the mind during illumination. Although the principles are changeless and righteous, the human mind is changeable and sometimes unjust; so, considering the wicked, Augustine argues that even corrupt human nature can still attain knowledge of goodness. The notions thus exist in the divine light and may illuminate the human mind even while it is turned away. There are levels of divine illumination; we must open up our minds to God for full illumination. The impression of a notion on the human mind requires divine illumination and the cooperation of the human will. The notions truly become a part of human nature only among those who live up to their principles, that is, the just; thus, Augustine specifies that the notions "pass into the heart of the just man." Although the unjust have access to knowledge of the principles of natural law, the just alone have a heart or conscience directed to fulfilling the dictates of the law.[65]

According to Aquinas, in contrast, the first principles of speculative reason and practical reason enter human consciousness through abstraction of
sense data. The speculative reason, which is concerned with necessary relations, can derive primary principles as well as conclusions from them; however, the practical reason, which is concerned with contingent circum-
stances, can derive only primary principles. Thus, there are two distinct
roles in the development of moral principles and conclusions, and there is
a distinct role for both synderesis and conscience: synderesis derives general principles, and conscience applies them to the particular situation.[66]

In the following passage, Aquinas explains this parallel, borrowing the
Stoic phrase *common notions* from Boethius (d. ca. 524):

> Accordingly, then, in speculative matters truth is the same in all men, both as
> to principles and as to conclusions; although the truth is not known to all as
> regards the conclusions, but only as regards the principles which are called
> "common notions." But in matters of action, truth or practical rectitude is not
> the same for all as to what is particular, but only as to the common principles;
> and where there is the same rectitude in relation to particulars, it is not equally
> known to all.[67]

Aquinas views notions as common to humankind and stresses that the
problems and disagreements of opinion come from applying the notions to
particular cases, but he does not think that the difficulty in applying them
makes them any less common.[68] In holding that sense knowledge is necessary for the common notions to emerge, Aquinas emphasizes the Aristotelian strain in ancient Stoic thought. In a Senecan passage Aquinas says,
"There is naturally in man a certain aptitude to virtue, but the very perfection of virtue must come to man through training."[69]

Distinguishing between intellect, will, and emotions and using the Aristotelian concept of active potentiality, Thomas Aquinas comes to a different solution to Augustine's question, "How can the wicked know they are
disobeying eternal principles?"[70] He holds that the principles exist in all
persons, just or unjust, in potentiality. These principles develop easily
through abstractions of sense experience, but they remain ineffective unless
they are applied to specific cases and unless the will and emotions obey
the reason. In the wicked not all these potentialities for virtue are fully
developed.[71]

Despite the different methods for attaining knowledge of the common
notions, both Augustine and Aquinas think that the notions are common
and therefore that ignorance of natural law is inexcusable in an adult. Gratian's statement that "ignorance of natural law excuses no adult" becomes
the norm, and a controversy emerges among the canon lawyers over the
age of moral discretion.[72] The theologians go so far as to say that a child
sheltered from a young age from contact with Christians is still responsible
for his ignorance at the age of discretion. By following the dictate of his

natural reason, such a child could come to some notion of God and thus pray to God for help.[73]

Followers of Augustine or of Aquinas are in agreement that humans have an internal source of knowledge of the common notions of natural law. Augustine views the internal source of these notions as the indwelling of the divine light, whereas Aquinas looks to the potentials of the practical reason. Augustine thinks that God imprints the notions on human reason during illumination, but Aquinas thinks that God imprinted potential notions when he created humankind: "The first and common principles are written in the natural reason."[74] Both, however, hold that the notions are common to all humankind, and both recognize that some adults would not develop their notions and thus would remain sinfully ignorant of natural law.

Seeds. The Stoic phrase *seminales rationes*, "seminal reasons," passes into Christian vocabulary in the first century. Accepting Aratus's text on the fatherhood of God, Saint Paul says to the Athenians, "Yet he is not far from each of us, for 'In him we live and move and have our being,' as even some of your poets have said, 'For we are indeed his offspring.' "[75] Also in particularly Christian fashion, Paul uses the Stoic imagery of seeds to explain Christ's resurrection. The true reality of a human being, the seed may throw off both soul and flesh and assume a new body, as occurred when Christ was resurrected.[76] The terms *sperma* and *kokkos*, "grain," take on a specific Christian theological application.

The Greek apologist Justin Martyr develops the Stoic doctrine of God as the *logos spermatikos* more explicitly. Following Philo in identifying the divine *logos* with the *logos spermatikos*, he believes that human reason is the seed sown by the divine sower: "Christ, the divine logos, is the universal reason, the 'seminal logos' in which all rational beings participated; therefore seeds of truth are found in almost everyone endowed with reason, particularly in the most gifted."[77] Each person who thinks or acts rationally is participating in the Logos, that is, Christ. Each philosopher speaks the truth according to a share in the seed. This explains the disagreements among philosophers: each has only a seed of truth, whereas Christ contains the unity of these fragments, the whole of truth. By Justin Martyr's identification of logos in humanity with participating in Christ, Christianity takes credit for the brilliance of the Greek philosophers.[78] This perspective will be useful in later Christian justification for reading pagan authors.

Unlike Philo and the Stoics, Augustine does not view logos and seminal reason as equivalent. In fact, Augustine does not use the phrase in the singular; rather, he talks about *rationes seminales* or *rationes causales*. The seminal or causal reasons are not God; they are created by God. This concept enables Augustine to explain how God created all things simultaneously from nothing and so created both matter and form and created some things "invisibly, potentially as future things which have not been made are made."[79] As in Stoicism, the seminal reasons are the source for all matter and the source for the reason and pattern of all things. The material nature of the seminal reasons is important for enabling them to be active causes in the material world. According to Augustine, the material seminal reasons are between the eternal reasons and the physical world: the seminal reasons were created by God in the image of the *rationes* (eternal reasons) in order that the physical world would contain the forms of all things to be.

God as the creator of the seminal reasons is the ultimate cause for all things that develop: "Like mothers heavy with their offspring, the world is heavy with the causes of things still to be; and they are created in the world by no one except by that supreme being in whom there is no birth and no death, no beginning and no end."[80] Secondary causes are thus of little importance; the forms of things to come are latent in matter.[81]

Just as the physical world is dependent on the seminal reasons and ultimately on God, humans are dependent on the eternal reasons in the Godhead. Augustine's phrase *rationes aeternae*, a phrase that recalls Seneca's concept of seminal reason, are the forms on which the seminal reasons are created.[82] We come to know these eternal reasons through illumination. Creation of ideas in our mind does not come indirectly through the *logoi spermatikoi* but directly through the Logos.

Secondary causes are no more important in the intellectual and moral order than in the physical order. God alone is the Creator: "For our good, the supreme good that is the subject of dispute among philosophers, is nothing but to cling to him, the sole being by whose incorporeal embrace the intellectual soul is, if we may put it so, impregnated and made to give birth to true virtues."[83] Derived from the Stoic concept of God as seminal reason and from the Pauline concept of humans as the offspring of God, Augustine's imagery of divine impregnation applies to causality in the moral and physical orders alike. Although Augustine does not here explicitly use the phrase *seeds of virtue*, later Augustinians do, sometimes in the Stoic or Thomist sense that such potential for virtue is in human nature from birth.[84] Étienne Gilson interprets Augustine as meaning that the seeds of virtue derive from participation in Jesus Christ: "It is God who fecundates our thought by His Word." God is not only the interior master, the light and the food of our soul; he is also "the living seed that enters the womb of thought," and thus God "espouses and fecundates it that it may conceive the truth."[85] In order for a mutable and contingent mind to attain universal and eternal truths, "it is necessary, clearly, that I receive the seeds of the virtues in the Divine embrace just as I receive the seeds of science."[86]

In *On Truth* Aquinas links the Augustinian doctrines of causality in the physical, moral, and intellectual orders and then rejects them all. In Gilson's words, "Both these theses suffer from the same inconvenience, for whether all is ready made in the womb of nature, or whether all is effected for it from outside, nature itself, in either case, does nothing at all."[87] In Aquinas's view, the doctrine of seminal reasons attributes all efficacy to an internal source, and the doctrine of illumination attributes all efficacy to an external source; Aquinas rejects both doctrines in their Augustinian form because he attributes some efficacy to nature. God out of his immensity of goodness created natural efficacy in order to make his creatures similar to him.[88] Turning to the physical world, Aquinas accepts the Aristotelian view that matter is "pure potentiality," requiring secondary causes in order to be actualized.[89] In Aquinas's view, the role of divine grace in the universe does not detract from the efficacy of nature and natural causes.[90]

To express the view that we have the potential to attain virtue, Aquinas sometimes uses the phrase *seminal principles*, which he rejects for the physical world: "We might also say that although not all men have these virtues in complete habit, yet they have them according to certain seminal principles in the reason, in force of which principles the man who is not virtuous loves the virtuous man, as being in conformity with his own natural reason."[91] In this passage, *seminal principles* indicates Aristotelian potentiality. More commonly, Aquinas talks of the *semina scientiarum* (seeds of knowledge), which he equates with the first principles from which we attain knowledge of natural law.[92] Comparable to the seeds of knowledge are the *semina virtutum* or *virtutes naturales* (seeds of moral virtue), which give humans a natural tendency to seek the good.[93] Aquinas constantly refers to the fact that "the principles of common law are called 'the seeds of virtues.'"[94] The definition occurs in these two passages: "Certain seeds or principles of the acquired virtues pre-exist in us by nature"; and in the afterlife too, "neither will these virtues be actually, but only in their root, i.e., in the reason and will, wherein are certain seeds of virtues, as we have stated above."[95] Thomas Aquinas thus makes ample use of the Stoic phrases *seeds of virtue* and *seeds of knowledge* and in doing so equates the concept with the first principles, or common notions, by which one knows natural law.

After the Thomist mention of *semina virtutum*, the phrase appears in the Augustinian tradition. The thirteenth-century Franciscan Matthew of Aquasparta (d. 1302), a disciple of Bonaventure, explicitly identifies the concept of seed plots of all the arts and science with the doctrine of seminal principles in nature. His thorough comparison of epistemologies is to become the style adopted by Bodin, Montaigne, and Charron. After rejecting the Platonic doctrine of innate ideas in a preexistent soul and Avicenna's doctrine of an external agent intellect, Matthew presents the view that the natural intellect has "connatural to itself, certain imparted and innate seed plots [*seminaria*] or roots and, as it were, an active potentiality with respect to all intelligible forms of all the arts and sciences." He immediately indicates that he is drawing an analogy between human and physical nature. Whereas in Aristotelian fashion he indicates that learning takes place through sense perception and moves from latency or potentiality to activity, in Augustinian fashion he insists on the relationship between humans and God: "Unsuitable it seems according to them, that the intellectual soul, which is like the image of God, be bare." But his wording emphasizes what is in human nature at birth—the gifts at Creation.[96]

Matthew not only provides the important expression of *seminaria* (seed plot) but also provides the important argument by authority. In chapter 6 we shall see Erasmus, in his argument with Luther over the freedom of the will, cite the church fathers as authorities to prove that there are seeds of virtue. The gathering of such citations is already a factor in thirteenth-century Franciscan writing: "In favor of this position was Augustine, II, *On Free Will*, where he said that the soul has in itself a seed plot of virtues; and in VIII, *On Trinity*, he said that there is an impressed notion in human nature; and Boethius, III, *On Consolation*: 'It remains inside some seed of truth, which skillful learning does excite,' and in V: 'Meanwhile it excites sleeping forms.'"[97] Matthew rephrases Augustine's words "regulas et quaedam lumina virtutum" [rules and certain lights of virtue] as "seminaria virtutum" [seeds of virtue]. He perceives that *seeds* and *lights* refer to the same issues. In addition, Matthew's use of the word *seed* turns Augustine's meaning away from illumination toward potency of the natural intellect. Matthew's reinterpretation of Augustine as proclaiming potency of the natural intellect is a precedent to the range of interpretations of Augustine possible during the succeeding centuries.

Sparks. Augustine's view of natural law makes ample use of the image of light, drawn from the Joannine Gospel. The Logos, or "Word," which contains the forms from which all was created, is Christ. Existing eternally with God and substantially one with God, Christ is the exemplar, the pattern for creation. The Word is the "true light that enlightens every man."[98] The true object of knowledge is the eternal reasons (*rationes aeternae*), which exist in the divine intelligence. Divine illumination is the medium by which the subject, the individual, participates in the eternal reasons and gains certain knowledge.[99]

The phrase *scintilla conscientiae*, "spark of conscience," is introduced into Christian literature by Saint Jerome (ca. 345–420) in his interpretation of the four creatures in the vision of Ezechiel. Accepting Plato's classification of the soul, Jerome says that the lion symbolizes the irascible faculty, the ox the concupiscent faculty, and human beings the rational faculty. Over these animals hovers the eagle, "which is above and beyond the three, which the Greeks call *synteresis*, that is, the spark of conscience which was not extinguished even in Cain's breast, after he was ejected from paradise, and by which when we are overcome by passions or fury and when we are meanwhile deceived in reason similarly by this same spark, we perceive ourselves sinning."[100] Symbolizing to Christians postlapsarian humanity, Cain still retains *scintillam conscientiae*, despite having killed his brother. Even when overcome by sin, we retain our consciences to the extent that we can realize that we are doing wrong.

In his influential *Sentences*, Peter Lombard (ca. 1095–1160) is the first theologian to utilize Jerome's text: "It is rightly said that because man was created good and just in will, he naturally discerns the good; for as says St. Jerome, the higher spark of reason referred to the superior part of reason, otherwise called the spark of superior reason."[101] Interpreted as natural goodness, sparks have been extinguished entirely in devils, but interpreted more correctly as superior reason, sparks have not been extinguished even in devils and the damned; for both can distinguish good from evil and judge that they have merited their punishment.[102]

Thus, *scintilla conscientiae* or *scintilla rationis* comes to be an equivalent for *synderesis*. Both synderesis and the spark of conscience are sources of human knowledge of natural law. William of Auvergne (d. 1249) writes that synderesis is the "light of natural law,"[103] and Aquinas declares that "the light of our reason is able to show us good things, and guides our will, in so far as it is the light of (i.e., derived from) Thy Countenance."[104] He clearly identifies this "light" with natural law: "The light of natural reason, whereby we discern what is good and what is evil, which is a function of natural law, is nothing else than an imprint on us of the Divine light."[105] Thus, the light of natural reason, the light of reason, and the light of natural law are all images equivalent to the spark of conscience.

Generally, late medieval nominalists, exemplified by Gabriel Biel (d. 1495), accept this identification of the various images for expressing natural law within human nature. Biel defines *synderesis* as *scintilla conscientiae*. *Synderesis*, *synteresis*, and *syneidesis* are interchangeable with *scintilla conscientiae*. Biel defines sin as acting contrary to right reason: "Let it not be thought that something is a sin because divine reason is divine. A sin is such because it is against divine reason and because that reason is right."[106] Likewise, it is a scholastic commonplace in the Middle Ages and the Renaissance that natural law is acquired through the natural light of the intellect.[107]

The term *spark* appears in a different form in writings of German mystics. The visions of Hildegard of Bingen (1098–1179) are influential. Hildegard's *Scivias* (1150) visualizes the sparks created by God that enter the human soul. An important idea common to Jewish and Christian medical writings as well as religious works is that the soul is divinely implanted in the human womb sometime after the conception of a human embryo.[108] Whereas the debate on natural law concerns exactly where it is and how it develops, the debate on the implantation of the soul concerns when it enters and how it animates the body. God's implantation of the soul takes on visual expression in the twelfth-century miniature in the Lucca manuscript of Hildegard (see fig. 2.4). I interpret this miniature, which has been called "The Original Blessing: The Golden Tent," as "Descent of the Soul." A treelike umbilical cord reaches down from the divine four-sided and tripartite source in heaven to implant a soul in a human embryo in the womb;[109] the descending soul contains numerous circular and eyelike formations. The divided-up soul stuff correlates in visual terms to the multiplicity implied by the twin concepts seeds of virtue and sparks of divinity. Although

2.4. Descent of the soul, central panel of miniature in Hildegard of Bingen, *Scivias*, ca. 1200.

Hildegard's text does not use the precise Stoic term *semina*, it does apply light images; in particular she refers to what enters the soul as "fireballs," that is, sparks, and she discusses the virtue expected from those so created by God. There is in fact a diversity of aspects that humanity needs to receive from the divine breath in order to fulfill the image of God.

Hildegard's vision of the divine implantation of the soul corresponds to another of her visions of God's greening power, *viriditas*. Building upon scriptural vegetative imagery, she expresses God's words as "I am the breeze that nurtures all things green. / I encourage blossoms to flourish with ripening fruits."[110] Likewise, her vegetative symbolism merges with light imagery in a macrocosmic-microcosmic meditation on a vision of cultivating the cosmic tree. "All living creatures are, so to speak, sparks from the radiation of God's brilliance, and these sparks emerge from God like rays of the sun. . . . For no creature exists that lacks a radiance—be it greenness or seed, buds or beauty. Otherwise it would not be a creature at all" (48).

In her commentary on her vision of the rooting of the soul in the human embryo she explains that the red balls descending are fireballs, the fire of human understanding, which animates the body. These fireballs "give the greenness of the heart and veins and all the organs to the entire body as a tree gives sap and greenness to all the branches from its root" (55). The onlookers carry cheese because ancient belief likened conception to curdling. A demon touches one of the cheeses, but the soul descends well protected by a vinelike cord. Hildegard thus follows the metaphor of the human tree rooted in the Divine in both her prose and her portrayal. Her confidence in human origins from the divine gift boosts her confidence in times of despair. Likewise, she applies the picture to the Christian rebirth, when a human is regenerated in Jesus (57).

Hildegard is a possible influence on Meister Eckhart (ca. 1260–ca. 1328), who writes of the free agency of the soul: "Sometimes I have called it the tabernacle of the Spirit. Other times I have called it the Light of the Spirit and again, a spark [*vunkelín*]. . . . It is at once pure and free, as God itself."[111] The *vunkelín* is not the natural intellect stressed by Aquinas and Biel; it is closer to the divine light of illumination theory. Eckhart borrows from Proclus's phrase "flower of the intellect" in speaking of "this same power of which I Eckhart have spoken, in which God is verdant and flowering with his entire Divinity."[112] In fact Eckhart adopts neo-Platonic doctrine when he suggests that "God lies hidden in the soul's core."[113] The statement, "There is in the soul something which is uncreated and uncreatable, and that is its intellect," earns him a condemnation in 1329 for failing to distinguish human intellect from God.[114]

In sum, the Stoic concepts reason, common notions, seeds, and sparks are common in medieval thought, and the latter two vegetative and light images lend themselves to mystical vision and artistic portrayal. Both Augustine and Aquinas agree that the participation of the rational creature in the eternal law is natural law, though they disagree on the method. In the Augustinian tradition, one participates in the Logos, Christ, who is the interior master of one's soul. This viewpoint is mentioned less frequently by scholastic theologians, who debate the location of natural law in the human mind. The Thomist and nominalist viewpoint is that human practical intellect, synderesis, has as its end knowledge of natural law. Whereas Augustine sees God imprinting common notions on the human soul during illumination, Aquinas argues that God imprinted on the human reason at Creation common notions that develop through abstraction of sense data. Augustine thinks that one contemplates the external reasons, the immutable rules of goodness, in God, but Aquinas thinks that one develops the seeds of virtue by exercising natural faculties. Medieval theologians refer to the remnant of human natural goodness that has survived original sin as the "spark of conscience." However, Augustine recommends that we seek knowledge of morality through the divine light illuminating the intellect with lights of virtue; Aquinas thinks we attain knowledge of morality through developing the gift at Creation of the natural light of reason.

Medieval and Renaissance Vegetative Images

THIS CHAPTER explores the visual metaphors of trees that enhance medieval and Renaissance acceptance of Seneca's and Thomas Aquinas's views that the mind grows naturally as a plant does from seeds of virtue and knowledge. Visual vegetative metaphors influence the neo-Platonic reformulation of the Stoic imagery. Both neo-Platonic philosophy and trees of ascent (often biblical trees of life) redirect the human intellect from sensual concerns upward to contemplation of God.

The paradigm of the mind growing like a plant used by artists, philosophers, and humanists alike finds support in Plato's one work that was available throughout the Middle Ages, the *Timaeus*, which describes God the Creator, the Demiurge, in macrocosmic organic imagery and the human being as an upside-down plant whose soul is rooted in God:

> And we should consider that God gave the sovereign part of the human soul to be the divinity of each one, being that part which, as we say dwells at the top of the body, and inasmuch as we are a plant not of an earthly but of a heavenly growth, raises us from earth to our kindred who are in heaven. And in this we say truly; for the divine power suspended the head and root of us from that place where the generation of the soul first began and thus made the whole body upright.[1]

This model of the soul as rooted in God is an image compatible with the Lucca artist's illustration of Hildegard's vision of the divine implantation of the human soul (fig. 2.4).

To organize this inquiry of vegetative imagery it is useful to develop the typology of the two wisdoms as discussed by both Thomas Aquinas and Pierre Charron and to suggest that visual imagery sometimes blurs such precise distinction.[2] A seeker of divine wisdom aims to contemplate God, whereas a seeker of human wisdom aims for virtuous, knowledgeable active governance of this life on earth; to either seeker one may propose one or both paths—the natural path of human effort and the path of divine illumination. The Greek Stoics, as pantheists and materialists, do not distinguish between the two paths: a divine spark causes upward ascent, and a divine seed is at the root of human virtue. Cicero, Seneca, and Philo, in Platonizing Stoic concepts, turn physical descriptions into figurative metaphors and paradigms of the mind's potential for growth. Cicero and Seneca stress the natural path to achieve human wisdom, which includes piety and contemplation of divine reason ordering the universe. Heir to both the Greek Bible and Hellenistic thought, Philo in his usage of *logos* as divine reason, human reason, and the ordering of the universe fuses divine and human wisdom and the divine and natural paths to wisdom. Philo emphasizes human reason and effort, but with awe before the divine presence in human history and nature. The young Augustine considers various human techniques of classical education and philosophy, but the mature Augustine turns from human wisdom to focus on divine wisdom, redefining *Logos* as Jesus Christ. While using some Stoic vocabulary that was originally inclusive and cosmopolitan, he transforms the meaning in an exclusionary manner by concluding that both human and divine wisdom derive from the interior master, Jesus Christ, who works in Christian souls.[3]

The master of precision and hierarchy is Thomas Aquinas, who argues that human effort may lead to natural law but that divine illumination, or the interior master, Jesus Christ, is needed in order for the effort to lead to salvation. Both Augustine and Aquinas as theologians are precise; in accord with Hildegard of Bingen and Meister Eckhart, who represent a mystical tradition that blurs the distinctions between humanity and the Divine, this chapter discusses important currents of medieval and Renaissance theological thought that are not precise. Linguistic and visual metaphors are appropriate for those who experience awe in exploring what derives from divinely created nature and what derives from divine aid.

Nevertheless, metaphor is an educational instrument. Some of the illustrations here, such as the forest of trees in Raymond Lull's books of wisdom, although credited to inspiration of the Holy Spirit, once presented in texts encourage human attempts to attain human and divine wisdom. Ficino's *De amore*, his commentary on Plato's *Symposium*, is addressed not to scholars but to Cosimo de' Medici and the emergent book-reading public to encourage attainment of human and divine wisdom through education and love.[4] Both the wide-ranging exploration of medieval tree imagery in this chapter and the narrowly focused case study of this most influential commentary in the next emphasize the powerful impact, intended or not, of the blurring of distinctions between the goals of human wisdom and divine wisdom and between human and divine paths.

The Stoic epistemology is especially meaningful to those accustomed to vegetative imagery and thought patterns. In the context of the abundance of visual vegetative images for knowledge, virtue, and ascent from the twelfth century onward, an author's easy acceptance of the epistemology of seeds of virtue and knowledge may indicate a distinctive *mentalité*[5] or "symbolic language" in which one views God as the ultimate creative source, the seed-giver, of all that is and one views one's mind as growing upward as a plant grows toward its root of origin, the Divine. We shall explore writers and artists who intentionally are not precise, who in awe before the search for divinity resort to analogy, to metaphor, and to image.

The phrase *seeds of virtue* as symbolic language suggests possibly related visual imagery supplementing the obvious abundance of nature itself and of an agricultural economy. Some insight can be gained by considering the image of plants of virtue as part of Western vegetative symbolic language, and visual images are particularly important when literacy is low.[6] Seeing with the mind's eye is part of medieval conceptualization of knowledge.[7] Visual and literary images of symbolic trees of virtue, trees of knowledge, and trees of ascent abound in manuscripts; these images suggest a pattern of visualizing in trees, that is, of showing the paths to virtue, knowledge, and ascent as vegetative growth.

The synagogue tree illustrations in fourth-century Dura Europos, not excavated until the 1930s, suggest the powerful presence of visual forms of the tree of life in the centuries leading to the Babylonian Talmud and to the church fathers' writings. Analysis of the iconography of the murals in relationship to Philo's tree imagery is the most vivid way to introduce Philo's metaphoric language, available in manuscripts in Rome, Florence, and elsewhere before its Paris publication in Latin (1552) and in French (1575).[8]

Trees of ascent, of virtue and vice, and of knowledge have a biblical basis in Genesis. Arborescent images for ascent to the Divine interpret the tree of life of Genesis but also relate to worldwide symbolism for the tree at the center. Trees that provide classificatory detail of the virtue and vices are related to the tree of knowledge of virtue and vice in Genesis. Trees of knowledge, which are classificatory schemes for knowledge (*science*) or for areas such as the liberal arts or medicine recall the knowledge aspect of the tree of knowledge of virtue and vice. In presenting these medieval tree images, I distinguish Judaic from Christian sources: the issues dividing Judaism and Christianity are reflected in vegetative imagery, and the medieval Christians' vegetative imagery varies from exclusive, which suggests that pagans or Jews may not be virtuous, to inclusive, which respects the virtue possible to Jews and Muslims but aims for conversion (as in Raymond Lull). Of the abundant tree symbolism of ancient civilizations, I consider scholars in gardens or under trees and pagan metamorphosis of a person into a tree. Scholars under trees takes us briefly into the forest of Raymond Lull, designed for Muslim, Jewish, and Christian readers, and in the next chapter to the garden of Careggi in Florence, where Ficino and his associates converse. Images of trees emerge that are harmonious with universal evidence of visual vegetative symbolism as well as with passages from the Hebrew Bible, the Greek Gospels, and classical literature.

JUDAIC TREES

The Hebrew Bible abounds in trees. On a practical level, God rewards the Hebrew people with the fruit trees of Palestine, and in a mystical vision that unites vegetation and light God's unique appearance to Moses occurs in a theophanous event, a burning bush that is not consumed.[9] Separating

Jewish ritual from that of neighboring peoples and distinguishing the God the Creator from natural creation, Mosaic law forbids worship of trees and vegetation.[10] Ritual objects, commanded by God, are presented instead. One of the most important is a tree of light, a menorah.

The seven-branched golden menorah, established to accompany the Holy Ark, is patterned explicitly by divine instruction on the model of the almond tree (Exod. 25.31–40). Although, the physical conquest of the temple menorah is commemorated on the Arch of Titus (fig. 2.3) and also appropriated into Christianity, the menorah has a continuous history as a major ritual symbol for Judaism from ancient times to the present. The most famous menorah today stands outside the Knesset in Jerusalem.[11]

Two trees that have different meanings in Judaism and Christianity are those in the Garden of Eden in Gen. 2.9, about which God gives commands (2.16–17) and whose violation causes the first human couple to leave Eden (2.22–23): the tree of life and the tree of knowledge of good and evil. Jews view as the tree of life both their oral tradition and the Hebrew Bible; the Torah teaches obedience to God's commandments in order to serve God and one's neighbors in a righteous life on earth. That tradition is to aid humans in their ability to choose to control the evil inclination (*yezar ra*) and to enhance the good inclination (*yezar tov*) within human nature.[12] The key Jewish text for interpreting the tree of knowledge of good and evil is Gen. 3.20, in which God recognizes that the human, having eaten of that tree, knows good and evil. Despite the sins of Adam and Eve, the text praises the righteousness of Enoch, Methuselah, and Noah; God's punishment of Noah's generation for their sins indicates that goodness is still expected of humans (Gen. 5).

While Genesis 1 repeats that God found the Creation good, it also stresses that after creating humanity in the divine image (Gen. 1.26), "God saw everything that he had made, and behold it was very good" (Gen. 1.31). In positive affirmation of the goodness in the natural world and in humanity, an analogy develops between a righteous person and a fruitful tree. For the Hebraic tradition, the law given by God to Moses for the people's governance is the path to righteousness, symbolized as fruitfulness. Psalm 1 makes this analogy:

> Happy is the man that hath
> not walked in the counsel of the wicked,
> Nor stood in the way of sinners,
> Nor sat in the seat of the scornful.
> But his delight is in the law of the Lord;
> And in His law doth he meditate day and night.
> And he shall be like a tree planted
> by the streams of water,
> That bringeth forth its fruit in its season.
>
> ·   ·   ·   ·   ·   ·   ·   ·   ·   ·   ·   ·   ·

> Not so the wicked;
> But they are like the chaff which the
> wind driveth away.   (Ps. 1.1–3, 4)

Vegetative analogies continue in the Prophets. Recognizing the special breath of life that the Divine gave the human (Gen. 2.7), the Hebrew Prophets expect much from humanity and lament the misbehavior that defies God's original good Creation:

> Yet I had planted thee a noble vine,
> Wholly of right seed,
> How then art thou turned into the degenerate plant
> Of a strange vine unto Me?   (Jere. 2.21)[13]

Jeremiah makes clear that humans are of "right seed," planted by God, and depart from their maker when they depart from virtue. That the external deeds of virtue are the fruit of the human tree allows for development of extensive symbolism related to fruits. Seed imagery is particularly prevalent with the multiseeded pomegranate, for instance, when rabbinical commentary suggests that a person is "full of good deeds as a pomegranate." The abundance of seeds in the pomegranate stand for good deeds: "[Even the] transgressors of Israel are full of good deeds as a pomegranate of seeds." The path to righteousness is through studies: "The pomegranate flowered—these are the children who sit and work at the Torah and sit in row after row like the seeds of pomegranates."[14]

These Hebrew comparisons of a human to a tree and of good deeds to fruit derive fundamentally from a biblical ritual culture of harvest festivals in which firstfruits are presented to God; and modern Judaism continues the ritual use of symbolic vegetation on specific holy days, for example the etrog and lulav and palm tree huts for Sukkah, commemorating the sojourn in the Sinai desert. Anticipating Seneca's analogy of a developing student to a tree, ancient Hebrew popular culture encourages the planting of a tree at a child's birth, so the Hebraic analogy between a righteous person and a tree develops in this ritual context. Jews in the Graeco-Roman period in Palestine, as well as in Rome, often represent the palm branch on tombs, perhaps, as Erwin Goodenough suggests, to indicate hope for an afterlife; in Jewish Wisdom literature the tree of life, which is a symbol of wisdom, becomes also a symbol of immortality.[15]

A synthesis of Hebraic and Graeco-Roman tree symbolism appears in the first-century writings of Philo of Alexandria, who comes under the influence of Stoicism and Platonism. To understand Philo's vegetative symbolism it is helpful for us to look at a visual image that is symbolically resonant, as his texts are. Situated above one another on the same site are the second- and third-century synagogues of Dura Europos on the Euphrates, produced by a Greek- and Aramaic-speaking Jewish community. Of particular interest is the vegetative symbolism above the niche for the Torah (scrolls of the five books of Moses) of the second Dura Synagogue, built in 256 C.E. Erwin Goodenough's account, which shows that the wall was decorated in stages, is the accepted historical reconstruction.[16] Although a variety of scholars have debated intricacies of Goodenough's interpretations, the consensus is that "the Jewish symbols [should] be taken seriously, and not be dismissed as mere decoration."[17]

In the first rendition the placement of a niche for the scrolls under a vegetative design emphasizes the rabbinical view of the Torah as the tree of life, a path to righteousness.[18] While rabbinical commentary on gardens is rare, one might think of the comparable second-century saying of Rabbi Judah ben Rabbi Ilai, who interprets Song of Songs 6.8 as "sixty companies of the righteous who sit in the Garden under the tree of life and study Torah."[19] The first design shows a tree growing out of a vase, its branches resembling a vine. The palm tree and the vine combine two symbols associated with the Torah as a path to the righteousness of following God's commandments. The ascending vegetative growth above the Torah is suggestive to me of the midrash "And by the tree of life the souls of the righteous are going up and down to heaven and from heaven to the Garden of Eden, like a man going up and down a ladder."[20] Possibly this midrash, obviously echoing Jacob's ladder, may be basic to the fusion that Marion Kuntz and Paul Kuntz have noted between trees of ascent and ladders of ascent in medieval imagery for the path to divine wisdom.[21]

In the second overlay (fig. 3.1) Goodenough argues that Philo's fully worked out allegory *Concerning Noah's Work as a Planter* comes to dominate.[22] I extend his suggestion further to emphasize Stoic influence and Philo's expansive notion of the garden of the soul. From the biblical text of Noah planting a vineyard Philo draws the analogy of God as planter, sowing the cosmos and all living things. Philo views all creation as part of a cosmic vegetative growth of tree and vine, the logos:[23] "He [the Everlasting Word] it is, who extending Himself from the midst to its utmost bounds and from its extremities to the midst again."[24] Likewise, incorporating the Stoic ethic of conforming one's reason to the reason of the universe, Philo views humans who turn away from animal passions as becoming engrafted on the upward thrust of the tree of the universe. Correspondingly, the final design of the painting places on branches of the tree the synthetic figure of Orpheus-David playing a lyre to control the passions, portrayed as animals. Also, a throne room above the treetop shows the goal of human ascent up the tree to the Divine, obviously through the Torah scrolls in the ark below.

If one views the synagogue wall fully in Philo's multivalent mode of allegorizing, the painted tree poses an upward path to the Divine, a theophanous or arborescent representation that serves also as a mirror of the internal spiritual growth of the observers, the congregants in prayer. Philo views the "trees of Life, of Immortality, of Knowledge, of Apprehension, of

3.1. Torah Shrine, Dura Synagogue, third century. Reconstruction after
Erwin R. Goodenough.

Understanding, of the conception of good and evil" as growing in the human soul, for "bountiful God plants in the soul as it were a garden of virtues and of the modes of conduct corresponding to each of them, a garden that brings the soul to perfect happiness."[25]

From Plato's organic image of the human soul rooted in the Divine of the *Timaeus* and from Philo's vision of the universe as vegetative and creation as planted, it is not a very large step to the macrocosmic trees of the Kabbalah; the most basic Kabbalah is in the thirteenth-century *Zohar*, viewed in Jewish and Christian circles before the seventeenth century as a book of ancient origin. In fact, Louis Jacobs has traced the first Jewish spiritual conception of the soul to Philo and views Philo as the source of the notion of "divine spark" among early Kabbalists. In the neo-Platonic poem of Gabirol (d. 1058) the soul is described as "pure radiance," fashioned from "fire of the Intelligence." One passage of the *Zohar* refers to the highest part of the soul as *neshamah*, the same name as an aspect of the Deity in the sefirotic realm of divine attributes. While the natural part of the soul, *nephesh*, can sin, the *neshamah*, the spark of the divine within the human soul, cannot.[26]

One might also notice that the most important holy chariot poem about the soul's ascent of R. Simeon mixes vegetative and light imagery:

> The secret Garden
> In worlds of light hidden
> —Two hundred and fifty
> Encompassing worlds—
> Where Shekinah's splendour
> From splendour proceeding
> Its splendour sends forth
> To the ends of creation
> In the fullness of glory
> Is revealed in its beauty
> To the eyes made seeing—
> The garden of Eden.

Possibly Philo influences the combining of vegetative and light imagery in the mystical vision "to the eyes made seeing" of a garden in the human soul lit by the blazing light of the Divine. A later stanza continues,

> Who sees those mighty ones
> High in the Heavens
> Mighty in beauty?
> Who sees the Chariots
> Holy and glorious? . . .
> Blessed are the souls of the righteous who perceive it![27]

The individual mystical gazes of the righteous combine to create "a closed garden": an earlier commentary of R. Jose declares that the closed garden

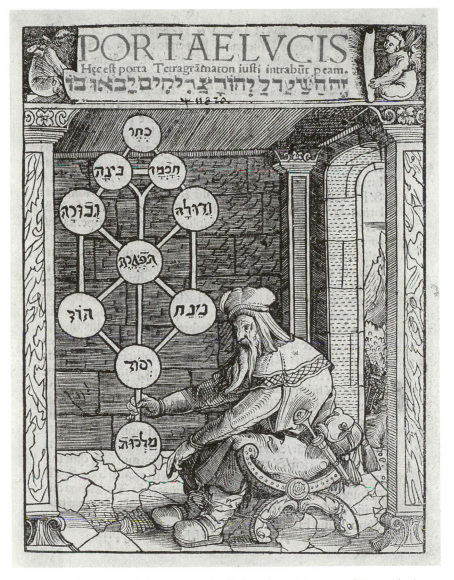

3.2. *Sefirot* (tree with names of God). Woodcut title page of *Portae lucis* (Gates of light), 1516.

refers to Song of Songs 4.12, and R. Eleazar explains that "as the garden has to be tended, ploughed, watered, and trimmed, so has the Community of Israel to be tended, nurtured and trimmed."[28] The neo-Platonic circle in Florence knows other Jewish commentaries on the Song of Songs as well, for Pico commissions the rabbi Yohanan Alemanno (ca. 1433–ca. 1504) to write one; by 1492 Alemanno completes *Shir ha-Ma'alot le-Shlomo* (The

Song of Solomon's ascents), which becomes one source of attention to Solomon as the embodiment of wisdom.[29]

Jewish and Christian devotees of the "very ancient" Kabbalah receive vegetative imagery for the Divine also from the vision of the Divine as a spiritual tree—an organic macrocosmic image. The woodcut title page of *Portae lucis* (Gates of light, 1516) introduces a Latin text published by the Christian convert Paul Ricius derived from a manuscript by Joseph ben Abraham Gikatilla (1248–ca. 1305) (fig. 3.2). In the woodcut, a mature Jewish man (one must be forty years old and married before attempting Kabbalah) grabs this *sefirot*, which is, strangely, suspended in the space of the closed room. The *sefirot* is composed of circles indicating the ten names of the emanations of the Divinity. The text elucidates the relationships of Keter (crown), Binah (intelligence), Hokhmah (wisdom), Gedullah (love), Gevurah (justice), Tiferet (beauty), Nezah (firmness), Hod (splendor), Yesod (foundation), Malkhut (kingdom), and Shekhinah (divine halo).[30] In the common medieval and Renaissance belief that Hebrew is the original language of humanity, there is enchantment in the recital of multiple Hebrew names for the divine attributes—the *sefirot*—in a mnemonic system that aids the Kabbalist's mystical experience of ascension and contemplation of the Divine.

Pico is fascinated by the magical power of Hebrew words; he rearranges the letters of the first four verses of Genesis to read "father, in the Son and through the Son, the beginning and end or rest, created the head, the fire, and the foundation of the great man with a good pact." The Trinity appears, as does the macrocosmic, anthropomorphic figure of the cosmos! This is a good example of Christian Kabbalah, employed for missionary work among Jews.[31] Also, Pico gives to Italian literature the idea of the kiss of divinity, the *morte di bacio*, which he finds in Kabbalist Recanati's *Commentary on the Pentateuch* as well as in Plato. As Recanati reinterprets a death without pain as the ultimate experience of the soul cleaving to and coming to union with the divine presence, he applies the fruit metaphor of Abraham ibn Ezra's commentary on Psalm 1: "Know that, just as the ripe fruit falls from the tree, it is no longer needing its connection (to the tree), so is the link between the soul and the body."[32]

Whereas in Ricius's version the figure of divine emanations appears upright and either anthropomorphic or treelike with a crown at the top, in other versions the *sefirot* appears distinctly as the macrocosmic tree, with its roots in heaven and its trunk reaching downward to draw the believer upward.[33] That image is very evident in Robert Fludd's engraving of 1621 in which the roots are lit up by the heavenly presence and the palm branches reach downward to aid the believer's ascent (fig. E.1).

Since vegetative symbolism for the seminal growths of the human mind may appear in vision, art, or text, I would like to suggest that Philo's allegorical interpretation of nature as a fertile human mind may have been one factor in the emergence of Renaissance landscape painting and one aspect of the enthusiasm for garden design. Konstantin Bazarov noted the revolutionary change in landscapes in the first decade of the sixteenth century; the origins might be sought in his suggestion with regard to Mathias Grünewald's *Two Hermits*, "that Grünewald's religious pictures are internal landscapes of the mind."[34] The genre of a saint in a landscape is a significant transitional stage to the "pure landscape," which has no figures.[35] As the ascetic saint is alone contemplating nature and seeking God, the saint figures for *adam* (human nature). For one who is aware of Philo's allegory of the garden of Genesis as the vegetative human mind it is not a large step to explore one's own mind through the artist's vision of divinely created nature. The landscape then reveals the vegetative abundance of the powers of the mind; animals included symbolize specific animal passions that tempt one away from an idyllic transcendent vision.[36] A purely vegetative Eden heightens the paradisal vision (see fig. 8.1).

CHRISTIAN TREES OF ASCENT

Exactly who is compared to a good tree has changed by the time we come to the Gospel of Matthew.[37] There the Jewish followers of the law who do not follow the coming new world order (the Pharisees and Sadducees) are scorned and tree imagery is abundant. John the Baptist says: "Even now the axe is laid to the root of the trees; every tree that does not bear good fruits is cut down and thrown into the fire" (Matt. 3.10). And reporting Jesus' words, Matthew declares, "Whoever speaks against the Holy Spirit will not be forgiven, either in this age or in the age to come. Either make the tree good, and its fruit good; or make the tree bad, and its fruit bad; for the tree is known by its fruit. You brood of vipers! how can you speak good, when you are evil?" (Matt. 12.32–34).

In the early church, the tree of life in Paradise is identified with Jesus on the cross and with the cross as a prefiguration.[38] Isaac of Antioch in the fifth century declares, "Come, marvel at the Tree / that groweth without watering / and on which the fruit of Light hangeth."[39] Gerhart Ladner explains that the ancient tree is substituted for the tree from which the cross was cut, conceptually related to the fall of Adam in Paradise and his rebirth in Christ, diachronically related to the time sequence of sacred history, and in a relationship of mutual participation in the divine process ending in redemption. Giovanni da Modena portrays Christ crucified directly on the tree from which Adam and Eve ate the fruit of the Fall.[40]

Early versions of the cross as the tree of life include a sixth- or seventh-century design of palm leaves of victory sprouting from the cross and the twelfth-century mosaic apse of San Clemente, Rome, in which an acanthus scroll winds around the large cross with Jesus. An inscription implies that the tree that was made dry by human transgression becomes green again by means of the cross; this may be a unification of the two trees of Paradise into the one tree at the center known in civilizations worldwide, or, as Ladner suggests, it may be an elliptical reference to the tree of knowledge of good and evil made dry by the human transgression and to the tree of life of Paradise prefiguring the cross.[41] Like the Dura Europos mural, this mosaic combines vine and tree, but the Christian inscription states that the acanthus symbolizes a vine, and the symbolism of the vine and the tree would be apparent to those in prayer in the church, as declares "I am the vine" (John 15.5).[42]

The tree of Jesse, representing the ancestry of Jesus, is important to Christian visualization of trees. Starting in the twelfth century, illustrations of the tree of Jesse become numerous in medieval and Renaissance church decoration and manuscript illumination.[43] For example, in the twelfth-century psalter of Henry of Blois in Winchester, Jesus is portrayed at the top, and his maternal ancestry from Jesse, through King David and Mary, is presented according to Isaiah 11.1: "There shall come forth a rod out of the stem of Jesse, and a branch shall grow out of his roots and the Spirit of the Lords shall rest upon him."[44] This early example of an upright tree winding gracefully like a vine from Hebrew Jesse upward to Jesus influences Joachim of Floris's "tree of history" (fig. 3.3).

The tree of Jesse is well known in the Italian Renaissance. The panel of Pacino di Bonaguida (active 1303–20), whose iconography is derived from Saint Bonaventure's (1221–74) *Lignum vitae* (The Tree of Life), expresses a fascination with symbolic harmonies of number.[45] Raymond Lull (1232–ca. 1316) might be background to this transformation of the tree of Jesse into an elaborate scheme that works on the harmony of numbers and the art of mnemonic memory. Jesus hangs on a tree that has six branches on each side. This tree of life of the Apocalypse has forty-eight narrative medallions containing "three times sixteen phases of Christ's salvific action."[46]

The Franciscan Raymond Lull, who was born in Majorca and grew up familiar with Moorish and Jewish cultures, wrote his *Arbor scientiae*, which contains most of his tree illustrations, in 1295 in Rome. He tried to interest Boniface VIII in this work.[47] Lull presents ascent in multiple ways. In his forest of the sciences, eight trees represent mainly human wisdom, and eight present mainly divine wisdom. Particularly interesting is his illustration *Celestial Tree*, which, like the tree in *Timaeus*, has its roots in heaven; the branches are the twelve signs of the zodiac, and the twigs are the seven planets.[48]

Lull's drawings, as well as drawings in printed versions of his works, are the simple introduction to his art, which takes the initiate into intricate paths of analogical thinking. His idea to show the trees of knowledge as both vegetative trees and classificatory systems may itself rely on some

3.3. A "tree of history" from the *Liber figurarum* of Joachim of Floris (ca. 1135–1202), ms., Dresden, A. 121, fol. 93v.

earlier trees of knowledge. The process of ascending to the heavenly sphere and beyond to God he disclosed in drawings prepared for his manuscript on ascent and descent. As we saw in the Talmudic midrash, ladders and trees both function in medieval religious thought as paths of ascent and descent.[49] In the drawing from *Liber de ascensu et descensu* (Valencia, 1512) that Frances Yates reprints the schematic drawing of labeled stairs with pictorial representation invites the initiate to proceed upward.[50] Following instruction on the graded scale of knowledge, one steps first to the level of stone and then to that of fire, progresses through the vegetative, animal, and human levels, and then proceeds to the heavenly realm, to the angelic realm, and to God, for whom there is no pictorial representation. The sun shines brightly on the door to the castle of wisdom. In contrast to eleventh- and twelfth-century manuscript illustrations, which show devils clawing down men and women who attempt to climb the ladder to God, drawings to Lull are optimistic, with no obstacles on the path upward. In the illustration reprinted by Frances Yates a teacher points the way and the door to wisdom is wide open. According to Lull's neo-Platonic viewpoint, no evil is there: evil is simply the absence of good.[51] It is intriguing that a later artistic interpretation inserted in an eighteenth-century edition from Palma, Majorca, shows a closed door; on the side a large palm tree bends in harmony with the stairs of ascent.[52]

CHRISTIAN TREES OF KNOWLEDGE

Tree diagrams are useful visual teaching aids that medieval schoolmen inherit form antiquity. The Greek scholar Porphyry's (ca. 234–ca. 305) *Isagoge* introduces the *scala prediamentalis* into medieval logic books, and the simple format of the tree diagram aids in the teaching of universals.[53] In the twelfth century, as genealogical trees become common in legal documents, the first visual illustrations of trees classify the various disciplines of learning. Their emphasis on the knowledge aspect of the forbidden tree of knowledge of good and evil gives them an ambiguous biblical allusion. The innovative portrayals that follow of the trees of knowledge, which encourage ascending to the heights of knowledge, counteract a taboo on knowing "high things."[54] In the *Arbor sapientiae* at the Beinecke Rare Book Room, Yale University, an abstract rising tree formation charts the areas of learning.[55]

The "tree of history" of Joachim of Floris (1135–1202) follows the same structural format as does the tree of Jesse but is an apocalyptical presentation of three ages of history—of the Father, the Son, and the Holy Ghost (see fig. 3.3). From the head of Noah arise two stems, Shem and Japhet, from whom ancient civilizations of Jews and Gentiles arise. The civilizations intersect above the head of Jesus, joining again over the head of the dove, representing the Holy Spirit. The branches wind around each other there, indicating conversion (euphemistically, "reconciliation") among Jews and Gentiles as they join in knotted branches above.[56] Joachim of Floris applies the dichotomy of withered tree and fruitful tree to visualizing the transference of the status of children of God from the Hebrew people to the Christians who follow the Gospels. Whereas before Jesus God's people, the Jews, flourish and their branch on the left bears fruit, the situation is reversed when they do not follow Jesus in the middle stage of history. In the reconciliation, which Joachim expects soon, all branches bear fruit.

Joachim's tree of history is not a classification scheme that happens to be in tree form but an organic vegetative image of historical development. The gestation period for the first stage of history extended from Adam to Abraham; for the second, from Elijah to Jesus; and for the third, from the foundation of monasteries under Saint Benedict to Joachim's own time. According to Roger Cook, "What was really new was Joachim's idea of the overlapping of these periods. For just as each new shoot on the tree grows out of the one preceding it, so the periods of history overlap, each stage germinating out of the one preceding it."[57] We shall see that Italian and northern humanists create notions of cultural rebirth that also use organic vegetative images for historical development.

Sixteen trees form the organic imagery for Lull's encyclopedia *Arbor scientiae*. Yates reprints illustrations from the edition printed in Lyons in 1515.[58] Lull appears with a monk under the branches of the "Tree of all the sciences." Of particular interest to humanists would be the "Arbor humanalis" (Tree of humanity), which comprises all the human capacities, including branches of elemental, vegetative, sensitive, and imaginative capacities, spiritual branches of memory, intellect, and will, and branches of arts and sciences that derive from the above capacities. The illustration of the "Arbor moralis" (Tree of morality) shows eighteen good roots and five bad roots and divides into two trees, one of the virtues and one of the vices. Lull's images show the root, trunk, branches, leaves, blossoms, and fruits of knowledge.

Although Lull's fullest forest of trees of knowledge is in his *Arbor scientiae*, trees appear as educational devices in his other books as well. One of the most interesting is Lull's diagram showing a horizontal cross section of the trunk and the fully flowering tree of medicine from his book on the principles of medicine (fig 3.4). He thus applies both meanings of *arbor*, "tree" and "shaft of a wheel." The core of the trunk shows his analogical system, in which letters are associated with the elements, the signs of the zodiac, the planets, and the temperaments. The four temperaments—hot, dry, humid, cold—also proceed up the main shaft of the tree of medicine. In this case the structure of a tree is a motivating educational strategy that guides the student of medicine to the full text of the book.[59]

3.4. A "tree of medicine," indicating steps and principles (core and trunk), from the *Liber principiorum medicinae* of Raymond Lull (1232–ca. 1316).

CHRISTIAN TREES OF VIRTUE AND VICE

The tree of knowledge of good and evil becomes graphically illustrative of Christian dichotomies among the virtues and vices. The abundance of human potential that can merely be guessed at in Hildegard's visualization of the multiplicity in the descending soul becomes clearly delineated among her contemporaries who classify and neatly label the leaves of the virtues and the leaves of the vices. The first trees of virtue and vice of the twelfth century are both organic vegetative images and graphical charts with labeled and pictorial medallions.

In the "Arbor bona" (good tree) and the "Arbor mala" (evil tree) of Lambert of Saint-Omer's *Liber floridus* (Flowery book) (fig. 3.5), two distinct trees branch out from the central roots. The tree of virtue springs from charity, the mother of all virtues. The trunk bears branches with twelve medallions of virtues, which produce sprouts and distinct buds. Thus, virtues are paired with trees: continence with the rose, sobriety with the fir, peace with the plane, faith with the pine, and so on. Such symbolism is commonplace in literature of herbals.[60] The root of the tree of evil encircles an inscription on cupidity; the medallions have no pictures to tempt us, only inscriptions of twelve evils; the branches wither, and the leaves lack the vitality of the tree of virtue.[61] In this rendition, which excludes Jews from fellowship among the virtuous, the tree of virtue is labeled to indicate faith in *ecclesia* and the tree of vice is labeled conspicuously *synagoga*, indicating that the path to virtue is a divine path through membership in the church; the biblical passages quoted are Gal. 5.19–22ff. and Matt. 21.18ff.

Another version with two distinct trees appears in the tract by Pseudo-Hugo, *De fructibus carnis et spiritus* (Salzburg, second quarter of the twelfth century). The tree of vice has medallions containing busts of the major vices and drooping leaves detailing the subsidiary vices. At the pinnacle is Adam crossing his arms with shame. The tree of virtue has medallions containing busts of the cardinal virtues and busts of theological virtues and flourishing leaves reaching upward like hands in prayer. At the top of the tree the new Adam, Christ, gives a benediction.[62] By the late thirteenth century, illustrations of trees of virtue and vices appear in handbooks for clergy. Churches are decorated with symbolic vegetation, as noted by Wilhelmus Durandus in 1284: "Sometimes flowers are portrayed, and trees: to represent the fruits of good works springing from the roots of virtues."[63] The level of detail in the listing of subsidiary vices seems to correspond to the intricate church management of sin, as evidenced also in the development of manuals for confession and pastoral care.[64]

In contrast to the portrayal of the tree of vice as a synagogue, Lull's trees of virtue and vice are ecumenical. In Lull's *Liber de Gentili et de tribus sapientibus* (The book of the Gentile and the three wise men), which is an ecumenical conversation, as is Peter Abelard's *Dialogue of a Philosopher*

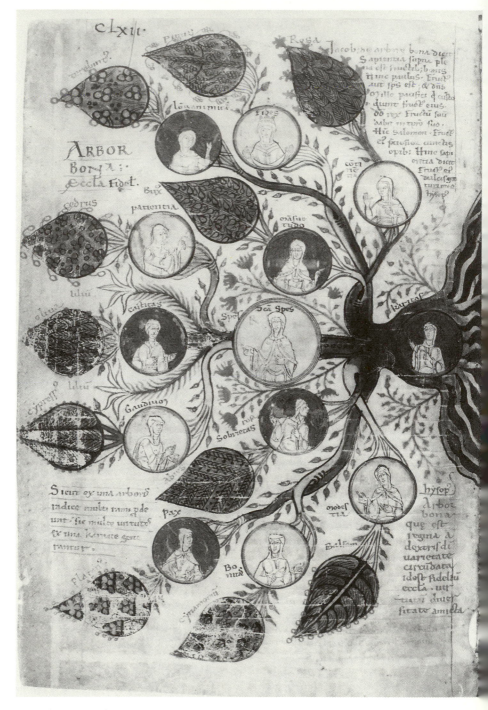

3.5. "Arbor bona; eccla. fidet." and "Arbor mala; synagoga," tree trunk splitting into branches blossoming with flowers of virtue and branches decaying with wilted leaves of vice. From Lambert of Saint-Omer's *Liber floridus*, twelfth century, Ghent University Library, ms. 92.

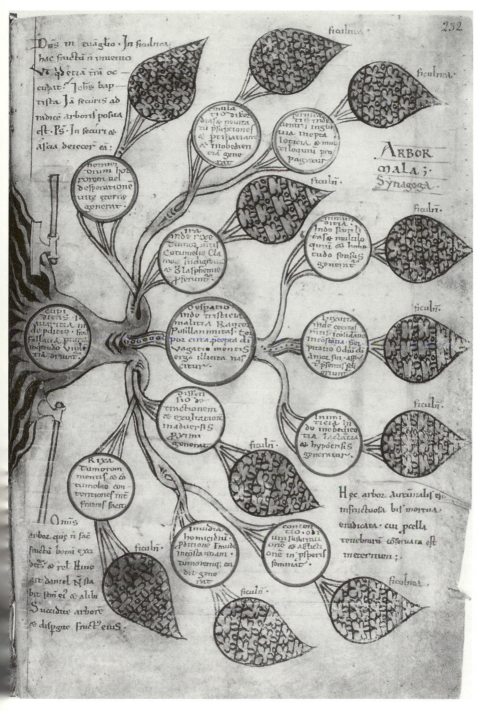

3.6. A Jew and a Gentile under a tree of virtues and vices, from the *Book of the Gentile*, by Raymond Lull, ms. 1732, Biblioteca Universitaria di Bologna.

with a Jew and a Christian, a Gentile and a Jew sit under a tree of virtues and vices (fig. 3.6), and in another, Saracen and Christian sit under a tree of virtues.[65] Situated like philosophers disputing in a garden in Epicurus's Athens or Cicero's Rome, members of different religions conduct a disputation under a tree—a possibility in the Iberian Peninsula in the fourteenth century. A Christian, a Jew, and a Muslim each politely tries to convince a Gentile of the best path to God; Lull's overall structure is polemical and evangelical in order to make the Christian faith the obvious right choice. He cites Aquinas's *Summa contra Gentiles* in another work in 1309, and his intent is in the spirit of the prevalent conversionary tactics.[66] Nevertheless his most important point—that the Jew, the Muslim, the Christian, and the Gentile all believe that they can agree on the same virtues and vices— indicates Lull's belief that human wisdom, knowledge for governing oneself morally in society, can be shared ecumenically and is not limited to those who receive Jesus Christ.

Vegetative and spark imagery are combined in Lull's works. As discussed by J. N. Hillgarth, the Muslim, the Jew, and the Christian compare sparks and seeds, seeing the analogy between sparks, which become fire, and seeds, which grow into trees. In the *Liber de meravelles* (ca. 1284) a philosopher sits under a tree contemplating God through the study of vegetation. Asked how a tree can grow from a small seed, he explains that a fire grows great on account of its *virtus*, converting to itself material that had less *virtus*. The philosopher then praises the questioner for drawing the parallel of the greatness of the *virtus* of Jesus Christ in relationship to other individuals. Lull thus links multiple meanings of *virtus*, especially "vigor" and "moral virtue."[67]

Lull's tree illustrations survive in fourteenth-century manuscripts in Catalonia, Paris (where he visited), in the libraries of Lorenzo de' Medici's physician, Pier Leoni, and Pico della Mirandola in Florence, and in German areas where Nicholas of Cusa worked. In sixteenth-century Paris, Lefèvre d'Étaples publishes Lull manuscripts and arranges for the Franciscan Bernard de Lavinheta to fill a chair of Lullism at the Sorbonne.[68] The illustrations of the 1515 Lyons printed edition of the *Arbor scientiae* are evidence of the abundant vegetative imagery for learning, virtue, and ascent available in the French Renaissance. For Lull the visual images are important "so that the senses can help the imagination and the imagination the intellect." They are also mnemonic "so that the memory can more easily recall the universal principles of the Art."[69]

VISUAL AND VERBAL VEGETATIVE SYMBOLISM

Arborescent imagery of the Divine as a tree or vine, showing a divine path to divine wisdom through participation in Jesus Christ, may be functional and educational in aiding illumination theories. Certainly the tree of Jesse plays this orthodox role, compatible with Augustine's vegetative imagery. From the perspective of the Christian view of participation or illumination, some of the images of the tree of ascent that do not point to a path through Jesus may be disturbing. Especially threatening are images of the Divine as a tree or vine that onlookers are encouraged to ascend naturally, by their own efforts. The illustrator, like the author, may be intentionally obscure about which path is designated; in terms of theological orthodoxy that obscurity is one of the values of symbolic language and imagery.[70]

My examples of visual vegetative imagery suggest varieties of verbal vegetative symbolism. The tree of Jesse suggests a divine path to divine wisdom (requiring baptism to participate), and Lull's trees of sciences suggest a natural path to human wisdom (available to those who try). There also are challenging trees, such as the *sefirot* tree (fig. 3.2), which is enticingly ambiguous concerning whether there is a human or a divine path to divine wisdom but very clear that there is a divine path open to non-Christians, in fact taught best in Hebrew. There are variations in Christian perspective: some illustrators indicate that the tree of virtue is limited to members of the church, whereas others present the trees of virtues and vices as a natural or human path to human wisdom available to people of diverse faiths. Lull's trees of divine wisdom in his forest of the sciences, and especially the upside-down celestial tree and the 1512 ladder of ascent, might suggest to some that his educational strategy is a natural path to divine wisdom. Lull invites adherents of many faiths to learn how to ascend either the ladder or the tree to God.

Within this cultural context of tree images a Stoicizing epistemology of seeds of virtue and knowledge, which implies a vegetative growth pattern of the human mind, is easily appropriated into diverse medieval and Renaissance texts. In fact the educational strategies in the visual images of trees that emerge in the twelfth century are aimed at enhancing God-given human powers. Trees of genealogical and legal descent, trees of virtue and vice, and trees of knowledge develop concomitantly with the increase in confidence in human reason and in seeds of virtue and knowledge evident in humanists such as John of Salisbury and in scholastics such as Thomas Aquinas. In a cultural milieu that favors vegetative imagery for knowledge, virtue, and ascent, confidence in the potential of the natural growth of the human mind increases among some in the thirteenth century as Stoicizing epistemology spreads even to such Augustinians as Matthew of Aquasparta and the *Zohar* and Lull's mnemonic art enter European culture.

The Renaissance fascination with vegetative symbolism is more extensive than these examples show. Particularly rich are the tree images deriving from ancient mythology. We shall consider only a few of the numerous images of trees that come into Renaissance civilization from ancient polytheistic civilizations. As individuals in the Renaissance overcome Christian fears of corruption from pagan rituals, they revive the ancient custom of recognizing talent and achievement by the appearance of a laurel wreath sprouting from a poet's brow.[71]

MYTHOLOGICAL ARBORESCENT IMAGES OF INDIVIDUAL VIRTUE

In the circle of Ficino, Platonic myths such as the myth of the cave or the myth of the androgyne express philosophical mysteries wherein beauty and truth fuse. Likewise, Renaissance renditions of pagan gods, goddesses, heroes, and heroines abound. In Boccaccio's *Genealogiae* (Venice, 1494), a key guidebook for Renaissance writers and artists, the amorous adventures of divinities with humans are aided by full-page, vine-like genealogical charts of descent from the god above to the heroes and heroines below; particularly suggestive of divine impregnation of humans is portrayal of the nude Neptune at the top of a vinelike tree branching into the names of his descendants below.[72] Humor and playfulness are essential to the myth-making in the intellectual, literary, and artistic circle of Lorenzo de' Medici and Marsilio Ficino. Renaissance writers and thinkers enjoy paradox, enigma, and particularly metamorphosis.

Ovid's *Metamorphoses* repeatedly exemplifies the idea of *arborescere*, "to grow into a tree." The best-known example is Daphne becoming a tree as she flees from Apollo. Even though Daphne flees in a way that hinders Apollo from a sexual relationship, their names are linked in memory as lover and beloved. A Renaissance observer might identify either with Apollo, who receives a laurel, or with Daphne, who experiences vegetative flowering. In a culture that views propagation of plants as an asexual process, the vegetative conclusion of the Apollo-Daphne myth suggests turning from a human sexual relationship to a higher path, as in a tree growing toward the heavens. In the miniature *L'Épître d'Othéa* by Christine de Pizan a tranquil serenity dominates the scene, as Daphne, whose skirt is as modest as a tree trunk, grows branches from her waist upward, while Apollo looks on in awe.[73] A more passionate version, a fresco painted in the early sixteenth century in the Palazzo della Farnesina in Rome, joins Apollo to Daphne in an upward embrace as her legs dissolve into a tree trunk and her head and arms sprout branches (fig. 3.7).[74] Daphne's metamorphosis may be background to Botticelli's rendition of Chloris. In the frieze decoration surrounding Botticelli's *Calumny of Apelles*, Botticelli renders Daphne's metamorphosis as only her head becoming treelike behind a figure of Venus; Venus points upward, as does Mercury in the *Primavera*.[75]

Ovid's *Metamorphoses* fascinates Renaissance readers with the multifold possibilities of transformations. Vegetative transformation, considered asexual and rising to the Divine, symbolically suggests a superior path for humanity. "The Garden," a poem by the seventeenth-century English poet

3.7. Peruzzi or Giulio Romano, fresco of Apollo and Daphne,
Palazzo della Farnesina, Rome, 1510–12.

Andrew Marvell, reinterprets the myth in such a way that both Daphne and
Apollo get what they wish for:

> Apollo hunted Daphne so,
> Only that she might laurel grow.
> And Pan did after Syrinx speed,
> Not as a nymph, but for a reed.[76]

Ficino: Neo-Platonic Ascent through Love and Education

MARSILIO FICINO (1433–99), the leading philosopher of the neo-Platonic Academy under Medici patronage in Florence, reformulates the Stoic phrases in relationship to Platonic and neo-Platonic texts, applying the models of vegetative growth and sparks rising to explain the soul's ascent to God. We shall focus on Ficino's commentary on Plato's *Symposium*, which influences literature, art, philosophy, educational theory, and religion. Both Ficino and his fellow neo-Platonic philosopher Giovanni Pico della Mirandola (1463–94) pride themselves on syncretism.[1] Ficino aims to harmonize Platonic and neo-Platonic texts with Christianity, as in his *Theologia platonica*, which, as we shall see, accords with major points of his *De amore* (On love, based on commentary on Plato's *Symposium*).

Starting in 1559 in the Medici Florentine villa built by Michelozzo in the gardens of Careggi, Cosimo de' Medici (1389–1464), inspired by recent Latin translations of some of Plato, encouraged Ficino (1433–99) to produce a Latin translation of the complete dialogues of Plato.[2] Ficino builds around him a scholarly community who converse like philosophers of antiquity in a garden setting.[3] In *De Christiana religione*, written after he becomes a priest in 1473, Ficino admits that he plays a lyre and sings Orphic hymns at holy festivities such as the celebration of Plato's birthday. Artists learn to imitate nature's beauty in the garden of Careggi,[4] which one can visit in Florence today. When Lorenzo de' Medici (1449–92) succeeds his father as ruler of the republic of Florence, the Platonic Academy of Ficino and his associates becomes well known throughout Europe for its original philosophical productions and its influence on the arts.

Ficino's key works appear in large printed editions: *Theologia platonica de immortalitate animae*, his Platonic theology proving the immortality of the soul (1482), and *Platonis opera omnia* (1484), containing his translations of Plato's dialogues and commentaries on the *Timaeus* and the *Symposium*. Ficino also translates and comments on Plotinus and translates Porphyry, Proclus, and Dionysius the Areopagite. The *Opera omnia* (Basel, 1561) becomes a major vehicle for spreading Plato's and Ficino's thought in France.

The vegetative symbolism we shall see in Ficino is compatible with Medici patronage. Janet Cox-Rearick has fully documented how the Medici family in particular applies vegetative symbolism in the fifteenth century in imprese (seals or devices with mottos) and how after restoration of the Medici dynasty in 1512 the imagery expands into a political program

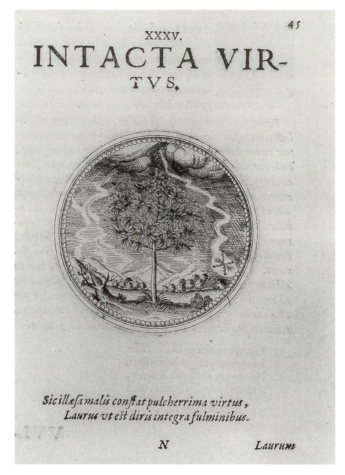

4.1. "Intacta virtus" (Uninjured virtue), emblem from
Joachim Camerarius's *Symbolorum et emblematum*, Nuremberg, 1590:
"Thus the fairest virtue stands firm, unharmed by evil / Just as the
laurel tree is untouched by the fearful lightning bolt."

supporting Medici rule. We might consider the associations of the laurel
branch with Lorenzo as early as 1459 in Gozzoli's *Procession of the Magi*.
Because it serves as a pun on *Lauro* and because of its appropriateness for
poets, the laurel becomes the device of Lorenzo the Magnificent after the
death of Cosimo de' Medici in 1464.[5] The laurel is an evergreen that grows
more vigorously when cut; the poet Poliziano repeats Pliny's account that
it can never be struck by Jupiter's lightning but is ever constant, as in the
emblem "Uninjured virtue" (fig. 4.1). Lorenzo's laurel is interpreted as a
symbol for the Medici's beneficence to Florence: Luca Pulci's 1464 poem
concludes with the line, "Florida fronda a far fiorir Fiorenzia" [A florid
leafage to make Florence flourish] (18).

With the Medici restoration the vegetative symbolism expands into monumental images to proclaim the flourishing of the dynasty, as in the abundant genealogical tree of Pope Leo X. Such a tree might be viewed as proclaiming the nobility derived from the seed of a lineage that is traced with care, as well as the nobility evinced by the eminent accomplishments derived from Medici seeds of virtue. "Le tens revien" [The time returns] proclaims the association of Lorenzo's laurel and the regrowth of a golden age. The Medici shield of balls or oranges echoes actual orange groves and reverberates in the orange grove in the *Primavera*; the illustration of the restoration of 1512 renews a version created under Lorenzo the Magnificent, highlighting Flora both carrying a flaming laurel branch and sitting under a flourishing laurel tree (17–24).

In the sixteenth century, scholars and artists in Florence and throughout Europe will look back with nostalgia on the Medici golden age of Ficino's Academy in Careggi. A fitting symbol for the generous Medici patronage of scholarship in the garden of Careggi is an image by Moreni showing Apollo and the Muses under a laurel tree, which is the frontispiece of a manuscript dedicated to the younger Lorenzo during the restoration (fig. 4.2).

In 1513 the younger Lorenzo, the duke of Urbino (1492–1519), stages a triumphant pageant that takes its name from the laurel branch, *broncone*. The frontispiece of the manuscript presented to him honors him as "il magnifico Laurentio Medici secundo" and portrays him as Apollo, surrounded by Muses, ushering in another golden age (26–27).[6] Nardi's song accompanying Lorenzo's pageant includes the lines, ". . . the happy Age returns and the phoenix is born from the stump of the old laurel, / and thus from the Iron Age is born the Gold" (27). The phoenix, a symbol for both the renewal of time and the renewal of life after death, is associated here with the restoration of the Virgilian Golden Age.[7] The vegetative symbolism of this frontispiece includes not only the laurel tree at the center, rising above Apollo/Lorenzo and one Muse's head, but also the distinct laurel branches sprouting upward above the heads of each of the eight seated liberal arts. The semicircle of arts leads to fertility and growth of the soul, and Cupid's bow suspended on the laurel indicates that love helps draw one's spirit upward. Apollo/Lorenzo's lyre brings harmony to Florence, and the pleasant music leads one's soul up the laurel, a tree of virtue, to the phoenix ushering in a new age. This image alludes to the golden age under Medici patronage of philosophers, writers, and artists who created in harmony beauty, truth, and virtue in the garden of Careggi.

Ficino's most influential single commentary, the one on Plato's *Symposium*, enables Stoic vegetative imagery to pass into the Renaissance as "Platonic" and "Academic." Ficino's commentary expresses Stoic concepts within a cosmic hierarchical framework taken from Plotinus and uses garden imagery to point the way to the natural ascent to God along the paths of love and education. *De amore*, to use its short Latin title, is a major

4.2. Apollo and the Muses under a laurel tree, by Moreni, frontispiece to
Lauretum, sive carmina in laudem Laurentii Medicis, ms. 23.2.52,
Biblioteca Laurenziana, Florence.

contribution to Renaissance theories of knowledge and pedagogy.[8] In particular, the use of Platonizing Stoic and Stoicizing Platonic spark and seed imagery in descriptions of the human soul gives renewed emphasis to the potent capacities of the human soul to strive for knowledge and virtue and to contemplate the ideas in the Godhead.[9] Ficino's vivid imagery of divine radiating light renews the neo-Platonic strand in Augustinian illumination theory; while respectful of human dependence on God's grace for illumination, Ficino's version interprets grace as abundantly available and places emphasis on human efforts, initiated by the indwelling light in the human soul, to ascend to the Divine.[10]

What follows is not a summary of Ficino's commentary but rather an intentionally concise analysis of the systematic and hierarchical seed and light theory contained in the seven speeches of the commentary. My citations indicate evidence of this seed and light theory elsewhere in Ficino's works to encourage further scholarship.

The first speech establishes the four Plotinian hypostases, namely, that from the Unity of God (*deus*) comes, second, the angelic mind (*mens angelica*); third, the world soul (*anima mundi*); and fourth, the material world (*machina*).[11] This treatise on the origin of love thus focuses on the second hypostasis, angelic mind, wherein are the Platonic ideas or models for the created world described in the *Timaeus*. Light imagery explains the relationship of the three hypostases to God, their author and creator: "But because [mind] is born from God, it turns toward God, its beginning, through a certain innate [*ingenitu*] appetite. Turned toward God, it is illuminated by His ray" (38; 1.3.4v). The light and splendor of light are what attract mind to God, and in that attraction comes the illumination of mind, the imprinting of the natures of all things to be created. Following Plotinus in his conceptualization of stages in the emergence of angelic mind from the One, Ficino's gradations of light imagery clarify the stages from potentiality to actuality, how the dark unformed angelic mind turns back to God and becomes the illuminated angelic mind from which proceeds inflammation, a clinging to God, and the emerging of the ideas of things to be.[12] This treatise on love is about attraction or love for divine beauty, which on the cosmic level brought about the created world and on the individual human level has the power to turn the human soul back to God for illumination with true knowledge.

In the second speech, comparing the longing of lovers to human longing for God, Ficino applies *The Republic* 6.508a–509b to point out the need for the light of truth to warm our souls (46; 2.2.10v). Recognizing that both Dionysius (*De Div. nom.* 4) and Plato compare God to the sun and that the divine light is what allows the visible light to be seen by the eyes, Ficino, like Leone Ebreo subsequently, interprets the sun as a light lesser than the divine light of truth.[13] Ficino ends this section with a traditional Augustinian comment to the effect that God illuminates and infuses souls with grace (47; 2.2.10v).

Speech 2, chapter 3, based on the fifth book of Plotinus's *Enneads*, clarifies the five levels in the hierarchy of images related to illumination. In describing the fourth level—the material world—the speech distinguishes nature (*natura*) from matter (*materia*):

> If the goodness of all things is the one God Himself, through whom all things
> are good, then beauty is the ray of God, infused in those four circles revolved
> around God in a certain way. This ray forms in those four circles all the species
> of all things. Those species we are accustomed to call in the mind, ideas; in the
> soul, reasons; in nature, seeds; and in matter, forms. Therefore in the four
> circles there seem to be four splendors. The splendor of ideas in the first, of
> reasons in the second, in the third of seeds, of forms in the last. (49; 2.2.12r)

This explanation helps to clarify creation-emanation as radiating in concentric circles from God, who initiates both the creation of ideas and the subsequent creation of material imitations through the seminal principles:
from God come the angelic mind's ideas, from which come reasons in the
world soul, and from these come the generative seeds in nature, and from
the seeds come the forms in matter.[14] Then in a scholastic argument Ficino
argues that these last are valued least as a path to the Divine and thus
human cognition arising from the senses is not the path to judge divine
things, that is, ideas and reasons. The human soul (*humanus animus*) is
kindled with desire to know what the ideas and reasons are but is mistaken
if it judges such divine things by the nature of material forms (51; 2.4.15v).
Ficino draws a parallel between human and divine love, indicating that the
passion of lovers, evidence of the heavenly ray (*celestis radius*), makes them
see more clearly (53; 2.4.16v). Having shown the causative progression of
the material world from the spiritual world, Ficino moves on with the
proem "The divine beauty shines through all things and is loved in all
things" (51; 2.4.15v).

The emanation of seeds in nature from reasons in the soul are basic to
the allegorical distinction between the two Venuses that appears in speech
2, chapter 7. The heavenly Venus, who in the Hesiodic account sprung
without a mother from the seed of Uranus, is the intelligence in the angelic
mind. The earthly Venus, who in the Homeric account is the daughter of
Jove and the mortal woman Dione, is the power of procreation in the
world soul.[15] Botticelli is to be influenced by the neo-Platonic discussions
of the two Venuses and paints both, the heavenly in his *Birth of Venus* and
the earthly in his *Primavera*. Ficino teaches that the beauty in the material
world derives from sparks (*scintillae*) from the earthly Venus that she in
turn received from the heavenly Venus, who embraced divinity. When a
human soul loves beauty in the form of a body, its power of understanding
(figuratively, its heavenly Venus) is aroused to seek through those sparks
the divine beauty, whereas its power of procreation (figuratively, its second
Venus) seeks to procreate a similar form in a corporeal body. While respecting the perpetuation of the human species through marital love, in the

ninth chapter Ficino explains that true reciprocal love aims to approximate the first Venus's love of intellect alone.

The third speech, which focuses on natural philosophy, equates love with the principle holding the cosmos together, as in *Enneads* 4.4.31–32, and foreshadows Diotima's speech in its comparison and distinction of natural procreation and artistic creation.[16] Ficino deems legitimate the propagation by seeds throughout nature, and he parallels that process with God giving light from the stars to all elements (64–65; 3.2.24r). Likewise, God as artist of the world is compared to human artists, craftsmen, and governors, and the dynamic in all creation is shown to be love. A student's thirst for learning derives from love, as does a teacher's concern for students (66; 3.3.25r). Ficino credits to the divine Creator the source of the fecundity of all things, that is, "the desire of propagating one's own perfection," and draws the inference that all works of the same Creator are bound to each other by reciprocal love. Fascinated by "coming to be," genesis—the origin of nature and humanity, the regular succession of growth of plants, the birth of animals and humans, and the cultural creations by humans—Ficino describes the bonding and reciprocal love that perpetuates the biological and physical world as "nodus perpetuus et copula mundi" [eternal knot and link of the world] (67–68; 3.3.27r).

Ficino's positive image of sexual union as a knot is an important precedent to a visual illustration in Barthélemy Aneau's emblem book *Picta poesis, ut pictura poesis erit,* whose title rewords Horace to draw reciprocal comparisons between poems and paintings, verbal images and visual images.[17] In the emblem of marriage (fig. 4.3) the central tree unites male and female. While the satyr, on the viewer's right, suggests the animal passions, Moses, on the viewer's left, points approvingly to the marriage under law. The lover's knot ties the couple to the tree of life; lovebirds and their young connote both souls and procreativity.[18] The male and female knotted together as one tree of life correlate also with Spenser's vegetative imagery in his description of the two lovers Britomart witnesses in the woods: "No word they spake, nor earthly thing they felt / But like two senceles stocks in long embracement dwelt." Britomart interprets them as a "faire Hermaphrodite" in accord with the ancient legend of the fusing of Salmacis with Hermaphroditus: "So seemed these two, as growne together quite. . . ."[19] The related ancient concept of male and female as an androgyne is in fact the topic of the following speech of Ficino on the legend of Aristophanes.

In speech 4 Ficino interprets the legend that there were three original kinds of human beings, a legend that Plato attributed to his speaker, Aristophanes. These spherical beings with four hands and legs and two faces came in three varieties: male and male, female and female, and male and female. Ficino takes the legend to indicate "human beings, that is, human souls" [homines, id est, hominum anime] (73; 4.2.30), a definition that Kristeller attributes to Plotinus. In the *Theologia platonica* Ficino quotes

4.3. Arboreal love knot in an emblem of marriage,
from Barthélemy Aneau, *Picta poesis*, 1552.

Plotinus: "*Homo* is the rational Soul itself, which remains in itself and generates the animal under itself," and one of Ficino's philosophical letters to
Giovanni Cavalcanti, his speaker in the first three orations, is entitled *Homo
est animus* and amplifies the *topos* of speech 2, chapter 8, on the exchange
of souls in reciprocal love.[20] Viewing a human as a soul is consistent with
the proem of speech 4, chapter 3, "The human being is the soul itself, and
the soul is immortal." Ficino makes clear that it is the soul (*anima*) that
procreates, nourishes, runs, and speaks, although we say that the "human
being" (*homo*) does these things (74; 4.3.31r). The soul alone is the human
being, and the body only its tool. In the most important intellectual activity, that of understanding incorporeals, the soul functions without the
body. Despite body changes from infancy to old age, we are called *homines*
throughout, for the term applies to souls, not bodies (74–75; 4.3.31–32).
"Who therefore, will be so foolish as to attribute the appellation of
'human,' which is firmly fixed in us, to the body, which is always flowing
and everywhere changed, rather than to the most stable soul? From these
things it can be clear that, when Aristophanes said humans, he meant our
souls, in the Platonic way" (75; 4.3.32v). Ficino's discussion of this myth
indicates that the current standard translation of *homo* as "man" would be

more appropriately retranslated in gender-free, body-free language as "human soul." In Plato's *Timaeus* any individual soul could be joined with either a male or female body.

Ficino allegorizes the mystery of Aristophanes' legend of the spherical beings into an image of bipartite nonmaterial souls. As in Philo's allegory of Genesis, the human soul has two intellects, one directed toward God and the other toward this world. Similarly, human souls when first created by God in the perfect shape had two lights—innate (*lumen ingenitum*), to perceive equal and inferior things, and infused (*lumen infusum*), to perceive superior things. Wishing to be like God, the souls used only the innate lights, the innate lights were divided from the infused lights, and the divided souls fell into bodies. Humans in adolescence are inspired by their natural, innate lights to seek through study the infused, divine light. On becoming whole they will receive a vision of God (73; 4.2.30–31r).

The notion that a spark of God is in human nature appears in speech 4, chapter 4. Ficino comments on the poem, "That the soul was created furnished with two lights and why it descends into the body." This account of the divine creation and enlightenment of the human soul parallels the account in speech 1 of the divine creating and sparking of the world mind and subsequently of the angelic soul. Likewise, the description of descent of human souls into bodies may parallel the account in speech 2 of the generation of animate matter. What descends may ascend; the physical principle that a small spark can ignite a bright flame and that fire rises is background to the image of the newly born soul turning to God and receiving illumination from God's rays. The soul turns or converts to God— the parent who gave it birth—and receives the first *scintilla*, which is sufficient for the soul to see itself and things inferior to itself but is not sufficient to see God. As fire rises, so the spark raises the human soul to God and enables it to receive the infused light and so perceive heavenly things. In order that there will be rational animals in accord with God's providence, often the *scintilla* dims in its contraction in a human soul, and the soul does not experience conversion back to its parent but acts as if its natural light is sufficient to itself; weighed down by its desire for a body, it descends into a human bodily form (75–76; 4.4.33r–34r). This account applies Aquinas's distinction between the natural and infused lights of the intellect (*Sum. theol.* 1–2.63), a distinction that is not present in Plotinus but is important for the Christian notion of divine illumination and grace in human lives.

Speech 4, chapter 5, indicates that humans may prepare themselves to receive infused light by practicing the four cardinal virtues—prudence and then courage, justice, and temperance. The distinctions in Aristophanes' fable are allegorized, so that courage is the masculine original being, temperance is the feminine being, and justice is the mixed male and female being; individuals vary in their predilection for one of these virtues. In stating that prudence leads us to another appropriate virtue, Ficino recognizes at least three lifestyles that lead to bliss. He labels ancient philosophers such as Epicureans and Stoics as having not only disregarded the divine light but spoiled their natural light through arrogance and thus as having been divided again as in Aristophanes' fable. One might interpret Ficino as separating Plato and his followers from the other ancient philosophers because he sees Plato as inspired by the Holy Spirit; if so, what Plato attributes to human potentiality for knowledge, as well as to the daemon inspiring Socrates, Ficino might be crediting to the divine inspiration from a trinitarian Christian perspective.

Ficino's severe criticism of the Stoics distinguishes him from many scholastics and humanists who attribute the natural light of moral virtues to pagan philosophers who aim for virtue and perhaps has encouraged neglect of the Stoic element in Ficino's overall Christian, neo-Platonic worldview. The Platonized Stoic image of the spark that inspires virtue distinguishes Ficino's "Platonic" commentary from the materialist Greek Stoics' view of God as a body, a divine fire leaving sparks of divinity in humankind.[21] Ficino advises his readers to recognize their limits, that is, the mutilation of natural light in its division from infused light, and to purge their souls in order that God might restore the soul through conjunction with the divine infused light (76–79; 4.5).

In speech 5, commenting on Plato's speech of Agathon, Ficino elaborates a comparison between the generation of goodness in a soul and generation of fecundity in a plant, a comparison that we have seen Seneca make evocatively in his epistle 124. Ficino may very well be drawing the analogy secondhand, for it is a commonplace among Italian humanist educators, as we shall see in my chapter 5. For example, Aeneas Sylvius Piccolomini, Pope Pius II (1458–64), writes in his book on education of 1450: "A master thus qualified will be competent to fulfill his duty, which is to fence in the growing mind with wise and noble precept and example, as a careful gardener hedges round a newly-planted tree. For in right training of the boy lies the secret of the integrity of the man."[22]

Any of the images in manuscripts by Raymond Lull might have suggested Ficino's vivid imagery. Lull shows that the roots of his trees of sciences and of virtues are the sources for the fecundity of the trees' blossoms.[23] Ficino, comparing the external manifestations of that beauty to that of a flowering plant, points out that the fecundity of the roots and stems generates the foliage, as the goodness of the soul causes the virtuous beauty of words and deeds: "There is as much difference between goodness and beauty as there is between a seed and a flower, and that just as the blossoms of plants, having originated in seeds, also produce seeds themselves, so this beauty, this blossom of goodness, as it originates from goodness, so it also leads lovers to goodness" (84; 5.1.40r).

Despite similarities to Seneca's epistle 124, Ficino's argument differs from Seneca where he parallels the beauty of the human person and that of the plant. Although Ficino accepts Plato's exceptional model of Socrates for the case of physical appearance belying internal beauty, he accentuates the medieval neo-Platonic tradition of recognizing in the physical manifestation of visible beauty the divine realm of invisible beauty.[24] Ficino's hierarchy of beauty relates back to speech 1, chapter 4, where Ficino states that love of a beautiful soul brings desire not for physical intercourse but for virtuous behavior. For Ficino love and educational pedagogy go hand in hand. Love expresses itself through intellect, eyes, and ears, not through smell, taste, or touch. In speech 5 he elaborates more fully that smell, taste, and touch are lower, corporeal senses, in contrast to the higher powers of reason, which have no specific location in the body. Without stating it here directly, Ficino clearly rejects the scholastic Aristotelian dictum that "all knowledge comes from the senses."

The lover needs to realize that the thirst is for God, whose rays shine most brightly in the angelic realm, secondarily in the realm of souls, and thirdly in the body of the world. Sometimes a mature individual through contemplation can find the reflection of the face of God by looking within. One might also see the incorporeal reflection of the face of God in a particular human who has the *scintilla divini* particularly bright, whose form corresponds very closely to the idea of the human species that our soul received from God. Beauty is "a certain lively and spiritual grace infused by the shining ray of God" that "inflames them [our souls] with burning love" (95; 5.6.52). Here Ficino links the double meaning of grace, the Christian infused gift of God and the aesthetic grace characteristic of a delightful vision, a harmonious melody, or virtuous human relationships.

Ficino's literary flair for combining vegetative and light symbolism lends his ideas to visual expression. In a 1621 Alciati emblem "Anteros, that is love of virtue," we find an epigram in which Cupid indicates that he sends arrows not to direct the passions to love of the common Venus but to spark burning love of the higher Venus: "I kindle in the pure minds the fires of learning. . . . And I weave out of virtue itself the four garlands."[25] Vegetative imagery appears also in the illustration: the leaves on Anteros's brow symbolize the wisdom developed by the love of the four cardinal virtues, and Cupid is shown alone pointing upward in harmony with the vertical thrust of a flourishing tree.

In speech 6 Ficino uses Diotima's account of the myth of Porus (plenty) lying with Penia (poverty) in the Garden of Jupiter to contrast the heavenly and earthly capacities for love. Going further than Plotinus in interpreting the allegory as one explaining earthly fecundity (*Enn.* 3.5.8–9), he explains that darkness of intellect, Penia, is compensated by the natural instinct in understanding to turn to God, its parent, from whom it receives the divine ray, Porus. "In this ray, as though in a kind of seed [*semen*], the reasons [*rationes*] of all things are contained" (116; 6.7.70r). The images light and seed are thus identified as in ancient Stoic thought. Adding to the discussion in speech 2 of the two Venuses, Porus thus is what the higher Venus receives, and her love puts the reasons in order. Meanwhile the lower

Venus "strives, through the fertility of its divine seeds, to reproduce in the matter of the world the beauty which is divinely conceived within itself" (118; 6.7.72r). The image of fertility is most fitting for the garden setting, encouraging further amplification of the comparison of the human soul to a plant.[26]

In speech 6, chapter 12, inspired by Diotima's contrast of procreativity and creativity, Ficino compares the pregnancy of the soul and the pregnancy of the body:

> If the body is fecund or fertile with seeds, the soul, which is more excellent than the body, is much more fertile, and it possesses the seeds of all of its own things from the beginning. Therefore the soul long ago was allotted the reasons of the customs, arts, and disciplines, and from them, if the soul is properly attended to, it will bring its own progeny into the world at the proper time. That the soul possesses innate reasons of all its own things we know from its desires, its seeking, its finding, its judging, and its comparing. (132; 6.12.88r)

In his *Philebus* commentary Ficino likewise discusses the soul's generation from itself of "laws, artifacts, books, words, morals" (producing them according to the rule of its rational principles) in the context of animal and plant propagation.[27] In *Theologia platonica*, a similar discussion of the "progeny" of the human mind culminates in one of the most optimistic passages in the Renaissance on the historically proven human capacities to invent technology, to create the fine and practical arts, to mold human and animal societies, and to cultivate the earth. Ficino proclaims that "the power of man, therefore, is very similar to that of the divine nature, seeing that man by himself, that is through his own decision and art, rules himself without being in the least limited by his physical nature, and imitates individual works of the higher nature."[28]

Discussing Diotima's speech in the *Symposium* and recognizing that the body is equipped at birth with the potential for teeth to develop at a specific time and for the seeds of procreation to flow at a later time, Ficino concludes that the mind is likewise equipped with a potential to grasp truth. Providing examples of each of the soul's faculties, he suggests that there must be innate ideas in the soul: "Some humans are said to become very learned even in youth, others with no teacher at all, and many others from a few rudiments of knowledge shown to them. This could never have happened, as we have said, except with nature helping a great deal. Socrates clearly proved this to the boys Phaedo, Theatetus, and Meno. . . . they are endowed by nature with the reasons of all the arts and disciplines" (133; 6.12.88r). In this eloquent account Ficino utilizes Plato's and Plotinus's examples of proof of innate ideas gained through prebodily reminiscence to proclaim the view found among Middle Stoics such as Posidonius and among Middle Platonists such as Cicero's teacher Antiochus that there are seeds or reasons of virtue and knowledge in human souls that give humans the potential through education for wisdom.[29] Ficino's Platonizing use of Stoic phrases serves well to maintain Christian orthodoxy. Sixteenth-century French readers of Plotinus and Ficino likewise modify Plato's doctrine of reminiscence in accord with Christian doctrine of the divine creation and implanting of each human soul.[30] While Aquinas's discussion of seeds of virtue and knowledge and natural law within human reason encourages scholastic theologians to think of Stoic epistemology as "Aristotelian," Ficino's reference to Phaedo, Theatetus, and Meno, coupled with references to Cicero's *Academica*, enables humanists to think of Stoic epistemology as "Platonic" or "Academic."

In speech 7 the points are summed up and the problems of vulgar love are discussed. A hierarchy of knowledge is presented for the soul's descent from its creator, God, to the body. Shining with a "ray of Divine Mind," the human soul contemplates ideas. As it contemplates itself, it reasons from universal reasons and draws conclusions. In studying bodies, the human soul acquires opinions through the senses. As it relates to matter, it uses nature to move and form matter (169; 7.13.120v). By divine madness, of which amatory madness is the most excellent, the soul can rise back up to the Divine. The book closes in the manner of an educational treatise: "But humans from a tender age, like plants from their younger years, must be cared for and directed towards the best fruit" (172; 7.16.122v). Echoing Seneca's epistle 124, Ficino here proclaims the paradigm of the mind developing like a plant.

We have seen that the ancient concepts seeds of virtue, sparks of divinity, reason, and common notions appear in a spectrum of texts and that these concepts are transformed either to indicate the divine path to divine wisdom through Jesus Christ, as in Augustine's epistemology or in visual images of the tree of Jesse, or to indicate the human path to human wisdom, as in Aquinas's mode of applying the natural light of the intellect to abstracting from sense data or as in the abstract classification schemes of Lull's visual trees of the virtues and the sciences. In the neo-Platonic view of Ficino the phrases appear as levels in a spherical organic universe. God the Creator is at the center, emanating the beauty of pure light, infusing four concentric circles with rays. Divine rays appear as ideas in the angelic mind, as reasons in the world soul, as seeds in nature, and as forms in matter. Since it is the progressively dimmed ray of the Divine that appears in mind, soul, nature, and body, human beings may admire the splendor of God by loving the beauty in any of these levels. Ficino recommends the practice of both active and contemplative virtues in the ascent to the divine light. To explicate this educational theory, he contributes to the contemporary humanist agricultural analogy between a student and a plant the evocative painterly image of the seed of virtue and knowledge blossoming under the warmth of the natural and infused lights and sparkling with love for the divine parent.

In book 11 of the *Theologia platonica* Ficino develops further the same epistemological assumptions—reasons of all arts and sciences, seeds of virtue, and sparks—that he credits to the founder of the Academy, Plato, as proof of the immortality of the soul.[31] His positive view of the potential of the human intellect to rise in contemplation of the Divine rests on a belief, derived from neo-Platonism and affirmative theology, of "the correspondence between the knowing mind and the object of its knowledge."[32] When the object of knowledge is God, Ficino's words, like the mystical trees of ascent, might suggest to an observer a human path to divine wisdom: "Thus the knowing mind and the thing known become one, since the form of that thing, as such molds the mind."[33]

Kristeller states for Ficino, "Immediate knowledge of God ... is achieved, not by the Soul's own force, but by an active intervention of God" (248), and he cites Ficino as follows: "The mind is not brought by its own power to assume divine substance as its own form, but is drawn by divine action" (246) and "So ungrateful men assert that they see true things through their own and natural light, whereas they really see them in the common divine light" (248). Nevertheless, Ficino's affirmative theology does suggest that one can rise far by effort before receiving the divine illumination that is preliminary in Augustine's mature epistemology. As Kristeller concludes regarding Ficino's approach to "knowledge of God": "Ficino's whole epistemology therefore converges, as we see into the knowledge of God. All thought is a steady ascent of the Soul toward God, in whom every particular and empirical knowledge unconsciously has a part and whom, in the supreme act of contemplation, the Soul finally perceives by intuition in His fullness of essence, face to face" (255).

Adapting the Senecan recommendations for cultivating the seeds of virtues and sciences and the spark of divinity to his commentary, Marsilio Ficino steers Renaissance educational theory and practice in the direction of spiritual reciprocal love between teacher and student as a path to reunion with the Divine. The title page of the 1561 *Opera omnia* provides an image that is to symbolize the neo-Platonic philosophy: while the heavenly wind blows, a hammer striking an anvil causes sparks to fly upward.

The influence of Ficino's epistemology of light is evident in Leone Ebreo's *Dialoghi d'amore* (1501) and, in less philosophical format, in Bembo's *Gli Asolani* (1505) and Castiglione's *Il Cortegiano* (1518). Leone Ebreo draws an analogy between God and light: "As the intellectual faculty is more excellent and its perception more perfect and true than that of the eye, so the light illumining the intellectual vision is more perfect and more truly light than that of the sun which illumines the eye of the body."[34] This passage clarifies the notion of light not simply as a metaphor but as a term for the ultimate divine intellect, for which the sun is a copy. The Hermit in Bembo's *Gli Asolani* states in his culminating speech: "But as all the stars draw light from the sun, all beauties which exist outside of the divine, eternal beauty are derived from it; and when our minds perceive these secondary beauties, they are pleased and gladly study them as likenesses and sparks of it, but they are never wholly satisfied with them be-

cause they yearn for that divine, eternal loveliness which they remember
and for which they are ever secretly spurred on to search."[35] The passage
brings up the influential image of sparks that are fragments of true divine
beauty. The stars and the sun are there to remind us each night and day of
our divine origin. At the close of Castiglione's *Il Cortegiano*, Bembo declares that the soul of the happy lover "sees in itself a ray of that light which
is the true image of the angelic beauty communicated to it." Rising higher
on a ladder of love, "the soul, aflame with the most holy fire of true divine
love, flies to unite itself with the angelic nature."[36]

Scholars have noticed the influence of Ficino's light imagery more than
that of his vegetative imagery; in chapter 5 we shall see that Ficino's vegetative and light imagery builds upon humanist sources. Humanist horticultural techniques for human education combine with Ficino's neo-Platonic
philosophy of love and education in the garden vision of Botticelli's *Primavera*, as well as in the historical concept of a rebirth of culture.

Italian Renaissance Humanism:
Rebirth and Flowering of
the Seeds of Virtue and Knowledge

RENAISSANCE SCHOLARS today are beginning to recognize that the Ciceronian belief that "the seeds of virtue are inborn in our dispositions and, if
they were allowed to ripen, nature's own hand would lead us on to happiness of life" gave humanists confidence that there was a standard of judgment at the foundation for oratory and prudent conduct.[1] Generally,
however, scholarship on Renaissance humanism, humanist education, or
individual humanists does not pay much attention to the seeds of virtue
and knowledge, this "tiny little something," in Martin Luther's words;[2] as
a result, the epistemological and philosophical foundations of Renaissance
humanism have not been fully appreciated.

My subject is the way the vegetative language of seeds of virtue and
knowledge among humanists and artists contributes to the formation of a
concept of a renaissance of arts and letters. Visual imagery, as well as written texts, make explicit the vegetative symbolism inherent in humanist
models of how the human mind develops. Humanist educators stress a
morally focused rhetoric that will inspire virtue in a lay public.[3] Let us keep
in mind many aspects of the model for the orator-sage, as proposed by
Quintilian:

> We are to form, then, the perfect orator, who cannot exist unless he is above
> all a good man. We require in him, therefore, not only consummate ability in
> speaking but also every excellence of mind. . . . Let the orator, therefore be
> such a man as may be called truly wise, not blameless in morals only (for that,
> in my opinion, though some disagree with me, is not enough), but accom-
> plished also in science, and in every qualification for speaking—a character
> such as, perhaps no man ever was. But we are not the less, for that reason, to
> aim at perfection, for which most of the ancients strove; though they thought
> that no wise man had yet been found, they nevertheless laid down directions
> for gaining wisdom.[4]

Of the five main subjects of humanist curricula—grammar, rhetoric, poetry, history, and moral philosophy—the first four together teach the fifth,
that is, applications of *recta ratio* to life.[5] The curricula, as well as individual, family, civic, or religious activity inspired by humanist writings and
speeches, encourage *imitatio* and *aemulatio* of exemplary men and women
of literature and history.

EPISTEMOLOGICAL CONFIDENCE AMONG FEMALE AND
MALE HUMANISTS

Before we look at Italian humanist educational theory, it is important to recognize that Cicero (106–43 B.C.E.) and Quintilian (ca. 35–ca. 100) had already had an earlier impact upon the humanist movement in the twelfth-century renaissance.[6] The *Metalogicon*, by the English educator John of Salisbury (1120–80), shows the influence of manuscripts of Quintilian (though defective ones) in northern France.[7] In his defense of the trivium John blends a Ciceronian perspective and the Christian qualification, all the time stressing that education builds on what is natural to a human being.[8]

Seed and fruit imagery in John of Salisbury helps us to show that the fourteenth-century discussion of rebirth and flowering is an established part of the liberal arts justification for education:

> Reason, the mother, nurse, and guardian of knowledge, as well as of virtue, frequently conceives from speech, and by this same means bears more abundant and richer fruit. Reason would remain utterly barren, or at least would fail to yield a plenteous harvest, if the faculty of speech did not bring to light its feeble conceptions, and communicate the perceptions of the prudent exercise of the human mind. Indeed, it is this delightful and fruitful copulation of reason and speech which has given birth to so many outstanding cities, has made friends and allies of so many kingdoms, and has unified and knit together in bonds of love so many peoples. (11)

John's gender play[9]—a teasing and gendering of words that ultimately show the fertility of the human mind through the copulation of male speech and female reason—is in harmony with twelfth-century habits of thought. Overall, John highlights the need for masculine speech, and especially dialectic, to fertilize feminine reason.[10]

Petrarch's (1304–74) writings and other early quattrocento humanist tracts on education indicate a Stoic strain, which explains how a refined educational program would encourage virtuous behavior. Petrarch's belief that his age was the dawn of a new period of cultural growth may be familiar, but his assessment of reason to proclaim the source of that emerging cultural rebirth is less well known. In his *Secretum*, of the 1340s, Petrarch searches his own soul in dialogue between Franciscus and Augustinus. Since there are Stoic concepts in Augustine's early works, we need not be surprised that the speech of the fictional Augustine analyzes a Stoic model for the wise person. At one point Augustinus places before us the Stoic belief in the nobility of human reason and recommends that human reason be applied to the practical moral goal of guiding one's life:

> If you see a human so potent in reason that he runs his life according to reason, subordinates his appetites to this alone, and checks his emotions by the

brake of reason, and knows that he distinguishes himself from the wildness of animals by this alone and deserves this very name of human in so far as he lives according to reason; moreover if he is a human so conscious of his mortality that he will have it daily before his eyes, regulate himself by it, and despising these perishable things, aspire to that life where, by a great increase of reason, he ceases to be mortal; he alone, you should say, has true and useful understanding of the definition of human. And concerning this last, since we talk about it, I said that very few attain a suitable understanding of it.[11]

Petrarch struggles so that he might have such strength of reason and will to govern his life, so that he might join the rare few talked about in classical texts; yet in his retrospective view of his life he recognizes, as does Thomas Aquinas, that the limited virtue of the pagan schools is not the ultimate goal for a Christian: "But we to whom, not by our own merit but by celestial gift, the light of truth more vividly appeared, where they stop we begin, for we strive not toward virtue as an end but toward God through virtues."[12] Fully within the Catholic tradition, Petrarch stresses that effort toward virtue is one important path to God.

In taking this perspective, Petrarch appreciates that ancient pagan literature also reflects a religious quest and that poetry has its origins "when at one time rude men, but burning with that desire which is innate in man for knowing the truth and for discovering the divine, began to think that there was some higher power by which mortals are ruled."[13] This view proclaims that the Divine is a common notion natural to humanity, a view basic to ancient Stoic moral theory; Petrarch validates reading pagan poetry through this recognition of the commonalty in the human quest for the moral and the Divine. In *De sui ipsius et multorum ignorantia* (On his own ignorance and that of many others) (1368–70) Petrarch recommends Cicero's proof of the divine ordering of the cosmos through the rational pattern of nature and goes on to recommend pagan moral philosophers who do not "merely teach what virtue and vice are and hammer into our ears the brilliant name of the one and the grim name of the other but sow in our hearts love of the best and eager desire for it and at the same time hatred of the worst and how to flee it."[14]

Generations of humanists are to implement Petrarch's plea and establish the liberal arts curricula. In *De ingenuis moribus et liberalibus studiis adulescentiae* (On noble customs and liberal studies of youth) (1404), written for use in Padua but widely distributed, Pier Paolo Vergerio (ca. 1368–1444) stresses parents' responsibility to give children a liberal arts education. Unlike the parental gifts of name and place of birth, "progress in learning . . . as in character, depends largely on ourselves, and brings with it its own abiding reward." He recognizes that a youth "is not of an age to be stimulated by the dictates of reason, which would be, doubtless, (as Plato and Cicero said) the surest motive, but emulation, going along with obedience, supplies that which reason is as yet too weak to give."[15] Later he glows with praise of human capacity, implied already in the use of *ingenuus* (natural, inborn, worthy of a noble) in his title: "We call those studies *liberal* which are worthy of a free man; those studies by which we attain and practise virtue and wisdom; that education which calls forth, trains and develops those highest gifts of body and of mind which ennoble men, and which are rightly judged to rank next in dignity to virtue only" (102).

Leonardo Bruni (c. 1369–1444), who serves as chancellor of Florence from 1415 until his death, shares with Vergerio a common educational vocabulary; for example, Bruni's *Dialogi*, addressed to Vergerio in the early 1400s, begins by lamenting that Vergerio could not be with him in Florence: "It is eminent for its numerous inhabitants, its splendid buildings and its great undertaking: and, in addition, some seeds of the liberal arts and of all human culture, which once seemed completely dead, remained here and grow day by day and very soon, I believe, will bring forth no inconsiderable light."[16] This passage stresses the natural potential of the inhabitants and the likelihood of one scholar's developing amid conversations with others and in an environment that cultivates the "seeds of the liberal arts."

In a letter to Battista Malatesta (1383–1450) entitled *De studiis et litteris liber* Bruni encourages her to emulate the best of those educated in former times. He quotes from Virgil and in order to defend such readings against contemporary Christian attacks on pagan literature immediately cites Lactantius's view that there was divine inspiration in Virgil. Bruni's selection is *Aeneid* 6.723–32, on the inner nature of the soul (discussed at the close of ch. 1 above). With emphasis on the soul's "flame," "bright intelligence," and "fiery force," Virgil's poetic description of human potential enables Bruni to provide the epistemological justification that Plato and Aristotle "were not Christians, indeed, but consistency of life and abhorrence of evil existed before Christianity and are independent of it."[17]

Despite Bruni's advice that women study rhetoric but not publicly display themselves as rhetoricians, Battista Malatesta delivers her own Latin oration to Emperor Sigismund in Urbino in 1433.[18] That both the humanist education of women and Stoicizing take root can be seen in a letter of 1443 or 1444 written by Battista Malatesta's granddaughter, Costanza da Varano (1426–47), educated in the humanist tradition, praising an accomplished humanist, Isotta Nogarola: "This statement from our Cicero's work *On Duties* you have also respected: For we are all drawn and led to the desire for knowledge and science, in which we think it fine to excel." She cites Quintilian, *Institutio oratoria* (On the orator) 1.1: "For just as birds are born for flight, horses for the race, wild beasts for savagery, so to us is distinctive a certain vitality and swiftness of mind [*mentis agitatio atque sollertia*]."[19] Her respect for the energizing quality—the activity, potency, ingenuity—of the mind echoes Virgil's "fiery force."

The first four paragraphs of chapter 1 of Quintilian's *Institutio oratoria* contain important Stoicizing material: the idea that the mind originates in heaven ("origo animi caelestis creditur"), the praise of the Stoic

Chrysippus for hiring knowledgeable nurses for infants, and the commendation of educated and eloquent Roman mothers and daughters. Nogarola and other humanists apply Quintilian's educational theory to female as well as male offspring, universalizing from Quintilian's androcentric ideal student, presumed from the first line to be a *filio* (son) raised by nurses and prepared by a male pedagogue for a usually male public school and for an eventual public role. Nevertheless, in Quintilian's first-century Rome, as in many city-states of quattrocento Italy, there is some primary education in combined classes for girls and boys, and an elite of well-to-do girls are tutored along with their brothers at home.[20]

In 1444, in an oration to Bianca Visconti, heir to Milan and spouse of Francesco Sforza, Costanza da Varano writes with renewed confidence in general human potential: "For there is no one, no matter how wild, how barbarous his character, how alien and remote the country of his birth, who would not flame with the fire of the love of your many virtues. Oh happy Italy, who from her womb has given birth to such a radiant light!"[21] Yes, this is political rhetoric, but it also attests to Costanza's belief that there is a spark of goodness in all humans that would inflame on contact with a person embodying true virtue. Likewise, Costanza's sexualizing of Italy as a womb reveals the growing sentiment among Italian humanists that the landscape of Italy, the center of the great Roman civilization, is the womb in which the seed of learning is flowering.[22]

There is good reason for new enthusiasm for Quintilian in the early quattrocento. In 1416 Poggio Bracciolini, attending the Council of Constance, discovers the complete text of *Institutio oratoria* in the tower of a Swiss monastery at St. Gallen, whereupon he immediately copies the manuscript and shares his newly found riches with Leonardo Bruni and Vittorino da Feltre, among others.[23] The abundance of manuscript copies attests to the text's immediate influence, which extends throughout Europe after the first printed edition in Rome in 1470.[24] Poggio also finds several previously unknown orations of Cicero; but of significance equal to the Quintilian discovery is Bishop Gerardo Landriani's discovery at Lodi in 1421 of the complete text of Cicero's *De oratore*, which also circulates in manuscript before publication in the 1470s.[25] In reading so many "new" works of Cicero, humanists gain a greater familiarity with the Stoic themes of the natural law within. Together these two "reborn" texts on oratory present an orator who embodies an encyclopedic breadth of knowledge and a moral capacity to seek and inspire practical wisdom.

A third major discovery, one not often mentioned in the context of humanism, is the finding in the Vatican archives of manuscripts of Theophrastus's *Historia plantarum* and *Causae plantarum*. Theophrastus (ca. 370–285 B.C.E.) was a botanist who worked closely with Aristotle and succeeded him as director of the Lyceum; he rejected spontaneous generation and focused on the importance of seeds, and in the case of the date palm he distinguished male from female trees. In the Florentine Academy, which enjoys its botanical garden at Careggi, humanists and artists are aware that Theodore Gaza (1400–1476), the first professor of Greek at the University of Ferrara and later a professor of philosophy at Rome, is translating from Theophrastus's Greek into Latin; the printed edition appears in 1483.[26]

Under the influence of these books, quattrocento educators increasingly realize the importance of learned and caring nursing for the young, whether plant or person. The Latin *nutricius*, similar to *nurse* in English, may mean one who cares for a child or one who rears plants. The analogy between a child and a plant is a traditional linguistic thought pattern that takes on new significance in the fifteenth and sixteenth centuries. In Quintilian a child, like a vine, can grow tall if it is attached to a tree that stretches out its lower branches—the introductory lessons for learning grammar, rhetoric, and morality (Quint., *Inst.* 1.2.26–27).

Cassandra Fedele (1465–1558), a humanist tutored in Venice, writes in her "Oration in Praise of Letters": "Moreover, simple men, ignorant of literature, even if they have by nature this potential seed of genius and reason, leave it alone and uncultivated throughout their whole lives, stifle it with neglect and sloth and render themselves unfit for greatness. For like wanderers they walk in darkness to all [life's] actions."[27] Fedele recognizes that the seeds of human reason are present not only in the upper classes but may be present in commoners and the uneducated as well. Her viewpoint reflects the debate in humanist circles over whether nobility derives from the seed of lineage or from the seed of virtue.[28]

Drawing the parallel between agricultural and educational cultivation, Fedele is suggesting that if ignorant men's (and women's) seeds of reason had been cultivated, they might have attained culture. She goes on: "But learned men, filled with a rich knowledge of divine and human things, turn all their thoughts and motions of the mind toward the goal of reason, and thus free the mind, [otherwise] subject to so many anxieties, from all infirmity. . . . The study of literature polishes intelligence, illuminates and shapes the force of reason, either nearly erases or completely washes away every blemish of soul."[29] With that statement on the baptismal powers of literature Fedele hedges close to a view of the full potency of human intellect. She adds the image that fields left wild can become fertile and fruitful. She finds an educational function for individual virtue, but more importantly for the virtue of a state, as in her oration at the University of Padua in 1487, she indicates how learning would make Padua "flourish" (73).

Four years later Fedele receives a letter from Angelo Poliziano (1454–94), who compares her to his friend Pico della Mirandola and concludes, "May a founder and consort be near who is not unworthy of your virtue, so that now that the spark of natural intellect has almost flamed by its own will, so hereafter a fuller flame, fed by breath or by kindling, may shoot forth brightly. Thus the cold night of sluggish stupidity in letters may be completely dispersed from the hearts and souls of our people" (127). Overexcited by the extraordinary nature of a woman intellectual "as rare, as

new, as if violets took root amid ice, roses in snow or lilies in frost" (127),
he uses the example to prove the spark of natural intellect in the unlikeliest
of surroundings and the possibility that learning might flourish in others
as well.

Likewise, Laura Cereta (1469–99), in responding to a severe critic of
education for women, proclaims the natural gifts of reason in men and
women. In answer to that critic's question why outstanding women are a
rarity, she claims that women have chosen lesser goals:

> But those in whom a deeper integrity yearns for virtue, restrain from the start
> their youthful souls, reflect on higher things, harden the body with sobriety
> and trials, and curb their tongues, open their ears, compose their thoughts in
> wakeful hours, their minds in contemplation, to letters bonded to righteous-
> ness. For knowledge is not given as a gift, but [is gained] with diligence. The
> free mind, not shirking effort, always soars zealously toward the good. . . .
> Nature has generously lavished its gifts upon all people, opening to all the
> doors of choice through which reason sends envoys to the will, from which
> they learn and convey its desires. The will must choose to exercise the gift of
> reason.[30]

Her answer implies the freedom of will and the naturalness of wisdom in a
willing woman. A friar advises her to read religious works rather than to
pursue pagan letters, symbolized by the word *flowers*: "If Laura has been
given such a talent as she has, she should use it to such a noble purpose as
this (reading Ambrose, Macharius, Augustine, Anthony, Jerome) rather
than merely to buy flowers."[31]

In the writings of clerical humanists, as well as in those of secular humanists, we find ample use of vegetative language—both the concept seeds
of virtue and knowledge and the agricultural imagery of cultivation. Aeneas
Sylvius Piccolomini, later Pope Pius II, writes in his tractate on education
De liberorum educatione (1450, reprinted 1551): "A master thus qualified
will be competent to fulfill his duty, which is to fence in the growing mind
with wise and noble precept and example, as a careful gardener hedges
round a newly-planted tree. For in right training of the boy lies the secret
of the integrity of the man."[32] His phrasing incorporates many of Quintilian's agricultural metaphors, for example, when he advises the tutor to dis-
courage precociousness and likewise discourages severe correction on the
grounds that "the knife must not be applied to tender shoots, as they appear to shrink from the steel, and to be unable as yet to bear an incision."[33]

To indicate how to select reading from pagan antiquity, Piccolomini
suggests the proverb on thorns and roses: "In handling Martial one cannot
gather the roses for the thorns" (151). He clarifies the proverb by citing
Seneca's analogy of the reader to a bee:

> Other creatures enjoy the colour, or the scent, of the flower; they, however,
> are wise to extract its lurking sweetness. Thus they choose where they will

settle, and are content with just that fruition of their choice which serves their end. . . . Herein is laid down an admirable principle by which we may be guided in reading all authors of antiquity. Wherever excellence is commended, whether by poet, historian or philosopher, we may safely welcome their aid in building up the character (150).

Piccolomini rejects ancient superstitions and seeks out ancient praise of virtue and condemnation of vice. And he insists in "God before all else" that the student be grateful for the gifts that we have received through no merit of our own (142). In his concluding statement on inculcating wisdom in youth he advises students to read, particularly Cicero, Seneca, and Boethius (158). Likewise, in an earlier passage he recommends reading Stoic preachers of moral philosophy (150). A youth is a sapling, encouraged in growth by reading and instruction. Flowers of wisdom, that is, the statements of classical authors, work as the fencing to help the tree grow erect with dignity and grace.

FLORILEGIA: GATHERING THE FLOWERS OF THE WISE

To aid in the internalization and dissemination of learning humanists create commonplace books, a genre appropriately named *florilegia*, for the titles and decoration often evoke the ancient and medieval analogies between vegetative and mental growth. Some Renaissance educators involve their students in gathering the worthiest sentences of great authors in order to encourage the emergence of common notions within the students. Such pedagogy draws on Quintilian's idea of transplanting seeds of wisdom from the wise to the student and on Seneca's idea of the maturing of the seeds of virtue and knowledge inborn in the student.

Various editions of the *Fior di Virtu* (Flower of virtue) introduce the sayings of the philosophers with a woodcut title page showing a monk gathering flowers in his robe.[34] In the first illustrated Venice edition (1487) the monk stands between two pairs of trees in an open field and picks a flower from a tree; in the influential Venetian edition of 3 April 1490 the monk, framed by two trees, picks a flower from a plant, and a peacock stands on the archway of the enclosed monastery garden.[35] That enclosure suggests that moral teachings are compatible with a Christian life; the two trees recall the tree of life and the tree of knowledge of good and evil. An alternative version, first produced in Florence in 1491, adds a Christian border to the woodcut (see fig. 5.1). Above is God the father with angels, and below is Christ resurrected with angels.

Nevertheless, the image's main referent is not the theological context of the new Florentine frame. Let us be clear about what is rarely stated in scholarship on Renaissance humanism: the monk appears here not in contemplation but in the action of picking a flower, symbolizing any one of the

5.1. Titled frontispiece with Venetian woodcut and Florentine frame, *Fior di virtù* (Florence, 1491). A popular vernacular book of flowers.

many virtuous exempla and sayings, that is, flowers, sprouting out from the *folia* (literally "leaves") of this lap-size book. (The title appears above only in small print so as not distract from the visual enactment of the gathering of flowers.) I say that the flowers are "sprouting out" for they are to be transplanted into the reader's mind, where they will bloom again. This title page invites the reader to follow. What could be more natural!

How much easier to sample this Italian book of flowers than to explore the multivolume Greek anthology compiled in the fifth century by Stobaeus, pouring off the Aldine Press from 1503 under the title *Florilegium diversorum epigrammatum*.[36] In a 1559 edition the dedicatory epistle praises this collection of illustrious *sententiae*, histories, and examples as "a work most sweet and flowery, a workshop or storehouse filled with diverse kind[s] of pleasing spaces."[37] The Plantin Press in 1575 produces Willem Canter's edition of Stobaeus, containing Latin translations of the fragments of the five hundred Greek authors as well as some critical study of Stobaeus's borrowings.[38] Henry Peacham in his *Garden of Eloquence* asks the reader to value the sentences "as the most beautiful flowers in gardens and fields, and as the most glorious lights in the firmament."[39]

The titles often make vivid the analogy of sayings to flowers and fruit; other titles in the genre include Thomas Hibernicius's *Flores omnium . . .* (1576), *Florio His First Fruites* (1578), and Jan Gruter's *Florilegium ethicopoliticum . . .* (1610).[40] Picture a cornucopia in the midst of a floral arrangement on a Renaissance banquet table, and you recognize the environment in which aristocratic readers savor these books. The scholar could forgo these tidbits and read the originals from which the selections are taken!

It is possible for readers of florilegia from antiquity to the present to be oblivious to the title's allusion to "flowers of wisdom," but at particular times in the transformations of the genre the metaphor is neither silent nor dead but especially alive and creative.[41] Within the current flourishing of reproductions of images from early printed books, the flower-decorated pocketbook *German Proverbs* opens with the line, "A book is like a garden that you can put in your pocket."[42] The twelfth-century expansion of the florilegium as a genre[43] occurs concomitantly with the calligraphic development of leafy and floral decoration stemming from initial letters and with the emergence in manuscript illumination of trees of virtue and vice.[44] The emergence of printed books—first illustrated using woodcuts and then featuring engravings—encourages artistic renderings of the analogy of culture with horticulture and encourages an educational strategy of imprinting images on the mind of the reader. In fact at the end of the sixteenth century so vivid is the allusion to a display of beautiful flowers that in my opinion the title *florilegium* transfers to the new genre of botanical books that picture a flower on each page (related to flowers dried in a book).[45]

Humanist educators encourage florilegia based on fresh readings of classical authorities and encourage thinking of ethics in the context of historical exempla. The process of storing uplifting quotations molds both the mind and the character, and characters so molded articulate memorized sayings and worthy examples for emulation at the moment of important ethical decisions.[46] More important than the published versions, which simplify the secondhand acquisition of classical culture, is the training of students to make their own copybooks from their readings of the classics.

Educated under the Byzantine schoolmaster Manuel Chrysoloras (ca. 1350–1414), Leonardo Bruni, Guarino dei Guarini (1374–1460), and other Italian educators advise their humanist students to keep copybooks for recording rhetorical forms and general information. Subheadings, such as "the virtues and vices," "youth and old age," and "monarchy and democracy," are to be devised. Records by Guarino's son Battista in 1459 indicate the techniques taught by Guarino;[47] and some later student notebooks are extant.[48]

Vegetative symbolism helps Battista Guarino in *De ordine docendi et studendi* (Upon the method of teaching and reading) explain the conjunction of words and ideas, speech and thought: "Whilst in Nature we find some animals which are content to feed upon flowers, like bees; others on leaves, like goats; others again on roots, like swine; the appetite of the Scholar demands the best of each and every kind of mental food." He goes on in an analogy of style to flowers, deeds to leaves, and thoughts to roots: "In purity and grace of style, in worthy deeds worthily presented, in noble thoughts nobly said,—in all these, and not in one alone, he finds the nourishment of his mind and spirit" (175). The analogy is itself a commonplace, derived from the fifth- and fourth-century B.C.E. sayings of Isocrates on the roots and fruit of education that are included in second-century C.E. rhetoric handbooks.[49] Adopting the notebook technique used by ancient writers, Pliny and Boethius, Guarino's student is to accumulate knowledge day by day, bit by bit, as in Guarino's rendition of Hesiod's *sententia*: "The heap after all is only an accumulation of tiny grains" (175). The result is not artificial; from ideas growing within the student's reason develop the speech and deeds that reflect his or her character.

In Renaissance humanist education there are some explicit linkages of the commonplace tradition in pedagogy to the Stoic epistemology of common notions. For example, the following appears in a Renaissance English translation of Aphthonius: "A Common place is a [*sic*] Oracion, dilatyng and amplifying good or evill, whiche is incidente or lodged in any man. This Oracion is called a common place, because the matter conteined in it, doeth agree uniuersally to all menne, whiche are partakers of it, and giltie of the same."[50] The Ciceronian version also clarifies the identification of common notions with commonplaces. The wax-and-impress image is used to describe both the seats of argument on a wax writing tablet[51] and the imprinted common notions in the mind. Since the orator is expected to memorize the commonplaces, these in fact add to such common notions as the idea of God or the idea of goodness, which without formal instruction arise in the mind naturally.[52]

In Renaissance theory, commonplaces are often viewed as flowers and fruits, as well as jewels, stars, and vestments. Sister Joan Marie Lechner, recognizing the humanist images of flowers and light in commonplace books, declares with enthusiasm: "The Renaissance writers sincerely culti- vated their flowers of rhetoric, laid on the gayest colors, and brightened their language with dazzling lights."[53] In our contemporary age of Strunk and White's *Elements of Style*, we might refer disparagingly to "flowery lan- guage."[54] But the Italian Renaissance abounds with flowers both literary and visual, in real and imagined gardens.[55]

LISTENING TO CHLORIS'S RHETORIC IN BOTTICELLI'S *PRIMAVERA*

As we consider the most famous such garden, Sandro Botticelli's (1445– 1510) *Primavera* (fig. 5.2), let us recall that Petrarch and his humanist followers appreciate the complex parallels between the senses of hearing and sight, between the evocative sounds of rhetoric and the sights, espe- cially of inner vision. Petrarch's words inspire: "Everyone who has become thoroughly familiar with our Latin authors knows that they stamp and drive deep into the heart the sharpest and most ardent stings of speech, by which the lazy are startled, the ailing are kindled, and the sleepy aroused." Citing a quotation from Plato in Cicero's *De officiis* 1.5.14, Petrarch imag- ines that "virtue and 'the shape, and as it were, the face of honesty' are beheld by the inmost eye 'and inspire miraculous love' of wisdom and of themselves, 'as Plato says.' "[56] Marsilio Ficino in his 1478 letter to Lorenzo di Pierfrancesco de' Medici likewise describes with the inmost eye "Hu- manity Herself," "a nymph of excellent comeliness, born of heaven and more than others beloved by God all highest. . . . Oh what exquisite beauty! How beautiful to behold!"[57]

Botticelli's *Primavera* has often been seen as symbolic of the humanist concept of a springtime of civilization. Like a medieval tapestry, its fore- ground is covered with attractive flowers and the figures stand in a grove of a dark forest of trees sparkling with bright, tempting oranges. Scholar after scholar has admired the painting with a particular text in mind (Ovid, Seneca, Andreas Capellanus, Ficino, etc.) and has duly found reverbera- tions, for the painting is literally a florilegium and cornucopia of classical references and resonances.[58] Botticelli fulfills Leon Battista Alberti's re- quest in *De pictura* for a "painter, so far as he is able, to be learned in all the Liberal Arts" and to enjoy ornaments shared with poets and orators.[59] My contribution to the abundant *Primavera* scholarship is to draw attention to the vegetative growth from Chloris as a clue to Renaissance fascination

5.2. Sandro Botticelli's *Primavera*, Uffizi Gallery, Florence.

with seeds in botany, biology, theology, and education and to present the *Primavera* as one particularly vivid educational vision of the nurturing of seeds of virtue and knowledge.

At the far right the wind god Zephyr pursues and breathes on the lightly veiled Chloris, transformed into Flora. As wind spreads vegetative seeds, Zephyr is symbolic of generation; although his pursuit of Chloris is often interpreted as carnal love, the lowest stage of love in the neo-Platonic ascent, even the portrayal of this love stresses the ethereal element. We have seen Poliziano compare a mentor to a hearth blower in that he might further kindle the divine spark in a gifted scholar.[60] Zephyr's insemination of Chloris, the root of the fertility in the *Primavera*, is portrayed by the lines of his breath,[61] a visual expression of the *seminales rationes*,[62] which provide for the temporal unfolding of both normal events, such as the decomposition of flowers into seeds, and abnormal or miraculous events, such as the transformation of Chloris into Flora in pagan legend[63] or the miracle of the incarnation of Christ. Several scholars have pointed out that the pose of Venus's right hand in the *Primavera*, a welcoming gesture, is similar to that of the Virgin in Renaissance Annunciations.[64]

In that transformation of Chloris another ethereal event occurs: flowers flow from the mouth of Chloris, adding to the decorative vestment of Flora (see the frontispiece). In an age that conceived of thoughts as flowers—from the flowers in the *Little Flowers of St. Francis* (*fioretti*, "little flowers" in the title, also means "little gift")[65] to the flowers of wisdom spoken by Ficino and his circle in the gardens of Careggi[66]—what might be more natural than petals of wisdom gracefully and eloquently descending from the mouth of Chloris as she looks back at her pursuer. In the quattrocento imagination thus appear flowers of eloquence sprouting in a garden devoted to Venus and the personification of Spring herself colorfully bedecked in new vestments as if connoting the transformation of naked plain speech into the colorful vestment of rhetorical tropes.

Perhaps it is because the language for discussing the pursuit of love and the pursuit of wisdom is intertwined with the poetics of gardens[67] that commentators have rarely explicated the metaphorical allusion in Chloris's utterance of flowers. Yet such a conclusion is in accord with Ficino's letter of 1478 to Lorenzo di Pierfrancesco de' Medici, the youthful patron and recipient of the painting. Ficino treats the painting as a visual educational program leading the young Medici to put order into the "fiery vigour" of the heavens within him.[68] From my perspective of educational theory, the carpet of "flowers" abounding in humanist libraries provides a grounding for the observer to contemplate the hidden meanings under the veils of Chloris and the Graces, as well as the astrological and mythological allusions in Ficino's letter. Seneca interprets the graces as giving, receiving, and returning benefits, a relationship that Alberti cites as a perfect painterly representation of liberality.[69] Amid the dialogues evoked by the paintings, the sheer beauty of Venus draws one upward to, in Ficino's words, "Humanity herself . . . a nymph of excellent comeliness, born of heaven and more than others beloved by God all highest."[70]

Looking from bottom to top, one sees the vegetative realm, seeds germinating in soil and blossoming in flowers; the animal realm of impregnation, humanized by the institution of marriage; personifications of the Deity in classical religious form; and then, in the upper realms, the fruit—oranges symbolic by their many seeds of fertility and in their goldness of immortality—and the clouds, through which one gains a hint of the divine realm.

The painting is both ethereal and resonant with erudite wit. On the right there is the divine insemination at the cerebral level: Zephyr's head, lips, and breath asexually impregnate Chloris's lips with vegetative growth. While in the newly cleaned *Primavera* we gaze at the sheerly veiled female beauty presented greater than life size we might consider the figure of Mercury on the left—the student of the liberal arts managing to turn his back to all the divine female pulchritude. Mercury, the pathmaker, pointing upward, encourages the viewer to share his awe at the beauty that is beyond sense perception. Yet a medieval literary tradition identifies Mercury of *The Marriage of Mercury and Philology* with Zephyr, the disseminator of seed by wind; the seed clusters surrounding Mercury's earth-tone boots remind us of the continuum between Zephyr's propagating love and Mercury's higher love.[71]

The receipt of this edifying painting as a wedding gift encourages the young Medici groom to continue his studies after marriage.[72] Compared with the medieval tradition according to which only those of clerical status attended the universities, how very Jewish an idea.[73] Might the intellectual associations of Jewish scholars (almost always married) with Christian scholars, as well as the emergence of a lay intelligentsia, have anything to do with these changing attitudes toward the compatibility of scholarship with family life in Italian Renaissance communities, already evident in Alberti's *On the Family*?[74]

The *Primavera* is not the only painting Botticelli painted for a marriage, nor is it his only painting that is comparable to an educational treatise. In the Louvre are two frescoes painted by Botticelli in celebration of a marriage in Fiesole. In one the groom is presented by Grammar to the Liberal Arts and their queen, Prudentia. In the adjoining fresco the bride receives a gift of flowers from Venus, accompanied by three figures who are most likely the Graces (fig. 5.3).[75] This historical document reminds us how rare women humanists are and also reminds us of the more typical restriction of women to the little gift of flowers, whereas men receive the flowers of the liberal arts. The association of the Graces with Venus in a marital painting reinforces the association of Flora with married love amid Venus and the Graces. Likewise, the introduction of the groom to the Liberal Arts in a clear pedagogical fresco reinforces the more complex intent in the *Primavera* to make an introduction to learning—sending the groom to the books

5.3. Botticelli, *Venus and the Graces Offering Flowers*, Musée du Louvre, Paris.

to figure out the conflicting resonances and the bride to a procreative and nurturing role.

Botticelli's literal rendering of the accurate detail of buds and flora from the Tuscan countryside adds to, rather than detracts from, the symbolic assemblage in the *Primavera*. As Levi D'Ancona has amply proved, in the progression from right to center we move from a scene symbolic of carnal love, fertility, and vegetative growth to a personification of human love—from Flora, with her marital symbols periwinkle, myrtle, and rose, to the central Grace's white campion plant, symbolic of human love. We are drawn on to Mercury, who stands amidst flax, asters, pinks, and cress, symbolizing divine love.[76] Noting the abundance of flames near and on Mercury's cloak near his groin, Levi D'Ancona explains Botticelli's careful rendering of the linen as both flame and seed—a seed that according to Pliny is planted before the arrival of Zephyr.[77] Mercury attracts our attention up with his caduceus reaching through the clouds, and the garments of Mercury and Venus both sparkle with embroidered flames of love. These "flames" appear also as the linen plant at the lower left. Drawing an analogy to the two loves from the attraction between fire and linen, Ficino suggests, in *De amore* 7.4, that flames both descend to linen, symbolizing human love, and ascend from linen, symbolizing divine love.

SAVORING THE FRUIT AND DISPERSING THE SEEDS

The fragility and time-boundedness of flowers draws in the topic of sexual defloration as a *topos* of contrasts to even this most Platonic of paintings. Poetry written in the circle of Lorenzo de' Medici makes the themes evident. Lorenzo de' Medici's "Triumph of Bacchus and Ariadne," which highlights sexual fulfillment and concludes with the refrain "What's to come is still unsure. How fair is youth that flies so fast!"[78] Exfloration and defloration are close behind wherever flowering is mentioned, as in Angelo Poliziano's "Ballata": "Let no damsel be proud / Toward her lover, for it is May" and "Who will be tardy the least to give him the flower of May?"[79] In his "Dance Song" he plucks blossoms of great variety until Love admonishes him to pick the "rarest and fullest blossom on the thorny spray."[80]

The contrast between thorns and flowers, like the contrast between the earthly and the heavenly Venus, is a common *topos*, as in the preface to Boccaccio's *De claris mulieribus*, which tells the reader not to be offended by offensive matters; "rather persevere, just as on entering a garden you put out your ivory hands for the flowers after moving the thorns aside."[81] For the two famous women Venus and Flora flowers are conspicuously mentioned along with offensive matters. Venus is presented as an adulteress in her relationship to Mars and as the founder of public prostitution. The Cypriotes are said to send their girls to lie with foreigners and "be seen offering the flower of their virginity to Venus and earning the dowry for their marriage."[82]

Flora was a wealthy Roman woman who was said to spend "all the flower of her youth and the beauty of her body in brothels." For fame she established yearly games in her honor wherein naked prostitutes did pantomines. To wipe out this disgraceful reputation in Rome the Senate invented a fiction that there once had lived a nymph named Chloris loved by the wind Zephyrus, whom the Romans viewed as a god. As a wedding dowry he "granted that she be a goddess with the duty of adorning trees, hills, and meadows with flowers in the spring" and that she be known as Flora. A prostitute in her life as in later, especially Venetian paintings such as Titian's *Flora*, Flora was honored as a goddess with sanctuaries and altars for imploring "that she would grant these flowers in great profusion and would let them be followed by fruit."[83] The *Primavera*, honoring the goddess whose name is associated with Florence, features Flora's role in the spreading of flowers and of seeds. The powerful propagative imagery and suggestiveness in the *Primavera* may have contributed to Botticelli's reputation as "a most excellent painter, both on panel and wall. His works have a virile air and are done with the best judgement and perfect proportion."[84]

My interpretation of the transformation of Chloris to Flora focuses on listening to the vegetative language rising from Chloris's lips. Less than three-quarters of a century after the *Primavera*, Guillaume de la Perrière

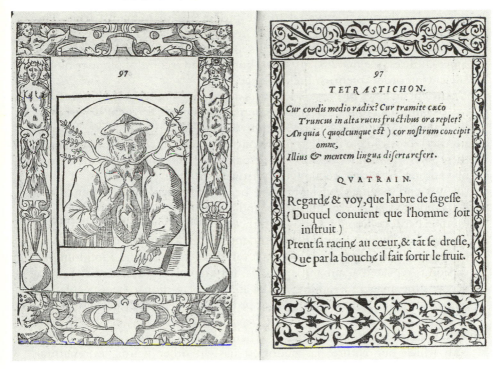

5.4. Guillaume de la Perrière, *La moroscopie*, 1553. "Why the root in the center
of the heart? Why does the / rising trunk fill the mouth with fruits by a
hidden path? / Our heart conceives all, whatever it may be, and the rhetorical /
tongue expresses the thought. / Look and see how the tree of wisdom /
(by which it is appropriate that the human being be taught) / Takes its root in
the heart and raises itself up, / Making fruit come out of the mouth.

creates an emblem that boldly corroborates such an interpretation of vegetation emerging from open lips (fig. 5.4). He portrays an old man whose
heart gives growth to a sturdy plant, which sprouts forth from parted lips.
The Latin quatrain explains that through language our mouths express the
thoughts conceived by our hearts, and the old man points to an empty
book where he might write such thoughts. The French quatrain labels the
vegetative growth a tree of wisdom and suggests that words will be the
fruit of wisdom.[85] Peggy Simonds views Horace's *Ars Poetica* as the most
important classical source for this emblem, for Horace equates words with
leaves;[86] Horace, long recognized as a source of the *Primavera*, contributes greatly to the vegetative analogies in Italian Renaissance aesthetic
theory.

   That fruit might follow from the dispersing of seeds in the gathered
flowers of wisdom is an essential premise of humanist educational method:
there is exfloration of the great books of antiquity in the humanist technique of dispersing ancient seeds of virtue and knowledge in florilegia, and

this seed-gathering is essential to the production of humanist fruit. The popularity of the biblical adage of stealing from the Egyptians and of Roman commemorative monuments parading Roman appropriation of other cultures (see fig. 2.3) attests to humanist awareness of plundering the ancients in order to enrich their own culture.

Ancient analyses of bees and flowers are at the bedrock of humanist theory of *imitatio*. From Lucretius the humanists repeat *De rerum natura* (On the nature of things) 3.10–12: "From your pages, as bees in flowery glades sip every blossom, so do I crop all your golden sayings."[87] Horace echoes these lines in *Carmina* 4.2.27–32, expanding Lucretius's borrowing from one author (Epicurus) to a poet's borrowing from several authors: "I, after the way and manner of the Matinian bee, that gathers the pleasant thyme with repeated labor around groves and banks of well-watered Tibur, I, a humble bard, fashion my verses with incessant toil."[88] We have already seen Aeneas Piccolomini compare the student to the bee in this eclectic Horatian sense of gathering flowers from a variety of authors; and Piccolomini's version is repeated again and again, as, for example, by Ronsard.[89] Seneca deepens the imagery in adding to the analogy of author to bee speculation on the sifting and blending stages of production of honey: "We also, I say, ought to copy these bees, and sift [*separare*] whatever we have gathered from a varied course of reading . . . then, by applying the supervising care with which our nature has endowed us,—in other words, our natural gifts,—we should so blend those several flavors into one delicious compound that, even though it betrays its origin, yet it nevertheless is clearly a different thing from whence it came."[90] Stressing the transformation the author makes from his *imitatio*, Seneca inspires creativity. Petrarch admonishes, "This is the substance of Seneca's counsel, and Horace's before him, that we should write as the bees make sweetness, not storing up the flowers but turning them into honey, thus making one thing of many various ones, but different and better."[91]

ANALOGY BETWEEN HORTICULTURE AND CULTURE

Petrarch has been credited with the transformation of the religious metaphor contrasting the pre-Christian age of darkness with the Christian age of light into a secular metaphor contrasting the intellectual darkness of his times with the light of antiquity. Although his is a pragmatic usage, calling for a scholarly restoration of ancient learning and light, it employs the traditional imagery as well, as when he expresses his pity for Cicero, who died too soon to see "the dawn of the light." Using vegetative imagery, he forecasts "Helicon green again with new growth" and the flourishing of the "sacred laurel."[92] His opportunity comes in Rome in 1341, the grand occasion when he accepts the classical laurel wreath, acknowledging that poets and Caesars share "a wreath from a fragrant tree, symbolizing the fragrance of good fame and glory."[93] Petrarch talks of a new (*nova*) age and of a previous age of barbarism and darkness (*tenebrae*). The fourteenth-century chronicler Villani picks up the imagery: "Poetry, therefore, lying prostrate without honor or dignity, that great man Dante Allagherii [*sic*] recalled it as from an abyss of shadows into the light, and giving it his hand, set the fallen art upon its feet."[94] Shortly after Petrarch's death his French disciple Nicolas de Clamanges, born in 1355, referred to *la renasci* together with *floribus*. There are numerous examples from such early French humanists as Jean de Montreuil, Guillaume Tradif, and Robert Gaguin of the transformation of the religious metaphor of light and darkness into a description of cultural regeneration in their own day.[95]

In his *Secretum* Petrarch states that sense perceptions and worldly cares distract one from ascending to the "only and supreme light" because "when too many plants are sown in a narrow ground, namely that their growth is prevented by crowding, the same thing happens to you, so that no useful roots are put down in the soul that is too occupied and nothing fruitful grows."[96] Drawing on the analogy between the soul and a garden, Petrarch, an experienced practical gardener, takes pride in his botanical skills and in his copy of Virgil's *Georgics and Eclogues*. The frontispiece, by Petrarch's friend Simone Martini, places Petrarch in the tradition of associating scholars with gardens (see fig. 5.5). Petrarch, seated under trees conversing with a shepherd, represents the *Eclogues*, and the caretaker of a vineyard represents the *Georgics*. Petrarch's written inserts refer to the Italian origin of the poet Virgil, his commentator Servius, and Simone Martini; Petrarch compares painting and poetry and praises Servius for showing Virgil's wisdom through shepherds and farmers (as does Martini).[97] Both the poet Virgil and the poet Petrarch share an interest in both the art of horticulture and the art of poetry; Petrarch draws heavily on the analogy between horticulture and culture for his comments on the times in which he lives.

Although much scholarship has delved into images of cultural renaissance, further understanding can be gained by recognizing the epistemological basis in the concepts of natural light of reason and seeds of virtue and knowledge. Gerhart Ladner has shown that vegetative growth combines with the contrasts of light and darkness, birth and death, and the return of a golden age in a cluster of ideas that forms the Italian and German notion of a cultural renaissance.[98] Citing J. Trier's study of 1950, Ladner gives evidence that in descriptions of images of vegetative growth and rebirth the Latin *renasci* in fact mean "to grow again" as well as "to be reborn" (731). The vegetative images of a broken clover regrowing (*renascetur*) occur in the older Cato, *De re rustica* 54, and humanists would find ample examples in Pliny of vegetative matter regrowing as shoots from stalk or trunk (*stirps*) (732 n. 15).

5.5. Simone Martini (Sienese artist in Avignon, 1336–44), allegory in Petrarch's Virgil manuscript, Pinacoteca Ambrosiana, Milan. The laborer at the lower left cuts a root for replanting, while Petrarch, upper right, borrows from his Virgil and writes.

The comparison of cultural to vegetative growth takes two visual forms: pruning shears encouraging new sprouts to emerge and spontaneous regrowth in spring. Trier emphasizes the former, whereas Ladner finds more evidence of the latter. Spontaneous growth, molded through fencing or guidance, as we have seen, is what is stressed in Italian humanist educational theory. The horticultural analogy in educational theory supports the paradigm of the mind developing in the way that a plant does.

Missing from the discussions of vegetative symbolism is the subject of seeds. Aristotle and Pliny both teach the possibility of spontaneous generation, that is, that some plants may grow without seeds. In contrast, Theophrastus and such church fathers as Ambrose are skeptical of spontaneous generation and teach instead that all growth derives from seeds. Botanists of the fifteenth century experiment with planting a variety of seeds and revive interest in Theophrastus.[99] A parallel appears to exist between the renaissance of botany and the concept of a renaissance: both focus on rebirth from seeds. Our examination of the amplification in humanist educational treatises of ancient theories of cultivating seeds of virtue and knowledge in the fourteenth through the sixteenth century and of the visualization of that notion in such images as Chloris's vegetative growth helps explain the emergence of the concept of a renaissance.

As Ladner shows, ancient Romans provide precedents for drawing metaphoric and political implications of the vegetative imagery; for example, Machiavelli in his history of *Roma rinata* after the pope's residence in Avignon (*Istorie Fiorentine* 1.31) echoes Livy's discussion of the regrowth of Rome from a trunk (*stirps*) after capture by the Gauls (Livy, *Hist.* 6.1.372–73). Secular and political usage of the visual imagery of trees resprouting abounds in seals, emblems, and insignia of Renaissance organizations. As we saw in chapter 4, Janet Cox-Rearick has fully documented how in the fifteenth century the Medici family utilizes vegetative symbolism in imprese and how after the Medici restoration the family expands the imagery into a monumental tree of a flourishing dynasty. In Duke Cosimo I de' Medici's seal a broken branch renews itself, and the imprese of many Italian academies show green branches or trees emerging from old roots. In retrospect, the most famous vegetative image, of course, is Leonardo da Vinci's drawing of a tree stump with a sprig reemerging.[100]

By the late quattrocento Ficino repeats the humanist refrain of the rebirth of arts and letters in an Italian context, and Erasmus in the Netherlands adapts the refrain to application in northern Europe. Ficino states: "It is undoubtedly a golden age which has restored to the light the liberal arts that had almost been destroyed: grammar, eloquence, painting, architecture, sculpture, music. And that all in Florence."[101] This Italian motif is echoed and expanded upon by Erasmus (ca. 1466–1536) in a letter to Cornelius Gerard in about 1489 in which he recites the revival of eloquence in Germany and the Netherlands, as well as Italy, and mentions not only letters but also painting, sculpture, and architecture. Erasmus declares that after a period of decline, all the arts are again "flourishing."[102]

The process of reading or contemplating and ultimately digesting fruits of virtue and knowledge helps one to cultivate one's own seeds of virtue and knowledge. Faith in this process is at the basis of the burgeoning belief wherever humanist studies are cultivated—Oxford, Cambridge, and Paris in the twelfth century; Italy in the fourteenth and fifteenth centuries; northern Europe in the fifteenth and sixteenth centuries; and European colonies in the seventeenth and eighteenth centuries—that a rebirth and flowering of culture will occur. Nevertheless, we shall see in the next chapter that already in the twelfth century there are opponents to the powerful, positive vegetative imagery for the natural growth of the human mind.

Vegetative Language of Virtue and Vice in Discourses on the Dignity or Depravity of Humankind

ALTHOUGH THE humanist educational treatises, letters, and orations concerning education proclaim a Stoic confidence in human potential for knowledge and virtue, Christians experience ambiguity and tension in their attempts to reconcile Stoic epistemology with their Christian lives.[1] It is significant for the sixteenth-century Reformation that in the Renaissance the ancient Roman Stoic version of the optimistic epistemology, the neo-Platonic version dispersed through Ficino's publications, and the Thomist formulation discussed and modified in the scholastic curriculum are in tension with the Augustinian emphasis on original sin and trust in divine illumination.

The much-publicized Reformation debate on the freedom or servitude of the will is in fact a continuation of the medieval and Renaissance debate on the dignity or depravity of humankind. I shall prove this contention by showing the continuity in the use of vegetative imagery, both the minuscule *seeds* of virtue and knowledge and the large *trees* of virtue or vice. From the collections of *flowers* culled from pagan, Jewish, Muslim, and Christian authors we move on now to the *forests* of manuscripts by those authors collected, copied, and illuminated for the papal libraries in Avignon and Rome. By looking at the debate on the extent to which human life is depraved or dignified from the late twelfth through the late sixteenth century, we shall study a dispute about *how the soul best grows* from the High Middle Ages to the Italian Renaissance, through the Northern Renaissance as it intermingles with the Protestant Reformation and the Catholic Reformation, and into my main area of focus—the later French Renaissance.

When we see that the published debates between Erasmus and Luther and between Sadoleto and Calvin concern differing estimations of seeds of virtue and knowledge, we shall come to understand better the relationship between humanist and evangelical trends during the age of the Renaissance and Reformation. In particular, tree imagery reveals attitudes toward the relationship between the Hebrew Bible and the New Testament and toward the relationship between humanly devised cultivation techniques (for gardening, for education, for civic virtue) and human dependence on divine illumination. As we saw in examining Lull, the Christian Kabbalah, and Ficino, and as we shall find in looking at Pico della Mirandola and Cardinal Sadoleto, some Christians apply vegetative language suggestive of attaining divine wisdom. From Innocent III to Martin Luther, other Christians reject the implication that humans may naturally develop their seeds of virtue and knowledge to attain divine wisdom; in rejecting a confidence in human potentiality derived from classical philosophy they suggest that not only salvation but also human wisdom is attained only through Jesus. On the other hand, the landscaped Chambre du Cerf in the papal palace at Avignon, the writings of Erasmus, and the teaching of civic ethics in Protestant schools share a common Christian respect for human cultivation of human wisdom.

FROM POPE INNOCENT III's TREE OF VICE TO THE MEDITATIVE FOREST STUDY OF THE AVIGNON POPES

The best-known work on the *contemptus mundi* is Innocent III's *De miseria condicionis humanae* (On the misery of the human condition). Cardinal Lotario dei Segni (1160–1216) writes the work in 1195—three years before assuming the papacy.[2] By that time the Stoicizing of John of Salisbury has already yielded the potent image of the "fruitful copulation of reason and speech," and visual images have appeared in manuscripts illustrating the specific leaves of virtue of the tree of virtue (fig. 3.5). Innocent III very vividly contrasts the fruits of humans to the fruits of trees: "Investigate the plants and the trees: they produce flowers, foliage and fruit from themselves, and you nits and lice and worms from yourself" (104–5). Likewise, he contrasts in use and in aroma the fruits of oil, wine, and balsam with the human fruits spittle, urine, and excrement. Then, ignoring Matthew's division of humans into trees of vice and trees of virtue, Innocent adopts Matthew's words: "As the tree is, so is the fruit, 'for an evil tree cannot bring forth good fruit'" (106–7).

Directly following that citation, he gives a gross materialistic rendering of the inverted tree, which in Plato's *Timaeus* and in mystical writings shows man's head rooted in the Divine: "For what is man in his shape but a tree turned upside down? Its roots are the hair, its base is the head along with the neck, its trunk is the chest along with the belly, its branches are the arms along with the legs, its foliage is the fingers and toes along with the joints. This is the leaf that is carried away by the wind and the straw that is dried by the sun" (107). The negative image of humanity as a fragile leaf is similar to Innocent's later quote from Job, highlighting in the human flower its short life: "[Humanity] commeth forth like a flower and is destroyed and fleeth as a shadow and never continueth in the same state" (160–61). Let us compare Innocent's image to Psalm 1:

> He is like a tree
> planted by streams of water,
> that yields its fruit in its season,
> and its leaf does not wither.

> In all that he does, he prospers.
> The wicked are not so,
> but like chaff which the wind
> drives away.   (Ps. 1.3–4)

Innocent's last line on humans echoes the psalmist's statement on the wicked, but in Innocent there is no image of a human tree that yields positive fruits. Lest one think that the positive fruit is the *humanum semen* (human seed), in fact—as Innocent III teaches in his book 1, chapter 3—the human seed is unclean in its nature, in its release in an act of passion, and in its development in the polluted womb of a woman, where it is nourished by menstrual blood. This view reflects biblical taboos on menstruation, Aristotelian embryology, and Christian views of original sin. In response to Job, who says, "For behold I was conceived in iniquities, and in sins did my mother conceive me," he explains, "Not in one such sin, not in one such transgression, but in many sins and in many transgressions: in her own transgressions and sins, in the transgressions and sins of others" (94–95).

With regard to potentiality and actualization Innocent III views the grown offspring as fulfilling in evil deeds the contamination through sinful origins and fleshly existence of the rational ability to distinguish good from evil, of the irascible ability to reject evil, and of the appetitive desire to be good (98–101). As the human tree grows tall, it grows haughty, and the consequence will be as in Isaiah 2.12–15, 17: "The day of the Lord of Hosts shall be upon one that is proud and highminded and upon everyone that is arrogant, and he shall be humbled; and upon all the tall and lofty cedars of Libanus, and upon all the oaks of Basan, and upon all the high mountains, and upon every high tower, and upon every fenced wall, . . . and the loftiness of men shall be bowed down, and the haughtiness of men shall be humbled" (188–89). Citing Isaiah 5.14, Innocent interprets that passage as an indication that hell shall open its mouth and humans will enter. The closing section of *De miseria* describes the judgment day: providing no discussion at all on those to be saved, the future pope graphically dwells on the rightful eternal punishment of the damned. In what becomes the model of the fire-and-brimstone sermon, associated by many Americans with Calvinist Puritans in colonial New England, the closing words of this late twelfth-century Catholic work concern "brimstone and fire burning forever and ever" [sulphur et ignis ardens in secula seculorum] (232–33).

Despite this negative vegetative symbolism and the association of fire with hell, we do find an admission of human reason and human conscience and positive imagery for the spark. Quoting Ecclesiastes, Innocent discusses the vexations of the spirit that accompany the search for prudence and learning, but in that description he admits the strivings and the possibility of recognizing—through doubt and folly, of course—the truth of human limitations. He cites Solomon's view that God created humanity upright but that certain knowledge and prudence elude confused human beings.[3] In the tradition of finding conscience in the pricks of Cain that remind him of his great sin, we learn about conscience: "It is not for the sinful to rejoice, says the Lord, because 'by what things a man sinneth, by the same also is he tormented.' For the truth of conscience [*Veritas consciencie*] never dies, and the fire of reason [*ignis racionis*] is never quenched."[4] He recites the biblical adage that those who "sow sorrows" [seminant dolores] will reap them. An example is his assurance that there is no one who has spent a delightful day of pleasure who has not that day experienced the "guilt of conscience" [reatus consciencie] or anger or concupiscence (128–29). This insight provides the basis of a frequently copied English poem of the fourteenth century, the *Pricke of Conscience*; evidence of the widespread influence of Innocent III can be found in the "Monologue of Law's Prologue" and in the "Pardoner's Prologue" and "Pardoner's Tale" in Chaucer's *Canterbury Tales* (5, 6–12).[5]

Among the commentaries on Innocent III's treatise are humanist works by Petrarch, Antonio da Barga, and Bartolomeo Facio, as well as Giannozzo Manetti's reply.[6] Let us consider Petrarch and Manetti particularly in relationship to the vegetative symbolism. Despite the visible misery all around him of the first wave of the Black Death of the mid-1350s,[7] Petrarch writes *De remediis utriusque fortunae libri II (Remedies for Fortune Fair and Foul)*, which confronts Innocent III's imagery:

> For what does obscenity of origin detract from human dignity? Do not tall and leafy trees, grown from filthy roots, cover the green earth with welcome shade? Are the fields of grain not made fruitful by the vilest dung? The vilest origin of the best things is not something disgusting. You are the grain fields of God to be winnowed in the plains of judgement, and to be placed in the granary of the greatest head of a household. Earthly was man's origin, although partly noble and celestial. But whatever his origin and however difficult his progress, his final seat is heaven.[8]

Charles Trinkaus is right in saying that Petrarch overcomes "medieval fastidiousness about the facts of bodily life by turning the equally medieval closeness to the soil and vegetation into a metaphor of the flowering of man."[9] Petrarch stresses the divine origin of the human soul (partly noble and celestial) and provides a biblical balance in considering human beings in the classifications of good grain and evil grain.

Coluccio di Piero Salutati (1331–1406), chancellor of Florence 1374–1406,[10] presents an activist ethic and an optimism based on human self-control in a passage focused on human dignity:

> Moreover moral goodness is a quality of man alone, and this is gathered solely through virtuous actions, for either God infuses virtue into us, or He potentially inserted it by nature and through the frequency of actions excited and perfected it. By this excellence of goodness, which from the beginning has

been common to us and the angelic creature and so will be common in the fatherland, human nature excels all corporeal creatures, and any man surpasses every dignity of his own body. By this goodness mortals ascend beyond themselves and in the merits of one man, the mediator namely of God and man, Jesus Christ, and of the Virgin Mary, and perchance in other things, surpass the glory of all the angels.[11]

Salutati likens humans in their origins to angels and does not mention original sin. He focuses on human virtuous actions as either fulfilling potential capacity or further activating God's infusion of grace. Salutati praises human dignity of mind by comparing it to the dignity of body unthinkable in Innocent III's scheme and expresses confidence that humans rise from their own merits, assume the merits of the son of God, and ascend to heaven. Both Petrarch and Salutati influence the culture of the papal court in the fourteenth century: Petrarch resides in and near Avignon from 1327 to 1362, and his Latin works are acquired by Pope Gregory XI (1370–78),[12] and the prestige of Salutati's humanist Latin correspondence influences papal hiring of humanist scribes and secretaries, such as Nicolas de Clamages.[13]

It is important to emphasize that Innocent III's vegetative imagery does not speak for the papacy as a whole and that he may have intended to balance his statements on human misery with additional ones on human dignity. Contributing to the vegetative imagery in the debate on human dignity and depravity are Thomas Aquinas's (d. 1274) Stoicizing proclamations of a concept of *semina virtutum* and *semina scientiarum* by which human reason can attain knowledge sufficient for natural law and for the virtue of a pagan in this life. Even some who come under the label "Augustinian," such as Matthew of Aquasparta (d. 1302), interpret Augustine as supporting the idea "that the soul has in itself a seed-plot of virtues."[14] Pope John XXII officiates in the canonization of Thomas Aquinas in Avignon in 1323. Furthermore, there are forest of trees under which ecumenical dialogue may take place and by which one may ascend, as in the books of Raymond Lull.

From the time of the reign of Pope Clement VI, 1342–52, vegetative frescoes decorate the pope's Chambre du Cerf of the Tour de la Garde-Robe and the adjoining Chambre du Pape of the Tour du Trésor, also known as the Tour des Anges in the Palais des Popes, Avignon, where the papacy is located from 1309 to 1378 (see figs. 6.1 and 6.2) and where schismatic popes continue to live until 1422 and which serves as an ecclesiastical center until 1791.[15] Artists and writers in the ambience of Avignon influence both the Italian and the French Renaissance: Petrarch in 1336 ascends nearby Mont Ventoux, and Simone Martini (in Avignon, 1336–44) both decorates Petrarch's Virgil (fig. 5.5) and brings the influence of Sienese painting to the papacy.[16] Often thought to be derived from tapestry designs popular with French royalty, continuous landscape frescoes in

the pope's private room depict hunting for rabbits in a dark woods opposite fishing in an open artificial pond and education in the art of falconry
opposite a man in a tree demonstrating the hawking for birds and the
much-faded hunt with dogs for a deer. A common modern response to
these images has been surprise at their secular nature and delight at the
early evidence of landscape painting. The images of persons standing in
abundant vegetation looking up at birds in a flourishing tree do express the
beauty of observed nature, as Kenneth Clark notes.[17] I have counted ten
distinct vines encircling the pope in the fresco in the Chambre du Pape
and about twice as many trees in the forest scene of the Chambre du Cerf.
In this landscape decoration of the papal chambers the image of trees, of
humans, and of animals does suggest natural potency; nevertheless, Boniface VIII, while in Rome in the late 1290s, was one of the first to see Lull's
Arbor scientiae,[18] and the forest of trees in the later papal residence in Avignon is likely to resonate in vegetative symbolism, especially the analogy
between vegetative and spiritual growth. In figure 6.1 the student observer
watching the tutor falconer pointing upward to the treetops with bird
ready for flight is suggestive of the deeper educational intent in the function of the room as a *studium*.[19]

The birds seem particularly significant, as the Chambre du Cerf and the
adjoining Chambre du Pape were structured to contain large birdcages in
the window recesses. In fact the recent restoration reveals that in the
Chambre du Pape wall paintings of birdcages decorate the window recesses.[20] Birds commonly symbolize the soul or spirit, and high up in a tree
they are associated with the soul's ascent. In these large images of trees the
hawker may be the church seeking out new souls for the Christian fold, but
in the private chambers of the pope the hawker is more likely beckoning the
Christian observer to the verdant growth possible in the exploration of the
soul. Medieval culture abounds in falconry symbolism; for example, a thirteenth-century manuscript illumination portraying a dove above a priest
reading and a hawk above a mounted nobleman conveys the moral to aim
for the balance between the contemplative and active lives.[21]

As one thinks of these landscapes for private meditation, one recalls also
the genre of trees of mystical ascent, to which the wall decoration in the
Dura Europos Synagogue belongs.[22] In fact the walls of the pope's public
adjoining room, where on the papal throne he welcomed visitors, are completely covered with a unifying vegetative imagery of vines and foliage and
acorns of the oak. As Joinville tells of King Louis IX (1226–70, canonized
1297) going after mass to sit under an oak tree to settle cases of justice, the
pope sits on a throne fully encircled by vines with leaves rising as if from the
midst of a tree of virtue (see fig. 6.2).[23]

The Avignon papal palace is a center for accumulation of manuscripts,
and the decor of the Chambre du Cerf may be a symbolical forest analogous to the forest of books there and in nearby rooms. Before the decorat-
ing of the Chambre du Cerf, Pope Benedict XII (1334–42) uses the room

6.1. Fresco on education in falconry in the Chambre du Cerf, Tour de la Garde-Robe, Palais des Papes, Avignon, ca. 1345.

as his *studium* and builds another, more well-lit *studium* in the Tour de l'Étudé, on the other side of the Chambre du Pape.[24] In fact, the Chambre du Pape is bounded by studies on four sides: Benedict XII's first *studium* (the Chambre de Cerf in the Tour da la Garde-Robe), the *studium* in the Tour de L'Étudé, and, in the Tour du Trésor, the Grande librairie adjoining the Trésor haut (above), and the Ancienne chambre du camérier (below), where scribes work. The visual design of the Chambre du Cerf seems appropriate for a room Benedict XII utilized for reading and contemplation, which leads by means of circular staircases to other rooms of study. The distinctive techniques of hunting with birds (fig. 6.1), hunting with dogs, fowling in trees, and fishing in ponds portrayed on the four

6.2. Wall-covering design, vines and oak leaves, Chambre du Pape,
Tour du Trésor, Palais des papes, Avignon.

walls of the Chambre du Cerf would help a cleric to locate a manuscript in
the room,[25] at the same time serving in a complex symbolical scheme connoting memory and learning.

Mary Carruthers has suggested that "the language that describes the formation of associations as 'hooking' material to other things leads to a
metaphor of recollecting as fishing; as one pulls up one's line, all the fish on

one's hooks come with it."[26] Might I suggest that one of the most explicit walls of the Chambre du Cerf shows a fishing scene in which four men use four distinctive tools to catch fish from a well-stocked, artificial rectangular pond. This interior wall, backing to the Chambre du Pape, is a clear place-maker, with its jutting corner on the left and entranceway on the right. Mary Carruthers continues, "The idea also informs the common meta-phorical extension in Latin of the word *silva*, 'forest,' to mean 'a mass of unrelated and disordered material,'" and she quotes Quintilian's *Institutio oratoria* for the notion of a trained student as a huntsman finding the loca-tions of the hidden rabbits and deer.[27] These quests are evident on the walls of the Chambre du Cerf, and precious game each in its own habitat (deer, rabbits, fish, and birds) may refer by analogy to the precious manu-scripts within this and other papal chambers. The function of the Chambre du Cerf as a study makes explicit the patterns of commonality in the educa-tion for venery[28] and for letters, and encourages the hunt for manuscripts by individuals of high rank.

The Avignon papacy, influenced by Petrarch's hunt in monasteries for manuscripts, is recognized as a center for artistic and intellectual patron-age, including the humanist movement; less well known to art historians is the use of the Chambre du Cerf as a *studium*. An extant inventory proves that Pope Benedict XIII (1394–1414) keeps a well-equipped private li-brary including a wheel of books and room dividers in the Chambre du Cerf.[29] Benedict XIII is following his predecessors in keeping in the Cham-bre du Cerf manuscripts, particularly their personal collections, that are not catalogued for the *magna libraria* above; for example, a list of 1369 for Urban V situates sixty-four manuscripts in the room beneath the Chapelle Saint-Michel, which is the Chambre du Cerf.[30] A list completed for Clem-ent VII in 1379–80 refers to the room as the "camera Cervi Volantis" and lists many classical works.[31] I notice that the room label reflects a Latin pun, for the Latin genitive of *cervus*, "deer," is also the nominative plural meaning "branches of a tree stuck in the ground as a palisade, to impede the advance of the enemy."[32] The books ranging beyond the ecclesiastical collection of the *magna libraria* inform the papacy of pagan authors, reli-gious controversies, and current literary trends, and the fresco wherein the deep forest of intertwining branches is painted does in fact serve as the ex-ternal southern defense wall of the Tour de la Garde-robe.

The reciprocal influences between the papal palace in Avignon and the French royal palaces expand the cultivation of arts, letters, and gardens that influence the French Renaissance. Saint Louis houses manuscripts from the Crusades with his royal treasures in Saint Chapelle. Manuscript collector King John II the Good (1350–64) commissions courtly wall frescoes on the château of Vaudreuil in 1349 and visits the papal court in 1351. King Charles V (1364–80) commissions an inventory of his 910 volumes four years after Pope Urban V's inventory reveals more than 2,000 manu-scripts.[33] Especially significant for the cross influences in the papal and royal hunts for books and in the fashion for tower libraries is Charles V's decision in 1367 to move the royal library from the Palais de la Cité to the northwest tour of the Palais du Louvre. The excavations in the basement of the Louvre now reveal the circular fortress of the Tour de la Fauconnerie, which Charles V renames the Tour de la Librairie to house three floors of books (as in Avignon). Whereas the popes imitate royal and aristo-cratic falconry in adding cages to send birds out of tower windows, King Charles V adds trellises in the former Tour de la Fauconnerie, where hunt-ing gear had been stored, to keep out "birds and other beasts."[34] In his commissioned 1372 illumination of *Policratique* by John of Salisbury Charles V appears seated before a circular, turning desk containing manu-scripts—a fashion to be followed by Pope Benedict XII in the Chambre du Cerf. Popularizing symbolical ideas and images in fifteenth-century vernac-ular writing, Christine de Pisan (1364–ca. 1430) notes the beauty and order of King Charles V's library and garden and contributes her manu-scripts to the royal collection.[35] King Charles VI (1380–1422) contributes to French royal symbolism the image of the *cerf-volant*, the winged deer.[36]

The educational function and symbolism of the "camera Cervi Volantis" is integral to the ethical and Christian symbolism. The room serves as a pastoral retreat devoted to the deer's taste for solitude and its embodiment of prudence; Pliny recounts that a deer's swiftness and flight may entangle its horns in shrubs, and thus it learns prudence by ruminating and looking around.[37] Especially if one identifies with the deer, as legend says Pope Clement VI did,[38] this pastoral retreat, furnished with manuscripts, pro-vides lessons for papal learning of prudence.

Those serving the successor of Saint Peter (a fisher of men)[39] might fish out manuscripts from many localities in this well-stocked room, texts that might help in gathering believers (little fish) for the baptismal font. Leg-ends of Saint Louis indicate the importance to him of Psalm 41.1–2, "As the hart panteth after the water banks, so panteth my soul after thee, O God,"[40] a text in which Saint Jerome interprets the deer as a soul disposing itself for baptism.[41] The conciliatory approach to welcoming converts con-forms with Clement VI's inviting Jews back to Avignon in 1342 and pro-tecting them from popular persecution in the aftermath of the Plague.[42]

PICO DELLA MIRANDOLA ON CULTIVATING FREE WILL IN THE FERTILE SOUL

Without reference to the positive vegetative imagery on the walls of the papal palace in Avignon but clearly influenced by papal support for the hu-manist movement, humanists of the fifteenth century continue to respond to Innocent III's negative vegetative imagery in their dialogues defending human dignity. In the jubilee year of 1450, considered the date of the founding of the Vatican Library, Pope Nicholas V employs copyists and illuminators to make human intellectual achievements visible and available;[43] the invention of printing and the proliferation of presses greatly expands the human capacity to make texts available. Giannozzo Manetti's (1396–1459) *De dignitate et excellentia hominis* (On the dignity and excellence of humankind) (ca. 1450–53) refutes Innocent III's view that whereas trees produce wholesome fruits, man only produces ugly, smelly excretions: "But the fruits of man are not properly those kinds of foul and superfluous filth and fetidness alleged above [Innocent III, *De miseria*, lines 104–7], but rather the manifold human operations of knowing and action are held to be and are the fruits of man for which man as though a tree for fructifying is naturally born."[44]

In response to Innocent III, the most famous hunter of lost manuscripts Poggio Bracciolini echoes Innocent's title with his *De miseria humane conditionis libri duo* (Two books on the misery of the human condition) (1455). During his brief time as the chancellor of Florence (1453–56) under Cosimo de' Medici, Poggio's main task is to write the history of Florence from the close of Bruni's *Historiarum florentini populi libri XII*. *De miseria* is a dialogue between Cosimo de' Medici and Matteo Palmieri about the recent fall of Constantinople to the Turks. Whereas Matteo expresses a pessimistic view of avarice as the root of human evil and an awareness that the rich have comforts that the poor cannot afford, Cosimo presents the Christianized Stoic position that has become fashionable in quattrocento Florence: "For since we have neglected reason, that is virtue which is right reason, and we are slaves to many kinds of desires adverse to reason. . . . That certainly happens by our own fault, not by nature's; we turn her gifts given to us for living well into our own ruin." Likewise, the ancients serve as an example of the possibility of guiding one's conduct by right reason: "They were held to be just and also wise, and they lived with virtue which drove all misery far away from them." Countering this confident viewpoint stressing gifts of nature rather than grace, Matteo alleges that the mythic Stoic sage does not meet the needs of the masses of humanity: "I do not make words about something unique like a phoenix or a sage of the Stoics who never has been found, but I speak of mankind. . . . We are all feeble by nature and oppose by no wisdom the boldness of fortune."[45]

Giovanni della Pico della Mirandola's *Oratio*, written in 1486 to accompany his nine hundred theses, gathers together individual truths from many civilizations. His library and the Medici collections attest to the diversity of texts available.[46] He begins with traditional praise of human dignity as containing discernment of reason and the light of intelligence (*intelligentiae lumine*), but his view is "that with freedom of choice and with honor, as though the maker and molder of thyself, thou mayest fashion thyself in whatever shape thou shalt prefer."[47]

In Pico's statement of the divine instruction to Adam one finds the vegetative symbolism common to the notions of the tree at the center, to the
notions of *axis mundi*.[48] As Mircea Eliade has explained this common symbol, the cosmic axis extends through the underworld, the earth, and the
sky, which it often reaches there at the North Star. Originating in the
fourth or the third millennium B.C.E., this concept is embodied in three
main images—a pillar or pole, a tree, or a mountain.[49] In that tradition,
Pico views God as a divine architect who has built this cosmic home (*mun-
danam domum*) as a temple according to laws of his wisdom (*legibus sapientiae*). In fact, in the passage the free will, *arbitrium* (from *arbiter*,
"judge") appears as what is at the center of the world, at the location where
traditionally stands the giant *arbor*, or tree. While the God of Genesis commands Adam not to eat of the tree of life and the tree of knowledge of good
and evil, the God of the *Oratio* commands Adam to use human free will.
The associations are vivid, as the command occurs following his creation of
the world: "The nature of all other beings is limited and constrained within
the bounds of laws prescribed by Us. Thou constrained by no limits, in
accordance with thine own free will [*arbitrio*], in whose hand We have
placed thee, shalt ordain for thyself the limits of thy nature. We have set
thee at the world's center [*medium mundi*] that thou mayest from thence
more easily observe whatever is in the world" (225; 106). That humanity
is a microcosm at the center of the macrocosm is emphasized throughout
the oration but particularly in analyzing the Apollonian "Know thyself,"—
for the "nature of man is both the connecting link and so to speak, the
'mixed bowl.' For he who knows himself in himself knows all things" (235;
124).[50] Both Ficino and Pico view the human being as the bond and knot
(*vinculum et nodus*) of celestial and earthly things.[51]

Further amplification on the human as "mixing bowl" and on God's creation of Adam in the divine image is in the *Heptaplus*, which Pico defines
as a "Sevenfold Narration on the Six Days of Genesis," in which he cites
Plato's *Timaeus* 41d to explain that the rational soul is "mixed" from the
same elements as is the soul of the heavens. Like Ficino, Pico views God's
creation of "male" and "female" as referring to the "male" upper part of
the soul, which contemplates, and the "female" lower part of the soul,
which rules the body.[52] The Adam described in the *Oratio* and the *Heptaplus* conforms to Genesis 1.26–27 as viewed by Philo Judaeus of Alexandria, Origen, and other Christian followers—the one being God created
before forming it into two bodies. "Let us make humankind [*adam*] in
our image, after our likeness, and let them have dominion. . . . And God
created humankind in his own image, in the image of God created he him;
male and female created he them."[53] Pico's Adam is a spiritual being,
an immaterial being in the image of God. In the *Heptaplus* Pico explicitly
cites Philo's, Origen's, and others' allegorical interpretations (68, 72;
170, 178), indicating that he is not looking at the "rough outer bark of
its words" [*rudi cortice verborum*] of the book of Moses but at the

inner, spiritual meanings (70; 176). In the *Heptaplus* he makes known his knowledge of such medieval Jewish thinkers as Rashi (1040–1105), the thirteenth-century Kabbalist Menahem ben Recanati, and Gersonides (1288–1344), among others (73; 180), and his own desire to make his own interpretation.

In Pico's tenth thesis, to which the *Oratio* is an introduction, God places in the center of Paradise "the great Adam who is *Tiferet*" [magnus Adam qui est Tepheret]; Pico borrows this identification from Menahem ben Recanati, who utilizes the Hebrew *Tiferet*, meaning "glory" or "beauty," in the standard way, as the sixth emanation in the Kabbalistic *sefirot*.[54] Thus, the Adam of the *Oratio* is influenced by the very large hermaphroditic Adam of Talmudic lore interpreted with a spiritual inner eye as the *Adam Kadmon* of the Kabbalah, whose spirit extends from earth to heaven in the shape of *sefirot* (fig. 3.2). Thus, the human free will that allows the spirit to soar upward to the Divine or downward to material creation is a central immaterial axis—a tree at the center—of Pico's universe.

The next paragraph in the *Oratio*, of thanks and praise for the divine generosity, utilizes an overarching paradigm of seeds as the source in all living things for physical and spiritual growth:

> On man when he came into life the Father conferred the seeds of all kinds [*omnifaria semina*] and the germs of every way of life [*omnigenae vitae germina*]. Whatever seeds each man cultivates will grow to maturity and bear in him their own fruit. If they be vegetative, he will be like a plant. If sensitive, he will become brutish. If rational, he will grow into a heavenly being. If intellectual, he will be an angel and son of God. And if, happy in the lot of no created thing, he withdraws into the center of his own unity, his spirit, made one with God, in the solitary darkness of God, who is set above all things, shall surpass them all. (225; 106)[55]

Vegetative imagery takes two forms here: as a lower form compared to sensitive and rational growth in accord with Aristotle and as the divinely given pattern by which all living growths germinate from seeds in accord with the Stoic *logos spermatikos*. In addition to describing Aristotle's three forms of organic life as three kinds of seeds—vegetative, sensitive, and rational—Pico subdivides the rational into three—rational, intellectual, and contemplative. The last path is traditional in mystic literature as the direct line upward along the central axis of the world to God. As Pico says of the intellectual and then of the contemplator, "If you see a philosopher determining all things by means of right reason [*recta ratione*], him you shall reverence. . . . If you see a pure contemplator, one unaware of the body and confined to the inner reaches of the mind . . . he is a more reverend divinity vested with human flesh" (226; 108, including Hebrew). A tree, the great chain of being, and Jacob's ladder are interchangeable as physical images of this notion of spiritual ascent (229–30; 114–16).[56] Likewise, Pico describes ascent through the wings of Mercury (231; 118), the pagan deity we saw in Botticelli's *Primavera* as the epitome of contemplative ascent.

Light imagery abounds—there is "the light of natural philosophy" (229; 114), by which we prepare our souls to ascend the ladder to the Divine, and there is the divine light shining above, spiritually and visibly in the heavenly stars and planets. There are alternative paths to ascent paralleling the three techniques—the active life and good deeds of the rational life, the intellectual observation of the mirror of the Divine in the natural world, and the withdrawal into the soul, as noted in chapter 2 in Meister Eckhart, into love of the Creator alone. Light imagery occurs in Pico's description of human striving through love and through intelligence, as well as in images of the goal of the Divine: "we shall speedily flame up with His consuming fire into a Seraphic likeness" (227–28; 110). Planetary light, divine light, and spiritual light combine in Pico's citation of Moses advising people not to enter the tabernacle until they have prepared by controlling their conduct and by study of holy teachings. Then they are to contemplate the lights in the heavens, the palace of the Lord, and look at the candelabra divided into seven lights (233; 120) (see fig. 2.3). Given his deep knowledge of the Kabbalah, which he proclaims later in the *Oratio* and in his exclamation in the Second Proem of the *Heptaplus* that the seven branches are a microcosm of the seven planets (76; 222), he appears to be aware of the vegetative aspects of the menorah. A ritual object prominent in Jewish worship in Medici Florence, the menorah culminates Pico's use of light imagery and highlights his indebtedness to Jewish lore.

Citing Hebrew, Chaldean, Christian, Delphic, and Pythagorean traditions, Pico in the *Oratio* emphasizes that they all show us "the benefits and value of the liberal arts" (233; 120). He wants learning to be available to as many as possible (237–38; 130). Philosophy teaches us to rely on conscience (*conscientia*) (238; 132). Pico proclaims his important belief in synthesis, the in-gathering of light of many different sects and schools of learning. He cites Plato's *Epistles*, which suggests that through a dialogue between teacher and pupil a light may inflame itself, providing truth (244; 142).[57]

Pico also teaches that one should not rely simply on the opinions of others; then he satirizes the custom (established by Guarino) of students' keeping commonplace books: "What were it to have dealt with the opinions of others, no matter how many, if we are come to a gathering of wise men with no contribution of our own and are supplying nothing from our own store, brought forth and worked out by our own genius? It is surely an ignoble part to be wise only from a notebook (as Seneca says)" (244; 142–43, citing Sen., *Ep.* 33.7). Emphasizing the "power of nature" within us, he uses vegetative symbolism: "For if a tiller of the soil hates sterility in his field, and a husband in his wife, surely the Divine mind joined to and associated with an infertile soul will hate it the more in that a far nobler offspring is desired" (244–45; 144). Comparing the fertility of "soul" and "soil," he justifies adding to his borrowings some "theses in natural philosophy and in divinity, discovered and studied by me" (245; 144).

The debate on the potentialities for intellectual, ethical, and spiritual growth in human nature becomes seriously divisive just before the Reformation. The collecting of diverse manuscripts by rulers and churchmen, even more than the gleaning for florilegia, implies that there is independent value to cultivating the human intellect. The seeds, buds, flowers, trees, and forests of learning that are cultivated in Florence, Avignon, Paris, Rome, and many other locations during the Renaissance suggest paths to wisdom beyond the one unique incarnation of divine seed.

A focus on the issue of the freedom of the will by Lorenzo Valla, as well as by Martin Luther, brings to a crisis the contrast between the optimism of Italian, especially neo-Platonic humanists and Pauline pessimism.[58] As the dialogue concerning human dignity and depravity focuses on free will, reconsideration of Augustine plays an important role. Augustine's *De libero arbitrio* (On the freedom of the will), written in response to the Manichaeans, who claim that there are rival powers of good and evil in the universe, emphasizes that the soul is not barren but that, like a "young and tender sapling" not bearing fruit for several seasons, it contains "a kind of beginning that enables it to mature with the fruits of wisdom and justice by its own efforts and growth." In response to Pelagius (ca. 354–ca. 418), Augustine's *Retractationes* (Retractions) takes on the then new Pelagian heretics, "who would assert the free choice of the will so as to leave no place for God's grace."[59] Both Giovanni d'Andrea and Teoldoro de' Lelli (d. 1464) mistakenly include the exposition of faith of Pelagius in the collected works of Saint Jerome, and this mistake continues to influence early-sixteenth-century printed editions.[60] Pelagius's name appears often in the texts of Luther and Calvin, as it does in Augustine's *Retractationes*, seemingly as the embodiment of a threatening live theological position.[61]

The dialogues on misery versus dignity in the sixteenth century, especially the famous ones between Erasmus and Luther and between Sadoleto and Calvin, focus on how to reconcile freedom of the will with God's providence and whether the freedom of the will is instrumental for salvation. Vegetative symbolism, especially seed and tree images, is a clue to the continuity between the fourteenth- and fifteenth-century dialogues on human dignity and the sixteenth-century debates on the freedom of the will. We shall note the evangelical turn first in the circle of Lefèvre d'Étaples and then in Martin Luther's confrontation with Desiderius Erasmus. In an early work of Marguerite de Navarre we find an image of the tree of sin as powerful as Innocent III's. In French-born Calvin and in Princess Elizabeth in the court of King Henry VIII we shall hear echoes of Marguerite's vision of the sinful soul. The voices of fifteenth-century Stoicizing Italian humanists and neo-Platonists echo in the sixteenth-century voices of such neo-Platonists as Cardinal Sadoleto as well as in those of such neo-Stoics as Du Vair and Lipsius.

DIVINE OR HUMAN GARDENING OF THE SOUL?
LEFÈVRE D'ÉTAPLES, LUTHER, AND ERASMUS

The intellectual atmosphere in Paris in the early sixteenth century reveals the tensions at work in the reevaluation of human nature. The intellectual transformations of Jacques Lefèvre d'Étaples (1455–1536) illustrate the changing attitudes toward human efficacy in achieving virtue and reaching God, which have an impact on Marguerite de Navarre (1492–1549) and Martin Luther (1483–1546). Lefèvre moves through stages of confidence in human reason toward an interest in mysticism and finally, under the influence of Paul and then Luther, toward full reliance on Christian faith.

As stated in 1506 in his commentary on Aristotle's *Politics,* Lefèvre's educational program is to teach natural and moral philosophy, study the works of Aristotle, and then rise up to higher philosophy through Aristotle's *Metaphysics.* An arts professor introducing a secular work, he goes on to indicate how Christians should properly complete their studies:

> Turn from this to a reverent reading of Scripture, guided by Cyprian, Hilary, Origen, Jerome, Augustine, Chrysostom, Athanasius, Nazianus, John of Damascus, and other fathers. Once these studies have purified the mind and disciplined the senses (and provided one has extirpated vice and leads a becoming and upright life), then the generous mind may aspire to scale gradually the heights of contemplation, instructed by Nicholas of Cusa and the divine Dionysius and others like them.[62]

Distinctive here is Lefèvre's valuing of Christian over pagan antiquity: Aristotle can help one to extirpate vice and guide one to virtue, but the Christians of antiquity may be of greater help. Likewise, his concern for the area of contemplation of the Divine starts with Aristotle's *Metaphysics* but culminates with Nicholas of Cusa (1401–64), of whom Lefèvre produces an edition in Paris in 1514.[63] There is both irony and humility in this recommendation.

In *De docta ignorantia* (1440) Nicholas of Cusa takes a position of humility on the powers of reason, suggesting, in Pauline Watts's words, that "the essential condition of human existence is that man is metaphysically and epistemologically disjoined from both his creator and from the natural world in which he lives."[64] Like Augustine, Nicholas emphasizes a fusion of faith with reason in intellectual cognition and in preparing the soul for divine illumination. We find a parallel viewpoint in Pico della Mirandola. Nicholas of Cusa's illumination theory is worked out more fully in *Idiota, de sapientia,* where in dialogues between a man on the street and an orator he teaches that Wisdom, that is, Logos, is the second person of the Trinity, Christ, and is accessible only by grace. In fact, it appears that those who spend their days amid books, as does the "arrogant Renaissance orator," may be less apt to receive the illumination than those who live "virtuously and humbly in a simplicity enforced by poverty and manual labor."[65] Although Lefèvre values reading of Aristotle for its limited preparatory use in the liberal arts, he recommends reading Nicholas of Cusa, this archcritic of scholastic Aristotelian rationalism, in preparation for rising to the Divine.

The early Lefèvre differs from his own, Luther's, and Calvin's later positions on the estimation of free will. For example, in *Corpus Dionysiacum* Lefèvre argues against predestination. If those who are not written into the "book of life"—the list of those to be saved—give up their evil ways and are penitent, God may give them the grace of reconciliation, allowing them to strive to be virtuous, to obey divine command, and to attain salvation.[66]

Lefèvre undergoes an evangelical change. According to Lewis Spitz, as early as in the *Commentary on the Epistles of St. Paul* (1512) Lefèvre expresses a belief that man is saved only by God's grace, which cannot be won by works or merit. Viewing Lefèvre as a rigid predestinarian, Spitz stresses that Lefèvre's emphasis on grace and faith influences Luther's reading of Saint Paul. When Luther prepares his Epistle to the Romans as lectures at the University of Wittenberg in 1515–16, he makes marginal notes on grace and faith in his copy of Lefèvre's *Commentary.*[67] On the other hand, Eugene F. Rice in a recent summary claims that "a common devotion to the Epistle to the Romans gave his doctrine of justification a superficial resemblance to Luther's"[68]; Rice emphasizes Luther's influence on Lefèvre, whose evangelical shift occurs by 1519.[69]

In the preface to his *Commentary* Lefèvre declares:

> The ground which is uncultivated and receives no rain from heaven produces nothing fit for human consumption, only thorns, prickles, thistles, and useless herbs. In almost the same way, human minds which have not received the divine ray can produce nothing which is not more harmful than profitable and are incapable of giving souls a vivifying nourishment. Indeed, works of an intelligence deprived of grace from above are worth scarcely more than thorns and thistles.[70]

The image of rain from heaven as essential for the growth of the human tree appears in emblem form as well as in evangelical circles (see fig. 6.4). Lefèvre's *Commentary* makes available to the general public Paul's two crucial statements, namely, "For by grace are ye saved through faith; and that not of yourselves: it is the gift of God: Not of works, lest any man should boast" (Eph. 2.8–9) and "Therefore we conclude that a man is justified by faith without deeds of the law" (Rom. 3.28).[71] Luther's *Ninety-five Theses* of 1517 transform the issues raised in Lefèvre into major political and ecclesiastical ones with implications throughout Europe.

A crucial turning point in Luther's development occurs in the years 1515–16. While Luther's reading of Lefèvre contributes to reciprocal influences, his reading of Gabriel Biel in the same years shows his departure from the scholastics' stand on reason and conscience. Biel thinks we lead a virtuous life by doing what is within us: "Knowledge is the root and foundation of all the virtues."[72] Like Aquinas, Biel holds that sinning goes against reason and thus against natural law as well as against eternal law.[73]

Luther makes marginal commentary on his edition of Biel's *Sententiae* and departs from viewing synderesis as a vestige of our pure nature enabling us to obey natural law and execute the will of God. As Steven Ozment points out, in contrast to Biel, who believes "one is able to love and enjoy God above all things from his natural powers," Luther writes that in Biel "grace is denied, and he argues absurdly, presupposing a healthy will."[74] Luther's argument with Biel is precedent to his debate with Erasmus.

Let us look at the controversy between Luther and Erasmus that stirs hearts all over Europe, and then at the combined influence of Luther and Lefèvre on Marguerite de Navarre's poem about the sinfulness and bondage of the soul. In 1519 Luther and Erasmus begin to correspond, and many expect Erasmus to join the reformers. Nevertheless, taking up argument with Luther's major theological position that justification is by faith alone, in September 1524 Erasmus publishes *De libero arbitrio* (On the freedom of the will), which is countered in 1525 by what is to be one of Luther's most influential works, *De servo arbitrio* (On the bondage of the will).

In terms of the centuries of dialogue on the relative depravity or dignity of human life, Luther's position is comparable to Innocent III's hell-oriented perspective, in which the only issue in this specific theological treatise is the human condition from the perspective of God's glory. On account of Luther's view that all human acts, even virtuous deeds, are sinful in God's eyes, Erasmus narrows his focus to the defense of the efficacy of the will in relationship to justification: the freedom of the will he defines as "a power of the human will by which a man can apply himself to the things which lead to eternal salvation, or turn away from them."[75] It is fascinating that in this narrow context the phrase *seeds of virtue* appears in Erasmus on the authority of church fathers as evidence of human free will to act rightly and is disputed and ridiculed by Luther, for "a man can receive nothing unless it is given him from heaven."[76] This much publicized literary exchange turns the phrase *seeds of virtue* into an Erasmian formulaic sign evidencing human cooperation in grace:

> ERASMUS: I shall make full use of the authority of the Fathers who say that there are certain seeds of virtue implanted in the minds of men by which they in some way see and seek after virtue. (*De libero arbitrio*, 1524)[77]
>
> LUTHER: "Meanwhile" you seek to "make full use of" the authority of the Fathers who say that "there are certain seeds of virtue implanted in the minds of men." First, if that is what you want, as far as we are concerned you may use or abuse the authority of the Fathers; but you should take note of what you believe when you believe men who are expressing their own ideas without the word of God. (*De servo arbitrio*, 1525)[78]

Erasmus mentions the phrase *seeds of virtue* following a discussion of the highest part of the human soul, the Stoic *hêgemonikon*. He claims that there are among philosophers those who strive for virtue and would recommend that one die a thousand deaths before committing evil even if God would forgive the deed and the deed were unknown to society. Clearly, Erasmus's context is ancient philosophy and his respect, shared by many church fathers, of the possibilities that pagan advice might help one achieve virtue (77). Although original sin inherited by all humans has obscured reason, reason has not been erased. By such internal means were the first generations of humans able to fulfill God's expectations before the written law was handed down to Moses. Thus, like classical antiquity, Genesis provides a parallel source of examples of humans striving for righteousness without the full benefits of religion.

Erasmus's confidence in human reason is evident in his reading of Psalm 4.6—"The light of thy countenance is impressed upon us, O Lord!"—which Erasmus interprets, as do Thomas Aquinas and the nominalists Biel, Gerson, and Tauler, as the law of nature engraved on all human minds that teaches the Golden Rule (47). Luther turns to an Augustinian interpretation of Psalm 4.6, stating that in 1518 "this verse cannot be understood of natural reason, synteresis, as it is the opinion of many who say that first principles in morals are self-evident, as in matters of speculation. This view is false, Faith is the first principle of all good works." "The light of thy countenance is impressed upon us" becomes to some Protestants, "Lift thou up the light of thy countenance upon us."[79]

Erasmus distinguishes three levels of grace: the gifts of God implanted in us by nature, which give us freedom to act; peculiar or operative grace, available to all who pray, which arouses a sinner to repent; and cooperating grace, which makes the will effective to complete an act justifiable in God's eyes (51–53). The agricultural analogy helps Erasmus indicate the way humans cooperate in their own salvation: although on the subject of the productivity of crops the Bible may give credit to God as the giver of rain, in fact without the laborer working the fields of good earth the crops will not grow. In such a biblical fashion it is proper for humans to attribute their works to God in order to avoid arrogance, but "our will might be a *synergos* ('fellow-worker') with grace" (81).

Peter Lombard and his successors in the late twelfth century are important sources for this agricultural analogy. In the anonymous *Summa sententiarum* the gifts of the Holy Spirit are "the first motions in the heart, as it were, like seeds of virtue" [primi motus in corde, quasi quaedam semina virtutum].[80] Peter Lombard, in his own *Summa sententiarum*, transforms the imagery of God sowing without human collaboration into an image of God and the human husbandman working together to grow the crops. Lombard compares free will to the soil and divine grace to rain (which some successors call "dew"). He distinguishes between virtue as a mental disposition to the good and virtue as good intentions and actions, and reassigning the role of seeds, he views the seed of virtue as a mental disposition to the good. The moral agent, appropriately disposed by the seeds of virtue, is a husbandman cultivating the fruit—virtue manifested in good intentions and actions. The production of the fruit of virtue thus depends on the "synergistic" interaction between grace and free will.[81]

In his citation of "the authority of the Fathers" Erasmus does not cite a specific church father. Nevertheless, we have seen Matthew of Aquasparta cite Augustine's *De Trinitate* (On Trinity), as well as *De libero arbitrio*, to proclaim a "seed-plot of virtue" in the soul, "common notions," and "natural light of reason." Ambrose is a particularly good direct source for vegetative imagery of the kind Erasmus uses to proclaim God's expectation that humans till the soil of their souls in preparation for grace.[82] Likewise, the following from Augustine's *De libero arbitrio* aids Erasmus's argument in his own *De libero arbitrio*: "Why, then, should the soul's Creator not be praised with all due reverence if He has given the soul a kind of a beginning that enables it to mature with the fruits of wisdom and justice by its efforts and growth, and when He has so dignified it that it is within its power to reach out for happiness, if it wills to do so?"[83] Only a few years after Luther's public response to Erasmus's seed imagery and "synergistic" interplay of nature and grace, Erasmus publishes the major ancient source of imagery of seeds of virtue and knowledge, an edition of Seneca's letters (Basel, 1529), which is often reprinted as the dominant edition until Justus Lipsius's edition of Seneca at the beginning of the seventeenth century.[84]

Luther answers Erasmus point by point: Luther glowingly praises Philip Melanchthon's *Loci communes* (Commonplaces) of 1519, which sums up Lutheran theological teaching in bold assertions and advises Erasmus, the writer of the *Adages*, that given his recalcitrance to accept the truth, "even though it were by recourse to thousands of books a thousand times over . . . you might as well plow the seashore and sow seed in the sand." Erasmus's "highly decorative arguments" might appeal to those without the spirit, who "are shaken like a reed by every wind" (Matt. 11.7; 103). Luther directly answers Erasmus's agricultural metaphor, indicating that without spirit one cannot properly interpret Scripture: "For although the subject before us demands more than an external teacher, and besides him who plants and waters outwardly (1 Cor. 3.7), it requires also the Spirit of God to give the growth and to be a living teacher of living things inwardly" (104). Later dismissing the "little thing" of "certain seeds of virtue," he ridicules Erasmus's argument by authority to an audience who all know Luther's opinion of the invalidity of a millennium of fathers, papal decrees, and councils. As Victoria Kahn has pointed out, Luther discredits human' ability to attribute free will to the self; in fact, he discredits their ability to give evidence of even one work arising from free choice that has "done anything alongside God."[85] Yet Erasmus, in choosing to write a humanistic discourse, highlights the humanist rhetorical strategy of motivating good human conduct; dialogue or debate is evidence itself of the praxis of human discrimination, judgment, and choice of paths.[86]

Luther rejects Erasmus's distinctions among graces, as well as his gradualist cooperative approach, in which prayer, charity, and good deeds aid in a lifelong reception of grace. The crux for Luther is that original sin has left humanity in a state of evil, entrapped by Satan, and the only human recourse is to be regenerated through Christ's redemption (329–33). By arguing with both Erasmus and the Pelagian position (the attribution of the lowest to grace and the highest to free will in attaining salvation), Luther uses the two positions to dismiss each other. In Erasmus's indication of some free will through "seeds of virtue" Luther ridicules the "tiny spark of desire," "the little bit of endeavor in man," "the little particle of it [free choice]." If Erasmus truly is to interpret the statement in Ecclesiasticus that "if thou wilt keep the commandments, they shall preserve thee" to credit humans with power of keeping the commandments, the diminutive potential would not be sufficient (186–87). Luther's stark contrasts appear again in Christ's words from Matthew 7.18 ("A sound tree cannot bear evil fruit, nor can a bad tree bear good fruit") and in accordance with Romans 14.23 ("whatever doe not proceed from faith is sin"). To bear good fruit, one needs first to begin by believing, since faith is the source of goodness. "Sinners," says Luther, "are 'bad trees' and cannot do anything but sin and 'bear bad fruit'" (317).

Lucas Cranach the Elder illustrates Luther's teaching in large painted panels that Carl Christensen interprets as a series on "The Law and the Gospel." These doctrinaire symbolical paintings turn Luther's ideas into folk culture, and Karl Meier and Oskar Thulin have found their motif imitated in innumerable panel paintings, altarpieces, Bible illustrations, stained glass, and wedding chest carvings.[87] At the center of the 1529 canvas in the Schlossmuseum, Gotha, Germany (fig. 6.3), is a composite of the tree of life and the tree of good and evil, on the left side dead and on the right side alive.[88] On the left (unproductive) side of the canvas, Moses, accompanied by three prophets, teaches the Ten Commandments to a man whom a demon and skeleton escort downward to a black pit; in the background are Adam and Eve sinning and the Old Testament scene of the encampment and the brazen serpent. The observer is to learn that the Old Testament and the law alone are not productive for human nature stained by original sin; the way of the old law is a dead tree, by which one may not ascend. On the right side, where the tree produces leaves, we see John the Baptist pointing out the Crucifixion to a penitent man who looks upward, hearing the saving word of the gospel. The viewer is to learn that the New Testament and the saving grace of Jesus is a fruitful tree growing toward salvation.

New Testament inscriptions on the Gotha panel support the contrast between the law and the gospel.[89] Another 1529 version of the panel, in the National Gallery in Prague, concentrates the drama at the base of the tree by showing one representative individual spoken to by Moses on the left and John the Baptist on the right.[90] Since the individual is choosing between Old and New Testaments, he may be appropriately viewed as a Jew whom Lutherans seek to convert. Hoping for mass conversion, in

6.3. Lucas Cranach the Elder, *The Law and the Gospel*, 1529, Schlossmuseum, Gotha.

1523 Luther writes a pamphlet called *That Jesus Christ Was Born a Jew*, but by August 1536, when Elector John Frederick of Saxony, Luther's patron, expels Jews from his principality, Luther refuses to intercede on their behalf.[91] The 1529 canvases, whose dates coincide with Luther's publication of his two catechisms, reveal important aspects of the Lutheran viewpoint. Contrasting with Lutheran frustration at the unresponsiveness of Jews to the evangelical appeal,[92] in the Prague canvas the victory is obvious: the individual turns away from Moses, whose beard bifurcates like two horns, and looks up to the Christian signs of grace on the right.

Luther accuses the Catholic Church of Judaizing: Catholics who believe in the efficacy of their fulfilling laws, rituals, and good deeds are in a similar position to followers of Mosaic law. The detailed elaboration of the vices developed in the medieval illustrations of trees of the vices and in the penance books for confessors suggest parallels between Mosaic and ecclesiastical law.[93] The tree represents the key choice from a Lutheran perspective, namely, between seeking Jesus in one's soul and following intricate legal detail. Old Testament law, canon law, and natural law are inadequate in comparison with the evangelical faith in the atoning death of Jesus Christ. Even all Christians in respect to their humanity are like the old Adam on the left side of figure 6.3. Luther presents the Ten Commandments at the beginning of his *Large Catechism*, noting, "*Thou shalt not covet*, etc. For He would especially have the heart pure, although we shall never attain to that as long as we live here; so that this commandment will remain, like all the rest, one that will constantly accuse us and show how godly we are in the sight of God" (74).[94]

For Luther, human capacity as implied by the Stoic phrases is merely the capacity to experience the prick of conscience, as in Jerome's formulation, and to know that we are sinning;[95] the popularity of Thomas à Kempis's *Imitatio Christi* attests to a continuing spirituality in accord with Augustine.[96] Only God-given faith transforms the old Adam into the new. As Thomas McDonough describes Luther's doctrine on law and gospel, "The just man, the one made righteous by the 'power of God's Word,' is bound to observe the Law as a living tree is bound to bring forth good fruit; his observance of the Commandments, his good deeds, flow from his heart as a matter of course."[97] In sum, Luther, like the mature Augustine, attributes the evidence of human capacity to be righteous to human participation in Jesus Christ; Luther presents a divine path not only to divine wisdom but also to human wisdom, to the obedience to law and the following of ethics.

Luther's patronage of Cranach reflects an accommodation with didactic art after some Lutherans' iconoclastic interpretation of his statement that "the chapels in forest and churches in fields, such as Wilsnack, Sternberg, Trier . . . which recently have become the goal of pilgrimages, must be leveled. . . . The miracles that happen in these places prove nothing, for the

evil spirit can also work miracles, as Christ told us in Matthew 24[.24]."[98]
The statement reflects both concern about idolatrous attitudes toward sacred objects that he finds in the cult of the saints and concern about pagan
nature cults. Some of his followers, particularly Andreas Bodenstein von
Karlstad, interpret his concerns in an iconoclastic manner and encourage
the destruction of venerated images.[99] On the subject of worship in forests
one might contrast Seneca's sentiment in epistle 41, "If ever you have
come upon a grove that is full of ancient trees which have grown to an
unusual height, shutting out a view of the sky by a veil of pleached and
intertwining branches, then the loftiness of the forest, the seclusion of the
spot, and your marvel at the thick unbroken shade in the midst of the open
spaces, will prove to you the presence of deity."[100]

MARGUERITE DE NAVARRE AND ELIZABETH I ON UPROOTING
THE TREE OF VICE

A Lutheran and evangelical impact comes to be felt in significant quarters
in France. Marguerite de Navarre, sister of King Francis I, writes and publishes in 1531 *Le Miroir de l'ame pechereuse*; the full title translates as "The
Mirror of the Sinful Soul, in which she recognizes her faults and sins as well
as the graces and benefices made to her by her spouse Jesus Christ." She is
directly influenced by Lefèvre, who publishes numerous editions of medieval women mystics, including Hildegard of Bingen's *Scivias*, and presents
her with his French translation of the Bible. His publication of *Regula
monacharum*, which he introduces as Jerome's, provides an entrance for
Marguerite de Navarre, and subsequently princess Elizabeth of England, to
write on the sinful soul in quest of illumination.[101]

Marguerite's work progresses from her detailed account of her sins as an
exemplum for human sins in general and moves on to show how not
through merits but through God's divine aid her sinful soul will be transformed into a capacity to love God.[102] I shall focus especially on her plant
imagery. Feeling her sins overweighing her soul, giving her no power of
knowledge, blocking out the light, she attributes the situation to a tree
rooted in her soul that produces branches, flowers, leaves, and fruit that
prevent her from seeing the light. The overall point is that the tree of sin
suffocates her senses: one branch closes her eyes, a bitter fruit chokes her
mouth, leaves stop up her ears, flowers get in her nose.[103] Her soul in
prison, its feet tied by concupiscence and its arms by bad habits, has no
remedy except to cry out for help. Salvation, grace, comes in the form of
light images, illumination.[104] In a passage summarizing the crux of Innocent III's lament on human misery, we learn also that her condition is generic for humankind, for it is derived from "the sin of Adam."[105]

Marguerite's description of the ugly vegetation within herself continues
the tradition of a tree of vice, but the particularly vivid way in which she

describes the blocking of her orifices may be derived from seeing medieval sculpted leaf masks with branches emanating from mouth and nose. The demonic versions of the "green man" abound in Romanesque churches, especially on capitals but also on corbels, fonts, and tympana; they also are evident in wood carvings and book illuminations.[106] The portrayal of horrid sights is a rhetorical device for redirecting the mind to God, perhaps even more effective than the portrayal of the beautiful. Giuseppe Manetti, interpreting the intended impact of Dante's frightening images, points out that in the aesthetics of Hugh of St. Victor and in Alexander of Hales beauty may tie the mind to the sensible world, "but what one experiences as ugly forces one away from the contemplation of itself and urges one to transcend it."[107] Marguerite de Navarre's image of a tree capturing her senses is in the tradition of *Purgatory* 22–23: an apple tree (evoking Eve's temptation) tapering downward blocks the path and the light of the sun, and captured there are some emaciated souls afflicted by their appetites for what appears to be sweet, fragrant fruit; Dante seeks the path upward by pointing to the sun.[108]

Marguerite's conclusion emphasizes further the illumination of the repentant soul by divine light. There is in the heart "a spark" [une scintille] of love for God, which senses the enormity of the direct sunlight of God's love for the soul (lines 1330–45). With a multitude of biblical references, she concludes with a hopeful prayer of praise to the divine king of heaven.

In 1544 eleven-year-old Princess Elizabeth translates this text into English. Anne Prescott has insightfully examined Elizabeth's inaccuracies and explored her discomfort with Marguerite's discussions of God's relationship to humanity in terms of familial relationships. On the crucial passage in which Marguerite suggests that some husbands from revenge upon wives have had them judged and put to death Elizabeth writes, "There be inoughe of them, wiche for to avenge their wronge, did cause the judges to condemne hym to dye." Her first version mistranslates *les* as "him" and then crosses out "him" and translates *les* properly as "them" above the line. As Prescott suggests, Elizabeth's "pen at first brought the man, not the woman, to the block,"[109] which is an irony given that Elizabeth's mother, Anne Boleyn, was beheaded in 1536, Henry VIII's fifth wife, Catherine Howard, was executed in 1542, and the person to whom Elizabeth dedicates and presents this translation in her hand-embroidered blue corded silk covering[110] is her father's sixth wife, newly wed in 1543, who in fact is to outlive him—Katherine Parr.[111]

The next surviving piece of Elizabeth's writing, from 1554–55, ten years after *The Mirror of the Sinful Soul*, is etched on a window where she is held prisoner: "Much suspected by me, / Nothing proved can be; / Quoth Elizabeth prisoner."[112] This declaration of innocence is supplemented by her shutter poem, based on Boethius, which laments that fortune sometimes rewards the guilty and punishes the innocent, concluding, "So God send to my foes all they have taught."[113]

In contrast to Elizabeth's response to an actual imprisonment, her earlier translation of Marguerite echoes Augustine's self-deprecatory dependency on divine illumination. Possibly the shift reflects not only a new task at hand—to declare her innocence for posterity if writing is all that remains of her—but also a confidence in human capacity and a knowledge of the fortunes and misfortunes with which history abounds, likely derived from her humanist education under Sir John Cheke and Roger Ascham, which began under Katherine Parr's direction only a year before the translation of Marguerite's poem. Nevertheless, Elizabeth attributes the credit for the good she can do to the Divine: "Shall I ascribe anything to myself and my sexly weakness? I were not worthy to live then; and, of all, most unworthy of the mercies I have had from God, who hathe given me a heart that yet never feared any foreign or home enemy. And I speak it to give God the praise."[114] The words "home enemy" take on double resonances with regard to her early family life and her later exclusive attachment to the family of England.

Elizabeth translates Marguerite's passage on the tree of sin quite literally and accurately:

> I fele well that the roote of it is in me and outwardly i se no othere effecte but all is eyther braunche leaffe or els frutte that she bringeth furth all aboute me. If i thinke to loke for better, a braunche cometh and doth close myne eyes. and in my mouth doth fall when i wolde speake the frutte wich is so bytter to sualowe down. If my spirite be styrred for to karken [harken]: that a great multitude of leaffes doth entre in myne eares and my nose is all stoped wityh flowres.[115]

Likewise, distinct from and preceding the translation itself, in her address to Katherine Parr from "a humble daughter" she writes very eloquently for an eleven-year-old about "her symple witte" and "small lerning." Elizabeth stresses in her summary of Marguerite's poem that the soul "can do nothing that is good" or "for saluation onles it be through the grace of God."[116] Likewise, "To the Reader" modestly indicates that such a work coming from a woman—she does not distinguish woman author from woman translator—indicates "what the gifte of god doth when it pleaseth hym to justifie the harte of a man. For what thinge is a man (as for [*sic*] bys owne strength) before that he hath receyved the gift of fayth."[117]

Marguerite and Elizabeth, while in keeping with the humility *topos* common to medieval and Renaissance women writers,[118] contrast strikingly with Italian women humanists of the quattrocento, who, while they are willing to voice the expected gracious, self-deprecatory references to their position as females, credit their accomplishments to the sparks and seeds of virtue and knowledge. Even in 1514 the Italian humanist Cassandra Fedele tries to argue to a Dominican that Saint Gregory's view that few will be saved contradicts divine mercy, as she thinks that all would accept Christ and thus be saved. Girolamo Campagnola, a secular poet, sympathizes with her concern and interprets Gregory to mean that "without the mercy of god the human species could be saved" and recollects his vernacular poem "in which I represent the wicked soul penitent of its sins and fleeing to the divine mercy."[119]

In contrast, the young princess Elizabeth thinks that the gifts of nature are not sufficient even for the task of writing: although God gave a gift, still the Creator never rests until He makes him Godly who puts his trust in God. Using vegetative symbolism as part of illumination theory rather than as a growth from natural endowment, she concludes her appeal to her readers with the invocation to put their trust in God and patiently to study this book, whose "fruit" would be the praising of God, and with the prayer that God "plant" in their hearts "the lively faith."[120] Clearly, the formal presentation of this translation at the court of King Henry VIII indicates the kind of religious sensibility with regard to nature and grace that is acceptable in England ten years after the separation of the Church of England from Rome.

Do the Seeds of Virtue Grow to Heaven? Calvin versus Sadoleto and Resolutions of Melanchthon and the Council of Trent

There is no better example of the historical significance of the broadening spectrum of Christian views on the issues of dignity and depravity than the 1539 public letters to Genevans written by Cardinal Jacopo Sadoleto (1477–1547) and Jean Calvin (1509–64). The participants, both well educated in the humanist curriculum, come from two extremes of sixteenth-century thought, Sadoleto participating in the neo-Platonism of the circles of Marsilio Ficino at Florence and then Pietro Bembo at Rome and Calvin participating in the evangelicalism of Paris and Geneva. Nevertheless, both know Stoic texts firsthand, and both utilize vegetative images in educational and theological contexts. In considering the relationship of Stoic texts to this debate, we may properly take caution: Sadoleto comes closer to some Stoic texts in his confidence in the human potential for religious and ethical strivings, but Calvin comes closer to other Stoic texts in his belief in the chain of causality that limits free will, an aspect of Stoicism that has not been our focus in this book. In truth, Sadoleto's and Calvin's complex, learned, and eloquent statements highlight the diversity of mainstream Christianity in the sixteenth century.[121]

Jacopo Sadoleto, educated at Ferrara and an ecclesiastic under Oliviero Caraffa (1476–1559) in Rome, serves along with Pietro Bembo as secretary to Medici Pope Leo X, participates in the Oratory of Divine Love, which seeks moral reform within the Catholic Church, and proclaims the compatibility of classical letters and Christian knowledge. In 1533 he publishes his treatise *De pueris recte instituendis* (On the education of boys), and under the administration of Pope Paul III he culminates his career as a cardinal after 1536.[122]

Jean Calvin, educated in the trilingual curriculum at the University of Paris, publishes a commentary on Seneca in 1532; becomes an evangelical in 1533, taking refuge in the circle of Marguerite de Navarre and Lefèvre d'Étaples at Angoulême; and flees to Basel, where he completes his *Christianae religionis institutio* in March 1536. Passing through Geneva in July 1536, he accepts Guillaume Farel's invitation to stay as a professor of theology and preacher. After Calvin becomes a leading personality in the city and tightens regulations on morals, in 1538 the city council orders both Farel and Calvin to leave. Cardinal Sadoleto in March 1539 addresses the government and citizens of Geneva, asking them to return to Catholicism. In August, urged by friends in Geneva, Calvin, in Strasbourg, writes a reply to Sadoleto. The upshot is that Calvin's defense of Protestantism helps win him support in Geneva, and after opposition becomes severe against the anti-Calvin party in power, Calvin returns to Geneva in September 1541, the year his *Institution de la religion chrestienne* is printed for the French-reading public.[123] Here we shall consider the role of seed and light imagery and tree imagery in Sadoleto's theory of education and in the public exchange of letters between Sadoleto and Calvin.

In a dialogue with his nephew Sadoleto states, "For no one can be properly trained as a youth, who has been badly brought up as a child; for as the character and quality of a tree come from its roots, so a well-conditioned, well-balanced youth is the fruit of childhood" (7).[124] In contrast to Plato's *Laws*, he laments that there is insufficient legislation on the rearing of children. Sadoleto views the Roman Twelve Tables as "that seed-plot of all equity and right" [totius aequitatis ac juris seminarium], as are the Greek city-state codes of Solon for Athens and Lycurgus for Sparta (8–9). That ancient heritage of law reveals to Sadoleto "that it was owing to the seeds of learning so wisely sown, to the assiduous cultivation of the fallow land of children's fresh young minds, that there grew the harvest of high character and conduct which so richly blessed the days of old" (10). Disliking leaving education to the freedom or carelessness of individual parents, he praises public legislation for education: "In general human creatures are ignorant and need the light of law, a light by which they may be guided, if they will, or even constrained, against their inclination" (10).

In accordance with Cicero's *De oratore*, line 69, Sadoleto praises moral and literary training. He follows the humanist belief that such learning or art perfects nature: "We receive from Nature what is central in ourselves, what indeed makes us truly and individually what we are, but in a rough and unfinished form; it is the function of letters to bring this to its highest perfection and to work out in it a beauty comparable to its divine original" (12). The words "divine original" refer both to the idea of humanity in the image of God by which God created the first human and to the Platonic notion that the soul, not the body, is the true self. Pico's portrayals of Adam in his *Oratio* and *Hexameron* are background to Sadoleto's mode of thinking. For judging moral character Sadoleto distinguishes the imitation of human models in childhood from the character one acquires oneself in adulthood in accordance with one's own will. He views children as malleable and utilizes a plant image to explain: "As with plants, so with characters; while they are soft and impressionable, any form you will may be easily put upon them; but when this form by use and time has grown hard, it becomes practically unchangeable" (18). The tutor ensures that the child's passions obey the exterior reason and are molded by good habits until the child's reason becomes capable of taking charge.

Sadoleto gives attention to external influences on the child: he views the maxims to be memorized as seeds to be implanted in the child. The child is a "soil fitly prepared." The "first and fairest seed, the most rich and fruitful in true happiness, that should be cast into the soul, is the name and thought of Almighty God" (26). The implantations of teachings go into "untenanted ground" (28). Echoing Petrarch, Sadoleto states:

> For seeds, which at the first sowing are set well apart, are not yet crowded into a narrow space by a forest of other growths. Of course, all that is human must at times go astray and fall; but if pure love and worship of God have once grown like a tree within the heart, then, just as weeds may spring up and flourish for a while in sunless places, but assuredly cannot come to maturity nor bear fruit, so the deadliest sins will be destroyed by the shadow of religion (28).

The tree of religion grows from a seed sown by the parents and shades out other sinful growths, which also seem to be planted externally. Likewise, Sadoleto stresses the nurturing of the parents rather than their lineage: the nobility of a young lad appears to come from observing a father whose reason controls his passions and his decorum. "If a boy from his earliest years has been steeped in this tradition in the example of his father, he will have taken into his heart the noble seed of a virtue which will come to a splendid fruition in his own character" (33). The image of a young sapling is again brought up: "For just as letters are easily cut upon the tender bark of young trees, so it is our hope that our faint outline of virtue marked upon a boy's nature may be deepened, strengthened, and made permanent by time" (37). He emphasizes that the goal is imprinting from outside, for "all teaching of virtue depends upon example or upon precept—that is, if the seed of virtue is borne into the mind either by the ears or by the eyes" (37). The memorization of "pregnant maxims" is important, for "the impressionable mind may well receive and carry [them] with it through the rest of life" (91).

Sadoleto utilizes light imagery and illumination in a neo-Platonic sense of natural path to wisdom: "This light, which is the reason implanted in every man, kindled and fed by the most trustworthy forms of knowledge and learning, which points out the path for itself in every plan and every action, standing in no need of guidance from any other source—this light, I say philosophy keeps in her breath" (71). This natural light within is a path to absolute Truth, as in Plato's *Republic* 6.509–10. He clearly is not talking about Augustinian illumination, for he says that it needs help from no other source and he refers for full amplification to his third section of the treatise, which discusses philosophy. The precepts, examples, and discipline of earlier education he views as "a ray" or "a borrowed gleam" from the natural light of philosophy (71). Much of Sadoleto's discussion revolves around the concept of imitation, the child's imitation of parent or tutor and, through each model, an imitation of what is ultimately good, beautiful, and true. His phraseology is Platonic, but it is not incompatible with a Platonizing found in Seneca.

One might easily extrapolate to education what Seneca says in epistle 65 about an artist and a sculpture. Seneca utilizes Aristotle's four-causal theory to proclaim that for an artist making a sculpture the bronze is the matter, the workman is the efficient cause, the formal cause is the shape emerging, and the final cause is the purpose of the artist, perhaps fame or money.[125] Seneca adds a fifth cause—the exemplar, or design according to which the sculpture is molded. With Quintilian and Erasmus as precedents, Sadoleto describes the ideal educator as the father—the natural father as biological progenitor and the artistic father as sculptor of the habits and character of the child. Sadoleto goes farthest in the direction of proud perfectionism reminiscent of the Senecan passage: "This is a spectacle than which the world offers nothing more God-like. For what can the eye discover so rare, so noble, so splendid in its rounded and beautiful dignity as the sight of virtue controlling and ordering the impulses and affections of the mind, or fitly adjusting them to the rule of reason" (33). The person of the father strives to imitate an idea of a perfect human, embodying in word and deed rational order; whereas the youth imitates this imitation, the young adult comes to recognize the idea of humanity itself. Sadoleto shares with Seneca a lack of concern whether the exemplar is internal or external in humans; as writers, both participate in literary prescriptions, which are meant to be internalized. The external model of the Godlike human fosters not mere imitation but character development in the pupil. Sadoleto uses *spark* in the Stoic sense, to indicate the natural intellect itself, which grows from within. He finds evidence of this light at a young age: "As soon as a boy has learnt to speak correctly . . . and to throw out some little sparks of boyish wit," the father must teach him to read (86–87).

Sadoleto cites the deathbed lament of botanist and moralist Theophrastus that some birds and beasts have a longer life, while humans die before giving full use to the "Light of man, born for knowledge and contemplation" (126), and again mentions "fertile intelligence" (132). Stressing the influence of virtuous friends, he particularly praises his friends Bembo, Erasmus, and Alciati (133). Especially apropos to his situation is the example of Gianfrancesco Pico della Mirandola, nephew of Pico della Mirandola, who follows in his uncle's footsteps. Like Ficino and Pico della Mirandola, Sadoleto contrasts the life of activity with the life of contemplation and invites his nephew to "enter the broad and open plains of philosophy, so fruitful and fertile in all" (138), and to find "a nursing mother in philosophy" (141).

Likewise, in his *De philosophia*, written in 1533, Sadoleto argues that, in Eugene F. Rice's words, "the natural man can acquire a knowledge of divine things by his own, unaided efforts," proof that Sadoleto applies this theoretical view is his conviction that Socrates, Plato, Theophrastus, Cicero, and other non-Christians reached the highest perfection.[126] In this conviction that knowledge of divine things can be acquired by human means, Sadoleto emphasizes natural intellect more than does Ficino, who holds that although humans may make great strides upward, the ultimate wisdom is an infusion or illumination of the divine light.[127]

When Cardinal Sadoleto takes on the task of writing a letter to the Genevans to reeducate them and call them back to Catholicism he employs some of the same images we have examined in his educational treatise to show his respect for what human effort can achieve.[128] He comes to Genevans' aid for "I thought I heard the groans of the Church our mother, weeping and lamenting at being deprived at once of so many and so dear children" (31). He is confident that he can explain truth so that they will understand, "for it both shines in darkness and is perspicuous to every man, and is most easily perceived alike by learned and unlearned, and especially in matters of Christian doctrines, rests not on syllogism, or quibbles on words, but on humility, reverence, and obedience to God" (32). Possibly thinking of Luther's stand at the Diet of Worms, Sadoleto's defense of clear humanist reason and dispute with scholastic "quibbles" is in harmony with humanistically educated brethren Protestants. However, the application immediately differs: he agrees with evangelicals that first the foundation in faith must be laid, but then, like Erasmus respecting the agricultural laborer in his debate with Luther, he proclaims that "we must cast seed into the earth, that we may afterward be able to reap in heaven; and in whatever works, or whatever studies we have exercised ourselves here, may ultimately obtain similar and fit fruits of our works and labors in another life" (32). Sadoleto praises works and studies and is confident that they will be rewarded, for Christ died for the resurrection of the "whole human race" (33) and "raised the whole human race from sin" (34).

Sadoleto's optimism on the possibilities of salvation corresponds to his optimism on the internal ability to choose and reach out for faith and piety: the mind "inwardly prepared of itself for well-doing and shows a prompt desire to obey God in all things, and this in us is the true habit of divine justice" (35). Even before Calvin gives his reply, Cardinal Gasparo Contarini finds fault with Sadoleto's emphasis in this statement on the early role of human charity as a step to faith.[129] A year earlier, in the summer of 1538, in a letter to Luther, Melanchthon, and their German followers Sadoleto views "justification by faith" as false doctrine contrived for rebellion and argues for human movements toward God as evinced by good works.[130] In his letter to the Genevans Cardinal Sadoleto alters his strategy somewhat: he claims to accept "justification by faith alone," for he views good works as a sign of a people preparing themselves for the Divine (35–36).

Praising Sadoleto for his humanist learning, Calvin criticizes him for appealing to the Genevans to consider their personal salvations rather than their obligation to sanctify and worship God (50). He claims that the Word has been misused and that the church has confused doctrine, discipline, sacraments, and ceremonies (59–63). He protests Sadoleto's attempt to claim for the Catholic Church "justification by faith alone" and emphasizes the necessity of placing one's "conscience before the tribunal of God" and recognizing that one has "no merit of his own" (66–67). "But what notion, does the very term *righteousness* suggest to us if respect is not paid to good works? I answer, if you attend to the true meaning of *justifying* in Scripture, you would have no difficulty. For it does not refer to man's own righteousness, but to the mercy of God" (67). Clearly for Calvin, righteousness stemming from human action, as in Stoic virtue in accord with nature, or Hebrew justice in accord with revealed law, or Catholic good works in accord with church doctrine, is not instrumental for human salvation. On the other hand, Calvin views these human efforts as fully relevant to life on this earth: "We deny that good works have any share in justification, but we claim full authority for them in the lives of the righteous" (68).

Calvin ridicules Sadoleto's Christian and neo-Platonic view that "love is the first and chief cause of our salvation." "Undoubtedly the very blind, while in darkness, feel the mercy of God too surely to dare to claim for their love the first cause of their salvation, while those who have merely one spark of divine light feel that their salvation consists in nothing else than their being adopted by God" (69). In terms of its ability to ignite by itself in love toward God, the "spark" of the Divine in the natural intellect appears to be just one step away from blindness. Like Sadoleto, Calvin uses seed imagery for external sowing, but he turns it around, accusing the church of creating monsters out of the "seeds of superstition" sown in antiquity (73). He accuses Sadoleto of having "too indolent a theology, as is almost always the case with those who have never had an experience in serious struggles of conscience" (78).

Calvin's use of the image of wax and seal and the image of light follow in the tradition of Augustine's theory of illumination or participation: Christian faith is "engraven on our hearts by the finger of the living God"; "it is God alone who enlightens our minds to perceive His truth, who by His Spirit seals it in our hearts, and by His sure attestation to it confirms our conscience" (78–79). Both Sadoleto and Calvin utilize the Stoic phrases primarily as externals, but for Calvin the imprinting, the sowing, the enlightening comes not from education or custom but from God alone. The one clear aid is the revealed word of God, which is "like a lamp" (87); Calvin accuses the church of not sharing this lamp with the congrega-

6.4. "Florebit rigante Deo" (It will bloom by God's watering), from
Jacob à Bruck's *Emblemata*, 1652. "It will spring up from a dry root—Look!
a flourishing little plant; / Which one day will bear fruit and welcome
seeds. /Often God awakens its offspring when the root seems to
have perished, /That it may grow into a new generation."

tion but instead delegating authority to a few to cause obedience in the
many (87).

One might view Calvin's viewpoint on human dependence on God as
that of the emblem "Florebit rigante Deo" (It will bloom by God's watering) (fig 6.4). A hand from heaven waters a plant that appeared to be dead,
and from the dry root a new generation grows. Similarly, in Romans 11.23
Paul discusses God's kindness in grafting back to the olive tree of the children of God Hebrews who turn to God in true faith. The viewpoint of this
emblem is the view I think Calvin applies to the issue of attaining divine
wisdom; he often refers to the divine hand reaching down to help humans
attain faith.

But Calvin does not think humans are entirely dependent on God for attaining human wisdom. His suggestion to Sadoleto that the lives of the righteous are aided by human effort is confirmed by many passages in his *Institutes* and his biblical commentaries.[131] An analysis of chapter 2 of his first French edition shows that "reason," "common notions," "seeds," and "sparks" are commonplaces to Calvin, as well as to Catholics in sixteenth-century France.[132] Calvin reduces the complex psychology of Plato, Cicero, and Aristotle to two major human capacities of *l'esprit*—intelligence and will. Intelligence judges what to approve or condemn, and will is to follow the intelligence in seeking what is judged good and to flee what is judged evil. Thus, all virtues are in the will or in the understanding. While on one page (99) Calvin cites ancient philosophers for claiming that we have a "divine light" in us, on the next page he more modestly cites Cicero, *Tusculanae disputationes* 3, for the view that there are "small sparks of goodness, lighting up naturally in our mind, which we corrupt easily by false opinions and bad customs."[133] Likewise, he talks about the "small spark" that gives humans "a natural love of truth," which brute beasts do not have.[134] Then, in words common to Montaigne and Charron, he applies images of the turning and twisting of the intellect to describe human troubles in seeking truth (114–15).

A resolution is reached that functions importantly in Calvin's writings and in those he inspires when he explains that intelligence has an earthly terrain. Although it is not sufficient for reaching God or immortality, it is useful for developing political doctrines, for governing city and home, for medicine, for the mechanical arts, for philosophy, and for the liberal disciplines. Citing a distinction between heavenly and earthly subjects, Calvin indicates that intelligence has some use for terrestrial subjects.[135] Intelligence figures in his advice for government and for liberal arts education. We learn that honesty and civil order derive from notions "imprinted on the understanding of all humans."[136] Following the Stoic natural-law doctrine, Calvin accepts that there are laws for which "there is some seed in us, which proceeds from nature without ruler or legislator";[137] he confirms his conviction that there is a "seed of nobility in our nature" that encourages justice and honesty.[138] The capacity for grasping natural law is evident in Calvin's emphatic summary of Moses' two tablets: "The first is that we love God with our whole heart, our whole mind and our whole strength; and the second: that we love our neighbors as ourselves" (117).

In support of liberal education[139] Calvin notes that ancient pagan writings expose that some pagans have "this admirable light of truth," which shows that despite the fall and corruption humans still retain some gifts of God.[140] He praises all the disciplines as coming from God, who gives gifts to whomever he wishes. The discussion of gifts blurs the distinction between nature and grace, as Calvin asks his contemporaries to be grateful that God has given gifts to some for the benefit of all humans (119). There is the implication that some of these gifts, such as classical writings, are products of the natural development of intelligence, for Calvin stresses that the virtue of understanding lesser things, such as knowledge of this earth, is "a frivolous thing and of no importance before God."[141] Human learning is simply a small thing in relationship to God's glory and can give humans false pride if they value it too highly. That sentiment corresponds to Erasmus's recognition in *Praise of Folly* of the follies of the pompous scholars compared with the more valuable spiritual Christian piety of the commoners. In Augustinian fashion, by contrasting the city of God to the earthly city Calvin can allow and even encourage studies of pagan letters. Humorously he points out concerning the need to create commonplace books, "These small drops of truth that we see scattered in the books of philosophers, by how much more horrible lies have they been obscured?"[142] In fact Calvin quite accurately observes that the florilegia are formed by winnowing the concise, rhetorically pleasing, and perceptive sentences of wisdom from the bountiful texts that exist.

From Innocent III to Martin Luther, some Christians reject the implication that humans may naturally develop their seeds of virtue and knowledge to attain either divine wisdom or human wisdom; in rejecting a confidence in human potentiality derived from classical philosophy they suggest that not only salvation but human wisdom as well comes from Jesus. Nevertheless, the distinction between a human path, built upon classical and biblical texts, to human wisdom and a divine path, dependent upon divine grace, to divine wisdom is an option. In practice, Protestants as well as Catholics accommodate to Augustine's distinction between the earthly city and the city of God. Luther's successor Philip Melanchthon adjusts Lutheran educational theory to fully accommodate the powers of human reason and the "seeds of virtue and knowledge."[143] The institutionalization of the humanist curricula in Protestant as well as Catholic schools and universities encourages the implantation of seeds of virtue and knowledge through florilegia as well as the strengthening of reason (the Senecan inborn seeds of virtue and knowledge) to build the human wisdom essential for orderly government.[144]

The debates on free will, good works, and justification between Erasmus and Luther and between Sadoleto and Calvin are background to the decisions of the Council of Trent in January 1547. In fact both Erasmus's and Sadoleto's views come under criticism within the Catholic Church before Trent.[145] Erasmus during his lifetime receives abundant criticism from all sides, and after his death his works are put on the first *Index librorum prohibitorum* by Pope Paul IV. The early criticism of Erasmus in the 1520s by Alberto Pio to the Roman Curia does include a section on justification that assumes a formula close to the one later adopted by the Council of Trent.[146]

After the mid-sixteenth-century proceedings of the Council of Trent, Catholics are expected to uphold the doctrine that original sin has weakened but not extinguished free will. According to Trent, Gentiles following nature and Jews following the law of Moses cannot be liberated or begin to rise:[147] in our own time, Erasmus and Sadoleto are background to the spirit of Vatican II.[148] Trent declares that the Passion of Christ, which was intended for all, applies only to those who are reborn again in Christ through holy water. The preparation for justification comes through predisposing grace of Jesus Christ, from an "illumination of the Holy Ghost" (6.5) rather than from a grace present from the Creation, as Erasmus argues. Cooperation in grace becomes assenting and not refusing it. The image of a good coming from outside is clear in 6.7: "whence man, in the said justification through Jesus Christ, into whom he is grafted, receives together with remission of sins, all these things infused at once, faith, hope, and charity. For faith, unless to it be added hope and charity, neither unites (man) perfecting with Christ, nor makes him a living member of His body. For which reason it is most truly said, that *faith without works is dead.*"

There is a gradualism in the post-Tridentine Catholic position, but unlike the gradualism of Erasmus and Sadoleto, which precedes and follows faith, this gradualism comes not before but after faith: "*From strength to strength* (Ps: 83.8) *they are renewed*, as the Apostle says, *day by day* (2 Cor. 4:16) and are still more justified, as is written, *He that is righteous, let him be made righteous still* (Apoc. 22:11)" (6.10). Likewise, the Council of Trent, although on the defensive against criticism of good work done for reward and seeking authority in the Scriptures, rejects Pietro Pomponazzi's and Protestants' discomfort with instrumental virtue and follows Thomas Aquinas in viewing it as proper that humans act justly in hope of eternal reward (6.11). Canon 1 holds anathema anyone who argues that one can be justified by natural powers, by free will, or by law without divine grace through Jesus Christ. Canon 24 opposes the view that works are merely "the fruits and signs of justification." The Council evokes the image of Jesus as the holy vine infusing strength into the branches (the church members) around which it winds (6.16).

Northern Renaissance Humanism: Cultivating and Transplanting the Seeds of Virtue and Knowledge

REVERBERATING humanistic themes within their distinct regional cultures, northern humanists apply Seneca, Cicero, and Quintilian to a strategy for nourishing, cultivating, and also transplanting seeds of virtue and knowledge. The Stoic phrase *seeds of virtue and knowledge* is especially common in Erasmus's educational treatises and textbooks. His friend Alciati creates poems to explain ancient mottos, to which the publishers add woodcuts. Vegetative imagery is very much in vogue in the sixteenth century as printing techniques advance the popular genre of illustrated herbals. The educational strategy of speeding student growth by implanting seeds of knowledge and virtue gains potency through the power of sentence-image-poem. In particular, Alciati's vegetative emblems, showing trees standing for particular virtues in human nature, exemplify the natural paths to wisdom encouraged by Seneca, Cicero, and humanist educators. Stoic ideas are elaborated in the major moralist tradition of late-sixteenth-century France and the Low Countries: neo-Stoicism. While Du Vair writes distinct books to separate his teaching of Christian religion from his teaching of ethics, Justus Lipsius builds a systematic Stoic ethic. Writing carefully in the atmosphere following the Council of Trent and in the midst of religious warfare, the neo-Stoics build upon the confidence in human potentialities of Erasmus and his predecessors to encourage choosing virtue and fulfilling the requirements of human dignity.

RESPROUTING OF THE SEEDS IN ERASMIAN HUMANISM

Sixteenth-century French humanists such as Guillaume Budé, Clément Marot, François Rabelais, and Louis le Roy continue the contrast of light and previous darkness and stress the rebirth (*renaître*) of letters.[1] Jacques Amyot credits King Francis I with causing good letters to be reborn ("renaistre") and to flourish,[2] and Jean Trithème writes of the reflowering of letters.[3] Guillaume Budé is most direct in his recognition of the role that rulers play in the cultural renovation, and he appeals directly to King Francis I to liberally revive French culture and provide rewards to royal lecturers and scholars.[4] The themes rebirth, reflowering, and fruitfulness pervade rhetoric, as well as the visual arts,[5] honoring the king, who commissions the château and garden in the forest of Fontainebleau.

Historians generally credit Giorgio Vasari with giving the age the name *la rinascità*, "rebirth," in 1550, in his first edition of *Lives*, in which he compares a historical epoch to the birth and death of a human body.[6] More typically, three years later, the naturalist Pierre Belon (1517–64) in his dedicatory epistle makes a direct Petrarchan comparison between the rebirth of culture and the rebirth of plants in the spring: "The minds of men . . . have begun to wake up and to leave the darkness where for so long they have remained dormant and in leaving have put forth and put in evidence all kinds of good disciplines which to their so happy and desirable *renaissance*, all as the new plants after a season of winter regain their vigor in the heat of the Sun and are consoled by the mildness of the spring."[7] The correspondence between awakening after sleep and the regrowth of plant stock after the winter cold is a natural one, indicating the continued vitality that was hidden during a period of dormancy. The darkness of human minds (*esprits*, suggesting both reason and will) in the period after antiquity now is lit up again by the vivid image of the sun.

The image of rebirth comes into general European usage by the mid-sixteenth century. The botanical image of Belon strikes me as most typical of both the literary and the visual evidence of this time period, for Belon follows the Italian and French humanists in comparing cultural growth to vegetative growth. We have seen abundant examples of imagery of seeds of virtue and knowledge at the basis of humanist confidence in a rebirth, the Medici restoration's visual usage of vegetative symbolism to explain their own renewal, and the French humanist association of Francis I with the rebirth and reflowering of letters.

The edition of Erasmus's adages published in 1571 in Paris by Jacques Charron typically gives credit to Erasmus as "the first to raise up good letters at the time when they were being reborn (*renascentes tum jam bonas litteras*)."[8] Erasmus himself often uses the phrase *renascantur bonae literae* in recognition of the rebirth of good literature in Italy and the north and traces the history of that literature in his 1528 *Ciceronianus* (Dialogue entitled the Ciceronian).[9] In accord with Cicero and humanist *imitatio*, Erasmus suggests that one draw from models that suit one's natural gifts, "so that your mind . . . may give birth to a style which smells not of any flower, shrub, or grass, but of your own native talent and feeling."[10] Eramus's *Adages* and *De copia* provide models for making honey from the flowers of the ancients.

There continues the tension we have seen in the medieval period between divine light as in the Joannine Gospel, the light of Christ, and the secular notion of human learning as the light. Ferguson finds Erasmians in northern Europe using light as well as birth metaphors, but he finds Italians avoiding light imagery except for religious thought, using instead revival, restoration, awakening, reflowering, and return to light. Protestant reformers view the period from the fifth century to their own time as an age of darkness for the church, for the idea of rebirth of the primitive church is essential to reformation. Protestant humanists call for a revitalization of the whole age, not just revival of learning and arts. They interpret humanist revival as "inspired by Divine Providence in preparation for the acceptance of the gospel."[11]

Seed imagery takes on new forms in an age of religious warfare: consider the sixteenth-century epigram that Erasmus laid the egg that Luther hatched.[12] With an agricultural image of the printing press sowing seeds, sixteenth-century Frenchman Jean Fernel recognizes that human ingenuity in creating machines increases humans' power to attain knowledge and appreciates the power of the printing press to disseminate knowledge: "The world sailed round, the largest of Earth's continents discovered, the printing-press sowing knowledge, gunpowder revolutionising the art of war, the ancient manuscripts rescued and the restoration of scholarship, all witness to the triumph of our New Age."[13]

Erasmus talks of seeds in his "The Sileni of Alcibiades," which refers to ancient statuettes that are ridiculous or ugly on the outside but contain a figure of a god within. "In trees, it is the flowers and leaves which are beautiful to the eye; their spreading bulk is visible far and wide. But the seed, in which lies the power of it all, how tiny a thing it is! . . . Gold and gems are hidden by nature in the deepest recesses of the earth. . . . In living things, what is best and most vital is secreted in the inward parts. In man, what is most divine and immortal is what cannot be seen."[14] Erasmus recognizes the parallel in generative source of the acorn to the oak and seminal fluid of animals to the process of generation; however, for the human being he draws the implication that what is most vital is what is divine and immortal, that which according to Christian as well as Jewish biological traditions gives "soul" to the human gamete.

From these examples Erasmus draws the implication that "in the universe, the greatest things are those not seen, like substances, which are called separate. And at the highest point of these there stands what is furthest removed from the senses, namely God, further than our understanding or our knowing, the single source of all things." "Seeds" connote to Erasmus the heavenly; for example, he says that "the kingdom of heaven has as its symbol a grain of mustard seed, small and contemptible in appearance, mighty in power."[15] Thomas M. Greene has appropriately interpreted Erasmus's comparison of seeds to gems as revealing "his fascination with the hard, secret, precious time-resistant capsule of signification."[16] I agree with Greene that for Erasmus and other humanists the seed image implies a non-Derridean "determinate power of its beginning,"[17] and I would add that the Renaissance comfort with nonclosure is a comfort in the continued seminal vitality of an ancient text to generate commentary and thought by germinating the seeds of knowledge and virtue in the reader.

The method is fully elaborated in Erasmus's *De copia*, which is an exemplary notebook. The goal for the humanist is to read the whole of classical literature at least once and record examples under subheadings for use in writing. For headings Erasmus advises an abundance of expressions, such as metaphor, allegory, and varieties of negatives, and an abundance of subject, such as commonplaces, likenesses, fables, and scriptural allegories.[18]

Quintilian's ideal of the eloquent, knowledgeable, and virtuous individual is important to Erasmus. In *De copia* Erasmus describes such an ideal individual in abundant examples of predications of equal weight: "est vir doctus simul et integer" [the man is learned and at the same time upright]; "vir est in litteris egregius, neque sui dissimilis in moribus" [the man is outstanding in learning, and his own equal in character]; "vir pari doctrina ac probitate" [a man of equal learning and probity].[19] After not three *sententiae* but three pages of such drill, the student senses from rhetorical rhythm the harmony of the balanced life and understands better the development of seeds of virtue and knowledge. Throughout his educational tracts Erasmus consistently treats as harmonious Quintilian's concept of the tutor planting a seed—an idea or a phrase—in the student's mind and the Stoic concept of developing the seeds naturally present there. Citing Quintilian, as Costanza da Varano and Battista Guarino do, Erasmus holds that "so also every human being can be taught virtue without any great hardship. The seeds that nature has implanted in us to attain to this goal are bursting with life; the only thing that is required, in addition to this natural inclination, is the effort of a dedicated teacher."[20]

VEGETATIVE IMAGERY IN ALCIATI'S EMBLEMS

Andrea Alciati's (1492–1550) first printed emblem collection, of 1531, starts a vogue that enhances the tradition of florilegia by adding printed images and poems to commonplaces. For the 1531 innovation in genre the Augsburg publisher Heynrich Steyner adds the woodcut illustrations to help less educated readers understand the poems.[21] The commonplaces and poems accompanying the images create emblems that are instructional devices for arousing right reason and virtuous conduct in the reader-viewer. Following up on Augustin Renaudet's calling Alciati's emblem collections "an ingenious complement" to Erasmus's *Adages*, Virginia Callahan has documented Alciati's friendship with Erasmus, especially Alciati's admiration for Erasmus and the influence upon Alciati's emblems of Erasmus's ideas.[22] We have already noticed that Sadoleto links Alciati, Erasmus, and Bembo together in praise for friends who inspire a striving for human virtue. Alciati, like Erasmus, from whom he borrows wording and whom he emulates, treats as harmonious the planting of a seed in the student's mind and the developing of the seeds naturally present there at birth.

Emblems in books printed in France and elsewhere in Europe contain numerous images of trees of virtue and trees of knowledge in bloom.[23] I shall use Alciati's name for emblems that appear in editions bearing his name. Significantly, Alciati's collection does not contain any emblems that give credit for vegetative blooming to divine intervention,[24] unlike "Florebit rigante Deo" (fig. 6.4), which suggests an Augustinian belief that illumination by God precedes truly good works, a viewpoint supported by Luther's most influential work, *De servo arbitrio*. Instead, Alciati's model of the natural growth of plants and trees symbolizes the natural growth of humanity, and his emblem books apply strategies to aid in that natural human instruction. Translators of his work also experiment with strategies for communicating the moral lessons to the public.[25]

Alciati's trees growing in natural sunlight seem to be consistent with the revival of botanical studies—both the printing of Theophrastus's botany in Latin translation in 1483 and, more directly, the appearance of botanical illustrations in Brunfels's *Herbarum vivae eicones* of 1530. It takes a major advance in printing technology for such realistic drawings to be produced.[26] Emphasizing the living plants of the title, this herbal does not copy plants from previous herbals but contains new representations from living plants by the artist Hans Weiditz. What makes the book an immediate success is not Brunfels's routine text, describing plants and discussing their virtues, but the illustrations, which show even withered species of plants.[27] Although the designs for Alciati's emblems are more traditional, being in the mode of the medieval and early Renaissance herbals, they imply, as Brunfels's do, the natural growth of vegetation by the natural light of the sun, the realm Thomas Aquinas would call "secondary causation."

Sixteenth-century culture values plants, whether in herbals, emblem books, collections of dried plants (simples), or actual gardens. The exploration of the Americas leads to an expansion of the taxonomy of known plants; and instructive botanical gardens, in Padua in 1525 and in Pisa in 1544 and then elsewhere, open to display the abundance of God's creation. Under the auspices of King Henry IV, in 1593 Pierre Richer de Belleval gains a chair at the renowned medical school in Montpellier and directs the first French royal botanical garden.[28] Less than three hundred years later in a monastery botanical garden Gregor Mendel (1822–84) will systematically study wrinkled versus round seeds, yellow versus green seeds, and seven other pairs of traits of garden peas, and through analysis of the pattern of trait inheritance he will found the modern field of gene research.[29] The 1596 illustration of Montpellier (fig. 7.1) shows that the newly acquired royal botanical garden is divided into several distinct sections. Starting at the foreground, the *seminarium* allows the acclimatization of seeds that come from afar to the nearby port at Marseilles; the *herbarium* is for herbs or dried plant specimens; the *planta quarum in*

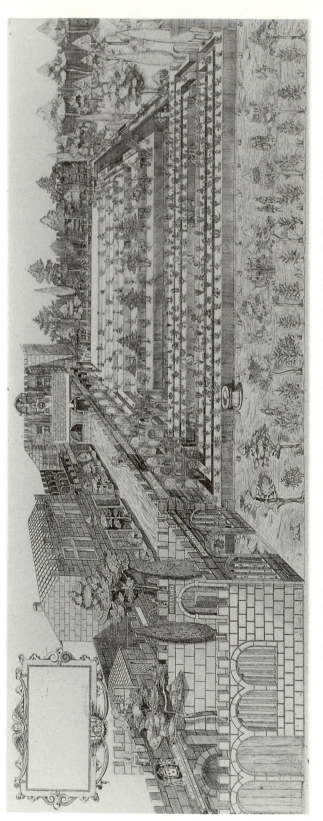

7.1. Jardin des Plantes, Montpellier, France, an etching attributed to Richer de Belleval, 1596. Note the label "Seminarium" for the courtyard of seedbeds at the lower left.

medicina provides for prescriptions of the medical school; and the *planta odorata* disperse odoriferous pleasure. Richer de Belleval demonstrates to his medical students from the expanding collection of dried plants. The preservation of dried plants between papers in large cabinets and with other exotic items in *cabinets de curiosité* allows one today to see some flowers from the Renaissance.[30]

It is not surprising that Alciati chooses to use plants in many illustrations.[31] The herbal is one of the most popular genres of the sixteenth century. "Leafing" through Agnes Arber's *Herbals* gives one a sense of the variety and vitality of the illustrations in this genre. *Der Gart der Gesundheit* was a model for others, and the *Hortus sanitatis* is a comprehensive encyclopedia, a guide to flora from the biblical tree of knowledge to known plants in 1491 as well as a guide to the medicinal arts.[32] The herbals explain the "virtues" of plants, their potency in a medicinal sense to cure human disorders. Alciati's poems on his plant illustrations, as well as others, explain the "virtues" of human beings that may overcome common vicious human disorders.

In fact, Alciati's *Emblemata*, published in Lyon in 1551, uses Balthasar Arnoullet's illustrative woodblocks of trees from Leonhart Fuchs's *L'histoire des plantes*. In the 1577 Antwerp edition of Alciati, Christophe Plantin uses the same woodblocks that he used for Rembert Dodoens's herbal *Cruydt-Boech* in 1557 and 1565 to illustrate fourteen trees of Alciati.[33] Joachim Camerarius the younger (1534–98), whose father (1500–1574) was both Melanchthon's biographer and a professor of classical texts, first edits a herbal in 1586 and then in 1590 prints the first volume of his four-volume *Symbolorum et emblematum*, in which some plants of his herbal illustrate moral and Christian truths through Camerarius's citation of classical authors and church fathers (see fig. 9.1).[34] These examples emphasizes for us both that the genres of herbal and emblem collections overlap and that there is a particularly classical and secular tone to Alciati's emblems.

The reading audience thus is familiar with plant lore when it confronts Alciati's images of trees. In his vegetative symbolism plants symbolize the moral virtues of particular human beings, but no exotic magic or miraculous features detract from Alciati's outlook that virtue is living in accord with nature. Natural light and human potency appear to be the sources for growth of the almond, who is precocious and never fully matures (fig. 7.2), as well as of the mulberry, who is not dumb, as some believe, but merely a slow bloomer (fig. 7.3)[35] I use *who* rather than *which* because these trees appear as personifications of various skills and subfields needed for full knowledge. Other trees of knowledge include the ivy, who reflects the poet's enduring fame, and the moly plant, who proclaims that eloquence is difficult.[36] The laurel, so valued in Florence, is a reward for the removal of ignorance.[37]

The full analogy between horticulture and culture appears in the emblems drawing a parallel between transplanting a plant and transplanting a

190 *ARBORI.*

MANDORLO.

Troppo anzi tempo i fior questa produce:
E i troppo anzi l'età maturi ingegni
Dirado Phebo a somma altezza adduce.

7.2. "Almond tree," from Alciati, *Diverse imprese*, Lyon, 1551. "This tree produces flowers too early; / And seldom does Apollo bring to great heights / Indications of genius that mature before their time."

230 ARBORES. *EMBL.*
Morus.

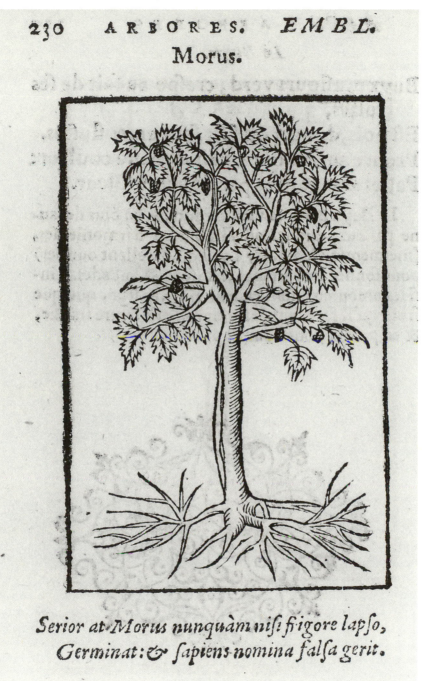

Serior at Morus nunquàm nisi frigore lapso,
Germinat: & sapiens nomina falsa gerit.

7.3. "Mulberry tree," from Alciati, *Emblemes*, Paris, 1561. "The wise mulberry
is wrongly named in Greek (numskull), / For it does not bloom
until after winter is over."

scholar. In this age when many seeds are brought from the Americas and planted in the new botanical gardens of Europe and when Italian humanists and artists seek employment for their skills across the Continent, an emblem proclaims: "The transplanted scholar bears better fruit" (fig. 7.4). Alciati himself spends his career as a legal humanist and an emblematist in both Italian and French cities and knows firsthand the different ways in which a person is appreciated.[38]

In the vegetative imagery of Alciati's emblem books the medieval trees of knowledge of virtues and vices (and the offshoot trees of knowledge) fuse with the medieval tradition of characters, personifications of particular virtues or vices or of particular arts and sciences. A very famous set of characters is Giotto's personifications of charity, envy, prudence, and folly in the Arena Chapel at Padua.[39] In Botticelli's *Lorenzo Tornabuoni presented by Grammar to Prudentia and the other Liberal Arts* the key virtue, Prudence, symbolizes the goal of the liberal arts; and in *Venus and the Graces Offering Flowers* (fig. 5.3) Venus and her court provide a wedding gift to a bride, likely Giovanna degli Albizzi. In both of these a person is honored by receiving gifts from the classical personifications. In Alciati one individual tree personifies a human being who embodies a specific virtue or vice, skill, or expertise. Theophrastus himself writes both a book of plants and a book of characters, and the two sides of Theophrastus here fuse.

Examples of individual trees of virtue and vice are particularly abundant in the Padua, 1621, edition of Alciati. They include "The prudent abstain from wine," in which an olive tree resists the embrace of the grape-bearing vine, a dangerous source of drunkenness. In "One Must Be Steadfast under Pressure" a palm is capable of bending under the weight. The poem clarifying the Stoic motto indicates that a person who is persistent and constant despite pressure will gain the sweet dates of the palm tree. The motto "On brief happiness" describes a gourd vine rising high and proud on top of a pine tree. The poem criticizes the pride of the gourd, who will be brought down when winter sets in.[40]

In "The Fig Tree Eaten by Crows" prodigals waste the wealth of the unwise. Likewise, in "On Fertility That is Harmful to Itself" boys throw stones at a nut tree, which laments that its fertility has attracted harm and so envies the sterile trees.[41] The parable of the nut tree appears in the *Florilegium diversorum epigrammatum* and in Ovid; by placing it in a section on parent-child relationships, Alciati shows Ovid's attention to the ungratefulness of children.[42] Alciati's language also shows his awareness of Erasmus's letter of 1523 (published 1524) to Thomas More's son John in which he applies the story of the nut tree to encourage him to pursue virtue and knowledge and to emulate his father with gratitude.[43] Another example of ruin derives not from others but solely from oneself; in Alciati's "Self-love" (emblem 69, Padua, 1621) Narcissus is portrayed in a forest looking at his reflection with admiration and turning into a flower as a warning to others.

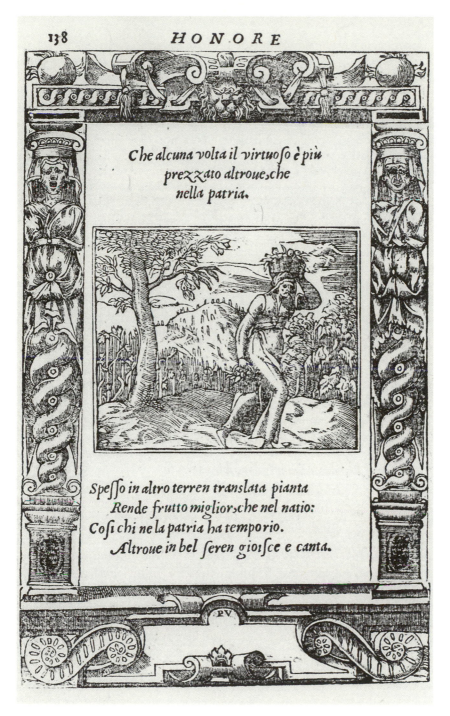

Che alcuna volta il virtuoso è più
prezzato altroue, che
nella patria.

Spesso in altro terren translata pianta
Rende frutto miglior, che nel natio:
Così chi ne la patria ha temporio.
Altroue in bel seren gioisce e canta.

7.4. "The transplanted scholar bears better fruit," from Alciati, *Diverse imprese*,
Lyon, 1551. "Often plants transplanted in other soil / Give better fruit than
in native soil. / So one who faces adversity in one's own land / May
enjoy and sing amid beautiful serenity of another land."

Other vegetative images show the positive rewards of clear virtue actively applied to public service. In "The Best Citizen" (fig. 7.5) a hero who liberates his homeland of Athens is rewarded with the olive garland. Likewise, in "The Oak" we see inscriptions on either side of a flourishing oak: the words "by senate decree father of his country for saving citizens" and a head of Jupiter with a garland wreath.[44] Alciati's example of the garland wreath as the reward for civic virtue is a common *topos* mediating between the contemplative virtues of solitude in nature and in study and the active virtues of service to one's community. Poets such as Andrew Marvel speak eloquently of the striving for such garlands and bemoan the banishment of civic virtues as a loss of the "civic crown."[45]

The emblems under Alciati's name raise several issues that are current in the sixteenth century, and these issues are also raised by the emblems of other collectors. Two Stoic themes are the nobility of virtue, rather than birth, and the difficulty of achieving virtue. Thus, in "Poverty Hinders Talent" Alciati shows a figure buoyed up by wings on one side and weighed down on the other; the epigram declares, "By virtue of my genius I could have flown through lofty citadels, were it not that despised poverty held me down."[46] "By Sweet Virtue" in Johannes Sambucus's *Emblemata* (Antwerp, 1564) portrays the hearth of a humble home, and the epigram is suggestive of the sparks of later success:

> Those who know how to untangle the obscure knots of nature and
>   seek the causes usually mark out the whole matter.
> These say that a flame is smoke kindled from light, for often the
>   matter is proved by the knowledgeable.
> Thus call it smoke, the origins of those born in a stable from
>   lowly parentage, whom virtue makes old.
> Light ennobles these, it enriches them with deserving and
>   honorable things.
> Thus they become illustrious, those who drove ignorance from
>   their home.[47]

Closely related to the theme of nobility of virtue and talent is the Stoic theme "virtue difficult, but fruitful," the title of an emblem showing a pinecone as the fruit of Cybele (fig. 2.2). Traditional tree imagery appears in "About to Pluck Sweet Fruit from a Bitter Root," in which a boy attempts to climb a palm tree; its rough bark hurts his skin, but he endures the ascent. "For those aiming at it, virtue first presents those approaches to itself, and the steep path shows the hardships. But the summit itself will give the best to those who reach it: perpetual relief and glory and honor await those."[48] Michel de Montaigne questions whether the difficult Stoic upward road is the best path by a vivid reference to a standard emblem on ascending the mountain of Stoic virtue to receive the victory palm and laurel wreath (fig. 9.1).

Most amusing from a botanical standpoint is Alciati's emblem of friendship, symbolized by a vine growing on a tree even after the tree is dead.

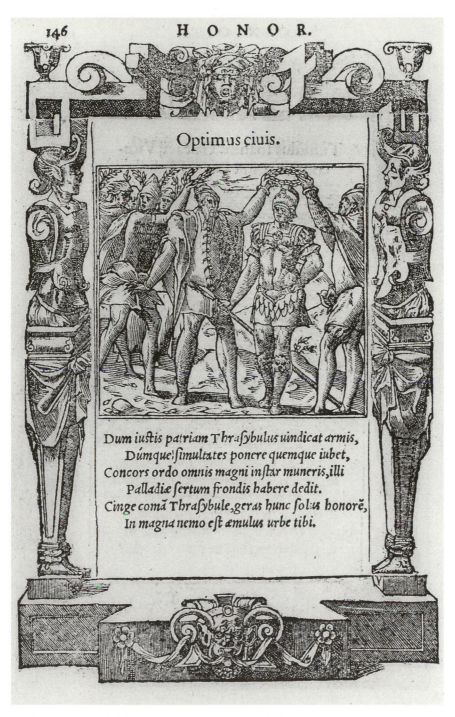

Optimus ciuis.

Dum iustis patriam Thrasybulus uindicat armis,
    Dúmque simultates ponere quemque iubet,
Concors ordo omnis magni instar muneris, illi
    Palladiæ sertum frondis habere dedit.
Cinge comã Thrasybule, geras hunc solus honorẽ,
    In magna nemo est æmulus urbe tibi.

7.5. "Optimus civis" (The best citizen), from Alciati, *Emblemata*, Lyon, 1550.
"While with just arms Thrasybulus was liberating his homeland / And ordering
each to put aside animosities, / All the citizens with one mind gave him an
olive-leaf garland of / Pallas Athena to wear instead of a great reward. / 'Crown
your hair, Thrasybulus, you alone should have this honor: / In the
great city, Athens, no one surpasses you.'"

This emblem shows that emblem trees sometimes do not necessarily reflect the growing field of botanical investigation, as botanists already understood that a too abundant vine can kill a tree! Nevertheless, the image is fully secular, as is the vine of inebriating grapes.[49] Both tree and vine represent ordinary humans clasped in friendship.

Seed theory receives increased attention in the sixteenth century in both natural and moral philosophy in both Catholic and Protestant lands. The herbal illustrators Conrad Gesner and Camerarius show the seeds simultaneously with the plants on the theory that the different phases of the life history of a plant should be shown.[50] The botanist Pierre Belon (1517–64), quoted above for his contribution to historical periodization in the analogy between horticultural rebirth and cultural rebirth, receives the patronage of the bishop of Le Man in 1535 at his garden in Touvoie, and the bishop encourages him to study botany with Valerius Cordus at the University of Wittenberg. One senses the camaraderie of botanists of Lutheran as well as Catholic persuasion. After studying botany and conversing with Luther, Belon in 1544 learns acclimatization techniques at the botanical gardens in Padua under Venetian dominion, works on the gardens of Fontainebleau under King Francis I, and in 1546 joins a delegation to Constantinople. Returning to the France of Henry II, Belon tries to replant and acclimatize a multitude of seeds from his travels in Turkey, Lebanon, Palestine, and Egypt. At Touvoie Belon does not succeed in planting the spruce, the strawberry tree, or the holm oak—the tree that divides in two, like some symbolical trees of virtue and vice (see fig. 3.5), but he does succeed in making flourish in French gardens the manna tree, along with the flowering ash, the olive tree, the oleander, and the plane tree (*Platanus orientalis*).[51] The plane is Belon's favorite: in Plato's *Phaedrus* Socrates walks out from Athens to converse with Phaedrus, who is sitting at a sacred sylvan site under a plane tree; Ficino's commentary emphasizes the sacredness of the setting.[52]

The lore for gathering the seeds of unusual and rare plants is humorously treatment by Rabelais (ca. 1490–1553) in *Gargantua and Pantagruel*, bk. 3, ch. 49, "How Pantugruel did put himself in a readiness to go to sea; and of the herb named Pantagruelion." As book 3 is not finished until 1552, it may very well reflect popular interest in Belon's quest for medicinal drugs in the Levant. Rabelais describes an amazing tall plant, the Pantagruelion, which grows higher than some trees. He explains how the Pantagruelion is to be prepared and describes its many virtues.[53] One recollects Machiavelli's play on the mandrake, a plant associated with fertility. Rabelais makes several outrageous claims about the Pantagruelion. Most outstanding is that fire cannot consume it; like asbestos, it covers the Abbey de Thélème so that it cannot burn (bk. 3, ch. 52). Rabelais suggests the possibility of sex division in plants. Every year the Pantagruelion dies in truth and root, but it propagates from seed from the male, while the female produces useless flowers. Deriding the custom of bringing plants to France from afar he proclaims:

Arabians, Indians, Sabaeans,
Sing not in Hymns and Iö Paeans;
Your Incense, Myrrh, or Ebony:
Come, here, a nobler Plant to see;
And carry home, at any rate,
Some Seed [*grène*], that you may propagate.
If in your Soil it takes, to Heaven
A thousand thousand Thanks be given;
And say with France, it goodly goes
Where the Pantagruelion grows.   (bk. 3, ch. 52)

In Catholic and Protestant lands, as botanists work on transplanting seeds from one soil to another, so moral theorists work to transplant seeds of wisdom from one text to another. Yet increasingly the revival of ancient Stoic texts builds human confidence in the seeds within all human beings, seeds that may be nourished by natural and human means for the development of human wisdom. A key message of the neo-Stoic revival is that in seeking to cultivate the most important seeds one does not need to explore faraway lands. The one seed that is native to all lands is the seed of virtue.

NEO-STOIC STRATEGIES OF DU VAIR AND LIPSIUS: SEPARATE FIELDS FOR ETHICS AND CHRISTIANITY OR ONE COMMON FIELD?

In approaching neo-Stoicism we shall begin with two thinkers upon whom there is a scholarly consensus that they are neo-Stoics: Guillaume du Vair (1556–1621) and Justus Lipsius (1507–1606). Our understanding of their approaches to ancient Stoic authors will help us see the problems in defining neo-Stoicism and in labeling writers as "neo-Stoic." Scholarly agreement on the Stoic influence on Du Vair and Lipsius contrast with scholarly debate on the more controversial Bodin, Montaigne, and Charron.

Historians have labeled "neo-Stoic" a movement emanating from France and the Low Countries in the late sixteenth century, although more and more scholars are confirming an eclecticism in the absorption of ancient philosophy by Christian authors. The prefix *neo-* may refer to a synthesis of Christianity with ancient philosophy, as in Ficino's *Theologia platonica*, a neo-Platonic synthesis that boosts the confidence of Pico della Mirandola, Costanza da Varano, and Sadoleto that humans may will to rise toward God and yet utilize pagan philosophy in the process. Theological or religious synthesis is not characteristic of the neo-Stoic movement; instead, the focus is on applying Stoic teachings for the benefit of the ethical and communal conduct of persons who do not agree on theology. *Neo-Stoicism* refers to an explicit revival of Stoic philosophical texts; except in the case of Lipsius, the synthesis combines Stoic ethics—not Stoic religion—with Christianity. As *Stoic* derives largely from titles and authors' praise of ancient Stoic belief or practice, there is much unlabeled Stoicism in medieval and Renaissance thought.[54] As we have seen, Stoic texts are influential throughout the Christian centuries; the belief in seeds of virtue, sparks of divinity, and reason contributes to the Christian confidence in human nature of Erasmus, and of Saint Ambrose, Saint Thomas Aquinas, and Pope Pius II before him.

The debate on the dignity or depravity of humankind takes on a distinctly Stoic, rather than biblical, framework in the late sixteenth century. To a generation for whom every passage in the Bible becomes a subject for violent contention, new editions of the texts of ancient Stoics are printed for the potential soothing effect they may have on souls impassioned by religious conflict.[55] Nevertheless, the issues of God's gifts by Creation versus God's grace in this life, free will versus predestination, and the path to justification remain issues upon which persons are burned amid civic and religious turmoil. By writing about morality in Christianized Stoic prose rather than in Christian theological disputation, a humanist might communicate not only to Jesuits and other Catholics but also to Calvinists, Lutherans, Anglicans, and other Protestants, and Jews and Muslims might benefit as well. The use of eclectic Hellenistic and Roman philosophy, especially Stoic texts such as those of Epictetus, who is heavily influenced by Platonizing, salvages the argument for human dignity in a time of wrenching discord in public life.

My focus is the French Renaissance, as I am interested especially in the vogue of Stoic texts among Du Vair, Jean Bodin, Michel de Montaigne, and Pierre Charron. There are fascinating reciprocal influences among these authors during the last decades of the sixteenth century. As the 1560s bring war in France between Catholics and Calvinists, and Christians are killed in the name of Christianity, moderates seek a foundation for moral behavior that might restore peace. Practical Stoic advice contributes to the cultural milieu of the *politiques*, moderates who have faith that a common human source for virtue would facilitate peace among warring factions of Catholics and Calvinists. Ultimately, the Edict of Nantes in 1598 provides an opportunity for a temporary working out of such a civic peace in early-seventeenth-century France.

Exemplary in France of the fashionable trend of neo-Stoicism is *La philosophie morale de Stoïques* (The moral philosophy of the Stoics), which Du Vair publishes in 1585, a year after his French translation of Epictetus's *Manual*. A self-conscious neo-Stoic movement emerges. The title *La philosophie morale des Stoïques*, appearing to limit Stoicism to ethics, sets the trend followed by Montaigne and Charron. In 1594 Du Vair, influenced by Justus Lipsius's *De constantia* (On constancy) of 1584, publishes his own *De la constance et consolation es calamitez publiques*, which comments upon his strivings for moderation in his own life and for a politics of reconciliation amid the struggles of the French Religious Wars.

Du Vair applies the full Stoic cluster of natural law within human nature: right reason, seeds, sparks, and principles of law. "The happiness and goodness of humanity depend on the application of right reason, that is, on applying the will to do what is right and honorable."[56] Du Vair combines the Stoic images of seeds and sparks, applying the concept of nature sowing sparks that can enflame with enlightenment: "Good, in truth, is not so placed that all the world may see and perceive it; nature has sowed and scattered here below only certain weak and feeble sparklings of it, which, notwithstanding, being rightly applied to our mind, are able to kindle a pure light in them and enable us to know the good as it is."[57] Making vivid the parallel between the natural world, where vegetative life grows, and the soul, where virtue may grow, he points out that plants do not grow where gold is mined and that no virtue grows where souls are dominated by lust for gold: "For she [Nature] has made that in those parts where it [gold] grows nothing prospers, neither herbs, nor plants, nor anything else that is of any value, as it were informing us that in the spirits of those men in whom the desire of this metal will rule there will live no sparkle of honor or virtue."[58]

Du Vair, however, does talk about vices, even about the seeds of vice that begin to grow early in a child's life. Referring to the ancient Stoics scorned by ancient Epicureans, Du Vair asks, "Should not they reverence and honor sobriety as the very foundation of all other virtues, and such a one as stifles all other vices in the cradle, and chokes them in the seed?"[59] The focus on infancy as a time when education for virtue must begin echoes Erasmus and Quintilian. The Stoic cluster adds up to obedience to "divine and inviolate law, promulgated from the beginning of the world, by which, if we wish to acquire what is good, it is necessary that we rule ourselves."[60]

Du Vair directly influences Charron, for example, in this optimistic passage, which Charron repeats almost verbatim: "She [Nature] is such a wise mistress that she has disposed all things toward the best state that they can be and has given to them the first movement toward the good and the end to which they must strive, so that whoever will follow her without doubt will obtain it."[61] Nature is sufficient for reaching one's end, and all who persevere are able to follow nature. Yet, as a Christian, Du Vair stops short after expounding "the principal laws" of the Stoics to introduce a prayer in the mode of an ancient song. He does not invoke Christian grace, but he asks that we appreciate our divine gifts at birth and prepare our souls so that they will be ready to obey God. In the final sentences he asks for something that Stoicism cannot give: "the light of your divine truth," which clears reason to follow "the true and everlasting good."[62]

Du Vair's neo-Stoic works have a reciprocal relationship with Montaigne's *Essais* and not only reflect but also influence the spread of Stoic thought patterns, especially in France and England.[63] Du Vair's writings are characterized by the ambiguity typical of the neo-Stoic attempts to combine Christianity with Stoicism: important passages suggesting Stoic self-sufficiency to fulfill the natural goal of human virtue are framed or at least followed by others focusing on the human need for grace to attain higher goals. Such religious passages occur typically toward the end, as a "last word," as in the prayer above. An obvious precedent is Michel de Montaigne's close of his longest essay, "Apologie de Raimond Sebond" (Apology for Raymond Sebond). Available to Du Vair is Montaigne's 1580 or 1582 *Essais*, which applies the commonplace image of God's hand (common in Calvin as well), which cannot be confused with ancient divine immanence.[64] In 1580 Montaigne writes, "He will rise, if God by exception lends him his hand; he will rise by abandoning and renouncing his own means, and letting himself be raised and uplifted by divine grace, but not otherwise."[65] After 1588, after reading Du Vair among others, Montaigne adds, "It is for our Christian faith, not for his Stoical virtue, to aspire to that divine and miraculous metamorphosis."[66]

Needless to say, Montaigne's appeal to divine grace has aroused a storm of controversy. In such an essay, which maximizes its use of human reason to dispute human reason, are the closing words merely lip service? Or does the closing indicate the earnest Christian life in which ancient philosophy is allowed to play a role? Or might Montaigne be reflecting awe before the complexity of the human condition and the world order itself?[67] We have seen Italian humanists struggle with the same issues—visually evident in the Florentine Christian frame of the Venetian frontispiece to *Fior da Virtù* (fig. 5.1). The image of God's hand reaching out to lift humanity clearly distinguishes Montaigne from Ficino, who uses the more ambiguous light imagery for the divine kindling of the sparks already making their upward ascent. Light may be natural or divine. If divine, light may refer to explicitly Christian and Augustinian illumination of the Trinity or may suggest any variety of pagan sun god or philosophical enlightenment.[68] Du Vair's use of light in his prayer appears to have some neo-Platonic origins (the focus on cleansing of ignorance) and is a generic divine light. Light imagery helps Du Vair's ecumenical mode of writing, which accepts as authentically religious ancient pagans as well as Christians of diverse denominations who pray to a personal God.

An obvious Christian conclusion precedent to both Du Vair and Montaigne is *De immortalite animae* (On the immortality of the soul) (1516), in which Pietro Pomponazzi states his Stoicizing view that "those who claim the soul is mortal seem better to save the grounds of virtue than those who claim it to be immortal. For the hope of reward and the fear of punishment seem to suggest a certain servility, which is contrary to the grounds of virtue, etc."[69] At the close he turns from natural reason to revelation, which allows him to proclaim with certainty, "Since therefore such famous men disagree with each other, I think that this can be made certain only through God," and then he cites the New Testament and Thomas Aquinas for the soul's immortality (377–78). Pomponazzi's theological ending occurs after a statement of Stoicizing ethical self-sufficiency that is precedent to Du Vair's *La philosophie morale* and after disputational evidence of the incapacities of human reason for truth that is precedent to Montaigne's "Apologie de Raimond Sebond."

Montaigne does not write a theological book, but both Du Vair and Pierre Charron do. Du Vair's *La saincte philosophie* (The holy philosophy), written before 1585, is explicitly dedicated to adapting to Christianity the best of ancient philosophical tradition. Du Vair discusses "our ruin" and the "light of wisdom" sent "to prepare souls of those who ought to participate in his grace and contemplate the splendor of his glory."[70] Influenced by Augustine and Ficino, Du Vair describes the sage radiating in a mirror reflection of the divine light, with reason guided by truth (6–7). He also dwells on the confession of sins and faults that lead us to "cultivate the faith that he has sowed in us" (11). "The seed is our will, which according to whether she comes to germinate to good or bad, produces good or bad actions."[71] The "fruit" of germinating good is a "divine and immortal life." His prayers in this work indicate much greater humility than do those in *La philosophie morale*.[72] With its emphasis on the role of conscience in examining one's failings, humility before the divine source of faith, and a focus on the one command—to love God with all one's heart and to love one's neighbor as oneself—Du Vair's nonsectarian style, although he is a Catholic, illustrates the influence of such works as Calvin's on the French-reading public.[73]

Du Vair is confident that God has provided right reason to guide the will to do what is good. In *De la constance et consolation* Du Vair proclaims that a person, as well as a state, is best when ruled by the one law "the light of nature."[74] Like those medieval authors who do not share Aquinas's precise distinctions, Du Vair refers to both natural law and revealed law and interprets obedience to right reason as being in part natural and in part supernatural. Grace is needed to help humans pursue what is beyond natural law, that is, the divine precepts directing us to the ultimate and supernatural end.[75] Later Charron is to write both a treatise on Christianity and a separate treatise on human wisdom suggesting that morality is the educational base upon which religion is added.

Du Vair's Stoicism is a support for his own *politique* position; he takes an active role in the politics of his day and writes many practical political statements.[76] One of his earliest involvements is serving in the Parlement of Paris in 1586. One example will suffice: on the Day of the Barricades protesters mount wooden barricades in the streets of Paris to protect the Guises, and Du Vair writes a plea to the king and to the people for moderation. In his oration "Après les barricades . . ." he talks of a tree growing in ancient Athens under which citizens took shelter during rain; during fair weather they frivolously decorated their hats with its leaves.[77] He extrapolates that the carelessness with which the French treat the tree of their state has left France no protection in time of bad weather (564–65). He returns to the image at the close of his oration as the only hope of unity: "The king being our trunk, the princes its branches, the people its leaves, the tree glorifies itself in its branches, and the branches and the leaves take their vigor and greenness from their trunk."[78]

The tree of state ia a popular image in the late Renaissance. Guillaume de la Perrière (1503–53), author of the first French emblem book and chronicler of his city of Toulouse, uses tree diagrams throughout his *Le miroir politique* (1555) as aids for following the intricacy of his presentation of the civic virtues.[79] He begins by employing the traditional dichotomy between a tree of vice and a tree of virtue to portray Aristotle's dichotomy between the three bad forms of government and the three good forms. In figure 7.6 one can see in the tree of good government excellent government of the best people, very good government of monarchy, and the less worthy government of the wealthy.[80] A detailed engraving in Charles de Figon's *Discours des estats et offices* (1579) indicates the titles of French officials and counsels on the roots, trunk, and branches of a highly bureaucratic tree of French government.[81] Francis Bacon (1561–1626) makes ample use of vegetative language in his *Essays*; he refers to the Roman Empire as the "Roman plant" growing in other soils and sprouting constitutions, and he favors a liberal naturalization process in order that the trunk of the "tree of monarchy be great enough to bear the branches and the boughs."[82]

The neo-Stoic of greatest cosmopolitan stature as a systematic synthesizer is Justus Lipsius (1547–1606), whose *De constantia* (1584) expresses Stoic philosophy as a way of moderation at a time of religious war in his Flemish homeland. Lipsius presents us with our first opportunity to see a full revival of the Stoic terms *reason*, *sparks*, *seeds*, and *common notions* in original Greek and Latin texts, understood in their relationship to Stoic natural philosophy. *Manuductio ad stoicam philosophiam* and *Physiologia stoicorum*, a Stoic philosophy in which the ethical and physical theory interrelate, appear in 1604, the same year Lipsius publishes the collected works of Seneca. Du Vair's mode of separating spheres of life contrasts with Justus Lipsius's mode of synthesizing. Lipsius's hermeneutics for Christianizing Stoicism is effective and subtle: "No one should place the End or happiness in Nature, as the Stoics do; unless by the interpretation which I gave, namely in God."[83] This formula not only allows Lipsius to turn the seeking of virtue into the seeking of God but also restores the ancient Stoic equivalency of God and nature—Romanized and Christianized to be God's immanence or participation in nature.

The English translator of Lipsius's *De constantia*, Sir John Stradling, reassures the reader by providing a Christian frame for the work of Lipsius:

Hee acknowledgeth the only direct path-way to salvation to be comprised in those sacred bookes: but that good letters withal, and the writings are both an ease and help for us to attain unto the understanding of them, and do further us in the way of vertue and godliness, howsoever som new Domitians maintaine the contrary, seeking to abolish all good arts & knowledge in humanity. That he writeth so highly in commendation of RIGHT REASON, although som

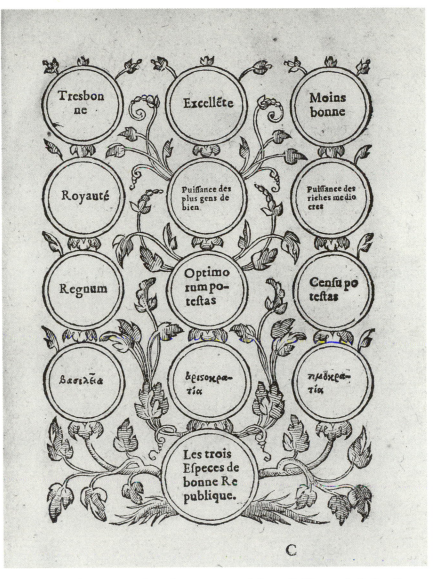

7.6. "The three types of good government," from Guillaume de la Perrière, *Le miroir politique*, 1555, which illustrates civic virtue and vice through a forest of trees. The book opens with this arboreal rendition of Aristotle's three types of good government.

times with the words of the Auncients: yet he accompteth no reason pure or right except it be directed by God & illuminated by faith.[84]

The decade of the 1590s is particularly important for neo-Stoic influences arriving in England from the Continent. Lipsius's *Two Books of Constancy* is published in English in 1594, and Du Vair's *Moral Philosophy of the Stoicks* appears in English in 1598.[85] Lipsius does not dwell on trees of vice, certainly not of the kind that tormented Marguerite de Navarre, but rather visualizes learning as a tree, as in various educational traditions from Raymond Lull (1236–1315) to Petrus Ramus (1515–73), who views discovery and judgment as "roots" of the divinely "implanted" reason.[86] In Lipsius's *Manuductio* Stoicism is a tree that may grow within us: the roots imply living in accordance with nature, the trunk suggests understanding the good, and the branches point to the axioms common to the ancient philosophical schools.[87]

Stoicism in Justus Lipsius appears to his reading public as a constancy in the midst of religious turmoil and political pressure. Educated at Louvain and living through the Dutch wars against Spain, Lipsius publicly turns to Lutheranism while at the University of Jena (1572–75) and to Calvinism while at the University of Leiden (1579–91).[88] Then as he prepares to return to the Louvain he returns to Catholicism. Three years later his *De constantia* appears.[89]

Lipsius begins by telling of his desire to travel to avoid "the troubles in the Low Lands, of the insolence of the governors and the soldiers" (1; 98). He tells of a man who asked Socrates why travel did him no good. "Because," Socrates said, "you did not leave yourself behind" (2; 101). The book then trains the readers to control themselves through reason. The full Stoic cluster of reason, sparks, seeds, and God within provides a "spring of wholesome counsel and sound judgment."

> For this good part in man may sometimes be pressed down, but never extinguished; and these fiery sparks may be cooled, but never wholly put out. These little coals shine always and show themselves forth, lightening our darkness, purging our uncleanness, directing our doubtfulness, and guiding us at the last to constancy and virtue. As the marigold and other flowers are by nature always inclined toward the sun, so has reason a respect to God and to the fountain whence it sprang. . . . To obey it is to bear rule; and to be its subject is to have sovereignty in all human affairs. God, by this image of himself, comes to us—indeed, what is more, even into us. (5; 107)

Lipsius's Christianized Stoic phraseology is full of vivid natural metaphors, emphasizing the flowering of the seeds and the enflaming of the sparks under the divine light. An overall Christian framework continues to dominate. He calms those bewailing the suffering of their native country in civil war not by the Stoic argument that one is a citizen of the world but by the Christian argument that one's home is heaven and the order of events that one laments occurs under the aegis of divine providence. His concern about the issue of free will focuses on the Stoic conception of fate; he argues that Stoics never make God subject to fate, but "God to God, so to speak" (18; 136). And the following "commendation" is part and parcel of the late Renaissance vogue for reading "the Stoics," ancient and contemporary, including Calvin's commentary on Seneca's *De Clementia*: "I give this commendation to the Stoics in good earnest: that no sect of philosophers avowed more the majesty and providence of god, nor drew men nearer to heavenly and eternal things than they" (18; 137).

Lipsius is farther from Augustine and closer to Aquinas (and to Stoics and Aristotle, for that matter) in stressing secondary causation:

> Yes, but it [Stoic destiny] is the first and principal cause, which is so far from excluding middle and secondary causes that (ordinarily, and for the most part) it does not work except by them; and your will is among the number of these secondary causes. Do not think that God constrains it, or wholly takes it away. . . . For God, who created all things, uses these wills without corrupting them. . . . He would that corn and trees grow: and so they do, without any force being exerted upon their nature. He would that men use deliberation and choice: and so they do, without force, of their free will. (20; 141–42)

One senses in Lipsius the natural harmony between humans and vegetative growth. Lipsius views even poisonous growth as a natural development: "The earth, with one universal and same juice nourishes all trees and fruits, some of which grow to be profitable and some poisonous." Responsibility lies not in the earth but in "the nature of those trees that convert such good nutriment into poison." He argues that "it comes of God that you are moved; but it is of and in yourself that you are moved to evil" (20; 143). The crux of Lipsius's teachings places upon humans the responsibility to form their own nature in according with Nature and God.

In 1604 Lipsius reattaches Stoic ethical theory to its origins in the Greek Stoic pantheistic, materialistic theory of the cosmos.[90] It may be no coincidence that in his attempt to be distant as a historian presenting the doctrines in their original context and involved as a Christian intellectual in adapting the Stoic texts to contemporary use, he publishes in the same year the complete works of Seneca, who had Platonized Stoicism. Recognizing that the Stoics view God as the divine fire and as the *Logos spermatikos*, Lipsius stands back as a Christian, quoting church fathers, and upholds the distinction between eternal God and God's creation. He stresses that the ancient Stoics, in Lactantius's words, "comprehended under the one name Nature the most diverse things, God and the World, the Artificer and the Work done . . . as if Nature were God, intermingled with the World."[91] As a historian of thought, Lipsius is able to present the Stoic ideas in their ancient framework and as a Christian making use of ancient thought, he is able to reject the ancient Greek Stoic pantheism and apply Augustine's neo-Platonic explanation that just as the wise man is called "wise" solely on account of his mind, so the world is called "God" solely on account of the presence of the mind of the Divine.[92]

Lipsius expands upon the metaphor of God as the gardener of the cosmos to aid the reinterpretation. Citing Hermes Trismegistus, he understands *logos spermatikos* as the adaptable and malleable creative reason by which God governs the universe: "Do you see the farmer, having sown the earth with seed, on one occasion with corn, on another with barley, and on another with something else? . . . Such a person is God, who produces immortality in the heavens, change on the earth, and motion and life in the universe."[93] In terms of the creation of humans, Lipsius with historical and Christian distance recognizes that the Stoics, like the Manichaeans and followers of Marcion, view the soul as derived from the substance of God—*Logos spermatikos* and Fire. While admitting that to Stoics God is fire, Lipsius gives evidence of Hebrews and Christians speaking of God in images of fire and light—God's appearance to Moses in the burning bush and to the Hebrews as "a column of fire" and Jesus called the "Lucidum verbum," the word of Light.[94] For Christian use Lipsius reinterprets the texts so that he can maintain that God is artisan of humans and that semen is "'that which is capable of generating offspring like the parent,' i.e. God" and that for each child born God has inserted a soul separate from the matter.[95]

Lipsius understands the origins of the Stoic ethical images of sparks of divinity and seeds of virtue in Stoic physics. He follows Cicero in upholding that "the general view is that the soul, or mind of man, is the dwelling-place of the Spirit or Vital Breath. This Spirit is linked by the Stoics to the Fiery Breath of the world; being animate, it contains warmth."[96] Lipsius also understands that the reason in humanity is an offshoot of the reason in the Divinity and that for Seneca reason in man grows like a seed, sprouting, plant, and tree. Lipsius cites Seneca's closing epistle, which states that goodness does not yet exist in a newborn nor even in a student but only in the height of maturity of a rational wise human being.[97]

Among those educated in humanist curricula there is considerable awareness of the ancient Stoic confidence in the powers of education to develop the seeds of reason and virtue divinely implanted in the human mind. Reading the ancient texts in Renaissance Greek and Latin editions, as well as in new vernacular translations, presents an alternative perspective that may have influenced behavior and private thoughts more than public writing.[98] Whereas the historical controversies have focused on the extent to which there is historical evidence for libertinism—free licentious behavior based on free thought—in the sixteenth and seventeenth centuries, the issue before us is the less sensational one of the extent to which a striving for rational development and virtuous behavior based on classical thought is in abundance in the sixteenth century. Calvin recognizes the subtle distinction between Aristotle's praise of virtue for its use and the Stoic praise of "virtue for its own rewards."[99] Calvin regularly expresses scorn for Pelagius of Augustine's day as if there are Pelagians among his acquaintances—apparently those who view salvation as derived from a maximum of human effort and a minimum of divine grace.[100]

Anyone who could read could find arguments in ancient texts for virtue for its own sake and for human perfectibility by human means alone,[101] but this is not a new phenomenon in the Renaissance. In twelfth-century Paris the bishop condemns a professor of the arts faculty of the university for taking his teaching of Aristotle out of the appropriate Christian framework: Boethius of Dacia in *De summo bono* proposes that "There is no more excellent state than to devote oneself to philosophy" and "Therefore, it is easier for the philosopher to be virtuous than for another. So it is that the philosopher lives as man was born to live, and according to the natural order."[102] In the sixteenth century one need not have the training of a professor of philosophy to take on this line of reasoning, for texts are available, literacy is increasing, and private reading and thinking is on the upsurge, especially in urban or Protestant areas.[103]

Let us for a moment try to relive the experience of privately reading afresh what Seneca says about how to achieve the highest good in his concluding epistle, which we have seen Lipsius cite. Even in the nonmaterialist, nonpantheistic Senecan form the Stoic worldview goes well beyond Erasmus, Du Vair, and Lipsius in stressing the human capacity to reach perfection through education.[104] Seneca argues that goodness can not be in the delicate frame of the human infant, any more "than in a seed. . . . Just as Nature in general does not produce her Good until she is brought to perfection, even so man's Good does not exist in man until both reason and man are perfected. And what is this Good? I shall tell you: it is a free mind, an upright mind, subjecting other things to itself and itself to nothing" (*Epistulae* 124.10–12).[105]

In Seneca there is neither praise for Hebrew obedience to divine command nor praise for Christian faith and openness to receive divine grace. The divine command in Genesis not to eat of the tree of knowledge of good and evil is from another worldview: some Gnostics teach that a God who would forbid learning must be the Devil in disguise![106] In Seneca both humans and God have reasoning power—in God it is "Nature that perfects the good; of the other—to wit man—pains and study do so."[107] Extrapolating from Seneca's comments, one might realize that trees can reach a greater physical erectness—in both height and girth—and a longer duration for bearing fruit and a longer life span, but humans can study the natural order, perceive its laws, and seek to attain happiness not in their time of physical prime but in old age through "long and concentrated study."[108]

We have become familiar with the intellectual atmosphere in France and the Low Countries in the sixteenth century: the Erasmian trilingual curriculum influences Catholics, including the French evangelical circle, and Calvin and the growing Huguenot community; in lands torn by wars over religious issues, people concerned for ethical conduct seek out commonplace books, emblem books, neo-Stoic treatises, as well as ancient Stoic texts. In the next three chapters we explore in depth philosophically educated French humanists who make significant reformulations of the Stoic theory of seeds of virtue and knowledge. In confronting the civil wars in

180 • *C H A P T E R 7* •

France between Huguenots and Catholics and in considering the Skeptical doubts about the mind's resources, Jean Bodin, Michel de Montaigne, and Pierre Charron apply the now eclectically supported Stoic belief system in "seeds of virtue and knowledge" for the purpose of restoring the individual and civic moral order.

CHAPTER EIGHT

Bodin: "All the Ancient Hebrews and Academics Have Held"

JEAN BODIN (1529/30–1596) is a French thinker who contributes to historiography, jurisprudence, comparative religion, demonology, natural theology, political philosophy, and economics. In the Renaissance and Reformation discussions of depravity and dignity Bodin is one of the strongest advocates of human dignity and of the freedom of the will (both God's will and human will).[1] As J. B. Bury states, "Bodin asserts the principle of the permanent and undiminishing capacities of nature" with the implication that "his own age was fully equal, and in some respects superior, to the age of classical antiquity, in respect of sciences and arts."[2] A clue to Bodin's viewpoint is his application of the phrase *seeds of virtue and knowledge* to the epistemology throughout his works;[3] as we shall see, in none of Bodin's usages of the phrase does he modify it by mention of original sin. Agreeing with the Stoics that sages are few, Bodin exhibits a high assessment of human potential, such as, for example, in his citation of the Stoicizing and Platonizing allegorical commentaries on Genesis of Philo of Alexandria (before the codification of rabbinical law) and of *De libero arbitrio* (Augustine's book on free will before his debate with Pelagius and before his refinement of the doctrine of original sin). Bodin wonders how it could be that a God who provided all of nature with its sources for growth and development would not provide the human soul with the seeds for its flowering.

Jean Bodin's life and religion have been a matter of controversy,[4] partly because his name is a common one in the historical records.[5] There is general agreement among historians that Bodin was born in Angers and studied in a Carmelite house in Paris in the mid-1540s. Like Erasmus, Lèfevre d'Étaples, and Calvin, Bodin sought proficiency in the trilingual humanist curriculum of Latin, Greek, and Hebrew texts. Some contemporaries reported that Bodin's mother was a Jewish refugee from Spain, and seventeenth-century readers of the *Colloquium* often thought Bodin's religious views were those of the Jewish speaker Salomon. Nevertheless, documents published in 1933 indicate that his family's background was Catholic,[6] and Bodin took an oath to Catholicism in 1562, joined the Catholic League briefly the same year as Charron, 1589, and received a Catholic burial in 1596. As early as the 1580s Bodin's books received criticism for unorthodoxy, and several of his books appeared on the *Index librorum prohibitorum*.[7]

SEEDS OF VIRTUE, KNOWLEDGE, AND RELIGION

Bodin's view that God has provided human nature with the potentiality for virtue, truth, and piety is the inner functional epistemology upon which his human, natural, and divine types of history attain unity. As he declares in the *Methodus*:

> In accordance with these divisions arise history's three accepted manifestations—it is probable, necessary, and holy—and the same number of virtues are associated with it, that is to say, prudence, knowledge and religion. The first distinguishes good from evil, the second true from false, the third piety from impiety. The first, from the guidance of reason and the experience of practical affairs, they call the "arbiter of human life." The second, from inquiry into abstruse causes, they call the "revealer of all things." The last, due to love of the one God toward us, is known as the "destroyer of vice." From these three virtues combined grows true wisdom, the highest and final good of man and those who participate in that good in this life are called blessed.[8]

Bodin believes that God has distributed appropriate seeds for these three realms. In the *Epitome, Methodus, République,* and *Paradoxon,* where Bodin examines reason and experience in human life, his trust in the seed of virtue as the source for prudence or *honnesté* is evident.[9] In the *Theatrum*, we shall see Bodin's confidence that the God-given seeds of knowledge will enable humans to distinguish truth from falsity in natural philosophy; yet Bodin also hopes that the seed of knowledge will make comparative study of law, history, and government into a science (*Distributio, Methodus, République*). From his first publicly delivered and published oration to his secret manuscript copied for private reading, Bodin expresses his confidence that despite human disagreements on specific doctrines or rituals, the seeds of religion may be cultivated to create piety and civic harmony.

Bodin follows the copybook method of collecting great sayings from antiquity, as evidenced by his publication in 1588 of the *Sapientiae moralis epitome,* containing 210 Latin maxims with French translations that are often transforming interpretations.[10] The purported author is Bodin's twelve-year-old son, Elie; a letter from Bodin of 1586 explains how children in his household learn through recitation of moral sentences as well as of sentences on natural philosophy.[11] These simple maxims reveal some of the essential building blocks of Bodin's worldview. The first maxims, on the education of infants, teach how nurture builds upon nature. "Virtutum natura animis sua semina iecit" [Nature has placed its seed of virtues in the soul] is translated into French as "Nature en nostre ame a ietté, la semence d'honnesté et d'honnesteté" (13). That saying reveals Bodin's originally Stoic and abundantly eclectic premise that the seed of virtues stems from nature and is in the human soul and his sharing in the sixteenth-century

French usage of *honnesté* as an equivalent for virtue, especially prudence. His translation of "Autor naturae sit deus" [Granted that the author of nature is God] as "le rayon de dieu" (14) shows that Bodin emphasizes God's role as creator and views the ray from God not as special illumination but as the gift at Creation. Nevertheless, the human cultivation of nature requires artisanship and doctoring (11, 12, 14).

The comment that among many people only the shadow of truth remains is followed directly by the statement that good changing into evil corresponds to Satan letting loose an angel (18, 19). While in another collection the sentence might be taken figuratively, Satan's minions are credited with distorting human minds in the *Démonomanie*, *Theatrum*, and *Colloquium*. In a multitude of verses of the *Epitome* encouraging modest and self-controlled virtue, one learns that it is better to have a healthy conscience ("recta conscientia" and "la conscience saine") than a vainglorious reputation. Although he attributes good deeds to a source within human nature, Bodin is not averse to alluding to angelic influence: "Praestat virtus gloriae" [Virtue is preferable to glory] appears in French as "La vertu belle comme un ange, passe devant toute louange" [Beautiful virtue like an angel exceeds all praise] (78).

There is ample elaboration of vegetative imagery. "Pace vigent leges, & florent pace coloni" translates as "On void en paix les champs florir, Et les sujetz leurs fruicts cueillir" [In peacetime one sees the fields flourish and the subjects gather their fruits] (107). Adding the figurative image of flowering to the Latin original, Bodin's French sentence states "To command and obey well causes the entire community to flourish [*fleurir*]" (123), and another claims, "The flower of the moral virtues is great courage without fear" (143).[12] The concluding Lucretian poem sums up the mysterious potential impact of this small florilegium: "As the bees savor all the flowers of the green groves: thus a marvel, we flourish from the golden words of all the sages" (210).[13]

The first words of Bodin's dedication of the *Methodus* state that "In this *Method* I planned to deal with the way in which one should cull flowers from history to gather thereof the sweetest fruits."[14] After telling of his plan to gather the general principles of jurisprudence from the many historical states, he explains the condition of the commentaries on Roman law before humanists improved legal scholarship: "Youth were called from the fairest flowers and gardens of eloquence and philosophy to those thickets and rocky crags," and what they found was "this discipline half closed by brambles and thorns."[15] Likewise, he refers to "the neglected forests of commentaries."[16] In discussing the restoration of legal studies, he regrets the loss of King Francis I: "Although he dispersed seed in the field of letters, those who ought to have gathered the flourishing harvest and hanging fruits of the sciences preferred to let them decay."[17] Here, as well as in the *Oratio*, Bodin expands upon the vegetative images of cultural growth developed among Italian humanists and spread by such Frenchmen as

Jean Trithème and Pierre Belon. Like Guillaume Budé, Louis Le Roy, and Jacques Amyot, Bodin repeats the refrain of crediting King Francis I with the reflowering of letters.[18]

In his 1559 address to the senate and people of Toulouse on education, Jean Bodin, a teacher at the Faculty of Law, discusses "the works of our generation, their discoveries and inventions and expresses appreciation to God for renewed knowledge of letters" (9b24).[19] He often talks of culture flourishing under King Francis I (10a), and he expresses concern that religious controversies are directing attention away from the peaceful arts. Trying to arouse moral and economic support for the college, Bodin praises what the city has so far accomplished (11). He asks his audience to draw the implications from the analogy between horticulture and culture. Just as a field left fallow sometimes sprouts up (11a5–6), Toulouse, which was once barbaric, became a center for legal studies. He asks for continued support for the college so that the light of knowledge ("scientarum lucem") will not be covered by ignorance (11a18–20).

Later in the *Oratio* Bodin follows Quintilian and Erasmus, but more harshly, on the deleterious impact women have on infants and children.[20] He expresses concern that by the time a tutor arrives in a household the child's "right reason is [already] obscured and with it all the natural light" (22a19). The example of Cyrus educated under Xenophon shows how natural appetite submits to reason under strict discipline, "which is the main point of all justice and of a natural law" (23b14–16). Bodin speaks eloquently for public education of all children, rich and poor, in the belief that all societies, laws, religions, and cultures teach that communities need to live happily in reciprocal relationships. Encouraging common Catholic education, he exclaims: "For in each of our souls some seeds of piety and religion have been placed by God, so deeply rooted that one would not be able to pluck them out without destroying in the same blow honor, faith, integrity and this justice without which God himself would not be able to rule well."[21] Although his practical pressing concern is for a uniformity of civic culture that might prevent religious warfare, this passage makes clear that Bodin's moral system, encompassing the individual, the family, the community, and the divine order, relies on a presupposition of divinely implanted seeds in the human soul.

In Bodin's dedicatory letter to his *Iuris universi distributio* (Order of universal law), of 1580, he cites "the Stoics" for the idea that justice accords with nature and claims that "the seeds of law and justice planted by the immortal God in the souls of each of us await being awoken by reason."[22] He attributes his ability to delineate the field of jurisprudence to the development of his reason, especially through experience and knowledge. While applying the Ciceronian vocabulary, he is groping to prove jurisprudence a science that might distinguish the true from the false. The bulk of this short treatise focuses on the *ius gentium*, the law of peoples, which he views in both its written and unwritten forms as positive law produced by a sovereign legislator.

Commenting on the *Digest*, he defines law in a Ciceronian mode as "a light of goodness and divine prudence distributed to humans for the utility of human society."[23] In comparison to the distinctions in Roman law between *ius civile*, *ius gentium*, and *ius naturale*, Bodin, like his contemporary François Connan, views the civil law as a regional expression of the law of peoples and makes his important distinction between this combined human law, which he calls *ius humanum*, and natural law, which he calls *ius naturale*.[24] His citation of Paul is significant here, for Bodin disregards the medieval commentators, who view *ius gentium* as a remedial law of nature, a remedy for original sin; instead, Bodin returns to Rom. 1.14–15, which attributes lawful or virtuous behavior of Gentiles to the law "written in their hearts," to which their "conscience bears witness."[25] Likewise, he cites Aristotle's *Nicomachean Ethics* 5 and Plato's *Laws* 2 for the distinction between justice according to law, *nomos*, and justice according to nature, *physis*.[26]

It is helpful to examine these references to the two major Hellenic philosophers,[27] for Bodin cites Plato other times for evidence that the human mind may grasp true principles, and Aristotle's argument that virtue is a mean between extremes is the starting point for Bodin's ethical treatise *Paradoxon*. Although Aristotle does not link *physis* (nature) with *nomos* (law), as the Stoics do, he does distinguish between natural justice and justice by convention. According to book 5 of Aristotle's ethics, "Of political justice part is natural, part legal—natural, that which everywhere has the same force and does not exist by people's thinking this or that" (5.10.1134b18–20). He makes clear that a justice governing persons needs to take into account different constitutions and multiple factors. A sentence declares that legal justice is different from true justice (1136b34–1137a1). Equity allows a judge to handle a specific case for which the law speaks universally: "What creates the problem is that the equitable is just, but not the legally just but a correction of legal justice" (1137b10). According to Plato's *Laws* 2, the best laws would derive from sages, who exceed all others in virtue and knowledge (659a), whereas in many states the laws habituate people to licence (656c). Plato recognizes the linguistic problem of popular usage: justice and virtue accord with the sages' standards; what people who seek only pleasure call "good" would be recognized as evil, and only that leading to virtue would be called "good" (661d). Likewise, in book 4 Plato explains that "we deny that laws are true laws unless they are enacted in the interest of the commonweal" (715b). Pointing out a universal common agreement, Bodin's citations thus synthesize Aristotle, Plato, Paul, Cicero, and the Roman law tradition to establish that human law does not always conform to justice or natural law. This distinction helps Bodin to be jurist, historian, and ethicist.

Bodin's viewpoint parallels that of the opening of Gratian's *Decretum*, which distinguishes between natural law, "which is contained in Scripture and Gospel," and customary law; however, unlike Gratian, Bodin does not mention canon law as an elaboration of natural law. In his *République* Bodin takes an antipapalist position, rejecting the subordination of a monarch to a pope and making the monarch personally responsible to the "law of God and of nature."[28] Bodin claims that natural law is in each of us from the origin of the species ("primordio sui generis insitum") and teaches religion, piety, reward, and punishment.[29] Likewise, his definition of human law reflects in its telic purpose the Ciceronian influence of his general definition of law above: human law is established to conform to nature and for social utility.[30]

Bodin's comparative global historical perspective puts a distance between him and Justinian's justifiers of Roman law: he does not claim in the *Distributio* that social laws do in effect achieve the Ciceronian goal. In differing from the Justinian Code by the sharpness of his distinction between natural law and law of peoples, Bodin views even the most universal of laws as a human product, capable of defying natural law.[31] For example, in the *République*, book 1, chapter 5, Bodin argues against Aristotle's view that slavery accords with nature. To Bodin, as for ancient Stoics, slavery is unnatural and inhumane.[32] The numerous abuses of human societies, such as cannibalism and human sacrifice, show "that one must not measure the law of nature by human behavior, however inveterate, nor conclude for that reason that the servitude of slaves is in accord with natural law or, even less, that there is charity in preserving captives for the purpose of taking gain and profit as from beasts."[33] Bodin's examples of cannibalism and human sacrifice are the very ones that are at issue in proving a people "barbaric" and thus worthy of slavery according to Aristotelian argument in Juan Ginés de Sepúlveda.[34]

Whereas the relationship of master to slave is one in which Bodin can distinguish natural law from customs of long and universal duration, in the relationship of husband to wife he mixes divine and natural law with such customs. Fundamental to his defense of inherited monarchy as the best form of government is the biblical model of patriarchy in the family. Nevertheless, by viewing the relationship of head of the family to wife, children, and slaves as political, governed by a variety of regional laws, Bodin reveals that the micropolitics of the family is a domain subject to legal change.[35] In accordance with his view that the patriarchal family is the natural and divinely instituted model for government, he views the French Salic law, which in 1464 prevents any woman from assuming the royal crown, as a "natural law." He goes farther than others in claiming that it originated among the Salian Franks.[36] His fundamental grounding for patriarchy is the divine law of Genesis 2, which Bodin interprets as God commanding the first husband to rule over the first wife.

Genesis is fundamental to Bodin's thought. He reads the text literally as a command for legal marital patriarchy, and he reads it morally as the rule of the soul over the body and reason over desire.[37] We shall see that the latter, Hellenistic philosophical interpretation of Genesis, which originated in Philo, is particularly important for Bodin's proof of the authority of seeds of virtue and knowledge, as well as for his system of analogies among hierarchies in the universe.[38]

In the *Methodus*, Bodin indicates many ways in which humans change from divinely created human nature. History is a realm of the probable and of human arbitration, for humans often do not conform their wills to God-given nature, namely, right reason: "Human actions are always involved in new errors, unless they are directed by the guidance of nature, that is right reason."[39] Significantly, he refrains from mentioning the doctrine of original sin as an explanation.[40]

In chapter 5, "On the Exact Judgment with Regard to Historians," he considers how *disciplina* (training) changes human nature. His examples of *disciplina* come from education, laws, customs, and government and imply the whole range of social training, socialization, or acculturation. In *Distributio*, *Methodus*, and *République* Bodin gives much attention to social mores and custom, by which people transform human life. Distinguishing between the divine law, which is right, and the human varieties of law, which may be right or wrong, he affirms that either divine or human influence may transform human nature. His analogy is to plant domestication:

> Now if Hippocrates truly thought all species of plants may be domesticated, how much more is this true for the human species? Was there even a nation of people so monstrous and barbaric, which having obtained leaders, was not led to the humanities? Or what people imbued with the most polished arts, but neglecting cultivation of the humanities, did not degenerate into barbarism and savagery? There are infinite examples of this.[41]

The difference between replanting a plant and replanting a human is that plants rapidly make adaptations to a different soil, whereas humans adapt and change their nature much more slowly.[42]

Bodin gives numerous examples of peoples who had a flourishing civilization that then declined. The prime example is the ancient Romans: "but there is not natural goodness so unbounded that it may not be corrupted by perverse training."[43] Bodin suggests that religious institutions and customs can contribute to the corruption of human nature:

> But if the influence of custom and training is so great in natural and human affairs that gradually they develop into mores and take on the force of nature, how much more true is this in divine matters? We see that the power and influence of religions is such as to change profoundly the mores of men and the corrupt nature, although it can hardly happen that the traces of our earlier dispositions can be altogether obliterated.[44]

Bodin's wording is very subtle and effective. A reader might find a hint there of the Christian explanation of human corruption, but in fact Bodin mixes custom in his discussion of the corruption of human nature, "mores humanum & corruptam naturam," and refers by "naturae prioris vestigia," associated with the myth of the golden age, to values of true human nature. The careful, even humorous wording disguises the radical impact, derived from Plato's *Laws* 2, that echoes in Montaigne and Charron:[45] even though the divine is always true, human corruption can stem from "religious" customs and training, which resemble natural and human customs except that they have additional authority in their alleged sanctity.

PHILO'S GARDEN OF THE SOUL IN THE BOOK OF NATURE

Both the *Methodus* and the *République* indicate Bodin's plans to explore natural philosophy. The *Methodus* declares that admiration of the splendor of the created universe leads to religious awe for God, the original source of the eternal laws of nature ("naturae leges aeternas").[46] Likewise, the *République* claims that it is important for the welfare of a state that some men not only study the causes of the rise and fall of states but also turn to the contemplation of the beauty and hierarchy of natural order.[47] The last book Bodin publishes is in fact a comprehensive encyclopedia of natural philosophy, first composed as a commonplace book[48]: the *Universae naturae theatrum* (The theater of universal nature).[49] A French translation appears posthumously.[50]

The metaphorical use of the phrase *theater of nature* in both the Latin and the French title connotes the importance of human observation of the beauty of divinely created nature. For Bodin's study of created nature as a path to the highest level of contemplation of God there are many precedents in Christian, Jewish, and Muslim medieval philosophy and mysticism.[51] The engraved title page frames an expansive scene of ocean surmounted by a miraculous rainbow symbolic of God's promise to Noah not to destroy humanity again; above the frame the four Hebrew letters radiate with light. The audience is expected to experience religious awe in beholding the magnificence of the divinely created theater, to appreciate both the underlying principles that sustain the world and the special divine acts (earthquakes or outstanding harvests) that exhibit God's continuing justice. Similarly, when Bodin sets the stage for the dialogues of the *Colloquium* on religion, he describes a learned and virtuous household environment wherein there is a physical model of the *theatrum mundi*. A wooden pantotheca in Coronaeus's house contains likenesses of the stars, planets, comets, stones, metals, fossils, plants, and living forms; by its classification scheme the model helps Coronaeus remember each natural item as well as things he hears and reads.[52]

The *Theatrum* contains five books, on the principles of nature, the minerals, the plants and animals, the soul, and the heavenly bodies. It appears to be designed for both erudite and popular audiences: while the margins contain numerous book references, the text is a dialogue between Theorus, an adult student who asks troubling questions, and Mystagogue, a mystical natural philosopher who generally claims to know the answers. They expound on everything from the abundant plenitude of plants and animals to the God-given human capacity to contemplate the divine order in nature. In an overall tone of appreciation for the divine blessings of life in this world, Bodin's work proclaims human dignity, in contrast to Pierre Boaistuau's frequently republished *Le théâtre du monde* (1558), which laments the misery of the human condition amid diseases and disasters.[53] Our focus will be on book 4, titled "On souls," which makes this book not only a natural philosophy but a natural theology.[54]

Book 4 especially challenges Bodin to support his view that truth is singular, consistent in all disciplines. Upholding the position of the Catholic Church in rejecting the doctrine of the double truth (suspected in Boethius of Dacia and Pomponazzi), Bodin in his *Theatrum* states, "What is true must be the same for physicists, theologians, dialecticians, and medical doctors, and there cannot be more than one truth."[55] His example is that human, angel, and demonic souls must have a *natura corporea*, "corporeal nature," so that God's punishment in hell of those who do evil will involve real suffering. His path to consistency is to uphold the immortality of the individual human soul while rejecting the long Christian tradition upholding the incorporeality of the soul. Whereas medieval Christian theologians often discuss the soul as "spiritual matter," which is created, noncorporeal, nonperceptible to the senses, the belief in the corporeality of the soul, which we have seen in Greek Stoicism, is condemned by the early church after Tertullian, under the influence of the Stoic Soranus, advocates the corporeality of the soul.[56] Possibly Bodin's position on corporeality has some compatibility with the position of medical practitioners, as in his statement above mentioning physicists and medical doctors and as evidenced by the translation of his work by Fougerolles, a medical doctor in Lyon. The corporeality of the soul is important to Bodin, author of *Démonomanie*, for it explains how demons can copulate with witches.[57] There are other implications of Bodin's sharp distinction between the immaterial Creator and the material Creation: in the *Colloquium* the natural philosopher Toralba declares that the divine mind, which is immaterial, cannot mingle with a human mind, which is corporeal: "Christ will be nothing other than a man."[58]

In book 4 of the *Theatrum*, in the ninth section, "On intellection and on the intellect, truth, the sciences, and cognition," Bodin raises the issue of the path to knowledge by having Theorus inquire of Mystagogue about his thoughts on the Aristotelian dictum "Nihil esse in mente, quod non prius fuerit in sensu" [Nothing is in the mind that is not first in the senses] and the corresponding notion that the mind is a tabula rasa.[59] This epistemological discussion has origins in the Stoic debates with other schools that we have seen recorded in Aëtius and Diogenes Laertius.[60] The issue is topical in late-sixteenth-century France: Henri Estienne's publication of Sextus Empiricus in Latin in 1562 and in a complete edition of 1569 increases scholarly attention to the deceptions of the senses.[61] The issue of the path to knowledge comes under notorious discussion in relationship to natural theology in Michel de Montaigne's "Apologie de Raimond Sebond," in *Essais* 2.12 (1580), following his earlier French translation of Sebond's *Theologia naturalis* (1568, reprinted in 1581).[62] In 1581 Bodin confronts the Pyrrhonian evidence of natural sources for faulty sense knowledge: in his 1581 preface to *Démonomanie* he suggests instead that there is evidence of demonic distortion of the senses.[63] Books 4 and 5 of the *Theatrum* likewise testify that the human soul is the battleground between the temptations of demons and the encouragement of angels.

Nevertheless, in considering the Aristotelian dictum, both Bodin's student and teacher give examples of the senses' helping one to achieve understanding. Very significantly, in a passage that is to influence Pierre Charron's departure from Montaigne's "Apologie," the teacher uses light and seed images to proclaim that the understanding has its own resources. There is a light within that has an affinity with the natural world of light; thus, in accord with Empedocles' principle "that similar things are known by their similars," man can recognize colors. Then Mystagogue proposes that God provided a seedbed in the human soul by which the soul comes to know the virtues and the sciences. As we have already noted, Bodin uses the Stoic epistemological concept seed—"semina virtutum" in his *Epitome* and "semina pietatis ac religionis" in his *Oratio.* Yet, here in the *Theatrum* the Stoic seed appears in the full context of garden imagery to indicate the extent of possible development of the human soul. The image of the developed soul, fully blossoming as a garden, is particularly evocative:

> Likewise we recognize that the seeds of all the virtues and sciences have been Divinely sown in our souls from their origins, in order to permit humans to live delightfully, as in the middle of a garden odoriferous with flowers and trees, and most abundant with all sorts of fruits.[64]

Thus he explains that a little cultivation of the mind will make it grow in abundance, and he cites for support Empedocles from Aristotle's *De anima* 1, Plato's *Meno*, Philo Hebraeus's *Legum allegoriae* 1, Andelandus's *De anima*, and the Academics. He opposes that string of authorities to Aristotle's view "that there are not any inborn notions of the sciences and virtues in our souls."[65] It might be noted here that Bodin's natural philosophy does not require the concept of seeds to explain origins; citing Aristotle, Theophrastus, Pliny, and Virgil, Bodin thinks some plants grow by spontaneous generation.[66] As Bodin's *hortus animae* passage above from the *Theatrum* does argue for its sources, we shall evaluate the evidence for each one of his so-called authorities.

Unlike Erasmus, who defends seeds of knowledge to Luther by citing "Church Fathers," Jean Bodin cites by name Greek philosophers, a Hellenistic Hebrew, and an Arab philosopher. His argument from authority stresses common consent from authorities from multiple traditions.[67] Pierre Charron (1541–1603), a Catholic priest, author of *Les trois veritez contre tous athées, idolatres, juifs, mahumetans, heretiques, & schismatiques* (1593), is to be influenced by Bodin's proof by authority, and he simplifies Bodin's list into the words "all the sages have said" in his *De la sagesse* (1601 and 1604).[68] We shall examine each of the authorities Bodin cites, for they influence several of his supporting arguments. Particularly interesting is the swift condensation of the allegorical interpretation of Adam and of Paradise. That allegory was originally made by Philo Hebraeus, and although Bodin might have cited church fathers such as Ambrose, who borrow the allegory from Philo, it is significant for Bodin's fresh reading of the allegory that Bodin cites Philo directly.

Philo's texts are translated into Latin for printed editions of 1552 in Paris, 1554 in Basel, and 1555 in Lyon and appear for the first time in French in Paris in 1575. The French edition opens with the allegory on Genesis.[69] The interest in Philo is accentuated by the translation of Leone Ebreo's *Dialoghi d'amore* into French by both Pontus de Tyard and Denys Sauvage in 1551.[70] A passage in Leone particularly apropos describes Adam in the garden of Paradise, amid "beautiful and aromatic trees . . . as in the mind full of wisdom," experiencing the perfect intellectual life and the felicity of eternal knowledge, that is, the distinction of true and the false.[71] Perhaps there are echoes of that condensation in Bodin, especially in the *Paradoxe*, where his argument by authority simplifies to "all the Hebrews and Academics have held for an assured thing, that we have souls inseminated by a divine seed of all virtues, that we can lead very close to the very happy life."[72]

That Philo and Leone appear to a Christian audience with *Hebrew* in their name is a good indicator that they are thought of together. In addition, Leone's work is a dialogue between a Hebrew Platonist Philo and his beloved Sophia, in which there is plentiful influence of the author Philo. That is one of several tutorial dialogues that are background to Bodin's mode in the *Theatrum*; Bodin shares Leone's major focus on love of the Creator. Nevertheless, Bodin relies on Philo directly as far back as in his *Methodus* of 1566.[73]

It should be mentioned here that Philo does not influence the Talmudic rabbis and only indirectly influences the rabbinical Jewish tradition before the sixteenth century. Leone also is outside the rabbinical mainstream as a neo-Platonic Jewish philosopher. Nevertheless, Philo's writings provide one example of first-century creative Jewish responses to Hellenistic culture, and Leone (Jehudah Abrabanel in Hebrew) is a good example of the creative synthesis of several streams of Italian Renaissance culture in the circle of Marsilio Ficino.[74]

Bodin shares in historical beliefs, found especially among neo-Platonists, that the oldest ideas are the wisest and that the streams of ancient diverse thought intersected in ancient times. Of course forgeries and false datings of the antiquity of some texts contribute confusion. From Philo and Leone, Bodin confirms that the Greeks borrowed their wisdom from the more ancient Hebrews, in particular that Plato's myths disclose in fable the secret wisdom of the Hebrew Bible and the Hebrew oral tradition.[75] Bodin's fascination with Hebrew as God's language, which he inserts in his books, is reflected in his interest in Hebrew names for God; his citation of Kabbalist Paul Ricius indicates likely viewing of the *sefirot* tree in the title page of Ricius's Latin translation *Portae lucis* (1516) (fig. 3.2).[76] His decision to have seven speakers in the *Colloquium* may well reflect the seven-branched candelabra, especially the versions of Postel in which the divine names of the *sefirot* appear.[77] In considering the correspondence between Greek and Hebrew planetary lore, a correspondence important for both the *Colloquium* and the *Theatrum*, Bodin states in the *Methodus* that "the Greeks took this idea, as they did all good things, from the Hebrews."[78] There Bodin quotes Hebrew terms for virtues in an attempt to show that the Latin names of the gods are derivatives from the Hebrew, the divinely given original language of humankind. Ironically, those insights occur in *Methodus*, chapter 5, under the title "The Correct Evaluation of Histories."

In his marginal references to what I shall call his garden-of-the-soul passage in the *Theatrum*, Bodin specifies that the reference is to "Philo Hebraeus, Allegories on the Paradise of Adam, Book 1" and that "it concerns the soul sown by virtues and sciences."[79] Philo's *Legum allegoriae* supplements his literal reading of Genesis. Philo provides an inspirational allegory that suggests moral lessons for humanity borrowed from Hellenistic philosophy. By incorporating the Philonic text into an epistemological dialogue within a book on natural philosophy Bodin obviously transforms the meaning and implications; nevertheless, he reads Philo with a sensitivity to the text. In Bodin's condensation Philo's presentation of the first human molded from the earth becomes a literal description of all created human souls. Philo's text is moving away from the Jewish scriptural tradition of viewing human nature as a psychosomatic whole, from which the hope for resurrection derives,[80] and Bodin is moving away from the Christian tradition of viewing the soul as incorporeal and distinct from the body: the two meet. Differing from Christian tradition by emphasizing the corporeality of the soul, Bodin reads Philo accurately as talking in *Legum allegoriae* 1 about *anthropos* molded from the earth, whose soul is breathed in, rather than archetypal *anthropos* in the image of God. Bodin transforms Philo's insights into proof that God, in animating each human being, provides the human mind with seeds of the virtues and sciences.

Philo in *Legum allegoriae* analyzes the description of God's creation of heaven and earth in Gen. 2.4–5: "In the day in which God made the heaven and the earth and every green thing of the field before it appeared upon the earth and all grass of the field before it sprang up." He suggests that this is symbolic language in which *heaven* stands for the mind and *earth* stands for sense perception; *every green thing of the field* stands for the intellectually perceptible, growing from the human mind, and *the grass of the field* (*grass* referring to the food of unreasoning creatures) refers to the sensibly perceptible, growth from the unreasoning part of soul.[81] There is an archetype of the intellectually perceptible and an archetype of the sensibly perceptive before objects come into being and before the intellect and the sense perceptions are present intellectually and sensibly to perceive.

Philo distinguishes the archetypal human (*anthropos*, from *adam*, meaning "human nature" in Hebrew) from the human molded from the earth (*anthropos*), but his insistence on the importance of its being the latter, bodily *anthropos* who receives the breath of life encourages readers to apply to humans as we know them Philo's comments on the human soul. Philo clarifies the moral application. "He created no soul barren of virtue, even if the exercise of it be to some impossible" (1.13, line 34). The inbreathing of the soul is important for Bodin and stems from other books of Philo as well. Philo interprets "God . . . breathed into his nostrils the breath of life" (Gen. 2.7) as a "divine spark," as a "besouling," as an "effulgence of the blessed, thrice blessed nature of the Godhead."[82] It is significant that Philo explains that his discussion of Adam applies to the descendants: "Every man, in respect of his mind, is allied to the divine Reason, having come into being as a copy or fragment or ray of that blessed nature, but in the structure of his body he is allied with the world."[83]

As Philo reads Gen. 2.8, "And God planted a pleasaunce in Eden toward the sun-rising, and placed there the man whom He had formed," he views God as planting virtue in the human soul, which will rise just as right reason rises. Ambiguous at this point on whether Eden is in the soul or around the soul, Philo interprets God as placing humans as gardeners amid virtues, which they are to cultivate. Bodin applies that latter interpretation in his garden-of-the-soul passage, viewing the human soul as in a garden. Philo goes on: "And God caused to spring out of the ground every tree fair to behold and good for food, and the tree of life in the midst of the garden, and the tree of knowledge of good and evil (Gen. ii. 9). Moses now indicates what trees of virtue God plants in the soul." Philo interprets these virtues in a Stoic sense as common duties, in accord with Cicero's *De officiis* 1.3.8 and 3.3.14. His inclusive interpretation includes theoretical arts and sciences, such as geometry and astronomy, and practical and mechanical arts, such as carpentry. To attain virtue, not only logic, ethics, and physics but also conduct are needed;[84] Bodin accurately draws from Philo the idea that the plants of Eden stand for the arts and sciences.

The ambiguity whether the tree of good and evil is inside or outside the garden highlights for Philo the human choice between being spiritually in the garden, that is, virtuous, or out of the garden, that is, evil. To Philo, "the tree of life is virtue in the most comprehensive sense," and he views it as in the garden (1.18.59). A human being is in the garden and becomes the tree of life when the ruling part of the intellect holds to its stamp of perfect virtue; when a human thinks of evil, the human is likened to the tree of good and evil outside the garden. Even a person in a desolate place who thinks and lives virtuously is in the garden (1.18). Philo explains that God's command to eat of all trees but the tree of good and evil goes to the Adam molded from the ground, for the archetypal human is virtuous instinctively, without instruction (1.30.92). This helps to corroborate Bodin's Stoic dictum, already present in the *Epitome*, that the seeds of virtue and knowledge need to be cultivated.

A book illumination from a seventeenth-century botanical encyclopedia may help us to see the choice between visualizing the soul-in-a-garden and visualizing the garden-of-the-soul. Like Bodin's title page of *Theatrum*, John Parkinson's title page for *Paradisi in Sole: Paradisus Terrestris* (fig. 8.1) shows the Tetragrammaton radiating above. The scene in Parkinson is one of luxurious and abundant vegetative growth. Parkinson's letter to the reader suggests symbolical biblical readings, for he draws analogies between a gardener and God as Planter and between the blossoming and decline of flowers, humans, and states. The tree of good and evil stands in the center of the design, and Parkinson's text indicates his belief that from Adam to Noah and from Noah onward humans have the capacity to comprehend natural truths.[85] Just as the title suggests a *double entente*, a pun on Parkinson's name—"Park in sun"—as well as an earthly paradise, the illustration suggests a double vision. The design corresponds to the ambiguity we have seen in Philo's text. Catching sight of Adam and Eve in the large expanse of nature, one might view human souls as immersed in a macrocosmic, splendiferous garden. Or one may view the egg-shaped oculus as a magnifying glass presenting a vision of the microcosmic garden-of-the-soul: from a Philonic interpretation one sees upright reason (Adam holding firm to a tree) and sense perception (crouching Eve in flux) immersed in the vegetatively abundant garden-of-the-soul. My phrase *garden of the soul* is intended to allow for the interplay between both interpretations.

Bodin's main alteration of Philo's text is to transform the imagery of trees in our souls to seeds in our souls and to choose Philo's option of viewing the human soul as being in a garden of trees. Thus Bodin further Stoicizes Philo's Stoicizing commentary on Genesis. Drawing from Philo's allegorical interpretation of Paradise, and specifically from his statement that "Moses now indicates what trees of virtue God plants in the soul," Bodin proclaims that "the seeds of all the virtues and sciences have been divinely sown in our souls from their origins, in order to permit humans to

8.1. A title page in John Parkinson's *Paradisi in Sole*, 1629. Seventeenth-century illustrators played with optical illusion. Through the oculus, do you see the soul-in-a-garden or the garden-of-the-soul?

live delightfully, as in the middle of a garden odoriferous with flowers and trees, and most abundant with all sorts of fruits."[86]

Clarification of Philo's commentary in the *Questions and Answers on Genesis* further elucidates Bodin's general philosophy.[87] Paradise is symbolically "wisdom or knowledge of the divine and human and of their causes. . . . His ideas the Creator planted like trees in the most sovereign thing, the rational soul. But as for the tree of life . . . it is the knowledge, not only of things on the earth but of the eldest and highest cause of all things. For if anyone is able to obtain a clear impression of this, he will be fortunate and blessed and truly immortal" (1.6). This corresponds to Bodin's indication in his *République* and *Methodus* that the culminating path to wisdom is knowledge of nature. As a source for Bodin's stress on the seed of piety in *Oratio* and *Colloquium*, consider Philo's general emphasis on piety: "But worthy and excellent men say that the tree of life is the best of the virtues in man, namely piety, through which pre-eminently the mind becomes immortal" (1.10, p. 7). The other tree Bodin refers to as "the tree of knowing the science of good and evil," clarifying, as Philo does, the broader definition of the disciplines of knowledge (1.11, Greek in 7n). Bodin may also have been influenced by any number of illustrations of trees of knowledge or of virtue and vice (see above, chs. 3 and 7).

Bodin's other references in his garden-of-the-soul passage help elucidate the synthetic way in which he builds his epistemology. The reference to Empedocles is to book 1 of Aristotle's *De anima* and thus uses Aristotle's text itself against the Aristotelian dictum; Bodin cites Empedocles, rather than Aristotle, for Empedocles is one of the authorities Bodin cites in support of his argument that the soul is material. Aristotle, of course, opposes Empedocles' position that the soul's composition from physical elements allows it to perceive external physical objects. Aristotle's discussion reveals the similarity of Empedocles' position that "by earth we see Earth, by Water Water . . . Love by Love, and Strife by bitter Strife" to Plato's *Timaeus*, wherein "from these first beginnings [from the resemblance of like to like] grow the things which we perceive."[88]

François de Fougerolles, the translator of the posthumous French edition of the *Theatrum*, there translates *Adelandus* as "Andelandus," which may indicate that he is as unknown then as now. Bodin may have received this reference from Pico della Mirandola's *Conclusiones*, which, according to Ann Blair, "include one 'Adelandus the Arab' who reportedly held that 'the soul has itself the *species* of things and is only excited by external things.'"[89] The obscure source allows Bodin to cite Arabic authority, so important in the field of commentary on Aristotle, while avoiding the Christian controversy surrounding the better-known Averroes and Avicenna.[90] Bodin also departs from the focus of Renaissance Aristotelian psychology, which defines *species* as the image of the object on the sense organ, metaphorically as a seal on soft wax.[91] The position of Andelandus, as cited by Pico della Mirandola, is similar to that of the concluding speaker in Ficino's *De amore*. The soul, in addition to abstracting universals from sense knowledge, can compare particulars with *species*, inborn universals, as in the contrast between lusting after a particular human being through sense perceptions and contemplating the beauty of the human species as a whole: "There immediately appears in the intellect another species of the image, which no longer seems to be a likeness of one particular human body . . . but a common reason or definition of the whole human race equally. . . . so from the intellect's universal species or reason, which is very remote from the body."[92] This example, or one like it, is background to Bodin's next example in the *Theatrum*, which distinguishes the very capacity to comprehend "the human" in the intellect from the abstraction of "human" from observation of individual humans. In rejection of the Aristotelian dictum, Mystagogue gives empirical evidence that even beasts can make universals from a singular; for example, animals can spot the dangerous species man and flee from danger. He cites Cicero, Plutarch, and Galen for evidence that animals have some reason (exactly Sextus Empiricus's and Montaigne's main technique for lowering human self-estimation) in order to argue that humans must have even greater human reason.[93]

Generally scholars translate Bodin's *academicos* (which Fougerolles translates as "Académiciens") as "academicians"; more specifically, the term well known among humanists from Cicero's *Academica* implies Plato's Academy, a nine-hundred-year-old institution, and Platonic philosophers to Bodin's day.[94] In Bodin's citation of authorities to support that the garden of the soul might be cultivated he answers the skepticism of the New Academy by citing the founder Plato's crucial book on whether virtue can be taught or comes by nature—the *Meno*. During the dialogue by which Socrates draws truth out of Meno, a young male slave is brought as a test of how anyone may discover within the mind the fundamental principles of geometry. This dialogue is useful, for it gives only the preliminary suggestion of the doctrine of reminiscence, by which the mind has notions previous to birth, while exemplifying how a tutorial dialogue may bring forth principles from the mind. Particularly useful for Bodin is that Plato extrapolates from the example that "you see, he can do the same as this with all geometry and every branch of knowledge."[95] Mathematics to Bodin implies both a number mysticism of microcosm-macrocosm correspondences and an organizing principle by which a field of study approaches a science where true and false may be distinguished.[96] His works seek the kinds of principles that *Meno* finds. The ultimate truth, the comprehension of the Divine, appears most simply and clearly to the human mind as the geometrical figure of the holy Tetragrammaton, the unutterable four consonant name YHWH; through the four-sided figure opposition and discord are resolved in one harmony.[97]

After showing that humans have reason to a greater extent than do animals, Mystagogue rhetorically asks whether the creator of nature has equipped humans even better than animals through the "seeds of the sciences and virtues"? Fougerolles, marking his French translation with an asterisk, adds that light in the human mind aids in understanding; for this addition, Fougerolles cites the Vulgate Latin of Psalm 4.6: "Signasti super nos lumen vultus tui" [The light of thy countenance is impressed upon us].[98] Thomas Aquinas, nominalists, and Erasmus utilize that passage as a reference to the natural light given by the Divine. Like other light images, it allows a reader's Augustinian, neo-Platonic, or Lutheran interpretation as illumination, although advocates of that position in the early seventeenth century would be more likely to reject the Vulgate historical account for the prayer, "Lord, lift thou up the light of thy countenance upon us."[99]

Still Theorus is not satisfied, but insists on the Aristotelian dictum. Furthermore, he questions whether it is true that if the seed of all the sciences and virtues were in humanity, then all humans would understand all the sciences (477; Fougerolles, 4.9.689). He cites Aristotle's *Historia animalium* for the observation that some humans do not differ from brutes. The mystical teacher responds by citing Psalm 8, which declares that infants chant God's praise, an example that shows that prayer to God is natural and that not only are some humans like animals but others are like angels.

The teacher returns to the seed and light imagery to draw out an analogy from the student: the soil of the earth would not yield plants if there were not seeds hidden within, and ashes would not light up if there were not sparks hidden within (478; 4.9.690). Even though one may not see the seeds hidden in the ground, nature is inseminated: "by the succession of time it will bear plants, according that nature has inseminated it: I leave to you to make the same judgment on the understanding of humans."[100] What might the student learn about the human understanding from that analogy? Obviously, that the human understanding would not yield growth and light if it were not provided by God, who provided nature so well. Citing arguments of Augustine, *De Trinitate*, book 9, and John Duns Scotus, Bodin proclaims that "all force and power of the senses depends so on the soul."[101] Thus, in the context of the dialogue, Mystagogue's stand on the special wisdom of the sages allows him to declare that the intellect can understand separately from the senses and to put the student on the defensive by suggesting that without the soul's activity the senses can do nothing. In section 10, entitled "Of sentences of Greeks, Egyptians, Latins, Arabs who have differed rightly on the soul," Bodin goes on to reject the view popular among Arabic Aristotelians that the active intellect, which is immortal, is not distinct for each soul and to declare the immortality of the individual soul (530; 4.10.764). In section 15, "On the active and passive intellect," Bodin suggests the alternative explanation that what has been called the "active intellect" is in fact separate from the person. Commands issue out from either a good angel, or daemon (like Socrates'), or a bad angel, or demon (as in witchcraft), and humans have free choice whether to follow the commands (527–28; 4.15.760–61).

Bodin's description of the soul as a garden, which combines Philo's allegory of Genesis with the originally Stoic epistemology of seeds sprouting as plants and maturing as trees (amplified by Philo and Renaissance neo-Platonists, whom Bodin cites), is important enough to reappear in the last pages of the *Theatrum*. Discussing "On Platonic ideas," he cites Ficino's *Platonic Theology* and Aristotle's *Metaphysics* 1 to sum up his dismissal of the concept of the mind as a blank tablet. He views God as the immaterial locus of the Ideas for the formation of all things. Bodin interprets Genesis 2.5, the very passage important for his garden-of-the-soul epistemology, as " 'God had created every seed of the field before it was in the land,' which cannot be interpreted in any other way than as the archetype and eternal example in the mind of the Creator."[102] Distinguishing precisely between the immaterial eternal deity and the material created human being, Bodin ridicules theorizing about intellectual essences or substances in the human mind; the kind of neo-Platonic theorizing on levels of participation in the Ideas that we have examined in Ficino appears not in Mystagogue but in Theorus's question. Mystagogue says in summary that, "as we have demonstrated above," the mind has "notions of universals collected from singulars," by which are engendered knowledge of principles and sciences.[103]

Bodin's epistemology incorporates not only Stoic seeds but Stoic common notions, so useful in antiquity for mediating between Peripatetic and Academic epistemologies. His citation of the Academy for defense of the Stoic doctrine indicates the influence of Ficino's Stoicizing in the guise of neo-Platonic commentaries on Plato. Posing as an Academic idea, one supported by the *Meno*, seeds of knowledge and common notions transform the Platonic Ideas into a more readily acceptable form. Two other vehicles to Stoic epistemology for Bodin are Cicero and Philo, both of whom absorb Stoic epistemology in the Middle Platonic tradition of Antiochus of Ascalon.[104] One advantage to Bodin of citing the "Academics" and of thinkers he mistakenly considers as Academics is that Stoic seeds of virtue and knowledge enter free from association with the Stoic doctrine of deterministic causation.

A fundamental viewpoint of Bodin is that nature is good. Bodin is able to view the soul as corporeal because he rejects all theories that view matter as evil: "Evil is nothing other than the lack or absence good." By Bodin's view of the gap between the Creator and the physical realm of creation, which includes souls, the subjects he treats in book 4 do belong to natural philosophy. Bodin's view of the goodness of all of nature and of God's creation is founded on a traditional Jewish reading of Genesis, common to Philo, the rabbinical tradition, and Kabbalists. Gen. 1.12, 18, 21, and 24 declare, "And God saw that it was good"; after God's creating humanity and commanding the human dominion over living things, the biblical text culminates with the summation statement "And God saw everything that he had made, and behold, it was very good." Soon after recalling the candelabra of seven lights and the analogous seven planets, Bodin cites in Latin the culminating repetition in Genesis 1.31, "All that God had made was very good," and adds that the Hebrews said it elegantly; "tov me'od" [very good].[105]

ECUMENICAL CONVERSATIONS ON DIVINELY IMPLANTED VIRTUE

In the *Colloquium* we meet the Catholic host, Coronaeus, who conforms to the Council of Trent; a strict Lutheran, Fredericus; a moderate Calvinist, Curtius; a Jew, Salomon; a natural philosopher and advocate of natural theology, Toralba; a congenial doubter and religious universalist, Senamus; and a tolerant convert to Islam, Octavius.[106] Non-Christians outnumber Christians in a discussion that concludes with a criticism of religious persecution and an agreement to nourish their piety in peaceful harmony (Kuntz 471; Noack 358).

In the conversation at the close of the dialogues, Senamus declares the minimum beliefs necessary for religion that are shared by all present: that God is the parent of all gods and creator of nature and that prayer to God from a good heart will please God and lead to knowledge of true religion (465; 354–55). In the criticism of the persecution of the Jews in Spain and Portugal emerges the notion that religious belief cannot be forced but must stem from freedom of the will (469; 357). Senamus in some ways expresses the spirit of the work in declaring, "But I, lest I ever offend, prefer to approve all the religions of all rather than to exclude the one which is perhaps the true religion" (465; 354).

Encouraged by Senamus's seeking a common religion, Toralba and Salomon agree with him that the oldest religion is the best, and they cite the religion of the biblical patriarchs (182–83; 1140–42). Utilizing a Stoic cluster of terms—*reason, light, innate, planted*—Toralba views the law of nature commanding the worship of one God: "Indeed as I view the almost infinite variety of sects, Christians differing with Ismaelites [Muslims] and pagans differing among themselves, no standard of truth seems more certain than right reason, that is, the supreme law of nature, planted in men's minds by immortal God" (337; 257. See also 185; 142). This view meets the approval of the Calvinist and the Catholic. Later Toralba adds, "Indeed reason, which is divine light, innate to the mind of each man, sees, feels, and judges that which is right, that which is wrong, that which is true, that which is false" (359; 259). After a debate about the doctrine of reward and punishment in an afterlife, Senamus suggests tolerance to disagreement, and Toralba concludes, "Is it not better to embrace that most simple and most ancient and at the same time the most true religion of nature, instilled by immortal God in the minds of each man from which there was no division (I am speaking of that religion in which Abel, Enoch, Lot, Seth, Noah, Job, Abraham, Isaac, and Jacob, heroes dearest to God, lived) than for each one to wander around uncertain?" (462; 351–52).

A fuller discussion by Toralba, Senamus, and Salomon of this ancient religion focuses on the Decalogue, that is, the Ten Commandments. Salomon suggests a correspondence between the divine laws and hidden secrets of nature, such as have been uncovered by Philo Hebraeus, Abraham ibn Ezra, King Solomon, and Leone Hebreus, and he cites Ibn Ezra for the Decalogue as natural law (191; 147).[107] Ezra's (1089–1140) biblical commentaries are known to reveal "secrets." Toralba confirms that the two tablets are the law of nature and that all the commands except resting on the sabbath are common to other nations (193; 148). Toralba boldly declares a Pelagian view: "If true religion is contained in the pure worship of eternal God, I believe the law of nature is sufficient for man's salvation" (225; 172).

Against Curtius's citation of Paul, "The law was given by Moses, but grace has been given through Jesus Christ" (410; 311), both the Jew and the Muslim argue for the benefits of obeying divinely granted law (Mosaic law or the Koran, respectively) for attaining a life of virtue and a life worthy of salvation (415, 420; 315, 319). Toralba and Senamus go further into free thinking in suggesting that neither revealed law nor faith in Jesus Christ is necessary. Toralba avows the outstanding virtues of ancient philosophers and denies that they could be eternally suffering (421; 319). Voicing the civic religion of Bodin's *Oratio*, Senamus suggests that those who are most natural and most worthy are religious to the gods, pious to their country, loyal to their parents, charitable to their neighbors, and kind to those in need (422; 320–21). Putting Christians on the defensive, the new Muslim, Octavius, argues that Muslims are superior to Christians in acts of virtue (426; 323–24). Salomon proclaims:

> What lawgiver was ever so cruel that he commanded his people to do something which was impossible? . . . It is so far removed from God's nature for Him to command anything which cannot be done as for Him to blame a man for breaking all the law when he had erred from one commandment, and even a man who has violated all the commands of the law and returned to honor after repentance, attains pardon for all his sins (430; 327).[108]

Salomon on several occasions indicates God's praise for people after Adam such as Noah, Enoch, and Moses (407; 308). However, in answer to Toralba's plea for that natural religion Salomon suggests that common folk and even the educated remain more constant in religion through rites and ceremonies (462–3; 352). As in Philo's *De decalogo*, Salomon views the Mosaic law code as a detailing of the four commandments of worship to God and of the six commandments of duty to other humans (186–87; 143).[109] Toralba finds those special laws unnecessary, and other participants reject some details of Jewish law. If we use Bodin's categories of law in the *Distributio*, Bodin is categorizing the Decalogue as *ius gentium*, the Decalogue excepting the sabbath command as *ius naturale*, and the specific laws as particular *ius civile* of one historical people. Thus, Bodin is suggesting that all humans need for living a good life—the natural law indicating that one should worship God and treat other human beings well—is contained in the divine law, and explicitly in the divinely revealed Decalogue.

In the *Colloquium* the doctrine of original sin receives refutation not only from a Jew, a Muslim, and a doubter but also from a natural philosopher expounding principles declared in the *Theatrum*. When Philo Judaeus comes up for discussion Salomon corrects the church fathers' formative Christianization of Philo, refusing to identify Philo's *logos*, the word, with Jesus (368–69; 279–380). Likewise, Bodin repeats Philo's allegory of Genesis 1–2 to explain Adam's sin as the turning of the intellect (Adam) away from contemplation toward temptations of the senses (Eve) and of pleasures (serpent). This time the allegory is an opportunity to argue that neither sins nor virtues are passed down from parents to children and that "there is no original sin" (392–93; 297). Coronaeus cites the Council of Trent anathema against those who would deny original sin, identifying that view as the Pelagian heresy; Fredericus cites Augustine's support for original sin; and Curtius cites the Jewish and Christian Scriptures. However, in support of Salomon, the Muslim Octavius and the naturalist Toralba argue that the doctrine would credit to the Creator evil in a newborn infant (392–96; 296–300). The natural philosopher cites Christians, Muslims, and Hebrews for concurring that the soul is created clean and pure from God (396–402; 299–305). Toralba's denial of the possibility of original sin passing from generation to generation utilizes principles found in the *Theatrum*: sin originates not in the body but in decisions in the soul; the human soul does not come in the seed but is directly created by God;[110] sin therefore cannot be passed down from parent to child (399–400; 302–3). The *Theatrum*, book 4, chapter 11, cites Augustine's *De libero arbitrio* for the argument that each has freedom of the will, the power within to control passions; one can not only prevent evil deeds but also restrain one's eyes and thoughts.[111] Fredericus cites Augustine to argue that the contagion of the flesh defiles the souls, but as we already know from *Theatrum*, Bodin denies evil in matter.

What follows next from the natural philosophy of Toralba, which is consistent with the principles of the *Theatrum*, is an argument against the possibility of the union of the Divine and the human in Jesus. Toralba views God as "eternal essence, one, pure, simple, and free from all contact of bodies, of infinite goodness, wisdom and power" (325; 248). The gap between Creator and created is too great for a union of the infinite, immaterial Divine and the finite, bodily human (351; 267). Likewise, Salomon borrows the same technique from Bodin's *Methodus* to suggest how religion can corrupt humankind: "All this discussion about the Fall of origin, which I think is no fall, has its beginnings in the leaders of the Christian religion. . . . Hence the seeds of errors began to creep far and wide through men's minds" (404–5; 306). He then refers to God ordering Noah after the flood to be good as commanding only what is possible (430; 327).

The dialogue on evil takes on an arborescent flavor. Lutheran Fredericus argues that "with whatever color the root is imbued, it imbues the trunk, branches, leaves, flowers, and fruits with the same flavor, odor, color, and poison. So it is that the nature of man, overturned from the foundation, seems to have no spark of any good or virtue" (396; 299). Returning to Philo's allegory, Salomon discusses Adam's recovery as mind regaining control over senses. That clue to Philo's allegory reminds us of the passage in the *Theatrum* where Empedocles explains how we perceive color and Philo describes the human soul as a garden containing fruit trees of virtue and knowledge. While Fredericus's argument is evocative of gospelist Matthew's trees of vice influential on Marguerite de Navarre and Martin Luther, it would not be convincing to Mystagogue.

Salomon utilizes Philo's allegory in viewing Adam's (and any human's) turn from the senses toward contemplation of intelligible things (true wisdom) as a perpetuation of the tree of life (405; 306. See also Prov. 3.13–18). Fredericus reinterprets the tree as referring to the cross (405; 306–7), but Salomon proclaims that all humans may repent, that God will help restore their right reason, and that Adam's repentance for eating of the tree of knowledge of good and evil was rewarded by eternal salvation (405–6; 307). Octavius reads a verse in which "the wrong doing of the father does not harm the son" and "the figure of trees displays this secret of hidden wisdom" (406–7; 307–8). Octavius suggests a metaphor of ascent to the Divine that is pleasurable, like a Muslim paradise: through love of God, one "plucks the sweetest fruits of happiness. This is that faith, or rather a unique trust in God, which, having embraced all virtues, nourishes and safeguards them" (422; 320).

For all their tolerance amid diversity of belief, all seven agree that if a storm breaks out on the Mediterranean Sea and a nearby ship carries on board a mummy from an Egyptian tomb, it would be wise to throw the mummy overboard to be rid of the demons.[112] In fact Bodin's natural philosophy consistently differs from Aristotle's in attributing storms, earthquakes, and plagues not to natural causes but to divine punishment (66–67; 51). Thus, Bodin need not burden the laws of natural causation with all the haphazard and troublesome happenings of nature.[113] Demons represent no Manichaean evil force separate from God's providence and creation; rather, they are instruments of God's justice. Likewise, God can intervene to reward individuals or whole societies. Bodin refers to Aristotle and Theophrastus to support his belief that plants and animals sometimes grow without seed, for example, by spontaneous generation,[114] and Curtius proclaims that some fish grew in the sea without seed (67; 51). In the *Response . . . à M. de Malestorict*, Bodin tries to get the French to eat more fish since

God has blessed their seas with such abundance. Bodin's biblical view that the created universe and the work of the sixth day, human beings, are "tov meod" is the fundamental source for his need to explain natural disaster and human wrongdoing as brought about by demons.

Bodin emphasizes free will in achieving virtue, as well as the belief that divine help would be given to anyone who turned to God. In assessing that human beings have full capacity to choose between right and wrong, Bodin, satirizing Aristotle, attributes full free agency to God. "Yet what more impious, more arrogant, finally, more mad than to give free will to himself, but wish to take it from God? The consequence is that God cannot stay the course of the sun, or check the power of the celestial stars, or change anything in universal nature; nor even the impulses and the volitions of man can He impel whither He wishes."[115] One of the reasons why Bodin is reluctant to cite Stoics in the context of free will and virtue is his rejection of their doctrine of determinism. God might have created humankind to pursue virtue always, and he might have created the world in such a way that in no mind or matter could there exist a seed of evil ("semen malorum"), but God chose to grant humans the greater good of free will.[116]

In seeking out the philosophical and theological position of Bodin's writings I am accepting as sincere his claims to present consistent truths in his multiple works. The reading of all his works for their treatment of seeds of virtue and knowledge reveals one philosophical and theological framework with regard to the issues of education for morality and religion, free will and human dignity, the relationship of the human soul to angels and demons, and the supplement of God-given natural law by the God-given Decalogue admired by the common consent of all nations. A short ethical treatise published at the close of Bodin's life brings us full circle to his earlier prescriptions for a child's moral education.

Bodin's *Paradoxon*, written in 1591, is published in 1596, and his French translation (1596) is published in 1598, when the *politique* movement is culminating in King Henry IV's Edict of Nantes, which legally establishes freedom of conscience and public office for Calvinists throughout France and allows public Calvinist religious services in some areas of Catholic France.[117] Like Du Vair, Bodin in his dedicatory letter indicates that he is providing a moral discipline that might serve well in time of civil war.[118] Unlike Du Vair's *La constance* (1594), Bodin's *Paradoxe* does not Christianize his philosophical ethic but presents it in a way that is suitable to individuals of not only different Christian denominations but also different world religions, as would become apparent to readers of the manuscript *Colloquium*. Bodin very succinctly presents a moral system based on ancient moral philosophy.

The dialogue form proceeds in a conversation between father and son. In answer to the question whether the virtues and vices are in our souls, the father responds: "Nature has not planted vices in us: that is why the wise would say that he was well born, and that his soul, being good, will find a body pure and dry: but all the Hebrews and Academics have held for an assured thing, that we have souls inseminated by a Divine seed of all virtues."[119] He continues that all of the Hebrews and Academics have also held

> that we can lead very close to the very happy life if we allow them to take their development: and for the proof, we see that tender minds that have never before learned, suddenly conceive the principles and foundations of all fields: and also the earth is filled naturally with an infinity of plants, metals, minerals, and precious stones, which she produces without seed and without labor, the sea produces the fish, which are sustained by celestial influences: thus it is that the soul, which is inseminated by an infinitude of beautiful sciences and virtues, which, being aroused by the divine influence, produce the sweet fruits that grow to be trees of prudence and of knowledge: but one should not stop at the fruits of prudence, one should go further to the fruits of life, that wisdom. (63)

Here Bodin sums up his view that the natural world, including human nature, is good, basing his claim on the two ancient fountains of wisdom—the Hebrew scriptures and the Platonic Academy. That argument by authority supports the reality of the seeds of virtue and knowledge in the human soul. Further proof is a child stating fundamental principles, as in the geometry lesson in Plato's *Meno*. Bodin declares that the observation of nature shows that the earth and sea can produce without seed as well, demonstrating the Creator's continuing active providence. Readers may differ in interpreting the relative impact of the God-given seeds, the natural sunlight, the celestial astrological influence, or divine aid. Nevertheless, in this garden-in-the-soul passage Bodin emphasizes both God's Creation and God's continuing influence in the growth of the trees of virtue and knowledge in the human mind. Bodin views the ultimate goal to be wisdom, symbolized, as in the Hebraic tradition, as the tree of life; Leone Hebreo and Philo view archetypal *adam* in Paradise, as well as a human being whose reason is in proper order, as comprehending the wisdom of the tree of life. The coalescence of Hebraic, Stoic, and Platonic imagery is apparent.

Montaigne: Seeds of Virtue in
Peasants and Amerindians

HISTORIES of natural-law theory generally ignore the essayist Michel de Montaigne (1533–92), yet in his description of peasants dying on his estate and of the Topinambá tribes of Brazil Montaigne claims that there is a natural law, born within human nature, which is a source of their human virtue. Our focus will be his two essays 3.12, "De la phisionomie" (On physiognomy), and 1.31, "Des cannibales" (Of cannibals), in which the epistemology of seeds of virtue and knowledge plays a pivotal role in proving natural goodness. Montaigne's titles for those essays echo common European prejudices: amusement at the facial features across the ranks of society and horror at the "savage" customs of tribes in the Americas. Tackling prejudices in his day against peasants and against tribes of the Americas, Montaigne applies the Stoic phrases primitivistically to describe peoples whose conduct evokes literary images of the Stoic golden age. In Montaigne's rendition of nobility derived from virtue, from the "seed of universal reason," Montaigne blends Epicurean and other philosophical insights with Stoic philosophy: he levels the steep mountain of the Stoic vision of virtue into a sloping hillside strewn with flowers.

Such use of natural-law theory is rare in Montaigne's *Essais*; one finds instead evidence of the diversity of human laws and the relativity of customs and belief to particular times and places.[1] Like Bodin, Montaigne describes the laws of various peoples, but unlike Bodin, he does not strive for a universalist *ius gentium*. While Montaigne's first published work, of 1569, is a translation of a theologian in the Thomist tradition, Raymond Sebond, Montaigne in his essay "Apologie de Raimond Sebond" (Apology for Raymond Sebond) applies Pyrrhonian evidence of the deception of the senses to question the ability of human reason to abstract natural law from sense data. Montaigne's *Essais* as a whole are at a crossroads in natural law-theory. Montaigne poses a full theoretical rejection of the human capacity to find natural law[2] and some bold insights, which he presents as merely his own individual judgment, against torture and against unnecessary violence to humans or animals. His insights place him at the beginning of the modern field of international law and in keeping with modern conceptions of natural and human rights.[3] The metaphor Montaigne chooses for visualizing judgment is an agricultural one: a sieve (see fig. E.3).

SIFTING FOR TRUTH

It does not surprise me that early readers and friends of Montaigne, such as Pierre Charron and Marie de Gournay, are inspired by some of his brilliant moral insights and that they cull sayings from Montaigne to include in their own works or that others create abridged versions of the *Essais*.[4] Montaigne's insights or seminal ideas are hidden like gems, or more precisely like seeds creative of his copious, adage-style, innovative essay writing. Equivalent to the classical sentences collected in florilegia, they often appear in great books of quotations. Montaigne's first essays themselves are evidence that he works using the copybook approach, carefully accumulating notes on a specific theme. Working in the upper level of the tower of the château de Montaigne, especially in the 1570s he carves his favorite classical sentences on the wooden beams of his ceiling.[5] In his French essays he intersperses Latin and Greek sayings (which are not precisely referenced until Marie de Gournay's later editions). Especially in the essays of book 3, published in 1588 and written after the publication of books 1 and 2 in 1580, in the act of creating concise, rhetorically pleasing French *sententiae* within his own cornucopian essay writing, Montaigne in effect vies as a modern with the ancients in the sixteenth-century educational battle between creativity and mere imitation.

Hugo Friedrich in 1948 concludes his study of Montaigne's *Essais* by emphasizing the "vegetative-like growth that distinguishes the spirit of its author."[6] A likely influence is Montaigne's friend Étienne Pasquier, who expresses the value of the open form of his *Recherches de la France*, which continuously grows from 1560 to his death in 1615: "Here is a miscellany. It is not said that a prairie variegated with an infinite variety of flowers, Nature's disordered products, be not just as pleasing to the eye as the Gardeners' artistically tilled parterres."[7] George Huppert comments that Pasquier's history of France, which extends beyond political and military events into social mores and popular culture, is based on "hunting down out-of-the-way evidence" and that Pasquier's comparison of his work to wildflowers "does not mean their growth is haphazard or casual; the laws of nature are far more rigorous than the rules of gardeners."[8] Another influence on Montaigne's creation of the essay form is the ancient Stoic Seneca; in 1597 Francis Bacon, the first English essayist, comments on Montaigne's resemblance to Seneca: "for Seneca's Epistles to Lucilius . . . are Essais, that is dispersed Meditacions."[9]

Montaigne's own imagery, like Seneca's, abounds in vegetative symbolism. For example, to express the rejuvenation of the mind in old age Montaigne suggests, "Let it grow green, let it flourish meanwhile, if it can, like mistletoe on a dead tree."[10] In a post-1588 description added to his essay on the education of children, Montaigne rejects the Stoic image of virtue

as a steep and rugged mountain and suggests instead that virtue is in a
flowering plain approachable by easy and natural paths up a gradual, flowering hill. One can see the image of virtue he opposes in the 1590 emblem
"Ardua virtutem," or "Virtue with difficulty" (fig. 9.1). On a steep mountain stand the laurel and the palm trees: "If you desire to pluck the laurel
wreath or victory palm, / You must first ascend to virtue with as much
difficulty as climbing a mountain."[11] In contrast, Montaigne declares
about education:

> She has virtue as her goal, which is not, as the schoolmen say, set on the top
> of a steep, rugged, inaccessible mountain. Those who have approached virtue
> maintain, on the contrary, that she is established in a beautiful plain, fertile
> and flowering, from where, to be sure, she sees all things beneath her; but you
> can get there, if you know the way, by shady, grassy, sweetly flowering roads,
> pleasantly, by an easy smooth slope, like that of the celestial vaults.[12]

Such a contrast might reflect Epicurean delight in the higher pleasures in
preference to the Stoic difficult path of virtue, yet Montaigne's phrasing
resembles Sadoleto's in *De pueris recte instituendis* (1533), which invites
the student "to enter the broad and open plains of philosophy, so fruitful
and fertile to all."[13]

Another important aspect of Montaigne's vegetative symbolism is his
use of the metaphor of a sieve, *l'estamine*, to describe the human capacity
for critical judgment. A farmer uses a sifter to shake seeds, letting the
smaller ones fall through. The Bible uses the image of a sieve realistically
and metaphorically for the separation of wheat from weed. Friedrich cites
two important examples of Montaigne's application.[14] In "Of the Education of Children" Montaigne suggests that the child learn to be a sieve for
ideas: "Let the tutor make his charge pass everything through a sieve and
lodge nothing in his head on mere authority and trust: let not Aristotle's
principles be principles to him any more than those of the Stoics or Epicureans. Let this variety of ideas be set before him; he will choose if he can;
if not, he will remain in doubt."[15] In assessing both Stoic and Epicurean
sources for Montaigne's ideas of nature, we shall keep in mind this caution-
ary warning. In the "Apology for Raymond Sebond" Montaigne suggests
limits to the possibilities of the human judgment functioning as a sieve:
"And yet our overweening arrogance would pass the deity through our
sieve."[16] Disputes about what God can or cannot do are beyond the scales
of human judgment.

Through his mental sieve Montaigne judges some behavior to be in accord with nature, for example, the Topinambá Indians' living without institutions that Europeans assume are natural (1.31), French peasants'
burying themselves during mass death from the plague (3.12), or Socrates'
presenting himself to his jury (3.13). As Montaigne very rarely utilizes the
phrases *laws of nature* and *seeds of universal reason* as sources for natural

V.

ARDVA VIR-
TVTEM.

15

Qui laurum & palmam victricem carpere gaudes,
Montis, si nescis, ardua scande prius.

E 3 *Montes*

9.1. "Ardua virtutem" (Virtue with difficulty), from Joachim Camerarius's
Symbolorum et emblematum, Nuremberg, 1590. "If you desire to pluck the laurel
wreath or victory palm, / You must first ascend to virtue with as much
difficulty as climbing a mountain."

virtue, their appearance in the 1588 description of French peasants and his 1580 descriptions of the Topinambá tribe are all the more striking. These two case studies show Montaigne's complex techniques for creating new exempla of virtue that provoke thought and for evoking moral conviction through a sparkling *sententia*.

PEASANT VIRTUE IN GARDEN AND FIELD

To what end do we keep forcing our nature with these efforts of learning? Let us look on the earth at the poor people we see scattered there, heads bowed over their toil, who know neither Aristotle nor Cato, neither example nor precept. From them Nature every day draws deeds of constancy and endurance purer and harder than those that we study with such care in school. How many of them I see all the time who ignore poverty! How many who desire death, or who meet it without alarm and without affliction! This man who is digging up my garden, this morning he buried his father or his son.

See these people: because they are dying in the same month, children, young people, old people, they are no longer stunned, they no longer bewail one another. I saw some who feared to remain behind, as in a horrible solitude; and found them generally to be concerned only about their burial. It pained them to see the bodies scattered amid the fields, at the mercy of the animals that promptly appeared in swarms. . . . Here a man, healthy, was already digging his grave; others lay down in them while still alive. And one of my laborers, with his hands and feet, pulled the earth over him as he was dying. . . . In short, a whole nation was suddenly, by habit alone, placed on a level that concedes nothing in firmness to any studied and premeditated fortitude.[17]

These poignant, value-laden descriptions reflect what Montaigne claims he saw from his library window and while walking on his estate during the plague in Périgord in 1586–87.[18]

"On Physiognomy" has frequently been compared to the 1580 version of Montaigne's essay "That to Philosophize Is to Learn to Die" (1.20). Whereas passages from book 1, chapter 20, written in 1572–74, emphasize the value of reading Stoic philosophers to prepare for death and ridicule those who do not think ahead to death, passages from book 3, chapter 12, written in 1585–88, praise his peasant neighbors for their serenity before sudden death and ridicule readers of Cicero's *Tusculanae disputationes*. This contrast was one basis for Villey's theory that the *Essays* evolved from Stoicism through Skepticism to Epicureanism;[19] and subsequently, critics of Villey's historicist method have emphasized the unity and subtle interplay of the two essays.[20] Montaigne's shifting emphasis may be traced not so much to different readings, but to the temporary suspension of reading as he looks out from his library window and sees the effects of brigandage and plague and to his later identification with the deaths that continue to take place at the château de Montaigne while he and his family are in flight, far from his library and his essay writing.

Overall, however, there are underlying consistencies between Montaigne's contrast of the fearsome imagination of death with the acceptable reality of experiencing death, his contrast of vicariously preparing for death through reading with observing and facing death; and his contrast of the artificial death rituals of the upper classes with the common folk's natural process of dying. The passages on peasant death from the plague represent the culmination of Montaigne's respect for Stoic virtue, learned and attained not from books but from "following nature."

Michel de Montaigne meditates much about death and preparation for death. In book 1, chapter 20, he talks about preparing for death with Stoic strength and stresses that philosophy helps to prepare us not to fear death. He scorns those who do not prepare for it: "The remedy of the common herd is not to think about it. But from what brutish stupidity can come so gross a blindness!"[21] Because they do not think about death, the vulgar cross themselves at even the mention of death, just as they do at the mention of the devil.

The "common herd" or "the vulgar" for Montaigne make up the masses, whom he contrasts with the man of understanding ("l'homme d'entendement"). To the extent that the terms describe class categories, it is likely that the "common herd" in the above passage from book 1, chapter 20, are not peasants at all but those who are wealthy enough to summon notaries and doctors, for he cites their not writing a will until a doctor has determined their imminent death.[22] At the close of that early essay Montaigne notes that humble village folk manage more serenely than those in great houses, who have elaborate rituals to prepare for.[23] The later essay reveals fuller experiential understanding of that tranquility that had made him ponder before: peasant neighbors do not cogitate over the last hour until it is there; the exercise of imagination expands anticipatory suffering.[24] The worker placidly planting the garden during the plague of 1586 was Montaigne's ideal back in the 1570s: "I want death to find me planting my cabbages, but careless of death, and still more of my unfinished garden."[25] As with his friend Pasquier, Montaigne's writing is his garden and his choice of the vegetable cabbage, used in greetings to friends in the sixteenth century, makes Montaigne's respect for workers on his estate, including himself, all the more evident.

Literacy, as well as imagination, is subject to criticism. In his essay "Of Physiognomy" Montaigne ridicules Cicero's *Tusculanae disputationes*, used by him for the title and main theme of book 1, chapter 20, on the grounds that dying would be no more cheerful if one had read Cicero's work than it would be if one had not.[26] Echoing his highly intellectual critique of intellectuality in book 1, chapter 25, "On Pedantry," and book 2, chapter 12, "Apology for Raymond Sebond," Montaigne proclaims the chasm between words about death and the reality of dying. His opening to the important first passage above contrasts our "efforts of learning" with peasants acting according to nature. And in the second passage he shows that the peasants accept the universal sentence of death, learning from one another, from common experience, how to accept it. He contrasts their naturalness with "studied and premeditated fortitude."[27]

In that vicarious experiencing of a dying unaided by books, Montaigne passes from the book-lined, closed circle of his study to the wide open spaces of his fields; he interprets his observations, however, in the language of his Stoic philosophical readings. Directly after describing the mass deaths of peasants in his time, he remarks that "we have abandoned Nature and we want to teach her her lesson, she who used to guide us so happily and so surely. And yet the traces of her teaching and the little that remains of her image—imprinted, by the benefit of ignorance, on the life of that rustic, unpolished mob—learning is constrained every day to go and borrow, to give its disciples models of constancy, innocence, and tranquility."[28] Montaigne applies Stoic phraseology for the common notions of goodness "imprinted" on those who live closer to nature.[29] He conforms to the traditional Stoic identification of "imprinted notions" with "seeds of virtue" and "reason," but his phraseology is innovative when he emphasizes "virtue" as the source of true law, but without directly mentioning natural law, and when he speaks of a "seed of universal reason": "What I like is the virtue that laws and religions do not make but perfect and authorize, that feels in itself enough to sustain itself without help, born in us from its own roots, from the seed of universal reason that is implanted in every man who is not denatured."[30] The Stoic image of the "imprinted" notions reinforces the imagery of natural "seeds" of virtue having "roots" in the natural human being. Furthermore, "On Physiognomy" begins with the admonition that we need clear sight to find the secret light hiding underneath our artifice of opinions; *secret light*, indicating, for example, the true remains of nature in the soul and the words of Socrates, is a standard abbreviated Stoic phrase for the light of virtue shining in human nature.[31]

Throughout the *Essais* Montaigne applies the terms *raison*, "reason," which appears 472 times, and *conscience*, which appears 174 times, to indicate the source within human nature for virtue.[32] This vocabulary, indicative of Montaigne's role as a natural-law theorist, is worthy of further investigation. Nevertheless, missing is a consistent epistemological theory to explain how the human mind attains knowledge of virtue. "On Physiognomy" is unusual since a full-blown statement of Stoic confidence in human capacity to know and achieve virtue such as occurs in that essay is rare in the *Essais* as a whole. The obstacle for Montaigne is his Skepticism explicated in book 2, chapter 12, "Apology for Raymond Sebond": applying the ancient test for common notions that they be ideas or customs universally upheld, Montaigne despairs of finding any such notion. Not knowing how to distinguish natural law amid the morass of human law, he suggests that we might find such law among animals.[33] That clue to where to look for natural law helps elucidate the passage on peasant death; the image of peasants dying in tranquility leads him to discuss animal behavior, for in peasants and animals he finds traces of constant and universal nature uncorrupted by cultures.[34] Skeptical of the intricacies of highly educated human reason, Montaigne's best passage incorporating the Stoic intertexts for the internal source for rational conduct describes an apparently silent communal self-burial. He speaks of "traces . . . imprinted" and a "seed of universal reason" in "On Physiognomy" to highlight his discovery of humans living and dying "in accordance with nature."

In contrast to those who hold that the seeds of virtue require careful cultivation and schooling and reach full development only in an elite of sages, Montaigne gives anecdotal evidence that nature's teaching is present in laborers and animals. His presentation of the virtuous nobility of peasants stresses the egalitarianism in ancient Stoicism, the school that includes alike Epictetus the slave and Marcus Aurelius the emperor. Montaigne's vegetative imagery of peasant nobility in the fields contrasts strikingly with vegetative imagery of peasant folly evident in contemporary visual arts. A typical example of the latter is a German pen-and-ink drawing of about 1525, possibly by Hans Weiditz, showing a woman shaking an abundant tree and watching the peasant fools fall out.[35] This illustration incorporates the proverbs that anything in ample supply is said "to grow on trees" and the expression of folly as a "a tree of fools," evocative of Adam and Eve's eating fruit of the forbidden tree; it is a concise illustration for us of the massive upper- and middle-class prejudices against peasants with which Montaigne contends in his portrayal of peasant nobility of character. In the debates on nobility during the Italian and the Northern Renaissance, Stoics are often cited on the side of virtue deriving from character rather than from birth;[36] Montaigne especially highlights the egalitarian side of Stoicism through his portrayal of noble peasants and noble Amerindians.

AMERINDIANS AND NATURAL-LAW THEORY

"These nations, then, seem to me barbarous in this sense, that they have been fashioned very little by the human mind, and are still very close to their original naturalness. The laws of nature still rule them, very little corrupted by ours."[37]

To emphasize the above passage is to reemphasize the normative and universalistic aspects of Michel de Montaigne's use of the classical dictum "Follow nature." In the variety of sources eclectically used by Montaigne, it is a challenge to specify the exact type of natural-law theory he uses in a particular case. For example, he applies the originally Stoic phrase "good seeds that nature had produced in them" in discussing the Amerindians' natural sources of virtue;[38] yet Montaigne's adaptation of the Stoic phrase *seeds of virtue* takes on a distinctly modern twist, moving away from the Stoic dichotomy between the elite sage and the people and toward seeking wisdom especially in simple people. Montaigne applies the vocabulary of natural-law theory primitivistically to describe peoples whose conduct evokes literary images of a presocietal "golden age"; however, as indicated by evocation of several ancient utopias at the beginning of "Of Cannibals," the term *golden age* connotes more than one model to Montaigne. The exemplum of people living in accordance with the laws of nature is particularly important in Montaigne's opening "To the Reader," where he claims his naturalness and sincerity: "Had I been placed among those nations which are said to live in the sweet freedom of nature's first laws, I assure you I should very gladly have portrayed myself here entire and wholly naked."[39] I shall suggest that the laws referred to in this passage, as well as in the one above from "Of Cannibals," appear to absorb some of the Epicureans' or Ulpian's version of natural-law theory—a law common to humans and animals, a law for personal survival.

In the passage from "To the Reader" it is significant that Montaigne writes in the conditional: if he had been born in another society, he would have conformed to its pattern. He does not break French social custom and describe himself completely naked; Montaigne's restraint is typical of his admonitions to respect and conform with the customs and positive law of one's locale.[40] Montaigne's reference to the "sweet freedom of nature's first laws" suggests that he is thinking of the law common to humans and animals. This view is reminiscent of Ulpian's view of the state of nature as a time when "everyone was born free under the law of nature." Also famous from the *Digest* is Ulpian's view that the *ius naturale* is "what nature teaches to all animals."[41]

Another significant aspect of the reference to the law of nature in "To the Reader" is the use of "on dict": the statement of these nations living in accordance with nature's law is reported from others. Likewise, the report of Amerindian culture in "Of Cannibals" is presented as a report of a simple man in Montaigne's employ.[42] More problematic is what occurs before the details of that report, namely, Montaigne's praise of this society in what appears to be the first-person voice:

> These nations, then, seem to me barbarous in this sense, that they have been fashioned very little by the human mind, and are still very close to their original naturalness. The laws of nature still rule them, very little corrupted by ours; and they are in such a state of purity that I am sometimes vexed that they were unknown earlier, in the days when there were men able to judge them better than we. I am sorry that Lycurgus and Plato did not know of them; for it seems to me that what we actually see in these nations surpasses not only all the pictures in which poets have idealized the golden age and all their inventions in imagining a happy state of man, but also the conceptions and the very desire of philosophy.[43]

Montaigne draws on the primitivistic theme in ancient Stoicism: of a time before development of reason, when natural law, rather than positive law, ruled the human species. Montaigne in his own words is accepting a description of these people as in accord with natural law. But there are several signs that the speech may not be taken at face value as complete, naked sincerity. First of all, Montaigne takes superlative praises of ideal societies and compares them to one another in the language typical of that tradition, which he admits is embellished. Second, as his opening sentence indicates, he is arguing against the simple assessment "barbarous" embedded in the French sixteenth-century label *cannibales*[44] and laments that Lycurgus and Plato are not available to make an assessment. The overall statement is in a cadenced rhetoric designed for such ancient authors. The irony is that without the benefit of either a lawgiver creating written law or philosopher-rulers contemplating justice, these simple tribesmen appear to have the military valor of the ancient Spartans and the congenial communal sharing of Plato's guardians. Montaigne's rhetoric informs Plato that vicariously experiencing the Topinambá life cycle surpasses the conception and desire for philosophy, suggesting that observation of human behavior, part and parcel of Montaigne's appreciation of "experience," might be a better method for learning what is possible than Plato's contemplation of abstract forms.

Subsequently, Montaigne's rhetoric shifts to direct address to Plato and culminates in a section imitated by Shakespeare in *The Tempest*, often praised as Montaigne's unique phrasing:

> This is a nation, I should say to Plato, in which there is no sort of traffic, no knowledge of letters, no science of numbers, no name for a magistrate or for political superiority, no custom of servitude, no riches or poverty, no contracts, no successions, no partitions, no occupations but leisure ones, no care for any but common kinship, no clothes, no agriculture, no metal, no use of wine or wheat. The very words that signify lying, treachery, dissimilation, avarice, envy, belittling, pardon—unheard of.[45]

In fact, though, there are several possible sources for his succession of *nuls*. Both the negative portrayals of New World people and the rarer positive portrayals defined these people by what they lacked.[46] A particularly similar rendition to Montaigne's, and a possible source for it, is one of the first New World travelogues, by Peter Martyr of Anghiera: "Naked without weights or measures or death-dealing money, [they] live in a Golden Age without laws, without slanderous judges, without the scales of the balance. Contented with Nature, they spend their lives utterly untroubled for the future. . . . Theirs is a Golden Age; they do not enclose their farms with trench or wall or hurdle; their gardens are open. Without laws, without the scales of the balance, without judges, they guard the right by Nature's light."[47] Although this passage seems most similar to Montaigne's thought in its attitude to scales of balance, leisure, lack of property, and its use of natural-law theory in reference to a New World people, both Peter Martyr and Montaigne had multiple ancient precedents.

Cicero's succession of *non*s in *De inventione rhetorica* tells of a time previous to the development of reason, when humans lived like animals: "There was as yet no ordered system of religious worship nor of social duties; no one had seen legitimate marriage nor had anyone looked upon children whom he knew to be his own nor had they learned the advantages of an equitable code of law."[48] Montaigne's high-styled prose, like Cicero's, contrasts with the evocation of humans living before the development of *l'esprit*. Further proof of the imitable rhetoric of golden-age descriptions is that Montaigne echoes his words of 1580 in 1588 but now adds that "not fifty years ago it knew neither letters, nor weights and measures, nor clothes, nor wheat, nor vines";[49] and again after 1588 Montaigne admits to using multiple sources for his information about "What they tell us of the Brazilians . . . as people who spent their life in admirable simplicity and ignorance, without letters, without law, without king, without religion of any kind."[50]

Montaigne concludes his discussion of the lacks of the primitive society by referring to Virgil's *Georgics* 2.20 and Seneca's epistle 90. The citation of Virgil, important for basic views of natural processes of vegetative growth and of husbandry as in Petrarch and other humanists, refers specifically to the section on natural growth before cultivation. Before the 1588 edition, Montaigne adds reference to Virgil through "the modes nature imparted first," that is, that the poplar grows spontaneously, the oak grows from seed, and the elm sprouts from the root.[51] After 1588, Montaigne adds the quotation from Seneca, "Men fresh sprung from the gods."[52] Montaigne, whose favorite childhood book is Ovid's *Metamorphoses*, would know also the golden-age passage—which influenced Italian humanists and artists—in which the Creation is described:

> The nobler Creature, with a mind possest
>
> . . . .
>
> That Maker, the best World's originall,
> Either Him fram'd of seed Caelestiall;
> Or Earth, which late he did from Heaven divide,
> Some sacred seeds retain'd, to Heaven ally'd.[53]

Seneca's important letter 90 is about the transition from primitive life to the golden age and then to corrupt society. Seneca clarifies the distinction between naive goodness, possible in the golden age, which lacks temptation, and virtue, which is possible only under practice and discipline (lines 37, 44). In epistle 90 Seneca encloses his narrative of historical development with an explanation of the emergence of philosophy, a gift of the gods that it requires human effort to acquire, in which the contemplation of the difference between innocence and virtue appears to be productive; the influence of Seneca may help explain Montaigne's strange comment that the observation of these people goes beyond "the conceptions and the very desire of philosophy."

Seneca rejects Posidonius's idea that the mechanical arts were produced by the wise, for Seneca views a simple life without luxury as the wiser life and distinguishes "right reason" governing conduct from the broader capacity of "reason," which produces the mechanical arts (line 24). The wise understand the "eternal Reason which was imparted to the whole, and to the force which inheres in all the seeds of things" (line 29). Seneca concludes, "Virtue is not vouchsafed to a soul unless that soul has been trained and taught, and by unremitting practice brought to perfection. For the attainment of this boon, but not in the possession of it, were we born; and even in the best of men, before you refine them by instruction, there is but the stuff of virtue, not virtue itself" (line 46).

Nevertheless, despite evidence of the influence of ancient authors praising the "golden age," there is an additional reason not to take seriously Montaigne's claim to find people living by nature's laws as his whole, sincere view. The idyllic description tricks the reader into not expecting the subsequent detailed description of war as the regular work of men, cannibalism for vengeance, and polygamy as a reward for valor; such social mores are not part of Seneca's golden age.[54] Furthermore, one of Montaigne's very important points is that the people have developed reason. There are letters, for Montaigne gives examples of love poetry and poetry of valor; and the Topinambá are capable of making value judgments such as those they make about French society. Montaigne views their activities as leisurely yet shows the men preoccupied with warfare for honor's sake. There is deception as the prisoner is fattened up for the community feasting. The last line of "Of Cannibals," which spoofs the tribesmen for not wearing trousers, encourages one to see the entire essay in a humorous vein, as a satire on both the Amerindians and the French.

In addition, Montaigne very skillfully dissimulates, hiding behind the "simple" narrator; and to add further complexity, the narration is an elaborate achievement of ethnographical observation and literary art.[55] The not-at-all-simple narrator is skillful in the utopian author's trick, which Montaigne exposes in the case of Lycurgus and Plato, of making the social institutions appear to be the cause for the happiness artistically portrayed. The narrator, by taking the victim's point of view, doubly tricks the reader: the prisoner sings of his happiness—he anticipates his enemies eating him and thus eating their own relatives, whom he has previously eaten—and the wives appear happy to find other wives for a valorous and deserving husband. Montaigne emphasizes that the eating of a prisoner derives not from hunger but from culture and ritual. What might be more unnatural—that is, against personal survival—than the prisoner's casuistic reasoning of happiness before his plight?

How might one reconcile the contradiction of a society living by nature's laws and at the same time practicing cannibalism for vengeance on its neighbors? There is a precedent for that conception within the Epicurean tradition in antiquity that might help us to resolve how Montaigne both proclaims that some Amerindian tribes live by nature's laws in "Of Cannibals" and questions the Stoic concept of a natural moral law in the "Apology for Raymond Sebond." "But they are funny when, to give some certainty to the laws, they say that there are some which are firm, perpetual, and immutable, which they call natural, which are imprinted on the human race by the condition of their very being. . . . Now the only likely sign by which they can argue certain laws to be natural is universality of approval. . . . Let them show me just one law of that sort—I'd like to see it."⁵⁶ Finding diversity of law and custom and no example of universal consent, Montaigne explores stimulus and response wherein human reason plays a minor role. For example, he contrasts the philosopher, whose reasoning makes the issue of sensory response to cold and hot problematical, with the simple person, who knows that fire is hot and snow is cold. "If they [philosophers] had left us in our natural state, receiving external impressions as they present themselves to us through our senses," then it would be accurate to judge fire and water by touching them. "This answer would be good among the cannibals, who enjoy the happiness of a long, tranquil, and peaceable life without the precepts of Aristotle and without acquaintance with the name of physics. . . . Not only we ourselves, but all the animals, and everything over which the domination of natural law is still pure and simple, would be capable of using this answer; but they [philosophers] have renounced it."⁵⁷

Still further evidence that Montaigne's positive assertions of natural law refer to the possibility of a law common to humans and animals is his concession in the "Apology." "If there is any truly natural law, that is to say, any instinct that is seen universally and permanently imprinted in both the animals and ourselves (which is not beyond dispute), I may say that in my opinion, after the care every animal has for its own preservation and the avoidance of what is harmful, the affection that the begetter has for his begotten ranks second."⁵⁸ Self-preservation and affection for offspring are to be important in seventeenth- and eighteenth-century philosophical conceptions of the state of nature.

Montaigne's criticism of Plato's philosophical foundation of justice and Montaigne's questioning of the Stoics' cosmopolitan doctrine of natural law founded on common consent have precedent in antiquity among Academic and Pyrrhonian Skeptics and among Epicureans. Of particular interest is that the Epicureans were the first to suggest as criticism of Stoic natural-law theory that without positive law humans might live like beasts and eat one another. Plutarch reports that according to the Epicurean viewpoint, those who have created society by law have given life security, and if one did not have kings and magistrates and laws, "we would live the life of beasts, and anyone of us, depending on fortune, would eat, one might say, anyone else."⁵⁹

Both the perspective that nature alone would not prevent cannibalism and the view that mutual agreement was at the formation of justice influence seventeenth-century natural-law theorists. Pufendorf is to claim that "if there were not any justice, each of us would eat one another"; and Grotius says almost exactly the same thing.[60] Montaigne supports that trend by his view that positive social law is necessary for the establishment of justice. Montaigne's rhetorical claims that the Topinambá people live in accordance with nature's laws and yet are cannibals (not for natural reasons of hunger but for vengeance) plays with the natural-law tradition in satiric and ironic ways. Yet in the essay "Of Cannibals" Montaigne explicitly cites "Chrysippus and Zeno, heads of the Stoic sect" for the position that "there is nothing wrong in using our carcases for any purpose in case of need, and getting nourishment from them."[61] The ambiguity of Montaigne's literary statement—his shaking Stoic and Epicurean notions through the sieve of his own critical reason and presenting them as a tutor developing the reader's ability to judge—is at the root of its power and varied influence.

It may be that Michel de Montaigne is a transitional figure in the great transformation that natural-law theory undergoes in the early modern period: the seventeenth-century *libertins*, such as La Mothe Le Vayer, read Montaigne in a way that undermines a universalist foundation for ethics,[62] Pierre Charron employs Montaigne's text to build a natural-law theory on "preud'hommie,"[63] and J. J. Rousseau adopts Montaigne's primitivistic idealization of the Amerindians as a path to build a natural-rights ethic.

As a transformer of natural-law theory Montaigne follows up on the issues exposed in the debate at the Spanish court in 1550 between Bartolomé de las Casas and Juan Ginés de Sepúlveda, a debate summarized briefly in the 1579 French translation of Bartolomé de las Casas, *Les tyrannies et cruatez des Espagnols*.[64] The French moral theorist Michel de Montaigne echoes some of the positions of the Spanish moral theorist Las Casas in his defense of the humanity of the Amerindian against the so-called natural-law theory of Juan Ginés de Sepúlveda. Las Casas's Latin writings make explicit the application to race relations of natural-law tradition: "The law of nations and natural law apply to Christian and gentile alike, and to all people of any sect, law, condition, or colour without any distinction whatsoever."[65] Likewise, he utilizes the agricultural imagery to indicate that the Amerindians, like all humans, have natural virtue, which needs cultivation to yield fruit.

Therefore, since uncultivated soil produces only thistle and thorns but possesses the innate goodness to yield useful fruit if it is cultivated, so all manners of men, however barbaric or bestial, possess the use of reason and are capable of being taught. Consequently, no man and no nation in the world, however barbarian or inhuman, is incapable of bearing the reasonable fruit of excellence, if taught in the manner required for the natural condition of man, especially with the doctrine of Faith.[66]

The Catholic missionary Las Casas's tone is more patronizing than Montaigne's, for Las Casas excerpts the apostle Mathew's term *thorns* to stress the unseemly culture of the Amerindians prior to the impact of Christian cultivation. On the same topic, Montaigne applies vegetative imagery to suggest that nature without the art of human cultivation produces virtue in both plants and people:

> These people are wild, just as we call wild the fruits that Nature has produced by herself and in her normal course; whereas really it is those that we have changed artificially and led astray from the common order, that we should rather call wild. The former retain alive and vigorous their genuine, their most useful and natural, virtues and properties.[67]

Montaigne's praise of both the vitality and the virtue of plants and peoples of the Americas leads to his statement that the laws of nature rule them, as they are not yet corrupted by European laws.

Nevertheless, Las Casas provides the most famous precedent for Montaigne's use of the argument that cannibalism is natural and in accordance with natural law to undermine the Aristotelian natural-law argument (associated with Sepúlveda and Francisco de Vittoria) that a war of conquest is justifiable over a people who eat human flesh and thus by definition are barbarians or, in Aristotle's terminology, "natural slaves."[68] In this context Montaigne's raising the estimation of the animals as creatures who reason from sense knowledge in his "Apology for Raymond Sebond" (1.12) and his protest against torture to animals likewise undermine the morality of those who would treat a race of humans as if they were animals. During Montaigne's visit to Rome in 1581 inquisitors read his book and criticize him "for esteeming as cruelty whatever goes beyond plain death"; in 1582 Montaigne adds to his essay "On Cruelty" the account of the mob strangling a robber and chopping him up, which he had witnessed in Rome on the same trip. His condemnation of pain and cruelty extends to animals for their sake and for the sake of humanity; he admits his own emotional and rational distress at seeing "a chicken's neck wrung" and at reading accounts of the ancient Roman Colosseum, where cruelty proceeded from slaughter of animals to slaughter of humans. The anecdotes build to a natural-law assertion, a statement of conscience, that is applicable to events in the Americas: "Still there is a certain respect, and a general duty of humanity, that attaches us not only to animals, who have life and feeling, but even to trees and plants. We owe justice to men, and mercy and kindness to other creatures that may be capable of receiving it."[69]

The series of lacks that Montaigne views as signs of the Amerindian's natural virtue is proof to Sepúlveda of the need to be ruled by others who have a system of government:

> The greatest philosophers declare that such wars may be undertaken by a very civilized nation against uncivilized people who are more barbarous than can

be imagined, for they are absolutely lacking in any knowledge of letters, do not know the use of money, generally go about naked, even the women, and carry burdens on their shoulders and backs like beasts for great distances.[70]

Montaigne's spoofing of this kind of thinking takes myriad forms, including his ridicule of the thought of a death sentence for demonic possession to a man who dreamed he was an animal carrying burdens for soldiers[71] and his heroic portrayal at the close of his later essay "On Coaches" (1585–88) of a human coach—the Amerindians defying their European conquerors as they take on the burden and stand in the place of compatriots killed carrying the last king of Peru in a seat of gold.[72] He admires the way Amerindian art in such cities as Cuzco and Mexico City imitates and enhances nature, as in "the garden of that king in which all the trees, the fruits, and the herbs were excellently fashioned in gold, and of such size and so arranged as they might be in an ordinary garden," concluding that "the beauty of their workmanship in jewelry, feathers, cotton and painting, show that they were not behind us in industry either." One of the few authors to echo Las Casas's bold admission of the genocide of the population in the Americas by exposure to European disease and warfare, Montaigne laments that Europeans "hastened the decline and ruin of this new world by our contagion."[73] The only evidence of condescension is in his view that the Greeks or Roman conquerors would have been better suited for "adding the Greek and Roman virtues to those originally in that region," for Montaigne appreciates "the good seeds that nature had produced in them" and "such fine natural beginnings" evident in virtues such as "devoutness, observance of the laws, goodness, liberality, loyalty, and frankness . . . boldness and courage . . . firmness, constancy, resoluteness against pains and hunger and death."[74]

Montaigne's ambiguity, his style of writing designed to encourage a reader's judgment,[75] would lead to different judgments by different readers.[76] The interpretation presented here indicates that Montaigne's statements that these nations live in accordance with the laws of nature belong to a long rhetorical tradition common to Cicero and Peter Martyr; to the extent that he amplifies the meaning of the concept of laws of nature he is blending Epicurean and Stoic natural law. He refers to the law common to humans and animals, the law of personal survival, proclaimed by the Epicureans and by Ulpian; yet even regarding eating of human flesh Montaigne cites Stoics as authorities. He uses the phraseology "bonnes semences que nature y avoit produit" in a Stoic manner to proclaim that Amerindian cultures express natural goodness and the beginnings of the rational, artistic labor of human cultivation and education that leads to virtue.[77] Even cannibalism is a cultural aspect of their idea of heroic virtue rather than a purely natural trait. Montaigne's matter-of-fact acceptance that cannibalism is characteristic of people, no matter how "idyllic," living without positive law and his protest at European wars of conquest of Amerindian tribes place him in line with the seventeenth-century founders of international law.

Montaigne's vegetative descriptions of the easy and natural development of plants and people in book 1, chapter 31, and of the easy and natural self-burial of peasants in the fields in book 2, chapter 12, correspond to his indication in his essay "Of the Education of Children" that one finds the path to virtue not by ascending a difficult mountain but by following the flowered, sloping path in the open plains. His approach both negates the elitism that is sometimes found in the image of the Stoic sage and affirms universal human dignity: whereas some of his contemporaries find only wretchedness among European peasants and only barbarism among American tribes, Montaigne provides evidence of their virtuous character.

Charron: Seeds of Virtue for Virtue's Own Sake

IN THE FOLLOWING passage of his major work, *De la sagesse*, Pierre Charron (1541–1603), a Catholic priest, vividly expresses the war-weary mood of late-sixteenth-century France and his concern to build a foundation for morality independent of religion:

> Whoever is a good person by religious restraint and scruple, beware of him and do not value him: and he who has religion without virtue, I do not mean to say that he is more wicked, but he is more dangerous than he who has neither the one nor the other. . . . It is not that religion in any way teaches or favors evil, as some out of foolishness or malice would like to object or conclude from what I have said: even the most absurd and false religion does not do that. I say this because people having no taste, image, or conception of virtue, except as the result and in the service of religion, and thinking that being a good man is nothing else than advancing and promoting their religion, believe that any activity whether it be treason, perfidy, sedition, rebellion, and any offense against anyone is not only allowable and permissible, under the colors of zeal and concern for religion, but moreover is praiseworthy, meritorious, and worthy of canonization.[1]

Charron is a thinker who, having seen what he believes to be immorality condoned by religious ideologues, searches for an independent source for ethics. He bases human wisdom upon the seeds of virtue and knowledge.

Like Guillaume du Vair, Charron applies ancient Stoic ethics to support the *politique* sentiment. For a half-century the *politiques*, the moderates who prefer law, order, and peace to sectarian strife, try to establish some form of compromise and religious toleration between the Huguenots and the Catholics.[2] When finally the French Religious Wars subside, King Henry IV promulgates the Edict of Nantes, which grants the Huguenots religious liberty in protected towns and estates and civil liberties throughout France. There is a close coincidence in timing between publications of the preparing of the edict in 1598–99 and Charron's writing of the *De la sagesse*, from February 1597 through April 1599.[3] In his avoidance of polemical attacks on Protestant beliefs and of polemical defenses of Catholic beliefs, in his exposition of the similarity of all religions, in his reliance on God's revelation and grace for right belief, in his advocacy of Skepticism on metaphysical and theological questions about which there was no agreement, in his repudiation of dogmatic partisanship, and in his main purpose of founding an autonomous ethic that might be shared by all, Pierre

Charron in *De la sagesse* expresses the *politique* sentiment of the contemporaneous document *L'Edict du Roy*.[4] Horrified by the great variety of sins
committed in the name of particular theological doctrines, Charron
preaches doctrinal humility and Skepticism and advises that his contemporaries give their prime attention to acting in accordance with prudence,
justice, courage, and temperance.

SEPARATE BOOKS FOR HUMAN WISDOM AND FOR DIVINE WISDOM

Published in 1601, Pierre Charron's *De la sagesse* purports to teach
"human wisdom" by analyzing human nature, setting forth the principles
of wisdom, and applying the four cardinal virtues to the details of everyday
and civic life. As the first edition is met by a storm of religious criticism of
his intention, Charron in his revised preface justifies his decision to omit
discussion of divine wisdom on the grounds that it is distinctly different
from human wisdom, is best treated separately, and is already treated in his
earlier works.[5] The contrast with his 1593 and 1595 publication of the polemical tract, *Les trois veritez*, which sets out to prove that God exists, that
Christianity is the true religion, and that the Catholic Church alone keeps
the truth pure, is striking.[6] We saw in chapter 7 that Charron is a careful
reader of Du Vair and, like him, intentionally separates his ethical treatise
from his religious treatise.

In *De la sagesse* Charron defines human wisdom as "integrity, a beautiful
and noble composition of the entire man, in his insides, his outsides, his
thoughts, his words, his actions, and all his movements; it is the excellence
and perfection of man as man."[7] Living in the late Renaissance, Charron is
a beneficiary of the arduous work of scholarly discovery, translation, and
interpretation of works of antiquity. Eclectically borrowing from a medley
of Renaissance, medieval, and antique writings, he seeks to present the essence of humanist wisdom.

In his preface Charron distinguishes human wisdom not only from "divine wisdom" but also from "worldly wisdom."[8] For Charron, worldly wisdom is a result of corrupted human life and reflects the folly of the worldly.
He refers to 1 Corinthians 3.19, as does the Alciati emblem that shows a
snake-man wallowing in the mud of earthly possessions yet looking upward
and imagining that his life will please God.[9] For divine wisdom Charron
refers his readers to *Les trois veritez*. The 1604 posthumous edition of *De
la sagesse* supplements the textual description of the nature of his topic,
human wisdom, with a carefully delineated visual title page. Charron's decision is recorded in his letter of 27 April 1603 to Gabriel Michel de la
Rochemaillet requesting a frontispiece and in his description in the 1604
preface. The 1606 edition adds a sonnet, and the 1646, 1656, and 1662
editions of this very popular work add a few more words.[10] I shall focus on
Charron's intention in the 1604 edition, although the addition of a poem

to the picture with its inscribed sayings illustrates the growing popularity of emblems in the baroque period.

Léonard Gaultier's engraving (fig. 10.1) emphasizes the vertical column on an open field: at the base is the inscription of this book of wisdom; on the base is a cube of justice, to which four figures are chained. Above, standing upright and wearing only a laurel and olive wreath, is the female figure Wisdom.[11] On Wisdom's right the observer reads, "I do not know," and to her left are the words "peace and prosperity" below an accompanying olive-laurel device. Autonomous and self-reflective, Wisdom looks at herself in a mirror; the dictum "Know thyself" obviously meets the approval of the heavenly hand holding the mirror. The engraving has more vegetative symbolism than Charron describes: the upright tree at the center evoked by the crown of olive and laurel on Wisdom's head, the open spaces of the fields of learning, which the mid-seventeenth-century editions view as signifying liberty, and the animation of each of the figures, including Wisdom, as live personifications rather than as statues.

The engraved title page conveys wisdom as the serene ability constantly to put in their place the lower aspects of human nature: passion, opinion, superstition, and pedantry. In the text Charron describes passion with features altered hideously, but the illustration, which shows a woman urgently pointing upward at the lady Wisdom, accords more closely with the 1606 sonnet, which describes Passion as impetuously demanding. In accord with Charron's description, Opinion literally stands upon the heads of the popular crowd, Superstition is gripped in fear, and Pedantry—"pedantic virtue, *preud'hommie*, or science"—reads in a book of "yes" and "no."

One might very well ask how Charron, who, as so many of his earliest critics and recent commentators have maintained, is a Skeptic, purports to teach wisdom.[12] Charron's work does reflect the influence, through Montaigne especially, of Pyrrhonian and Academic Skepticism and is instrumental in its further spread; however, Charron's Skepticism is epistemologically limited by his belief—stated in both editions of *De la sagesse* in a manner reflecting the influence of Bodin particularly but also compatible with Montaigne—that the seeds of virtue and knowledge are present in the human being from birth.[13] The major motive for Charron's advocacy of Skepticism is the purpose it might achieve: mental tranquillity, which would allow the individual to concentrate his or her attention on leading the good life. In fact, *Skepticism* is a misleading term, for the liberty Charron recommends affects the will as much as the judgment. In the context of *De la sagesse*, the purpose is to free the judgment from the lesser purpose of pursuing truth and to free the will from the adherence to superfluous or harmful truths in order that the *esprit* in judgment and in will might guide one in the conduct of one's individual and public life.

That Charron's Skepticism is a preliminary to the good life is evinced by the organization of book 2 of *De la sagesse*. Book 2, chapter 2, on "Universal and full liberty of the *esprit*, as much in judgment as in will," is a

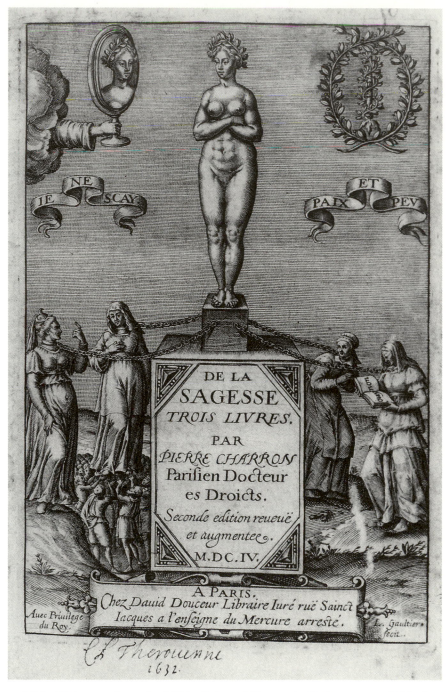

10.1. Title page from the 1604 edition of Charron's *De la sagesse*, published posthumously. Léonard Gaultier's engraving of Wisdom trapping Passion, Opinion, Superstition, and Pedantry was requested by Charron in a letter of April 1603.

"disposition to wisdom," to be directly followed by a chapter on "the first and fundamental part of wisdom." Book 2, chapter 3 is thus the most important chapter of the work because it teaches the fundamental principle of wisdom, without which no one can be wise. This principle is "true and essential *preud'hommie*." The foundation stone of Charron's conception of *preud'hommie* is the concept of the natural law within. Charron restores natural law to its original Stoic context as a base for an autonomous ethic.

CULTIVATING EXEMPLARY VIRTUOUS INDIVIDUALS

We have seen that there is a large variety of Christian and classical sources from which Charron could derive his belief that natural law is implanted in man. He admits as much when he simplifies Bodin's list of authorities into the statement, "It is proven first of all by the saying of the greatest philosophers, who all have said that the seeds of the great virtues and knowledge have been scattered naturally in the soul."[14] A typical writer of the Renaissance, influenced by the copybook method of collecting *sententiae*, Charron brings together concepts, opinions, and information from a variety of authors in what J. B. Sabrié calls "an anthology of humanism."[15] Yet for his doctrine of seeds of virtue and knowledge Charron is most indebted to Bodin, Montaigne, and Du Vair and to the ancient Stoics.[16]

Following Seneca and Cicero, Charron views wisdom as the art of "living well and dying well." Cicero had said that "the art of living is prudence." Charron considers prudence, which he defines as knowledge of what to desire and what to reject, as the guide to all the virtues, and he therefore calls wisdom "*preude prudence*, a supple and strong *preud'hommie*, a well-advised probity."[17] Thus, for Charron the man who follows the Stoic art of living well is the *preud'homme*. Huguet's dictionary defines *preud'homme* as *homme honnête*: *honnête*, meaning "honest," and *sage*, meaning "wise," are as packed with meaning as *preud'homme*.[18] Widely used in the sixteenth and seventeenth centuries, *preud'homme* means, most simply, "man of integrity." When other authors consider *preude'femme*, "woman of integrity" as well, the *preud'homme* may take on a generic connotation for "good human being," with goodness adapted, as Charron suggests, to one's station in life. *Preud'hommie*'s connotations depend on the user's philosophy of living. For Charron the major characteristic of the *preud'homme* is independence from one's times, the source of which is the internal integrity of judgment and will.[19] Like the sage described in Epictetus's *Manual*, Charron's *preud'homme* has a noble constancy and self-sufficiency, directing attention to the realm of life that is within one's own control.[20]

In emphasizing *preud'hommie* as the first and fundamental part of wisdom, Charron is emphasizing the internal, natural source from which true wisdom flows. A person may not become a *preud'homme* by outward actions alone, for actions might be motivated by fear of the law, fear of divine wrath, desire for divine reward, desire for public approval, or desire for glory or profit. All these causes for motivation are external and therefore subject to change. Some of his comments are a response to Protestant criticism of Catholic doctrine of justification. True *preud'hommie*, deriving its source from human nature, is stable, essential, and unchanging. In order to discover who is a true *preud'homme*, it is necessary to look within at the source and motivation of the external actions.[21]

> The source of this *preud'hommie* is nature, which obliges all persons to be and to become what they ought, that is, to conform and rule themselves according to her. Nature is to us both the teacher who enjoins and commands *preud'hommie* and the law or instruction which teaches it. . . . A person should not in any way expect or seek any other cause, obligation, source, or motive for one's *preud'hommie*, and one will find none more just and legitimate, more powerful, or more ancient, as it is as old as one and born with one. All humans ought to be and want to be good humans because they are human.[22]

Like the ancient Stoics, Charron equates the terms *nature* and *natural law*: "Since this law and light is essential and natural in us, it has been called nature or law of nature."[23] Charron calls this law by its many Stoic equivalents: *universal law, fundamental law,* and *equity.* To explain how humans have a source within themselves for knowledge of universal law, Charron makes ample use of three of the Stoic terms for natural law in man: *reason, seeds,* and *sparks.*[24]

Charron's Ciceronian advice to live according to nature is advice to live according to reason. Charron's conscious indebtedness to the ancient Stoics for this doctrine is indicated by his statement that "the doctrine of all the sages states that to live well is to live according to nature . . . 'by taking nature as guide, you will not err':—'the good is what is according to nature':—'all the vices are against nature':—'it is the same thing, to live happily and to live in accordance with nature,' understanding by nature the equity and universal reason which shines in us."[25] Charron thus cites Cicero and Seneca as authorities on the virtuous life, and in his own words he indicates his comprehension that the Stoic life "according to nature" is life according to the universal reason that is in everyone: "For this law of equity and natural reason is perpetual in us, 'a perpetual proclamation'; it is inviolable, and can never be extinguished or erased."[26] Thus, in order to be virtuous one should look within to find the sure standard of natural law.

Thus, despite Charron's doubts about the power of human reason, he still views reason as the standard and source of human knowledge of natural law. Freedom of the mind in judgment and in will restores human nature to its natural harmony and order. Once one's own human nature is in order, one is then in a better position to put it in harmony with the order of the universe. No longer believing all the opinions and laws of the locality, the Skeptic is a "citizen of the world" and has a mind open to accept natural law. The human being, as a microcosm of the world, may also be said to contain a government. When the soul is in its natural order, the sovereign understanding rules the lower faculties by the law of nature.[27] The will submits itself to right reason for the proper ordering of the passions.[28] Thus, when human nature is in its proper order, human reason is able to follow the instructions of universal reason.

When one's mind is in its natural condition, one will find by looking inward the divine "light of thy countenance" and the "law written in our hearts."[29] Charron's equation of Psalms 4.7 and Romans 2.15 places him as a successor of Erasmus, Biel, and Aquinas, and distinct from Luther, in the belief in the natural light of the intellect. These phrases draw upon the traditional biblical passages used by medieval Christian writers to prove the existence of natural law in humans. Like the early church fathers, Charron quotes Romans 2 directly without much comment.[30] The passage itself is his Christian proof that God wrote a law into the human being at Creation. However, that Charron shows no scholastic concern for specifying the nature of reason's access to natural law indicates his distance from the scholastic natural-law tradition and his closeness to the Stoic original.[31] Not distinguishing between natural reason and conscience and not indicating the exact location of natural law, Charron occasionally uses the term *conscience* to indicate the source of *preud'hommie*.

Whereas in medieval writers the reference to "the law written in the heart" is usually a basis for discussion of the concept of common notions, Charron rejects this concept for explaining human knowledge of natural law. In doing so he refers not to the medieval interpretation of common notions as first principles of practical reason but to the Stoic concept of ideas for which there is universal consent. Like the Academic Skeptic Carneades in his attack on the Stoic school, and indebted to Montaigne for many of his examples, Charron compares customs from different lands as well as arguments from different so-called authorities to show that there is no notion that is universally accepted. Furthermore, he proclaims that because the number of fools far exceeds the number of sages, the ideas commonly held are likely to be false. But as with Cicero before him, Charron's recognition of the Skeptical attack does not stop him from believing that natural law is within. He argues that if the nature of humankind were ordered according to reason, then common consent would be a trustworthy guide.[32]

The Stoic image of seeds of virtue forms the basis for many of Charron's figurative descriptions of internal natural law. It is by using the image of seeds that Charron refutes the Aristotelian assumption that all knowledge comes from the senses and asserts, as does Bodin, that the *esprit* without instruction and by its own resources can think and reason.[33] Another passage, referring to "all the sages," defines nature as "the equity and universal reason which shines in us, which contains and nurtures the seeds of all virtue, probity, justice, and is the womb from which are born and come all good and beautiful laws, all just and equitable judgments that even an idiot will pronounce."[34] This passage clearly indicates that the seeds of virtue are nurtured by universal reason and thus are an internal natural-law source for true judgments and laws, one result of which is that some thoughts arise naturally and spontaneously by nature, not by art.

That the seeds are a source of human knowledge of natural law and that they germinate into *preud'hommie* is shown by the following passage: "Here is an essential, radical, and fundamental *preud'hommie*, born of its own roots, from the seed of universal reason, which is in the soul like the spring and balance in a clock ... by which one acts according to God, according to oneself, according to nature."[35] Charron applies Montaigne's phrase *seeds of universal reason*. The analogy stated here between the seed and the balance of a clock explains Charron's use of the term *balance* in other places to indicate the source of natural law in man.

The doctrine of seeds of virtue is stated by Charron without reference to the doctrine of seminal reason. However, in the above passage he equates seeds with roots, and in the following passage the use of *roots* is derived ultimately from the concept *logos spermatikos*: "By the mind [*l'esprit*] there is a parentage between God and humanity; and in order that the mind remember him he has turned its roots toward the sky, so that it always will have its sight turned toward the place of its birth."[36] As the evidence in chapter 3 shows, in this passage Charron follows Plato's *Timaeus* and the mystical traditions in viewing humanity whose face looks upward to God as an upside-down tree rooted in the Divine.

Like Seneca, Charron interprets the seeds of virtue and knowledge not as full-blown wisdom but as the potentiality for wisdom. While from the seeds themselves some true propositions can emerge naturally, Charron emphasizes that cultivation helps the seeds to grow. In discussing prudence, the major of the four cardinal virtues, Charron says that the seed of prudence is in us by nature; in order for this seed to develop into a full-blown virtue, we need theoretical guidance and practical experience.[37] Since Charron quotes heavily from Seneca's *Epistles* and *De beneficiis*, he may very well have borrowed his concept of seeds from a passage such as the following: "How do we first acquire the knowledge of that which is good and that which is honourable? Nature could not teach us this directly; she has given us the seeds of knowledge, but not knowledge itself."[38]

Charron sometimes mixes the image of seeds with the images of sparks or light. Thus, natural law is said to light the seeds, incubating them and causing them to blossom. Charron equates sparking the internal light with reviving the seeds. Both processes restore us to the natural order. The image of light also appears alone. As a noun, *light* refers to the natural light put in the human species at the Creation. The human being as the image of God contains the light of the divine countenance.[39] For our navigation through the stormy waters of life, God has given us "this natural, divine, original law which is an internal and inner torch."[40]

Charron's use of the term *light* in verb form, however, is misleading. Natural law is said to light or shine in us: "reason, original and universal law and light inspired by God, which shines in us."[41] Interpreted out of context, Charron's use of the image of light might seem to imply in an Augustinian sense God's active illumination of man in the precepts of natural law. However, such an interpretation would not accord with Charron's clear-cut statement that natural law is in us at birth; nor would it accord with his claim, often repeated, that *preud'hommie* is of the realm of nature, not of grace, or with his recommendation of the study of philosophy for helping one gain knowledge of natural law. The method for becoming a person of integrity is very different from the method for becoming a Christian. The only thing both have in common is the preliminary emptying of the mind of all beliefs and opinions. In discussing the reception of Christianity by the emptied mind, Charron describes in Augustinian terms the "impression of the Holy Spirit" and the reception of God's "revelation."[42] In discussing the appearance of natural law in the emptied mind, he speaks of turning inward to the "nature," which "in each of us is a sufficient and gentle teacher."[43] His use of the Christianized Stoic image of light thus is influenced more by Christian Aristotelian discussions of the natural light of the intellect. The light of natural law shining in humanity is, in Charron's words, "the law and light which God has put within us from our origin."[44]

The verbal use of the image of light may also indicate a Stoic belief that God is in the soul, enlightening it with wisdom. In reference to the highest part of the human mind, Charron says, "I do not object to calling it [*l'esprit*] an image of the living God, a particle of the immortal substance, an emanation of divinity, a heavenly light to which God has given reason."[45] If this sentence is interpreted literally, Charron falls heir to the error of Meister Eckhart in suggesting that the soul is partly uncreated, therefore preexistent.[46] He also seems to imply that God is partly material. However, after discussing the human being as a tree rooted in the Divine, he concludes: "These are all plausible words with which the schools and pulpits resound."[47] Thus, it is unclear whether Charron is proposing that the human mind emanates from God rather than having been created by him or whether he is just using the emanation vocabulary figuratively, as did many Christian writers in order to suggest the affinity of humanity to God.

The following long passage exemplifies Charron's eclectic merger of Stoic and Christian expressions for the doctrine of natural law:

> I say that it is this equity and universal reason which shines and lights in each of us; whoever acts according to it, acts truly according to God, for it is God, or else his first, fundamental and universal law, which has put it into the world and from which it was first to originate; for God and nature are to the world

what to a state are its king, author, and founder and the fundamental law which he has made for the conservation and rule of that state. It is a spark and ray of divinity, and emanation and dependence of the eternal law which is God himself and his will: "what is nature if not God and the divine reason inserted in the entire world and in each of its parts?"[48]

In this passage the pantheistic statement that nature is God appears twice— once in a quotation from Seneca and once in Charron's own words. However, like the words in Gratian's *Decretum*, "natura, id est deus," Charron's words may have been intended to indicate that God is the ultimate source of natural law.[49] For he does qualify his statement that nature is God with a reference to the Christianized Stoic concept of God as the author, founder, and ruler of a world state, for which there are plentiful examples in Jean Bodin. For the ruling of the universe God has the eternal law. Natural law, which is a part of the eternal law, originated in God and thus may figuratively be said to be God. However, perhaps Charron is literally saying that nature is God: the emanationist vocabulary implies that the law literally comes out of God. Charron's concept of natural law within at times comes very close to the authentic Stoic idea that the presence of a part of God in humans allows them to know natural law.

Again combining ancient with Christian concepts, Charron goes on to state that this law is constant, not changing with place or time. The law of Moses and the Decalogue are external copies of it, as are the law of the Twelve Tables, Roman law, the moral teachings of theologians and philosophers, the advice of jurisconsults, and the edicts of sovereigns. Any law that goes against natural law is not authentic.[50] Charron indiscriminately combines two traditions: the canon lawyers' tradition of viewing revelation as a copy of natural law and the tradition inherited from the Roman lawyers of viewing positive law as a copy of natural law.[51] As in most medieval Christian writings, the qualification that only an exact copy of natural law is a true law is not applied in practice: Charron stresses that the sage should obey and observe the laws, customs, and ceremonies of his own country, even when he internally recognizes that they go against natural law.[52]

It is significant that in stating that the law of Moses was a copy of natural law Charron does not give the common medieval explanation for why God gave us an external copy of the internal natural law. He does not mention original sin in this context or in his description of God's creation of humanity.[53] Furthermore, he does not suggest that we should look to revealed law as more fully and purely expressed natural law. Not clarifying whether he is including revealed law in his statement, Charron says that all laws are merely copies of natural law disguising, hiding, and distorting the authentic natural law.[54] He asks us, "Why do you seek elsewhere for the law or rule of the world? What can one say or propound to you that you would not find inside yourself if you were willing to probe and listen?"[55] Charron thus briefly discards the claim made by political and religious institutions that in our present condition we need their guidance to find natural law. Viewing these external sources as an encumbrance to the development of true internal integrity, Charron recommends that we begin by looking within ourselves.

However, like the ancient Stoics, Charron recognizes that social conditions and bad upbringing have caused a "general and universal alteration and corruption" of human nature.[56] There is no longer common consent to the law of nature, for people hold highly divergent ethical principles. We have allowed our seeds of virtue to lie dormant and our light of divinity to be covered over by corruption. Like the ancients, Charron recommends as a solution to the general decay of humanity the study and practice of philosophy.[57] Since we are no longer in the natural state, the instructions found in *De la sagesse* are necessary to point out to us how to find and develop the natural law lying dormant within ourselves.

The major reason for my contention that Charron's concept of the internal natural law is Stoic is his restoration of the Stoic and Christianized Stoic images of natural law to an authentic ancient context. Despite disagreement on whether the cardinal virtues could be attained without God's help, there is general Christian agreement that the infused theological virtues are a necessary preliminary for attaining the true moral virtue meritorious of salvation.[58] As stated by St. Thomas Aquinas, "It is possible by means of human works to acquire the moral virtues. . . . But in so far as they produce good works in relation to a supernatural last end, thus they have the character of virtue truly and perfectly and cannot be acquired by human acts, but are infused by God. Such moral virtues cannot be without charity."[59] Whereas in Aquinas's view all persons could be truly virtuous only by directing their actions to meriting salvation, in Charron's view they could be truly virtuous only by directing their actions toward achieving the natural end, virtue.

In satire, Charron writes, "They want one to be a good person, because there is a paradise and a hell. . . . You guard yourself from being evil, for you do not dare, and fear to be beaten; and already in that you are evil."[60] Deleted from the second edition was the statement, "You become a good person so that one pays you, and that one gives you great thanks."[61] Charron is reviving an authentically "classical" or "pagan" theory of morality: "I would like you to be a good person, even though you were never to go to paradise, but because nature, reason, that is to say God, wishes it, because the law and the general order of the world, of which you are a part, requires it so; and you can consent to be other only by going against yourself, your being, your end."[62] For Charron, as for the ancient Stoic Chrysippus, virtue means bringing one's life into harmony with the nature of the universe and thus fulfilling one's human nature. For Charron, as for Pomponazzi, reason argues cogently that virtue is its own reward.[63]

Charron thus distinguishes moral from religious motivation. Probity, *preud'hommie*, and conscience go together, as do piety, religion, and devotion. He advises those seeking to be wise to distinguish between probity and piety; the wise have both, but independently of each other. Charron does not want a person to do without either. He criticizes those who are religious without being virtuous, as well as those who are virtuous while being nonbelievers. Significantly, he accepts the latter phenomenon as a possibility and gives his harshest criticism to the religious extremist who self-righteously commits sins and crimes in the name of a fanatical faith. Not explicitly saying which extremes he thinks are worse, Charron says that religion without virtue is easy and common, whereas virtue without religion is difficult and very rare. Such virtuous individuals are "powerful and generous souls."[64]

Charron's perspective on morality is nothing less than a culmination of the Renaissance tradition of viewing the ancient Greeks and Romans as "paragons of human excellence."[65] While earlier generations of historians of the Renaissance attributed to the fourteenth- and fifteenth-century Italian humanists the accomplishment of erecting a secular ideal of virtue alongside the Christian ideal, the dominant trend of current scholarship is to view even the Italian humanists as "Christian humanists."[66] If we consider the essential belief of the ancient pagan philosophers that the wise have within themselves both the means and the goal of the good life, then indeed there are in the Renaissance few among Christians who are non-Christian humanists. Petrarch sets the keynote:

> But we, to whom the light of truth more vividly appeared, not by our own merit but by the celestial gift, where they stop we begin, for we strive not toward virtue as an end but toward God through virtue. . . . Thus when the illustrious pagan philosophers refer everything to virtue, the Christian philosopher refers virtue itself to the author of virtue, God, and by using virtue enjoys God, nor even stops with his mind before he has reached him.[67]

Charron, however, in his belief that God has provided us at birth with the means to achieve the good life and in his belief that the human virtue of pagans would be lessened by initially directing it to a divine end, keeps his Christianity in a separate compartment from his ethics and declares an ecumenical foundation for morality.

The 1601 edition of *De la sagesse* is under attack from the moment of its publication, and the 1604 edition is condemned by the Sorbonne and the Congregation of the Index. One study has tried to explain this condemnation as a product of factional politics.[68] While that may well be, it is also of great interest to know the intellectual reasons for the condemnation. We can gain some insight into the reasons for this attack from Charron's attempt in the "Petit traicté de sagesse" to answer complaints leveled against his book. These are: endangering religious belief by advising readers to judge all things; causing Pyrrhonian incertitude by admonishing readers to free themselves from dogmatic attachments; proclaiming to teach *preud'hommie* independently of thought of reward or punishment;

and stressing the sufficiency of natural law to the neglect of grace. Charron answers these complaints not by changing his views but by justifying what he has done and claiming that he has not intended these irreligious implications.[69] To appease his critics, he also makes omissions, modifications, and additions to the second edition of *De la sagesse*.[70] However, one is struck by how small the changes are in the sensitive area of the role of grace. Whereas in the first edition grace is not discussed at length, the discussion of it in the second edition clarifies even further the small role he attributes to it in the development of virtuous human behavior.

Charron's restriction of his Christianity to *Les trois veritez* and his other religious writings and his restriction of his ethics to *De la sagesse* is a compromise with precedent in Guillaume du Vair. Nevertheless, as the church fathers knew, the tension between Christianity and ancient thought is inescapable. A work more influential in the seventeenth century than Montaigne's *Essais, De la sagesse* antagonizes some who view themselves as "religious," that is, individuals who believe that one's relationship with the Divine must affect one's entire life; and it appeals to generations of secularists, individuals who focus on their human lives in society.

For in the end, by stressing the independence of religion and morality, Charron makes religion subordinate to virtue. He rejects the basic religious perspective that "religion is a generality of all good and of all virtue, that all virtues are comprised in it." Instead he claims that "it is in the reverse, because religion, which is posterior, is a special and particular virtue, distinct from all other virtues."[71] Justice, which requires giving to each his due, teaches obedience, service, and worship of God. True piety, as a particular part of justice, is a crowning achievement of *preud'hommie*. In Charron's view, there is a law that God put within us at Creation. This law, which is the source of human virtue, is thus anterior to religion.[72]

One of Charron's most blatant statements that *preud'hommie* precedes religion comes from the first edition of *De la sagesse*: "Religion is posterior to *preud'hommie*; it is also a thing learned, which needs to be heard, received by 'faith from the hearing and through the word of God,' by revelation and instruction, and thus cannot cause it. It is rather *preud'hommie* which ought to cause and engender religion; for it comes first, it is more ancient and natural."[73]

The idea expressed in this passage is repeated in more disguised form in the second edition; what is left out, though, is the unorthodox statement that religion cannot cause *preud'hommie*. In both editions, however, Charron expresses his view that virtue normally precedes religion: God created the human species with an internal source for morality; through this internal source for the four cardinal virtues, individuals learn their first concept of their obligations to God; through the external source of God's revelation, they acquire and extend their religious faith. As implied by Bodin's phrase *seeds of piety*, for Charron worship of God is part and parcel of the main purpose of leading a virtuous life.

Charron contrasts the internal source of *preud'hommie* with the external source of religion: *preud'hommie* is "au dedans," from within, while religion is "au dehors," from without. Divine wisdom is attained in part by speculation on first principles but mainly through the infused gifts of the Holy Spirit, whereas human wisdom is attained by acquisition of the principles of moral and natural philosophy and by developing one's natural gifts given by God to humankind at Creation.[74] Criticized for not discussing infusion and grace, Charron in his second edition explains his view of the relationship between nature and grace. Significantly, he still does not make the statement of the Council of Trent that infused virtue or grace precedes the acquisition of true moral virtue; instead he states that grace comes after *preud'hommie*, perfecting it and making it worthy of salvation:

> After all that I have said, there remains yet one thing to render the work complete and perfect, that is the grace of God through which such *preud'hommie*, goodness, virtue, is brought to life and vivified, animated, and receives its last visual trait, is raised up, Christianized, crowned, that is to say accepted, verified, confirmed by God, rendered meritorious and worthy of eternal reward.[75]

Charron goes on to state that without this last culminating act of grace an action still can be naturally, morally, and humanly good in itself. Thus the great philosophers and men of ancient times—Socrates, Cato, Scipio—had natural virtue, even though they did not have meritorious virtue. He clearly states here that *preud'hommie* can exist without grace:

> These also are *preud'hommie* and grace, the action naturally, morally, humanly good in itself [and] the meritorious action. The former can indeed exist without the latter, it has its value as can be seen in those philosophers and great men of antiquity, certainly admirable in nature and in every sort of moral virtue, but who nevertheless are counted among the unbelievers, but the latter cannot exist without the former.[76]

The last unorthodox statement, that grace cannot exist without virtue, Charron himself contradicts in passages where he admits that grace is a pure gift of God given to anyone who requests it. Without making too much of Charron's ambiguity on the issue of whether grace would engender *preud'hommie*, I think it is clear that Charron views such an order as an exception, not the general rule. A major cause for this new orientation is his belief that attaining salvation should not be the conscious reason that a person is virtuous. Charron's general view is that the fulfillment of one's natural end is a necessity for fulfillment of one's supernatural end; therefore, the best way to prepare for grace is to be a *preud'homme*.

In Charron's view, *preud'hommie* precedes and predisposes one for grace: "Human wisdom is a way to the divine, the law of nature to grace, moral and philosophical virtue to theological, human duty to divine favor and liberality."[77] He gives the examples of Abraham, Job, and the father of Saint Gregory, who as pagans and nonbelievers followed the natural law and thus as a "recompense for their moral virtues" were called to the faith.[78] The prayer Charron suggests for gaining grace is significant:

> O God! Deign by your immense goodness to look at me with a merciful eye, accept and receive my desire, my attempt, my small work, which originally comes from you, by the obligation and instruction that you have given me in the law of nature, which you have planted in me, in order that it return to you, and that you finish what you have begun, so that you may be my *A* and my *Ω*.[79]

The supplicant recognizes God's gift at Creation of natural law, which in Ciceronian terms is described as "implanted," and asks for the grace necessary for the soul to return to its Creator. As Charron states in the "Petit traicté," his book is not about actions meritorious but about actions naturally good. Unlike *preud'hommie*, which requires much long study and labor, grace "is a pure gift of God, which it is necessary to desire and request humbly and ardently, and to prepare for as much as one can by moral virtue and by obedience to natural law which I teach here."[80]

Pierre Charron's *De la sagesse* is a humanist treatise that attempts to motivate and guide individuals to cultivate their potential for developing integrity. The root for such *preud'hommie* is not grace or religion but nature. While Charron's phraseology reveals his eclectic borrowing from a variety of sources for his belief that natural law is within us, the phraseology and the context of his concept of seeds of virtue and knowledge are essentially Stoic. He is clearly greatly indebted to the neo-Stoic revival—to Du Vair, Lipsius, Bodin, Montaigne, and others—for arguing for an ancient reading of the ancient moral texts.[81] For Charron, as for the ancient Stoics, natural law is the basis for human self-sufficiency in achieving the good life. Like the cube of justice upon which Wisdom stands tall on the title page of *De la sagesse*, equity and universal reason constitute the foundation stone for an autonomous ethic. A society of such exemplary virtuous individuals would be crowned with the laurel branch of honor and the olive branch of peace.

SEEDS OF VIRTUE and knowledge—epistemology, strategy, paradigm, intertext, metaphor, language—continues into the seventeenth and eighteenth centuries. Two equivalent concepts—reason and light—in fact have traditionally given the period its name—the Age of Reason or Age of Enlightenment. Given the abundant evidence in the seventeenth and eighteenth centuries of the phrases we have been tracing,[1] we shall not be too surprised to find that the 1758–60 engravings of Cesare Ripa's *Iconologia* (first published with illustrations in 1603), as well as other visual images, support some of my key points.[2]

Ripa's engraved "Instruction" reveals the continuing respect for the founder of the ancient Greek Stoic school, Zeno, shown wearing a crown of laurel.[3] The Latin phrase *semina virtutis* (seeds of virtue) originates in ancient Stoicism, where it is a systematic component of the Stoic epistemology of natural law within humanity. In ancient Stoicism human nature is intimately linked to God and to the divine law of nature through the divine substance of the human soul. Human nature thus has direct access to the precepts of moral behavior. The Stoics have four major ways of expressing the relationship between humanity and the Divine. Law exists in nature as *logos*, *nous*, or *ratio*; humans come to know this law through their reasoning capacities, for right reason is the law of nature. Human reason is directed in its development by the *koinai ennoiai*, or common notions, which provide the potential to attain certain knowledge of the general notions of God, goodness, justice, and beauty. A more figurative expression of the relationship between God and humanity is the gendered belief that God as *logos spermatikos* inseminated the human species with *spermata*, seeds of knowledge and virtue, which direct human development in growth toward the trunk, branches, and treetop of human wisdom. The relationship appears also as God as *pyr*, fire, leaving within humans *igniculi*, sparks of divinity.[4]

The Stoics intermingle these four images, using each to give support to the truth of the others. At birth humans have the faculty to reason, the ability to form common notions, the seeds of knowledge, and the spark of divinity. This gift gives humans not the full-blown knowledge of natural law but the potential to attain it. The Stoic synthesis of the doctrine of natural law carries the conviction that natural law is knowable by those who develop their God-given faculties. Through the writings of Seneca, Cicero, and Philo in particular the ancient Stoic epistemology influences European thought in the Middle Ages and the Renaissance. The Stoic phrases appear in the writings of a number of thinkers, some of whom hold basic disagreements on epistemology, ethics, and assessment of humanity.

My visual symbol for the Christianization of the Stoic image of a seed of virtue is the papal placement of the ancient bronze pinecone in St. Peter's (fig. 2.1). My visual symbol for the appropriation by Rome and then by Christianity of Jewish culture is the candelabra, the biblical almond tree of light, on the Arch of Titus (fig. 2.3). In Philo's Hellenization of Jewish thought the Mosaic Decalogue is seen as an expression of natural law. In the Christianization of the Stoic images the Pauline *law written in the heart* becomes identified with Stoic natural law, and the *spark of divinity* is transformed by St. Jerome into the *spark of conscience*. The *seeds* and *sparks* by which the Stoics explained the self-sufficient ability to achieve goodness become diminutive expressions for the Christian belief that despite the Fall humanity still retains some remnant of natural goodness. The Christianized Stoic phrases enter into a variety of medieval theological, philosophical, legal, and literary works and become commonplaces of medieval thought. The Christian concept of *participation* or *illumination* emphasizes the divine—rather than the natural—light of the intellect through human participation in Christ. Ripa's *The Deity* shows Augustine attempting to explore the divine mystery, which is portrayed by the symbolism of light.[5]

It becomes traditional for Augustine and Thomas Aquinas to provide two poles of thought around which other authors cluster. Differences between Augustine's and Thomas Aquinas's formulations of Stoic light and seed imagery are consistently based on differences of epistemology. Both agree that the participation of the rational creature in the eternal law is natural law, but they disagree on the method of this participation. In Augustine's view, humans participate in the Logos, Christ, who is the interior master of the soul; in the Thomist view, the practical intellect, *synderesis*, has as its end knowledge of natural law. Augustine emphasizes that God imprints common notions on the soul during illumination; Thomas Aquinas emphasizes that God imprinted common notions on human reason at Creation, notions that develop through abstraction of sense data. According to Augustine, humans contemplate the eternal reasons, the immutable rules of goodness, in God; according to Thomas Aquinas, humans develop the seeds of virtue in their souls by exercising their natural faculties. Augustine stresses that knowledge of morality is attained through the divine light illuminating the intellect with lights of virtue; Thomas Aquinas stresses that we may attain a limited knowledge of morality through the development of the natural light of reason. In terms of the development of human wisdom, Augustine recognizes only a divine path, whereas Thomas Aquinas recognizes a natural path as well.[6]

The medieval period, during which literacy declines, is a time for the popularization of ideas through images. A very important idea common to Jewish and Christian authors is that the soul is divinely implanted by God after the conception of a human embryo. This idea takes on visual expression in a miniature designed in accord with Hildegard of Bingen's *Scivias* in which a treelike umbilical cord reaches down from heaven; the descending soul is portrayed as containing numerous circular and eyelike formations (fig. 2.4). The divided up soul stuff Hildegard calls "fireballs," gifts from God that allow the full human being to develop.

Seeing with the mind's eye is basic to the medieval conceptualization of what it is to know. Images emerge that are in harmony with worldwide evidence of visual vegetative symbolism as well as with specific biblical, classical, and Christian symbols. The Hebrew Bible abounds in trees, as in the literal reward of the fruit trees of ancient Palestine and the appearance of the Divine to Moses in a burning bush. Trees represent human strivings, as in the Psalmist's analogy of a righteous person to a flourishing tree and the Genesis narrative of the first human couple gaining knowledge of good and evil from eating of the tree of knowledge of good and evil.

The tree painted above the Torah Shrine of Dura Synagogue (fig. 3.1) emphasizes the mainstream Jewish view of the Torah as the tree of life, a path to righteousness,[7] as well as Philo's fully worked out allegorical reading of Genesis. The tree both corresponds to the macrocosmic tree of the divine gardener of the universe, and to the vegetative growths within each human soul striving upward. From Plato's *Timaeus* medieval readers learned that humanity itself is an upside-down tree rooted in heaven. The upside-down trees of the divine names aid the Kabbalist to ascend to the Divine, and they continue to fascinate Christian authors in the seventeenth century. The *sefirot* of the English physician Robert Fludd is an upside-down palm tree whose branches reach out to the mystic seeking ascent (fig. E.1).[8] Reflecting the alchemical movement's interest in male and female principles, this tree is a palm, the one tree to which ancient texts attribute sexuality.[9]

The tree of knowledge of good and evil becomes graphically illustrative of Christian dichotomies among the virtues and vices, and the tree design recurs for other areas of knowledge. The abundance that we can merely guess at in Hildegard's visualization of the descending soul becomes clearly delineated in twelfth-century labeling of the leaves of the virtues and the leaves of the vices (fig. 3.5). Raymond Lull expands upon that device in his numerous trees of virtues and vices as well as in his innovations concerning trees of the sciences and medicine.

Printed books of Lull and his followers spread awareness of arboreal graphics to such seventeenth-century writers as Athanasius Kircher;[10] the continuation of trees in books of medicine is evident in Lange's *Medina mentis* (1708).[11] A tree containing emblems of fourteen disciplines bound together in a chain of knowledge appears in the 1654 engraved title page of Athanasius Kircher's *Magnes sive De arte magnetica* (The magnet or the magnetic art) (fig. E.2).[12] The chains, indicating the magnetic attraction or bonding power that is the theme of the book, clockwise link the emblems of philosophy, physics, poetry, rhetoric, cosmography, mechanics,

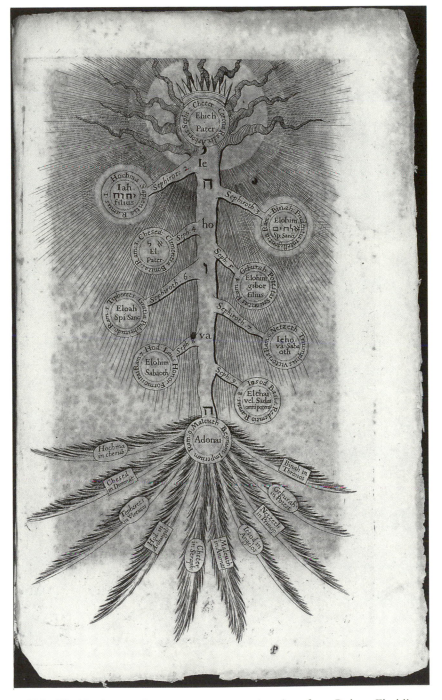

E.1. Upside-down palm tree as macrocosmic *sefirot*, from Robert Fludd's
Utriusque cosmi maioris scilicet . . ., Frankfort, 1621.

E.2. Engraving of tree with emblems of disciplines linked in a chain, first of two title pages from Athanasius Kircher's *Magnes sive De arte magnetica*, Rome, 1654.

perspective, astronomy, music, geography, arithmetic, natural magic, medicine, and theology. The symbol for natural magic is a flower blooming under the natural sunlight, and the central tree stands within a forest of knowledge. Throughout this scientific text sections begin with an initial floral capital and conclude with vegetative decor.

Personifications of the Muses, like trees of knowledge with branches, serve to systematize knowledge into disciplines.[13] A visualization of the circle of Apollo and the Muses under a laurel tree suggests the growth of many branches of culture under Medici patronage (fig. 4.2). Ficino's commentary on Plato's *Symposium* employs much garden imagery to teach the path to love and to education. His teaching becomes popularized within literature on love between men and women, as well as in treatises on education. Education in the new sciences adopts dialogues in the garden environment; the frontispiece of the seventeenth-century *Conversations on the Plurality of the Worlds* shows female student and male teacher conversing in a lushly growing garden under the enlightenment of the bright sunlight.[14]

The use of seed and light imagery in Ficino's *De amore* and *Theologia platonica* gives renewed emphasis to the potencies of the human soul to contemplate the ideas in the divine mind and reduces the Aristotelian emphasis on the senses as paths to knowledge. An underlying unity within all seven speeches of the *De amore* derives from the following Plotinian hierarchy of Ficino. From God come the ideas in mind; from the ideas in mind come reasons in the soul; from the reasons in the soul come the seeds in nature giving the power of procreation; and from seeds in nature come the forms in matter.

The concepts of rays of divinity and seeds of virtue, which in the Stoic worldview are identical, in Plotinus and in the Florentine neo-Platonic outlook appear as levels in a spherical universe. Ficino's epistemology of light and seed has immediate impact on Pico, Leone Ebreo, Bembo, Castiglione, and Sadoleto. The French translations of Ficino and of Leone are good examples of the entrance of neo-Platonic imagery of seeds and sparks into the discourse of the French Renaissance.

Recognition that the image and epistemology of seeds of virtue and knowledge evoke one of the most powerful metaphors from the fourteenth to the sixteenth centuries—the birth and growth metaphor—by which humanists declare a "rinascità" (rebirth) of arts and letters, helps us to realize that seeds of virtues are aided in growth by florilegia, commonplace books containing flowers of wisdom, and through contemplation of gardens (real, painted, and imagined), in which, as in the human soul, flowers and trees of virtue can bloom. Botticelli's *Primavera*, often interpreted today as a symbol for the Renaissance, takes on added meaning when one considers Chloris's vegetative florescence (see the frontispiece to this volume) and Flora's disseminating flowers of knowledge and virtue to the viewer who seeks to rise through contemplation to enlightenment (fig. 5.2).

Attention today extends to the aesthetics of gardens in literary as well as visual settings.[15] Further research might explicate how the language of flowers permeates the language of virtues and of gender in the Middle Ages and the Renaissance, as we have seen in explicating Botticelli's and Boccaccio's renditions of Flora. The flower and herb imagery in Shakespeare, especially in *As You Like It* and *Romeo and Juliet* and in Ophelia's last speech in *Hamlet*, might be related to the tree imagery, as in the forest of soldiers that overthrow Macbeth and the resolution under an oak tree in *Merry Wives of Windsor*.[16] The cluster of Shakespeare's vegetative imagery shares in the larger cultural significance we have exposed of the language of vegetative growth to virtue and knowledge.[17]

Nevertheless, the language of flowers in the eighteenth and nineteenth centuries has been epitomized by the art of disguising expressions of love in floral valentines, as in Lady Mary Wortley Montagu (1690–1762), or in the nineteenth-century lapbook *The Language and Poetry of Flowers*.[18] Guidebooks to the flowers of Shakespeare and of the Bible are plentiful, and that tradition is one of the reasons, I think, for the relative lack of art historical interest in encyclopedias of Renaissance floral symbolism; those horizontal studies are a step toward exploring the more significant topic of the vertical transformations in the language of vegetative growth. Anthropological inquiry has begun on the history of cross-cultural influences among Islamic, Asian, European, and American cultures in flower cultivation, floral design, gardening, plant symbolism, and flower rituals.[19]

A very lively dialect of the language of flowers is the rationalist, feminist version initiated by Christine de Pizan, who comments on the misogyny of the *Roman de la Rose*: "Would to God this rose had never been planted in the garden of Christianity!"[20] The history of rationalism has not often been associated with the topic of vegetative symbolism; nevertheless, we have seen Italian women humanists founding their right to reason upon the inborn seeds of virtue and knowledge.[21] Within a distinctly women's culture, as well as in the broader culture as a whole, the rational tradition continues to build upon the distinctly Stoic language of flowers, as in Mary Collyer's (d. 1763) book of letters to a friend, as the subtitle declares, "tending to prove that the seeds of virtue are implanted in the mind of every reasonable being."[22]

A Ripa engraved page entitled "On the Distinction of Good and Evil" epitomizes the tradition of vegetative symbolism for *recta ratio*, "right reason," making judgments between right and wrong and good and evil (fig. E.3). It shows a mature woman sifting and separating bad seeds from good and removing useless weeds from healthful plants.[23] The female figure—the sifter—personifies right reason! There is no better illustration of Montaigne's direct mention of developing the student's and the reader's judgment, or more precisely, the "sieve" by which one's judgment distinguishes good from evil. Yet the engraving draws its imagery from the well-

DISTINCTIO BONI ET MALI.

Diuitis uber agri fruges cum foenore reddit,
Frugibus et careunt femina fparfa mala.

49.

Unterfcheidung deß Guten vom böfen.
Auf gute Saat folgt gleiche Frucht,
der Feind des Unkrauts Wachsthum fucht.

Eichler del.

J. Wachsmuth Sculps.

Hertel excud.

E.3. Sifting for seeds of virtue, Cesare Ripa's "Distinctio boni et mali" (The distinction between good and evil), engraving from Johan Georg Hertel's *Sindbildern und Gedancken*, Augsburg, 1758–69.

known biblical accounts of gardening in Palestine wherein a sieve is mentioned for sifting wheat seeds.[24]

Not surprisingly given the difference in their size, much more common than the visualization of seeds is the visualization of trees. In particular, the tree of the righteous of Hebrew Psalm 1 contrasts with the tree imagery in Matthew, wherein those who do not follow Jesus are viewed as bad trees to be cut down. Under the influence of the Protestant Reformation, the cutting down of the bad trees, those that bear no fruit, appears vividly in painting, Bible illustration, and emblem.[25]

Since the Stoic educational theory of seeds of virtue and knowledge and the Psalmist's tree of the righteous both predate the development of the Christian doctrine of original sin, it is important to explore the impact of those vivid ancient images in the conspicuous emergence in the Renaissance of outspoken proclamations of human dignity. When one considers the dialogue on the depravity and dignity of human nature from the late twelfth through the late sixteenth century, indeed one finds a debate about seeds and trees that reveals a tension between dependence on divine illumination or grace as a preliminary to human dignity and independence based on divinely created gifts in human nature that may be cultivated through the techniques of education.

The humanist curriculum encourages digesting exemplary fruits of virtue and knowledge to advance the growth of one's own seeds of virtue and knowledge; this approach reaches a crescendo in neo-Platonists Ficino and Pico della Mirandola, who believe not only that one can become educated through human art but also, like some medieval mystics and Kabbalists, that one might thus reach up to heaven. The hint of a human path to divine wisdom stirs strong responses. It is particularly ironic that Cardinal Sadoleto, who takes neo-Platonism to an extreme, is the man who writes the letter to the Genevans to which Calvin responds. Calvin's response, similar to Marguerite de Navarre's *Mirror of the Sinful Soul*, expresses serious concerns about brambles the human plant might produce in the absence of God's watering through grace (see fig. 6.4).

An examination of Luther's concept of *synderesis* in his formative Pauline lectures and of Calvin's departure from the Senecan commentaries indicates that the founders of the Protestant Reformation turn away from the Stoicizing, neo-Platonic, and Thomist trends to accentuate the Augustinian view of the tiny spark that reminds children of Cain that they are sinners. The much-publicized dialogue between Luther and Erasmus on free will transforms the Erasmian phrase *seeds of virtue* into a formulaic sign for Catholic confidence that humans may aid the process toward salvation. Nevertheless, the Protestant Reformation proliferates the establishment of the Erasmian curriculum in schools in Lutheran and Calvinist lands; the contrast between Luther and Erasmus and and between Calvin and Sadoleto regarding seeds of virtue and trees of virtue is greater on the subject of justification before God than on the subject of good works for the conduct of one's life and for the benefit of society. The pedagogy of planting seeds of wisdom through commonplace books influences humanist education in Protestant as well as Catholic schools.

For example, in colonial New England the debate between evangelical and moderate Calvinists concerns Quintilian's model of the tutor implanting seeds of virtue in a student. While evangelicals, believing in infant depravity, try to uproot seeds of vice, moderates try to prevent the tutor from implanting seeds of vice. The evangelical Anne Bradstreet (1612–72) advises: "But when by prudent nurture they are brought into a fit capacity, let the seed of good instruction and exhortation be sown in the spring of their youth, and a plentiful crop may be expected in the harvest of their yeares." Bradstreet views the seed as coming from outside, whether through parental moral instruction or from infused grace of God. She concedes that some children do not need the rod: they are "like tender fruits that are best preserved by sugar." An important source for the moderate Calvinist position is John Locke (1632–1704), raised in a Puritan family. In *Some Thoughts concerning Education* (1693) Locke expresses the Erasmian concern that parents should not indulge their infants. He advises parents who have been too indulgent of their children's whims "to get out those Weeds which their own hands have planted, and which now have taken too deep root to be easily extirpated." He is concerned for "seeds of vice," such as threats with violence, that parents mistakenly plant in impressionable children. Overall he attributes bad growths to nurture rather than to nature.[26]

The analogy of a student to a plant is basic to Abigail Adams's correspondence with Mercy Otis Warren in the 1770s: after visiting the Warren home and admiring the "happy fruits" in her well-ordered household, she writes her "to communicate to me the happy Art of 'rearing the tender thought, teaching the young Idea how to shoot . . .' that the tender twigs alloted to my care, may be so cultivated as to do honour to their parents and prove blessing[s] to the riseing generation." Warren responds to Adams that she herself is seeking aid for "the mighty task of cultivating the minds and planting the seeds of Virtue in the infant Bosom." In concern for their son John Quincy, Abigail writes her husband John Adams: "Every virtuous example has powerfull impressions in early youth. Many years of vice and vicious examples do not erase from the mind seeds sown in early life. They take a deep root, and tho often crop'd will spring again."[27] Supplementing the comparison of a child to a plant is the belief that external seeds of instruction and morality are best rooted during infancy and early childhood. Quintilian's recommendations thus are transplanted to Protestant English colonies and to two presidents of the United States.

Previous to the mid-sixteenth century and the Council of Trent, in some optimistic Catholic circles scholars attribute to inborn seeds of virtue and knowledge a role leading to a salvation about which Stoics never dreamed. Responding to the evangelical inquiry into nature and grace, the Council of Trent does not give to seeds of virtue and knowledge the role in preparing for salvation that we find in Erasmus or the even greater role we find in Cardinal Sadoleto. In the second half of the sixteenth century most Catholic writers, as well as Protestant writers, do not write about the possibility of salvation for non-Christians or even for those who are not members of their own brand of Christianity. Bodin's unpublished manuscript of *Colloquium heptaplomeres* spreads ecumenical thinking to some European intellectuals, and the subject of salvation outside one's church revives in La Mothe le Vayer's *De la vertu des païens* (On the virtue of pagans) of 1642. In the 1960s the Second Vatican Council reconsiders the issues, and its ecumenical conclusions renew the relevance of the French Renaissance Catholics Du Vair, Montaigne, Bodin, and Charron, who assume that the sparks of conscience reflect the natural moral law.[28]

In the Erasmian tradition of the sixteenth century the natural cultivation of inborn seeds of virtue into trees of virtue continues to be very important, and emblem books visually display a variety of tree imagery. Alciati's first printed emblem collection, of 1531, starts a vogue that enhances the tradition of florilegia by adding pictures and poems to commonplaces. The commonplaces and poems accompanying the illustrations create emblems that are instructional devices for arousing right reason and virtuous conduct in the reader-viewer. The medieval trees of virtue and vice merge with the anthropomorphic personifications of virtues and vices to create arboreal personifications, individual trees personifying specific virtues and vices. I wonder what Theophrastus would think of this merger of his book on characters with his books on plants. Alciati's collection does not contain emblems that give credit for the blooming to divine intervention, as in "Florebit rigante Deo" (fig. 6.4). Natural light and human potency appear to be the sources for growth of the personified mulberry, who is not dumb, as some believe, but merely a slow bloomer (fig. 7.3), and of the almond, who is precocious and never fully matures (fig. 7.2). Alciati's ethical concerns are evident in other collections of emblems as well; thus whether nobility is a product of birth or of merit is a common theme, as is the theme that virtue is difficult but fruitful. Alciati's enjoyment of natural vegetative growth as a symbol for human capacity is also characteristic of Guillaume de la Perrière, in emblems and especially in the abundant vegetative teaching devices of *The Mirrour of Policie*.

Whereas Cicero, Seneca, and Quintilian are influential on medieval humanism, Stoic texts especially influence the Italian Renaissance in the years before the Reformation controversies and wars, and their publication reaches a crescendo in the Northern Renaissance of the late sixteenth and early seventeenth centuries. Renaissance humanists read the Stoic texts in full and support Stoic imagery with the pre-Stoic texts of Aristotle, Plato, and the Hebrew Bible and with the Stoicizing texts of Quintilian, Philo, Paul, and the church fathers. Exemplary of this trend is *La philosophie morale des Stoïques* of Guillaume du Vair, which follows his French translation of the Stoic Epictetus. Using Stoic and neo-Platonic phraseology, his second paragraph asserts that "nature has sowed and scattered here below some weak sparks, which notwithstanding being rightly applied in our minds, are able to kindle a pure light in them and cause us to see good as it is." In Stoic fashion, he values both reason and will: "Nature has placed a storehouse in our mind: let us stretch the hand of our will, and we shall take as much as we will." Yet, as a Christian who recognizes natural infirmities, he stops short after expounding Stoic principles to conclude with a Christian prayer to restore the good that we continually waste, for "our forces would not be sufficient of themselves to keep us in this perfection."[29]

Du Vair is typical of the ambiguity of neo-Stoic attempts to combine Christianity with Stoicism, and the title *La philosophie morale des Stoïques*, with its attempt to limit Stoicism to ethics, is an appropriate symbol of the French neo-Stoic movement. *La philosophie morale des Stoïques* contains his ethical teachings, and *La sainte philosophie* contains his religious teachings; likewise, Charron's *De la sagesse* contains his ethical teachings, and *Les trois veritez* contains his religious teachings. Montaigne refrains from writing a book on his religious thought. Building upon precedents in classical, scholastic, and humanist exploration of moral and political philosophy, these late-sixteenth-century French writers explore new genres in which ethics for humanity, based on universal natural law, may be treated as a separate field from Christian theology.

Lipsius, the most internationally prominent neo-Stoic, comes to understand the materialism and pantheism underlying Greek Stoicism and exposes ancient systematic Stoicism in 1604. His earlier works, such as *De constantia*, of 1584, available to Bodin, Montaigne, and Charron and available in English in 1594, combine Christianity and Stoicism in a new synthesis that influences the fine arts as well as philosophy. Rubens's *The Four Philosophers*, portraying Lipsius and friends below a Stoic bust, is among many seventeenth-century paintings, heroic busts, and engraved title pages that encourage the vogue of Stoicism.[30] Lipsius's description of refreshing his mind in a friend's garden, inspired by the many philosophers and poets whose creativity was aided by walks in gardens, encourages an English vogue for philosophical garden poems.[31] The techniques of engraving allow the emergence of numerous highly detailed trees of knowledge, such as *The Laurus metaphysica* (1622), whose top reaches to God and whose roots are the three subdivisions of the ancient Stoics: physics, ethics, and logic.[32] Léonard Gaultier is the designer of this tree of wisdom, as well as of the wreathed Wisdom in *De la sagesse*.

The authorities who have trusted in seeds of virtue and knowledge become particularly important in the sixteenth century because the splitting up of church authority and the discovery of peoples of diverse moral beliefs and customs raise a question with religious, political, and social implications: Is there a sure and universal foundation for morality? This profound and practical question leads French authors living during the crises of the French Religious Wars, such as Bodin, Montaigne, Du Vair, and Charron, to seek a source for morality that is natural to humanity. On one hand, Justus Lipsius, the most internationally influential neo-Stoic, finds support of human dignity in ancient Stoicism, as he wavers between Protestantism and Catholicism to secure academic appointments; on the other hand, Jean Bodin functions in society as a Catholic but, to a greater extent than Pico della Mirandola before him, finds support of ethical optimism within the Jewish tradition.

Particularly fascinating is the concept of seeds in Jean Bodin, who in research on the diversity of values in world history emphasizes the ways human societies alter human nature. The Stoic seeds of virtue, knowledge, and piety become the fundamental epistemological premise of his diverse works in history, law, comparative government, comparative religion, educational theory, and natural philosophy. Bodin adds a new element in crediting the doctrine to the ancient Hebrews and the Academics: the Stoicizing in the texts of Philo and Ficino contributes to the Stoic epistemology of Bodin. Like Aëtius, Matthew of Aquasparta, and Ficino, both Jean Bodin and Pierre Charron directly utilize the imagery of seeds in our souls to question the Aristotelian view that all knowledge comes from the senses.

In his *Paradoxe* Jean Bodin declares that "all the ancient Hebrews and Academics have held as an assured thing, that we have souls inseminated with the divine seed of all the virtues," and he comes close therein to reviving the ancient Stoic doctrine of virtue for its own sake. His *Theatrum* indicates further that the Latin translation of Philo's commentary on Genesis is Bodin's source for the allegory between the human soul and the garden of Paradise, for "the seeds of all the virtues and sciences have been divinely scattered in our souls from their first origin" in order that humans might live as if in "a garden filled with fragrant flowers and trees and with all sorts of goods in great abundance." The Ripa engraving "The Rational Soul" illustrates the Philonic allegory basic to Bodin's presentation: the female personification of the soul points in the background to Adam (reason) and Eve (sense perception), and the interpretation of Genesis reads, "Man in God's image was created, By sense and reason regulated."[33]

The sixteenth and seventeenth centuries play with alternative designs, however. Original humanity as an androgyne, derived from Genesis and the *Symposium*, may be seen in the emblem of "On the Human Origin and Goal," which portrays Adam as the tree trunk rooted in the ground, symbolizing the body, and Eve sprouting out from him, symbolizing the soul seeking heaven.[34] The idea that the soul is fertile with vegetative growth, so important in Bodin's natural philosophy, takes on visual form in the image of the tree of the soul in the work of the eighteenth-century mystic William Law (see fig. E.4). The penitent person appears in miniature in the circle of the soul, from which grows a strong and upright palm tree reaching up to the light of God, portrayed in geometrical beauty by circles within and surrounding a triangle.

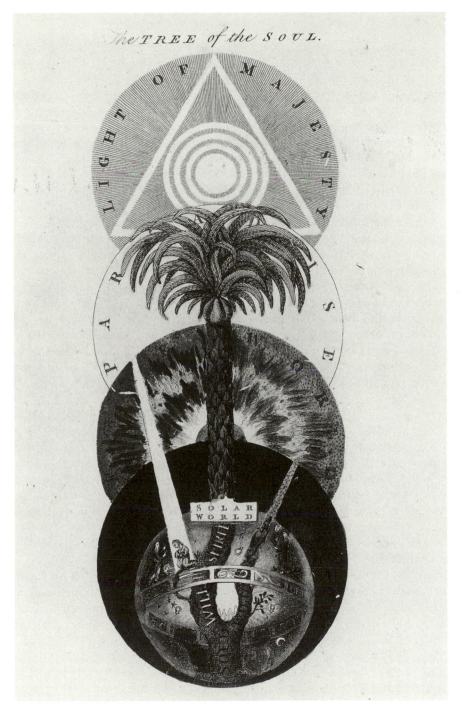

E.4. "Tree of the Soul" by William Law, from *The Works of Jacob Boehme*, London, 1764. Ambrose, *Paradise* 11.51, helps elucidate this illustration: "Many hold that by Paradise is meant the soul of man and that, while man was placed there as a worker and guardian, certain seeds of virtue sprouted forth."

Bodin's *République* links the notion of human reason to its ties with God's eternal natural law, which provides a normative guideline to the conduct of a sovereign monarch. The *Colloquium heptaplomeres* fulfills the universalist tendency of Bodin's thought in its conversation among seven men of different faiths.[35] The attribution to Hebraic sources of the Stoic concept of natural law and the fusing of natural law with the Decalogue culminates in the speeches of Salomon. Through his intertextual blending of Jewish, Christian, and classical sources Bodin contributes an important step in ecumenical application of the Stoic "seeds of virtue."

Michel de Montaigne in his *Essais* not only is influenced by evidence of the relativity of values to historical cultures, but also, under the influence of Sextus Empiricus, as well as Cicero, questions whether there is a secure source outside of revelation for human knowledge and virtue. To Montaigne, *seed of universal reason* is an expression for uneducated, uncorrupted goodness. Since he very rarely refers to such seeds, the occurrences in his descriptions of an Amerindian tribe (1.31) and in his description of peasants (3.12) are all the more striking. He applies this Stoic phrase in a primitivistic manner to describe peoples whose conduct evokes literary images of the Stoic "golden age," people whose character gives them nobility.

Montaigne's declaration of nobility based on virtue alone contributes to the controversy on whether nobility has its basis in birth or virtue. For example, among Florentine humanists, Landino writes of "the best seed which the best parent, nature, gave for the propagation of virtue,"[36] whereas noble and royal families by their decorated trees of lineage claim to perpetuate both seeds of lineage and virtue;[37] Poggio's *De Nobilitate* is a Ciceronian dialogue between the Stoic view that nobility is virtue and the Aristotelian and aristocratic view that nobility requires ancestry, property, position, and virtue.[38] In contrast, Montaigne seems not to debate this particular issue; rather, he applies *seed of universal reason* in recognition of the only true nobility. Historians have commented on the egalitarianism of Stoic influence, but one might seek out specifically *reason, seeds, common notions, rays of light* for the transformation of views on nobility that is background to Jean Jacques Rousseau's egalitarianism.[39]

In "Of Cannibals" Montaigne describes a people still ruled by the "laws of nature"; he combines an ethnographic description of a people in the Americas, philosophical accounts of the golden age before corrupt civilization, and statements in accord with reason and nature—three elements essential to John Locke's contributions to natural-law and natural-rights theory.[40] Likewise, regarding Montaigne's peasant neighbors facing death more nobly than nobles, he declares: "What I like is the virtue that law and religions do not make but perfect and authorize, that feels in itself enough to sustain itself without help, born in us from its own roots, from the seed of universal reason that is implanted in every human who is not denatured."[41]

Ironically, Montaigne's two most vivid applications of seeds of virtue and knowledge, the quotation in the preceding paragraph in a scene of peasants dying and "good seeds that nature has produced in them" in a description of an Amerindian culture in the process of destruction,[42] contrast with the early Renaissance buoyant associations of *seeds* with *rebirth* and mark Montaigne's vivid awareness of the closing of the epoch that featured the Renaissance culture of Francis I. Bodin laments that scholars let decay "the hanging fruits of the sciences"; Montaigne, writing of both horticulture and culture, echoes Virgil and Bodin in lamenting "grapes hanging on the vines." Because Montaigne's literary originality is so striking, it is important for us to appreciate that he builds on the florilegia tradition of the Italian and Northern humanists. The inscribed wood beams of his study are a fitting reminder of the bookish nature of his observations and of his techniques for building right reason by selecting the seeds of truth.[43]

Pierre Charron's *De la sagesse* reveals the imprint of his French contemporaries Du Vair, Bodin, and Montaigne, as well as the impact of ancient Stoics. In borrowing from Du Vair's vision of a Christian Stoic, Charron goes further in viewing religion as one office of true *preud'hommie*. In borrowing from Bodin's phraseology for his statement that "it is proven first of all by the saying of the greatest philosophers, who all have said that the seeds of the great virtues and knowledge have been scattered naturally in the soul," the priest Charron does not draw attention to Bodin's attribution of Jewish sources. The influence of Augustinianism and neo-Platonism is apparent in that even though he follows Montaigne in Pyrrhonian doubts on the reliability of the senses, Charron asserts the powers of the human mind, which he consents to call "a heavenly light" and "an emanation of the Divinity." Even though Charron uses such neo-Platonic expressions, the goal of *De la sagesse* is to teach human wisdom, distinct from the Christian wisdom of his *Les trois veritez*. The basic thrust of Charron's treatise is to stress the natural sources for human wisdom (see fig. 10.1). Although it borrows from Montaigne's *Essais*, *De la sagesse* is distinct in its tight pedagogical organization and in its restoration of the Stoic concept of natural law to its ancient role as the source for the human capacity to attain virtue for its own sake.

Both Thomas Aquinas's scholastic synthesis, which provides a hierarchy from ancient, limited virtue to Christian virtue imbued with divine grace, and Ficino's neo-Platonic theology, which combines ancient wisdom with holy Christian wisdom, contrast with Guillaume du Vair's and Pierre Charron's decisions to write humanist treatises on human virtue and wisdom separate and distinct from their works on holy Christian wisdom.[44] Thus, both structurally and intellectually French neo-Stoicism is filled with tensions between classical and Christian approaches to ethics. The compartmentalization of the mind aids the Catholic orthodoxy of Jesuits in the seventeenth century: the engraved frontispiece in Scheiner's *Rosa Ursina sive Sol* shows the upper paths of sacred authors and reason and the lower paths of profane authors and sense perception. Ironically, the telescope, dependent on sense perception, symbolizes the frailty of senses: in this anti-Galileo portrayal the telescope is projecting sunspots onto the image of the sun.[45]

In Renaissance editions of the ancient Stoics and in Pomponazzi, Bodin, Charron, Montaigne, Lipsius, and Du Vair there are passages implying that the seeds of virtue and right reason provide a foundation for human self-sufficiency in achieving the life of virtue. A study of the historically neglected topic of seeds of virtue and knowledge has shown that an originally Stoic optimistic assessment of human nature sometimes coincides in important Western thinkers with a deemphasis or omission of the Christian doctrine of original sin. The conspicuous role of seeds of virtue and knowledge in neo-Platonic and Erasmian circles is answered by a reassertion of original sin and of Augustinian illumination by Luther and his followers; yet seeds of virtue and knowledge play an important role in Melanchthon's and Calvin's Protestant teachings, as well as in Catholic teachings, in building the foundation for ethics and law on this earth.

The age of the Renaissance is known as an age when human dignity is proclaimed. Historians have recognized that the Western idea of human dignity builds upon the biblical idea that humanity was created in God's image and the classical idea that the human being is a microcosm of the macrocosmic world.[46] I document that the self-proclaimed dignity evinced in individual achievement and in the rebirth of arts and letters relies on the seeds of virtue and knowledge both in concept and in practice. This book shows that many Western theologians, humanists, educators, and philosophers apply the Stoic belief in an epistemology of seeds of virtue and knowledge (seeds, right reason, common notions, sparks of conscience) to provide details about the divine gift to humanity; likewise, they apply the specifically Stoic belief that human reason, the natural law within, stems from divine reason to elucidate how the human being, the microcosm, can grow to understand the rational and moral order extending from God throughout the universe.

The fusing together of a cluster of ideas from a multiplicity of sources allows creative thinkers to draw a variety of implications from the Stoic idea that human dignity is enhanced by the seeds of virtue and knowledge. Diverse applications of the language of vegetative growth during the Middle Ages, the Renaissance, and the Reformation allow individual thinkers to give evidence of free will, provide an epistemological foundation for the scholarly disciplines, encourage study of the natural efficacy of the created world, extend the humanist curriculum to women, recommend for leadership a nobility based on virtue rather than on birth, explain the natural virtue of peasants and Amerindians, argue against tyranny and slavery, and build a human ethic compatible with not only different sects of Christianity but also different religions.

Nevertheless, the ambiguous resonances of the phrases *seeds of virtue* and *sparks of divinity*, which from the Augustinian, neo-Platonic, and Kabbalistic traditions convey the pictorial image of the divine light enflaming the sparks in the human soul, allow Stoicizing passages in sixteenth-century authors to be interpreted either as consistent with a Christian belief in the presence of Jesus in the human soul or as exemplifying a universalist religious belief in the immanent presence of the Divine in human life. Nevertheless, the texts of Cicero, Seneca, Epictetus, and other Stoics, available in Latin and in the vernacular and amply quoted by fifteenth- and sixteenth-century authors, teach virtue not through grace or organized religion but through "following nature." The tension of epistemological positions on seeds of virtue and knowledge that reverberates between the positions of Augustine and Thomas Aquinas takes on new aspects in the debates between Erasmus and Luther and between Calvin and Sadoleto and in the confrontation of the *Index* with books by Bodin and Charron.

Faith that God implanted seeds of virtue and knowledge in humanity provides the confidence in the possibility of gathering flowers of wisdom for a rebirth of arts and letters—a renaissance. The intertext of "seeds of virtue in the human soul" in numerous texts of the Renaissance provides a path to Enlightenment optimism about the natural potentialities of human nature. The famous words "We must cultivate our garden," which Voltaire utilizes one and a half centuries later as closure to *Candide*,[47] a book as full of human suffering as Petrarch's *Remedies for Fortune Fair and Foul*, resonate with traditional imagery for our education for knowledge and virtue.

INTRODUCTION

1. See Arthur O. Lovejoy and George Boas, "Some Meanings of Nature," *Primitivism and Related Ideas in Antiquity* (New York: Octagon, 1973), 456–57; and Cicero, *De senectute*, ch. 19, quoted by Montaigne in the concluding pages of his *Essais* 3.13: "Everything that happens in accordance to nature should be considered good" [Omnia quae secundum naturam fiunt, sunt habenda in bonis] (Michel de Montaigne, *Oeuvres complètes*, ed. Albert Thibaudet and Maurice Rat [Paris: Gallimard, 1962], 1081; *The Complete Works*, trans. Donald M. Frame [Stanford: Stanford University Press, 1967], 845). Montaigne added this quotation after 1588.

2. For sayings on learnedness and goodness, see Erasmus, *De Copia*, trans. Betty I. Knott, in *Collected Works of Erasmus*, ed. Craig Thompson, vol. 24 (Toronto: University of Toronto Press, 1978), 365. For the operative definition of Renaissance humanism, see Paul Oskar Kristeller, *Renaissance Thought and the Arts* (Princeton: Princeton University Press, 1990); and Albert Rabil Jr., ed., *Renaissance Humanism: Foundations, Forms, Legacy*, 3 vols. (Philadelphia: University of Pennsylvania Press, 1988). I distinguish the gendered from the generic *man* in philosophical and educational texts by using *human* as a noun equivalent to *human being* for the generic *man* (see ch. 1, n. 1).

3. Hannah Arendt, *The Human Condition* (New York: Doubleday, 1959), chs. 13–16. I cite the humanists' use of biographical exempla as evidence of their classical tradition of combined moral and intellectual education: John D. Lyons, *Exemplum: The Rhetoric of Example in Early Modern France and Italy* (Princeton: Princeton University Press, 1988). Lyons begins by pointing out that *exemplum* in medieval Latin means a "clearing in the woods" (3).

4. For the extensive literature on natural law, see Paul Foriers, Léon Ingber, and P.-F. Smets, *Introduction bibliographique à l'histoire du droit et l'ethnologie juridique* (Brussels: Université de Bruxelles, 1982).

5. Louis Dupré, *Passage to Modernity: An Essay in the Hermeneutics of Nature and Culture* (New Haven: Yale University Press, 1993), esp. 23–24, 127–30, 135–44. The question of origins of *ius naturale* as "natural right" is raised in Leo Strauss, *Natural Right and History* (Chicago: University of Chicago Press, 1953).

6. "I think I do not err in stating that there is in our souls some native seed of reason, which if nourished by good counsel and training, flowers into virtue, but which, on the other hand, if unable to resist the vices surrounding it, is stifled and blighted" (Étienne de la Boétie, *The Politics of Obedience: The Discourse of Voluntary Servitude*, trans. Harry Kurz [New York: Free Life Editions, 1975], 55–56). For controversy on La Boétie's political views and Montaigne's, see Quentin Skinner, *The Foundations of Modern Political Thought*, 2 vols. (London: Cambridge University Press, 1978), 2:281–82; Gérald Nakam, *Les essais de Montaigne: Miroir et procès de leur temp, Témoignage historique et création littéraire* (Paris: Nizet, 1984), 178–83; and Daniel Martin as cited in David L. Schaefer, *The Political Philosophy of Montaigne* (Ithaca: Cornell University Press, 1980), 40–41 and n. 1, 387 n. 66.

7. Richard Tuck underplays the evidence of natural-law language among humanists yet astutely points to the 1580s as an important time of transition in *Natural Rights Theories: Their Origin and Development* (Cambridge: Cambridge University Press, 1979), 50, 33. Tuck is on the right track in investigating Barbeyac's belief that modern natural law emerged in replies to Skepticism, and he finds Montaigne and Charron important for Grotius's natural-law response to Carneades and Skepticism (see Richard Tuck, "The 'Modern Theory' of Natural Law," in *The Languages of Political Theory in Early-Modern Europe*, ed. Anthony Pagden [Cambridge: Cambridge University Press, 1987], 109–14; on Tuck's denial of natural law in Montaigne and Charron, see 116). In order to understand how the emergence of thinking about internal natural rights involves the vocabulary of the internal natural law, I suggest looking at seventeenth-century responses to neo-Platonists and neo-Stoics; see my epilogue notes for suggestions of database searches.

8. Genealogical trees were developed in Schleicher, *Compendium of Comparative Grammar of the Indo-European Sanskrit, Greek and Latin Languages*, 2 vols. (1874–77).

9. Jacques Derrida, *La dissémination* (Paris: Seuil, 1972), published in English as *Dissemination*, trans. and intro. Barbara Johnson (Chicago: University of Chicago Press, 1981); Jacques Derrida, *L'écriture et la différance* (Paris: Seuil, 1967), published in English as *Writing and Difference*, trans. Alan Bass (Chicago: University of Chicago Press, 1978), 8–12, 56–57, discussing Michel Foucault, *Folie et déraison: Histoire de la folie à l'âge classique* (Paris: Plon, 1961). See the discussion of Derrida's *La dissémination* below in the discussion entitled "Continuing controversy on assessing humanity." I thank François Rigolot for drawing my attention to *La dissémination*.

10. Foucault, *Les mots et les choses* (Paris: Gallimard, 1966).

11. See Steven E. Ozment, *Homo Spiritualis: A Comparative Study of the Anthropology of Johannes Tauler, Jean Gerson, and Martin Luther (1509–1516) in the Context of Their Theological Thought* (Leiden: Brill, 1969), 8–9, on hermeneutics: "Authors may say very different things with the very same words, phrases, and themes."

12. On the varieties of wisdom sought in the Middle Ages and the Renaissance, see Eugene F. Rice Jr., *The Renaissance Idea of Wisdom* (Cambridge: Harvard University Press, 1958).

13. Library of Congress, *The Circle of Knowledge: An Exhibition in the Great Hall of the Library of Congress Dec. 7, 1979–March 16, 1980* (Washington, D.C., 1979) (see the cover photograph of the rotunda, the core of the library, and fig. 18, an analytical encyclopedia guide via a detailed tree of knowledge, from Denis Diderot and Jean le Rond d'Alembert, eds., *Encylopédie*, 35 vols. [Paris: Briasson, 1751–80], vol. 1, "Table analytique"). See also Mortimer Adler, "Circle of Learning," *The New Encyclopaedia Britannica* (Chicago, 1994), *Propaedia*, 5–8.

14. This is an additional explanation for the popularity of female personifications and their later demise, discussed in Londa Schiebinger, *The Mind Has No Sex? Women in the Origins of Modern Science* (Cambridge: Harvard University Press, 1989), 119–56, with Renaissance illustrations, and 165–69. She gives examples of women scholars making a personal identification with a muse.

15. Virgil, *Georgics*, ed. Richard Thomas (Cambridge: Cambridge University Press, 1988).

16. Donald R. Kelley, ed., *The History of Ideas: Canon and Variations*, Library

of the History of Ideas (Rochester: University of Rochester Press, 1990) and *History of Ideas in the Twentieth Century* (Rochester: University of Rochester Press, 1992).

17. James Hankins, "The 'Baron Thesis' after Forty Years and Some Recent Studies of Leonardo Bruni," *Journal of the History of Ideas* 56, no. 2 (April 1995): 309–38; Ronald Witt, "Introduction *AHA* Forum: Hans Baron's Renaissance Humanism" and "The *Crisis* after Forty Years," *AHA Forum, American Historical Review* 101 (1996): 107–9 and 110–18; John M. Najemy, "Baron's Machiavelli and Renaissance Republicanism," ibid., 119–39; Craig Kallendorf, "The Historical Petrarch," ibid., 130–41; Werner Gundersheimer, "Hans Baron's Renaissance Humanism: A Comment," ibid., 142–44; Leonardo Bruni, *The Humanism of Leonardo Bruni*, trans. and intro Gordon Griffiths, James Hankins, and Craig Thompson (New York: Center for Medieval and Early Renaissance Studies, State University of New York, Binghamton, 1987), 15–21, esp. n. 30, and 402 for additional English translations; to examine Stoicizing passages in Bruni, follow the index to Seneca, Cicero, and Stoicism. Jerrold E. Seigel, *Rhetoric and Philosophy in Renaissance Humanism: The Union of Eloquence and Wisdom, Petrarch to Valla* (Princeton: Princeton University Press, 1968). Note the humor with which Anthony Grafton and Lisa Jardine use the very metaphors of humanists as they discuss them in *From Humanism to the Humanities: Education and the Liberal Arts in Fifteenth- and Sixteenth-Century Europe* (Cambridge: Harvard University Press, 1986), xii–xiii.

18. Leonardo Bruni, *Panegyric to the City of Florence*, in *The Earthly Republic: Italian Humanists on Government and Society*, trans. Benjamin G. Kohl (Philadelphia: University of Pennsylvania Press, 1978), 135–75.

19. J. G. A. Pocock, *Politics, Language, and Time: Essays on Political Thought and History* (New York: Atheneum, 1973), 99; William J. Connell, "The Republican Tradition in and out of Florence," in *Girolamo Savonarola: Piety, Patronage, and Politics in Renaissance Florence*, ed. Donald Weinstein and Valerie R. Hotchkiss (Dallas: Bridwell Library, 1994), 95–105.

20. Hans Baron, *The Crisis of the Early Italian Renaissance: Civic Humanism and Republican Liberty in an Age of Classicism and Tyranny* (Princeton: Princeton University Press, 1966).

21. Baldesar Castiglione, *Il libro del cortegiano* (Turin: Unione Tipografico-Editrice, 1981), bk. 2, ch. 3, p. 197: "il che non è maraviglia, perché niun male è tanto malo, quanto quello che nasce dal seme corrotto del bene." For the English, see Baldesar Castiglione, *Book of the Courtier*, trans. Sir Thomas Hoby (1561; reprint, New York: Dutton, 1974), 1.13 and 2.3 on the seed of good lineage and 1.14 and 1.16 on the seed of virtue. Translations and imitations of this work spread the debate on nobility by birth versus nobility by virtue. See examples of arguments for nobility through virtue in my selections from Cassandra Fedele (ch. 5), Alciati (ch. 7), and Montaigne (ch. 9).

22. Richard Pace, *De Fructu Qui Ex Doctrina Percipitur (The Benefit of a Liberal Education)*, ed. and trans. Frank Manley and Richard S. Sylvester (New York: Federick Ungar for the Renaissance Society of America, 1967), 113–15, 125 (quotation), and 178 n. 9 on "topos generositas virtus, non sanguis."

23. Skinner, *Foundations of Modern Political Thought*; Albert Rabil Jr., "The Significance of 'Civic Humanism' in the Interpretation of the Italian Renaissance," in *Renaissance Humanism*, 2:141–75, and articles on individual cities and states.

The controversy on ties between humanism and republicanism extends to J. G. A. Pocock, *The Machiavellian Moment: Florentine Political Thought and the Atlantic Republican Tradition* (Princeton: Princeton University Press, 1975).

24. Lucien Febvre, *Life in Renaissance France*, trans. Marian Rothstein (Cambridge: Harvard University Press, 1977), 6 (quotation), 24–25, 38; Fernand Braudel, "Daily Bread," in *The Structures of Everyday Life*, trans. Siân Reynolds (New York: Harper & Row, 1979), bk. 1, ch. 2, pp. 104–83.

25. Thomas Kuhn, *The Structure of Scientific Revolutions* (Chicago: University of Chicago Press, 1974).

26. For relevant examples of folk psychology, see Carol Delaney, "The Meaning of Paternity and the Virgin Birth Debate," *Man* 21 (1986): 494–513; and Marta Weigle, *Creation and Procreation: Feminist Reflections on Mythologies of Cosmogony and Parturition* (Philadelphia: University of Pennsylvania Press, 1989). See also Stephen P. Stitch, *From Folk Psychology to Cognitive Science: The Case against Belief* (Cambridge: MIT Press, 1983).

27. Aram Vartanian, "Man-Machine from the Greeks to the Computer," in *Dictionary of the History of Ideas*, ed. Philip P. Wiener, 5 vols. (New York: Scribner's Sons, 1973), 3:131–46. Charron compares the seed of universal reason to the spring and balance of a clock (see below, ch. 10, n. 35).

28. John Stuart Mill, *On Liberty*, 3rd ed. (London: Longman, Green, 1864), 107. I thank Allan Levine for drawing my attention to Mill's tree imagery.

29. Ibid., 112.

30. Antoine Compagnon, *La seconde main ou le travail de la citation* (Paris: Seuil, 1979); Mary B. McKinley, *Words in a Corner: Studies in Montaigne's Latin Quotations* (Lexington, Ky.: French Forum, 1981); François Rigolot, "Referentialité, intertextualité, autotextualité dans les *Essais* de Montaigne," *Oeuvres & Critiques* 8 (1983): 87–101.

31. Claude Levi-Strauss, *Anthropologie structurale* (Paris, 1958); Noam Chomsky, *Language and Mind* (New York, 1968). In modern terminology, my book is about the premodern nurture-nature debate. The seed imagery is about deep structures of our mind and the impact for later development of cultivating or stultifying one's mental potentialities.

32. The phrases *seeds of virtue* and *seeds of knowledge* may be metonymic, one word substituting for another on the basis of a material, causal, or conceptual relationship. See Quintilian, *Institutio oratoria*, trans. H. E. Butler, Loeb Classical Library, bks. 8 and 9; and Gerhart B. Ladner, "Medieval and Modern Understanding of Symbolism: A Comparison" (1979) and "Vegetation Symbolism and the Concept of the Renaissance" (1961) in *Images and Ideas in the Middle Ages: Selected Studies in History and Art*, 2 vols. (Rome: Edizioni di Storia e Letteratura, 1983), 1:239–82 and 2:727–63.

33. Roger Cook, *Tree of Life: Symbol of the Centre* (London: Thames & Hudson, 1974), recommended by Paul G. Kuntz and Marion L. Kuntz, in "The Symbol of the Tree Interpreted in the Context of Other Symbols of Hierarchical Order, the Great Chain of Being, and Jacob's Ladder," in *Jacob's Ladder and the Tree of Life: Concepts of Hierarchy and the Great Chain of Being*, ed. Marion L. Kuntz and Paul G. Kuntz (New York: Peter Lang, 1987). See also Joanna Drew and Roger Malpert, eds., *The Tree of Life: New Images of an Ancient Symbol*, catalog of exhibition organized by Common Ground (London: South Bank Centre, 1989).

34. Paul Friedrich, *Proto-Indo-European Tree: The Arboreal System of a Prehistoric People* (Chicago: University of Chicago Press, 1970), 23, 138–40. I thank C. Scott Littleton for drawing my attention to Friedrich's research.

35. Carlo Ginzburg, "Clues: Roots of an Evidential Paradigm," in *Clues, Myths, and Historical Method* (Baltimore: Johns Hopkins University Press, 1989), 118, citing Giovanni Morelli, *Della pittura italiana* (Milan: Treves, 1897), discusses the problematics of comparing art and ideas (17–60) and the dilemma of encountering long-term continuities of popular belief (vii–xiii). See also Carlo Ginzburg, *The Cheese and the Worms: The Cosmos of a Sixteenth Century Miller*, trans. John Tedeschi and Anne Tedeschi (New York: Penguin, 1982), xix–xx, xxiii–xxiv, 58–61.

36. Paul Watson, *The Garden of Love in Tuscan Art in the Early Renaissance* (Philadelphia: Art Alliance Press, 1979); Terry Comito, *The Idea of the Garden in the Renaissance* (New Brunswick, N.J.: Rutgers University Press, 1978).

37. James Hall, *Dictionary of Subjects and Symbols in Art* (New York: Harper & Row, 1974), 75; Terence Cave, *The Cornucopian Text: Problems of Writing in the French Renaissance* (Oxford: Clarendon, 1979), esp. 171–82; Pamela Berger, *The Goddess Obscured: The Transformation of the Grain Protectress from Goddess to Saint* (Boston: Beacon, 1985). See also the statue Fortune with Cornucopia, a Roman copy of the fourth-century B.C.E. Greek original, in the *Encyclopedia of World Art*, 17 vols. (New York: McGraw-Hill, 1958–87), vol. 13, pl. 338; and *Andreas Alciatus*, ed. Peter M. Daly, with Virginia W. Callahan and Simon Cuttler, 2 vols. (Toronto: University of Toronto Press, 1985), vol. 1, emblem 99.

38. Forrest G. Robinson, *The Shape of Things Known: Sidney's Apology in Its Philosophical Tradition* (Cambridge: Harvard University Press, 1972), esp. chs. 1–2, shows the domination of visual epistemology in Western thought. In ch. 3, 122–28, openly struggling to trace the origins of Philip Sidney's use of the noun *ground-plot* in the *Apology for Poetry or the Defence of Poetry* (1595), Robinson misses its origins in *seminarium*, "seed plot" or "seedbed," discussed in ch. 2, below, 'Seeds.' Throughout, cross references to sections of my text are by section titles.

39. Simon Schama, *Landscape and Memory* (New York: Knopf, 1995).

40. See the *Index of Christian Art* (1917–), journal produced by the Department of Art and Archeology, Princeton University, and card catalog index available at Princeton, UCLA, and other locations (computerization in progress); and Raimond van Marle, *Iconographie de l'art profane au Moyen-Age et à la Renaissance*, 2 vols. (New York: Hacker Art Books, 1971).

41. Maryanne Cline Horowitz, Anne J. Cruz, and Wendy A. Furman, eds., *Renaissance Rereadings: Intertext and Context* (Urbana: University of Illinois Press, 1988): Julie A. Smith, "The Poet Laureat as University Master: John Skelton's Woodcut Portrait," 159–83, and Paul F. Watson, "To Paint Poetry: Raphael on Parnassus," 113–41.

42. For Skinner, see James Tully, ed., *Meaning and Context: Quentin Skinner and His Critics* (Oxford: Polity Press, 1988); and David Boucher, *Text in Context: Revisionist Methods for Studying the History of Ideas* (Dordrecht: Nijhoff, 1985), esp. ch. 5, "The View from the Inside: Skinner and the Priority of Retrieving Authorial Intentions." For Pocock, see J. G. A. Pocock, "Introduction: The State of the Art," in *Virtue, Commerce, and History: Essays on Political Thought and History, Chiefly in the Eighteenth Century*, ed. J. G. A. Pocock (Cambridge: Cambridge University Press, 1985), 1–34; and "A Bibliography of the Writings of J. G. A.

Pocock," in *Political Discourse in Early Modern Britain*, ed. Nicholas Phillipson and Quentin Skinner (Cambridge: Cambridge University Press, 1993), 429–37.

43. William J. Bouwsma, "Intellectual History in the 1980s: From History of Ideas to History of Meaning," *Journal of Interdisciplinary History* 12 (1981): 277–91, reprinted in idem, *A Usable Past: Essays in European Cultural History* (Berkeley: University of California Press, 1990).

44. Donald. R. Kelley, "Horizons of Intellectual History: Retrospect, Circumspect, and Prospect," *Journal of the History of Ideas* 48 (1987), 143–69, reprinted in *History of Ideas: Canon and Variations*, quotation on 321.

45. John Toews, "Intellectual History after the Linguistic Turn," *American Historical Review* 92, no. 4 (October 1987): 881, citing Martin Jay, "Should Intellectual History Take a Linguistic Turn? Reflections on the Habermas-Gadamer Debate," in *Modern European Intellectual Tradition: Reappraisals and New Perspectives*, ed. Dominick LaCapra and Steven L. Kaplan (Ithaca: Cornell University Press, 1982), 87.

46. James J. Bono, *The Word of God and the Languages of Man: Interpreting Nature in Early Modern Science and Medicine* (Madison: University of Wisconsin Press, 1995); J. F. West and John Murray, *The Great Intellectual Revolution* (London: Cox & Wyman, 1965), ch. 9, "The Death of Metaphor."

47. For case studies showing the vitality and transformations of humanists as scientific methods developed, see Anthony Grafton, *Defenders of the Text: The Traditions of Scholarship in an Age of Science, 1450–1800* (Cambridge: Harvard University Press, 1991).

48. For an anthropologist's viewpoint, see Jack Goody, *The Culture of Flowers* (Cambridge: Cambridge University Press, 1993).

49. See below, Ch. 1, nn. 56 and 64. Pagden, *Languages of Political Theory in Early-Modern Europe*, 3. See also above, n. 7.

50. "Reason-of-state" philosophies define *reason* in the instrumental sense of preserving the state and involve a rejection of the Ciceronian *recta ratio* conforming to the universal principles of equity. See Maurizio Viroli, *From Politics to Reason of State: The Acquisition and Transformation of the Language of Politics, 1250–1600* (Cambridge: Cambridge University Press, 1992), definition on 4–5. Viroli focuses on Italy but recognizes parallels in France, England, Spain, and Germany (2). My discussion of Du Vair, Lipsius, Bodin, Montaigne, and Charron provides some northern European counterparts to his chapter "The Last Glimmering of Civil Philosophy." Exemplary of the current controversy is A. Enzo Baldini, ed., *Aristotelismo politico e ragion di stato* (Florence: Leo S. Olschki, 1995).

51. See Maryanne Cline Horowitz, "Aristotle and Woman," *Journal of the History of Biology* 9 (1976): 186–213. See also below, ch. 1, n. 1; and Marcia L. Colish, *The Stoic Tradition from Antiquity to the Early Middle Ages*, 2 vols. (Leiden: Brill, 1985), 1:36–41, on Stoic egalitarianism, and 1:344–45, on distinguishing ancient Stoic natural law from seventeenth- and eighteenth-century renditions.

52. For Ficino, see below, ch. 4, the discussion of speech 6, ch. 12, of Ficino's commentary on Plato's *Symposium*. For Bodin, see Jean Bodin, *Response . . . à M. de Malestroict* (1568) in *La vie chère au XVIe siècle*, ed Henri Hauser (Paris: Librairie Armand Colin, 1932), 34.

53. J. G. A. Pocock, "The Concept of a Language and the *Métier d'historien*: Some Considerations on Practice," in Pagden, *Languages of Political Theory in*

Early-Modern Europe, 23. See also Boucher, *Texts in Context*, ch. 4, "The Priority of Paradigms: The Pocock Alternative."

54. Luther questions Erasmus's proper use of that authority in their most important controversy on free will (see below, ch. 6).

55. Arthur Robinson, "Genetics and Heredity," in *The New Encyclopaedia Britannica*, 19:730–40.

56. In "Clues: *Roots* of an Evidential Paradigm," 71, Ginzburg relates Freudian analysis, Sherlock Holmes's detective method, and Giovanni Morelli's analysis of minor aspects of a painting to determine an artist's authenticity to ancient hunters' drawing inferences from the clues of animal footprints.

57. Walter J. Ong, "Latin Language Study as a Renaissance Puberty Rite," *Studies in Philology* 56 (1959): 103–24; Janet Backhouse, *The Illuminated Manuscript* (Oxford: Phaidon, 1979), figs. 63 and 64 (pp. 72–74); Edward Johnson et al., *Writing, Illumination, and Lettering* (London: Pitman, 1977), pls. 16–19 (pp. 165–67); Lucia N. Valentine, *Ornament in Medieval Manuscript* (London: Faber & Faber, 1965), 27–41, 85–89.

58. For focus on the lack of productivity in ethics, see John Bunyan (d. 1688), *The Barren Fig-Tree; or the doom and downfall of the fruitless professor, shewing, that the day of grace may be past with him long before his life is ended: the signs also by which such miserable mortals may be known*, in John Bunyan, *The Practical Works* (London: Aberdeen, 1841), 3:149–218.

59. A diversity of interpretations of Psalm 1 is discussed in chs. 3 and 6 below.

60. M. H. Abrams, *The Mirror and the Lamp: Romantic Theory and the Critical Tradition* (New York: Oxford University Press, 1953): 166–77, 218–25 (Coleridge), 204–5 (Herder), 206–7 (Goethe), 207–8 (Kant), 216–17 (Carlyle).

61. For example, there are pedigree, lineal, and binary trees. Applications include game trees and decision trees. See Ellis Horowitz and Sartaj Sahni, *Fundamentals of Data Structures in Pascal* (New York: W. H. Freeman, 1994), ch. 5, "Trees."

62. George Lakoff and Mark Johnson analyze current examples of the metaphors "ideas are people," "ideas are plants," and "creation is birth" (all relevant to my book) in *Metaphors We Live By* (Chicago: University of Chicago Press, 1980), 47 and 74–75, and they view metaphor positively in an experientialist synthesis between objectivity and subjectivity on 185–91. For an overview and some bibliography on the controversy on metaphor, see Alex Preminger et al., eds., *Princeton Handbook of Poetic Terms* (Princeton: Princeton University Press, 1986), 136–41.

63. Stephen Pepper, "Metaphor in Philosophy," in Wiener, *Dictionary of the History of Ideas*, 3:197–98. See also idem, *World Hypotheses: A Study in Evidence* (Berkeley: University of California Press, 1962), 113.

64. Quentin Skinner, "Meaning and Understanding in the History of Ideas," *History and Theory* 8 (1968): 3–58, reprinted in Tully, *Meaning and Context*, where organicism is critiqued on 34–35.

65. Joseph Huber, *Clusters of Grapes: Sow a Character and You Reap Destiny* (Gweru, Zimbabwe: Mamo, 1984), which juxtaposes proverbs from around the world on the virtues sincerity, patience, courage, etc.; Elliot Dorff and Arthur Rosett, *A Living Tree: The Roots and Growth of Jewish Law* (Albany: State University of New York Press, 1988). From a Conservative Jewish perspective, Dorff and Rosett focus on the general ethical principles at issue in Talmudic commentary and

interpretation of the laws presented in the Torah, the "tree of life," that is, the Hebrew Bible.

66. Beryl Cohon, *Introduction to Judaism* (New York: Block, 1942), 62–65, quotation on 64. Cohon compares Judaism to a four-thousand-year-old tree (3). My own earliest exposure to such ideas was through my parents' teaching inspired by Rabbi Beryl Cohon. See also idem, *The Small Still Voice* (New York: Behrman House, 1957).

67. See, e.g., Alasdair MacIntyre, *After Virtue: A Study in Moral Theory* (Notre Dame: University of Notre Dame Press, 1981), challenged by Gilbert C. Meilaender, *The Theory and Practice of Virtue* (Notre Dame: University of Indiana Press, 1984). Judith Shklar draws from Montaigne's concerns in *Ordinary Vices* (Cambridge: Harvard University Press, 1984). A contemporary florilegium groups stories and poems for inculcating in children ten virtues; William J. Bennett, ed., *The Book of Virtues: A Treasury of Great Moral Stories* (New York: Simon & Schuster, 1993).

68. Daniel Mark Nelson, *The Priority of Prudence: Virtue and Natural Law in Thomas Aquinas and the Implications for Modern Ethics* (University Park: Pennsylvania State Press, 1992), 146.

69. See Derrida, *La dissémination*, 319–407, and Johnson's English translation, *Dissemination*, 287–366; pages cited in the text refer to the French edition, followed by the English edition.

70. Maryanne Cline Horowitz, "The 'Science' of Embryology before the Discovery of the Ovum," in *Connecting Spheres: Women in the Western World, 1500 to the Present*, ed. Marilyn J. Boxer and Jean H. Quataert (New York: Oxford University Press, 1987), 86–94.

71. On medieval awareness and consideration of the problematics of referentiality, see, e.g., Augustine, *The Teacher*, in *The Teacher, The Free Choice of the Will, Grace and Free Will*, trans. Robert P. Russell, Fathers of the Church, 59 (Washington, D.C.: Catholic University of America Press, 1968), 7–61; J.-P. Migne, *Patrologia Latina*, 221 vols. (Paris: Garnier, 1841–1902), 32:1193–1220 (available in *Patrologia Latina Database* [Alexandria, Va.: Chadwyck-Healey, 1995]).

72. Archelaus, teacher of Socrates: "The noble and the base exist by convention [*nomos*] and not by nature [*physis*]," cited in Ernest Barker, *Greek Political Theory: Plato and His Predecessors* (London: Methuen, 1952); Antiphon, "On Truth," cited in ibid., 83–85; Plato, *Gorgias*, in *Lysis, Symposium, Gorgias*, trans. W. R. M. Lamb (Cambridge: Harvard University Press, 1953); Epicurus: "There never was an absolute justice, but only an agreement made in reciprocal intercourse in whatever localities now and again from time to time," in "Principal Doctrines," in *Greek and Roman Philosophy after Aristotle: Readings in the History of Philosophy*, ed. Jason Saunders (New York: Free Press, 1966), 53–57.

73. Arthur O. Lovejoy, *The Great Chain of Being: A Study of the History of an Idea* (Cambridge: Harvard University Press, 1936); Kelley, *History of Ideas: Canon and Variations*; idem, *History of ideas in the Twentieth Century*; Frances Oakley, *Omnipotence, Covenant, and Order: An Excursion in the History of Ideas from Abelard to Leibniz* (Ithaca: Cornell University Press, 1984).

74. James Kirwan deconstructs Derrida in *Literature, Rhetoric, Metaphysics: Literary Theory and Literary Aesthetics* (London: Routledge, 1990), 3, 15–34. Kirwan distinguishes between scientific metaphors, which are capable of extinction, and rhetorical metaphors, which can hide: "Likewise 'leaves of a book' is not metaphor-

ical because one does not have to think of leaves (botanical) in understanding or using it (though my placing it here, among other 'leaves', has probably made you do so)" (34).

75. J. B. Bury, *The Idea of Progress: An Inquiry into Its Growth and Origin* (London: Macmillan, 1920; reprint, New York: Dover, 1960).

76. See esp. Charles Trinkaus, *In Our Image and Likeness: Humanity and Divinity in Italian Humanist Thought*, 2 vols. (Chicago: University of Chicago Press, 1970); idem, "Marsilio Ficino and the Idea of Human Autonomy," in *Ficino and Renaissance Neoplatonism*, ed. Konrad Eisenbichler and Olga Zorzi Pugliese (Ottawa: Dovehouse, 1986); Rice, *Renaissance Idea of Wisdom*; Eugene F. Rice Jr., *St. Jerome in the Renaissance* (Baltimore: Johns Hopkins University Press, 1985); Paul Oskar Kristeller, *Renaissance Concepts of Man and Other Essays* (New York: Harper & Row, 1972); idem, *The Philosophy of Marsilio Ficino*, trans. Virginia Conant (Gloucester, Mass.: Peter Smith, 1964); idem, *Greek Philosophers of the Hellenistic Age* (New York: Columbia University Press, 1993); Maryanne Cline Horowitz, "Paul Oskar Kristeller's Impact on Renaissance Studies," *Journal of the History of Ideas* 39 (1978): 677–83; and Paul F. Grendler, *Schooling in Renaissance Italy: Literacy and Learning, 1300–1600* (Baltimore: Johns Hopkins University Press, 1989).

77. *New York Times*, 8 December 1985, Final report of the Second Vatican Council, 2nd ed., 7 December 1985, trans. from Latin, 8, citing Confer NAE 2 and Confer Lumen Gentium 16. Pope John Paul II reaffirms the inclusive, ecumenical viewpoint in *The Splendor of Truth* (Washington, D.C.: U.S. Catholic Conference, 1993), 6–7. The church's concern is that conscience has become dislocated from the natural moral law (84–98). Although this encyclical discusses both the natural and the illumined light of the intellect, it does not refer to the Thomist and Erasmian Catholic teachings on nourishing the seeds of virtue and knowledge.

78. Anne Frank (1929–45), *The Diary of a Young Girl*, trans. B. A. Mooyaart-Doubleday (New York: Doubleday, 1967), 287.

CHAPTER ONE

1. The best way to reflect and transform the historical ambiguity of the complex sex/gender patterns of moral philosophy is to focus our discussion on "human nature" while recognizing the ambiguities of traditional discussions of "man." The word *man* in published English translations, especially those in the Loeb Classical Library, remains in my quotations. My own text, in which I use *humankind, humans*, and *we*, acknowledges that the Stoics apply their expectations to both men and women. In Loeb texts *man* as an androcentric (male-focused) generic is sometimes used for the Greek *anthropos* or the Latin *homo* (as well as the Hebrew *adam*, which in the Septuagint is *anthropos*), the clearly generic *humankind*; other times *man* is a translation of the Latin *vir*, which, like the English *man* or French *homme*, sometimes applies to women as "a praise" for their character. The ambivalent *man* is sometimes the most accurate translation, since the educational treatises and educational institutions from antiquity to the Renaissance are often directed to male pupils, although tutors do apply the instruction to females as well. Nevertheless, today a feminist transformation of our traditional language of philosophical anthropology is in process, and Stoicism provides an important precedent. The phrases *seeds of virtue* and *seeds of knowledge* generally imply moral and intellectual agency

in women as well as in men, although as a problematic example influenced by Aristotle's biology, see n. 65, on Plutarch. We need both a more inclusive philosophical anthropology and a history of philosophy that is more aware of the contributions of women and the implications for women. In their sharp distinction between the wise few and the foolish many the Stoics do not differentiate humankind by race or sex (H. C. Baldry, *The Unity of Mankind in Greek Thought* [Cambridge: Cambridge University Press, 1965], 151–66, 177–203; A. W. H. Adkins, *From the Many to the One* [Ithaca: Cornell University Press, 1970], ch. 8, esp. 229–30). On *moral agency* as a Kantian term for autonomous Stoic ethics, see Bernard Williams, "The Idea of Equality," in *Problems of the Self* (Cambridge: Cambridge University Press, 1973), 230–39 (recommended by Marcia L. Homiak); and on the historical importance of feminist reworking of natural-law theory in the Renaissance as well as today, see Ginevra Conti Odorisio, "Natural Law and Gender Relations: Equality of All People and Differences between Men and Women," ch. 3 of *Women's Rights and the Rights of Man*, ed. A. Arnaud and E. Kingdom (Aberdeen: Aberdeen University Press, 1990); and Constance Jordan, *Renaissance Feminism: Literary Texts and Political Modes* (Ithaca: Cornell University Press, 1990), 65–133.

2. L. D. Reynolds, ed., *Texts and Transmission: A Survey of the Latin Classics* (Oxford: Clarendon, 1983), 374, for example, indicates that Seneca's letters are read from the twelfth century; the transmission of Cicero's speeches, philosophical works, and letters is discussed on 54–142. A key work on Stoicizing Platonism is John Dillon, *The Middle Platonists, 80 B.C. to A.D. 220* (Ithaca: Cornell University Press, 1977); the same philosophers may be discussed from either a Stoic or a Platonic perspective. This chapter discusses distinctly Stoic phrases that became Platonized. See below, ch. 4 for Quintilian, ch. 3 for Plotinus, chs. 2, 3, and 8 for Philo, and ch. 7 for Epictetus.

3. Clement of Alexandria, quoting Cleanthes, in Joannes von Arnim, *Stoicorum veterum fragmenta*, 4 vols. (Leipzig: B. G. Teubner, 1903–24), 1:180 (1:552) (hereinafter cited as SVF); Jason Saunders, *Greek and Roman Philosophy after Aristotle: Readings in the History of Philosophy* (New York: Free Press, 1966), 111. References to the Stoic fragments translated by Saunders will follow this form, indicating the author of the source and the reference to the Greek or Latin original in SVF, by volume and fragment number, with second fragment number in parentheses, followed by the page location in Saunders. Recent editions include K. H. Hülser, *Die Fragmente zur Dialektik der Stoiker* (Stuttgart–Bad Cannstatt, 1987), and A. A. Long and D. N. Sedley, *The Hellenistic Philosophers*, 2 vols. (Cambridge: Cambridge University Press, 1987). For a well-edited collection of Stoic statements translated into Italian, see Margherita Isnardi Parente, ed., *Stoici antichi*, 2 vols. (Turin: Unione Tipografico–Editrice Torinese, 1989). For a thorough bibliography, see Ronald H. Epp, "Stoicism Bibliography," *Southern Journal of Philosophy* 22 (1985): 125–71.

4. Cleanthes, "Hymn to Zeus," SVF 1:537; Saunders, 149–50. In the Stoic worldview logos is both the basis of the natural sequence of causes in the deterministic system and the basis of human free will and autonomous action. For a thorough study of these issues and others that concern later Christians, see Marcia L. Colish, *The Stoic Tradition from Antiquity to the Early Middle Ages*, 2 vols. (Leiden: Brill, 1985).

5. Diogenes Laertius, *Lives of Eminent Philosophers*, trans. R. D. Hicks, Loeb

Classical Library, 7.86; Brian Inwood, *Ethics and Human Action in Early Stoicism* (Oxford: Clarendon, 1985), 33. See chs. 8 and 10 below.

6. Lactantius, SVF 1:162a and b, 1:537; Saunders, 102, 149–50.

7. In the words of Heraclitus, "Those who speak with sense must rely on what is common to all, as a city must rely on its law, and with much greater reliance: for all the laws of men are nourished by one law, the divine law: for it has as much power as it wishes and is sufficient for all and is still left over" (Heraclitus, *The Cosmic Fragments*, ed. G. S. Kirk [Cambridge: Cambridge University Press, 1962], 48. See also M. R. Wright, *The Presocratics* [Bristol: Bristol Classical Press, 1985], 59, analyzing fragment 22 [114], Stobaeus 3.1.179).

8. Plato, *Lysis, Symposium, Gorgias*, trans. W. R. M. Lamb, Loeb Classical Library, *Gorg.* 483–84, 489–91; Plato, *Laws*, trans. R. G. Bury, Loeb Classical Library, 957c.714–15 and 890b; Glenn R. Morrow, "Plato and the Law of Nature," in *Essays in Political Theory*, ed. Milton R. Konvitz and Arthur E. Murphy (Ithaca: Cornell University Press, 1948), 21–24, 39.

9. See n. 14 on Hellenistic eclecticism.

10. Cicero, *De re publica, De legibus*, trans. R. G. Bury, Loeb Classical Library, *Rep.* 3.33.

11. Cic., *Leg.* 1.23.

12. Ibid., 1.33.

13. Ibid., 1.23.

14. Currently, scholars note the "eclecticism" of Hellenistic thought as well as of Renaissance thought. For the controversies concerning the emergence of natural-law theory in both Cicero and Philo in the first century B.C.E., see Helmut Koester, "NOMOS PHYSEOS: The Concept of Natural Law in Greek Thought," in *Religions in Antiquity*, ed. Jacob Neusner (Leiden: Brill, 1968), 421–41; Richard A. Horsley, "The Law of Nature in Philo and Cicero," *Harvard Theological Review* 71 (1978): 35–59; and H. E. Remus, "Authority, Consent, Law: *Nomos, Physis*, and the Striving for a 'Given,'" *Studies in Religion*, 1984, 5–18. Quotation from Philo, *De Josepho*, trans. F. H. Colson, in *Philo*, Loeb Classical Library, vol. 6, lines 29–31, cited in comparison to passage from Cicero by Horsley, 37.

15. Cic., *Leg.* 1.18–19. See Dillon, *The Middle Platonists*, 90; Dillon considers the influence on Cicero of Panaetius, Posidonius, and Antiochus, his direct teacher.

16. Diog. Laert. 10.33.

17. Saunders, 68n. For selections from Epicureans and Stoics on epistemology, see Long and Sedley, *Hellenistic Philosophers*, 1:78–102, 39–43 (English), 2:83–103, 238–63 (Greek and Latin).

18. The meaning of *phantasiai kataléptikei* (as well as their differences from ordinary *phantasiai*) is ambiguous in the Greek texts and has caused much controversy. See John M. Rist, *Stoic Philosophy* (Cambridge: Cambridge University Press, 1969), 133–51.

19. On the criterion of truth, see Rist, *Stoic Philosophy*, 133–51.

20. Diog. Laert. 7.54.

21. Aëtius, SVF 2:83; Saunders, 68.

22. Seneca, SVF 3:169; Saunders, 120. Seneca's influential *Epistles* are addressed to women as well as to men. He includes women in his high moral ideal (see Anna Lydia Motto, "Seneca on Women's Liberation," *Classical World*, January 1972, 155–57). A well-known example is Seneca in exile advising his mother

Helvia not to grieve, citing examples of women who have been virtuous in the face of husbands' and children's deaths or exiles and contrasting his expectations with those who use the "excuse of being a woman" (Seneca, "Consolation to Helvia," in *The Stoic Philosophy of Seneca*, ed. Moses Hadas [New York: Norton, 1958], 107–36).

23. Sextus Empiricus, SVF 2:56; Saunders, 64. Cicero, SVF 1:59b; Saunders, 62. A Stoic comparison of the upper part of the soul to a piece of papyrus that may receive inscriptions appears in *Des opinions des philosophes* 4.2, disputably attributed to Plutarch, quoted in Jean Brun, *Les stoïciens textes choisis* (Paris: Presses Universitaires de France, 1957), 79.

24. Emile Bréhier, *Chrysippe et l'ancien stoïcisme* (Paris: Presses Universitaires de France, 1951), 103. For more on the problematics of developing notions, see A. A. Long, "Dialectic and the Stoic Sage," and G. B. Kerford, "What Does the Wise Man Know?" in *The Stoics*, ed. John M. Rist (Berkeley: University of California Press, 1978).

25. Bréhier, *Chrysippe et l'ancien stoïcisme*, 67. The ancient Stoics, like the later scholastic theologians, inquire in detail about the process of developing reason and the age when a child achieves the ability to reason (see Inwood, *Ethics and Human Action*, 71–79).

26. Cic., *Leg.* 1.27.

27. Ibid., 1.30.

28. Cicero, *Topica* 7.31, in Cicero, *Philosophica omnia*, ed. R. Klotz, 2 vols. (1840), as cited in Vernon Arnold, *Roman Stoicism* (Cambridge: Cambridge University Press, 1911), 137 nn. 58 and 61: "nobis notitiae rerum imprimuntur, sine quibus nec intellegi quicquam nec quaeri disputarive potest."

29. Seneca, *Ad Lucilium epistulae morales*, trans. Richard M. Gummere, Loeb Classical Library, 3 vols., *Ep.* 117.6.

30. Cicero, *De natura deorum. Academica*, trans. H. Rackham, Loeb Classical Library, *Nat. d.* 1.63.

31. Cicero, *Tusculanae disputationes* 1.13.30, cited in Arthur Lovejoy and George Boas, *A Documentary History of Primitivism* (Baltimore: John Hopkins Press, 1935; reprint, New York: Octagon, 1973), 256.

32. R. D. Hicks, *Stoics and Epicureans* (New York: Russell & Rusell, 1962), 67; Eduard Zeller, *The Stoics, Epicureans, and Sceptics*, trans. Oswald J. Reichel (New York: Russell & Russell, 1962), 81.

33. John Locke, *An Essay concerning Human Understanding*, ed. A. C. Fraser (Oxford: Clarendon, 1894), 37. Cf. Locke's view in the preface to the 2nd ed., xxiii.

34. For preachers and authors whom Locke is refuting, see John W. Yolton, *John Locke and the Way of Ideas* (Oxford: Clarendon, 1968). For mixing of Platonic and Stoic epistemologies in Ficino and Bodin, see below, chs. 4 and 8.

35. Sen., *Ep.* 49.12.

36. For the differences between Epictetus and other Stoics, see Frances Devine, "Stoicism on the Best Regime," *Journal of the History of Ideas* 21 (1970): 328–29, 332–36. For Du Vair's translation of the *Manual*, see below, ch. 7.

37. Epictetus, *Discourses*, trans. W. A. Oldfather, Loeb Classical Library, 2 vols., 1.22.1.

38. Ibid., 1.22.1–10, 4.1.41–43.

39. Ibid., 2.11.3.

40. Ibid., 2.11.17–18, 2.16.6–8, 1.17.11–12.

41. Hicks, *Stoics and Epicureans*, 62–63.

42. Diog. Laert. 7.139.

43. For a discussion of Aristotle's procreation theory, see the following articles in the *Journal of the History of Biology*: Maryanne Cline Horowitz, "Aristotle and Woman," 9 (1976): 186–213, esp. 197–98; Anthony Preuss, "Galen's Criticism of Aristotle's Conception Theory," 10 (1977): 65–85; Johannes Morsink, "Was Aristotle's Biology Sexist?" 12 (1979): 83–112; Michael Boylan, "The Galenic and Hippocratic Challenges to Aristotle's Conception Theory," 17 (1984): 83–112; and idem, "Galen's Conception Theory," 19 (1986): 47–77.

44. Sen., *Ep.* (trans. Gummere) 65.3–11, at 65.7, English and Latin cited in Arthur F. Kinney, *Continental Humanist Poetics: Studies in Erasmus, Castiglione, Marguerite de Navarre, Rabelais, and Cervantes* (Amherst: University of Massachusetts Press, 1989), 35–39.

45. Kinney, *Continental Humanist Poetics*, 38, citing Wesley Trimpi, *Muses of Our Mind* (Princeton: Princeton University Press, 1983), xv–xvi. Timothy Hampton brings new attention to the exemplum in *Writing from History: The Rhetoric of Exemplarity in Renaissance Literature* (Ithaca: Cornell University Press, 1990). See below, ch. 6, on Sadoleto and Calvin.

46. The Aristotelian biological basis for Stoic cosmology has been argued cogently by David E. Hahm in *The Origins of Stoic Cosmology* (Columbus: Ohio State University Press, 1977), esp. 44–48, 72–82. Thomas Laqueur, *Making Sex: Body and Gender from the Greeks to Freud* (Cambridge: Harvard University Press, 1990), contends that until the eighteenth century the basic worldview was a one-sex theory.

47. Diog. Laert. 7.148–49.

48. Zeller, *Stoics, Epicureans, and Sceptics*, 172.

49. Diog. Laert. 7.135–36.

50. Ibid., 9.9; Saunders, 84–85.

51. Arnold, *Roman Stoicism*, 161. Another example is Proclus, SVF 2:717; Saunders, 96.

52. Proclus, SVF 2:717; Saunders, 96.

53. William Leslie Davidson, *The Stoic Creed* (Edinburgh: T. and T. Clark, 1907), 91.

54. Stobaeus, SVF 1:87a; Saunders, 80–81.

55. φύσει δὲ πάντες πρὸς ἀρετὴν γεννώμεθα, καθ' ὅσον ἀφορμὰς ἔχομεν (SVF 3:214, citing *Anecdota Graeca e codd. manuscriptis bibliothecae regiae parisienses*, ed. John Anthony Cramer, 4 vols. [Oxford, 1839; reprint, Hildesheim: G. Olms, 1967], 1:371). The passage does not contain the phrase *seeds of virtue*, as mistakenly indicated by Saunders, 123. In the sentence quoted above, there is use of the verb γεννάω (to produce from, to bear). I thank John Walsh for translating this passage. For Aristotle's citations of Empedocles and Jean Bodin's reconsideration of the materialist viewpoint, see below, ch. 8, n. 87.

56. Cic., *Rep.* 1.41.

57. Cicero, *De finibus* 5.21.58–60, cited in Boas and Lovejoy, *Documentary History of Primitivism*, 248–49. For a full discussion of Cicero's epistemology and ethics, see Colish, *Stoic Tradition*, 1:104–9, 126–52.

58. Sen., *Ep.* 65.4, 65.12.

59. Ibid., 90.29.

60. Ibid., 92.27.

61. Ibid., 76.9.

62. Ibid., 85.36–37, 92.30.

63. Ibid., 49.12.

64. Ibid., 120.4.

65. Ibid., 90.46. While Seneca views women as having "seeds of virtue" (see n. 22), Plutarch's views are atypical for Stoics when he is influenced by Aristotelian texts (*De generatione animalium* 4.7 in the following example): "Great care must be taken that this sort of thing [tumorous growth] does not happen in women's minds. For if they do not receive the seed[s] (*spermata*) of good doctrines and share with their husbands in intellectual advances, they, left to themselves conceive many untoward ideas and low designs and emotions" ("Advice to Bride and Groom," in *Moralia*, trans. Frank Cole Babbitt, Loeb Classical Library, 2:339–40, lines 145D–145E). See Laqueur, *Making Sex*, 59. See also France Le Corsu, *Plutarque et les femmes dans les Vies parallèles* (Paris: Belles Lettres, 1981); Mary E. Waithe, *A History of Women Philosophers: Volume 1, Ancient Women Philosophers, 600 B.C.–500 A.D.* (Dordrecht: Nijhoff, 1987); Ethel M. Kersey, *Women Philosophers: A Bio-Critical Source Book* (New York: Greenwood, 1989), which has short biographies of the following "Stoicists": Arria the Elder (d. C.E. 42, Rome), Arria the Younger (fl. C.E. 66, Rome), Fannia (first century C.E.), and Eudocia Athenais, Christian empress, Constantinople (ca. 401–60); and Anthony J. Close, "Commonplace Theories of Art and Nature in Classical Antiquity," *Journal of the History of Ideas* 32 (1971): 177–79.

66. Sen., *Ep.* 124.10–11. See also below, ch. 7.

67. Quintilian (30–ca. 96), though indebted to Stoicism, is a rhetorician (see Colish, *Stoic Tradition*, 1:327–28; see also below, chs. 5 and 6).

68. "Cacumen radicis loco ponis" (*Ep.* 124.8).

69. *Ep.* 124.14.

70. Zeller, *Stoics, Epicureans, and Sceptics*, 152; Diog. Laert. 7.135–36.

71. Augustine, SVF 2:423; Saunders, 85.

72. Eusebius, SVF 1:98; Saunders, 92. See also Robert B. Todd, "Monism and Immanence: The Foundations for Stoic Physics," in Rist, *The Stoics*, 145–46; and above, quotation cited in n. 49.

73. Stobaeus, SVF 1:107; Saunders, 93.

74. Cic., *Leg.* 1.33.

75. Censorinus, SVF 1:124; Saunders, 97.

76. Cicero, SVF 2:421; Saunders, 85.

77. Virgil, *Aeneid*, in *Virgil in English Verse*, trans. Charles Bowen (London: John Murray, 1887), 6.729–32, p. 297. See Arnold, *Roman Stoicism*, 256–65; and Virgil, *Publi Virgili Maronis Opera*, commentary by John Conington (London: Harper Brothers, 1884), 2.6.728–32.

78. Virgil, *Aeneid* 6.744–47, p. 298.

79. "Igneus est ollis vigor et caelestis origo seminibus" (ibid., 2.6.731). See Bruni's citation to Battista Malatesta in ch. 5, n. 17.

CHAPTER TWO

1. *Ius naturale* is translated here as "natural law," not as "natural right," since Roman, medieval, and Renaissance usages of *ius naturale* differ significantly from early modern fully developed natural-rights theories, in accord with Allessandro

Passerin d'Entrèves, *Natural Law: An Introduction to Legal Philosophy*, rev. with new introduction by Cary Nederman (New Brunswick, N.J.: Transaction, 1994), 30. Nevertheless, scholars researching the origins of natural rights would do well to consider my evidence of the widespread belief in the internal *ius naturale*. See also Richard Tuck, *Natural Rights Theories: Their Origin and Development* (Cambridge: Cambridge University Press, 1979), esp. 1–32; Brian Tierney, "Marsilius on Rights," *Journal of the History of Ideas* 52 (1991): 3–17; idem, "Origins of Natural Rights Language: Texts and Contexts, 1150–1250," *History of Political Thought* 11 (1990): 1–32; Stephen E. Lahey, "Wyclif on Rights," *Journal of the History of Ideas* 58 (1997): 1–20; and Dom Odon Lottin, *Le droit naturel chez Saint Thomas d'Aquin et ses prédécesseurs*, 2nd ed. (Bruges: Charles Bayaert, 1931).

2. For example, attention to Stoic writings might be helpful for emphasizing Aquinas's use of the cardinal virtues and prudence (see Daniel Mark Nelson, *The Priority of Prudence: Virtue and Natural Law in Thomas Aquinas and the Implications for Modern Ethics* [University Park: Pennsylvania State University Press, 1992]).

3. *Inst.*, 1.2.11, cited in Passerin d'Entrèves, *Natural Law*, 32; Gratian, "The Concordance of Discordant Canons of Decretum," in *Natural Law in Political Thought*, ed. and trans. Paul E. Sigmund (Washington, D.C.: Winthrop, 1971), 48, from *Corpus juris canonici* (Leipzig: B. Tauchnitz, 1879).

4. Since C. A. Maschi, *La concezione naturalistica del diritto e degli istituti guiuridici romani* (Milan: Vita e Pensiero, 1937), scholars have questioned the causative historical theory that Roman law transmitted Stoic natural law (see the substantive scholarly evidence in Marcia L. Colish, *The Stoic Tradition from Antiquity to the Middle Ages*, 2 vols. [Leiden: Brill, 1985], 1:341–89, where she concludes that Cicero and other orators are the main transmitters of the legal theory of Stoic natural law and ethics). On the other hand, for the continuing tradition that Christian natural law developed from the church fathers, Roman law, and canon law, a tradition that still influences norms in theology and political theory, see Ewart E. Lewis, *Medieval Political Ideas*, 2 vols. (New York: Knopf, 1954), 1:6; and Gérard Verbeke, "Aux origines de la notion de la loi naturelle," in *La filosofia della natura nel medioevo* (Milan: Vita e Pensiero, 1966), 164–67. See below, ch. 6, "Do the Seeds of Virtue Grow to Heaven?" and chs. 8 and 10.

5. For Augustine's development, see Peter Brown, *Augustine of Hippo: A Biography* (Berkeley: University of California Press, 1967). The best account of Stoic influences on the early church and church fathers is Colish, *Stoic Tradition*, vol. 2. Whereas this chapter focuses on Augustine's mature theological viewpoint, Stoicizing humanists of the Renaissance gain support from Augustine's early writings, discussed below, in ch. 6. On Augustine's changing views on the Stoics, see esp. Colish, *Stoic Tradition*, 2:147, 154–55, 212–20, 234–38.

6. Recent scholarship has substantiated that Augustine views Adam as the true parent (seed-giver) of the child and that his one-seed theory is important in his claim of the inheritance through the father of original sin through concupiscence; see *De civitate Dei* 14.18–20. See also Elizabeth A. Clark, "Vitiated Seeds and Holy Vessels: Augustine's Manichean Past," and Elaine Pagels, "Adam and Eve and the Serpent in Genesis 1–3," in *Images of the Feminine in Gnosticism*, ed. Karen L. King (Philadelphia: Fortress, 1988); and Kari Børreson, *Subordination and Equivalence: The Nature and Rôle of Woman in Augustine and Thomas Aquinas* (Washington, D.C.: University Press of America, 1981), 57–68. Although there is extensive theological discussion of how Mary's virginal body passes on no pollution to baby Jesus,

the official promulgation in 1854 of the Dogma of Immaculate Conception, by which Mary full of grace merited by her son on the cross is declared exempt of original sin, postdates Karl Ernst von Baer's (1792–1876) discovery of the mammalian ovum in 1827 (Maryanne Cline Horowitz, "The 'Science' of Embryology before the Discovery of the Ovum," in *Connecting Spheres: Women in the Western World, 1500 to the Present,* ed. Marilyn J. Boxer and Jean H. Quataert [New York: Oxford University Press, 1987], 86–94).

7. Eugene F. Rice Jr., *The Renaissance Idea of Wisdom* (Cambridge: Harvard University Press, 1958), 2, 4–6, on Augustine's transformation of the Stoic "sapientia est rerum humanarum divinarumque scientia."

8. See "Wisdom of Solomon" and "Ecclesiasticus or the Wisdom of Sirach," in *The Apocrypha,* trans. Edgar J. Goodspeed (New York: Random House, 1989). The Greek version of the Jewish Scriptures, the Septuagint, contains these books, which are translated into Latin in Saint Jerome's Vulgate. Although *The Apocrypha* aims to teach *torah* (wisdom) (*torah* in Hebrew is translated as *sophia* in Greek), these are later works, after the scrolls of the Five Books of Moses, the *Torah* per se, and the additional scrolls of the canonical Hebrew Bible.

9. Phyllis P. Bober and Ruth Rubinstein, *Renaissance Artists and Antique Sculpture* (Oxford: Oxford University Press, 1986), 187–88, is the most up-to-date analysis. Inquiry continues on the original location of this bronze pinecone. I thank Eric Frank and Regina Stefaniak for bibliographical suggestions.

10. Richard Krautheimer, *Corpus Basilicarum Christianarum Romae, Early Christian Basilicas in Rome (IV–IX Cent.),* 5 vols. (Rome: Città del Vaticano, 1933–77), 5:229–30 (figs. 211, 212) and 263. An early-seventeenth-century drawing (fig. 211) shows the pinecone in an open structure in the atrium of old St. Peter's.

11. Bober and Rubinstein, *Renaissance Artists,* 188.

12. Peter Gun, *The Churches of Rome* (New York: Simon & Schuster, 1981), 43.

13. For two examples of the importance of flowing water in Paradise, see Philo of Alexandria, *Philo,* trans. F. H. Colson and G. H. Whitaker, 10 vols. plus 2 suppl. vols., Loeb Classical Library, vol. 1, *De opificio mundi* 45, lines 131–34; and John 22.1–2 Revised Standard Version.

14. Campo Calvesi and Maurizio Calvesi, *Treasures of the Vatican* (Geneva: Skira, 1962).

15. J. N. Adams, *The Latin Sexual Vocabulary* (Baltimore: John Hopkins University Press, 1982). The term *seminales rationes* is usually discreetly left in Latin. It is a delicate matter to sail through texts, avoiding shipwreck on either the Scylla of euphemism concerning the sexual imagery or on the Charybdis of outrage at the sexism.

16. Elizabeth Goldsmith, *Ancient Pagan Symbols* (New York: Putnam, 1929); J. G. Frazer, *The New Golden Bough,* abr. ed. (London: Criterion, 1957), 314.

17. Jean Seznec, *The Survival of the Pagan Gods* (Princeton: Princeton University Press, 1953).

18. Theophrastus, *Enquiry into Plants (Historia plantarum),* trans. Arthur Hort, Loeb Classical Library, 2 vols., 1:79–85 on seeds, 163 on doubts about spontaneous generation, 177 on male trees defined as those without fruit, 211–21 on firs, including pines, 219 on seeds within cones. See also below, chs. 5 and 7. A. G. Morton thinks that manuscripts by Theophrastus disappear from use in the West from the late second century to the fifteenth century; Pliny's *Natural History*

and Dioscorides' list of medicinal plants dominate (see A. G. Morton, *History of Botanical Science: An Account of the Development of Botany from Ancient Times to the Present Day* [London: Academic Press, 1981], 23, 28, 33, 37–38, 42, 82–85).

19. The influence of Theophrastus continues through the hexameral literature; for example, Ambrose doubts spontaneous generation and claims that living things come from seeds (see Ambrose, *Hexameron, de paradiso*, ed. C. Schenkl, *CSEL* 32.1; and *Hexameron, Paradise, and Cain and Abel*, trans. John J. Savage, Fathers of the Church, 42 [Washington, D.C.: Catholic University of America, 1961], 3.66, p. 118, quotation 3.68, p. 119–120.

20. Jeremy Cohen, *"Be Fertile and Increase, Fill the Earth and Master It": The Ancient and Medieval Career of a Biblical Text* (Ithaca: Cornell University Press, 1989), 231–34, 262–63.

21. See, e.g., Robert Grosseteste, *Hexaëmeron*, ed. Richard C. Dales and Servus Gieben (London: Oxford University for the British Academy, 1982), 6.12.1; 193.

22. Personal communication from Regina Stefaniak.

23. Ambrose, *Hexameron* 32.1.

24. See *Roman Altar Priests of Cybele Bearing Her Litter*, Fitzwilliam Museum, Cambridge, and Mantegna, *The Cult of Cybele*, National Gallery, London, in *Mantegna, with a Complete Catalogue of Paintings, Drawings and Prints*, by R. W. Lightbown (Berkeley: University of California Press, 1986), plates 148 and 146, respectively.

25. The Great Goddess takes many varieties worldwide. See Marija Gimbutas, *The Goddesses and Gods of Old Europe* (London: Thames & Hudson, 1982); and Frazer, *The New Golden Bough*, on Attis, 309–16.

26. Philippe Ariès, *L'homme devant la mort* (Paris: Seuil, 1977), ch. 1.

27. Leon Yarden, *The Tree of Light: A Study of the Menorah, the Seven-Branched Lampstead* (Ithaca: Cornell University Press, 1971); idem, *The Spoils of Jerusalem on the Arch of Titus: A Reinvestigation* (Stockholm: Svenska, 1991).

28. See below, ch. 3, for images from the Kabbalah, and ch. 6 for the *Oratio*. Frazer's phrase "golden bough" stresses the merger of vegetative and light symbols, as in the mistletoe described by Virgil in the *Aeneid*, 6.202–4: "whence shone a flickering gleam of gold" (Frazer, *New Golden Bough*, 589–609; for Virgil, 605).

29. Ernst Robert Curtius, *European Literature and the Latin Middle Ages*, trans. Willard R. Trask (New York: Bollingen Foundation, 1953), 319–26.

30. Philo of Alexandria, *Philo*, trans. F. H. Colson and Reverend G. H. Whitaker, Loeb Classical Library, vol. 7, *De decalogo*. See also Thomas Conley, ed., *"General Education" in Philo of Alexandria* (Berkeley: Center for Hermeneutical Studies, 1975); John Dillon, *The Middle Platonists, 80 B.C. to A.D. 220* (Ithaca: Cornell University Press, 1977), 139–84; Ronald Williamson, *Jews in the Hellenistic World: Philo* (Cambridge: Cambridge University Press, 1989); and Roberto Radice and David T. Runia, *Philo of Alexandria: An Annotated Bibliography, 1937–1986* (Leiden: Brill, 1988).

31. R. W. Carlyle and A. J. Carlyle, *A History of Medieval Political Theory in the West*, 6 vols. (New York: G. P. Putnam's Sons, 1903–36), 1:102–6.

32. Maryanne Cline Horowitz, "The Image of God in Man—Is Woman Included?" *Harvard Theological Review* 72 (1979): 190–95 on Philo and Origen, 199–200 on Augustine departing from Ambrose.

33. Augustine, *De Trinitate* 12.7.10 (Migne *PL* 42:1003), cited without this section in the misleadingly titled *Not in God's Image: Women in History from the*

Greeks to the Victorians, ed. Julia O'Faolain and Lauro Martines (New York: Harper & Row, 1973). *PL* refers to Jacques P. Migne, ed., *Patrologiae cursus completus: Series Latina*, 221 vols. (Paris: Garnier, 1841–1902), available also in *Patrologia Latina Database* (Alexandria, Va.: Chadwyck-Healey, 1995). References will include standard English translations as cited.

34. David Winston, *Logos and Mystical Theology in Philo of Alexandria* (Cincinnati: Hebrew Union College Press, 1985), 9–26.

35. Horowitz, "Image of God in Man," 190–95.

36. Justin Martyr, *Apology*, 1.46, in Étienne Gilson, *History of Christian Philosophy in the Middle Ages* (New York: Random House, 1955), 13.

37. See D. M. Crossman and C. J. Peter, "Logos," in *New Catholic Encyclopedia*, 15 vols. (New York: McGraw-Hill, 1967); and R. A. Markus, "Marius Victorinus," in *The Cambridge History of Later Greek and Early Medieval Philosophy*, ed. A. H. Armstrong (Cambridge: Cambridge University Press, 1967), 332–37.

38. Vernon Arnold, *Roman Stoicism* (Cambridge: Cambridge University Press, 1911), 417, 419–20.

39. "Lex intima, in ipso tuo corde conscripta" (Augustine, *Enarrationes in Psalmos* 57.1 [Migne *PL* 36:673–74]). Gerard O'Daly, *Augustine's Philosophy of Mind* (London: Duckworth, 1987), emphasizes Augustine's view that illumination is the one secure source of truth. For another viewpoint, see James Wetzel, *Augustine and the Limits of Virtue* (Cambridge: Cambridge University Press, 1992). See also above, n. 5.

40. Étienne Gilson, *The Christian Philosophy of Saint Augustine*, trans. L. E. M. Lynch (New York: Random House, 1960), 210–11.

41. John 1.9 RSV. Augustine in his *Confessions*, bk. 7, ch. 9, blends the neo-Platonic doctrine of illumination with the Joannine Gospel. Plotinus's theory of illumination may be found in Plotinus, *Enneads*, trans. A. H. Armstrong, 6 vols., Loeb Classical Library, 1:6, 9; 5:5, 7.

42. Matt. 23.10; Augustine, *De magistro* 11.38 (Migne *PL* 32:1216), 14.46 (32:1220). For feminine imagery of Jesus, see Matt. 23.37 and Bernard of Clairvaux (d. 1153) and other Cistercians of the twelfth and thirteenth centuries, cited in Caroline Walker Bynum, *Jesus As Mother: Studies in the Spirituality of the High Middle Ages* (Berkeley: University of California Press, 1982), 110–69, esp. 138, 151. On John of Salisbury, see below, ch. 5.

43. "Quando autem bene recordatur Domini sui, Spiritu eius accepto sentit omnino, quia hoc discit intimo magisterio" (August., *De Trin.* 14.15.21 [Migne *PL* 42:1052]).

44. "Illuminatio quippe nostra participatio Verbi est, illius scilicet vitae quae lux est hominum" (ibid., 4.2.4 [Migne *PL* 42:889]).

45. Rom. 2.14–15.

46. Carlyle and Carlyle, *History,* 1:83, 105–6.

47. Joseph Le Cler, *Toleration and Reformation*, trans. J. L. Weston, 2 vols. (New York: Association Press, 1960), 1:9–14. *Syneidêsis, syntêrêsis,* and *synderesis* (the last a variant pronunciation not originally in Greek) are identical. Rabbinical commentary draws out the moral implications of a good heart, *lev* (Avot 2.9, Ber. 54a, cited in *Encyclopedia Judaica*, 16 vols. [New York: Macmillan, 1972], s.v. "Heart," by Louis Isaac Rabinowitz). The claim that Judaism lacks a concept of conscience has slanderous overtones (see Robert T. Wallis, *The Idea of Conscience in Philo of Alexandria* [Berkeley: Center for Hermeneutical Studies, 1975], 1–8,

19–23). There have been creative responses among reform Jews; see introduction, n. 66; and Milton Konvitz, *Judaism and Human Rights* (New York: Norton, 1972).

48. Le Cler, *Toleration and Reformation*, 1:14; M. W. Hollenbach, "Synderesis," *New Catholic Encyclopedia*. St. John Chrysostom (ca. 347–407) writes that natural law is promulgated through the human conscience. St. John Chrysostom, *Ad. Pop. ant.* 12, cited in B. F. Brown, "Natural Law," *New Catholic Encyclopedia*.

49. Augustine, *De libero arbitrio* 3.5.17 (Migne *PL* 32:1279); Augustine, *Epistulae* 157.3.15 (Migne *PL* 33:681).

50. Augustine, *De diversis questionibus* 83.31.1 (Migne *PL* 40:20).

51. *Digest* 1.1.1, cited in Passerin d'Entrèves, *Natural Law*, 29;. Victor Goldschmidt, *La doctrine d'Épicure et le droit* (Paris: Vrin, 1977); Michael B. Crowe, "St. Thomas and Ulpian's Natural Law," in *St. Thomas Aquinas, 1274–1974: Commemorative Studies*, ed. Armand A. Maurer, 2 vols. (Toronto: Pontifical Institute of Mediaeval Studies, 1974), 1:261–82.

52. Abelard, *Epist. ad Rom.*, 1.2.813–14, cited in D. Luscombe, "Nature in the Thought of Peter Abelard," in *La filosofia della natura nel medioevo* (Milan: Vita e Pensiero, 1966), 317. One of the important ecumenical dialogues, along with Lull's, ch. 3 below, and Bodin's, ch. 8 below, is Abelard, *A Dialogue of a Philosopher with a Jew and a Christian*, trans. Pierre J. Payer (Toronto: Pontifical Institute of Mediaeval Studies, 1979).

53. Dom Odon Lottin, *Psychologie et morale aux XIIe et XIIIe siècles*, 3 vols. (Louvain: Abbaye du Mont César, 1949), 2, pts. 3, 4, and 5.

54. Saint Bonaventure, II. *Sent.* d. 39, art. 1–2, d 24 part 2a, art. 1, qu. 1, cited in Lottin, *Le droit naturel*, 52–53; Bonaventure, "Commentary on Peter Lombard's Books of 'Judgements' 2.39," in *Conscience in Medieval Philosophy*, ed. Timothy C. Potts (Cambridge: Cambridge University Press, 1980), 110–22 and commentary, 32–44.

55. Aquinas, *Summa theologiae* 1, qu. 90, art. 1, quoted in Étienne Gilson, *Moral Values and the Moral Life: The Ethical Theory of St. Thomas Aquinas*, trans. L. R. Ward (1961; reprint, Westport, Conn.: Greenwood, 1979), 193–94.

56. Aquinas, quoted in Harry V. Jaffa, *Thomism and Aristotelianism: A Study of the Commentary by Thomas Aquinas on the Nicomachean Ethics* (Chicago: University of Chicago Press, 1952), 172–73. In Jaffa's view, Aquinas is here distorting Aristotle: "One thing, however, is perfectly clear, namely: that there is not mention of synderesis (or any possible equivalent) by Aristotle."

57. Lottin, *Le droit naturel*, 63–73.

58. Ibid., 103, my translation.

59. Heiko A. Oberman, *The Harvest of Medieval Theology: Gabriel Biel and Late Medieval Nominalism* (Cambridge: Harvard University Press, 1963), 475.

60. Ibid., 63–64, 108–10.

61. Ibid., 65–66.

62. August., *De lib. arb.* 2.9.26 (Migne *PL* 32:1254–55).

63. August., *De Trin.* 8.3.4 (Migne *PL* 42:949).

64. Ibid., 14.15.21 (Migne *PL* 42:1052). A translation of the full passage appears in R. A. Markus, "Augustine: Sense and Imagination," in Armstrong, *Cambridge History*, 368–69.

65. August., *De Trin.* 14.15.21 (Migne *PL* 42:1052), quotation from Markus, "Augustine," 368–69; Gilson, *Saint Augustine*, 89–94. I concur with O'Daly,

Augustine's Philosophy of Mind, 184–85, on how Augustine's *notio impressa* differs from Stoic doctrine. See 92–105, 162–71, for O'Daly's more detailed discussion of Augustine's views of ancient epistemologies known especially through Cicero's *Academica*. Augustine's response to the Skeptical onslaught is a precedent to later responses; for the late Middle Ages and Renaissance, see Charles B. Schmitt, *Cicero Scepticus: A Study of the Influence of the Academica in the Renaissance* (The Hague: Nijhoff, 1972).

66. Frederick Copleston, *A History of Philosophy*, vol. 2 (Westminster, Md.: Newman, 1952), 388–97; Aquinas, *Sum. theol.* 1, qu. 79, "Of the intellectual powers." Unless otherwise indicated, the English translation of *Summa theologiae* accords with *Basic Writings of St. Thomas Aquinas*, ed. A. C. Pegis, revision of part of Dominican Fathers' English translation, 2 vols. (New York: Random House, 1945).

67. Aquinas, *Sum. theol.* 1–2 (first part of the second part), qu. 94, "On the natural law," art. 4; the translation modifies A. C. Pegis, who suggests Boethius's impact (Pegis, *Basic Writings*, 2:777). See also Boethius, *De Hebdomadibus*, in John Wippel and Allan Wolter, *Medieval Philosophy: From St. Augustine to Nicholas of Cusa* (New York: Free Press, 1969), 97.

68. Cf. Epictetus in ch. 1, above; and D. J. O'Connor, *Aquinas and Natural Law* (London: Macmillan, 1967), 62–63, 73–77. Aquinas does not sufficiently elucidate how the particulars are derived from principles.

69. Aquinas, *Sum. theol.* 1–2, qu. 95, "Of human law," art. 1; Gilson, *History*, 377. On the influence on Aquinas of Stoic notions of reason and nature, particularly through the texts of Seneca, see Gérard Verbeke, "Saint Thomas et le Stoicisme," in *Mensch und natur in Mittelalter*, ed. P. Wilpert, Miscellanea meddiaevalia 21 (Berlin: Walter, 1962), 1:48–68.

70. See above, nn. 65 and 66.

71. Thomas Aquinas, *Questiones Disputatae*, ed. R. M. Spiazzi (Turin, 1949–64), vol. 1, qu. 1, art. 8, translated in *The Disputed Questions on Truth*, 3 vols., trans. James McGlynn et al. (Chicago: H. Regnery, 1952–54).

72. Lottin, *Psychologie et morale*, 3:59–89, idem, *Le droit naturel*, 34–35; *Psychologie et morale*, 2:97.

73. Lottin, *Psychologie et morale*, 3:92–96.

74. Ibid., 2:97.

75. Acts 17.22, quoted in Arnold, *Roman Stoicism*, 409.

76. 1 Cor. 15.27–38.

77. H. Chadwick, "Justin Martyr," *New Catholic Encyclopedia*, citing *Dialogue with Trypho the Jew*, trans. A. L. Williams (New York: McGraw-Hill, 1930). His works do not appear in print in Latin until 1554.

78. Justin Martyr's syncretist viewpoint echoes in Pico della Mirandola, *Oratio* (see below, ch. 6). See also Justin Martyr, *Apol.*, 2.10–13, cited in H. Chadwick, "The Beginning of Christian Philosophy: Justin: the Gnostics," in Armstrong, *Cambridge History*, 162–63; and Gilson, *History*, 13.

79. Gilson, *Saint Augustine*, 206; Jules M. Brady, "St. Augustine's Theory of Seminal Reasons," *New Scholasticism* 38 (1964): 141–58. For a full analysis of Augustine's view of seminal reasons and a bibliography, see Colish, *Stoic Tradition*, 2:203–7, 204 n. 160.

80. Gilson, *Saint Augustine*, 206.

81. Étienne Gilson, *The Spirit of Medieval Philosophy*, trans. A. H. C. Downes (New York: Charles Scribner's Sons, 1936), 134–36.

82. See above, ch. 1, as well as the discussion of Seneca in relationship to Sadoleto in ch. 6.

83. Augustine, *The City of God*, trans. D. Wiesen, Loeb Classical Library, bks. 8–11, quotation at 10.3.2.

84. Matthaeus ab Aquasparta, *Quaestiones disputatae de fide de cognitione* (Karachi: C. Bonaventure, 1957), 257–58. Matthew of Aquasparta paraphrases Augustine's phrase "regulas et quaedam lumina virtutum" as "seminaria virtutum."

85. Gilson, *Spirit*, 137.

86. Ibid., 137–38.

87. Ibid., 138–40.

88. Aquinas, *De veritate*, qu. 11.

89. Étienne Gilson, *The Christian Philosophy of St. Thomas Aquinas*, trans. L. K. Shook (New York: Random House, 1955), 181.

90. Gilson, *History*, 382. The Thomist view of the impact of secondary causation is echoed in the "Garden of Adonis" in Edmund Spenser, *The Faerie Queene* 3.6.33, in *Edmund Spenser's Poetry*, ed. Hugh Maclean, 2nd ed. (New York: Norton, 1982), 272.

91. Aquinas, *Sum. theol.* 1–2, qu. 27, "Of the cause of love," art. 3, obj. 4.

92. Aquinas, *De veritate*, qu. 11, art. 1 reply.

93. Lottin, *Psychologie et morale*, 3:570.

94. Aquinas, *Sum. theol.* 1–2, qu. 51, "Of the cause of habits, as to their formation," art. 1.

95. Ibid., qu. 63, "Of the cause of virtues," art. 2, reply obj. 3; qu. 67, 'On the durations of virtues after this life," art. 1, reply obj. 3.

96. Aquasparta, *Quaestiones disputatae*, 257–58. The late Julius Weinberg drew my attention to this passage.

97. Ibid., 258.

98. John 1.9.

99. C. E. Schützinger, "Illumination," *New Catholic Encyclopedia*.

100. "Quartamque ponunt quae super haec et extra haec tria est, quam Graeci vocant συντηρησιν, quae scintilla conscientiae in Cain quoque pectore, postquam ejectus est de paradiso, non extinguitur, et qua victi voluptatibus vel furore, ipsaque interdum rationis decepti similitudine, nos peccare sentimus" (Saint Jerome, commentary on Ezek. 1.6–10 [Migne *PL* 25:22], quoted in Lottin, *Psychologie et morale*, 2:104, my emphasis and translation. See an alternative translation and discussion in Potts, *Conscience in Medieval Philosophy*, 79–91).

101. Marcia L. Colish, *Peter Lombard*, 2 vols. (Leiden: Brill, 1994), 1:383.

102. Lottin, *Psychologie et morale*, 2:120–22. Potts, *Conscience in Medieval Philosophy*, 90–93, translation of *Magistri Petri Lombardi Sententiae in IV libros distinctae* 1, pt. 2. Robert A. Greene, "Synderesis, the Spark of Conscience, in the English Renaissance," *Journal of the History of Ideas* 52 (1991): 194–99, points out the influence of Jerome's commentary through Lombard's *Sentences*, as well as through the *Glossa ordinaria*; see also M. T. Gibson, "The Place of the *Glossa ordinaria* in Medieval Exegesis," in *Ad literam: Authoritative Texts and Their Medieval Readers* (Notre Dame: University of Notre Dame Press, 1992), 5–27.

103. Lottin, *Psychologie et morale*, 2:135.

104. Aquinas, *Sum. theol.* 1–2, qu. 91, art. 2, translated by Michael Baylor in *Action and Person: Conscience in Late Scholasticism and the Young Luther* (Leiden: Brill, 1977), 158, 173, 177, cited in Greene, "Synderesis," 203 and n. 20.

105. Aquinas, *Sum. theol.* 1–2, qu. 91, art. 2.

106. Gabriel Biel, *Sententiae*, 2.35, cited in K. McDonnell, "Nominalist Natural Law Theory Revisited," in *The Medieval Tradition of Natural Law*, ed. Harold Johnson (Kalamazoo: Medieval Institute, 1987), 130.

107. Oberman, *Harvest of Medieval Theology*, 471, 475.

108. Samuel S. Kottrek, "Embryology in Talmudic and Midrashic Literature," *Journal of the History of Biology* 14 (1981): 299–315; I. Jakovits, *Jewish Medical Ethics* (New York: Bloch, 1975), 174–91; John T. Noonan, *Contraception: A History of Its Treatment by the Catholic Theologians and Canonists* (Cambridge: Harvard University Press, 1966), 89–90. The early church condemns Tertullian (ca. 160–ca. 220) for "traducianism," the view that only Adam's soul was created by God and other human souls derive from generation (*New Catholic Encyclopedia*, s.v. "Traducianism").

109. David Maclagan, *Creation Myths* (London: Thames & Hudson, 1977), 24. Note how Hildegard prescribes a visual rendition of the tension between viewing the soul as having four parts (Ezekiel's vision) and viewing it as having three parts (Plato and Augustine's trinitarian view), which Jerome confronts in his interpretation of Ezekiel (see above, n. 100). Visions of the Divine sometimes emphasize quaternity. Four-sidedness corresponds to the number of letters in the unutterable name YHWH; for Hebrew letters in mysticism, see below, chs. 3 and 8.

110. Hildegard of Bingen, *Illuminations of Hildegard of Bingen's*, ed. Matthew Fox (Santa Fe: Bear, 1985), 32; the page references that follow in the text are from this source. Lefèvre d'Étaples produces the first printed edition of Hildegard's *Scivias* after finding a manuscript in Rupertsberg in 1510 (reprinted in Migne, *PL* 197:383–738) (Eugene F. Rice Jr., "Lefèvre d'Étaples and Medieval Christian Mystics," in *Florilegium historiale*, ed. J. G. Rowe and W. H. Stockdale [Toronto: University of Toronto Press, 1971], 114). Hildegard's mysticism is discussed in Gerda Lerner, *The Creation of Feminist Consciousness: From the Middle Ages to Eighteen-seventy* (New York: Oxford University Press, 1993), esp. 52–64. A full recent translation is *Hildegard of Bingen: "Scivias,"* trans. Columba Hart and Jane Bishop (New York: Paulist Press, 1990); see chapter titled "Vision Four: Body and Soul," 109–29, esp. 124 (the analogy of the tree) and 121 (the intellect "sifting" the good from the bad).

111. *Meister Eckhart*, trans. Raymond Blakney (New York: Hopper & Bros., 1941), 210–11.

112. Eckhart, sermon entitled "Jesus Entered," using Proclus, *flos intellectus*, from *De Providentia et Fato*, cited in *Meister Eckhart, Mystic and Philosopher*, trans. Reiner Schürmann (Bloomington: Indiana University Press, 1978), 44.

113. *Meister Eckhart*, treatise 10, p. 14.

114. Gilson, *History*, 441.

CHAPTER THREE

1. Plato, *Timaeus* 90, in *The Dialogues of Plato*, trans. Benjamin Jowett, 2 vols. (New York: Random House, 1937), 2:66. A neo-Platonic translation helps to understand Renaissance references to the upper part of the soul as "daemon": "But with respect to the most principal and excellent species of the soul, we should conceive as follows: that divinity assigned this to each of us as a daemon" (*The Cratylus, Phaedo, Parmendides, Timaeus, and Critias of Plato*, trans. Thomas Taylor [London: B. and J. Whit, 1793], 369).

2. See the introduction, pp. 5–6, and ch. 2, p. 36.

3. There are important issues involved in defining *exclusionary* as an opposite of *ecumenical*. Compare Vatican II, discussed at close of the introduction, with Louis Capéran, *Le problème du salut des infidèles* (Toulouse: Grand Séminaire, 1934). Additional issues arise related to the peoples of the Americas (see Richard H. Popkin, *Isaac La Peyrère [1596–1676]: His Life, Work, and Influence* [Leiden: Brill, 1987]).

4. The neo-Platonic movement in Florence gains enormous influence from the coincidence of its foundation at the beginning of the era of the printing press. On the printing revolution, see Elizabeth L. Eisenstein, *The Printing Press in Early Modern Europe* (Cambridge: Cambridge University Press, 1983).

5. Emmanuele Le Roy Ladurie, *Le territoire de l'historien* (Paris: Gallimard, 1973), esp. chs. 7 and 15; Patrick H. Hutton, "The History of Mentalities: The New Map of Cultural History," *History and Theory* 20, no. 1 (1981): 237–59. Carolyn Merchant, *The Death of Nature: Women, Ecology, and the Scientific Revolution* (New York: Harper & Row, 1980), ch. 4, discusses the neo-Platonic contribution to organicism. Jack Goody labels the early medieval period as "the decline of flower culture in Europe" and the twelfth-century renewal as "the return of the rose in medieval Western Europe" (*The Culture of Flowers* [Cambridge: Cambridge University Press, 1993], chs. 3 and 5). Through Tertullian, Minucius Felix, St. Bernard of Clairvaux, and English Puritans, he shows the taboos against ancient vegetative ritual and details the growing markets in horticulture that are the socioeconomic context of the Christian debate on flowers from the twelfth century on.

6. Gerhart B. Ladner, "Medieval and Modern Understanding of Symbolism: A Comparison" (1979), in *Images and Ideas in the Middle Ages: Selected Studies in History and Art*, 2 vols. (Rome: Edizioni di Storia e Letteratura, 1983), 1:239–82.

7. Forrest G. Robinson, *The Shape of Things Known: Sidney's Apology in Its Philosophical Tradition* (Cambridge: Harvard University Press, 1972), esp. chs. 1–2.

8. See Paul Oskar Kristeller, *Iter Italicum: A Finding List of Uncatalogued or Incompleted Catalogued Humanistic Manuscripts of the Renaissance in Italian and Other Libraries*, 6 vols. and suppl. (London: Warburg Institute, 1963–96); Philo, *Philonis Judaei in libros Mosis de mundi opificio, historicos, de legibus. Eiusdem libri singulares*, ed. A. Turnebus (Paris, 1552); and idem, *Les oeuvres de Philon Juif*, ed. and trans. P. Bellier (Paris, 1575).

9. Aseph Goor and Max Nurock, *The Fruits of the Holy Land* (Jerusalem: Israel University Press, 1968), is the best of many books on biblical botany and its symbolism. See also in James Strong, *Exhaustive Concordance of the Bible* (New York: Abingdon-Cokesbury, 1890), s.v. "seed" and "tree."

10. Martin Buber expresses his distancing I-and-Thou model as: "I contemplate a tree" (*I and Thou*, trans. Walter Kaufman [New York: Scribner's, 1970]). As we shall see, Philo draws less distinct boundaries between the observer and the observed.

11. L. Yarden, *The Tree of Light: A Study of the Menorah, the Seven-Branched* (Ithaca: Cornell University Press, 1971). See also above, ch. 2, "Tree of light."

12. See Louis Jacobs, *A Tree of Life: Diversity, Flexibility, and Creativity in Jewish Law* (London: Oxford University Press, 1984). See also *Encyclopedia Judaica*, 16 vols. [New York: Macmillan, 1972], s.v. "Man, nature of," by Theodore Friedman, and "Inclination, Good and Evil," by Samuel Rosenblatt.

13. *The Holy Scriptures* (Philadelphia: Jewish Publication Society, 1965).

14. Goor and Nurock, *Fruits of the Holy Land*, 81. See also Elliot R. Wolfson, introduction to *The Book of the Pomegranate: Moses de Leon's Sefer Ha-Rimmon*, ed. Wolfson (Atlanta, Ga.: Scholars Press, 1988), 16–20.

15. Erwin R. Goodenough, *Jewish Symbols in the Greco-Roman Period*, 13 vols., Bollingen Series (New York: Pantheon, 1953–68), vols. 7, 9, and 11; see esp. 7:121–26 and the illustrations in vol. 11, esp. figs. 73–77 and 93.

16. Kurt Weitzmann and Herbert L. Kessler, *The Frescoes of the Dura Synagogue and Christian Art* (Washington, D.C.: Dumbarton Oaks, 1990), reprinted Goodenough's reconstructions as figures 195–96. On pp. 157–64 Weitzmann and Kessler emphasize that the grapeless vine and the empty throne indicate the continuing Jewish waiting for the Messiah, when "the vine shall yield its fruit" (Zech. 8.12, quoted on 158).

17. Jacob Neusner, introduction to abridged edition of Goodenough, *Jewish Symbols in the Greco-Roman Period*, ed. Jacob Neusner (Princeton: Princeton University Press, 1988), quotation on xxx, reviews of Goodenough on xxxv–xxxvii; Joseph Gutmann, *The Dura-Europos Synagogue: A Re-evaluation (1932–1973)* (Missoula, Mont.: American Academy of Religion Society of Biblical Literature, 1973). The rabbinical and Philonic influence on the murals is an important area of contention.

18. Goodenough, *Jewish Symbols in the Greco-Roman Period*, 9:27–82 and 11: fig. 73.

19. I thank Rabbi Allan Schranz for drawing my attention to this midrash, Midrash Rabbah 7.2.1 commenting on *Song of Songs* 6.9.2, *Midrash rabbah*, trans. under H. Freedman (London: Soncino, 1939), 266, cited in Goodenough, *Jewish Symbols in the Greco-Roman Period*, 7:128.

20. *Bet ha-Midrash*, ed. Adolf Jellinek, 6 vols. (Jerusalem: Bamberser & Vahrman, 1938), 2:28, cited in Goodenough, *Jewish Symbols in the Greco-Roman Period*, 9:80.

21. Paul G. Kuntz and Marion L. Kuntz, "The Symbol of the Tree Interpreted in the Context of Other Symbols of Hierarchical Order, the Great Chain of Being, and Jacob's Ladder," in *Jacob's Ladder and the Tree of Life: Concepts of Hierarchy and the Great Chain of Being*, ed. Marion L. Kuntz and Paul G. Kuntz (New York: Peter Lang, 1987), 323–27.

22. Goodenough, *Jewish Symbols in the Greco-Roman Period*, 9:107.

23. Ibid., 9:107–10, 88–92.

24. Philo, *De plantatione*, trans. F. H. Colson and G. H. Whitaker, Loeb Classical Library, line 9.

25. Ibid., lines 36–37.

26. Louis Jacobs, "The Doctrine of 'Divine Spark' in Man in Jewish Sources," in *Studies in Rationalism: Judaism and Universalism*, ed. Raphael Lowe (London: Routledge & Kegan Paul, 1966), 87–114; see p. 93 citing Gabirol, *Kether Malkhuth*, and citing *Zohar* 2.174a. Whereas Pico and Bodin agree with Philo that Mosaic lore influenced Plato, current scholarship has shown ancient neo-Platonic influences on the Kabbalah.

27. *The Zohar*, trans. Harry Sperling, Maurice Simon, and Paul Levertoff, 2nd ed., 6 vols. (London: Soncino, 1984), 3:4a–4b.

28. Ibid., 3:3b–4a.

29. Arthur Lesley, "'The Song of Solomon's Ascents,' by Yohanan Alemanno: Love and Human Perfection according to a Jewish Associate of Giovanni Pico della

Mirandola" (Ph.D. diss., University of California, Berkeley, 1976); idem, "Jewish Adaptation of Humanist Concepts in Fifteenth- and Sixteenth-Century Italy," in *Renaissance Rereadings: Intertext and Context*, ed. Maryanne Cline Horowitz, Anne J. Cruz, and Wendy A. Furman (Urbana: University of Illinois Press, 1988), 51–66.

30. Joseph ben Abraham Gikatilla, *Gates of Light (Sha'are orah)*, trans. and intro. Avi Weinstein, foreword Arthur Hertzberg, historical intro. Moshe Idel (San Francisco: HarperCollins, 1994). S. K. Heninger, *The Cosmographical Glass: Renaissance Diagrams of the Universe* (San Marino, Calif.: Huntington Library, 1977), 88–90; see also "The Human Microcosm," 144–58. Moshe Idel, *Kabbalah: New Perspectives* (New Haven: Yale University Press, 1988), ch. 9, "Kabbalistic Hermeneutics," 209–10, points out that in the *Zohar* the feminine divine attribute the *shekhina* plays a feminine role toward the *zaddik*, the righteous human being. Nevertheless, in the ecstatic Kabbalah, influenced by Aristotelianism, which attempts to liberate the human soul (feminine) from the body to unite with either the active intellect or God (masculine), the *zaddik* functions as a female in relationship to God.

31. David Ruderman, *The World of a Renaissance Jew: Life and Thought of Abraham ben Mordecai Farissol (1981)* (Cincinnati: Hebrew Union College Press, 1981), esp. 51–52 on Pico. Ruderman modifies Cecil Roth's Burckhardtian portrayal of Jewish-Christian camaraderie in the neo-Platonic circle. See Cecil Roth, *The Jews in the Renaissance* (Philadelphia: Jewish Publication Society of America, 1959), chs. 4–7. See also Howard Adelman, "Rabbi Leon Modena and Christian Kabbalists," in Horowitz, Cruz, and Furman, *Renaissance Rereadings*, 271–86, esp. 278.

32. Idel, *Kabbalah*, 43–44, 291 n.34, citing *Commentary on the Pentateuch*, fol. 38b in Hebrew and referring on Pico to Chaim Wirszubski, *Three Studies in Christian Kabbala* (in Hebrew) (Jerusalem, 1975), 14–22.

33. Pauline Moffitt Watts, "Pseudo-Dionysius the Aeropagite and Three Renaissance Neoplatonists: Cusanus, Ficino, and Pico on Mind and Cosmos," in *Supplementum Festivum: Studies in Honor of Paul Oskar Kristeller*, ed. James Hankins, J. Monfasani, and F. Purnell (Binghamton, N.Y.: Medieval & Renaissance Texts & Studies, 1987), 293.

34. Konstantin Bazarov, *Landscape Painting* (New York: Octopus Books, 1981), ch. 2, quotation on 34. Note the emergence of pure landscapes in Durer's watercolors of 1503–11 and in the paintings of Albrecht Altdorfer's (d. 1538), as well as the remarkable landscapes with figures of the Venetians Piero di Cosimo, Giovani Bellini, and Giorgione (Kenneth Clark, *Landscape into Art* [New York: Harper & Row, 1976]). On indirect paths of Philo's influence, such as Ambrose, see below, ch. 6, n. 82.

35. Specifically, early landscapes often show a single saint in contemplation in nature, such as Johannes der Taufer's *Geertgen tot Sint Jans* (1460/65–1495), Staatliche Museum, Berlin, or Sano di Pietro's *The Penitent St. Jerome in the Wilderness* (1444) (see Eugene F. Rice Jr., *St. Jerome in the Renaissance* [Baltimore: John Hopkins University Press, 1985], fig. 5; Hieronymus Bosch, *St. Jerome in Prayer*, in Bazarov, *Landscape Painting*, 27). I have not found art historical discussion of a Philonic interpretation.

36. Note Bellini's *St. Francis in Ecstasy* and Giorgione's *The Tempest* face to face on pp. 24–25 in *Places of Delight: The Pastoral Landscape*, by Robert C. Cafritz, Lawrence Gowing, and David Rosand, catalog for Phillips Collection exhibit,

Washington, D.C., 1988 (New York: Potter, distributed by Crown, 1988). Some scholars have noted a possible biblical interpretation of *The Tempest*. All the elements needed for a specifically Philonic interpretation are present—male higher reason, female sense perception, lush growth, psychic turmoil symbolized by nature's storm. For iconography of biblical trees in Bellini, see John V. Fleming, *From Bonaventure to Bellini: An Essay in Franciscan Exegesis* (Princeton: Princeton University Press, 1982), 75–98, 154.

37. *Holy Bible*, Revised Standard Version (New York: Collins' Clear Type Press, 1952).

38. Ladner, "Medieval and Modern Understanding of Symbolism," 1:256 n. 57, 243 n. 44.

39. Folke Norström, *Virtues and Vices on the Fourteenth Century Corbles in the Choir of Uppsala Cathedral* (Stockholm: Almquist & Wiksell, 1956), 21.

40. J. C. Cooper, "Tree," in *An Illustrated Encyclopaedia of Traditional Symbols* (London: Thames & Hudson, 1978), 179, upper figure.

41. Gerhart Ladner, "Vegetation Symbolism and the Concept of the Renaissance" (1961), in *Images and Ideas in the Middle Ages*, 2:742, citing the inscription, "Ecclesiam Christi viti similabimus isti. . . . Quam lex arentem, set crus facit esse virentem."

42. Ladner, "Medieval and Modern Understanding of Symbolism," 1:257.

43. Ibid., 1:268–75, shows a twelfth-century increase in the number of tree formations, derived from genealogies in Roman law.

44. Roger Cook, *Tree of Life: Symbol of the Centre* (London: Thames & Hudson, 1974), fig. 53.

45. See Rab Halfield, "The Tree of Life and the Holy Cross: Franciscan Spirituality in the Trecento and Quattrocento," in *Christianity and the Renaissance: Image and the Religious Imagination in the Quattrocento*, ed. Timothy Verdon and John Henderson (Syracuse, N.Y.: Syracuse University Press, 1990), 132–60 and fig. 5.2. Saint Bonaventure exerted widespread influence on later medieval mystics both within his Franciscan order and elsewhere. See *The Tree of Life* and *The Mystical Vine: Treatise on the Passion of the Lord* in vol. 1 of *The Works of Bonaventure*, trans. José de Vinck, 5 vols. (Paterson, N.J.: St. Anthony Guild Press, ca. 1960–70).

46. Ladner, "Medieval and Modern Understanding of Symbolism," 1:258.

47. Frances A. Yates, *Lull and Bruno: Collected Essays* (London: Routledge & Kegan Paul, 1982), 43–45 and figs. 2, 8a–d, 10b, 11a, 17ab.

48. *Celestial Tree*, in Raymond Lull, *Arbor scientiae*, reprinted in Yates, *Lull and Bruno*, fig. 9.

49. Lina L. Cofresí, "Hierarchical Thought in the Spanish Middle Ages: Rámon Lull and Don Juan Manuel," in Kuntz and Kuntz, *Jacob's Ladder and the Tree of Life*, 152–59, esp. 154. For earlier illustrations, see Adolf Katzenellenbogen, *Allegories of the Virtues and Vices in Mediaeval Art: From Early Christian Times to the Thirteenth Century* (London: Warburg Institute, 1939), figs. 23–26 and ch. 3, "Man's Arduous Ascent to God (The Ladder of Virtue)."

50. Raymond Lull, *Liber de ascensu et descensu* (Valencia, 1512); figure reprinted in Frances A. Yates, *The Art of Memory* (Chicago: University of Chicago Press, 1966), fig. 4, and in *Lull and Bruno*, fig. 7a.

51. See Raymond Lull, *Felix and the Book of Wonders*, in *Selected Works of Raymón Lull (1232–1316)*, ed. and trans. Anthony Bonner, 2 vols. (Princeton:

Princeton University Press, 1985), 2:1069–72 on "Sin," and 2:1030–34 on "Conscience."

52. Lull, *Liber de ascensu et descensu* (Valencia, 1512). The Palma, Majorca, 1744, edition is in the San Francisco Theological Seminary.

53. Drawing of Porphyry's tree in the *New Catholic Encyclopedia*, 15 vols. (New York: McGraw-Hill, 1967), 11:593; Porphyry, *Isagogue*, trans. Edward Warren (Toronto: Pontifical Institute, 1975).

54. Carlo Ginzburg, "The High and the Low: The Theme of Forbidden Knowledge in the Sixteenth and Seventeenth Centuries," in *Clues, Myths, and Historical Method*, trans. John Tedeschi and Anne C. Tedeschi (Baltimore: John Hopkins University Press, 1989), 60–76. Ginzburg discusses the problems posed by the Vulgate translation of Paul's Epistle to the Romans 11.20 as "Noli altum sapere, sed time," often "misinterpreted" as a "rebuke" of intellectual quests. See alternative versions in Thomas à Kempis, *Imitatione Christi*, critical ed. (Vatican City: Libreria Editrice Vaticana, 1982), 2.13.

55. *Arbor sapientiae*, ms. 416, cited in the *Yale University Library Gazette* 52 (1978): 195ff.

56. Bernard McGinn, *The Calabrian Abbot: Joachim of Fiore in the History of Western Thought* (New York: Macmillan, 1985), 186–87.

57. Cook, *Tree of Life*, pl. 42 and pp. 28–29, quotation on 29. Joachim influenced the mosaics of San Marco in Venice (Otto Demus, *The Mosaics of San Marco in Venice* [Chicago: University of Chicago Press, 1984], vol. 2, suggested by Marion Kuntz).

58. Yates, *Lull and Bruno*, trees in fig. 8.

59. Ibid., 25–30 and pl. 2. The word *arbor* frequently occurs in medieval Latin as "mill shaft"; see, e.g., *Harper's Latin Dictionary* (New York: American Book Co., 1907); and *Dictionary of Medieval Latin from British Sources* (London: Oxford University Press, 1975).

60. Frank J. Anderson, *An Illustrated History of Herbals* (New York: Columbia University Press, 1977); A. G. Morton, *History of Botanical Science: An Account of the Development of Botany from Ancient Times to the Present Day* (London: Academic Press, 1981), ch. 4.

61. Katzenellenbogen, *Allegories of the Virtues and Vices*, 63–66 and fig. 64. Katzenellenbogen dates the drawing to 1120; Cook, *Tree of Life*, dates it to before 1192.

62. Katzenellenbogen, *Allegories of the Virtues and Vices*, 66–67, 72, and figs. 66 and 67.

63. Guillaume Durand, *Rationale Divinorum Officiorum*, trans. John Mason Neale and Benjamin Webb in *The Symbolism of Church and Church Ornaments* (London, 1893), 55; see also Folke Norström, *Virtues and Vices*, 23.

64. Thomas N. Tentler, *Sin and Confession on the Eve of the Reformation* (Princeton: Princeton University Press, 1977).

65. Lull, *Selected Works*, 1:110–304, pl. 10, tree 4; Peter Abelard, *A Dialogue of a Philosopher with a Jew and a Christian*, trans. J. Payer (Toronto: Pontifical Institute of Medieval Studies, 1979).

66. Lull, *Selected Works*, 1:97.

67. J. N. Hillgarth, *Ramon Lull and Lullism in Fourteenth-Century France* (Oxford: Clarendon, 1971), 36–38, 53. Hillgarth provides full bibliographical information and locations for Lull manuscripts.

68. Ibid., 280–90, 318–19. Yates, *Lull and Bruno*, 235, cites Pico della Miran-dola, *Apologia*, p. 180, of the *Opera omnia* (Basel, 1572), where Pico states that his thought owes much to the "Raymundus."

69. Lull, *Selected Works*, 1:64 n. 53, citing Lull's *Compendium artis demon-strativae*.

70. For my phrases "divine path to divine wisdom," "human path to divine wis-dom," "divine path to human wisdom," and "human path to human wisdom," see the introduction and the beginning of ch. 2, above.

71. Goody, *Culture of Flowers*, 66–69, 75–79, 157–59, 167–68.

72. Boccaccio, *Genealogiae* (Venice, 1494), facsimile in The Renaissance and the Gods, ed. Stephen Orgel (New York: Garland, 1976); Neptune on p. 7. This is the fourth printed edition of Boccaccio's manuscript of 1371. Following those of Venice 1472, Reggoi 1482, and Vicenza 1487, it is the first to include genealogical trees at the beginning of each book. Illustrations vary; for example, the 1531 Paris edition in French has woodcut illustrations but no genealogical trees.

73. Mary Barnard, *The Myth of Apollo and Daphne from Ovid to Quevedo* (Dur-ham: Duke University Press, 1987), fig. 8. Daphne is only one of the metamor-phoses of anthromorphic beings into trees; see Percy Preston, *Dictionary of Picto-rial Subjects from Classical Literature* (New York: Scribner, ca. 1983), s.v. "Tree," 275–76.

74. The subject matter at this villa focuses on "the mythological creation of the flowers, of nature, and of the cycle of time and nature" (David Coffin, *The Villa in the Life of Renaissance Rome* [Princeton: Princeton University Press, 1979], 87–109, quotation on 103).

75. See the detail of pl. 97, *Calumny of Apelles*, ca. 1494–95, in Ronald W. Lightbown, *Sandro Botticelli: Life and Work* (New York: Abbeville, 1989), 210.

76. Andrew Marvell, *The Poems and Letters of Andrew Marvell*, 2 vols., ed. H. M. Margoliouth (Oxford: Clarendon, 1971), verse 4, lines 29–32. Marvell's poem "The Garden" (and the Latin version, "Hortus"), pp. 51–55, has received much commentary, but it would be valuable to consider interpreting the full poem as an example of Philo's landscape of the mind.

CHAPTER FOUR

1. See the section on Pico della Mirandola below, in ch. 6, for an analysis of Pico's *Oratio* and *Heptaplus*. Pico's own manuscripts and books suggest the ecu-menical riches available in the Italian peninsula, where Hebrew and Arabic were spoken and whence an elaborate trade network extended throughout the Medi-terranean (see the list in Pearl Kibre, *The Library of Pico della Mirandola* [New York: Columbia University Press, 1936]).

2. For translations of Plato, see James Hankins, *Plato in the Italian Renaissance*, 2 vols. (Leiden: Brill, 1990), 2:738–85. The Museum of Naples has a small ancient mosaic showing philosophers conversing under a tree.

3. Terry Comito, *The Idea of the Garden in the Renaissance* (New Brunswick, N.J.: Rutgers University Press, 1978), 77–87; André Chastel, *Marsile Ficin et l'art* (Geneva: Droz, 1954), 8–9.

4. See the drawing by Giuseppe Zocchi, 1774, in James S. Ackerman, *The Villa: Form and Ideology of Country Houses* (Princeton: Princeton University Press, 1990), fig. 3.8.

5. Janet Cox-Rearick, *Dynasty and Destiny in Medici Art: Pontormo, Leo X, and the Two Cosimos* (Princeton: Princeton University Press, 1984); for the genealogical tree of Leo X, see fig. 44, and for the Medici shield, see fig. 10. Unless otherwise noted, pages cited in the text refer to this book.

6. F. Barberi, *Il frontispizio nel libro italiano del quattrocento e del cinquecento* (Milan, 1969), 110, 125, fig. 57. On earlier examples of Apollo and the Muses, see Jean Seznec, *The Survival of the Pagan Gods* (Princeton: Princeton University Press, 1953), 110, 135, 177, 203.

7. See R. Van den Broek, *The Myth of the Phoenix according to Classical and Early Christian Traditions* (Leiden: Brill, 1972), summaries on 146–47, 412, and 422.

8. Marsilio Ficino, *Commentaire sur le Banquet de Platon*, Latin and French edition, trans. Raymond Marcel (Paris: Belles Lettres, 1978); idem, *Commentary on Plato's Symposium on Love*, English trans. by Sears Jayne (Dallas: Spring, 1985). This commentary was published in Latin in 1469, in Italian in 1474, and in French in 1542. I cite the page number in Jayne, followed by the oration, chapter, and line numbers in Marcel. I adopt Jayne's translation except that I translate *homo* to mean a generic human being rather than as "man," and I omit capitalization foreign to the Latin text, and I include Ficino's Latin terms that indicate the impact of Stoic imagery.

9. Andreas Graeser, *Plotinus and the Stoics: A Preliminary Study* (Leiden: Brill, 1972), wrestles with the complexity of the Stoic influences on Plotinus and shows parallel light symbolism (23–24, 37), close competition on views of virtue (59–61), and a possible drawing from Posidonius's revision of Stoic views on causation (101–11). For reciprocal influences in the Middle Academy and the Middle Stoa, see P. Merlan, "The Stoa," in *The Cambridge History of Later Greek and Early Medieval Philosophy*, ed. A. H. Armstrong (Cambridge: Cambridge University Press, 1967), 124–32.

10. For the acceptance of this approach by a churchman influential at the Council of Trent, see John W. O'Malley, *Giles of Viterbo on Church and Reform: A Study in Renaissance Thought* (Leiden: Brill, 1968), 24–29, 49–53.

11. Plotinus, *Enneads,* trans. A. H. Armstrong, Loeb Classical Library, 3.5 ("On Love") and 5.1–4; and note the similar Plotinian structure in Ficino's commentary on Plato's *Timaeus*, Michael J. B. Allen, "Marsilio Ficino's Interpretation of Plato's *Timaeus* and Its Myth of the Demiurge," in *Supplementum Festivum: Studies in Honor of Paul Oskar Kristeller*, ed. James Hankins, J. Monfasani, and F. Purnell (Binghamton, N.Y.: Medieval & Renaissance Texts & Studies, 1987), 413–17, 419–20.

12. Michael J. B. Allen, "Cosmogony and Love: The Role of Phaedrus in Ficino's *Symposium* Commentary," *Journal of Medieval and Renaissance Studies* 10–11 (1980–81): 141–44.

13. Marsilio Ficino, *Théologie platonicienne*, Latin and French edition, trans. Raymond Marcel, 3 vols. (Paris: Belles Lettres, 1970), 12.1, further amplifies this comparison. See also the edited collection *Il lume del sole* (Florence, 1984).

14. Paul Oskar Kristeller, *The Philosophy of Marsilio Ficino*, trans. Virginia Conant (Gloucester, Mass.: Peter Smith, 1964), 138–39; Allen, "Marsilio Ficino's Interpretation of Plato's *Timaeus*," 411, 415.

15. Michael J. B. Allen, *The Platonism of Marsilio Ficino: A Study of His "Phaedrus" Commentary, Its Sources and Genesis* (Berkeley: University of California

Press, 1984), 127–32, discusses Ficino's allegorizing of the myths of the two Venuses.

16. Marsilio Ficino, *The Philebus Commentary*, ed. and trans. Michael J. B. Allen (Berkeley: University of California Press, 1975), 79–81. Allen points out the contrast between the Creation by God before ideas or matter and the generation by the angelic soul using *semina et rationes*.

17. Barthélemy Aneau, *Picta poesis, ut pictura poesis erit* (Lyons, 1552), discussed in S. K. Heninger, *The Cosmographical Glass: Renaissance Diagrams of the Universe* (San Marino, Calif.: Huntington Library, 1977), 149–50.

18. Elémire Zolla, *The Androgyne: Reconciliation of Male and Female* (New York: Crossroad, 1981), 72.

19. Edmund Spenser, *The Faerie Queene*, in *Edmund Spenser's Poetry*, ed. Hugh Maclean, 2nd ed. (New York: Norton, 1982), 1590 edition's concluding stanzas to bk. 3, 3.12, p. 350, note to Ovid, *Metamorphoses* 4:285–388.

20. Marsilio Ficino, *Opera omnia*, 2 vols. (Basel, 1561), 384, quoting Plot., *Enn.* 1.1, cited in Kristeller, *Philosophy of Marsilio Ficino*, 328; *The Letters of Marsilio Ficino*, trans. members of Language Department of the School of Economic Science, London, 5 vols. (London: Shepheard-Walwyn, 1975–94), 1:78–79.

21. Augustine, SVF 1:180; Censorius, SVF 1:124; Cicero, *De re publica, De legibus*, trans. Clinton Keyes, Loeb Classical Library, *Leg.* 1.33.

22. Aeneas Sylvius, *De liberorum educatione*, in *Vittorino da Feltre and Other Humanist Educators*, ed. and trans. William Harrison Woodward (1897; reprint, New York: Columbia University Press, 1963), 137, applying Quntilian, *Institutio oratoria*, trans. H. E. Butler, Loeb Classical Library, 1.3 and 2.4.

23. Manuscripts of Lull were in the libraries of Pico della Mirandola and of Lorenzo de' Medici's physician (J. N. Hillgarth, *Ramon Lull and Lullism in Fourteenth-Century France* [Oxford: Clarendon, 1971], 280–90, 318–19).

24. See above, ch. 1, "Seeds to Trees." See also Hugh of St. Victor, *Commentaria in hierarchiam coelestem Sancti Dionisii* (1137), cited in "Symbolism and Allegory," *Encyclopedia of World Art*, 17 vols. (New York: McGraw-Hill, 1958–87), 13:794–95; Dionysius the Areopagite, discussed in E. H. Gombrich, "Icones Symbolicae...," in *Symbolic Images: Studies in the Art of the Renaissance* (London: Phaidon, 1972), 145–60; and Richard C. Dales, "Medieval View of Human Dignity," *Journal of the History of Ideas* 38 (1977): 557–72.

25. *Andreas Alciatus*, ed. Peter M. Daly, with Virginia W. Callahan and Simon Cuttler, 2 vols. (Toronto: University of Toronto Press, 1985), vol. 1, emblem 110, my translation.

26. The mythological context helps to bring to the surface the ancient biological framework that permeates both Stoic and Plotinian cosmology (see above, ch. 1, n. 43). Plot., *Enn.* 4.3.23, 4.7.13, and 3.8.10, gives evidence of the Stoic defense of *panagenesis* (that the semen is drawn from all parts of the body) and of the Aristotelian distinction between the formative capacities of seeds in nature and the material contribution of unformed matter.

27. Ficino, *Philebus Commentary*, 202–4. In his introduction (52–56) Allen confirms Kristeller's view that both the *Symposium* commentary and *Philebus* commentary were written in 1469.

28. Charles Trinkaus, "Marsilio Ficino and the Ideal of Human Autonomy," in *Ficino and Renaissance Neoplatonism*, ed. Konrad Eisenbichler and Olga Zorzi Pugliese (Ottawa: Dovehouse, 1986), 141–53, quotation on 147, citing Ficino,

Theologia platonica, ed. Marcel, 2:224–25. Likewise, Ficino applies the model of the Demiurge who creates from Ideas, not *ex nihilo*, as a model for the human creator who applies ideas to fashioning matter (Allen, "Marsilio Ficino's Interpretation of Plato's *Timaeus*," 438–39). For the controversy over Trinkaus's interpretation, see Michael J. B. Allen, *Icastes: Marsilio Ficino's Interpretation of Plato's "Sophist"* (Berkeley: University of California Press, 1989), 147–54. For the possible influence of Philo, see below, ch. 8, "Philo's Garden of the Soul in the Book of Nature."

29. Plot., *Enn.* 4.7.1,8–10; John Dillon, *The Middle Platonists, 80 B.C. to A.D. 200* (Ithaca: Cornell University Press, 1977), 69–70, 80–81, 95; Seneca, *Ad Lucilium epistulae morales*, trans. Richard M. Gummere, Loeb Classical Library, *Ep.* 120.4–8; 90.46. See above, ch. 1, "Common Notions."

30. Françoise Joukovsky, *Le regard intérieur: Thèmes plotiniens chez quelques écrivains de la Renaissance française* (Paris: Nizet, 1982), 110, 152–56, 163–72.

31. See Fic., *Théol. plat.*, ed. Marcel, 2:97–98, 103, 105, 107, 110, 117, 119, 125, for examples from 11.3–4 alone.

32. Pauline Moffitt Watts, "Pseudo-Dionysius the Areopagite and Three Renaissance Neoplatonists: Cusanus, Ficino, and Pico on Mind and Cosmos," in Hankins, Monfasani, and Purnell, *Supplementum Festivum*, 295.

33. Kristeller, *Philosophy of Marsilio Ficino*, 50, citing *Theol. plat.* 11.1 in *Opera omnia* 1:230. The following parenthetical references in the text are to Kristeller's book.

34. Leo Hebraeus, *The Philosophy of Love*, trans. F. Friedeberg-Seeley and Jean H. Barnes (London: Soncino, 1937), dialogue 3, 207, 209. Two influential French editions are Léone Hébreu, *Dialogues d'amour*, trans. Pontus de Tyard (1551), ed. T. Anthony Perry (Chapel Hill: University of North Carolina Press, 1974), and *Philosophie d'amour*, trans. Denys Sauvage (Lyon, 1551). For the impact of Leone Ebreo's Judaism (his name was Jehudah Abrabanel) and his differences from Ficino, see Naomi Yavneh, "The Spiritual Eroticism of Leone's Hermaphrodite," in *Playing with Gender: A Renaissance Pursuit*, ed. Jean R. Brink, Maryanne C. Horowitz, and Allison P. Coudert (Champaign: University of Illinois Press, 1991), 85–98; and Arthur Lesley, "The Place of the *Dialoghi d'amore* in Contemporaneous Jewish Thought," in *Ficino and Renaissance Neoplatonism* (Toronto: University of Toronto Press, 1986), 71–86.

35. Pietro Bembo, *Gli Asolani*, trans. Rudolf B. Gottfried (Bloomington: Indiana University Press, 1954), 183–84 and 100 (quotation).

36. Castiglione, *The Book of the Courtier*, trans. Charles S. Singleton (Garden City, N.Y.: Anchor, 1959), 353–54.

CHAPTER FIVE

1. Victoria Kahn, *Rhetoric, Prudence, and Skepticism in the Renaissance* (Ithaca: Cornell University Press, 1985), 33–34, citing Klaus Oehler, "Der Consensus omnium als Kriterium der Wahrheit in der antiken Philosophie und der Patristik," *Antike und Abendland* 10 (1961): 110, and Cicero, *Tusculan Disputations*, trans. J. E. King (Cambridge: Harvard University Press, 1971), 3.1.2; Arthur F. Kinney, *Continental Humanist Poetics: Studies in Erasmus, Castiglione, Marguerite de Navarre, Rabelais, and Cervantes* (Amherst: University of Massachusetts Press, 1989), ch. 1, esp. 11, 35–39, 45. *Erasme. Declamatio de pueris statim ac liberaliter instituendis,*

ed. Jean-Claude Margolin (Geneva: Droz, 1966), 68 nn. 8–9, comes closest to recognizing common usage and significance of the phrase for Erasmus and his Italian humanist predecessors, but he does not recognize its Stoic origin. Nevertheless, Margolin finds the "gestation" and "fermentations" of "l'ingenuité naturelle" as proper merit for the name Renaissance (pp. 69, 74, 87).

2. See below, ch. 6, "Divine or Human Gardening of the Soul? Lèfevre d'Étaples, Luther, and Erasmus"; and Gordon Rupp et al., eds. and trans., *Luther and Erasmus: Free Will and Salvation* (London: SCM Press, 1969), 311.

3. Paul F. Grendler, *Schooling in Renaissance Italy: Literacy and Learning, 1300–1600* (Baltimore: Johns Hopkins University Press, 1989), 233–34, 263–65, 406–10, reaffirms the Italian humanists' thorough commitment to teaching ethics through the study of great sayings and deeds of the ancients.

4. James J. Murphy, ed., *Quintilian on the Teaching of Speaking and Writing* (Carbondale: Southern Illinois University Press, 1987), pref., lines 9–10, 18–20. Quintilian builds upon Cicero's *De oratore*; see Cicero, *De oratore*, trans. H. Rackham, Loeb Classical Library, esp. 1.4.17–6.23 and 3.19–20, and Robert R. Rusk and James Scotland, *Doctrines of Great Educators* (New York: St. Martin's, 1979), 35–45, esp. 36–37.

5. Paul O. Kristeller, "The Humanist Tradition," in *Renaissance Thought: The Classic, Scholastic, and Humanist Strains* (New York: Harper & Row, 1961). As Albert Rabil Jr. points out, "Kristeller's formulations constitute the most widely accepted paradigm of humanist studies today" (*Renaissance Humanism: Foundations, Forms, and Legacy*, ed. Rabil, 3 vols. [Philadelphia: University of Pennsylvania Press, 1988], 1:xii).

6. Robert L. Benson and Giles Constable with Carol D. Lanham, eds., *Renaissance and Renewal in the Twelfth Century* (Cambridge: Harvard University Press, 1982), indicates some of the controversy following C. H. Haskins, *The Twelfth Century Renaissance* (Cambridge: Harvard University Press, 1927). Two recent works stress the differences between medieval and Renaissance teaching of rhetoric: Grendler, *Schooling in Renaissance Italy*, 205–12; and John Monfasani, "Humanism and Rhetoric," in Rabil, *Renaissance Humanism*, 3:171–35.

7. Murphy, *Quintilian on the Teaching of Speaking and Writing*, xxxix–xl; James J. Murphy, *Rhetoric in the Middle Ages: A History of Rhetorical Theory from Saint Augustine to the Renaissance* (Berkeley: University of California Press, 1974), 123–30.

8. John of Salisbury, *The Metalogicon*, trans. Daniel D. McGarry (Berkeley: University of California Press, 1955), 9, 33. The works he cites, including works of Cicero, Seneca, Quintilian, and Virgil, are listed in R. R. Bolgar, *The Classical Heritage and Its Beneficiaries* (Cambridge: Cambridge University Press, 1954), 423 n. 219.

9. Maryanne Cline Horowitz, "Introduction: Playing with Gender," *Playing with Gender: A Renaissance Pursuit*, ed. Jean R. Brink, Maryanne C. Horowitz, and Allison P. Coudert (Champaign: University of Illinois Press, 1991), ix–xxiv.

10. Allegorical literature increasingly personifies the soul (*anima*) as female to emphasize the capacities that come to it from the masculine deity. See Joan Ferrante, *Woman As Image in Medieval Literature from the Twelfth Century to Dante* (New York: Columbia University Press, 1975); Londa Schiebinger, *The Mind Has No Sex? Women in the Origins of Modern Science* (Cambridge: Harvard University Press, 1989), ch. 5, which shows the predominance of feminine personifications of

science, wisdom, and the Muses in the Renaissance (loved by the male scholar) and discusses the Platonic origin of viewing the soul as female; and Caroline Walker Bynum, "Jesus As Mother and Abbot As Mother: Some Themes in Twelfth-Century Cistercian Writing," *Jesus As Mother: Studies in the Spirituality of the High Middle Ages* (Berkeley: University of California Press, 1982), esp. 110–25, 138–41, 150.

11. Francesco Petrarca, *Secretum*, in *Opere*, ed. Giovanni Ponte (Milan: Mursia, 1968); idem, *Petrarch's Secret: or, The Soul's Conflict with Passion (Secretum)*, trans. William Draper (1899; reprint, Westport, Conn.: Hyperion, 1977); Charles Trinkaus, *In Our Image and Likeness: Humanity and Divinity in Italian Humanist Thought*, 2 vols. (Chicago: University of Chicago Press, 1970), 1:13, Latin text on 330 n. 13. Translation by Trinkaus except that I have translated *homo* as "human" (see above, ch. 1, n. 1). See also William J. Bouwsma, "The Two Faces of Humanism: Stoicism and Augustinianism in Renaissance Thought," in *Itinerarium Italicum: The Profile of the Italian Renaissance in the Mirror of Its European Transformations*, ed. Heiko A. Oberman with Thomas A. Brady Jr. (Leiden: Brill, 1975), 19.

12. "At nos, quibus non nostro merito sed celesti munere vivacius veri lumen apparuit, ubi illi desinunt incipimus neque enim ad virtutem quasi finem, sed ad Deum per virtutes nitimur" (Petrarch, *Il "De Otio religoso" di Francesco Petrarca*, ed. Giuseppi Rotondi, Studi e Testi 195 [Vatican City, 1958], 91–92, cited in Trinkaus, *In Our Image and Likeness*, 45, Latin text on 342 n. 97).

13. "Quod cum olim rudes homines sed noscendi veri praecipueque vestigande divinitatis studio, quod naturaliter inest homini, flagrantes, cogitare coepissent esse superiorem aliquam potestatem per quam mortalia regerentur" (Petrarch, *Rerum familiarum* 10.4, in Trinkaus, *In Our Image and Likeness*, 690, Latin text on 863 n. 12).

14. Petrarch, "On His Own Ignorance and That of Many Others," trans. Hans Nachod, in *The Renaissance Philosophy of Man*, ed. Ernst Cassirer, Paul O. Kristeller, and John H. Randall Jr. (Chicago: University of Chicago Press, 1948), 80–88, on Cicero's *De natura deorum*, quotation on 104. In stressing Petrarch's awareness of reason in both humanity and the cosmos I differ from Robert Proctor, *Education's Great Amnesia: Reconsidering the Humanities from Petrarch to Freud* (Bloomington: Indiana University Press, 1988); see quotations on 23–24, 16–20, 82–83.

15. Vergerius, "Concerning Character," in *Vittorino da Feltre and Other Humanist Educators*, ed. and trans. William Harrison Woodward (1897; reprint, New York: Columbia University Press, 1963), 97. See also Grendler, *Schooling in Renaissance Italy*, 117–18.

16. Leonardo Bruni, *Dialogues*, in *The Three Crowns of Florence: Humanist Assessments of Dante, Petrarca, and Boccaccio*, ed. and trans. D. Thompson and A. F. Nagel (New York: Harper & Row, 1972), 19. On the controversy on rhetorical and civic aspects of Bruni's humanism, see my introduction, under "Strategy."

17. Leonardo Bruni, "Concerning the Study of Literature," in Woodward, *Vittorino da Feltre and Other Humanist Educators*, 122–33, quoting the *Aeneid*, 130.

18. Battista Malatesta, "Oration," in *"Her Immaculate Hand": Selected Works By and About the Women Humanists of Quattrocento Italy*, ed. and trans. Margaret L. King and Albert Rabil Jr. (Binghamton: State University of New York Press, 1983), 36–38 and introduction, 701–2. I am grateful to Albert Rabil for

sending me the women humanists' Latin texts. Although Woodward's date for Bruni's letter—1405, the year of Battista's marriage (ibid., 13)—still has influence, Hans Baron argued for the later date of 1423–26 in *The Crisis of the Early Italian Renaissance: Civic Humanism and Republican Liberty in an Age of Classicism and Tyranny* (Princeton: Princeton University Press, 1966), 554 n. 23. Grendler, *Schooling in Renaissance Italy*, 87, accepts Baron's dating, as does Proctor, *Education's Great Amnesia*, 4. It is indisputable that Battista's Latin oration to Emperor Sigismund in Urbino in the spring of 1433 postdates Bruni's treatise and disregards Bruni's limitation that "rhetoric in all its forms,—public discussion, forensic argument, logical fence, and the like—lies absolutely outside the province of woman" (Bruni, "Concerning the Study of Literature," 126).

19. Costanza da Varano, in King and Rabil, *"Her Immaculate Hand,"* 56.

20. Quintilian, *Institutio oratoria*, trans. E. H. Butler, Loeb Classical Library, 1.1; Stanley F. Bonner, *Education in Ancient Rome: From the Elder Cato to the Younger Pliny* (Berkeley: University of California Press, 1977), 28, 107, 135–36; Grendler, *Schooling in Renaissance Italy*, 93–102; Patricia Labalme, ed., *Beyond Their Sex: Learned Women of the European Past* (New York: New York University Press, 1984); Margaret King, "Thwarted Ambitions: Six Learned Women of the Early Italian Renaissance," *Soundings* 76 (1976): 280–314.

21. Costanza da Varano, in King and Rabil, *"Her Immaculate Hand,"* 40; I am grateful to Albert Rabil for sending me the Latin text. "Nemo enim est tam effrenis tam barbaris moribus & tam externarum gentium & disjunctissimarum natione, qui tantarum virtutum tuarum amoris non flagret incendio. O felicem Hesperiam, quae e suo gremio tam radiantissimum lumen oriri passa est!" (J. Lamius, *Catalogus codicum manuscriptorum qui in Bibliotheca Riccardiana Florentiae adservantur* . . . [Livorno, 1756], 146).

22. Jacob Burckhardt, *The Civilization of the Renaissance in Italy*, trans. S. G. C. Middlemore (New York: Harper & Row, 1958), 143–45 and 175–82 (bk. 2, ch. 1, and bk. 3, ch. 1). The influential Burckhardt is under the spell of such Italian humanist rhetoric (176). For ancient precedents of womb images one might note the allegorical panel of the Ara Pacis of Emperor Augustus (ca. 9 B.C.E.), which shows a woman associated with human, animal, and plant fertility flanked by two personifications of winds. Only in the sixteenth century are parts of the Ara Pacis found (David Castriota, *The Ars Pacis Augustae and the Imagery of Abundance in Later Greek and Early Roman Imperial Art* [Princeton: Princeton University Press, 1995]).

23. Murphy, *Quintilian on the Teaching of Speaking and Writing*, xli; Michael Winterbottom, "Quintilian: *Institutio oratoria*," in *Texts and Transmission: A Survey of the Latin Classics*, ed. L. D. Reynolds (Oxford: Clarendon, 1983), 332–34.

24. More than 250 manuscripts are extant, and a controversy continues concerning two or more that may be Poggio's (see Jean Cousin, *Quintilien institution oratoire*, 7 vols. [Paris: Belles Lettres, 1975–80], vol. 1, esp. xcv, cx).

25. Grendler, *Schooling in Renaissance Italy*, 121–23 and references in n. 31. See also Reynolds, *Texts and Transmission*, 102–9.

26. A. G. Morton, *History of Botanical Science: An Account of the Development of Botany from Ancient Times to the Present Day* (London: Academic Press, 1981), 100, 27–33; Theophrastus, *Enquiry into Plants* [*Historia plantarum*], trans. Arthur Hort, Loeb Classical Library; idem, *De causis plantarum*, trans. Benedict Einarson and George K. K. Link, Loeb Classical Library, 1976–90 (note that 1990

marks the first full publication in English of *De causis plantarum*); John Scarborough, "Theophrastus on Herbals and Herbal Remedies," *Journal of the History of Biology* 11 (1978): 353–85. Theophrastus has an impact on educational theory not only through the above botanical works but also through his moral treatise *The Characters*, which gives short, vivid descriptions of people embodying specific vices, such as "dissembling," "buffoonery," "boorishness," and "recklessness" (see *The Characters of Theophrastus*, trans. J. M. Edmonds, Loeb Classical Library.

27. Cassandra Fedele, "Oration in Praise of Letters," in King and Rabil, *"Her Immaculate Hand,"* 75. "Rudes autem & literarum expertes si quam ingenii & rationis sementem a natura inchoatam habent eam cum omni vitae tempore incultam deserunt, neglectu quodam, situque penitus interire cogunt, ac sese praeclaras ad res reddunt inutiles?" (*Cassandra Fidelis Venetae epistolae et orationes*, ed. J. F. Tomasini [Padua, 1636], 203).

28. For examples of seeds of virtue as the subject of debate in the quattrocento, see Albert Rabil Jr., ed. and trans., *Knowledge, Goodness, and Power: The Debate over Nobility among Quattrocento Italian Humanists* (Binghamton: State University of New York Press, 1991), e.g., 41, 44, 82–89, 114–15, 141, 217–18, 281–82, 325, and 223–24.

29. Fedele, "Oration in Praise of Letters," in King and Rabil, *"Her Immaculate Hand,"* 76. "At viri eruditi & multiplici rerum humanarum divinarumque cognitione referti omnes suas cogitationes & animi discursus ad rationem tanquam ad scopum dirigunt, ipsumque animum tot solicitudinibus obnoxium omni agritudine liberant. . . . Literarum studia ingenia pollunt, rationis vim illustrant, ac formant, omnem animi labem aut penitus eluunt, aut magna ex parte tollunt; & eius dotes cumulate perficiunt, fortuna corporisque commodis ornamenti plurimum addunt, et decoris" (*Cassandra Fidelis*, 204–5).

30. King and Rabil, *"Her Immaculate Hand,"* 83. "At illae, quibus ad virtutem integritas maior aspirat, frenant principio iuvenilem animum, meditantur meliora consilia, durant sobrietate & laboribus corpus, cohibent deinde linguam, observant aures, componunt in vigilias ingenium, & mentem excitant in contemplationem ad literas probitati semper obnoxias. . . . Donavit satis omnes Natura dotibus suis: Omnibus optionis suae portas aperuit, per quas ad voluntatem mittit ratio legatos a qua secum sua desideria reportent. Vestra est auctoritas; nostrum ingenium" (Laura Cereta, *Laurae Ceretae epistolae*, ed. J. F. Tomasini [Padua, 1640], 192–93).

31. King and Rabil, *"Her Immaculate Hand,"* 123. See also Albert Rabil Jr., *Laura Cereta Quattrocento Humanist* (Binghamton: State University of New York Press, 1981), esp. 75, 102–3, and quotation from Frater Thomas to Silvestro Cereto: "Tantumne talentum hoccine auri purgatissimi pondo tradidit, ut florea duntaxat commercemur? Ignosce obsecro, et Laura pariter indulgeat" (147).

32. Aeneas Sylvius Piccolomini, *De liberorum educatione*, in Woodward, *Vittorino da Feltre and Other Humanist Educators*, 137. Subsequent references in the text are to Woodward's translation.

33. Quint., *Inst.* 1.3 and 2.24.4.

34. *The Florentine "Fior di Virtu" of 1491*, trans. Nicholas Fersin with facsimiles of all the original woodcuts (Washington, D.C.: Library of Congress, 1953), illustrations on xiv and xvi. On fourteenth-century manuscripts, see Grendler, *Schooling in Renaissance Italy*, 278–80. I thank Paul F. Watson for suggesting that I look at the facsimile edition at the Clark Library.

35. The phrase *enclosed garden* (*hortus conclusus*) is used to describe actual monastery gardens or images of the Annunciation, as in "Hortus conclusus soror mea, sponsa, hortus conclusus, fons signatus," in Canticles for the Vigil of the Assumption, cited in Stanley Stewart, *The Enclosed Garden: The Tradition and the Image in Seventeenth Century Poetry* (Madison: University of Wisconsin Press, 1966), 31. To gain perspective on what is medieval and Christian about the interpretation of the Song of Songs by the artists and writers Stewart discusses, see a poet's new translation of the Hebrew Song of Songs: Marcia Falk, *The Song of Songs: Love Poems from the Bible*, illus. Barry Moser (New York: Harcourt Brace Jovanovich, 1977). Up until now most studies of the garden of the soul (*hortus animae*) have been Christian iconographical studies of the enclosed garden.

36. Stobaeus, *Florilegium diversorum epigrammatum in septem libros* (Venice: Aldus Manutius, November 1503), copy in the Special Collections, UCLA Research Library. For the English version, see *The Greek Anthology*, trans. W. R. Paton, Loeb Classical Library, 5 vols.

37. "Gravissimas et illustrissimas Graecorum sententias, interdum et historias elegantiores et exempla memorabilia, . . . ex vario genere florum quicquod inerat succi suavioris exhauriens, hanc . . . apothecam, diverso genere nobilium aromatum instar divitis pharmacopolae, singulis suis capsulis discernentes, implevit" (*Johannis Stobaei sententiae ex thesauris Graecorum*, cited in Sister Joan Marie Lechner, *Renaissance Concepts of the Commonplaces* [New York: Pageant, 1962], 149 n. 129; an influential edition is H. Estienne, *Epigrammata graeca selecta ex anthologia* [Paris, 1570]).

38. Anthony Grafton, "The Availability of Ancient Works," in *The Cambridge History of Renaissance Philosophy*, ed. Charles B. Schmitt et al. (Cambridge: Cambridge University Press, 1988), 791.

39. Henry Peacham, *The Garden of Eloquence*, ed. William G. Crane (Gainesville, Fla.: Scholars' Facsimiles and Reprints, 1954), 191.

40. Lechner, *Renaissance Concepts of the Commonplaces*, in which ch. 2, sec. 3, "Metaphorical Substructure of the Places," 131–52, gives a valuable analysis.

41. For further consideration of origin, variation, transformation, dormancy, and reinvigoration of figurative language, see in my introduction under "Metaphor" and "Language of vegetative growth," as well as my analysis of Derrida's ideas on the death of metaphors.

42. *German Proverbs*, ed. John Zug, woodcuts from *The Nuremberg Chronicle* (1493) (Iowa City: Penfield, 1988).

43. The expansion of the genre supplements such works as the sayings of Cato (compiled from the second through the fourth century), read from the seventh century on, so basic that Chaucer says of the foolish carpenter in "The Miller's Tale": "He knew not Catoun, for his wit was rude" (see *Dicta Catonis*, in *Minor Latin Poets*, ed. J. W. Duff and A. Duff [Cambridge: Harvard University Press, 1935], introduction and 585–89; and C. H. Talbot, Introduction to *Florilegium morale oxoniense*, Ms. Bodl. 633 [Lille: Giard, 1956], 5–31). For a good study of building one florilegium from another and of practical applications, as in sermon writing, see Richard Rouse and Mary Rouse, *Preachers, Florilegia, and Sermons: Studies on the "Manipulus florum" of Thomas of Ireland* (Toronto: Pontifical Institute, 1979).

44. Janet Backhouse, *The Illuminated Manuscript* (Oxford: Phaidon, 1979),

72–74 and figs. 63 and 64; Edward Johnson et al., *Writing Illumination and Lettering* (London: Pitman, 1977), 165–67, pls. 16–19; Morton Bloomfield, *The Seven Deadly Sins* (East Lansing: Michigan State College Press, 1952).

45. Adriaen Collaert, *Florilegium* ([Anvers]: P. Galle, [c. 1590]); Pierre Vallet, *Le jardin du tres chrestien Henry IV* (Paris, 1608); Jean Théodore Bry, *Florilegium Novum* (Kew: De Belder, 1611), listed in the *Catalogue of Botanical Books in the Collection of Rachel McMasters Miller Hunt*, ed. Jane Quinby (Pittsburgh: Hunt Botanical Library, 1858), vol. 1. See also Schuster Gallery, *The Flowering Garden: Florilegia 1600–1700* (London, 1988); and the discussion of botanical gardens below in ch. 7.

46. See Mary J. Carruthers, *The Book of Memory: A Study of Memory in Medieval Culture* (Cambridge: Cambridge University Press, 1990), ch. 7, "Memory and the Ethics of Reading."

47. Battista Guarino, *De ordine docendi et studendi*, in Woodward, *Vittorino da Feltre and Other Humanist Educators*, 161–78, esp. 168 and 175–76. The following text quotations from Guarino are from this text.

48. Anthony Grafton and Lisa Jardine, *From Humanism to the Humanities: Education and the Liberal Arts in Fifteenth- and Sixteenth-Century Europe* (Cambridge: Harvard University Press, 1986), analyze some student notebooks on 9, 15–17, 113–19. Their approach to cumulative humanist borrowings is reflected on 136: "When Agricola [in *De inventione dialectica*] combined 'grouping by headings,' as a means of ordering the fruits of one's reading, . . . he was broadly following Boethius. But packaged by Alardus, and marketed by Erasmus, the *De inventione dialectica* swept the educational board as the *system* which would transform the by now familiar process of collection and accumulation of 'matter' into a pathway to truth and salvation."

49. Bonner, *Education in Ancient Rome*, 259, citing rhetorical handbooks by Hermogenes and Aphthonius. Roman rhetoricians assign exercises based on Isocrates: see Arist., *Top.* 1.14.105b; Cic., *De or.* 2.86.364; and Quint., *Inst.* 10.5.1–14, discussed in Bonner, 65–90, 212–88.

50. Richard Rainolde, *The Foundacion of Rhetorike* (New York: Scholars' Facsimiles and Reprints, 1945), fol. xxxiijʳ, cited in Lechner, *Renaissance Concepts of the Commonplaces*, 17.

51. Cic., *De or.* 2.86.354, cited in Lechner, *Renaissance Concepts of the Commonplaces*, 164–65; see also above, ch. 1, "Common Notions."

52. Cicero, *De legibus* 1.30, cited above in ch. 1, n. 27 above.

53. Lechner, *Renaissance Concepts of the Commonplaces*, 136–37.

54. W. Strunk Jr. and E. B. White, *The Elements of Style*, 3rd ed. (New York: Macmillan, 1979).

55. Claudia Lazzaro, *The Italian Renaissance Garden: From the Conventions of Planting, Design, and Ornament to the Grand Gardens of Sixteenth Century Central Italy* (New Haven: Yale University Press, 1990).

56. Petrarch, "On His Own Ignorance and That of Many Others," in Cassirer, Kristeller, and Randall, *Renaissance Philosophy of Man*, 103–4; idem, *De sui ipsius et multorum ignorantia*, ed. L. M. Capelli (Paris: Champion, 1906), 68–69.

57. Marsilio Ficino, "Letter to Lorenzo di Pierfrancesco de' Medici," trans. E. H. Gombrich, in Gombrich, *Symbolic Images: Studies in the Art of the Renaissance* (London: Phaidon, 1972), 41–42. An alternate translation is in *Letters of*

Marsilio Ficino, trans. members of Language Department of the School of Economic Science, 5 vols. (London: Shepheard-Walwyn, 1975–94), letter 46, 4:61–63.

58. My interpretation is inclusive, validating the multitude of source studies, and not dependent on the issues of contention in the most up-to-date encyclopedic work on Botticelli by Ronald W. Lightbown, *Sandro Botticelli: Life and Work* (New York: Abbeville, 1989). Cf. the style of interpretation in E. H. Gombrich, "Botticelli's Mythologies," *Journal of the Warburg and Courtauld Institutes* 8 (1945): 7–60. Lightbown disputes the view that the painting was commissioned to be hung in Castello and dates the work as late as 1482–83 (143), rejects the association of the painting with Ficino's letter of 1478, disassociates the painting from neo-Platonic allegories (142), and dismisses Gombrich's view of Chloris and Flora as a metamorphosis. Although date and location are not important to my interpretation, the x-ray revealing a tree form in the underlayer beneath Chloris's face (145) supports, rather than contradicts, an important propagative/procreative and creative transformation taking place on the right-hand side of the painting (see the frontispiece). Liana Cheny presents a clear summary of a spectrum of interpretations in *Quattrocento Neoplatonism and Medici Humanism in Botticelli's Methodological Paintings* (New York: University Press of America, 1985), and Horst Bredekamp reaffirms the floral components and their place in Medicean culture in *Botticelli Primavera: Florenz als Garten der Venus* (Frankfurt am Main: Fischer Taschenbuch, 1988). Articles related to my interest include Paul Barolsky, "Botticelli's *Primavera* and the Tradition of Dante," *Konsthistorisk Tidskrift* 52 (1983): 1–6, which reaffirms Aby Warburg's comparison of Chloris's metamorphosis to Daphne's; and Dalia Haitovsky, "The Source of Botticelli's *Primavera,*" *Hebrew University Studies in Literature and the Arts* 13 (1985): 153–60, which reminds one to consider visual sources. Might Botticelli be referring to Chloris in rendering Daphne with branches flowering from her head in the painted low relief in the *Calumny of Apelles,* just behind the Venus who points upward in a similar pose to that of Mercury in the *Primavera?* See the illustration in Lightbown, *Sandro Botticelli,* 211.

59. Leon Battista Alberti, *On Painting and On Sculpture: The Latin Texts of "De pictura" and "De statua,"* ed. C. Grayson (London: Phaidon, 1972), 95–96, cited by Anthony Grafton in "The Choice of Zeuxis" [paper delivered at UCLA Center for Medieval and Renaissance Studies, Los Angeles, March 1995]).

60. The breath biblically is what animates living beings; and in ancient Delphi, divine vapors exhaled from nature "impregnated" the priestess with words of wisdom (*Longinus on the Sublime,* ed. W. Rhys Roberts [Cambridge: Cambridge University Press, 1935], cited in Thomas Greene, *The Light in Troy: Imitation and Discovery in Renaissance Poetry* [New Haven: Yale University Press, 1982], 79. Joanne Snow-Smith considers the divine breath in *The "Primavera" of Sandro Botticelli: A Neoplatonic Interpretation* (New York: Peter Lang, 1993).

61. Umberto Baldini, *Primavera: The Restoration of Botticelli's Masterpiece* (New York: Abrams, 1986), 50–51.

62. Augustine, *De Genesi ad litteram* 6 and *De Trin.* 3.8.13, discussed in R. A. Markus, "Augustine: God and Nature," in *The Cambridge History of Later Greek and Early Medieval Philosophy,* ed. A. H. Armstrong (Cambridge: Cambridge University Press, 1967), 398–401, and above, in ch. 2, "Seeds."

63. Edgar Wind, *Pagan Mysteries in the Renaissance* (New York: Barnes & Noble, 1968), 115–16.

64. Frederick Hartt, *History of Italian Renaissance Art* (Englewood Cliffs, N.J.: Prentice-Hall, 1962), 289, compares the pose to that of the Virgin in Alesso Baldovinetti's *Annunciation* of 1460. Also, he says that the gold lines indicate the divine source of the birth.

65. I thank Marcella Leigh for calling to my attention the Italian title of the words of wisdom of St. Francis of Assisi (d. 1226) written down by his followers.

66. Terry Comito, *The Idea of the Garden in the Renaissance* (New Brunswick, N.J.: Rutgers University Press, 1978), 77. It is likely that Botticelli observed the flowers in Medici gardens; the cleaning of the painting reveals the details of flowers that one sees in Florence in the spring today (Baldini, *Primavera*, 96–97, 100).

67. While I am simply suggesting a habitual linguistic usage, Comito, *The Idea of the Garden in the Renaissance*, citing Paul Piehler, *The Visionary Landscape* (London: Edward Arnold, 1971), suggests that gardens "are themselves the very language by which love manifests its nature to the human understanding" (92).

68. Ficino, "Letter to Lorenzo di Pierfrancesco de' Medici," in Gombrich, *Symbolic Images*, 41–42, and in Ficino, *The Letters of Marsilio Ficino*, 4:61–63. The importance of this tutorial relationship is reaffirmed throughout Snow-Smith, *The "Primavera" of Sandro Botticelli*.

69. Seneca, *De beneficiis* 1.3.2, and Alberti, *De pictura* 3.5496–97, discussed in Charles Dempsey, *The Portrayal of Love: Botticelli's Primavera and Humanist Culture at the Time of Lorenzo the Magnificent* (Princeton: Princeton University Press, 1992), 36–37. Dempsey's new synthesis correlates the painting to poetry.

70. Ficino, "Letter to Lorenzo di Pierfrancesco de' Medici," in Gombrich, *Symbolic Images*, 42.

71. Dempsey, *Portrayal of Love*, 38–41; Wind, *Pagan Mysteries in the Renaissance*, 125.

72. It was widely accepted that the groom is Lorenzo di Pierfrancesco de' Medici. Dempsey, *Portrayal of Love*, 20–24, raises doubts. For a rival claim that Lorenzo the Magnificent's younger brother Giulano Medici (d. 1478) commissions the painting for the birth of his child by Fioretta, see Mirella Levi d'Ancona, *Due quadri el Botticelli eseuiti per nascite in casa Medici* (Florence: Leo S. Olschki, 1992).

73. Robert Bonfil, *Jewish Life in Renaissance Italy*, trans. Anthony Oldcorn (Berkeley: University of California Press, 1994), 255–64 on marriage, 151–68 on Jews' and Christians' influences on each other; Moses A. Shulvass, *The Jews in the World of the Renaissance*, trans. Elvin I. Kose (Leiden: Brill, 1973), 148–55, 164–66, 346–59.

74. Leon Battista Alberti, *The Family in Renaissance Florence (I Libri della famiglia)*, trans. Renée Neu Watkins (Columbia: University of South Carolina Press, 1969).

75. Lightbown, *Sandro Botticelli*, 170–77.

76. Mirella Levi D'Ancona, *Botticelli's Primavera: A Botanical Interpretation Including Astrology, Alchemy, and the Medici* (Florence: Leo S. Olschki, 1983), 71–95.

77. Ibid., 19–21; Pliny, *Natural History*, 18.56.206.

78. "Di doman non c'è certezza. / Quant' è bella giovinezza / Che si fugge tuttavia!" (Lorenzo de' Medici, in *Lyric Poetry of the Italian Renaissance*, ed. L. R. Lind [New Haven: Yale University Press, 1954], 226–27).

79. "Nessuna stia superba / All' amadore il maggio"; "Qual sarà la più presta / A dargli e' fior del maggio?" (Angelo Poliziano, in ibid., 236–37).

80. "Va', cò' di quelle / Che più vedi fiorite in sullo spino" (ibid., 244–45).

81. Boccaccio, *Concerning Famous Women*, trans. Guido A. Guarino (New Brunswick, N.J.: Rutgers University Press, 1963), xxxiv.

82. Ibid., 17.

83. Ibid., 139–41.

84. Account to Lodovico il Moro, duke of Milan, on artists in Florence, cited in L. D. Ettlinger and Helen S. Ettlinger, *Botticelli* (New York: Oxford University Press, 1977), 11–12.

85. Guillaume de la Perrière, *La moroscopie* (1553), 97.

86. Horace, *Art of Poetry*, lines 60–62, trans. Francis Howes, in *The Art of Poetry*, ed. Albert S. Cook (New York: Stechert, 1926), 5, cited in Peggy Simonds, "The Green Man and Wise Words in a Renaissance Emblem" (paper delivered at the annual meeting of the Renaissance Society of America, New York, March 1995).

87. See Greene, *Light in Troy*, 307: ". . . tuisque ex, inclute, chartis, / floriferis ut apes in saltibus omnia libant. / omnia nos itidem depascimur aurea dicta."

88. See ibid., 68: "Ego apis Matinae / more modoque / grata carpentis thyma per laborem / plurimum circa nemus uvidique / Tiburis ripas operosa parvus / carmina fingo."

89. Terence Cave, *The Cornucopian Text: Problems of Writing in the French Renaissance* (Oxford: Clarendon, 1979). See also, Greene, *Light in Troy*, 199–200.

90. Seneca, *Ad Lucilium epistulae morales*, trans. Richard M. Gummere, Loeb Classical Library, *Ep.* 84.5. See below, ch. 9, "Sifting for Truth," and fig. E.3.

91. Petrarch, *Le familiare*, ed. Vittorio Rossi and Umberto Bosco, 4 vols. (Florence: Sansoni, 1933–42), 23.19, cited in Greene, *Light in Troy*, 98.

92. Petrarch, *Africa* 9.456–61, cited in William Kerrigan and Gordon Braden, *The Idea of the Renaissance* (Baltimore: Johns Hopkins University Press, 1989), 7–8 and 20; Peter Burke, *The Renaissance* (London: Longmans, 1964), 2.

93. Theodore E. Mommsen, "Petrarch's Conception of the 'Dark Ages,'" *Speculum* 17 (1942): 227.

94. Villani, *Liber de civitatis Florentiae famosis civibus*, ed. G. C. Galletti (Florence, 1847), 8, cited in Wallace K. Ferguson, *The Renaissance in Historical Thought: Five Centuries of Interpretation* (Cambridge: Houghton Mifflin, 1948), 20. Further amplification of the rebirth theme occurs on pp. 2, 3, 28, 31, 38, 39, 65, 307, and 309 of Ferguson.

95. Jean Plattard, "'Restitution des bonnes lettres' et 'Renaissance,'" in *Mélanges offerts par ses amis et ses élèves à Gustave Lanson* (Paris, 1922), 128–31. See also F. Simone, "La coscienza della rinascità negli umanisti," *La Rinascità* 2 (1939): 838–71 and 3 (1940): 163–86; Simone quotes from Nicolas de Clamanges, *Opera*, ep. 46: "Non proinde tamen aut in patria odio haberi aut ipsa pelli merui quod his ingeniosis studiis tanta superioribus saeculis celebrittae veneratis, operam aliquantam impendi atque ipsam eloquentiam olim sepultam, in Galliis quodammodo renasci, novisque iterum floribus licet priscis longe imparibus, repullulare laboravi" (2 [1939]: 850).

96. Petrarch, *Secretum*, cited in Trinkaus, *In Our Image and Likeness*, 1:14–16; Latin text on 331–32 n. 46.

97. Kenneth Clark, *Landscape into Art* (New York: Harper & Row, 1976), 9–10. Virgil's first commentator, Servius, introduced *polysemous* into critical discourse, and Annabel Patterson frames her book in the suggestiveness of Simone Martini's illumination: *Pastoral and Ideology: Virgil to Valéry* (Berkeley: University of California Press, 1987), esp. 19–30, 329–30, and color plate 1.

98. Gerhart B. Ladner, "Vegetation Symbolism and the Concept of Renaissance" (1961), reprinted in *Images and Ideas in the Middle Ages: Selected Studies in History and Art*, 2 vols. (Rome: Edizioni di Storia e Letteratura, 1983), 2:727–63, esp. 736 and fig. 1–19. Ladner cites J. Trier, "Zur Vorgeschichte des Renaissance-Begriffs," *Archiv für Kulturgeschichte* 33 (1950): 45ff.

99. On Theophrastus, see above, n. 26. For the label "renaissance in botany," see Morton, *A History of Botanical Science*. For embryological focus on rival seed theories (Galenic and Aristotelian) as background to the seventeenth-century notion that all comes from seed, see Ian Maclean, *The Renaissance Notion of Woman* (Cambridge: Cambridge University Press, 1980).

100. Ladner, "Vegetative Symbolism and the Concept of Renaissance," 730, 729 n. 5, 746, fig. 7 from Da Vinci.

101. Marsilio Ficino, "Letter to Paul Middelburg" (1492), in *Opera omnia* (Basel, 1576), cited in Ferguson, *The Renaissance in Historical Thought*, 28.

102. Erasmus, ep. 23 (June 1489?), in *Opus epistolarum Erasmi*, ed. P. S. Allen, 12 vols. (Oxford: Clarendon, 1906–58), cited in Ferguson, *The Renaissance Historical Thought*, 43.

Chapter Six

1. William J. Bouwsma, "The Two Faces of Humanism: Stoicism and Augustinianism in Renaissance Thought," in *Itinerarium Italicum: The Profile of the Italian Renaissance in the Mirror of Its European Transformations*, ed. Heiko A. Oberman with Thomas A. Brady Jr. (Leiden: Brill, 1975), 3–60; Charles Trinkaus, *Adversity's Noblemen: The Italian Humanists on Happiness* (New York: Columbia University Press, 1940); idem, *In Our Image and Likeness: Humanity and Divinity in Italian Humanist Thought*, 2 vols. (Chicago: University of Chicago Press, 1970).

2. Lotario dei Segni (Pope Innocent III), *De miseria condicionis humane*, ed. and trans. Robert E. Lewis (Athens: University of Georgia Press, 1978). Page references in the text are to this Latin and English edition.

3. Eccles. 7.30: "Fecit autem Deus hominem rectum, et ipse se infinitis immiscuit questionibus" (ibid., 110–11).

4. "Veritas enim consciencie numquam moritur, et ignis racionis numquam extinguitur" (ibid., 122–23).

5. Robert E. Lewis, introduction to Lotario dei Segni, *De miseria*, 5, 69 n. 30, and comparison of texts on 6–12.

6. Trinkaus, *In Our Image and Likeness*, 1:388 n. 4.

7. Millard Meiss, *Painting in Florence and Siena after the Black Death* (Princeton: Princeton University Press, 1951).

8. Petrarch, *De remediis*, cited in Trinkaus, *In Our Image and Likeness*, 1.193, Latin text on 399 n. 32. See also Letizia A. Panizza, "Stoic Psychotherapy in the Middle Ages and Renaissance: Petrarch's *De remediis*," in *Atoms, "Pneuma," and*

Tranquillity: Epicurean and Stoic Themes in European Thought, ed. Margaret J. Osler (Cambridge: Cambridge University Press, 1991), 39–66. See the new critical edition and translation, Petrarch, *Remedies for Fortune Fair and Foul*, trans. and commentary Conrad H. Rowski, 5 vols. (Bloomington: Indiana University Press, 1991).

9. Trinkaus, *In Our Image and Likeness*, 1:193.

10. See Ronald D. Witt, *Coluccio Salutati and the Public Letters* (Geneva: Droz, 1976).

11. Trinkaus, *In Our Image and Likeness*, 1:69.

12. Maurice Faucon, *La Librairie des papes d'Avignon*, 2 vols. (Amsterdam, Gérard Th. Van Heusden, 1969), 2:30, 138–39.

13. Marie-Henriette Jullien de Pommerol and Jacques Monfrin, "La bibliothèque pontificale à Avignon au XIVe siècle," in *Histoire des bibliothèques françaises*, ed. André Vernet, 4 vols. (Paris: Promodis, 1988–92), 1:165–66.

14. Matthaeus ab Aquasparta, *Quaestiones disputatae de fide de cognitione* (Karachi: C. Bonaventure, 1957), 257–58. See above, ch. 2, "Seeds."

15. Some scholars attribute the origin of the current decoration of the Chambre du Pape to Benedict XII's commission in account books of March 1337, but Michel Laclotte contends that Clement VI commissioned the vine-and-birdcage decoration. See Esther Moench, "The Palace Painters," in *The Palace of the Popes*, ed. Stéphane Guégan (Paris: Nuit et Jour, 1992), 52; and Michel Laclotte and Dominique Thiébaut, *L'École Avignon* (Paris: Flammarion, 1983), 32–33.

16. Petrarch, "Ascent of Mont Ventoux," in *The Renaissance Philosophy of Man*, ed. Ernst Cassirer, Paul O. Kristeller, and John H. Randall Jr. (Chicago: University of Chicago Press, 1969), 36–46.

17. Kenneth Clark, *Landscape into Art* (New York: Harper & Row, 1976), fig. 8 (pp. 12–13). See Laclotte and Thiébaut, *L'École d'Avignon*, color photographs on 28–29 and a naturalistic interpretation on 32–33.

18. Lull's books do not appear in Boniface's library catalog or in the Avignon catalog (Faucon, *La Librairie des papes d'Avignon*, index, and 2:3–18).

19. Education in the hunt serves in the fourteenth century as a vivid elementary example of tutor-tutored, master-apprenticeship instruction. The daughter of Sir James Berners (d. 1390), Juliana Berners, composes *Boke of Huntyng*, which begins as an educational lesson in the first person from a woman to a "dere chylde" (Julian Barnes, *Boke of Huntyng*, ed. Gunnar Tilander [Karlshamn, Switzerland, 1964], 22). The incunabula of 1486 binds it with books of falconry and heraldry: Dame Juliana Berners [or Bernes], *Book of hawking, hunting, and blasing of arms*, 1486, at Huntington Library.

20. Hervé Aliquot, *Avignon pas à pas* (Roanne/le Coteau: Editions Horvath, 1985), 138–40. Esther Moench, in "The Palace Painters," color photograph, 51, accepts Michel Laclotte's attribution of the cages to Matteo di Giovanetti da Viterbo. For literary evidence of expressing human characteristics through bird behavior and for symbolism and allegory, as in the bird figuring the lover's soul, see Baudouin van den Abeele, *La Fauconnerie dans les lettres françaises du XIIe au XIVe siècle* (Leuven: Leuven University Press, 1990), 194–249 and figs. 12 and 13.

21. John Cummins, *The Hound and the Hawk: The Art of Medieval Hunting* (London: Weidenfeld & Nicolson, 1988), ms. in the Heiligenkreuz monastery near Vienna, fig. 43 and 226.

22. See above, ch. 3, close of section "Judaic Trees," esp. nn. 34–36, on the emergence of landscape art. The pope amid the Avignon wall landscapes may be related to the vegetative manuscript illumination (ch. 5., n. 44) and then the painting of saints in the landscape.

23. Moench, "The Palace Painters," color photographs of the Chambre du Pape, 50–51, and of the Chambre du Cerf, 52–55; Sire de Joinville, *Mémoires de Sire de Joinville ou histoire et chronique du très-Chrétien roi Saint Louis* (Paris: Firmin Didot, 1871), 18–19. See above, the source cited in n. 34 to the introduction, on the long-term significance of the oak.

24. See a cross section of the building in Jullien de Pommerol and Monfrin, "La bibliothèque pontificale à Avignon au XIVe siècle," 1:152.

25. These four distinct arts become apparent in the title of William Gryndall, *Hawking, Hunting, Fouling, and Fishing* (London: Adam Islip, 1596). See also Alain Besson, *Medieval Classification and Cataloguing: Classification Practices and Cataloguing Methods in France from the 12th. to 15th. Centuries* (Biggleswade, Bedfordshire: Clover, 1980), 63–79 and notes, on medieval shelving procedure by pressmarks and wall inscriptions in the Cistercian abbey of Citeaux, the chapter library at Bayeux, and the library of Le Puy.

26. Mary Carruthers, *The Book of Memory: A Study of Memory in Medieval Culture* (Cambridge: Cambridge University Press, 1990), 62.

27. Ibid., citing Quintilian, *Institutio oratoria* 5.10.20–22.

28. Barnes, *Boke of Huntyng*. The hunting arts receive a bookish dimension in Albertus Magnus's *De Falconibus* and in bibliophile Emperor Frederick II's mid-thirteenth-century *De arte venandi cum avibus*, in which the illustrations in the margins show distinct birds, their habits, and human training procedures on land and up trees. Frederick's son's illustrated copy entered the papal collection as Cod. Vat. pal. lat. 1071. See illuminations in *De arte venandi cum avibus*, 2 vols. (Graz: Druck-u. Verlagsanstalt, 1969), facsimile and commentary.

29. Jullien de Pommerol and Monfrin, "La bibliothèque pontificale à Avignon au XIVe siècle," 1:157.

30. Franz Ehrle, *Historia bibliothecae Romanorum pontificum tum Bonifacianae tum Avinonensis* (Rome: Vatican, 1890), 428–32, cited in ibid., 1:161.

31. The list, entitled "Inventarium librorum que solebant esse in camera Cervi Volantis, nunc vero sunt in libraria turris," is in Faucon, *La Librairie des papes d'Avignon*, 2:27–33; Faucon evaluates the quality of the classical collection in ibid., 1:58–59.

32. Caes., *BGall.* 7.72.4, cited in *The Classical Dictionary* (Chicago: Follett, 1961), 93 and the *Oxford Latin Dictionary* (Oxford: Clarendon, 1982), 306.

33. Faucon, *La Librairie des papes d'Avignon*, 1:xiv, xviii. Faucon is one of the few scholars to relate the royal and papal collecting. The most complete royal inventory, including documents, of Charles V's collection is Léopold Delisle, *Recherches dur la librairie de Charles V, roi de France, 1337–1390*, 2 vols. (Amsterdam: Gérard Th. van Heusden, 1967). For book descriptions and illuminations, see Bibliothèque nationale, *La librairie de Charles V* (Paris, 1968).

34. Excavation in Musée du Louvre, cited in Pierre Quoniam and Laurent Guinamard, *Le Palais du Louvre* (Paris: Éditions Nathan, 1988), 26–27; Robert Brun, *Avignon au temps des papes* (Brionne: Gérard Monfort, 1983), 266–72.

35. Christine de Pizan, *Livre des fais et bonnes mœurs du sage roy Charles V* (1405), cited in *Mémoires relatifs à l'histoire de France* (Paris: Didier, 1654), vol. 2,

ch. 3, sec. 12, pp. 77–78; Denise Block, "La formation de la Bibliothèque du Roi," in Vernet, *Histoire des bibliothèques françaises*, 1:311–12.

36. Dominique Ravel, *L'oeuvre royale de Charles VI: Symbolique achimique et mystère royale* (Paris: Le Leopard d'or, 1984), figure on last page, "La tapisserie aux cerfs-volants," Musée départemental, Rouen.

37. See "Cerf," in Guy de Tervarent, *Attributs et symboles dans l'art profane, 1450–1600: Dictionnaire du'un langue perdu* (Geneva: Droz, 1988), 65–69, 417.

38. Legend has it that Clement VI requested that in his funeral procession his body be wrapped in the skin of a deer, as in ancient Gaulic dance ritual (Jean-Jacques Hatt, *Archeologia*, 9, 10, cited in J. P. Clébert, *Bestiaire fabuleux* (Paris: Albin-Michel, 1971), 86–88. The best history of Clement's tomb is Julian Gardner, *The Tomb and the Tiara: Curial Tomb Sculpture in Rome and Avignon in the Later Middle Ages* (Oxford: Clarendon, 1992).

39. See Luke 5.10. Since Pope Clement IV's innovation of 1265, each pope has an individual fisherman's ring for sealing private letters (*New Catholic Encyclopedia*, 15 vols. [New York: McGraw-Hill, 1967], 5:948).

40. See "Cerf," in Paul Imbs, *Trésor de la langue française*, vol. 5 (Paris: Éditions du Centre national de la recherche scientifique, 1974), 416.

41. See "Cerf," in *Dictionnaire d'archéologie Chrétienne et de liturgie*, by Fernand Cabrol and Henri Leclerq, 15 vols. (Paris: Librairie Letouzy, 1913–55), 2, pt. 2: 3301, citing Jerome (Migne *PL* 26:949). Jerome equates *catéchumenènes* with deer approaching water. *PL* refers to Jacques P. Migne, ed., *Patrologiae cursus completus: Series Latina*, 221 vols. (Paris: Garnier, 1841–1902), available also in *Patrologia Latina Database* (Alexandria, Va.: Chadwyck-Healey, 1995).

42. When in 1348 Christians blame Jews for the plague, Clement threatens excommunication to those who persecute Jews (Armand Lunel, *Juifs du Languedoc, de la Provence, et des Etats français du Pape* [Paris: Albin Michel, 1975], 72–73).

43. The Vatican Library, while having precedent in the Avignon collection, develops separately in the fifteenth century (see Leonard E. Boyle, "The Vatican Library"; Anthony Grafton, "The Vatican and Its Library"; and James Hankins, "The Popes and Humanism," all in *Rome Reborn: The Vatican Library and Renaissance Culture*, ed. Anthony Grafton [Washington, D.C.: Library of Congress, 1993], xi–xx, 3–86. This volume's 216 color plates exhibit the rich color illuminations commissioned and acquired by the papacy. For color illuminations commissioned at Avignon, see P. Pansier, *Histoire du livre et de l'imprimerie à Avignon du XIVme au XVIme siècle* [Avignon: Librairie Aubanel Frères, 1922]).

44. Trinkaus, *In Our Image and Likeness*, 1:256, Latin text on 428.

45. Ibid., 261, 262, 263; Latin texts on 430–31.

46. For Pico della Mirandola's library, see Pearl Kibre, *The Library of Pico della Mirandola* (New York: Columbia University Press, 1936), which shows Philo among Pico's manuscripts. For the Medici collections, see, for example, Frances Ames-Lewis, *The Library and Manuscripts of Piero di Cosimo de' Medici* (New York: Garland, 1985).

47. Giovanni Pico della Mirandola, *Oration on the Dignity of Man*, trans. Elizabeth Livermore Forbes, in Cassirer, Kristeller, and Randall, *Renaissance Philosophy of Man*, 225. The Latin reads: "Nec te caelestem neque terrenum, neque mortalem neque immortalem fecimus, ut tui ipsius quasi arbitrarius honorariusque plastes et fictor, in quam malueris tute formam effingas" (Pico della Mirandola, *De hominis dignitate, heptaplus, De ente et uno*, Latin and Italian texts, ed. Eugenio Garin

[Florence: Vallecchi, 1942], 106). References in the text are to Forbes's English translation followed by Garin's Latin.

48. See the discussion on Derrida's *La dissémination* above, in the introduction.

49. Roger Cook, *The Tree of Life: Symbol of the Centre* (London: Thames & Hudson, 1974), 9–10; Mircea Eliade, *Images and Symbols*, trans. Philip Mairet (New York: Sheed & Ward, 1969).

50. See S. K. Heninger Jr., "The Human Microcosm," in his *The Cosmographical Glass: Renaissance Diagrams of the Universe* (San Marino, Calif.: Huntington Library, 1977), 144–58.

51. For some differences between Pico and Ficino, see Paul Oskar Kristeller, *The Philosophy of Marsilio Ficino*, trans. Virginia Conant (Gloucester, Mass.: Peter Smith, 1964), 407–10, quotation on 410.

52. Pico della Mirandola, *Heptaplus* 2.6, in *On the Dignity of Man; On Being and the One, Heptaplus*, trans. Douglas Carmichael (Indianapolis: Bobbs-Merrill, 1965), 103–4; *De hominis dignitate, heptaplus, De ente et uno*, ed. Garin, 240–41. Page references in the text are to Carmichael's English translation followed by Garin's Latin.

53. Gen. 1.26–27. The Hebrew word *adam* refers to generic human nature, especially evident when Eve had not yet been separated from Adam. I translate *adam* as "humankind"; medieval and Renaissance interpretations of Gen. 1.26–27 are discussed in Maryanne Cline Horowitz, "The Image of God in Man—Is Woman Included?" *Harvard Theological Review* 72 (1979): 175–204.

54. Chaim Wirszubski, *Pico della Mirandola's Encounter with Jewish Mysticism* (Cambridge: Harvard University Press, 1989), 30, 190. The convert Mithradates' manuscript translations of the Kabbalah are available to Pico between May and October 1486, before he completes the theses in November.

55. In Zoroastrianism "the germs of every way of life" are the seeds of the tree of all seeds. See J. C. Cooper, "Tree," in *An Illustrated Encyclopedia of Traditional Symbols* (London: Thames & Hudson, 1978), 176–79 and the illustration of Scandinavian Yggdrasil on 197.

56. Paul G. Kuntz and Marion Leathers Kuntz, "The Symbol of the Tree interpreted in the Context of Other Symbols of Hierarchical Order, the Great Chain of Being, and Jacob's Ladder," in *Jacob's Ladder and the Tree of Life: Concepts of Hierarchy and the Great Chain of Being*, ed. Marion L. Kuntz and Paul G. Kuntz (New York: Peter Lang, 1987), 319–34, esp. 323–24.

57. Plato, *Epistles*, trans. Glenn Morrow (New York: Bobbs-Merrill, 1962), 7.341c–d (pp. 237–38). See also Cook, *Tree of Life*, 18–20, 119–20.

58. Lorenza Valla (1405–57) in his *De libero arbitrio* of 1438–39 states that in terms of who among unborn children are elected for salvation and who are not so elected, humanity is a lump of clay molded by the hands of the divine potter ("Dialogue on Free Will," trans. Charles Trinkaus, in Cassirer, Kristeller, and Randall, *Renaissance Philosophy of Man*, 176–77; *Laurentii Vallae de libero arbitrio*, ed. Maria Anfossi, in Opusculi filosofici, 6 [Florence: L. S. Olschki, 1934]). Luther cites Valla in his debate with Erasmus (see G. G. Coulton, *Infant Perdition in the Middle Ages* [London: Simpkin, Marshall, Hamilton, Kent, 1922]).

59. Augustine, *The Free Choice of the Will*, in *The Teacher, the Free Choice of the Will, Grace and Free Will*, trans. Robert P. Russell, Fathers of the Church, 59 (Washington, D.C.: Catholic University of America Press, 1968), 224–25; *De libero arbitrio* (Migne *PL* 32:1221–1503); *The Retractations*, trans. Mary Inez

Bogan, Fathers of the Church, 60 (Washington, D.C.: Catholic University of America Press, 1968) 1.3, p. 33. My translation. See also Augustine, *Four Anti-Pelagian Writings*, trans. John A. Mourant and William J. Collinge, Fathers of the Church, 86 (Washington, D.C.: Catholic University of America Press, 1992).

60. Eugene F. Rice Jr., *St. Jerome in the Renaissance* (Baltimore: Johns Hopkins University Press, 1985), 121–22.

61. On the labels "Pelagian" and "Semi-Pelagian" and on the continuation of a need to defend Erasmus and others against the labels, see B. A. Gerrish, "*De Libero Arbitrio* (1524): Erasmus on Piety, Theology, and the Lutheran Dogma," in *Essays on the Works of Erasmus*, ed. Richard L. DeMolen (New Haven: Yale University Press, 1978), 194–211.

62. *Politicorum libri octo*, ed. Lefèvre d'Étaples (Paris: Henri Estienne, 1506), fols. 123v–24r, cited by Eugene F. Rice Jr. in "Humanism in France," in *Renaissance Humanism: Foundations, Forms, and Legacy*, ed. Albert Rabil Jr., 3 vols. (Philadelphia: University of Pennsylvania Press, 1988), 2:112.

63. Eugene F. Rice Jr., *The Renaissance Idea of Wisdom* (Cambridge: Harvard University Press, 1958), 19.

64. Pauline Moffitt Watts, *Nicolaus Cusanus: A Fifteenth-Century Vision of Man* (Leiden: Brill, 1982), 224. Watts challenges Ernst Cassirer's contention in *The Individual and the Cosmos in Renaissance Philosophy*, trans. Mario Domandi (Oxford: Oxford University Press, 1963), 12, that Nicholas significantly influences Ficino and Pico della Mirandola.

65. Rice, *Renaissance Idea of Wisdom*, 23, also 19–22; Watts, *Nicolaus Cusanus*, 117–31.

66. Similarly, those written in the "book of life" may replicate the fall of Adam: "Then our names are crossed out; but nevertheless will again be found there if we try to rise once more; and we can rise (though not of ourselves). God raises us" Lefèvre, translated by Rice in "Jacques Lefèvre d'Étaples and Medieval Christian Mystics," in *Florilegium historiale: Essays Presented to William Ferguson*, ed. J. G. Rowe and W. H. Stockdale (Toronto: University of Toronto Press, 1971), 99.

67. Lewis Spitz, *The Renaissance and Reformation Movements* (St. Louis: Concordia, 1911), 285–86.

68. Rice, "Humanism in France," 2:111.

69. Rice, "Jacques Lefèvre d'Étaples and Medieval Christian Mystics," 104.

70. "Mentes autem humanae de se steriles sunt, quae si se posse credunt, praesumunt: et si quicquam pariunt, infructuosum est, grave, opacum et potius contrarium menti quam vitale pabulum animae vitaeque consentaneum. Ergo si sensibilis terra profert fructum humano corpori accommodum caelestis doni manifestissimum est indicium, at vero multo magis si humana mens foetum edit vitae ac saluti conducentem animarum" (translated in Rice, *Renaissance Idea of Wisdom*, 126; Latin text in idem, ed., *The Prefatory Epistles of Jacques Lefèvre d'Etaples and Related Texts* [New York: Columbia University Press, 1972], ep. 96 to Guillaume Briçonnet p. 296. See also part of letter translated by P. L. Nyhus in *Forerunners of the Reformation*, ed. H. A. Oberman [New York: Holt, Rinehart, Winston, 1966], 302–5).

71. Rice, *Renaissance Idea of Wisdom*, 126.

72. "Cognitio est radix et fundamentum omnium virtutum," cited in Heiko A. Oberman, *The Harvest of Medieval Theology: Gabriel Biel and Late Medieval Nominalism* (Cambridge: Harvard University Press, 1963), 65–66.

73. Ibid., 65–68, 106–9; Steven E. Ozment, *Homo Spiritualis: A Comparative Study of the Anthropology of Johannes Tauler, Jean Gerson, and Martin Luther (1509–1516) in the Context of Their Theological Thought* (Leiden: Brill, 1969), esp. 144, 149–68, 184–97.

74. Ozment, *Homo Spiritualis*, 208. Ozment provides full evidence of the early date at which Luther arrives at his theology of faith. The Stoic cluster of phrases are abundant in Ozment's quotations from Luther; Ozment gives evidence of Luther's increasingly Augustinian, or grace-focused, reinterpretation of the Stoic phrases.

75. Gordon Rupp et al., eds. and trans., *Luther and Erasmus: Free Will and Salvation* (London: SCM Press, 1969), 47. References to Erasmus's *De libero arbitrio* (35–97) and to Luther's *De serve arbitrio* (101–334) are to this edition.

76. Ibid., 287, Luther applying John 3.27.

77. Ibid., 76.

78. Ibid., 277. See the analysis of this confrontation about authorities in Victoria Kahn, *Rhetoric, Prudence, and Skepticism in the Renaissance* (Ithaca: Cornell University Press, 1985), 111–12.

79. Ps. 4.6; Thomas Aquinas, *Summa theologiae* 1–2, qu. 19, art. 4; Michael G. Baylor, *Action and Person: Conscience in Late Scholasticism and the Young Luther* (Leiden: Brill, 1977), 158, 173, 177, cited in Robert A. Greene, "Synderesis, the Spark of Conscience, in the English Renaissance," *Journal of the History of Ideas* 52 (1991): 203 and n. 20.

80. Marcia L. Colish, *Peter Lombard*, 2 vols. (Leiden: Brill, 1994), 2:490.

81. Ibid., 2:488–92, 747; Peter Lombard, *Sentences* 2, distinctio 27, chs. 1–2.3. Colish notes that although Peter relies on the *Summa sententiarum* and Augustine, he contributes the emphasis on a simultaneous division of labor, which she calls a "theandric, synergistic view of the interaction of grace and free will" (491).

82. Ambrose, *Hexameron, de paradiso*, ed. C. Schenkl, *CSEL* 32.1, 3–251, 267–336. Ambrose, *Hexameron, Paradise, and Cain and Abel*, trans. John J. Savage, Fathers of the Church, 42 (Washington, D.C.: Catholic University of America, 1961), *Paradise* 4.24, 4.25 (p. 303) cites Philo directly, as does 2.11 (p. 294) indirectly. Examples of vegetative imagery include: "Then Paradise has a certain vital force which receives and multiplies seeds in which each and every virtue is planted" (*Paradise* 1.6); "In tilling there is a certain exercise of man's virtue, while in keeping it is understood that the work is accomplished" (4.25); and "Many hold that by Paradise is meant the soul of man and that, while man was placed there as a worker and guardian, certain seeds of virtue sprouted forth" (11.51). See fig. E.4 below.

83. Augustine, *The Teacher, The Free Choice of the Will, Grace and Free Will*, ch. 22, sec. 65, p. 225 (Migne *PL* 32:1222–1303).

84. Pierre Villey, *Les sources et l'évolution des Essais de Montaigne*, 2 vols., 2nd ed. (Paris: Hachette, 1933), 1:237–42.

85. Kahn, *Rhetoric, Prudence, and Skepticism in the Renaissance* 111–12.

86. Ibid., 81.

87. Carl C. Christensen, *Art and the Reformation in Germany* (Athens: Ohio University Press, 1979), 124–25, citing Oskar Thulin, *Cranach-Altäre der Reformation* (Berlin: Evangelische Verlagsanstalt, 1955), and Karl Ernst Meier, "Fortleben der religiös-dogmatischen Kompositionen Cranachs in der Kunst des Protestantismus," *Repertorium für Kunstwissenschaft* 13 (1909): 415–35.

88. A precedent for a singular tree that divides into withered branches and

greening branches is Joachim of Floris's (d. 1202) "tree of history" (fig. 3.3), analyzed above, in ch. 3, "Christian Trees of Knowledge."

89. The quotations are from Rom. 1.18, 3.23, 4.15, 3.20, 3.28; 1 Cor. 15.54–55, 56, 57; Matt. 11.13; John 1.29; and 1 Pet. 1.2 (Christensen, *Art and the Reformation in Germany*, 234 n. 20).

90. Workshop of Lucas Cranach the Elder, *The Law and the Gospel*, 1529, in Christensen, fig. 3. I thank the National Gallery in Prague for a photograph.

91. Heiko A. Oberman, *Luther: Man between God and the Devil*, trans. Eileen Walliser-Schwarzbart (New Haven: Yale University Press, 1982), 292–93.

92. Haim Hillel Ben-Sasson, "Jewish-Christian Disputation in the Setting of Humanism and Reformation in the German Empire," *Harvard Theological Review* 59 (1966): 369–90; idem, "The Reformation in Contemporary Jewish Eyes," *Proceedings of the Israel Academy of Sciences and Humanities* 4, no. 12 (1970): 59–78; Jerome Friedman, *The Most Ancient Testimony: Sixteenth Century Christian Hebraica in the Age of Renaissance Nostalgia* (Athens: Ohio University Press, 1983); Heiko A. Oberman, *The Roots of Anti-Semitism in the Age of Renaissance and Reformation* (Philadelphia: Fortress, 1984). Erasmus's biases also have been explored; see Simon Markish, *Erasmus and the Jews* (Chicago: University of Chicago Press, 1986). For a recent overview, see Frank E. Manuel, *The Broken Staff: Judaism through Christian Eyes* (Cambridge: Harvard University Press, 1992).

93. See ch. 3 above, "Christian Trees of Virtue and Vice"; and Thomas N. Tentler, *Sin and Confession on the Eve of the Reformation* (Princeton: Princeton University Press, 1977). Calvin describes the confessional as a tree of vice: "First, they betook themselves to calculation, proceeding according to the formula given by the schoolmen, and dividing their sins into boughs, branches, twigs, and leaves" (*Inst.* 3.4.17, in *Institutes of the Christian Religion*, trans. Henry Beveridge, 2 vols. [Grand Rapids, Mich.: Eerdmans, 1957], 1:548).

94. Thomas M. McDonough, *The Law and the Gospel in Luther: A Study of Martin Luther's Confessional Writings* (Oxford: Oxford University Press, 1963), 74.

95. On Jerome, see ch. 2, n. 100.

96. Thomas à Kempis, *Imitation of Christ*, trans. Ronald Knox and Michael Oakley (London: Burns & Oates, 1959), 55.2 and 55.4, pp. 194–95, esp. on the "spark hidden among ashes" and "your grace is absolutely necessary for me for starting off some good act, for improving it, for making it perfect."

97. McDonough, *The Law and the Gospel in Luther*, 87, citing Luther's *On Good Works*. See above, ch. 2, n. 46, on the importance of *lev* (heart) in Jewish ethics.

98. *To the Christian Nobility of the German Nation* (1520), cited in Christensen, *Art and the Reformation in Germany*, 45. On Luther's relationship to the witch craze, see pt. 1, "The Witch as a Focus for Cultural Misogyny," in *The Politics of Gender in Early Modern Europe*, ed. Jean R. Brink, Maryanne Cline Horowitz, and Alison P. Coudert (Kirksville, Mo.: Sixteenth Century Essays & Studies, 1989), 13–90.

99. Christensen, *Art and the Reformation in Germany*, 52–109.

100. Seneca, *Ad Lucilium epistulae morales*, trans. Richard M. Gummere, Loeb Classical Library, *Ep.* 41.3.

101. Rice, *St. Jerome in the Renaissance*, 123; idem, "Jacques Lefèvre d'Étaples and Medieval Christian Mystics," esp. 91–92.

102. Anne Lake Prescott, "The Pearl of the Valois and Elizabeth I: Marguerite de Navarre's *Miroir* and Tudor England," in *Silent But for the Word: Tudor Women as Patrons, Translators, and Writers of Religious Works*, ed. Margaret P. Hannay (Kent, Ohio: Kent State University Press, 1985), 61–76.

103. "Bien sens en moy que j'en ay la racine, Et au dehors ne voy effect ne sign Qui ne soit tout branche, fleur, fueille, et fruict, Que tout autour de moy elle produict. Si je cuyde regarder pour le mieulx, Une branche me vient fermer les yeulx; Et en my bouche tombe, quant vueil parler, Le fruict par trop amer à avaller. Si pour ouyr, mon esperit s'esveille, Force fueilles entrent en mon aureille; Aussi mon naiz est tout bousché de fleurs" (Marguerite d'Angoulême, *Le miroir de l'âme pechereuse*, ed. Joseph Allaire [Munich: W. Fink, 1972]), 13–23). The passage is cited and discussed in Prescott, "The Pearl of the Valois and Elizabeth I," 67–68. Contrast the vegetative imagery with *l'Heptameron*, below, ch. 7, n. 5.

104. "Mais la grace que ne puis meriter / Qui poeut de mort chascun ressusciter / Par sa clarté ma tenebre illumine" (lines 33–35).

105. "Subjecte à mal, ennuy, douleur, et peine / Vie briefve, et la fin incertaine, / Qui soubz peché par Adam est vendu / Et de la loy jugé d'estre pendu" (lines 50–53).

106. Kathleen Basford, *The Green Man* (Ipswich: D. S. Brewer, 1978), 12–14 and plates, esp. 16, 31, 32; William Anderson, *Green Man: Archetype of our Oneness with the Earth* (London: HarperCollins, 1990), 23, on examples of "green women," and figures, esp. 19, 46, 69–70, 85. I thank Peggy Simonds and Giuseppe Mazzotta for their generous discussion of Simonds's "The Green Man and Wise Words in a Renaissance Emblem" (paper presented at the annual meeting of the Renaissance Society of America, Bloomington, Ind., March 1995).

107. Dante, *La Divina Commedia secondo l'antica vulgata*, ed. Giorgio Petrocchi, trans. Charles Singleton, 4 vols. (Princeton: Princeton University Press, 1970–76), *Purg.* 22.127–23.

108. Giuseppe Mazzotta, *Dante's Vision and the Circle of Knowledge* (Princeton: Princeton University Press, 1993), 237, interpreting Hugh of St. Victor, *In Hierarchiam coelestem* (Migne *PL* 175:978), and Alexander of Hales, *De pulchritudine universi*. See also above, ch. 4, n. 24.

109. Prescott, "The Pearl of the Valois and Elizabeth I," 70.

110. Elizabeth, *The Mirror of the Sinful Soul*, ed. Percy Ames (1544; facs. reprint, London: Asher, 1897), 14–15, shows a photograph of the design in gold and silver wire that contains four pansies, one for each corner, as well as Katherine Parr's initials in the center.

111. For a brief biography, see Frances Teague, "Elizabeth I: Queen of England," in *Women Writers of the Renaissance and Reformation*, ed. Katharina M. Wilson (Athens: University of Georgia Press, 1987); and for examples of cross-outs in Elizabeth's speeches, see Alison Heisch, "Queen Elizabeth I: Parliamentary Rhetoric and Exercise of Power," *Signs, Journal of Women in Culture and Society* 1 (1975): 31–56.

112. Cited in Teague, "Elizabeth I," 535. See *Boethius' Consolation of Philosophy*, trans. George Colville (1556), ed. Ernest B. Bax (London: David Nutt, 1897).

113. Teague, "Elizabeth I," 524, 535.

114. Ibid., 545.

115. See above, n. 103.

116. "To the Reader," in Elizabeth, *The Mirror of the Sinful Soul.*

117. Ibid., fol. 7.

118. Gerda Lerner, *The Creation of Feminist Consciousness: From the Middle Ages to Eighteen-seventy* (New York: Oxford University Press, 1993), esp. 51–52.

119. See above, ch. 5; and Margaret L. King and Albert Rabil Jr., eds., *"Her Immaculate Hand": Selected Works By and About the Women Humanists of Quattrocento Italy* (Binghamton: State University of New York Press, 1983), 128–29.

120. Elizabeth, "To the Reader," fol. 5: "Euen fo the gifte the wich oure creatour giueth at the beginninge. doth neuer reste, tyll he hath made hym godly, wich putteth hys trust in god. . . . Therfore reader, with a godly mynde i beehe befeche the to take it pacientely to perufe this worke wich is but lytell, and taste nothinge but the frutte of it praieng to god full of goodnes, that in your harte he will plante the liuely fayth."

121. George H. Williams, *The Radical Reformation,* 3rd ed. (Kirksville, Mo.: Sixteenth Century Essays & Studies, 1992), shows a multitude of ways of categorizing radicals depending on which belief or ritual is being considered.

122. Jacopo Sadoleto, *Sadoleto on Education: A Translation of De Pueris Recte Instituendis,* ed. and trans. E. T. Campagnac and K. Forbes (London: Oxford University Press, 1916), vii–xxiii.; text references are to this edition. The Latin text is in Jacopo Sadoleto, *Opera quae extant omnia,* 4 vols. (Verona, 1737–38), 3:66–126.

123. John Calvin and Jacopo Sadoleto, *A Reformation Debate: Sadoleto's Letter to the Genevans and Calvin's Reply,* ed. John C. Olin (New York: Harper & Row, 1966), 7–19.

124. "Nemo enim institui recte potest adolescens, qui nequiter fuerit eductus puer: nam ut radix indolem ingeniumque arboris, sic bene moratam & compositam adolescentiam pueritia ipsa producit" (Sadoleto, *Opera,* 3:68).

125. Sen., *Ep.* 65.3–11, cited in Arthur F. Kinney, *Continental Humanist Poetics: Studies in Erasmus, Castiglione, Marguerite de Navarre, Rabelais, and Cervantes* (Amherst: University of Massachusetts Press, 1989), 35–39. See also above, ch. 1, "Seeds to Trees."

126. Rice, *Renaissance Idea of Wisdom,* 80, with Latin quotation in n. 71, and 84.

127. Ibid., 85–91 and 67.

128. Calvin and Sadoleto, *A Reformation Debate.* Text references are to this updated version of Henry Beveridge's translation. The Latin text is in *Ioannis Calvini opera quae supersunt omnia (Corpus Reformatorum),* 59 vols. in 58 (Brunswick: C. A. Schwetschke, 1863–1900), 5:369–416.

129. Richard M. Douglas, *Jacopo Sadoleto, 1477–1547* (Cambridge: Harvard University Press, 1959), 145.

130. Ibid., 137–39. Note parallel developments in Thomas Elyot, *The book named the Governour* (1531; facs. Menston, Yorkshire: Scolar, 1970).

131. William J. Bouwsma, *John Calvin: A Sixteenth-Century Portrait* (New York: Oxford University Press, 1988).

132. Jean Calvin, *Institution de la religion chrestienne,* ed. Jacques Pannier, 3 vols. (Geneva, 1541; reprint, Paris: Belles Lettres, 1936–38). Chapter 2 focuses on the knowledge of God and of human will. I cite the edition that contains a dedication intended for bringing King Francis I into the evangelical camp (1:7–36)

in order to suggest Calvin's influence on Du Vair, Bodin, Charron, and Montaigne of the French Renaissance.

133. "Cicero dit que nous avons seulement des petites estincelles de bien, allumées de nature en nostre esprit, lesquelles nous corrumpons aisément par faulses opinions et mauvaises meurs" (1:100).

134. "C'est donc desja quelque estincelle de clarté en l'esprit humain qu'il ha une amour naturelle à la verité, le contemnement de laquelle ès bestes brutes monstre qu'elles sont pleines de stupidité et sans aucun sentiment de raison" (1:114).

135. "Ceste donc sera la distinction, que l'intelligence des choses terriennes est autre que des choses célestes" (1:115). We shall see that both Du Vair and Charron choose to separate their theological writings on divine wisdom from their lay writings on human wisdom.

136. "Pourtant nous voyons qu'il ya quelques cogitations géneralles d'une honnesteté et ordre civil imprimées en l'entendement de tous hommes" (1:116).

137. "[Il] y en a quelque semence en tous, qui procède de nature sans maistre ou législateur" (1:116). See Susan E. Schreiner, *The Theater of His Glory: Nature and the Natural Order in the Thought of Jean Calvin* (Durham, N.C.: Labyrinth, 1991).

138. "Toutesfois nous ne nyons pas qu'il n'y ayt quelque semence de noblesse en nostre nature, laquelle nous doibve inciter à suyvre justice et honnesteté" (1:83).

139. For three years following his expulsion from Geneva Calvin lectures on the New Testament in the Strasbourg Gymnasium, where he comes under the influence of Martin Bucer and a humanist curriculum following Wimpheling's *Adolescentia* and Erasmus's *De ratione studii*. For early Lutheran educational reform in Strasbourg, see Miriam Chrisman, *Lay Culture, Learned Culture: Books and Social Change in Strasbourg, 1480–1599* (New Haven: Yale University Press, 1982), 98–99, 192–201.

140. "Pourtant quand nous voyons aux escrivains payens ceste admirable lumière de verité, laquelle apparoist à leurs œvres, nous doibt admonester que la nature de l'homme, combine qu'elle soit decheute de son intégrité, et fort corrumpue, ne laisse point tousefois d'estre ornée de beaucoup de dons de Dieu" (1:118).

141. ". . . estre chose frivole et de nulle importance devant Dieu" (1:120).

142. "D'avantage ces petites gouttes de verité que nous voyons esparses aux livres des Philosophes, par combien d'horribles mensonges sont-elles obscurcies?" (1:121).

143. Philip Melanchthon, *Declamationes*, ed. K. Hartfelder (Berlin: Speyer & Peters, 1894). One might do a full study of the Stoic images in Melanchthon.

144. See Lewis W. Spitz, *The Religious Renaissance of the German Humanists* (Cambridge: Harvard University Press, 1963). Gerald Strauss emphasizes how the reformers' theological principles adapt to the already prevalent use of humanist educational tracts and to the necessity of building upon human potential in *Luther's House of Learning: Indoctrination of the Young in the German Reformation* (Baltimore: Johns Hopkins University Press, 1978), esp. 48–85. Rabil, *Renaissance Humanism*, vol. 2, focuses on national varieties of humanism beyond Italy, as its title indicates.

145. Both the Sorbonne and the Vatican criticize Sadoleto's commentary on

St. Paul's Epistle to the Romans in 1535, which precedes his letter to Calvin and his cardinalship (Olin, introduction to Calvin and Sadoleto, *A Reformation Debate*, 9–20).

146. Myron P. Gilmore, "Italian Reactions to Erasmian Humanism,"in Oberman and Brady, *Itinerarium Italicum*, 72–84.

147. *The Canons and Decrees of the Council of Trent*, trans. Theodore A. Buckley (London: George Routledge, 1851), sess. 6, "Decree on Justification," 30–50. References in the text are to session 6, chapters and canons in this session, which celebrated its achievements in January 1557.

148. See above, the concluding section of the introduction.

CHAPTER SEVEN

1. F. Simone, "La coscienza della rinascità negli umanisti," *La Rinascità* 2 (1939): 838–71 and 3 (1940): 163–86. Samuel Kinser provides evidence of greater French humanist innovation and confidence in "Ideas of Temporal Change and Cultural Process in France, 1470–1535," in *Renaissance Studies in Honor of Hans Baron*, ed. Anthony Molho and John A. Tedeschi (Dekalb: Northern Illinois Press, 1971), 703–56.

2. Wallace K. Ferguson, *The Renaissance in Historical Thought: Five Centuries of Interpretation* (Cambridge: Houghton Mifflin, 1948), 31.

3. Jean Trithème, *Epistolae* (1536), 175, cited in Simone, "La coscienza della rinascità negli umanisti," 855: "Haec sunt vere aurea tempora in quibus bonarum literarum studia, multis annis neglecta, *refloruerunt.*"

4. On Budé, his French treatise for the king, "On the education of a Prince," and his *De philologia*, see Kinser, "Ideas of Temporal Change," 750–51.

5. See Bibliothèque nationale, *The French Renaissance in Prints* (Los Angeles: Grunwald Center for the Graphic Arts, University of California, Los Angeles, 1994), 272, 274, 279, 301–2, 320–22. Note the images of fruit on the ornamental frames of the school of Fontainebleau (figs. 58, 59, 61). The vegetables, flowers, and fruit ornamenting the wall paintings of the Gallery of Francis I at Fontainebleau (fig. 72) resemble those in the ornamental garland of the engraving *Ceres Punishing Cupid* (fig. 85), a partner to *Flora and Zephyr Scattering Flowers*. In the first illumination in a manuscript of *l'Heptameron*, Marguerite de Navarre is portrayed seated between two trees, enjoying music in the circle of her court, like Apollo and the Muses (drawing on vellum inserted in Ms. 242, Pierpont Morgan Library, New York; I thank Myra Orth for this reference).

6. See Giorgio Vasari, *Le Vite de' più excellenti architetti, pittori, et scultori italiani da Cimabue insino a tempi nostri*, in *Le Opere*, ed. Gaetano Milanesi, 9 vols. (1878–85; reprint, Florence: Sanson, 1973), 1:243 for periods of art compared to stages of a human body ("corpi umani") and for the concept *rinascità*: "(è per conseguente, la natura di quest'arte simile a quella dell'altre, che, come i corpi umani, hanno il nascere, il crescere, lo invecchiare ed it morire), potrannao ora più facilmente conoscere il progresso della sua rinascita." This passage from Vasari's preface, translated by Mrs. Jonathan Foster, appears in *The Portable Renaissance Reader*, ed. James Bruce Ross and Mary Martin McLaughlin (New York: Viking, 1953), 145. For other commonly cited selections from the first awareness of renaissance, see Peter Burke, *The Renaissance: Problems and Perspectives in History* (London: Longmans, 1964), 2–6.

7. "Les esprits des hommes . . . ont commencé à s'esveiller et sortir des tenebres ou si long temps estoyent demeurez ensueliz et en sortant ont iecté hors et tiré en evidence toutes especes de bonnes disciplines lesquelles à leur tant eureuse et desirable renaissance, tout ainsi que les nouvelles plantes apres saison de l'hyver reprennent leur vigeur à la chaleur du Soleil et sont consolées de la doulceur du printemps" (Pierre Belon, *Observation de plusieurs singularitez et choses memorables, trouvées en Grece, Asie, Iudée, Egypte, Arabe, & autres pays estranges* [Paris: Corrozet, 1553]; also cited in Erwin Panofsky, *Renaissance and Renascences in Western Art* [New York: Harper & Row, 1972], 17 n. 4). For an account of Belon's collections of plants from the Orient, see Marguerite Duval, *The King's Garden*, trans. Annette Tomarken and Claudine Cowen (Charlottesville: University Press of Virginia, 1982), 9–18. On Petrarch, see Petrarch, *Secretum,* cited in Trinkaus, *In Our Image and Likeness,* 1:14–16; Latin text on 331–32 n. 46.

8. Ferguson, *The Renaissance in Historical Thought,* 32, citing Erasmus, *Adages,* ed. J. Charron (Paris, 1571), fol. a iii.

9. Simone, "La coscienza della rinascità negli umanisti," 840, 856–57, 862; Erasmus, *Opus epistolarum Des. Erasmi Roterodami,* ed. P. S. Allen, 12 vols. (Oxford: Clarendon, 1906–58), ep. 117, line 27, ep. 862, lines 2ff., ep. 967, lines 128, cited in Ferguson, *The Renaissance in Historical Thought,* 43.

10. Erasmus, *Ciceronianus or a Dialogue on the Best Style of Speaking,* trans. Izora Scott (New York: Teachers College, Columbia University, 1908), 81–82, cited in Thomas Greene, *The Light in Troy: Imitation and Discovery in Renaissance Poetry* (New Haven: Yale University Press, 1982), 182–83. See also above, ch. 5, "Analogy of Horticulture and Culture."

11. Ferguson, *The Renaissance in Historical Thought,* 65, 52, 83 (quotation).

12. Florimond de Rémond, *Histoire de l'hérésie de ce siècle* (Paris, 1605), 32, cited in ibid., 53: "Aussi disoient ordinairement les Allemans: Erasmus innuit, Lutherus irruit; Erasmus parit ova, Lutherus excludit pullos; Erasmus dubitat, Lutherus asseverat."

13. Burke, *Renaissance,* 6.

14. Erasmus, *The Adages of Erasmus,* trans. Margaret M. Phillips (Cambridge: Cambridge University Press, 1964), 274–75. *Sileni Alcibiadis* appears separately in 1517 and then in other editions in Spanish, German, Dutch, and English (ibid., 269 n. 1).

15. Erasmus, *Adages,* 275, 273.

16. Thomas M. Greene, "Erasmus's 'Festina lente': Vulnerabilities of the Humanist Text," in *Mimesis from Mirror to Method: Augustine to Descartes,* ed. John D. Lyons and Stephen G. Nichols Jr. (Hanover, N.H.: Dartmouth College Press, 1982), 135.

17. Greene, "Erasmus's 'Festina lente,'" 146–47. Derrida is discussed above, in the introduction.

18. Erasmus, *Collected Works of Erasmus,* ed. Craig Thompson, vol. 24 (Toronto: University of Toronto Press, 1978), *De copia,* Latin of pt. 1 with English translation by Betty I. Knott, table of contents, 290–94, and *De ratione studii,* trans. Brian McGregor, 672–75. See also R. R. Bolgar, *The Classical Heritage and Its Beneficiaries* (Cambridge: Cambridge University Press, 1954), 267–75.

19. Erasmus, *De copia,* in *Collected Works,* 24:365–67.

20. Erasmus, *De pueris instituendis (On the Education of Boys),* trans. Beert Verstraete in Erasmus, *Collected Works,* vol. 26 (Toronto: University of Toronto Press,

1985), 310; *Erasme. Declamatio de pueris statim ac liberaliter instituendis,* ed. Jean-Claude Margolin (Geneva: Droz, 1966), 68 nn. 8 and 9. See also above, ch. 5, n. 1. One might trace seeds of virtue and knowledge as a consistent principle throughout the works of Erasmus, as I have done for Bodin.

21. The first printed collection is *Viri clarissimi D. Andree Alciati iurisconsultiss* (Augsburg: H. Steyner, 1531); however, Alciati publishes some of his epigrams without illustration in 1529 (see Alison Saunders, "Alciati and the Greek Anthology," *Journal of Medieval and Renaissance Studies* 12 [1982]: 1–18, esp. 1–2).

22. See Virginia W. Callahan, "The Erasmus-Alciati Friendship," in *Acta conventus neo-Latini Louvaniensis* (Munich: Fink, 1973), 136 (citing A. Renaudet, *Erasme et L'Italie* [Geneva: Droz, 1954], 221); idem, "Andrea Alciati's View of Erasmus: Prudent Cunctator and Bold Counselor," in *Acta conventus neo-Latini Sanctandreani,* ed. I. D. McFarlane (Binghamton, N.Y.: Medieval and Renaissance Texts & Studies, 1986), 203–21; and idem, "The Mirror of Princes: Erasmian Echoes in Alciati's *Emblematum Liber,*" in *Acta conventus neo-Latini Amstelodamensis* (Munich: Fink, 1979), 183–96.

23. For emblems in books printed in France, see Alison Saunders, *The Sixteenth-Century French Emblem Book: A Decorative and Useful Genre* (Geneva: Droz, 1988); Jean Mesnard, "Les traductions françaises des *Emblèmes d'Alciat,*" in *Crossroad and Perspectives: French Literature of the Renaissance,* ed. Catherine Grisé and C. D. E. Tolton (Geneva: Droz, 1986), 101–20; Daniel S. Russell, *The Emblem and Device in France* (Lexington, Ky.: French Forum, 1985); C. Balvaoine, "Le statu de l'image dans les livres emblématiques en France de 1580 à 1630," in *L'automne de la Renaissance, 1580–1630* (Paris: Vrin, 1981), 163–78.

24. *Andreas Alciatus,* ed. Peter M. Daly, with Virginia W. Callahan and Simon Cuttler, 2 vols. (Toronto: University of Toronto Press, 1985). Unless otherwise noted, emblems are from this English translation of the Latin (vol. 1) and vernacular emblems (vol. 2). Emblem numbers refer to all examples of the emblem in both volumes.

25. Current scholarship is exploring subtle differences in strategies in the various emblem collections. See Jerome Schwartz, "Emblematic Theory and Practice: The Case of the Sixteenth-Century French Emblem Book," *Emblematica* 2, no. 2 (1986): 293–313; and Irene Bergal, "Discursive Strategies in Early French Emblem Books," ibid., 273–89. Especially interesting is Claude Mignault's French-Latin edition with commentary, produced in Paris by Richer in 1584, 1585, and 1587; see Alison Saunders, "Sixteenth-Century French Translations of Alciati's *Emblemata,*" *French Studies* 44, no. 3 (1990): 271–88, which highlights Mignault's highly decorative translations and his focus on stressing Alciati's moral lesson.

26. James Ackerman, "Artists in Renaissance Science," in *Science and the Arts in the Renaissance,* ed. John W. Shirley and F. David Hoeniger (Washington, D.C.: Folger Shakespeare Library, 1985), 103, 113.

27. F. David Hoeniger, "How Plants and Animals Were Studied in the Mid-Sixteenth Century," in ibid., 131.

28. Antoine Schnapper, *Le géant, la licorne, et la tulipe: Collections et collectionneurs dans la France du XVIIe siècle* (Paris: Flammarion, 1988), 40–41; Duval, *The King's Garden,* 27–28.

29. Gregor Mendel, "Experiments in Plant Hybridization" (1865), in *Classic*

Papers in Genetics, ed. James A. Peters (Englewood Cliffs, N.J.: Prentice Hall, 1959), 1–19.

30. The first use of the Latin term *herbarium* to describe a collection of dried plant specimens (simples) is in Cassiodorus, *Institutiones divinarum et humanarum* 1.31 (ca. 550); equivalents in late-sixteenth-century France are *l'hortus siccus* and the French *le jardin d'hiver, le jardin sec*, and lastly *l'herbier*. Visit the Museo Botanico, Florence, to view historical herbaria; a 1558 French collection belongs to the Muséum National d'Histoire, Paris (Schnapper, *Le Géant*, 37–40, 221).

31. One can get a sense of the frequency with which Alciati uses plant emblems in comparison with his use of other emblems from the systematic chart in Mason Tung, "A Concordance of Fifteen Principal Editions of Alciati," *Emblematica* 1 (1986): 319–38; the kinds of trees he uses are listed on 338. For flowers and plants by name, see idem, "A List of Flora and Fauna in Peacham's *Minerva Britanna* and Alciati's *Emblemata* Together with Possible Models in Contemporary Illustrations," ibid., 345–57.

32. Agnes Arber, *Herbals* (New York: Cambridge University Press, 1986), 33 and fig. 14, on the "Tree of knowledge" in *Hortus sanitatis* (Moguntia: Jacobus Meydenbach, 1491); there are hand-colored illustrations in a copy in the Biomedical Library, UCLA. The *Gart der Gesundheit* (Mainz, 1485), which has representations of plants, some copied from medieval manuscripts, others reproduced from nature, is a model for several other works; UCLA conference on *Hortus sanitatis*, UCLA Center for Medieval and Renaissance Studies, Los Angeles, November 1991.

33. Mason Tung, "From Natural History to Emblem: A Study of Peacham's Use of Camer[ar]ius's *Symbola et Emblemata*," *Emblematica* 1 (1986): 53–76, esp. 54 and n. 2, with citations from Claus Nissen, J. Baudrier, M. Funck, and M. Rooses. The fourteen emblems appear at the end of *Andreas Alciatus*, vol. 2, numbered 199–212.

34. Ibid., 54–55. There are multiple examples of the hand of god and of the divine sun signifying grace in plant emblems in Camerarius, *Symbolorum et emblematus ex re herbaria centuria* (Nuremberg, 1590).

35. *Festina lente*, which means "make haste slowly," is one of the most valued Renaissance sayings, expressed in visual form by the tortoise carrying a sail, the dolphin around an anchor, and the mulberry tree. Leonardo da Vinci's patron Ludovico il Moro wore a coat embroidered with a mulberry emblem. Pliny explains in his *Natural History* 16.25 that although the mulberry blooms slowly, it bursts forth with both fruit and flower (Edgar Wind, *Pagan Mysteries in the Renaissance* [New York: Barnes & Noble, 1968], 112, 98–101).

36. *Andreas Alciatus*, emblems 205 and 182.

37. Ibid., emblem 188 (Padua, 1621).

38. See the brief biography in *Andreas Alciatus*, 1:xix–xxii.

39. See James Stubblebine, ed., *Giotto: The Arena Chapel Frescoes* (New York: Norton, 1969), figs. 58–59, 68–69.

40. *Andreas Alciatus*, emblems 24, 36, 125.

41. *Andreas Alciatus*, emblems 73, 193.

42. Virginia W. Callahan, "Ramifications of the Nut Tree Fable," in *Acta conventus neo-Latini Turonensis*, ed. Jean-Claude Margolin (Paris: Vrin, 1980), 197–204, esp. 198–99.

43. Ibid., 199–200.

44. *Andreas Alciatus*, emblem 200 (Padua, 1621).

45. Annabel Patterson, *Marvell and the Civic Crown* (Princeton: Princeton University Press, 1978), esp. 16–19, 252. See above, ch. 3, n. 76.

46. *Andreas Alciatus*, emblem 121 (Padua 1621).

47. Joannes Sambucus, *Emblemata* (Antwerp: Christophe Plantin, 1564), 156; *Emblemata. Handbuch zur Sinnbildkunst des XVI. und XVII. Jahrhunderts*, ed. Arthur Henkel and Albrecht Schöne (Stuttgart: Metzler, 1967), 129.

48. Dionysius Lebeus-Batillius, *Emblemata* (Frankfort, 1596), 44, cited in Henkel and Schöne, *Emblemata*, 198.

49. *Andreas Alciatus*, emblems 125 and 24.

50. See fig. 54 from Simler, *Vita Conradi Gesneri* (1566), and figs. 58 and 119 from Camerarius, *Hortus medicus* (1588), in Arber, *Herbals*, 78, 110–12, 233–34.

51. Duval, *The King's Garden*, ch. 2, "Belon: First Botanist-Traveler," 9–18.

52. Michael J. B. Allen, *Platonism of Marsilio Ficino: A Study of his "Phaedrus" Commentary, Its Sources and Genesis* (Berkeley: University of California Press, 1984), 3–6.

53. Rabelais, *Gargantua and Pantagruel*, translated in the late seventeenth century by Sir Thomas Urquhart and Peter Mottenx (Philadelphia: George Barrie, 1900); idem, *Oeuvres complètes*, annot. Jacques Boulenger, ed. Lucien Scheler (Paris: Gallimard, 1955). Rabelais wrote bks. 1 and 2 in 1532–34, bks. 3 and 4 in 1546–52; and bk. 5 in 1552.

54. See for example, Louis Fothergill-Payne, *Seneca and "Celestina"* (Cambridge: Cambridge University Press, 1988).

55. For example, Seneca, *L. Annaei Senecae philosophi opera, quae exstant omnia, a J. Lipsio emendata et scholiis illustrata* (1605).

56. "Le bien donc de l'homme consistera en l'usage de la droite raison,—qui est à dire en la vertu, laquelle n'est autre chose que la ferme disposition de notre volonté à suivre ce qui est honnête et convenable" (Guillaume du Vair, *De la sainte philosophie, Philosophie morale des Stoïques*, ed. G. Michaut [Paris: Vrin, 1945], 64. The word *sainte* in the title is misleading; the text is Du Vair's *La philosophie morale des Stoïques*, a different work from Du Vair's *La saincte philosophie*, cited below, from Guillaume du Vair, *Oeuvres* [Paris: Sebastien Cramoisy, 1641; reprint, Geneva: Slatkine, 1970]. *La sainte philosophie* is on pp. 1–29 in the section "Treatises on Piety," and *La philosophie morale des Stoïques* is on pp. 255–58, in the section "Philosophical Treatises." Translations are mine, with consideration of Du Vair, *The Moral Philosophie of the Stoicks*, trans. Thomas James, ed. Rudolf Kirk [New Brunswick, N.J.: Rutgers University Press, 1951]).

57. "Le bien, en vérité, n'est exposé ici en vue à tout le monde; la nature n'en a semé ca-bas que de faibles étincelles, qui, toutefois, applicquées purement à nos esprits, s'enflamment en une pure lumière et le fond connaitre tel qu'il est" (ibid.).

58. "La nature semble, en la naissance de l'or, avoir aucunement présage la misère de ceux qui le devaient aimer; car elle a fait qu'ès terres où il croit, il ne vient ni herbes, ni plantes, ni fleurs, ni chose qui vaille: comme nous annoncant qu'ès esprits où le désir de ce métail naitra, il ne demeurera nulle scintille d'honeur ni de vertu" (ibid., 79). Note the common contrast of gold with vegetative growth, also found in the emblem "Vertu meilleure que richesse," in which a woman weighs a palm, symbolizing virtue, against a gold crown and scepter and finds that virtue is worth more and brings true nobility (emblem in Gilles Corrozet, *Hecatongraphie* [Paris, 1543], reproduced in Henkel and Schöne, *Emblemata*, 196).

59. "Puisqu'Epicure se glorifie de mépriser les délices, que doivent faire les Stoiques? Ne doivent-ils pas honorer et revérer la sobriété, comme le fondement de toutes les autres vertus, comme celle qui étouffe les autres vices au berceau et les suffoque en la semence?" (Du Vair, *La philosophie morale*, 76). Note Erasmus's concern for infant moral education in *De pueris instituendis*, in Erasmus, *Collected Works*, 26:299, 321.

60. "C'est une loi divine et inviolable, publiée dès le commencement du monde, que, si nous voulons avoir du bien, il fuat que nous nous le donnions nous-mêmes" (Du Vair, *La philosophie morale*, ed. Michaut, 67).

61. The passage in Du Vair reads: "Elle [nature] est si sage maîtresse qu'elle a disposé toutes choses au meilleur état qu'elles puissent être, et leur a donné le premier mouvement au bien et à la fin qu'elles doivent chercher; de sorte que qui la suivra, sans doute l'obtiendra" (ibid., 64). And the passage in Charron reads: "Nature a disposé toutes choses au meilleur estat qu'elles puissent estre, et leur a donné le premier mouvement au bien et à la fin qu'elles doivient chercher, de sorte que qui la soyvra ne fauldra point d'obtenir et posseder son bien et sa fin" (Pierre Charron, *De la sagesse*, ed. Amaury Duval, 3 vols. [Paris, 1827], 2:87). On Du Vair and Charron, see also below, ch. 10.

62. "Oh Dieu tout bon, tout sage & tout-puissant, qui nous avez donné un entendement pour gouverner le cours de nostre vie, faites-luy connoistre & aymer l'excellence dont vous l'avez orné, & l'aydez tellement que quand il viendra donner mouvement aux pussiances de nostre ame, il trouve nos membres & nos sens purgez de toutes passions, & prompts à obeir. Ostez des yeux de nostre esprit les troubles & nuages que l'ignorance & la cupidité y efleuent, afin que nostre raison esclairée par la lumiere de vostre divine verité, nous dresse tousjours vers ce qui est vrayement & sera eternellement bien" (Du Vair, *Oeuvres*, 288).

63. Pierre Villey, *Les sources et l'évolution des Essais de Montaigne*, 2 vols., 2nd ed. (Paris: Hachette, 1933), 1:31, 2:53, 56, 60, 66, 390.

64. The phrase *God's hand* is particularly prevalent in Calvin (William J. Bouwsma, *John Calvin: A Sixteenth-Century Portrait* [New York: Oxford University Press, 1988], 169).

65. Michel de Montaigne, *Essais*, 2nd ed. (Bordeaux, 1582; reprint, Cambridge: Harvard University Press, 1969), 610: "Il s'eslevera, si Dieu luy preste la main: il s'eslevera abandonnant & renonçant a ses propres moyens & se laissant hausser & soubslever par la grace divine, main non autrement." For the earlier, 1580 version, see Michel de Montaigne, *Oeuvres complètes*, ed. Albert Thibaudet and Maurice Rat (Paris: Gallimard, 1962), bk. 2, ch. 12, pp. 587–89. For the English see *Complete Essays*, trans. Donald M. Frame (Stanford: Stanford University Press, 1965), 457: "Il s'esle-vera si Dieu lui preste extraordinairement la main; il s'eslevera, abandonnant et renonçant à ses propres moyens, et se laissant hausser et soubslever par les moyens purement celestes"; see notes in both texts for variants.

66. Montaigne, *Oeuvres complètes*, bk. 2, ch. 11, p. 589; *Complete Essays*, 610: "C'est à nostre foy Chrestienne, non à sa vertu Stoïque de pretendre à cette divine et miraculeuse metamorphose."

67. On legitimate multiple readings of Montaigne's religious sensibility, see Maryanne C. Horowitz, "Montaigne's Doubts on the Miraculous and the Demonic in Cases of His Own Day," in *Regnum, Religio, et Ratio: Essays Presented to Robert M. Kingdon*, ed. Jerome Friedman (Kirksville, Mo.: Sixteenth Century Journal Publications, 1987), 81–91.

68. On Ficino's subtlety, see Eugene F. Rice Jr., *The Renaissance Idea of Wisdom* (Cambridge: Harvard University Press, 1958), 65–68, 210–11.

69. Pietro Pomponazzi, *On the Immortality of the Soul*, trans. William Henry Hay II, rev. John H. Randall Jr., annot. Paul O. Kristeller, in *The Renaissance Philosophy of Man*, ed. Ernst Cassirer, Paul O. Kristeller, and John H. Randall Jr. (Chicago: University of Chicago Press, 1948), xiv–xv, 375–81.

70. " . . . notre ruïne . . . ceste lumiere de sapience, il a envoyé . . . pour preparer les ames de ceux qui devoient participer à sa grace, & contempler la splendeur de sa gloire" (*La saincte philosophie*, in *Oeuvres*, 5).

71. "Il faudrat adviser d'y faire une semence, qui en fin produise pour son fruict une vie divine & immortelle. Cette semence est nostre volonté, laquelle selon qu'elle vient à bien ou à mal germer, produit de bonnes ou mauvaises actions" (ibid., 12).

72. "C'est celle [foi] avec laquelle nous humilions nos sens, & nous dementons nous-mesmes, pour donner creance à sa verité: reconoissons nostre infirmetié: avoüons sa toute-puissance" (ibid., 23).

73. See Jean Calvin, *Institution de la religion chrestienne*, ed. Jacques Pannier, 3 vols. (Geneva, 1541; reprint, Paris: Belles Lettres, 1936), which contains a dedicatory letter to Francis I, hoping for his conversion.

74. Rudolf Kirk, introduction to Du Vair, *Moral Philosophie of the Stoicks*, 13–25. Du Vair serves as a moderate *politique* again after the assassination of Henry III in 1589 and then after the siege of Paris by the duke of Parma. Under Henry IV, Du Vair serves on a special court in Provence and as president of the Parlement of Aix in 1598.

75. Du Vair, *Oeuvres*, 316.

76. Du Vair, *La saincte philosophie*, in *Oeuvres*, 12–13, 22–23. He uses the words "la lumière naturelle" as equivalent to "droite raison" and talks of "loy," with examples coming from revealed biblical law (Anthony Levi, S.J., *French Moralists: The Theory of the Passions, 1585 to 1649* [Oxford: Clarendon, 1964], 82–83).

77. Du Vair, "Apres les barricades. . . ," in *Oeuvres*, 563–67.

78. "C'est la seule union que nous devons, entant qu'il nous est possible, procurer & embrasser, afin que le Roy estant nostre tige, les Princes ses branches le peuple ses feuilles, le tige se glorifie en ses branches, & les branches & feüillages tirent leur vigueur & verdeur de leur tige" (ibid., 567).

79. Guillaume de la Perrière, *Le miroir politique, oeuvre non moins utile que necessaire à tous monarches, roys, princes, seigneurs, magistrats & authres surintendans* (Lyon: Macé Bonhomme, 1555; reprint, Paris, 1567), published in English as *The Mirrour of Policie* (London: Adam Jslip, 1598; reprint, 1599). See also Alison Saunders, introduction to Guillaume de la Perrière, *Le theatre des bons engins, La morosophie* (Hants, England: Scolar, 1993).

80. Continuing the tradition of applying mnemonic devices for remembrance of Aristotle's six forms of government, La Perrière substitutes branches and leaves of a tree for rooms of a building. See vignettes of six rooms in King Charles V's illumination of Aristotle, *Politiques*, reprinted in Bibliothèque nationale, *La librairie de Charles V* (Paris, 1968), pls. 22–23. For the most basic mnemonic of rooms establishing loci, see Quintilian, *Institutio oratoria* 11.2.17–22, quoted and discussed in Frances A. Yates, *The Art of Memory* (Chicago: University of Chicago Press, 1966), 1–4, 22–23.

81. Charles de Figon, *Discours des etats et offices* (Paris: Guillaume Auvray,

1579), illustration reprinted in Donald R. Kelley, *Foundations of Modern Historical Scholarship* (New York: Columbia University Press, 1970), 186.

82. Frances Bacon, *Essays*, in *The Moral and Historical Works of Lord Bacon* (London: Henry G. Bohn, 1852), 85–86, citing Dan. 4.10.

83. Justus Lipsius, *Manuductio, ad lectorem*, 4.617f., quoted in Jason Saunders, *Justus Lipsius: The Philosophy of Renaissance Stoicism* (New York, 1953), 55, 69.

84. John Stradling, "The Epistle to the Reader," in *Two Bookes of Constancie*, ed. Rudolf Kirk (New Brunswick, N.J.: Rutgers University Press, 1939), 67–68.

85. There is increasing scholarship today on English literary renditions of Stoic themes. See Gordon Braden, *Renaissance Tragedy and the Senecan Tradition* (New Haven: Yale University Press, 1985); Audrey Chew, *Stoicism in Renaissance English Literature: An Introduction* (New York: Peter Lang, 1988); and Thomas G. Rosenmeyer, *Senecan Drama and Stoic Cosmology* (Berkeley: University of California Press, 1989). For history of the medieval texts of ancient Stoic works, see L. D. Reynolds, ed., *Texts and Transmission: A Survey of the Latin Classics* (Oxford: Clarendon, 1983), which updates the history of Renaissance publication and translation gathered concisely in such works as Rudolf Kirk, introduction to Lipsius *Two Books of Constancie*, 13–30, and Léontine Zanta, *La renaissance du stoïcisme au XVIe siècle* (Paris: Champion, 1914), 1–29, 129–51.

86. Petrus Ramus, *Aristotelicae animadversiones*, in *Renaissance Philosophy: The Transalpine Thinkers*, ed. and trans. Herman Shapiro and Arturo B. Fallico (New York: Modern Library, 1969), 179: "Furthermore, since eternal reason has been divinely implanted and impressed into the minde of each man, natural dialectic can be intuited in the insights of men by leaning upon the twin roots of discovery and judgement, or (as it were) by leaning upon the arms of both."

87. Saunders, *Justus Lipsius*, 70.

88. The controversy during his lifetime over Lipsius's religion is discussed in ibid., 11–14, 18–20, 31–34, 36–39, 40.

89. See Justus Lipsius, *De constantia*, in *Opera omnia*, 4 vols. (Wesel, 1675), 4:526–607; idem, *Two Books of Constancie*; and idem, *On Constancy*, in Shapiro and Fallico, *Renaissance Philosophy: The Transalpine Thinkers*, 97–148. References are to chapter in any standard edition and to page in Shapiro and Fallico's condensed English translation.

90. For Stoic impact on the sciences, see Peter Barker, "Stoic Contributions to Early Modern Science," and J. T. Dobbs, "Stoic and Epicurean Doctrines in Newton's System of the World," in *Atoms, "Pneuma," and Tranquillity: Epicurean and Stoic Themes in European Thought*, ed. Margaret J. Osler (Cambridge: Cambridge University Press, 1991.

91. Lactantius, quoted in Lipsius, *Physiologia* 1.5 (4.841), cited in Saunders, *Justus Lipsius*, 125.

92. Augustine, *De civitate Dei* 7.6, cited in Lipsius, *Physiologia* 1.8 (4.849), cited in Saunders, *Justus Lipsius*, 132.

93. Hermes Trismegistus, *Corpus Hermeticum* 14.10, cited in Saunders, *Justus Lipsius*, 127.

94. *Physiologia* 1.6 (4.845), cited in Saunders, *Justus Lipsius*, 128.

95. Diog. Laert. 7.158, quoted in *Physiologia* 3.6 (4.977), cited in Saunders, *Justus Lipsius*, 211.

96. Saunders, *Justus Lipsius*, 212, showing the influence of Cicero's *De natura deorum* 3.14.35 on *Physiologia* 3.9 (4.987).

97. Lipsius, *Manu.* 2.22 (4.736), citing Seneca, *Epistulae* 124, cited in Saunders, *Justus Lipsius*, 105. Saunders does not himself link the Stoic theory of *logos spermatikos* to the ethical theory of *semina virtutum*. My development of the connection provides further evidence for Saunders's point that Lipsius returns Stoic ethics to its physical basis.

98. James Turner's recent *One Flesh: Paradisal Marriage and Sexual Relations in the Age of Milton* (Oxford: Clarendon, 1987) discusses libertinism derived from radical readings of the Bible. A long line of French scholars has taken seriously the evidence of such books as Marin Mersenne, *L'Impieté des deistes, athees, et libertins de ce temps, combattuë* . . . (Paris: P. Bilaine, 1624). The controversy reached summation and set scholars into new directions with Lucien Febvre, *Le problème de l'incroyance au XVIe siècle: La religion de Rabelais* (Paris, 1942). See Henri Busson's update of his 1922 book, *Les sources et développement du rationalisme dans la littérature française de la Renaissance (1533–1601)* (Paris: Vrin, 1957). Scholarship set off in a new direction—recognizing Christian fideism in Skeptical thinkers and not dwelling on behavior—with Richard H. Popkin, *The History of Skepticism from Erasmus to Descartes* (The Hague: Van Gorcum, 1960), as evidenced by his expanded *History of Scepticism from Erasmus to Spinoza* (Berkeley: University of California Press, 1979).

99. John Calvin, *Calvin's Commentary on Seneca's De Clementia*, ed. and trans. Ford Battles and André Hugo (Leiden: Brill, 1969), 25.

100. Calvin, *Institution de la religion chrestienne*, 1:87–92.

101. A view that there is a major historical movement of secular, rational, classically based free thinkers who are predecessors to Enlightenment thought may be found in H. A. Enno van Gelder, *Two Reformations in the Sixteenth Century: A Study of Religious Aspects and Consequences of Renaissance and Humanism* (The Hague: Nijhoff, 1964); dismissed by Lewis Spitz in "Humanism and the Protestant Reformation," in *Renaissance Humanism: Foundations, Forms, and Legacy*, ed. Albert Rabil Jr., 3 vols. (Philadelphia: University of Pennsylvania Press, 1988), 3:403. See also François Berriot, *Athéismes et athéistes au XVIe siècle en France*, 2 vols. (Lille: Université de Lille, 1984).

102. J. F. Wippel, "The Condemnations of 1270 and 1277 at Paris," *Journal of Medieval and Renaissance Studies* 7 (1979): 169–201.

103. Elizabeth Eisenstein, *The Printing Press As an Agent of Social Change*, 2 vols. (New York: Cambridge University Press, 1972).

104. John Passmore, *Idea of Perfectibility* (New York: Scribner's, 1970); of the three, only Erasmus is mentioned by Passmore, on 105. See ch. 2, "The Godlike Man: Aristotle to Plotinus."

105. See the full quotation above, in ch. 1, "Seeds to Trees."

106. Elaine Pagels, *The Gnostic Gospels* (New York: Vintage, 1979); Turner, *On Flesh*, 23. Also, the Vulgate version of Rom. 11.20, "Noli altum sapere, sed time," is interpreted as a taboo against overstepping limits of human knowledge, as in Thomas à Kempis. See above, ch. 3, n. 54, discussing Carlo Ginzburg, *Clues, Myths, and Historical Method*, trans. John Tedeschi and Anne C. Tedeschi (Baltimore: John Hopkins University Press, 1989), 60–76, esp. 64, 74. Ginzburg emphasizes Horace's Epistle to Lollius "Sapere aude" [Dare to be wise] as a corrective of traditional pre-Erasmian interpretations of Paul's epistle; likewise, Seneca's much quoted *Epistles* are a corrective.

107. "Ex his ergo unius bonum natura perficit, dei scilicet, alterius cura, hominis," trans. Gummere (*Ep.* 124.14). See above, ch. 1, long passage at n. 66.

108. "Hoc bonum adeo non recipit infantia, ut pueritia non speret, adulescentia inprobe speret: bene agitur cum senectute, si ad illud longo studio intentoque pervenit" (*Ep.* 124.12). Seneca shows that it is not physical beauty that is the good, for animals can surpass humans in physical beauty (*Ep.* 124.21–22).

CHAPTER EIGHT

1. Paul L. Rose reveals that Bodin's view of natural goodness is especially evident in the *Paradoxon* (see Rose's *Bodin and the Great God of Nature: The Moral and Religious Universe of a Judaiser* [Geneva: Droz, 1980]). See the succinct summary of Bodin as a natural theologian in François Berriot, *Athéismes et athéistes au XVIe siècle en France*, 2 vols. (Lille: Université de Lille, 1984), 2:775–97.

2. J. B. Bury, *The Idea of Progress: An Inquiry into Its Growth and Origin* (New York: Dover, 1960), 39, 43.

3. The following is a brief list of Bodin's works in the order of their first publication: *Oratio* (1559), *Methodus* (1566); *Response .. à M. de Malestorict* (1568); *République* (1576); *Distributio* (1580); *Démonomanie* (1580); *Epitome* (1588); *Paradoxon* (1596); *Theatrum* (1596); "Colloquium Heptaplomeres" (ms.).

4. See Jean Bodin, *Colloquium of the Seven about Secrets of the Sublime*, ed. and trans. Marion Leathers Daniels Kuntz (Princeton: Princeton University Press, 1975), xv–xxviii, esp. nn. 5–6, 25–15. A Latin version with Hebrew and Greek text is *Colloquium heptaplomeres de rerum sublimium arcanis abditi*, ed. Ludovicus Noack (Schwerin, 1857; facs. reprint, Stuttgart: Friedrich Frommann Verlag, 1966). My references to the *Colloquium* are to Kuntz's translation, followed by pages in Noack's book. Jean Bodin, *Colloque entre sept scavans*, ed. François Berriot with Katherine Davies, Jean Larmat, and Jacques Roger (Geneva: Droz, 1984), follows a 1923 French manuscript with variants; an international team of scholars currently is working on a critical edition. For source study, see Georg Roellenbleck, *Offenbarung . . . und juedische Ueberlieferung bei Jean Bodin* (Gütersloh: G. Mohn, 1964). For posthumous criticism of Bodin, see Pierre Bayle, selection from *Dictionnaire historique et critique* (1734) in Jean Bodin, *Oeuvres*, ed. and trans. Pierre Mesnard (Paris: Presses Universitaires de France, 1951), xxiii–xxxvii, esp. xxxiii; see also Mesnard's "Vers un portrait de Jean Bodin," vii–xxi. For an examination of aspects of the religious issue, see Maryanne Cline Horowitz, "La religion de Bodin reconsiderée: Le Marrane comme modèle de la tolérance," in *Jean Bodin: Actes du colloque interdisciplinaire d'Angers (24–27 Mai 1984)*, 2 vols. (Angers: Presses de l'Université d'Angers, 1985), 1:201–15, 2:568–73; and idem, "Judaism in Jean Bodin," *Sixteenth Century Journal* 13 (1982): 109–13.

5. For example, a Jean Bodin was tried as a heretic in Paris in 1548, and a Jean Bodin was noted in the marital records of Geneva in 1552.

6. Emile Pasquier, "La famille de Jean Bodin," *Revue d'histoire de l'église de France* 19 (1933): 457–62.

7. Books by Bodin that appeared on the *Index* include *De Republica libri XVI*, in 1592; *De Daemonomanie*, in 1594; *Methodus*, in 1596, and on the *Index* of Clement VIII, *Universae naturae theatrum*, 1633. For examination of documents showing the criticism that leads to book condemnation, see Françoise Berriot, "La fortune du *Colloquium heptaplomeres*," in Bodin, *Colloque entre sept scavants*, xviii–xxiv.

8. *Methodus*, ch. 1, in John Bodin, *Methodus, ad facilem historiarum cognitionem* (Paris: Martinus Juvenes, 1572), reprinted in Bodin, *Oeuvres*, ch. 1, 114.

The Latin text appears in *Oeuvres*, 112–269, the modern French translation by Pierre Mesnard on 278–473. The English translation is from Jean Bodin, *Method for the Easy Comprehension of History*, trans. Beatrice Reynolds (New York: Norton, 1945), 15. References to the *Methodus* give the page, column, and line of the Latin edition, preceded by the chapter number except for prefatory material. A precedent to Bodin's tripartite distinction appears in François Baudouin's *De Institutione historiae universae et eius cum jurisprudentia* (1561), as noted by John L. Brown, *The Methodus . . . A Critical Study* (Washington, D.C.: Catholic University Press, 1939).

9. See *La catégorie de l'honnesté dans la culture du XVIe siècle: Actes du colloque international de Sommières II, septembre 1983* (Saint-Étienne: Institut d'Études de la Renaissance et de l'Age Classique, Université de Saint-Étienne, 1965).

10. Jean Bodin, *Sapientiae moralis epitome*, in Bodin, *Selected Writings on Philosophy, Religion, and Politics*, ed. Paul L. Rose (Geneva: Droz, 1980), 21–30; see Rose's commentary, v–vi. I give the number of the maxim in parentheses.

11. Jean Bodin, "Épître de Jean Bodin," in Bodin, *Selected Writings*, 3–4; see also Rose's commentary, ii.

12. The Latin reads, "Publica res quaeque imperio, obsequioque" (123) and "Fortitudo decus moralium bonorum est" (143). It is possible that in the sixteenth century floral imagery and horticultural vocabulary for the cultivation of civilization become more extensive in the vernacular than in the Latin.

13. Bodin renders the apian metaphor of Lucretius, *De rerum natura* 3.10–12 (see above, ch. 5, "Savoring the Fruit and Dispersing the Seed"). In *Universae naturae theatrum; in quo rerum omnium effectrices causae & fines contemplantur & continua series quinque libris discutiuntur autore Jo. Bodino* (Lyon: Jacques Roussin, 1596), p. 276, Bodin emphasizes that the smallest seeds sometimes have the greatest power because their virtue, in the horticultural sense of potency, is concentrated.

14. "Quemadmodum flores historiarum legere, ac suavissimos decerpere fructus oporteret, hac methodo" (*Methodus*, 107a1–2).

15. "Cùm enim juventus à suavissimis eloquentiae ac philosophiae floribus & hortulis, ad illa senticeta, praeruptaque saxa vocaretur . . . vepribus ac spinis interclusus tenebatur" (108a45–51).

16. "Commentariorum squallens sylva" (108b45–46).

17. "Cùm enim sementem in literarum agros sparsisset, is qui florentem scientiarum segetem, ac fructus pendentes legere debuissent, putredine corrumpi maluerunt" (109a20–23). *Seed* appears here in Quintilian's usage. Montaigne echoes Bodin and the refrain of vegetative symbolism indicating the decline of humanistic culture with his description of desolation, "the grapes hanging on the vines" (*Essais* 3.12, *Oeuvres complètes* (Paris: Gallimard, 1962), 1025; *Complete Essays*, trans. Donald M. Frame (Stanford: Stanford University Press, 1965), 802 [b]).

18. See above, ch. 7, "Resprouting of the Seeds in Erasmian Humanism." Donald Kelley points out that the story of the transmission of studies from Italy to France under Francis I was "quasi-official doctrine," as Bodin would know from the preface to Budé's *De Asse* (1515), Le Roy's *G. Budaei vita* (Paris, 1540), 46ff. (Donald R. Kelley, "The Development and Context of Bodin's Method," in *History, Law, and the Human Sciences* [London: Variorum Reprints, 1984], ch. 8, 125–26).

19. Jean Bodin, *Oratio*, in *Oeuvres*, 7–30; Mesnard's French translation appears

on 34–65. My references are to page, column, and line. Mesnard's introduction, 1–2, discusses the fracas that leads Bodin to leave Toulouse the next year. The French translation interprets the text. For example, "literarum cognitione pervenerunt" (9b24) is translated "la renaissance des lettres" (36b35), and two added subdivision titles indicate modern periodization: "Tableau de la Renaissance" (34) and "Toulouse doit participer au réveil des belles-lettres" (38). Appropriately, the latter title introduces the following discussion of horticulture and culture.

20. See above, ch. 5, "Epistemological Confidence among Female and Male Humanists"; *Erasme. Declamatio de pueris statim ac liberaliter instituendis*, ed. Jean-Claude Margolin (Geneva: Droz, 1966), 380–81, 388–89; and Quintilian, *Institutio oratoria*, trans. H. E. Butler, Loeb Classical Library, 1.1.

21. "Etenim jacta sunt à Deo in uniuscujusque nostrûm animos, pietatis quaedam ac religionis semina, quae cùm altissimis defixa radicib[us] haerent, tum erui nullo modo possunt, nisi pudorem, fidem, integritatem, & eam, fine qua ne Deus quidem regnarit, justitiam unà convellas" (*Oratio*, 25a47–53, French on 57b32–37).

22. "At juris & justitiae semina in animis uniuscujusque nostrûm ab immortali Deo insita primùm à ratione excitantur: & cùm ratio in nobis adolevit, eaque perfectionem est assecuta, juris hanc quam quaerimus prudentiam parit: quae tandem usu & arte concluditur hunc in modum" (Jean Bodin, *Exposé du droit universel: Juris universi distributio* [Paris: Presses Universitaires de France, 1985], 10–11).

23. "Jus est bonitaris & prudentiae divinae lux hominibus tributa, & ab iis ad utilitatem humanae societatis traducta" (ibid., 14–15). This example of a ray of light clearly refers to what the Creator implanted in human nature.

24. See *Digest* 1.1.9, in Allessandro Passerin d'Entrèves, *Natural Law: An Introduction to Legal Philosophy*, rev. with new introduction by Cary Nederman (New Brunswick, N.J.: Transaction, 1994), 25–28. François Connan's commentaries, published in Paris in the 1550s, are discussed in Donald R. Kelley, "*Altera natura*: The Idea of Custom in Historical Perspective," *New Perspectives on Renaissance Thought*, ed. John Henry and Sarah Hutton (London: Duckworth, 1990), 95–96.

25. See Simone Goyard-Fabre's commentary in Bodin, *Exposé du droit universel*, 101–5, 113, 152–53, 170.

26. *Exposé du droit universel*, 17.

27. Aristotle, *Nicomachean Ethics*, trans. W. D. Ross, in *Works of Aristotle*, ed. Ross (London: Oxford University Press, 1942); Plato, *Laws*, trans. R. G. Bury (London: Heinemann, 1926).

28. See Gratian, "The Concordance of Discordant Canons of Decretum," in *Natural Law in Political Thought*, ed. and trans. Paul E. Sigmund (Washington, D.C.: Winthrop, 1971), 48, from *Corpus juris canonici* (Leipzig: B. Tauchnitz, 1879); Simone Goyard-Fabre, *Jean Bodin et le droit de la république* (Paris: Presses Universitaires de France, 1989), 110; and Jean Bodin, *Les six livres de la république* (Lyon, 1593; reprint, Paris: Fayard, 1986), 1.8.214.

29. *Exposé du droit universel*, 14–15. Likewise, in the *Colloquium*, bk. 6 (Kuntz, 462–71; Noack, 352–58), all the participants conclude that worshiping God is essential to human nature and that piety and reward and punishment are part of the essential minimum common religion. Charron likewise is to subordinate religion to an expression of human nature (see below, ch. 10, nn. 73–75).

30. "Humanum ius est, quod ab hominibus praeter naturam utiliter constitutum est" (*Exposé du droit universel*, 16–17).

31. Ibid., 16–21.

32. Miriam Yardeni suggests a correlation between Bodin's views and those of Las Casas in "Barbares, sauvages et autres: L'anthropologie de Jean Bodin," in *Jean Bodin: Actes du colloque Interdisciplinaire d'Angers*, 2:464–66 and n. 10. Léon Ingber suggests a correlation with Francisco de Vittoria in "Jean Bodin et le droit naturel," in ibid., 286–87, 296–97.

33. "qui monstre bien qu'il ne faut pas mesurer la loy de nature aux actions des hommes, quoy qu'elles soyent inveterees: ni conclure pour cela, que la servitude des esclaves soit de droit naturel, et encores moins y a de charité de garder les captifs pour en tirer gain et proffit comme de bestes" (Bodin, *Les six livres de la république*, 1.5.91–92).

34. For a brief example, see the selection of *Demócrates alter de justis belli causis apud Indios*, trans. J. L. Phelan, in *Latin American History: Select Problems*, by Frederick B. Pike (New York: Harcourt, Brace & World, 1969), 47–52. See also Tzvetan Todorov, *The Conquest of America: The Question of the Other*, trans. Richard Howard (New York: Harper & Row, 1982), esp. 154–57. On Juan Ginés de Sepúlveda, see below, ch. 9, 219–222.

35. *République*, 1.3. Using divine Mosaic law as a standard, Bodin recommends marital separation as more humane than Roman laws sanctioning the husband's right to punish a wife by death (56–60).

36. Ibid., 1.8.197, 6.5.228, 232–34, 248. See also the recent study by political scientist Genevra C. Odorisio, *Famiglia e stato nella "République" di Jean Bodin* (Turin: G. Giappichelli, 1993); Pierre-Louis Vaillancourt, "Bodin et le pouvoir politique des femmes," in *Jean Bodin: Actes du colloque interdisciplinaire d'Angers*, 1:63–74, esp. 68–70; and Janine Chanteur, "L'idée de la loi naturelle dans la république," in *Jean Bodin* (Munich: Beck, 1973), 201–6. For another contemporary account, see Claude de Seyssel, *The Monarchy of France*, trans. J. H. Hexter, ed. Donald Kelley (New Haven: Yale University Press, 1981). Marie de Gournay argues from historical precedent and from natural justice in disputing this particular law of the French in "Égalité des hommes et des femmes" (1622) (see Elayne Dezon-Jones, ed., *Fragment d'un discours feminin: Marie de Gournay, textes établis, presentés et commentés* [Paris: José Corti, 1988], 119–20).

37. *République*, 1.2.52. He cites Maimonides in interpreting Solomon's identification of women with desire as an allegory rather than a policy against women.

38. Ibid., 1.1.31–32. Citing Aristotle's *Politica* 7 and *Ethica Nichomachea* 10, Bodin views reason in the soul commanding the lower soul to govern the appetites as analogous to the sovereign commanding in a state and God ruling in the universe.

39. "Atque omnino humanae actiones novis semper erroribus implicantur, nisi à natura duce, id est, à recta ratione . . . dirigantur" (*Methodus*, 1.115a51–56).

40. Likewise, in *Methodus*, 7.226a1–35; Reynolds, 296, Bodin views the golden age as a myth, but a myth that in chronology corresponds to the period after Noah. God punishes the contemporaries of Noah for actions freely chosen, for "the evil deeds of humans" [scelera hominum] (line 15). Bodin reworks both Greek and Christian theories of human degeneration. His view of the life of the early patriarchs as exemplary, rather than as a product of original sin, finds support in the *Colloquium*.

41. "Restat igitur ut videamus quantùm disciplina possit, ad immutandum hominum naturam. Duplex est autem disciplina, divina & humana: haec prava aut

recta, utraque profecto tantam vim habet, ut saepius naturam vincat. nam si verissimè Hippocrates, omnia plantarum genera ἐφημερούσια putavit, quanto id verius est in hominum genere: aut quae natio tam immanis ac barbara, quae nacta duces ad humanitatem perducta non fuerit? aut quae gens politissimis artibus imbuta, quae humaniore cultu neglecto, in barbariem ac feritatem non aliquando degenerarit? atque ejus rei cùm infinita sint exempla" (*Methodus*, 5.164a1–14, my translation). Reynolds, 145, properly corrects Bodin's Greek from ἐφημερώσται (*ephēmerousia*), indicating that all the species of plants are for one day only, to ἐξημερῶσθαι (*exēmerōsthai*), indicating that the plants are capable of domestication.

42. "Neque enim ut stirpes, quae alio translatae, cito vim amittunt; & soli unde trahunt alimenta, naturam induunt: ita quoque homines, insitam suae naturae vim facilè mutant, sed longa temporis diuturnitate" (5.163b37–41; Reynolds, 144). Note the theme of comparing human and plant transplantation in the Alciati emblem of Lyon, 1551 (fig. 7.4).

43. "Sed nulla tanta naturae bonitas est, quae prava disciplina non corrumpatur" (5.164a48–50; Reynolds, 145–46).

44. "Quod si tanta consuetudinis ac disciplinae vis est in rebus naturalibus & humanis, ut paulatim abeat in mores, & naturae vim obtineat, quanto id verius est in divinis? videmus enim religionum tantam vim esse ac potestatem, ut mores hominum & corruptam naturam, penitus immutare videantur" (5.164b8–14; Mesnard, 5.345b45; Reynolds, 146). Mesnard's translation refers to "une seconde nature," which conforms to the Bartolist tradition of viewing custom as a second nature, an "altera natura," as described by Donald R. Kelley in "Law," in *The Cambridge History of Political Thought, 1450–1700*, ed. J. H. Burns (Cambridge: Cambridge University Press, 1991), 89, and in "*Altera natura*," 83–101. However, I think variety, multiplicity, and distortion from nature are Bodin's point, as is Louis Le Roy's in *De la vicissitude ou varieté des choses en L'Univers . . .* , first published in 1575; for Le Roy's influence on Bodin, see Bury, *The Idea of Progress*, 44–48.

45. Peter Burke, "Tacitism, Scepticism, and Reason of State," in Burns, *Cambridge History of Political Thought*, gives as radical examples Montaigne's statement that "the laws are maintained in credit not because they are just but because they are laws. That is the mystical foundation of their authority; they have not other" (*Essais* 3.13) and Charron's that "lawes and customs are maintained in credit, not because they are just and good, but because they are lawes and customs" (*On Wisdome* 2.8). Both could find backing in Bodin (*Methodus*, 5.226b43; Reynolds, 298). See also above, n. 44.

46. *Methodus*, 1.115, esp. a25.

47. *République*, 1.34–35.

48. Ann M. Blair, "Humanist Methods in Natural Philosophy: The Commonplace Book," *Journal of the History of Ideas* 53 (1992): 541–51.

49. Bodin, *Theatrum*. References are to the 1596 edition, followed by volume, chapter, and page in the French translation by Fougerolles. I have also consulted the 1605 Frankfurt edition published by Wechel. Fougerolles (see below, n. 50) numbers the topic changes as chapters and inserts in the text the numbered chapter headings. Ann M. Blair's "Restaging Jean Bodin: The 'Universae Naturae Theatrum' (1596) in its Cultural Context" (Ph.D. diss., Princeton University, 1990), revised as *The Theater of Nature: Jean Bodin and Renaissance Science* (Princeton: Princeton University Press, 1997), makes a major contribution to the history of this

book. See also Pierre Bayle's discussion of the *Theatrum* in his article on Bodin in *Dictionnaire historique et critique* (1734), reprinted in *Oeuvres*, xxii, xxiv; and W. H. Greenleaf, "Bodin and the Idea of Order," in *Jean Bodin* (Munich: Beck, 1973), 23–38, esp. 23–25.

50. *Le Théâtre de la nature universelle, auquel on peut contempler les causes efficientes et finales de toutes choses, desquelles l'ordre et continué par questions et responses en cinq livres*, trans. François de Fougerolles (Lyon: Jean Pillehotte, 1597), appears the next year, following Bodin's death. (I am grateful to the library of the Université d'Angers for a microfilm.) François de Fougerolles, a medical doctor, adds additional dedicatory letters, diagrams, and hierarchical charts of organization. Pierre Charron most likely uses the French translation. Most appropriately, in his foreword Fougerolles refers to the late Bodin as "a plant adorned with such beautiful flowers" (see Ann M. Blair, "The Languages of Natural Philosophy in the Late Sixteenth Century: Jean Bodin's *Universae naturae theatrum* and Its French Translation," in *Acta conventus neo-Latini Hauniensis* [Copenhagen, 1991], 6).

51. Further work might proceed on Arabic and Jewish precedents of discussions in the *Theatrum* and the *Colloquium*. Bodin's natural philosophy shows the influence of Abraham ibn Ezra's (1089–1140) "secrets," revealed in his biblical commentaries and his works on astrology and numbers (see Colette Sirat, *La philosophie juive au Moyen-Age* [Paris: Editions du Centre nationale de la recheche scientifique, 1985]; and idem, *A History of Jewish Philosophy in the Middle Ages*, trans. M. Reich [Cambridge: Cambridge University Press, 1985], 104–12). Several important Jewish books emerging in thirteenth- and fourteenth-century Provence are published in Hebrew in the mid-sixteenth century; for example, thirteenth-century Gershom ben Solomon's *Sha'ar ha-Shamayim*, published in 1547, translated into English as *The Gate of Heaven* by F. S. Bodenheim (Jerusalem, 1953): the book of minerals, plants, animals, and humans leads to a book on astronomy, followed by a book on metaphysics. The union of the active intellect is the gate to heaven. Gersonides Levi ben Gershom (1288–1344) is influential through the 1560 publication of *Milhamot Adonai*, translated into English as *The Wars of the Lord* by Seymour Feldman, 2 vols. (Philadelphia: Jewish Publication Society, 1984). He discusses prophecy as well as astronomy, and he discusses the active intellect to defend the individuation of immortality.

52. *Colloquium*, Kuntz, 4; Noack, 2.

53. Pierre Boaistuau, *Le théâtre du monde, ou il est faict un ample discours des miseres humaines* (1558), ed. Michel Simonin (Geneva: Droz, 1981). Boaistuau himself takes the optimistic side in *Bref discours de l'excellence & dignité de l'homme* included in editions after 1562.

54. A very general overview of book 4 appears in Pierre Mesnard, "The Psychology and Pneumatology of Jean Bodin," *International Philosophical Quarterly* 2 (1962): 244–64.

55. "Quamquam quod verum sit, idem Physicis, Theologis, Dialecticis, Medicis, verum esse oportet, nec plus uno verum esse potest" (Jean Bodin, *Universae naturae theatrum* [Frankfurt: Wechel, 1597], 521; on pp. 82 and 484 Bodin declares that there can be only one definition of the soul (cited in Blair, "Restaging Jean Bodin," 284–85).

56. A work influential because of its discussion of "spiritual matter" is *Fons Vitae*, influenced by Plotinus, *Enneads* 2.4; Proclus, *Elements of Theology*; and

Pseudo-Empedocles. See Solomon ben Judah Ibn Gabirol, *Fountain of Life*, bk. 3, trans. H. E. Wedeck (London, 1963); and *Avencebrolis Fons Vitae*, ed. C. Boeumker (Münster, 1892). As in Arabic philosophical literature and as in Bodin, the teacher-student dialogues allow the teacher to present his views. On Tertullian's advocacy of the Stoic doctrine of the soul's corporeality, "All things have one form of simple corporeality, which is a substantial thing," see Marcia Colish, *The Stoic Tradition from Antiquity to the Early Middle Ages*, 2 vols. (Leiden: Brill, 1985), 2:20.

57. Jean Bodin, *De la Démonomanie* (Paris: Jacques du Puys, 1581). In his 1588 and later additions to "Des Boyteux" (On cripples), in *Essais*, Michel de Montaigne spoofs the rationality of Bodin's system of causative explanation, especially regarding "eyewitness" reports of the "demonic flights" of humans. See Maryanne Cline Horowitz, "Un drogue médicinale où un ancien conte: L'histoire et la justice chez Montaigne, Bodin et Augustin," in *Montaigne et l'histoire*, ed. Charles G. Dubois (Bordeaux: Université de Bordeaux Press, 1991); and Raymon Escapez, "Deux magistrats humanistes du XVIe siècle face à l'irrationnel: Montaigne et Bodin," *Bulletin de la société des amis de Montaigne*, ser. 7, no. 7–8 (1987): 47–74.

58. *Colloquium*, 6 (Kuntz, 379; Noack, 286).

59. *Theatrum*, 475; 4.9.686. The section "De intellectione & intellectu, vero, scientiis, cognitione," appears on 470–82 in the Latin, 678–89 in the French. The medieval scholastic phrase has origins in Aristotle, *De anima* 432a5–11 (see P. Cranefield, "On the Origins of the Phrase *Nihil est in intellectu quod non prius fuerit in sensu*," *Journal of the History of Medicine* 25 [1970]: 77–80).

60. See above, ch. 1, "Common Notions."

61. Richard H. Popkin, *History of Scepticism from Erasmus to Spinoza* (Berkeley: University of California Press, 1979), 18–65.

62. See Raymond Sebond, *Theologia naturalis* (Lyon: Balsarin, 1484), translated as *Théologie naturelle de Raymond Sebond* by Montaigne (Paris: Jean Martin, 1568); Yvonne Bellenger, *Montaigne: Une fête pour l'esprit* (Paris: Balland, 1987), 95–106, 318–19; and Michel de Montaigne, *L'Apologie de Raymond Sebond*, critical edition of original text, annotated by Paul Porteau (Paris: Fernard Aubier, 1937), 244–45. See also Claude Blum, ed., *Montaigne, Apologie de Raimond Sebond: de la Theologia à la Théologie: etudes* (Paris: Champion, 1990).

63. Bodin, *De la Démonomanie*, preface; Richard H. Popkin, *The History of Scepticism from Erasmus to Descartes*, rev. ed. (New York: Harper & Row, 1968), 84.

64. "Sic etiam in animis nostris, virtutum ac scientiarum omnium semina divinitùs sparsa fuisse, ut quasi in hortis odoratissimis, floribus & arboribus, ac frugum omnium copia abundantissimis, homini iucundissimè vivere liceret" (*Theatrum*, 475; 4.9.687).

65. "Nam modicè culta mens abūndanti fertilitate luxuriat. In ea quidem sententia fuisse videmus Empedoclem, Platonem, Philonem Hebraeum, Adelandum, Academicos. Quod autem Aristoteles negat, ullam animis nostris insitam esse sciētiarum ac virtutum notionem" (*Theatrum*, 475–76; 4.9.687, citing Arist., *De an.* 3.1 and *Eth. Nic.*).

66. *Theatrum*, 276–77.

67. Blair, "Restaging Jean Bodin," 257–68.

68. See ch. 10, n. 14, and below.

69. Rose, *Bodin and the Great God of Nature*, 227; Philo, *Philonis Judaei in libros Mosis de mundi opificio, historicos, de legibus. Eiusdem libri singulares*, ed. A. Turnebus (Paris, 1552); idem, *Les oeuvres de Philon Juif*, ed. and trans. P. Bellier (Paris, 1575). Rose gives extensive evidence of Philo's influence on Bodin.

70. Léone Hébreu, *Dialogues d'amour*, trans. Pontus de Tyard (Lyon, 1551), ed. T. Anthony Perry (Chapel Hill: University of North Carolina Press, 1974). The other edition's publications indicate extensive popularity: Léone Hébreu, *Dialogues d'amour*, trans. Denys Sauvage (Lyon, 1551; reprinted in 1559, 1577, 1580, and 1595). See Arthur Lesley, "The Place of the *Dialoghi d'amore* in Contemporaneous Jewish Thought," and Eva Kushner, "Pontus de Tyard entre Ficin et Léon l'Hébreu," in *Ficino and Renaissance Neoplatonism* (Toronto: University of Toronto Press, 1986), 71–86 and 49–68, respectively.

71. "Or fut il mis en Paradis terrestre, auquel estoient tous les beaux et savoureux arbres . . . comme en l'entendement plein de sapience . . . sont toutes les eternelles cognoissances, et la divine sus toutes en sa pure unité" (trans. Pontus de Tyard, 250).

72. See below, n. 119.

73. In chapters 7 and 8 of the *Methodus*, citing Melanchthon as a precedent, Bodin trusts Philo as a major historian of the proper chronology from Creation and of the interrelationships of ancient peoples, as well as a reliable interpreter of Hebraic culture.

74. David Ruderman, "Italian Renaissance and Jewish Thought," in *Renaissance Humanism: Foundations, Forms, and Legacy*, ed. Albert Rabil Jr., 3 vols. (Philadelphia: University of Pennsylvania Press, 1988), 1:394–433, esp. 403–12.

75. D. P. Walker, *The Ancient Theology* (London, 1972), esp. 39–41.

76. *Theatrum*, 544, citing Ricius, *De agricultura coelesti*; Blair, "Restaging Jean Bodin," 93. Postel's drawings of the *sefirot* likely also directly influence Bodin (Paul G. Kuntz and Marion L. Kuntz, "The Symbol of the Tree Interpreted in the Context of Other Symbols of Hierarchical Order, the Great Chain of Being, and Jacob's Ladder," in *Jacob's Ladder and the Tree of Life: Concepts of Hierarchy and the Great Chain of Being*, ed. Marion L. Kuntz and Paul G. Kuntz [New York: Peter Lang, 1987], 220); see on 327 the illustration in Postel's hand, which uses biblical names for God rather than the standard *sefirot* (British Library, ms., *Resolutionum Diuinarum Exposito*). See also Marion L. Kuntz, "Jean Bodin's Colloquium Heptaplomeres and Guillaume Postel: A Consideration of Influence," in *Jean Bodin: Actes du colloque interdisciplinaire d'Angers*, 2:435–44.

77. Kuntz, introduction to Bodin, *Colloquium*, lxi, citing Guillaume Postel, *Candelabri typici in Mosis Tabernaculo . . . interpretatio* (1548). The illustration is from his previous Hebrew broadsheet *Or Nerot ha-Menorah* (1547?), in Biblioteca Ambrosiana, Milan, cited in *Encyclopedia Judaica*, 16 vols. (New York: Macmillan, 1972), s.v. "Kabbalah," where the Christian Hebraicists are discussed on 643–45.

78. "Quod Graeci cùm ab Hebraeis, ut optima quaeque, accepissent" (*Methodus*, 5.150b8–9). Reynolds, 111, does not give the Hebrew; however, her index is useful for tracing authors whom Bodin cites.

79. "Philo Hebraus libr. 1. Allegor. paradisū Adami, ad animā virtutibus ac disciplinis consitam refert" (476 margin; 687 margin).

80. See Ovey N. Mohammed, *Averroes' Doctrine of Immortality: A Matter of Controversy* (Waterloo, Ont.: Wilfrid Laurier University Press, 1984), section en-

titled "Christian Anthropologies," 40–53, presents the viewpoint of the Hebrew Bible from the perspective of its differences with Plato, the New Testament, Aristotle, Thomas Aquinas, and Averroes (similar to Bodin's points of comparison); *Theatrum*, 497; and *Encyclopedia Judaica*, s.v. "Man, Nature of." According to the latter, *nefesh* is associated with the blood (Gen. 9.4), as well as the person (Gen. 46.26); *ru'ah* implies both energy (Ex. 35.21) and the impulse to a higher life (Ex. 28.3); *neshemah* is the breath by which God vitalizes *adam* (Gen. 2.7). Bodin utilizes these three Hebrew terms in *Theatrum*, 497.

81. Philo of Alexandria, *Philo*, trans. F. H. Colson and G. H. Whitaker, 10 vols. plus 2 suppl. vols., Loeb Classical Library, vol. 1, *Legum allegoriae* 9–11, lines 21–30.

82. Philo, *De specialibus legibus* 4.24, cited in Louis Jacobs, "The Doctrine of the 'Divine Spark' in Man in Jewish Sources," in *Studies in Rationalism: Judaism and Universalism*, ed. Raphael Lowe (London: Routledge & Kegan Paul, 1966), 91.

83. Philo, *De opif. mund.*, ch. 51, line 145, discussed in Jacobs, "Doctrine of the 'Divine Spark,'" 91–92.

84. Philo, *Legum allegoriae* 1.17.

85. John Parkinson, *Paradisi in Sole: Paradisus Terrestris* (1629; reprint, London: Methuen, 1904). See also John Prest, *The Garden of Eden: The Botanic Garden and the Re-Creation of Paradise* (New Haven: Yale University Press, 1981), 7, 54. In the copy of the illustration reprinted in Prest, fig. 7 on p. 7, below this seventeenth-century image are handwritten lines from Milton's *Paradise Lost*.

86. Cited in n. 64 above.

87. Philo, *Questions and Answers on Genesis*, trans. Ralph Marcus, in *Philo*, suppl. 1.

88. Arist., *De an.* 1.2.404b12–20. Other references to Empedocles include 1.2.405b.10; 1.4.408a–b; 1.5.409b–411a; and, after bk. 1, 3.5.430a–b. Aristotle borrows some of Empedocles' expressions, as in the statement, "In general, the mind when actively thinking is identical with its objects" (3.7.531b). Bodin appears to be heir to a movement of analyzing the organic soul as material, identified with Averroism, followed by Melanchthon and by Bernardino Telesio (Katherine Park, "The Organic Soul," in *The Cambridge History of Renaissance Philosophy*, ed. Charles B. Schmitt, Quentin Skinner, Eckhard Kessler, and Jill Kraye [Cambridge: Cambridge University Press, 1988], 483). However, he differs from others in also viewing the highest part of the soul, both the active and the passive intellect, as material and corporeal yet individually immortal. Bodin may be expanding the notion of the organic soul to encompass the soul. For a parallel discussion, see Philip Melanchthon, "On the Soul" (1553), in *Melanchthon Reader*, trans. Ralph Keen (New York: Peter Lang, 1988), 254–68, 284–98, esp. 255–56, 260. Melanchthon discusses "seeds" (260), but the long physiological section on the organic soul is omitted (see Philip Melanchthon, *Melanchthons Werke in Auswahl*, ed. Robert Stupperich et al. [Gütersloh: C. Bertelsmann Verlag, 1951–75], 3:307–72]).

89. Blair, "Restaging Jean Bodin," 54 n. 97, citing Pico della Mirandola's *Conclusiones* in *Opera omnia* (1567; reprint, Turin: Bottega d'Erasmo, 1971).

90. Controversial issues include the Arabic interpretation of immortality as one universal immortal soul and the Arabic doctrine of double truth, as in Averroes's prologue to *Physics*, bk. 3: "Truth is the end of philosophy while the end of the religious lawgiver is neither truth nor falsehood but to make men good and well-

behaved" (Pomponazzi's citation of Averroes, in Martin Pine, "Double Truth," *Dictionary of the History of Ideas*, ed. Philip P. Wiener, 5 vols. [New York: Scribner's Sons, 1973], 2:37).

91. See Park, "The Organic Soul," 472–75, 483, on Arab influence.

92. Marsilio Ficino, *Commentary on Plato's Symposium on Love*, trans. Sears Jayne (Dallas: Spring, 1985), 7.1, p. 154. See above, ch. 4.

93. "Quantò verius igitur homines ab ipso naturae parente scientiarum ac virtutum semina hauserunt & expresserunt?" (*Theatrum*, 476). This contrast of humans and animals is consistent with the *Colloquium*, where in order to explain human belief in the power of statues, Senamus states, "Rude and ignorant men have a weaker mind and are concerned with only that which is at hand, just like animals who know nothing except that which the senses receive" (Kuntz, 442; Noack, 336).

94. *Theatrum*, 630.

95. *Plato*, trans. W. R. M. Lamb (London: Heinemann, 1924), *Meno*, esp. lines 70a, 81, 82–86, 89, quotation at 85e. See above, ch. 1, "Common Notions." Bodin may have been influenced by any Ficino citation of Meno's rapid learning to prove that the mind is fertile with seeds; see above, ch. 4, discussion on Ficino, *De amore*, speech 6, chapter 12.

96. Marion L. Kuntz, "Pythagorean Cosmology and Its Identification in Bodin's 'Colloquium Heptaplomeres,'" *International Congress of Neo-Latin Studies* 2 (1976): 685–796, esp. 689–90, citing *Colloquium*, 372–73 (Noack, 282), and *Theatrum*, 143–44. Plato, *Laws* 2, which Bodin cites in *Distributio*, concerns the importance of teaching the young proper musical harmony.

97. Philippe Desan, *Naissance de la méthode* (Paris: Nizet, 1987), 100–106. The unutterable Hebrew letters for God appear on the engraved title page of the 1596 edition; Salomon in the *Colloquium*, 372–73 (Noack, 282) argues that God as a quaternity is more meaningful than God as a trinity. See above, ch. 2, n. 109.

98. Fougerolles, 4.9.688, explains the seeds emerging by "moyenneant la lumière qu'il leur en a communiqué par son esprit." Rose, *Bodin and the Great God of Nature*, 132–33 n. 34, interprets this to transform Bodin's meaning to illuminated light. However, Bodin refers to natural light in citation of Empedocles. Likewise, Bodin in the *Epitome* utilizes "ray of light" to indicate what God implanted at Creation. Fougerolles marks his addition from Bodin's text by an asterisk at the addition and at the marginal note; he may have been influenced by reading the passage cited below from the *Paradoxon*. Another example is in *Theatrum* (1597), 190; Fougerolles, 261, cited by Blair in "The Languages of Natural Philosophy in the Late Sixteenth Century."

99. Robert A. Greene, "Whichcote, the Candle of the Lord, and Synderesis," *Journal of the History of Ideas* 52 (1991): 632, shows Benjamin Whichcote and Nathanael Culverwell, 1647–48, viewing Psalm 4.8 as, "Lift thou up the light of thy countenance upon us," and utilizing instead for the natural light Proverbs 20.27, "The spirit of the Lord is a lamp, searching out the hidden chambers of the heart."

100. *Theatrum*, 478; 4.9.691: "Illa verò stirpes sibi à natura congenitas promet: idem quoque de mentibus humanis relinquitur iudicandum, si vel levissimo sensuum adiumento utantur: neque tamen ab iis scientiarum perfectionem adipiscuntur." Note Philo's influence on Ambrose, *Paradise* 10.48, 11.51, in *Hexameron*,

Paradise, and Cain and Abel, trans. John J. Savage, Fathers of the Church, 42 (Washington, D.C.: Catholic University of America Press, 1961), 327, 329. Ambrose's student Augustine repeats the point in *Free Choice of the Will*, in *The Teacher, The Free Choice of the Will, Grace and Free Will*, trans. Robert P. Russell, Fathers of the Church, 59 (Washington, D.C.: Catholic University of America Press, 1968), 22.65: "We would be wrong to call the young and tender sapling barren, even though it goes through several summer seasons without bearing fruit until the proper time arrives to show its fruit. Why then, should the soul's Creator not be praised with all due reverence if He has given the soul a kind of beginning that enables it to mature with the fruits of wisdom and justice by its efforts and growth, and when He has so dignified it that it is within its power to reach out for happiness, if he wills to do so?"

101. *Theatrum*, 478–79; 4.9.691: "Cùm tamen sensuum omnium vis ac potestas ab anima dependeat."

102. *Theatrum*, 630, cited in Kuntz, *Colloquium*, xxxiii, as expressing a Platonic-Augustinian theme: "Sunt igitur Ideae exemplaria aeterna in Opificis aeterni mēte, vel, ut planiùs loquar, essentia causalis rerū omnium in esse intelligibili producta: quod his verbis significatur [Gen. 2], *Omne virgultum agri creaverat Deus antequam esset in terra*: quod aliò referri non potest, quàm ad ἀρχέτιπον & exempla aeternum in mente Creatoris."

103. *Theatrum*, 630–31; 5.11.912: "Ideas habuit in se expressas rerum omnium genitarum: in nobis verò Ideae sunt nihil aliud quàm notiones universorum ex singulis collectae, unde principia, demonstrationes, scientiae, atque notiones derivantur: quae accidentia non essentiae, aut substātiae intellectuales, cùm nulla sit preter Deum substantia corporis expers, ut superiùs demonstravimus."

104. Curtius mentions in passing in the *Colloquium* that "Cicero followed the philosophy of the Academicians" (Kuntz, 148; Noack, 115). Philo's epistemology uses Stoic terms: *epistêmê* for "knowledge," *katalêpsis* for "perception," *kataléptikê phantasia* for "criterion." See Robert M. Berchman, *From Philo to Origen: Middle Platonism in Transition* (Chico, Calif.: Scholars Press, 1984), "Epistemology," 167–200, esp. 170–76.

105. "Cùm disertè scriptum sit, *omnia quae Deus fecerat optimà fuisse*, quod elegantiùs Hebraei dicunt, טבה מוד. Itaque malum aliud nihil est quàm boni carentia, seu privatio" (*Theatrum*, 631; 5.12.914–15). (Gen 1.31 states: טוב מאד.) See also Blair, "Restaging Jean Bodin," 171–75.

106. For the influence of this manuscript, see Berriot, "La fortune de *Colloquium heptaplomere*" (see above, n. 7); Richard Popkin, "The Dispersion of Bodin's Dialogues in England, Holland, and Germany," *Journal of the History of Ideas* 49 (1988): 157–60; and idem "The Role of Jewish Anti-Christian Arguments in the Rise of Scepticism," in Henry and Hutton, *New Perspectives on Renaissance Thought*, 5–8.

107. A possible source for Bodin's knowledge of Abraham ibn Ezra (1089–1164) is *Aseret ha-Devarim Decalogus* (Lyon, 1566–68), a book by a Hebraicist with whom Bodin studied in Paris, Jean Mercier, which contains commentary by Abraham ibn Ezra in both Hebrew and Latin. Isaac Husik, *Medieval Jewish Philosophy* (New York: Macmillan, 1916), 194, confirms that Ibn Ezra holds that the Decalogue, with the exception of the seventh day of rest, consists of laws planted by God in the minds of rational beings; that is exactly the consensus of Bodin's seven

speakers. Technically, although he recognizes that the Decalogue is acknowledged by the intelligent of all nations, Ibn Ezra does not refer to it as natural law; likewise, Moses Maimonides (1135–1204) views the main principles of divine law to be derived from divine reason and to be knowable by the common consent of human reason (*Guide to the Perplexed*, trans. M. Friedländer [New York: Hebrew Publishing Co., 1881], 3.26–49). Joseph Albo (d. 1444) introduces into Hebrew the term for natural law, *dath tiv ith* (see Sirat, *La philosophie juive au Moyen-Age*, 243, 383, citing Joseph Albo, *Sefer ha-Ikkarim*, trans. I. Husik [Philadelphia: Jewish Publication Society of America, 1946]; and J. Guttmann, "Towards a Study of the Sources of the Book of Principles," in *Dat u-Maddah* [Jerusalem, 1955], 169–81 [in Hebrew]).

108. Salomon takes a position of full divine mercy for evildoers, a libertarian Jewish position of the Arabic period and libertarian Muslim philosophers (see Harry Austryn Wolfson, *Repercussions of the Kalam in Jewish Philosophy* [Cambridge: Harvard University Press, 1979], 198–233. See also Bodin, *Paradoxe*, in *Selected Writings*, 54, discussed in Rose, *Bodin and the Great God of Nature*, 145–47).

109. Philo, *De decalogo; De specialibus legibus*, trans. F. H. Colson, Loeb Classical Library, vol. 7.

110. Aristotle, *De generatione animalium* 2.3.736b.28.

111. Augustine, *The Free Choice of the Will* in *The Teacher, The Free Choice of the Will, Grace and Free Will*. Bodin is influenced by Augustine's Stoicizing phrase "eternal law impressed upon our nature" (85). For Augustine's praise of human free will and dignity, see 5.14–15.

112. *Colloquium*, Kuntz, 73, and Noack, 58; *Theatrum*, 143–44; as well as *Démonomanie*. See also Kuntz, *Colloquium*, xli n. 78.

113. Jean Céard, *La nature et prodiges: L'insolite au XVIe siècle en France* (Geneva: Droz, 1977).

114. *Theatrum*, 272–75; *Methodus*, 210b.

115. *Methodus*, 8.231b1–10; Reynolds, 310.

116. Joseph Dan, "'No Evil Descends from Heaven'—Sixteenth Century Jewish Concepts of Evil," in *Jewish Thought in the Sixteenth Century*, ed. Bernard Cooperman (Cambridge: Harvard University Center for Jewish Studies, 1983), 93, citing thirteenth-century *Sefer ha-Yashar* (Venice, 1544), for the natural process by which thorns are created along with the rose and dirt is created along with the fruitful seed of wheat. Bodin, likewise, views all aspects of nature, including poisons, as beneficial from the perspective of the totality of nature.

117. King Henry IV, *Edict du Roy & Declaration sur les precedent Edicts de Pacification* (Paris?: Royal Press, 25 February 1599). The king signs the edict in April 1598, but it not published by the Parlement of Paris until February 1599 (G. A. Rothrock, *The Huguenots: A Biography of a Minority* [Chicago: Nelson-Hall, 1979], 124–26).

118. *Paradoxon quod nec virtus ulla in mediocritate, nec summum hominis bonum in virtutis actione consistere possit; Le Paradox de Jean Bodin Angevin qu'il n'y a pas une seule vertu en mediocrité, ny au milieu de deux vices*, dedicatory letter 37 in *Selected Writings*, ed. Rose, 54; commentary on vii–x. See also Rose, *Bodin and the Great God of Nature*, 145–47. For an overview, emphasizing Bodin's view of salvation for non-Christians, see Pierre Mesnard, "Jean Bodin et la morale d'Aristote," *Revue Thomiste* 49 (1949): 542–62.

119. "Mais tous les anciens Hebrieux & Academiques ont tenu pour chose asseurée, que nous auōs les ames parsemees d'une semence divine de toutes vertus" (*Le Paradoxe*, 65, in *Selected Writings*,63. See also Rose, *Bodin and the Great God of Nature*, 108).

CHAPTER NINE

1. Eva Marcu, *Répertoire des idées de Montaigne* (Genève: Droz, 1965), s.v. "Conscience," "Universelle loi," "Loi."

2. Tzvetan Todorov, "L'être et l'autre: Montaigne," in *Montaigne: Essays in Reading*, ed. Gérard Defaux, Yale French Studies 64 (New Haven: Yale University Press, 1983), 117–20; Lawrence Kritzman, *Destruction/Découverte* (Lexington, Ky.: French Forum, 1980), 31–33; Yvonne Bellenger, "'Nature' et 'naturel' . . . (Livre III, chapitres 2, 6, 8 et 10)," *Bulletin de la Société des Amis de Montaigne*, 5th ser., no. 25– 26 (1978): 45–46; Henri Weber, "Montaigne et l'idée de nature," *Saggi e ricerche di letteratura francese* 5 (1965): 49–53.

3. James B. Scott, *The Spanish Origin of International Law: Francisco de Vitoria and His Law of Nations* (Oxford: Clarendon, 1934), 47–55, presents Montaigne as one of the first to use vernacular language to make a universal appeal for such principles; see, for example, 2.11, P. 414, S 318. Citations to the *Essais* are to book, chapter, and page. Page numbers are preceded by "P" (referring to the Pléiade edition: Michel de Montaigne, *Oeuvres complètes*, ed. Albert Thibaudet and Maurice Rat [Paris: Gallimard, 1962]) or "S" (referring to the Stanford English translation: Michel de Montaigne, *The Complete Works*, trans. Donald M. Frame [Stanford: Stanford University Press, 1967]). The designation "(a)" following the page number refers to text written before 1580, "(b)" refers to text written between 1580 and 1588, and "(c)" to text written following the 1588 edition. A sequel to Montaigne's concern for justice in the New World might include the *Inter-American Convention to Prevent and Punish Torture* (1985) (Washington, D.C.: Secretary General, Organization of American States, 1986).

4. See Marie de Gournay, *L'Ombre: Oeuvre composé de méslanges* (Paris, 1626); and Maryanne Cline Horowitz, "Marie de Gournay, Editor of the *Essais* of Michel de Montaigne: A Case-Study in Mentor-Protégée Friendship," *Sixteenth Century Journal* 17 (1986): 271–84. See also Françoise Kaye, *Charron et Montaigne: Du plagiat à l'originalité* (Ottawa: l'Université d'Ottawa, 1982).

5. For a list of these sentences, see Montaigne, *Essais*, P 1419–27. For photographs, see Jean-Yves Pouilloux, *Montaigne* (Paris: Gallimard, 1987), 48–49.

6. Hugo Friedrich, *Montaigne*, trans. Dawn Eng, ed. Philippe Desan (Berkeley: University of California Press, 1991), 350; originally published as *Montaigne* (Bern: A. Francke, 1949) and published in French as *Montaigne*, trans. Robert Rovini (Paris: Gallimard, 1968).

7. "Ce sont icy des meslanges. Il n'est pas dit qu'une prairie diversifiée d'une infinité de fleurs, que la Nature produit sans ordre, ne soit aussi agréable à l'oeil, que les parterres artistement labourez par les Jardiniers" (Étienne Pasquier, *Recherches* 5.41 [p. 703 in the 1611 ed.], cited in Friedrich, *Montaigne*, trans. Rovini, 366 and 419n; see the index to the Montaigne family for evidence of a close relationship. Mme de Montaigne sends Pasquier an account of his last days [see p. 40]).

8. Quotation in George Huppert, *The Idea of Perfect History: Historical Erudition and Historical Philosophy in Renaissance France* (Urbana: University of Illinois

Press, 1970), 63. See also D. Thickett, *Estienne Pasquier (1529–1615): The Versatile Barrister of Sixteenth-Century France* (London: Regency, 1979).

9. Friedrich, *Montaigne*, trans. Eng, 344.

10. *Essais* 3.5, S 641 (b), quoted in ibid., 370. See also Verg., *Aen.* 6.202–11; mistletoe is the basic vegetative and light image of Frazer's *Golden Bough.*

11. Joachim Camerarius, *Symbolorum et emblemetum ex re herbaria centuria* (Nuremberg, 1590), 15; *Emblemata: Handbuch zur Sinnbildkunst des XVI. und XVII. Jahrhunderts*, ed. Arthur Henkel and Albrecht Schöne, 2nd ed. (Stuttgart: Metzler, 1976), 202.

12. "Elle a pour son but la vertu, qui n'est pas, comme dit l'eschole, plantée à la teste d'un mont coupé, rabotteux et inaccessible. Ceux qui l'ont approchée, la tiennent, au rebours, logée dans une belle plaine fertile et fleurissante, d'où elle voit bien souz soy toutes choses; mais si peut on y arriver, qui en sçait l'addresse, par des routes ombrageuses, gazonnées et doux fleurantes, plaisamment et d'une pante facile et polie, comme est celle des voutes celestes" (*Essais* 1.26, P 160, S 119 [c]).

13. Jacopo Sadoleto, *Sadoleto on Education: A Translation of De Pueris Recte Institutendis*, ed. and trans. E. T. Campagnac and K. Forbes (London: Oxford University Press, 1916), 138, discussed above in ch. 6, "Do the Seeds of Virtue Grow to Heaven?"

14. Friedrich, *Montaigne*, trans. Eng, 361. The sieve is a more important vegetative concept to Montaigne than that expressed by the quotation "I have gathered a posie of other men's flowers and nothing but the thread that binds them is my own," citation of Montaigne without further comment in frontispiece with floral wreath in Lys de Bray, *The Art of Botanical Illustration* (Bromley, Kent: Helm, 1989).

15. "Q'il luy face tout passer par l'estamine et ne loge rien en sa teste par simple authorité et à credit; les principes d'Aristote ne luy soyent principes, non plus que ceux des Stoiciens ou Epicuriens. Qu'on luy propose cette diversité de jugemens: il choisira s'il peut, sinon il en demeurera en doubte" (*Essais* 1.26, P 150, S 111 [a]). The sieve metaphor helps us cope with the multiple philosophical influences on Montaigne. For an assessment of recent writing on Stoic, Epicurean, and Skeptical influences on Montaigne's politics, see John Christian Laursen, "Michel de Montaigne and the Politics of Skepticism," *Historical Reflections/Réflexions Historiques* 16 (1989): 99–133; on Montaigne's concerns about both Ulpian's and Stoic natural-law theory, see 100, 113–14. I dispute Laursen's claim that "Montaigne recognizes 'in universal consensus the only proof of the determination of laws of nature'" (114, citing Anna Maria Battista, *Alla origini del pensiero politico libertino: Montaigne e Charron* [Milan: Giuffre, 1966], 171). Whereas Quentin Skinner finds "stoic moralism" in Montaigne, Laursen finds "skeptical moralism" (John Christian Laursen, *The Politics of Skepticism in the Ancients: Montaigne, Hume, and Kant* [Leiden: Brill, 1992], 98, citing Quentin Skinner, *The Foundations of Modern Political Thought*, 2 vols. [Cambridge: Cambridge University Press, 1978], 2:276, 281).

16. "Et toutesfois nostre outrecuidance veut faire passer la divinité par nostre estamine" (*Essais* 2.12, P 509, S 393). See the precedent for sifting one's reading in Seneca, *Epistulae* 84.5.

17. "A quoi faire nous allons nous gendarmant par ces efforts de la science? Regardons à terre les pauvres gens que nous y voyons espandus, la teste penchante

après leur besongne, qui ne sçavent ny Aristote ny Caton, ny exemple, ny precepte; de ceux là tire nature tous les jours des effects de constance et de patience, plus purs et plus roides que ne sont ceux que nous estudions si curieusement en l'escole. Combien en vois-je ordinairement, qui mescognoissent la pauvreté? Combien qui desirent la mort, ou qui la passent sans alarme et sans affliction? Celuy là qui fouyt mon jardin, il a ce matin enterré son pere ou son fils" (*Essais* 3.12, P 1017, S 795–96 [b]).

"Voyez ceux cy: pour ce qu'ils meurent en mesme mois, enfans, jeunes, vieillards, ils ne s'estonnent plus, ils ne se pleurent plus. J'en vis qui craingnoient de demeurer derriere, comme en une horrible solitude; et n'y conneu communéement autre soing que des sepultures; il leur faschoit de voir les corps espars emmy les champs, à la mercy des bestes, qui y peuplerent incontinent. . . . Tel, sain, faisoit desjà sa fosse; d'autres s'y couchoient encore vivans. Et un maneuvre des miens à tout ses mains et ses pieds attira sur soy la terre en mourant. . . . Somme, toute une nation fut incontinent, par usage, logée en une marche qui ne cede en roideur à aucune resolution estudiée et consultée" (ibid., P 1025, S 802–3 [b]).

18. For an analysis of this passage in the context of Montaigne's biography, the events of the 1580s, and the class-based mentalities reflected in death rituals, see Maryanne Cline Horowitz, "Michel de Montaigne's Stoic Insights into Peasant Death," in *Renaissance Rereadings: Intertext and Context*, ed. Maryanne Cline Horowitz, Anne J. Cruz, and Wendy A. Furman (Urbana: University of Illinois Press, 1988), 236–52. See also Géralde Nakam, *Montaigne et son temps: Les événements et les essais, l'histoire, la vie, le livre* (Paris: Nizet, 1982), 13, 103, 169–84, 246; and idem, *Les essais de Montaigne: Miroir et procès de leur temps, Témoignage historique et création littéraire* (Paris: Nizet, 1984), 278–85, 304–10.

19. Pierre Villey, *Les sources et l'évolution des essais de Montaigne*, 2 vols. (Paris: Hachette, 1908), 2:390–98, esp. 392.

20. Floyd Gray, "The Unity of Montaigne in the *Essais*," *Modern Language Quarterly* 22 (1961): 79–86; Donald Stone, "Death in the Third Book," *L'Esprit Créateur* 7 (1963): 185–93. Jules Brody, "Montaigne et la mort: deux études sur 'Que philosopher c'est apprendre à mourir (I, 20),'" in *Lectures de Montaigne* (Lexington, Ky.: French Forum, 1982), 93–144, analyzing b and c additions as amplifications of ideas in 1.20 (a), rejects Villey's theory that Montaigne's attitudes toward death evolved.

21. *Essais* 1.20, P 82, S 57–58 (a). See Claude Blum, "La mort des hommes et la mort des bêtes dans les *Essais* de Montaigne: Sur les functions paradigmatiques de deux exemples," *French Forum* 5 (1980): 3–13.

22. *Essais* 1.20, P 82, S 58 (a).

23. Ibid., P 94–95, S 68 (a).

24. Ibid., 3.12, P 1029, S 805 (b).

25. "Je veux . . . que la mort me treuve plantant mes chous, mais nonchalant d'elle, et encore plus de mon jardin imparfait" (ibid., 1.20, P 87, S 62 [a]). The first passage quoted in n. 17, above, echoes this earlier one.

26. *Essais* 3.12, P 1016, S 794 (c).

27. See above, n. 17.

28. "Nous avons abandonné nature et luy voulons apprendre sa leçon, elle qui nous menoit si heureusement et si seurement. Et cependant les traces de son instruction et ce peu qui, par le benefice de l'ignorance, reste de son image empreint

en la vie de cette tourbe rustique d'hommes impolis, la science est contrainte de l'aller tous les jours empruntant, pour en faire patron à ses disciples de constance, d'innocence et de tranquillité" (*Essais* 3.12, P 1026, S 803 [b]).

29. For a methodological model, see Mary B. McKinley, *Words in a Corner: Studies in Montaigne's Latin Quotations* (Lexington, Ky.: French Forum, 1981). The seed image in Seneca's *Epistles* has a direct impact on Montaigne (see Camilla Hill Hay, *Montaigne: Lecteur et imitateur de Sénèque* [Poitiers: Société française d'imprimerie, 1938], 77–86, 120–24). Lipsius's *De constantia* appears in 1584, and Guillaume du Vair writes *La philosophie morale des Stoïques* around 1585 (see Guillaume du Vair, *De la sainte philosophie, Philosophie morale des Stoïques*, ed. G. Michaut [Paris: Vrin, 1945], 63–68).

30. "Je l'aime telle que les loix et religions non facent, mais parfacent et au- thorisent, qui se sente de quoy se soustenir sans aide, née en nous de ses propres racines par la semence de la raison universelle empreinte en tout homme non des- naturé" (*Essais* 3.12, P 1037, S 811 [c]).

31. "Il faut la veuë nette et bien purgée pour descouvrir cette secrette lumière" (ibid., P 1013, S 793).

32. Roy E. Leaky, *Concordance des Essais de Montaigne*, 2 vols. (Geneva: Droz, 1981), 1:226, 2:1060–63.

33. *Essais* 2.12, P 563–64, S 437–38.

34. Ibid., 3.12, P 1026, S 803.

35. Christiane Andersson and Charles Talbot, *From a Mighty Fortress: Prints, Drawing, and Books in the Age of Luther, 1483–1546* (Detroit: Detroit Institute of Arts, 1981), fig. 51 (158–59). Another tree of about 1530, one definitely by Hans Weiditz, shows the classes of society. Peasants are at both the roots and the treetop, providing the base of society and the sustenance of produce (Prints Division, New York Public Library, reprinted in Carolyn Merchant, *The Death of Nature: Women, Ecology, and the Scientific Revolution* [New York: Harper & Row, 1980], fig. 8).

36. See below, nn. 35–38 to the epilogue.

37. *Essais* 1.31, P 204, S 153 (a). The French is contained in the long quotation in n. 43 below. The sixteenth-century reader would be familiar with the labels *sav- age, barbarian*, and especially *cannibal* from travel literature and from graphic drawings circulating of cannibalism in the Americas, as in Amerigo Vespucci's letter of 1499 published in Theodor de Bry, *Peregrination in America* (Frankfurt-am- Main, 1597), and André Thévet, *Les singularitez de la France Antarctique, autre- ment nommée Amérique* (Paris, 1557) (see Santiago Sebastian, *Iconografía del indio americano, siglos XVI–XVII* [Madrid: Ediciones Tuero, 1992]).

38. "Bonnes semences que nature y avoit produit" (*Essais* 3.6, P 888, S 694 [b]). See also above, ch. 1, "Seeds to Trees."

39. "Que si j'eusse esté entre ces nations qu'on dict vivre encore sous la douce liberté des premieres loix de nature, je t'asseure que je m'y fusse très-volontiers peint tout entier, et tout nud" (*Essais* P 2, S 2 [a]).

40. Richard Sayce, *The Essays of Montaigne: A Critical Exploration* (London: Weidenfeld & Nicolson, 1972), 245.

41. Richard Tuck, *Natural Rights Theories: Their Origin and Development* (Cambridge: Cambridge University Press, 1979), 18, 34. See the discussion of Ulpian above, in ch. 2.

42. There is ample, increasing evidence of use of traveller reports supported by comparison with other passages. See, for example, Frank Lestringant, "'Des Canni-

bales' et le 'corpus huguenot' sur l'Amérique," in *Le huguenot et le sauvage* (Paris: Klincksieck, 1990), 143–45; B. Weinberg, "Montaigne's Readings for 'Des Cannibales,'" in *Renaissance and Other Studies in Honor of William Leon Wiley*, ed. George Bernard Daniel Jr. (Chapel Hill: University of North Carolina Press, 1968), 261–79; and Gilbert Chinard, *L'exotisme américain dans la littérature française au XVIe siècle* (1911; reprint, Geneva: Slatkine, 1970).

43. "Ces nations me semblent donq ainsi barbares, pour avoir receu fort peu de façon de l'esprit humain, et estre encore fort voisines de leur naifveté originelle. Les loix naturelles leur commandent encore, fort peu abastardies par les nostres; mais c'est en telle pureté, qu'il me prend quelque fois desplaisir dequoy la cognoissance n'en soit venuë plustost, du temps qu'il y avoit des hommes qui en eussent sceu mieux juger que nous. Il me desplait que Licurgus et Platon ne l'ayent eüe; car il me semble que ce que nous voyons par experience en ces nations là, surpasse non seulement toutes les peintures dequoy la poësie a embelly l'age doré et toutes ses inventions à feindre une heureuse condition d'hommes, mais encore la conception et le desir mesme de la philosophie" (*Essais* 1.31, P 204, S 153 [a]).

44. See Frank Lestringant, "Le nom des 'cannibales' de Christophe Colomb à Michel de Montaigne," *Bulletin de la Société des Amis de Montaigne*, 6th ser., no. 17–18 (1984): 61–74.

45. "C'est une nation, diroy je à Platon, en laquelle il n'y a aucune espece de trafique; nul cognoissance de lettres; nulle science de nombres; nul nom de magistrat; ny de superiorité politique; nul usage de service, de richesse ou de pauvreté; nuls contrats, nulles successions; nuls partages; nulles occupations qu'oysives; nul respect de parenté que commun; nuls vestemens; nulle agriculture; nul metal; nul usage de vin ou de bled. Les paroles mesmes qui signifient la mensonge, la trahison, la dissimilation, l'avarice, l'envie, la detraction, le pardon, inouïes" (*Essais* 1.31, P 204, S 153 [a]).

46. Olive Patricia Dickason, *The Myth of the Savage: And the Beginnings of French Colonialism in the Americas* (Edmonton: University of Alberta Press, 1984), 52.

47. Peter Martyr, *De rebus oceanicis et novo orbi, decades tres Petri Martyris ab Angleria, Mediolanensis* (Cologne, 1574), cited in Alfred Biese, *The Development of Feeling for Nature in the Middle Ages and Modern Times* (New York: Burt Franklin, 1905), 140.

48. "Nondum divinae religionis, non humani officii ratio colebature, nemo nuptias viderat legitimas, non ceros quisquam aspexerat liberos, non ius aequabile quid uilitates haberet, acceperat" (Cicero, *De inventione*, trans. H. M. Hubbell, Loeb Classical Library, 1.2. See also Cicero, *De oratore* 1.33).

49. "Il n'y a pas cinquante ans qu'il ne sçavoit ny lettres, ny pois, ny mesure, ny vestemens, ny bleds, ny vignes" (*Essais* 3.6, P 886, S 693 [b]).

50. "Ce qu'on nous dict de ceux du Bresil . . . comme gens qui passoyent leur vie en une admirable simplicité et ignorance, sans lettres, sans loy, sans roy, san religion quelconque" (ibid., 2.12, P 471, S 362 [c], for which Simon Goulard, *Histoire du Portugal* [Estienne, 1581; reprint, 1587], 2.23, is one source).

51. Virgil, *Georgics*, ed. Richard Thomas (Cambridge: Cambridge University Press, 1988); see also lines 1–34 and the editor's notes, indicating Seneca's use of Theophrastus.

52. Seneca, *Ad Lucilium epistulae morales*, trans. Richard Gummere, Loeb Classical Library, *Ep.* 90.44, quoted in *Essais* 1.31, P 204, S 153 (c). I have re-

considered the impact of this letter on Montaigne in the context of Carlo Ginzburg's seminar at UCLA in 1992.

53. Ovid, *Metamorphoses* 1.16 on childhood reading. Montaigne likely later uses the Basel edition of 1549 (Villey, *Les sources et l'évolution des essais de Montaigne* 1:206). Ovid, *Metamorphoses*, trans. George Sandys (1621), ed. K. Hulley and S. Vandersall (Lincoln: University of Nebraska Press, 1970). I choose to use this Elizabethan translation for its beauty and influence.

54. Raymond Lebègue, "Montaigne et le paradoxe des cannibales," *Studi di letteratura, storia e filosofia in onore di Bruno Revel*, 1st ser., 74 (1965): 359–63.

55. One of the best analyses of the complex shifting perspective of the essay is Edwin M. Duval, "Lessons of the New World: Design and Meaning in Montaigne's 'Des Cannibales' (I:31) and 'Des Coches' (III:6)," in Defaux, *Montaigne: Essays in Reading*, 95–112.

56. "Mais ils sont plaisans quand, pour donner quelque certitude aux loix, ils disent qu'il y en a aucunes fermes, perpetuelles et immuables qu'ils nomment naturelles, qui sont empreintes en l'humain genre par la condition de leur propre essence. . . . Car ce que nature nous auroit veritablement ordonné, nous l'ensuivrions sans doubte d'un commun consentement. . . . Qu'ils m'en montrent, pour voir, une de cette condition" (*Essais* 2.12, P 563–64, S 437 [a]).

57. "S'ils nous eussent laissé en nostre estat naturel, recevans les apparences estrangeres selon qu'elles se presentent à nous par nos sens. . . . Cette response seroit bonne parmy les Canibales, qui jouissent l'heur d'une longue vie, tranquille et paisible sans les preceptes d'Aristote, et sans la connoissance du nom de la physique. . . . De cette-cy seroient capables avec nous tous les animaux et tout ce où le commandement est encor pur et simple de la loy naturelle; mais eux, ils y ont renoncé" (ibid., 2.12, P 522–23, S 404 [a]).

58. "S'il y a quelque loy vrayement naturelle, c'est à dire quelque instinct qui se voye universellement et perpetuellement empreinct aux bestes et en nous (ce qui n'est pas sans controverse), je puis dire, à mon advis, qu'après le soing que chasque animal a de sa conservation et de fuir ce qui nuit, l'affection que l'engendrant porte à son engeance tient le second lieu en ce rang" (ibid., 2.8, P 365, S 279 [a]). Peter Martyr interprets natural law as avoidance of injury: "They leave their gardens open, without law, without records, without judges, but following a natural justice esteeming those wicked who would injure others" (*Extraict ou recueil des isles nouvellement trouvees* [Paris: Simon de Colines, 1532], 23, cited in Dickason, *Myth of the Savage*, 53).

59. "Ceux qui ont disposé les lois et coutumes, et établi les rois et les magistrats dons les Cités, ont placé notre vie dans une grande securité et paix, et ont écarté les troubles; mais si quelqu'un suprimait tout cela, nous mènerions une vie de bêtes, et n'importe qui, avec un peu de chance, mangerait, autant dire, n'importe qui" (Colotes, in Plutarch, *Adv. Colot.* 30.1124d, cited in Victor Goldschmidt, *La doctrine d'Épicure et le droit* [Paris: Vrin, 1977], 17–19, 246). Cicero, *De re publica, De legibus*, trans. Clinton Keyes, Loeb Classical Library, *Leg.* 3.16, and *De finibus*, trans H. Rackham, Loeb Classical Library, 1.16.53, report the Epicurean view that law is founded by a contract grounded in doing no harm to others.

60. Pufendorf: "S'il n'y avait point de Justice, on se mangerait les un les autres"; Grotius: "S'il n'y avait point de Magistrats on se mangerait les uns les autres" (Goldschmidt, *La doctrine d'Épicure et le droit*, 17–18 n. 4).

61. *Essais* 1.31, P 208, S 155.

62. Jeanne Haight, *The Concept of Reason in French Classical Literature, 1635–1690* (Toronto: University of Toronto Press, 1982), 101–8.

63. Erneste Seillière, "La doctrine de la bonté naturelle de Montaigne à Delisle de Sales," *Séances et travaux de l'Académie des sciences morales et politiques* 85 (1925): 371–85.

64. Bartolomé Las Casas, *Tyrannies et cruautez des Espagnols, perpetrées ès Indes Occidentales qu'on dit le Nouveau Monde . . .* (Paris, 1579), edition in Bibliothèque nationale. This French translation of *Brevísma relación* (1552) is followed by other translations, such as *Brief Account* (London, 1583).

65. Bartolomé de Las Casas, *Historia de las Indias* (1561), vol. 1, prologue, in *Obras completas*, Latin and Spanish, 14 vols. to date (Madrid: Alianza Editorial, 1988–), quotation translated by Lewis Hanke in *Aristotle and the American Indian: A Study of Race Prejudice in the Modern World* (Bloomington: Indiana University Press, 1959), 112. Las Casas's ideas come to Montaigne through other travel accounts utilizing Las Casas, but it is likely that they also come directly. Research has only recently begun on the echoes of Las Casas in Montaigne: Nakam, *Montaigne et son temps*, 40–41, suggests that Montaigne uses the 1580 *Tyrannies et cruautés des Espagnols. . .*; Juan Durán Luzio, "Las Casas y Montaigne: Escritura y lectura del Nuevo Mundo," *Montaigne Studies* 1 (1989): 88–106, suggests that he uses the 1582 *Tyrannies*. I thank Angelica Salas for work under a Ford Foundation faculty-student grant.

66. Bartolomé de Las Casas, *History of the Indies*, condensed, trans., ed. Andrée Collard (New York: Harper & Row, 1971), 6.

67. "Ils sont sauvages, de mesme que nous appellons sauvages les fruicts que nature, de soy et de son progrez ordinaire a produicts: là où, à la verité, ce sont ceux que nous avons alterez par nostre artifice et detournez de l'ordre commun, que nous devrions appeler plutost sauvages. En ceux là sont vives et vigoureuses les vrayes et plus utiles et naturelles vertus et proprietez" (*Essais* 1.31, P 203, S 152 [a]).

68. Francisco de Vittoria, *De Indis et De Jure Belli* 3.15.290, and Juan Ginés de Sépulveda, *Democrates Alter*, discussed in Tzvetan Todorov, *The Conquest of America: The Question of the Other*, trans. Richard Howard (New York: Harper & Row, 1982), 149–65.

69. *Essais* 2.12, S 330–58; *Travel Journal*, S 941–42, 955; "On Cruelty," 2.11, P 414, S 313 (a) on the chicken, S 318 (a) for the following quotation: "Y a-il un certain respect qui nous attache, et un general devoir d'humanité, non aux bestes seulement qui ont vie et sentiment, mais aux arbres mesmes et aux plantes. Nous devons la justice aux hommes, et la grace et la benignité aux autres creatures qui en peuvent estre capables."

70. Sepúlveda, *Democrates Alter* 1.4–5, cited in Todorov, *Conquest of America*, 156. See also the Dominican Tomás Ortiz's letter to the Council of the Indies, included in Peter Martyr, *De orbe novo* 7.4, cited in Todorov, *Conquest of America*, 151–52.

71. Maryanne Cline Horowitz, "Un drogue médicinale où un ancien conte: L'histoire et la justice chez Montaigne, Bodin et Augustin," in *Montaigne et l'histoire*, ed. Claude G. DuBois (Bordeaux: Université de Bordeaux Press, 1991).

72. *Essais* 3.6, P 887–88, S 693–95. After decades of incredulity about Las

Casas's statistics on genocide, historians have proved his to be the most accurate of the early accounts (see A. W. Crosby, *Columbian Exchange: Biological and Cultural Consequences of 1492* [Westport, Conn.: Greenwood, 1972]).

73. "Bien crains-je que nous aurons bien fort hasté sa declinaison en sa ruyne par nostre contagion" (*Essais* 3.6, P 887, S 693).

74. Ibid., P 887–88, S 694–95.

75. Duval, "Lessons of the New World," 111–12.

76. See also Gérard Defaux, "Un cannibale en haut de chausses: Montaigne, la différence et la logique de l'identité," *Modern Language Notes* 97 (1982): 919–57.

77. See above, n. 38.

CHAPTER TEN

1. "Qui est homme de bien par scrupule et bride religieuse, gardez-vous en, et ne l'estimez gueres: et qui a religion sans preud'hommie, je ne le veux pas dire plus meschant, mais bien plus dangereux que celuy qui n'a ny l'un ny l'autre. . . . Ce n'est pas que la religion enseigne ou favorise aucunement le mal, comme aucuns ou trop sottement, ou trop malicieusement voudroyent objecter et tirer de ces propos: car la plus absurde et la plus faulse mesme ne le fait pas; mais cela vient que n'ayant aucun goust ny image ou conception de preud'hommie, qu'à la suite et pour le service de la religion, et pensant qu'estre homme de bien, n'est autre chose qu'estre soigneux d'avancer et faire valoir sa religion, croyent que toute chose, quelle qu'elle soit, trahison, perfidie, sedition, rebellion et toute offense à quiconque soit, est non-seulement loisible et permise, colorée du zele et soin de religion, mais encores louable, meritoire et canonisable" (Pierre Charron, *De la sagesse*, ed. Amaury Duval, 3 vols. [Paris, 1827], 2.5.155). Unless otherwise stated, references to Charron refer by book, chapter, and page number to Duval's edition of *De la sagesse*. Authenticity has been judged by comparison with the three early editions of *De la sagesse*: Bordeaux: Simon Millanges, 1601; Paris: David Douceur, 1604; and Paris: David Douceur, 1607. Duval's critical edition follows the tradition of the 1607 edition in that it contains smaller works of Charron along with the 1604 text of *De la sagesse* and attempts, without succeeding completely, to list all passages from the 1601 edition that were modified or omitted later. For a selection of Charron in modern English (2.1–3), I recommend Pierre Charron, "Concerning Wisdom," trans. Herman Shapiro and Arturo B. Fallico, in *Renaissance Philosophy: The Transalpine Thinkers*, ed. and trans. Shapiro and Fallico (New York: Modern Library, 1969), 214–48.

2. Joseph Le Cler, *Toleration and the Reformation*, trans. J. L. Weston, 2 vols. (New York: Association Press, 1960), 2:3–191.

3. "Lettres de Pierre Charron à Gabriel Michel de la Rochemaillet," ed. L. Auvray, *Revue d'Histoire Littéraire de la France* 1 (1894): 318, 320.

4. King Henry IV, *Edict du Roy & Declaration sur les precedent Edicts de Pacification* (Paris?: Royal Press, 25 February 1599).

5. J. B. Sabrié, *De l'humanisme au rationalisme: Pierre Charron (1541–1603), l'homme, l'oeuvre, l'influence* (Paris: Félix Alcan, 1913), 53–65; Pierre Charron, "Discours Chrestien," in *De la sagesse*, ed. Duval, vol. 3, pp. 349–58.

6. Pierre Charron, *Les trois veritez contre tous athéés, idolatres, juifs, mahumetans, heretiques, & schismatiques*, 2nd ed. (Bordeaux: S. Millanges, 1595), reprinted in *Oeuvres de Pierre Charron* (1635; reprint, Geneva: Slatkine, 1970).

7. "Cette sagesse humaine est une droitture, belle et noble composition de l'homme entier, en son dedans, son dehors, ses pensées, paroles, actions, et tous ses mouvemens; c'est l'excellence et perfection de l'homme comme homme" (Charron, vol. 1, p. xlii).

8. Ibid., xliv–xlvi.

9. *Andreas Alciatus: The Latin Emblems*, ed. Peter M. Daly, with Virginia W. Callahan and Simon Cuttler, 2 vols. (Toronto: University of Toronto Press, 1985) vol. 2, emblem 5, example of Lyon, 1551.

10. "Lettres de Pierre Charron à Gabriel Michel de la Rochemaillet," 326, quoted in Eugene F. Rice Jr., *The Renaissance Idea of Wisdom* (Cambridge: Harvard University Press, 1958), 205 n. 88; Rice discusses the engraving on 205–7. The Duval edition contains the 1604 preface, the sonnet, and the expanded commentary but not the engraving. The engraving, the "explication," and the sonnet are contained in the edition of *De la sagesse* edited by Barbara de Negroni (Paris: Fayard, 1986); and the engraving was reproduced in Pierre Charron, *Of Wisdom* (before 1612; reprint, New York: Da Capo, 1911).

11. Léonard Gaultier (ca. 1561–ca. 1635) is also the designer of an engraving of a highly detailed tree of knowledge, *The Laurus metaphysica* (1616), whose top reaches to God and whose roots are the three subdivisions of the ancient Stoics: physics, ethics, and logic (see the 1622 enlargement, measuring 23¼ inches by 16⅝ inches, Hennin Collection no. 1307, in Bibliothèque nationale, *The French Renaissance in Prints* [Los Angeles: Grunwald Center for the Graphic Arts, University of California, Los Angeles, 1994], no. 174, pp. 432, 472).

12. Richard Popkin, *The History of Scepticism from Erasmus to Descartes*, rev. ed. (New York: Harper & Row, 1968), 57–63. On the early criticisms of Father Garasse and Father Mersenne, see Jean Daniel Charron, *The "Wisdom" of Pierre Charron: An Orthodox Code of Morality*, Studies in the Romance Languages, 34 (Chapel Hill: University of North Carolina Press, 1960), 22–30.

13. On Charron as a reader of Montaigne, see Maryanne Cline Horowitz, "Pierre Charron's View of the Source of Wisdom," *Journal of the History of Philosophy* 9, no. 4 (October 1971): 443–57. On Charron as a reader of Bodin, see above, ch. 8, nn. 29, 45, 68, and below, nn. 14, 33, 48. On Charron as reader of Du Vair, see above, ch. 7, "Neo-Stoic Strategies of Du Vair and Lipsius," and esp. n. 61. A recent study argues for Charron's blurring of Academic and Pyrhonnian Skepticism and the primacy of his commitment to natural law: Zachary Sayre Schiffman, *On the Threshold of Modernity: Relativism in the French Renaissance* (Baltimore: Johns Hopkins University Press, 1991), ch. 4, esp. 84–86.

14. "Elle se prouve premierement par le dire des plus grands philosophes, qui tous onct dict que les semences des grandes vertus et sciences estoisent esparses naturellement en l'ame" (Charron, 1:56 [1601 ed.]). Renée Kogel suggests that the wording of this statement reveals Charron's direct borrowing from Jean Bodin, *Le Théâtre de la nature universelle, auquel on peut contempler les causes efficientes et finales de toutes choses, desquelles l'ordre et continué par questions et responses en cinq livres*, trans. François de Fougerolles (Lyon: Jean Pillehotte, 1597), 687, quoted in Renée Kogel, *Pierre Charron* (Geneva: Droz, 1972), 112. Bodin's Latin text from the *Theatrum* appears above, in ch. 8, n. 64. Charron differs from Bodin in not mentioning "the Hebrews."

15. Sabrié, *Pierre Charron*, 3; R. R. Bolgar, *The Classical Heritage and Its Beneficiaries* (Cambridge: Cambridge University Press, 1954), 265–75, 295–301.

16. Aspects of Charron's Stoicism have been recognized and studied by Albert Desjardins, *Les moralistes français du seizième siècle*, 2nd ed. (Paris: Didier, 1870), 346–456; Sabrié, *Pierre Charron*, 255–84, 336–56; Fortunat Strowski, *Pascal et son temps*, 3 vols. (Paris: Plon-Nourrit et Cie, 1921–22), 1:1–126; Julien Eymard d'Angers, "Le Stoïcisme en France dans la première moitié du XVIIe siècle," *Etudes franciscaines* 2 (August and December 1951): 287–99, 389–410; Rice, *Renaissance Idea of Wisdom*, 179–207; Kogel, *Pierre Charron*. My interpretation of *De la sagesse* as the foundation of an autonomous ethic accords with the interpretation of Eugene Rice and Renée Kogel. I differ with Rice in my view that for Charron science leads to *sagesse*, that *preud'hommie* is in the will and the intellect (see Horowitz, "Pierre Charron's View of the Source of Wisdom," 454–57), and from both Rice and Kogel in my view that in *De la sagesse* religion is not merely separate but also subordinate to virtue.

17. "Bref c'est la vraye science de l'homme . . . elle apprend à bien vivre, et bien mourir, qui est tout; elle enseigne une preude prudence, une habile et forte preud'hommie, une probité bien advisée" (Charron, 1, preface, xlviii. See also Cicero, *De finibus* 5.16, influencing Charron, 2:283 n. 2: "Sic vivendi ars est prudentia").

18. Edmond Huguet, ed., *Dictionnaire de la langue française du seizième siècle*, s.v. "preud'homme."

19. Charron's book is in the tradition of educational treatises for males; he has little to say on *preude'femme* and treats women as unequal partners in 1.48–49, on marriage, parents, and children, and in 3.10, on flattery (see Constance Jordan, *Renaissance Feminism: Literary Texts and Political Models* [Ithaca: Cornell University Press, 1990], 269–70). The follower of Montaigne who discusses the *preude'femme* in depth is Marie de Gournay (see Maryanne Cline Horowitz, "Marie de Gournay, Editor of the *Essais* of Michel de Montaigne: A Case-Study of a Mentor-Protégée Friendship," *Sixteenth Century Journal* 17 [1986]: 271–84; and Marie de Gournay, *L'Ombre de la Demoiselle de Gournay* [Paris: Jean Libert, 1626]).

20. Charron, 2.3.78. *Le Manuel d'Epictète* becomes available in French translations by André Rivaudeau and Guillaume du Vair. Its philosophy is incorporated in Du Vair's *De la sainte philosophie*, from which Charron borrows directly. See Guillaume du Vair, *La sainte philosophie des Stoïques, Manuel d'Epictète, Civile conversation et plusieurs autres traictez de piété* (Lyons, 1600).

21. Charron, 2.3.75–81.

22. "Le ressort de cette preud'hommie est nature, laquelle oblige tout homme d'estre et se rendre tel qu'il doibt, c'est-à-dire se conformer et regler selon elle. Nature nous est ensemble et maistresse qui nous enjoint et commande la preud'hommie, et loy ou instruction qui nous l'enseigne. . . . L'homme ne doibt point attendre ny chercher autre cause, obligation, ressort ou motif de sa preud'hommie, et n'en sçauroit jamais avoir un plus juste et legitime, plus puissant, plus ancien, il est tout aussi tost que luy, nay avec luy. Tout homme doibt estre et vouloir estre homme de bien, pource qu'il est homme" (ibid., 79–80).

23. "Car cette loy et lumiere est essentielle et naturelle en nous, dont aussi est appellée nature et loy de nature" (ibid., 83).

24. See above, ch. 1.

25. "La doctrine de tous les sages porte que bien vivre, c'est vivre selon nature, . . . *naturam si sequaris ducem, nusquam aberrabis* [Cicero, *De officiis* 1.28]:

————*bonum est quod secundùm naturam*: ————*omnia vitia contrà naturam sunt*:
————*idem beatè vivere et secundùm naturam* [Seneca, *Epistulae* 118; Lucius An-
naeus Seneca, *De vita beata. Sénèque: Sur le bonheur*, ed. Pierre Grimal (Paris:
Presses universitaires de France, 1969), ch. 8; *Ep.* 122], entendant par nature
l'equité et la raison universelle qui luit en nous" (Charron, 2.3.86–87).

26. "Car cette loy d'equité et raison naturelle est perpetuelle en nous, *edictum
perpetuum*, inviolable qui ne peust jamais estre esteinte ny effacée" (ibid., 83).

27. Ibid., 2.2.55; 1.2.14–15.

28. Ibid., 3.6.444. Robert Hoopes studies antique, medieval, and Renaissance
uses of right reason in *Right Reason in the English Renaissance* (Cambridge: Harvard University Press, 1962). *De la sagesse*, which in the original and in *On Wisdome*, trans. Samson Lennard (London: Aspley, 1608), was influential in the "Renaissance rehabilitation" of right reason, is not mentioned in Hoopes's chapter by
that title.

29. "Signatum est super nos lumen vultûs tui" (Ps. 4.7) and "lex scripta in cor-
dibus nostris" (Rom. 2.15), quoted in Charron, 2.3.84.

30. R. W. Carlyle and A. J. Carlyle, *A History of Medieval Political Theory in the
West*, 6 vols. (New York: G. P. Putnam's Sons, 1903–36), 1:83, 105–6.

31. See above, ch. 2; and Dom Odon Lottin, *Le droit naturel chez Saint Thomas
d'Aquin et ses prédécesseurs*, 2nd ed. (Bruges: Charles Beyaert, 1931).

32. Charron, 1.8.59–63; 1.15.123, 127; 2.3.92. See also Cicero, *De natura
deorum* 1.63, and *De re publica* 3.7–33.

33. Charron 1.14.111–12; 1.15 (1601 ed.); 1.8.55–56 variant. See above,
ch. 8, "Philo's Garden of the Soul in the Book of Nature."

34. "Entendant par nature l'equité et la raison universelle qui luit en nous, qui
contient et couve en soy les semences de toute vertu, probité, justice, et est la ma-
trice de laquelle sortent et naissent toutes les bonnes et belles lois, les justes et
equitables jugemens que prononcera mesme un idiot" (Charron, 2.3.87).

35. "Voyci donc une preud'hommie essentielle, radicale et fondamentale, née
en nous de ses propres racines, par la semence de la raison universelle, qui est en
l'ame, comme le ressort et balancier en l'horloge . . . par laquelle l'on agit selon
Dieu, selon soy, selon nature" (ibid., 86).

36. "Que par luy [l'esprit] y a parentage entre Dieu et l'homme; et que pour le
luy ramentevoir il luy a tourné les racines vers le ciel, affin qu'il eust tousjours sa
veue vers le lieu de sa naissance" (ibid., 1.15.118).

37. Ibid., 3.1.285.

38. "Hoc nos natura docere non potuit; semina nobis scientiae dedit, scientium
non dedit" (Seneca, *Ad Lucilium epistulae morales*, trans. Richard Gummere, Loeb
Classical Library, *Ep.* 120.3–4).

39. See above, nn. 29 and 34.

40. "Cette loy premiere, divine, naturelle, qui est un flambeau interne et do-
mestique" (Charron, 2.3.94).

41. "Raison, premiere et universelle loi et lumiere inspiréé de Dieu, qui esclaire
en nous" (ibid., 1, preface, xliii).

42. Ibid., 2.2.53–55.

43. "Certes nature en chascun de nous est suffisante et douce maistresse" (ibid.,
2.3.88).

44. "Loy et lumiere que Dieu a mis au dedans de nous dès notre origine" (ibid.,
2.5.152).

45. "Je consens que l'on l'appelle image de Dieu vive, un desgoust de l'immortelle substance, une fluxion de la divinité, un esclair celeste auquel Dieu a donné la raison" (ibid., 1.15.118).

46. Étienne Gilson, *History of Christian Philosophy in the Middle Ages* (New York: Random House, 1955), 438–43. See above, ch. 2, nn. 110–13.

47. "Ce sont tous mots plausibles dont retentissent les escholes et les chaires" (Charron, 1.15.118). Here is French evidence parallel to Locke's English evidence on preachers' claims (see above, ch. 1, n. 34). H. A. Enno van Gelder, *The Two Reformations in the Sixteenth Century: A Study of Religious Aspects and Consequences of Renaissance and Humanism* (The Hague: Nijhoff, 1964), 21, 26, discusses the emanationist vocabulary of Pico della Mirandola and Marsilio Ficino. On the direct influence of Plotinus in France, see Françoise Joukovsky, *Le regard intérieur: Thèmes plotiniens chez quelques écrivains de la Renaissance française* (Paris: Nizet, 1982).

48. "C'est dis-je cette equité et raison universelle qui esclaire et luit en un chascun de nous; qui agit selon elle, agit vrayement selon Dieu, car c'est Dieu, ou bien sa premiere, fondamentale et universelle loy qui l'a mis au monde, et qui la premiere est sortie de luy; car Dieu et nature sont au monde, comme en un estat, le roy son autheur et fondateur, et la loy fondamentale qu'il a bastie pour la conservation et regle dudit estat. C'est un esclat et rayon de la divinité, une defluxion et dependance de la loy eternelle qui est Dieu mesme, et sa volonté: *quid natura nisi Deus, et divina ratio toti mundo et partibus eius inserta?*" (Charron, 2.3.82–83. See also Seneca, *De beneficiis* 4.7.1).

49. Brian Tierney, "*Natura Id Est Deus*: A Case of Juristic Pantheism?" *Journal of the History of Ideas* 24 (1963): 307–22.

50. Charron, 2.3.84; "Petit traicté de sagesse," in *De la sagesse*, ed. Duval, vol. 3, pp. 290–91. The "Petit traicté," 3:257–318, was found among Charron's writings after his death.

51. Ernst Troeltsch, *Social Teaching of the Christian Churches*, trans. Olive Wyon, 2 vols. (New York: Macmillan, 1931), 1:152–54, 193–94.

52. Charron, 2.8.211–12. See also Allesandro Passerin d'Entrèves, *Natural Law: An Introduction to Legal Philosophy* (London: Hutchinson University Library, 1961), 43–44.

53. Charron, 1.2.13–19; Ewart E. Lewis, *Medieval Political Ideas*, 2 vols. (New York: Knopf, 1954), 1:10, 27–28.

54. Charron, 2.3.84–85.

55. "Que vas-tu chercher ailleurs? loy ou regle au monde. Que te peust-on dire ou alleguer que n'ayes chez toy et au dedans, si tu te voulois taster et escouter?" (ibid., 84).

56. "Generale et universelle alteration et corruption" (ibid., 92).

57. Ibid., 89–98. For Charron's educational theory, see Horowitz, "Pierre Charron's View of the Source of Wisdom," 454–57.

58. See G. Grisez, "Man, Natural End of," and T. C. O'Brien, "Virtue," in *New Catholic Encyclopedia*, 15 vols. (New York: McGraw-Hill, 1967).

59. Thomas Aquinas, *Basic Writings of St. Thomas Aquinas*, ed. A. C. Pegis, 2 vols. (New York: Random House, 1945), *Summa theologiae* 1–2, qu. 65, art. 2.

60. "Ils veulent que l'on soit homme de bien, à cause qu'il y a un paradis et un enfer, . . . Tu te gardes d'estre meschant, car tu n'oses, et crains d'estre battu; et desja en cela es-tu meschant" (Charron, 2.5.152–53).

61. "Tu fais l'homme de bien affin que l'on te paye, et l'on t'en dise grand mercy" (ibid., 156–57 [1601 ed.]).

62. "Je veux que tu sois homme de bien, quand bien tu ne debvrois jamais aller en paradis, mais pource que nature, la raison, c'est-à-dire Dieu le veust, pource que la loi et la police generale du monde, d'où tu es une piece, le requiert ainsi, et tu ne peux consentir d'estre autre que tu n'ailles contre toy-mesme, ton estre, ta fin" (Charron, 2.5.153).

63. Diogenes Laertius, *Lives of Eminent Philosophers*, trans. R. D. Hicks, Loeb Classical Library, 7.87; Léontine Zanta, *La renaissance du stoicisme au XVIe siècle* (Paris: Champion, 1914), 34–46; Pietro Pomponazzi, *On the Immortality of the Soul*, trans. William Henry Hay II, rev. John H. Randall Jr., annot. Paul O. Kristeller, in *The Renaissance Philosophy of Man*, ed. Ernst Cassirer, Paul O. Kristeller, and John H. Randall Jr. (Chicago: University of Chicago Press, 1948), esp. 359–61, 374–75.

64. "Esprits forts et genereux" (Charron, 2.5.150).

65. Bolgar, *Classical Heritage*, 281.

66. Wallace K. Ferguson, *Europe in Transition, 1300–1520* (Boston: Houghton Mifflin, 1962), 297–98; Paul O. Kristeller, "Paganism and Christianity," in *Renaissance Thought: The Classic, Scholastic, and Humanist Strains* (New York: Harper & Row, 1961), 70–92.

67. See ch. 5. Petrarch, *De otio*, 92, quoted in Charles Trinkaus, *In Our Image and Likeness: Humanity and Divinity in Italian Humanist Thought*, 2 vols. (Chicago: University of Chicago Press, 1970), 1:45, Latin in note. Trinkaus also gives evidence that both Lorenzo Valla and Coluccio Salutati recognize and reject the implications toward an autonomous ethic in Stoicism (1:116–19, 2:670).

68. Alfred Soman, "Pierre Charron: A Revaluation," *Bibliothèque d'Humanisme et Renaissance* 32 (January 1970): 57–79.

69. Charron, "Petit traicté," 3:304–13.

70. "Lettres de Pierre Charron à Gabriel Michel de la Rochemaillet," 322–25, 328.

71. "Ils pensent que la religion soit une generalité de tout bien et de toute vertu, que toutes vertus soyent comprinses en elle, . . . Or c'est au rebours, car la religion qui est posterieure, est une vertu speciale et particuliere, distincte de toutes les autres vertus" (Charron, 2.5.151).

72. Ibid., 2.3.101; 2.5.152.

73. "La religion est posterieure à la preud'hommie: c'est aussi chose apprinse, receue par l'ouye, *fides ex auditu et per verbum Dei*, par revelation et instruction, et ainsi ne la peust pas causer. Ce seroit plustost la preud'hommie qui debvroit causer et engendrer la religion; car elle est première, plus ancienne et naturelle" (ibid., 2.5.157 [1601 ed.]). Note that this statement is direct and positive, whereas the following statement, in the second edition, is in the negative. The content, however, is essentially the same. "Ceux-cy veulent au rebours que l'on soit religieux avant preud'homme, et que la religion qui s'acquiert et s'apprend au dehors, *ex auditu, quomodo credent sine praedicante* [Rom 10:14], engendre la preud'hommie, laquelle nous avons montré devoir ressortir de nature, loy et lumiere que Dieu a mis au dedans de nous dès notre origine, c'est un ordre renversé" (ibid., 2.5.152).

74. Ibid., 2, preface, xxxvi–xxxviii.

75. "Ce'est qu'après tout ce que j'ay dit, il reste encores une chose, pour rendre l'ouvrage complet et parfait, c'est la grace de Dieu par laquelle cette telle

preud'hommie, bonté, vertu, est animée, mise à son jour, et reçoit son dernier trait visuel, est relevée, christianisée, couronnée, c'est-à-dire acceptée, verifiée, homologuée de Dieu, rendue meritoire et digne de recompense eternelle" (ibid., 2.3.100–101).

76. "Sont-ce deux que la preud'hommie et la grace, l'action bonne en soy naturellement, moralement, humainement, [et] l'action meritoire. Celle-là peust bien estre sans cette-cy, et a son pris comme en ces philosophes et grands hommes du temps passé, admirables certes en la nature et en toute sorte de vertu morale, et se trouve encores parmy les mescreans: mais cette-cy ne peust être sans celle-là" (ibid., 102–3; the bracketed word *et* is *est* in the original editions of 1601 and 1604).

77. "Parquoy je conclus que cette sagesse humaine est voye à la divine, la loy de nature à la grace, la vertu moral et Philosophique à la Theologale, le devoir humain à la faveur et liberalité divine" (Charron, "Petit traicté," 3:295).

78. "En recompense de leurs vertus morales" (ibid., 294).

79. "O Dieu! daignez par vostre immense bonté me regarder de l'oeil de vostre clemence, accepter et aggréer mon desire, mon essay, mon petit euvre, qui originellement vient de vous, par l'obligation et instruction que m'en avez donné en la loy de nature, qu'avez planté en moy, affin qu'il retourne à vous, et qu'acheviez ce que vous avez commencé, affin que soyez mon *A* et *Ω*" (Charron, 2.3.101. See the parallel in Du Vair, quoted above, in ch. 7, n. 62).

80. "Car c'est [cette grace] un pur don de Dieu, qu'il faut desirer ou demander humblement et ardemment, et s'y preparer tant qu'en nous est, par les vertus morales et observation de la loy naturelle que j'enseigne icy" (Charron, "Petit traicté," 3:313).

81. For political implications of the neo-Stoic movement, see Nannerl O. Keohane, *Philosophy and the State in France: The Renaissance to the Enlightenment* (Princeton: Princeton University Press, 1980).

EPILOGUE

1. For continuity, see Jeanne Haight, *The Concept of Reason in French Classical Literature 1635–1690* (Toronto: University of Toronto Press, 1982); Andrew Chew, *Stoicism in Renaissance English Literature: An Introduction* (New York: Peter Lang, 1988). For tension, see Michael Macklem, *The Anatomy of the World: Relations between Natural and Moral Law from Donne to Pope* (Minneapolis: University of Minnesota Press, 1958). For the use of data bases for exploring the history of ideas, see Donald R. Kelley, "Review of *Past Masters*," *Journal of the History of Ideas* 56, no. 1 (1995): 153–59. I have found abundant seventeenth- and eighteenth-century examples of phrases such as *semences des vertus, semences des sciences, l'equité et raison universelle,* and *la semence de la raison universelle,* as well as related vocabulary through the *ARTFL: A Textual Data Base* (Department of Romance Languages and Literature, University of Chicago). I invite colleagues to join me in further exploration.

2. Cesare Ripa, *Baroque and Rococo Pictorial Imagery: The 1758–60 Hertel Edition of Ripa's "Iconologia" with 200 Engraved Illustrations,* ed. Edward Maser (New York: Dover, 1971). Earlier editions of Ripa's illustrations are much more modest; see, for example, Cesare Ripa, *Iconologie,* trans. Jean Baudouin (Paris: Mathieu Guillemot, 1644; reprint, New York: Garland, 1976).

3. Ripa (Hertel ed.), fig. 22.

4. For more examples of the transformations in vocabulary and for a lengthier study of the Greek and Latin Stoics, I recommend use of the following full-text data bases: *Thesaurus Linguae Graecae CD-Rom* (School of Humanities, University of California, Irvine) and *Aureae Latinitatis Bibliotheca* (Zanichelli Editore s.p.a., Bologna). For more examples of *semina virtutis* in Seneca, see Mireille Armisen-Marchetti, *Sapientiae facies: Étude sur les images de Sénèque* (Paris: Belles Lettres, 1989), 148–50, 323–40. I thank Marc Wiesmann for handing me this book, alas after mine was in press.

5. Ripa (Hertel ed.), fig. 3.

6. For further research into individual medieval Latin authors' applications of *semina virtutum, semina scientarum, virtutes naturales, synderesis, notio impressa, scintilla conscientiae, ratio naturalis, consenus gentium*, and related vocabulary, I recommend the *Patrologia Latina Database* (Alexandria, Va.: Chadwyck-Healey, 1995).

7. Judaica is discussed only briefly in this book; for example, see references to biblical passages and to fruits in the well-indexed *Babylonian Talmud*, trans. Maurice Simon, ed. Isidore Epstein et al., 35 vols. (London: Soncino, 1952). Important new resources for such study include *The Soncino Talmud on Cd-Rom* in English and Hebrew (Davka Corporation, Chicago), the *Global Jewish Database*, and *Talkit-Shoot CD-Rom* (Bar-Ilan University, Ramat-Gan, Israel).

8. Roger Cook, *The Tree of Life: Symbol of the Centre* (London: Thames & Hudson, 1974), fig. 38, ascribes the illustration to *Philosophia sacra* (1626); however, it was not in copies I checked. Joscelyn Godwin, *Robert Fludd: Hermetic Philosopher and Surveyor of Two Worlds* (London: Thames & Hudson, 1979), fig. 36 (p. 38), reference to Robert Fludd, *Utriusque cosmi maioris scilicet . . . Tomi secundi, tractatus secundus. De preternatural utriusque mundi historia*, vol. 2 (Frankfort, 1621), 181, folded leaf; I am grateful to Judy Wilson, of the Houghton Library, who found the leaf in *Utriusque cosmi* 1, sec. 1, portion 2, pt. 1, opposite p. 156 of *De Primar. Microcos. Princip.*

9. In Babylonian Talmud, *Pes.* 4.8 discusses shaking the blossom from the male tree over the blossom from a female tree; *Gen. R.* amusingly tells of a female palm of Tiberias who "longed for" a palm in Jericho. Pliny also praises the palms of Jericho, in *Nat. Hist.* 13.45. See also *Encyclopedia Judaica*, 16 vols. (New York: Macmillan, 1972), s.v. "Palm tree." For alchemical androgyny, founded on Hermes Trismegistus, see Elémaire Zolla, *The Androgyne: Reconciliation of Male and Female* (New York: Crossroad, 1981), 78–81; and S. K. Heninger, *The Cosmographical Glass: Renaissance Diagrams of the Universe* (San Marino, Calif.: Huntington Library, 1977), 154–58.

10. For seventeenth-century neo-Lullians and Athanasius Kircher, see Wilhelm Schmidt-Biggemann, *Topica Universalis: Eine Modellgeschichte humanistischer und barocker Wissenschaft* (Hamburg: Felix Meiner, 1983), 156–89. Trees of knowledge reemerge today amid the revival of studies of Giambattista Vico. For the genesis of Tagliacozzo's 1959 "Tree of Knowledge" and his 1989 "doubly Vichian Tree of Knowledge," see Giorgio Tagliacozzo, *The "Arbor Scientiae" Reconceived and the History of Vico's Resurrection* (Atlantic Highlands, N.J.: Humanities Press, 1993), esp. 1–29.

11. Werner Schneiders, *Hoffnung auf Vernunft: Aufklärungsphilosophie in Deutschland* (Hamburg: Felix Meiner, 1990), 98.

12. For examination of Kircher's encyclopedic works, see Thomas Leinkauf, *Mundus combinatus: Studien zur Sruktur der barocken Universalwissenschaft am Beispiel Athanasius Kirchers SJ (1602–1680)* (Berlin: Akademie Verlag GmbH, 1993); and for evidence of his visual vocabulary, see Joscelyn Godwin, *Athanasius Kircher: A Renaissance Man and the Quest for Lost Knowledge* (London: Thames & Hudson, 1979), 79, on the tree of the society of Jesus, and 75, on the chain as magnetic attraction.

13. A contemporary rendering of personifications of the cardinal virtues—fortitude, temperance, prudence, and justice—symbolizes the 1990s movement for character education: see *Newsweek*, 13 June 1994.

14. Bernard Le Bovier Fontenelle, *Conversations on the Plurality of the Worlds*, trans. H. A. Hargreaves, intro. Nina R. Gelbart (Berkeley: University of California Press, 1990); the original frontispiece appears on the cover of this paperback. Fontenelle utilizes the full dialogue technique of the Platonic tradition that we have seen in Ficino to conduct scientific discourse along more modern lines than those of Bodin's *Theatrum*.

15. Terry Comito, *The Idea of the Garden in the Renaissance* (New Brunswick, N.J.: Rutgers University Press, 1978).

16. I am grateful to Edward Horowitz for his rendition of Shakespearian roles.

17. Robert F. Fleissner, *A Rose By Any Other Name: A Survey of Literary Flora from Shakespeare to Eco* (West Cornwall, Conn.: Locust Hill, 1989), 1–33 on Shakespeare, with extensive bibliography.

18. *The Language and Poetry of Flowers* (London: Milner, ca. 1871). The Huntington Library and Botanical Gardens collection includes Louise Cortambert, *Le Langage des fleurs*, 10th ed. (1876); Catherine Esling, *Flora's Lexicon* (1858); John Ingram, *Flora Symbolica* (1869); Leynadier, *Nouveau langage des fleurs* (1877); and Philippes, *Floral Emblems* (1877).

19. Jack Goody, *The Culture of Flowers* (Cambridge: Cambridge University Press, 1993), esp. chs. 4 on Islam, 7 on expanding markets with Asia, and 8 on the language of flowers.

20. See the chapters "The Debate on the *Roman de la Rose*," "The Order of the Rose," and "The Joy and First Fruits of Learning" in Enid McLeod, *The Order of the Rose: The Life and Ideas of Christine de Pizan* (Totowa, N.J.: Rowman & Littlefield, 1976), quotation on 70–71; Maryanne Cline Horowitz, "The Woman Question in Renaissance Texts," *History of European Ideas*, special issue on women's history, ed. Karen Offen, 8 (1987): 587–95; Judy Chicago, *The Dinner Party: A Symbol of Our Heritage* (Garden City, N.Y.: Anchor, 1979), esp. 144, 150, and 160, for Hildegard, Christine, and Elizabeth; Carolyn Merchant, "Isis' Consciousness Raised," *Isis* (1982): 398–99, 402–3, on the gendering in medieval garden symbolism, and 407, on the association of women with botany.

21. Italian women humanists' citations of seeds and sparks of knowledge is a mode by which women assert their claim to receive education and to be writers, a mode supplementing those explored in Gerda Lerner, *The Creation of Feminist Consciousness: From the Middle Ages to Eighteen-seventy* (New York: Oxford University Press, 1993).

22. Mary Collyer, *Felicia to Charlotte: being letters from a young lady in the country to her friend in town. containing a series of the most interesting events, interspersed with moral reflections; chiefly tending to prove that the seeds of virtue are*

planted in the mind of every reasonable being (London: Griffiths & G. Woodfall, 1749).

23. Ripa, fig. 49. The 1644 edition, p. 51, indicates that her age, not too young or too old, indicates her capacity for reason. It cites an Egyptian source and a biblical proverb for the sieve as a metaphor for the ability to distinguish virtue from vice. The rake is presented as a tool for ordinary laborers to root out harmful plants.

24. Gen. 4.18–19 explains God's punishment of Adam, including the curse of the ground yielding the generic "thorns and thistles" (*koz ve-dardar*). Winifred Walker, *All the Plants of the Bible* (Garden City, N.Y.: Doubleday, 1971), 190–91, explains that in ancient Palestine a sieve was applied specifically to retain the larger wheat seeds while shaking into refuse the smaller, poisonous darnel seeds. Matt. 13.24–29, cited in Ripa, discusses how an enemy can sow bad seeds in a field previously sown with wheat; the enemy is portrayed in the background of this engraving as a devil deceiving the sleeping farmer. Alastair I. MacKay, *Farming and Gardening in the Bible* (Emmaus, Penn.: Rodale, 1950), 138–40, indicates that a sieve for retaining corn seeds appears in Amos 9.9, confirming the Hebrews' knowledge of the role of wind in spreading seeds (both good and bad). Fans are applied to blowing chaff away (dry grass or hay) in Isa. 5.24, 33.11, Job 13.24, and Jer. 51.1–2. Interpreting Matthew 3.12, MacKay suggests that a pronged shovel is applied for tossing mixed seeds in order to aid the wind in sending away the lighter ones; possibly the rake in our illustration is an allusion also to Matthew.

25. See the emblem "Quae non facit bonos fructus" (That which does not bear fruit), in *Emblemata. Handbuch zur Sinnbildkunst des XVI. und XVII. Jahrhunderts*, ed. Arthur Henkel and Albrecht Schöne (Stuttgart: Metzler, 1967), 183.

26. Philip J. Greven, ed., *Child-Rearing Concepts, 1628–1861* (Itasca, Ill.: Peacock, 1973), 49 (Bradstreet) and 20, 22 (Locke). See also John Locke, *Some Thoughts concerning Education*, ed. John Yolton and Jean Yolton (Oxford: Clarendon, 1989), 104–5 and editors' intro., 14–28.

27. Philip J. Greven, *The Protestant Temperament: Patterns of Child-Rearing, Religious Experience, and the Self in Early America* (New York: Knopf, 1977), 171–72, 176, in the section "'Planting the Seeds of Virtue' in Childhood and Youth."

28. See the introduction, n. 77; and Maryanne Cline Horowitz, "Toleration and Skepticism in French Free-Thinkers in the First Decades after the Edict of Nantes," in *Early Modern Skepticism and the Origins of Toleration*, ed. Alan Levine, forthcoming.

29. "La nature en a mis le magazin en nostre esprit, portons-y la main de nostre volonté, & nous en prendrons telle part que nous voudrons" (Du Vair, *Oeuvres* [Paris: Sebastien Cramoisy, 1641; reprint, Geneva: Slatkine, 1970], 258); "nos forces ne seroient pas suffisantes d'elles-meme à nous conserver en cette perfection" (ibid., 288; see also ch. 7, n. 62).

30. Mark Morford, *Stoics and Neostoics: Rubens and the Circle of Lipsius* (Princeton: Princeton University Press, 1991).

31. Lipsius, *Two Books of Constancie*, trans. Sir John Stradling (New Brunswick, N.J.: Rutgers University Press, 1939), 135–36; Ilva Beretta, *"The World's a Garden": Garden Poetry of the English Renaissance* (Ph.D. diss., Uppsala University, 1993), 176–92.

32. *Laurus metaphysica*, 1622, enlargement of Léonard Gaultier's print of 1616, Hennin Collection no. 1307, in Bibliothèque nationale, *The French Renais-*

sance in Prints (Los Angeles: Grunwald Center for the Graphic Arts, University of California, Los Angeles, 1994), no. 174, p. 432.

33. Ripa (Hertel ed.), fig. 5.

34. Barthélemy Aneau, *Picta poesis* (Lyon: M. Bonhomme, 1552), 50, "Humana origo et finis"; Henkel and Schöne, *Emblemata*, 1843. See also *Playing with Gender*, eds. Jean R. Brink, Maryanne C. Horowitz, and Allison P. Coudert (Urbana: University of Illinois Press, 1991).

35. Pierre Magnard suggests that the image of a tree without foliage ("l'arbre sans son feuillage") expresses Bodin's recognition that the trunk of essential beliefs of the natural religion is preserved through the leafy flourishing of diverse rites and rituals (Pierre Magnard, *Le Dieu des philosophes* [Paris: Editions universitaires et editions Mame, 1992], 251). A new study of Bodin's contribution to toleration is Gary Remer, *Humanism and the Rhetoric of Toleration* (University Park: Pennsylvania State University Press, 1996), 203–30.

36. A good sample of texts defending nobility of virtue is contained in Albert Rabil, ed. and trans., *Knowledge, Goodness, and Power: The Debate over Nobility among Quattrocento Italian Humanists* (Binghamton, N.Y.: State University of New York Press, 1991), for example, on 41, 44, 82–89, 114–15, 141, 217–18, 223–24 (quotation), 281–82, 325.

37. See the manuscript of Leo X, genealogical tree of the Medici, Laur. ms. Palat. 225, fols. 3v–4r, fig. 44 in Janet Cox-Rearick, *Dynasty and Destiny in Medici Art: Pontormo, Leo X, and the Two Cosimos* (Princeton: Princeton University Press, 1984).

38. Renée Neu Watkins, ed. and trans., *Humanism and Liberty* (Columbia: University of South Carolina Press, 1978), 121–48.

39. In the controversies on whether to limit the noble class to traditional nobility (based on a century or two of noble status) or to expand it to include the new nobility (based on the upward mobility of the bourgeoisie) the phrase *seeds of virtue* supports the opening of noble ranks. For further investigation, one might start with the primary sources discussed in Kristen B. Neyschel, *Word of Honor: Interpreting Noble Culture in Sixteenth-Century France* (Ithaca: Cornell University Press, 1989); Ellery Schalk, *From Valor to Pedigree: Ideas of Nobility in France in the Sixteenth and Seventeenth Centuries* (Princeton: Princeton University Press, 1986); Domna C. Stanton, *The Aristocrat As Art* (New York: Columbia University Press, 1980); and Arlette Jouanna, *L'idée de race en France au XVIème siècle et au début du XVIIème siècle (1498–1614)* (Paris: Champion, 1976). Some emblems confront the issue of poverty and nobility of character: see Joannes Sambucus's "Virtute Duce," and Gilles Corrozet's "Vertu meilleure que richesse," in Henkel and Schöne, *Emblemata*, 129, 196.

40. See above, ch. 9, nn. 43 and 57, and case studies of John Locke in Maryanne Cline Horowitz, ed., *Race, Gender, and Rank: Early Modern Ideas of Humanity*, Library of the History of Ideas (Rochester: University of Rochester Press, 1992). Work remains to be done in elaborating Locke's development from *Essays on the Law of Nature* (1660) to *Two Treatise on Government* (1690). See *John Locke, Essays on the Late of Nature*, Latin text with translation, ed. W. Von Leyden (Oxford: Clarendon, 1954); and John Locke, *Two Treatises on Government*, ed. Peter Laslett (Cambridge: Cambridge University Press, 1971). See also the issues raised in John Colman, *John Locke's Moral Philosophy* (Edinburgh: Edinburgh University Press, 1983); and see above, the introduction, nn. 4–7, and ch. 1, nn. 32–34.

41. See above, ch. 9, n. 30.

42. See above, ch. 9, n. 38; and Claude Blum et al., eds., *Montaigne et le nouveau monde: Actes du Colloque de Paris, 18–20 May 1992* (Paris: Société Internationale des Amis de Montaigne, 1994).

43. See above, ch. 8, n. 17; ch. 9, n. 5. For Montaigne's creative use of commonplace agricultural imagery, see Carol Clark, *The Web of Metaphor: Studies in the Imagery of Montaigne's "Essays"* (Lexington, Ky.: French Forum, 1978), 42–43, 58–63, 124–25, 172–73.

44. The emergence of the "science de l'homme" is a theme of Demenico Bosco, *La decifranzione dell'ordine*, 2 vols. (Milan: Vita e Pensiero, 1987), which has a useful bibliography.

45. William B. Ashworth, *Jesuit Science in the Age of Galileo* (Kansas City, Mo.: Linda Hall Library, 1986), fig. 6.

46. For a fine analysis of a literary rendering of human dignity, see Marcia L. Colish, "The Mime of God: Vives on the Nature of Man," in Horowitz, *Race, Gender, and Rank*. For a brief overview and bibliography, see Charles Trinkaus, "The Renaissance Idea of the Dignity of Man," and George Boas, "Macrocosm and Microcosm," in *Dictionary of the History of Ideas*, ed. Philip P. Wiener, 5 vols. (New York: Scribner's Sons, 1973); Dorothy Koenigsberger emphasizes the "Renaissance analogy of nature" in *Renaissance Man and Creative Thinking: A History of Harmony 1400–1700* (Hassocks, Sussex: The Harvester Press, 1979). A November 1992 colloquium at the Sorbonne provided a lively reconsideration of the origins and paradoxes in Renaissance affirmations of human dignity (see Pierre Magnard, ed., *La Dignité de l'homme* [Paris: Champion, 1995]).

47. "Cela est bien dit, répond Candide, mais il faut cultiver notre jardin" (Voltaire, *Candide ou l'optimisme*, in *Romans et contes*, ed. Frederic Deloffre and Jacques van den Heuvel [Paris: Gallimard, 1979], 233).

This index contains names of authors and historical persons. For mythological characters and biblical figures, as well as for topics, please see the Index Rerum.

Barbeyac, Jean, 258n.7
Barga, Antonio da, 122
Barnard, Mary, 284n.73
Barolsky, Paul, 294n.58
Baron, Hans, 259nn.17, 20, 290n.18
Basford, Katherine, 305n.106
Bayle, Pierre, 322n.49
Bazarov, Konstantin, 281n.34
Bellenger, Yvonne, 329n.2
Bellini, Giovani, 281nn.34, 36
Belon, Pierre, xvi, 156, 184; gathering of
  seeds by, 168, 309n.7
Bembo, Pietro, 94–95, 287n.35
Benedict XII (pope), 124–25, 127, 128,
  298n.15
Bennett, William J., 264n.67
Ben-Sasson, Haim Hillel, 304n.92
Benson, Robert L., 288n.6
Beretta, Ilva, 345n.31
Bernard de Lavinheta, 77
Bernard of Clairvaux, 274n.42, 279n.5
Berners, Juliana, 298n.19
Berriot, François, 316n.101, 317nn.1, 4, 7,
  327n.106
Biel, Gabriel, 46, 47, 137; Luther's reading
  of, 135–36; on sin, 53
Blair, Ann M., 196, 321nn.48, 49
Blum, Claude, 323n.62, 331n.21, 347n.42
Boaistuau, Pierre, 189, 322n.53
Bober, Phyllis P., 272n.9, 11
Boccaccio, Giovanni: *De claris mulieribus*,
  112, 244; *Genealogiae*, 79, 284n.72
Bodenstein von Karlstad, Andreas, 142
Bodin, Jean: Augustine's influence on,
  328n.111; Calvin's influence on,
  307n.132; Charron's borrowings from,
  191, 225, 237, 253, 322n.50, 337n.14;
  early life of, 181; Ficino's influence on,
  326n.95; on foreign trade, 14; on free
  will, 199, 201, 202, 203; on goodness of
  nature, 199, 205, 317n.1; in *Index librorum prohibitorum*, 181, 255, 317n.7;
  on materialism, 269n.55; Philo's influence on, xiii, 42, 191, 324n.69; posthumous criticism of, 317n.4; religious beliefs of, 181, 317n.4; seed concept of, 8,
  181, 182, 184, 190–91, 194, 196, 198,
  204, 250; on the soul, 189, 190, 194,
  196, 240, 320n.38, 322n.56, 325n.88;
  synthesizing of, 185, 191, 196, 205; at
  Toulouse, 184, 319n.19; tree imagery of,
  196, 203, 205, 346n.35; use of Hebrew
  literature by, 325n.80, 327nn.105, 107;
  use of Stoicism by, 21, 170, 180, 232,

327n.104; vegetative imagery of, 183,
  187. Works: *Colloquium*, 183, 187, 200–
  203, 248, 326n.93, 327n.106; human
  mind in, 189; —, original sin in,
  320n.40; — seeds in, 196; *Démonomanie*,
  183, 189, 190; *Distributio*, 182, 184,
  187, 326n.96; — Decalogue in, 202;
  —, social law in, 186; *Epitome*, 190, 194;
  Methodus, 182, 183–84, 187, 196,
  320n.40, —, creation in, 188; —, Philo
  in, 191, 324n.73; *Oratio*, 184, 201;
  —, seeds in, 190, 196; *Paradoxon*, 185,
  204–5, 250, 317n.1, 326n.98; — seeds
  in, 182, 191; *République*, 3–4, 182, 186,
  187, 188, 196, 252; *Response à M. de
  Malestroict*, 203–4; *Sapientiae moralis*,
  182–83; *Universae naturae theatrum*,
  182, 183, 188–91, 196–99, 202;
  —, Philo in, 250
Bodin, Jean (heretic), 317n.5
Boehm, Jacob, fig. E.4
Boethius, 293n.48; on common notions,
  48; in educational curriculum, 103; influence on Aquinas of, 276n.67; on seeds,
  52
Boethius of Dacia, 179, 189
Boétie, Étienne de: *De la servitude volun-
  taire*, 4
Bonaventure, Saint, 46, 282n.45; *Lignum
  vitae*, 68
Bonfil, Robert, 295n.73
Boniface VIII (pope), 68
Bonner, Stanley F., 290n.22, 293n.49
Bono, James J., 262n.46
Børreson, Kari, 271n.6
Bosco, Demonico, 347n.44
Botticelli, Sandro: *Birth of Venus*, 79; *Cal-
  umny of Apelles*, 79; *Lorenzo Tornabuoni
  presented by Grammar*, 110, 164; *Prima-
  vera*, 7, 12, 86, 243, fig. 5.2; —, Chloris
  in, 107–10, 112, 117, 243, 294n.58,
  Frontispiece; —, Flora in, 111, 112, 243,
  244, 294n.58; —, Mercury in, 110, 111,
  132, 294n.58; —, orange grove of, 12;
  Venus and the Graces, 110, 164, fig. 5.3
Bouwsma, William J., 12, 297n.1,
  306n.131, 313n.64
Bracciolini, Poggio, 100; *De miseria humane conditionis*, 129; *De Nobilitate*,
  252; library of, 290n.24
Braden, Gordon, 296n.92
Bradstreet, Anne, 247
Bredekamp, Horst, 294n.58
Brown, Peter, 271n.5

For book titles, look in Index Nominum under author's name.

phallic symbolism, 6, 28, 37, 79, 87, 97, 101, 109, 112

phantasiai, 23, 267n.18

philosophy: Arabic, 323n.56, 328n.108; gender in, 42–43, 97; moral, 265n.1; political, xiii, 12; natural law in, 3; "reason-of-state," 262n.50

philosophy, pagan: Calvin on, 152–53; Ficino's use of, 81, 89–90; Lefèvre's change on, 134–35; Pico on, 129, 132; mythology in, 18; role in Christianity of, 169, 170, 172, 234

physics, Stoic, 178

Picta poesis, 87, 112–13

pinecone, bronze (Vatican), 37–36, 239, 272n.10, fig. 2.1

pinecones: emblems of, 39, 166, fig. 2.2; as seeds of virtue, 37–39, 239

plagues, 122; of 1348, 128, 300n.42; of 1586–87, 210, 211, 331n.18

plant propagation, 6–7, 37; Ficino on, 91, 87; in *Primavera*, 112; Rabelais on, 168–69. *See also* procreation; seeds

plants: asexual, 6–7, 37, 79; domestication of, 321n.41; in *Primavera*, 107–11; sex division in, 168, 240, 343n.9. *See also* flowers; trees

Platonism, influence on Stoicism of, 24, 57, 77, 83, 92–95, 119, 133, 177, 199, 253, 266n.2

poetry, Petrarch on, 97–98

politics, of church and state, xv, 128, 176, 204, 223–24, 249–50; of civic humanism, 8–9, 99, 129, 153, 166, 176; forms of, 9, 174, 314n.80; radical, 3–4; in state of nature, 214–17, 252; of world state, 22–23

politiques (moderates), 170, 204; compromise by, 223–24; Du Vair as, 173, 314n.74

Porus, myth of, 91

potency, ancient depictions of, 3

"Poverty Hinders Talent," 166

predestination, 135; and free will, 170

preud'femme, 227, 338n.19

preud'hommie, 253; Charron on, 219, 225, 227–31, 233, 235; conscience as source of, 229; definition of, 227; and religion, 235

Pricke of Conscience (poem), 122

Primavera, 107–14

printing press, xvi; seed imagery of, 157; and spread of neo-Platonism, 279n.4

procreation, 28–29; Aristotle on, 6, 27, 28, 117, 121, 269n.43, 286.26; Erasmus on,

157; spontaneous, 100, 117, 190, 203. *See also* plant propagation

prolêpseis, 23, 24; *physikai*, 26

Protestantism: of Calvin, 146; conscience in, 16; pedagogical debates in, 152–53; 247

proverbs, 263n.65

Psalms, 15; first, 60–61, 120–21, 263n.59; fourth, 137, 198, 229

punishment, divine, 203, 228

Puritans, English, 279n.5

pyr. See fire

races of humanity: seeds of virtue and knowledge in, xiii, xv, 19–20; Bodin on, 186–89; Las Casas on, 219–20; Montaigne on, 218, 221; *vs.* racism, 345n.28, 346n.40

rationalism, 18, 244

reason: in ancient Stoicism, 21–23; of animals, 197, 220, 326n.93; Aquinas on, 35, 47; Aristotle on, xv, 13, 131; Augustine on, 35, 47; Calvin on, 152; Charron on, 228–29; in Christian theology, 45–47; Cicero on, 13, 30; development in children of, 268n.25; epistemology of, 14; equivalence with seeds of, 3; Erasmus on, 137; as female, 97; gendered, 42–43; in John of Salisbury, 97; as law, 22; Lefèvre on, 134; Lipsius on, 174, 176; logos as, 30; Montaigne on, 208, 212, 213; and natural law, 45–47, 252; Petrarch on, 289n.14; Renaissance belief in, 21; Sadoleto on, 149; as source of creativity, 30; as source of virtue, 21; synderesis in, 47; universal, 230, 250; upper and lower, 42, 198, 254; and will, 48. *See also* right reason

reason, seminal, 27, 28, 272n.15; Aquinas on, 50–51; in Augustine, 5, 49–50, 276n.79; Charron on, 230; in *Primavera*, 109. *See also* genes; *logos spermatikos*

rebirth. *See* cultural rebirth

referentiality, 264n.71

Reformation, Protestant: Erasmian curriculum in, 246; growth of soul in, 119

religion: Charron on, 223, 231, 233–35, 319n.29, 338n.16; corrupting influence of, 202–3; independence from morality, 233–34, 235; natural, 201; and natural law, 200; subordination to virtue, 338n.16; vegetative symbolism in, 7

religious wars, xv, 179–80, 223, 249

Renaissance: concept of species in, 196–97; floral symbolism of, 244; Italian, 81,

synéidesis. See synderesis
synteresis. See synderesis

Talmud, 191; Adam in, 131; Babylonian, 59, 343nn.7,9; ethical principles in, 60, 263n.65
The Tempest, 281nn.34, 36
Ten Commandments. *See* Decalogue
Tetragrammaton, 194, 197, 278n.109
theios nomos. See divine law
tolerance, religious, xv, 19–20, 200, 204, 247–48, 345n.28; Bodin's contribution to, 346n.35; Charron on, 223. *See also* Vatican Council, Second
Topinambá Indians, 206, 208, 210, 215
Torah, 60, 272n8; as tree of life, 62, 240, 264n.65
Tour de la Garde-Robe. *See* Chambre du Cerf
Tour du Trésor. *See* Chambre du Pape
traducianism, 278n.108
transplantation, imagery of, 18, 321n.42, fig. 7.1, 7.4
tree imagery: of Alciati, 161; biblical, xiii, 59–61, 239, 246, 282n.36; of civic virtue, fig. 7.6; of Du Vair, 173–74; in educational strategy, 78; in Genesis, 59–60, 130; Graeco-Roman, 61; of Innocent III, 120–21; in J.S. Mill, 10; medieval, xiv, 58; of peasants, 332n.35; of Pico, 130; of Sadoleto, 147; of sixteenth century, xvi; visual, 57, 246
tree of Jesse, 11, 68, 93; in divine illumination, 78
trees: almond, 60, 161, 239, 248, fig. 7.2; ancient symbolism of, 10; of arts and sciences, 5–6, 240, 243, 249, fig. E.2; genealogical, 83, 258n.8; of history, 68, 70–71, 304n.88, fig. 3.3; of medicine, 71, 240, fig. 3.4; nut, 164; oak, 10, 216, 299n.23; orange, 110; palm, 62, 166, 240, 312n.58, 343n.9, fig. E.1; sexuality of, 240, 343n.9; of soul, fig. E.4; of state, 10, 173–74; upside-down, 57, 68, 231, fig. E.1
trees, *sefirot*, xiv, 66, 240, fig. 3.2, fig. E.1; influence on Bodin, 324nn.76, 77; and paths to wisdom, 78
trees of ascent, 57, 59, 70, 124; in illumination theory, 77–78
trees of fools, 213, 332n.35
trees of knowledge, 59, 240, 343n.10; in Alciati, 164; Christian, 70–72; and confidence in reason, 78; in core curriculum,

5–6, 258n.13, fig. 3.4; engraved, 249, 337n.11; in *Fior di Virtu*, 103; in Judaism, 60; Philo on, 193, 194
trees of life, xiv; Bodin on, 196, 203; of Cranach, 139–42, fig. 6.3; cross as, 67–68; in *Fior di Virtu*, 103; in Judaism, 60, 61; in Paradise, 67, 68; Philo on, 193; Torah as, 62
trees of light, 26, 39–42, 178, 207, 240, fig. 2.3, 4.1
trees of state, 10, 173–74
trees of vice and virtue, xv, fig. 3.5; in Alciati, 164; Bodin on, 196, 205; Calvin on, 304n.93; Christian, 73–77; Cranach's, 139–42, fig. 6.3; in emblem books, 159; in Gospel of Matthew, 203; holm-oak as, 168; in Lipsius, 176; literary images of, 12; in manuscript illumination, 120; Marguerite de Navarre on, 142–44; medieval, 141, 248
truth, criterion for, 23

United States of America: Library of Congress of, 6; presidents of, 247
universities: of Cambridge, 118; of Ferrara, 101; of Geneva, 146; humanist curriculum of, 8, 118; of Jena, 176; of Leiden, 176; of Montpellier, 159, fig. 7.1; of Oxford, 118; of Padua, 101, 159; of Paris, 46, 134, 146; teaching of Aristotle in, 179; of Toulouse, 174, 184; of Wittenberg, 138–39, 168

valentines, floral, 244
Vatican: bronze pinecone of, 37–36, 239, 272n.10, fig. 2.1; papal library of, 119, 129, 300n.43
Vatican Council, Second, 19, 20, 248, 265n.77, 279n.3
vegetation. *See* flowers; fruit; plants; seeds; trees
vegetative imagery, xv, 11, 13, 15, 36; of clerical humanists, 102; continuity in, 119; of cultural rebirth, 71, 95, 99, 156, 183, 243, 252; of the Divine, 77–78; of divine wisdom, 119–20; of Elizabeth I, 145; of Ficino, 6, 81, 93, 95; in florilegia, 106; gold in, 312n.58; of Hildegard of Bingen, 55; in human dignity debate, 133; humanist, xvi, 71; of Marguerite de Navarre, 142–43, 305n.103; Medicis' use of, 81–83, 117, 156; of menorahs, 41–42, 132; of Montaigne, 207–8, 213, 222, 318n.17; negative,

About the Author

Maryanne Cline Horowitz is a Professor of History at Occidental College and an Associate of the Center for Medieval and Renaissance Studies at the University of California, Los Angeles.